RELIGION FROM TOLSTOY TO CAMUS

RELIGION FROM TOLSTOY TO CAMUS

Selected, with an introduction and prefaces, by
Walter Kaufmann

HARPER TORCHBOOKS
The Cloister Library

HARPER & ROW, PUBLISHERS
NEW YORK AND EVANSTON

TO HERMAN AND SARAH WOUK

WHO LED ME TO LOVE

ST. THOMAS, V. I.

RELIGION FROM TOLSTOY TO CAMUS

Copyright © 1961 by Walter Kaufmann.
New material copyright © 1964 by Walter Kaufmann.

Printed in the United States of America.

All rights in this book are reserved. No part of this book
may be used or reproduced in any manner whatsoever
without written permission except in the case of brief quotations
embodied in critical articles and reviews.
For information address Harper & Row, Publishers, Inc.
10 East 53rd Street, New York 22, N.Y.

This book was originally published by
Harper & Brothers, Publishers, in 1961.

First HARPER TORCHBOOK edition published 1964 by
Harper & Row, Publishers, Inc.

Library of Congress catalog card number: 61-12838.

Grateful acknowledgment is made to the following publishers for permission to use selections from the works indicated:

THE BEACON PRESS, BOSTON: *Europe and the Jews,* by Malcolm Hay, copyright 1950 by The Beacon Press under the title *The Foot of Pride.*

BENZIGER BROTHERS, INC., NEW YORK: "Aeterni Patris" by Leo XIII, in *The "Summa Theologica" of St. Thomas Aquinas,* 1911; copyright 1947 by Benziger Brothers, Inc.

BASIL BLACKWELL, OXFORD: "Gods," in *Philosophy and Psycho-analysis,* by John Wisdom, 1957; copyright 1953 by Basil Blackwell. (Grateful acknowledgment is also made of Professor Wisdom's permission.)

THE DEVIN-ADAIR COMPANY, NEW YORK: Dogmatic Canons and Decrees by Pius IX, 1912.

GROVE PRESS, INC., NEW YORK: "Reflections on the Guillotine," in *Evergreen Review,* Vol. I, No. 3, by Albert Camus, translated by Richard Howard, copyright 1957 by Grove Press, Inc. (Grateful acknowledgment is also made of permission by the French publisher, Calmann-Levy, Paris.)

HARPER & BROTHERS, NEW YORK: *Christian Beginnings,* by Morton Scott Enslin, copyright 1938 by Harper & Brothers; *Approaches to God,* by Jacques Maritain, copyright 1954 by Jacques Maritain; *Dynamics of Faith,* by Paul Tillich, copyright 1957 by Harper & Brothers.

WILLIAM HODGE & CO., LTD., EDINBURGH: *The Gestapo Defied,* by Martin Niemöller, copyright 1941 by William Hodge & Co., Ltd.

HENRY HOLT AND COMPANY, NEW YORK: "The Dark Side of Religion," in *The Faith of a Liberal,* by Morris Cohen, copyright 1946 by Henry Holt and Company. (Grateful acknowledgment is also made of the permission of Harry N. Rosenfield, Executor of the Cohen Estate.)

LIVERIGHT PUBLISHING CORPORATION, NEW YORK, AND THE HOGARTH PRESS, LTD., LONDON: *The Future of an Illusion,* by Sigmund Freud, translated by W. D. Robson-Scott, Copyright 1928.

THE MACMILLAN COMPANY, NEW YORK: "The Conception of the Kingdom of God in *the Transformation of Eschatology*" by Albert Schweitzer, in *The Theology of Albert Schweitzer* by E. N. Mozley, copyright 1950 by A. & C. Black, Ltd., London; "Theology and Falsification," by Antony Flew, R. M. Hare, and Basil Mitchell, in *New Essays in Philosophical Theology,* 1955 edited by Antony Flew and Alasdair MacIntyre.

MCGRAW-HILL BOOK CO., INC., NEW YORK: "The Dark Side of Religion," by Morris Cohen, in *Religion Today, A Challenging Enigma,* copyright 1933 by Arthur L. Swift, Jr. (Grateful acknowledgment is also made of the permission of Harry N. Rosenfield. Executor of the Cohen Estate.)

OXFORD UNIVERSITY PRESS, NEW YORK: "A Reply to the Synod's Edict of Excommunication," in *On Life and Essays on Religion,* by Leo Tolstoy, translated by Aylmer Maude (World Classics Edition, 1934).

ROUTLEDGE & KEGAN PAUL, LTD., LONDON: *The Way of Man According to the Teachings of Hasidism,* by Martin Buber, copyright 1950 by Martin Buber.

STUDENT CHRISTIAN MOVEMENT PRESS, LTD., LONDON: *Against the Stream,* by Karl Barth, 1954; "Theology and Falsification," by Antony Flew, R. M. Hare, and Basil Mitchell, in *New Essays in Philosophical Theology,* 1955 edited by Antony Flew and Alasdair MacIntyre.

THE VIKING PRESS, INC., NEW YORK: *The Antichrist* in *The Portable Nietzsche,* by Friedrich Nietzsche, selected and translated by Walter Kaufmann, copyright 1954 by The Viking Press, Inc.

THE WESTON COLLEGE PRESS, WESTON, MASS.: *Humani Generis* by Pius XII, translated with commentary by A. C. Cotter, S.J., second edition 1952, copyright 1952 by The Weston College Press.

PREFACE

Most of the following selections are complete, whether they be short stories, fables, encyclicals, essays, fairy tales, poems in prose, sermons, letters, or even a short book. All deal with religion, some with its truth, some with its relation to morality and society.

The point is not to win friends for religion, or enemies, but to provoke greater thoughtfulness. Here are texts that deserve to be pondered and discussed. Some of them I have criticized in other volumes; in such cases, the references are given. But in the present book nothing is included merely to be disparaged, nor is anything offered only to be praised. The hope is that those who read this book will gain a deeper understanding of religion.

W. K.

PREFACE TO THE TORCHBOOK EDITION

*I*n this new edition nothing has been omitted, but three selections have been added at the end: two longish items to strengthen the philosophic content of this volume, and one short one to update the treatment of the Roman Catholic church.

The posture of the church has changed as radically under Pope John XXIII as it did under Pius IX a century before. Obviously, this does not render superfluous a study of the documents of Pius IX, Leo XIII, and Pius XII, which were included in the first edition: only those who have studied this material can fully appreciate the changes wrought since the death of Pius XII. What needs to be said about that, I have tried to say in the preface to the newly added selection by Pope John.

The new philosophical selections deal, respectively, with "God, Evil, and Immortality" and "Theology and Falsification." More material on the problem of evil, which continues to fascinate students of religion, requires no justification; but perhaps the choice of McTaggart's ideas on this subject does. The reasons were simple: this material is hard to come by, yet unusual in its clarity, vigor, and relevance.

Without the controversy on "Theology and Falsification," now included, the great significance of Wisdom's important but elusive essay on "Gods" is not likely to be fully appreciated by most students. The issues Wisdom raises—and those Flew poses in the opening statement of the controversy— richly merit discussion. While I am not satisfied with the discussion they get, it has the great merit of facilitating further discussion and thought. And it is a pleasure to be able to offer together in the same volume not only Clifford and James but also Wisdom's essay and the four pieces based on it.

The arrangement of this volume is largely chronological. This makes it easy for the reader who wants to trace the development "from Tolstoy to Camus," but it is not so obvious how this volume is best used in courses that proceed from problem to problem. Chiefly, two problems are considered from a great variety of points of view. The first of these is the *justification of faith*. Under this heading one might distinguish several subheads; e.g., as follows:

Faith and evidence: Clifford and James (a confrontation that is eminently suitable for the beginning of a course), and Freud, Cohen, and Maritain. *The problem of evil:* Dostoevsky and Wilde pose it, and Royce and McTaggart analyze it. *Faith and its meaning:* Tillich, Wisdom, and Flew, Hare, and Mitchell. The importance of these three topics is generally acknowledged, but it is customary to give much more attention to the old proofs of God's existence which are here represented only by Maritain. The proofs, however, are now discussed almost exclusively in college and seminary courses: for most Protestants and Jews, as well as unbelievers, they are at most of academic interest. It is far more common in the twentieth century to try to justify faith with an *appeal to Scripture*, though this sort of attempt is rarely studied. In this book, the problems posed by such appeals can be studied by comparing Tolstoy, Nietzsche, Enslin, Niemöller, Hay, Tillich, and Schweitzer. Those who discuss these four facets of the justification of faith will stay closer to the existential realities of faith and its justification than academic courses and discussions usually do.

The other major problem which is taken up again and again from different points of view is *the relevance of religion to morals and society*. Selections that are important in this context include Tolstoy, Dostoevsky, Nietzsche, Wilde, Cohen, Hay, Barth and Brunner, Schweitzer, Buber, and Camus.

Besides these two major topics—truth and morals—one could obviously suggest any number of other approaches. In the above enumerations, for example, the four popes represented in this book have been omitted. And there is obviously, as the title of the volume indicates, material germane to the study of "religion in literature."

W. K.

CONTENTS

* Complete

* Complete

The story of religion, whether in Biblical times or in the last three quarters of a century, is not reducible to the superficialities of the masses and the subtleties of priests and theologians. There are also poets and prophets, critics and martyrs.

It is widely recognized that one can discuss religious ideas in connection with works of literature, but exceedingly few poets and novelists have been movers and shakers of religion. Leo Tolstoy, who was just that, has not been given the attention he deserves from students of religion. With all due respect to twentieth-century poets and novelists who are more fashionable, it is doubtful that any of their works have the stature of Tolstoy's *Resurrection*. This novel does not merely illustrate ideas one might like to discuss anyway but aims rather to revise our thinking about morals and religion. To say that Tolstoy was a very great writer, or even that his stature surpassed that of any twentieth-century theologian, may be very safe and trite. But a much bolder claim is worth considering: perhaps he is more important for the history of religion during the century covered in this volume than any theologian; perhaps he has contributed more of real importance and originality and issues a greater challenge to us. That is why his name appears in the title of this book, and why he has been given more space than anyone else.

Those who follow are a heterogeneous group, selected not to work toward some predetermined conclusion but to give a fair idea of the complexity of our story. The work of the theologians has been placed in perspective, no less than that of the literary figures, philosophers, and others who are not so easy to classify.

Almost all the men included were "for" religion, though not the popular religion which scarcely any great religious figure has ever admired. Like the prophets and Jesus, like the Buddha and Luther, these men were critical of much that was and is fashionable; but their point was for the most part to purify religion. Only three of the twenty-three represented here wrote as critics of religion without being motivated by an underlying sympathy: Nietzsche, Freud, and Morris Cohen.

No effort has been made to give proportional representation to various denominations. As it happens, Roman Catholicism and the Greek Orthodox church, Judaism, atheism, and various forms of Protestantism are all represented by at least one adherent; but with the exception of the popes, these are not spokesmen. The point is not to appease everybody but to provoke thought.

The men included disagree with one another on fundamental issues.

Hence one cannot help disagreeing with most of them unless one refuses to think. These men did not aim to please but to make us better human beings. By wrestling with them we stand some chance of becoming more humane.

TOLSTOY

It is customary to think of Tolstoy as a very great novelist who wrote *War and Peace* and *Anna Karenina*, but who then became immersed in religion and wrote tracts. His later concerns are generally deplored, and many readers and writers wish that instead he might have written another novel of the caliber of his masterpieces. A very few of his later works are excepted: chief among these is *The Death of Ivan Ilyitch*, which is acknowledged as one of the masterpieces of world literature. And some of those who have read the less well-known fable, *How Much Land Does a Man Need?* have said that it may well be the greatest short story ever written. But these are stories. Such *direct* communications as *My Religion*, with their unmistakable and inescapable challenge, one prefers to escape by not reading them. This makes it likely that most admirers of the stories, and even of *Anna Karenina*, come nowhere near understanding these works—a point amply borne out by the disquisitions of literary critics.

Lionel Trilling, as perceptive a critic as we have, has said that "every object . . . in *Anna Karenina* exists in the medium of what we must call the author's love. But this love is so pervasive, it is so constant, and it is so equitable, that it created the illusion of objectivity. . . . For Tolstoi everyone and everything has a saving grace. . . . It is this moral quality, this quality of affection, that accounts for the unique illusion of reality that Tolstoi creates. It is when the novelist really loves his characters that he can show them in their completeness and contradiction, in their failures as well as in their great moments, in their triviality as well as in their charm." Three pages later: "It is chiefly Tolstoi's moral vision that accounts for the happiness with which we respond to *Anna Karenina*."

Happiness indeed! Love, saving grace, and affection! Surely, the opposite of all this would be truer than that! After such a reading, it is not surprising that the critic has to say, near the end of his essay on *Anna Karenina* (reprinted in *The Opposing Self*): "Why is it a great novel? Only the finger of admiration can answer: because of this moment, or this, or this. . . ." The point is not that Trilling has slipped for once, but that *Anna Karenina* is generally misread—even by the best of critics.

Any reader who responds with happiness to this novel, instead of being disturbed to the depths, must, of course, find a sharp reversal in Tolstoy's later work which is so patently designed to shock us, to dislodge our way of looking at the world, and to make us see ourselves and others in a new, glaring and uncomfortable, light. Even if we confine ourselves to *Anna*

Karenina, I know of no other great writer in the whole nineteenth century, perhaps even in the whole of world literature, to whom I respond with less happiness and with a more profound sense that I am on trial and found wanting, unless it were Søren Kierkegaard.

Far from finding that Tolstoy's figures are bathed in his love and, without exception, have a saving grace, I find, on the contrary, that he loves almost none and that he tells us in so many words that what grace or charm they have is not enough to save them.

Instead of first characterizing an apparently repulsive character and then exhibiting his hidden virtues or, like Dostoevsky, forcing the reader to identify himself with murderers, Tolstoy generally starts with characters toward whom we are inclined to be well disposed, and then, with ruthless honesty, brings out their hidden failings and their self-deceptions and often makes them look ridiculous. "Why is it a great novel?" Not on account of this detail or that, but because Tolstoy's penetration and perception have never been excelled; because love and affection never blunt his honesty; and because in inviting us to sit in judgment, Tolstoy calls on us to judge ourselves. Finding that most of the characters deceive themselves, the reader is meant to infer that he is probably himself guilty of self-deception; that his graces, too, are far from saving; that his charm, too, does not keep him from being ridiculous—and that it will never do to resign himself to this.

The persistent preoccupation with self-deception and with an appeal to the reader to abandon his inauthenticity links *Anna Karenina* with *The Death of Ivan Ilyitch,* whose influence on existentialism is obvious. But in *Anna Karenina* the centrality of this motif has not generally been noticed.

It is introduced ironically on the third page of the novel, in the second sentence of Chapter II: "He was incapable of deceiving himself." To trace it all the way through the novel would take a book; a few characteristic passages, chosen almost at random, will have to suffice. "He did not realize it, because it was too terrible to him to realize his actual position. . . . [He] did not want to think at all about his wife's behavior, and he actually succeeded in not thinking about it at all. . . . He did not want to see, and did not see. . . . He did not want to understand, and did not understand. . . . He did not allow himself to think about it, and he did not think about it; but all the same, though he never admitted it to himself . . . in the bottom of his heart he knew. . . ." (Modern Library ed., 238 ff.) "Kitty answered perfectly truly. She did not know the reason Anna Pavlovna had changed to her, but she guessed it. She guessed at something which she could not tell her mother, which she did not put into words to herself. It was one of those things which one knows but which one can never speak of even to oneself. . . ." (268) "She became aware that she had deceived herself. . . ." (279) "He did not acknowledge this feeling, but at the bottom of his heart. . . ." (334)

Here is a passage in which bad faith is specifically related to religion: "Though in passing through these difficult moments he had not once thought of seeking guidance in religion, yet now, when his conclusion corresponded, as it seemed to him, with the requirements of religion, this religious sanction to his decision gave him complete satisfaction, and to some extent restored his peace of mind. He was pleased to think that, even in such an important crisis in life, no one would be able to say that he had not acted in accordance with the principles of that religion whose banner he had always held aloft amid the general coolness and indifference." (335)

Later, to be sure, Anna's husband becomes religious in a deeper sense; but as soon as the reader feels that Tolstoy's cutting irony is giving way to affection and that the man "has a saving grace," Tolstoy, with unfailing honesty, probes the man's religion and makes him, if possible, more ridiculous than he had seemed before. And the same is done with Varenka: she is not presented as a hypocrite with a saving grace but as a saint—until she is looked at more closely.

Inauthenticity is not always signaled by the vocabulary of self-deception. Sometimes Tolstoy's irony works differently: "Vronsky's life was particularly happy in that he had a code of principles, which defined with unfailing certitude what he ought and what he ought not to do. . . . These principles laid down as invariable rules: that one must pay a cardsharper, but need not pay a tailor; that one must never tell a lie to a man, but one may to a woman; that one must never cheat anyone, but one may a husband; that one must never pardon an insult, but one may give one, and so on. These principles were possibly not reasonable and not good, but they were of unfailing certainty, and so long as he adhered to them, Vronsky felt that his heart was at peace and he could hold his head up." (361) Here, too, we encounter a refusal to think about uncomfortable matters. Here, too, as in the passage about religion, it is not just one character who is on trial but a civilization; and while the reader is encouraged to pass judgment, he is surely expected to realize that his judgment will apply pre-eminently to himself.

Such passages are not reducible, in Trilling's words, to "this moment, or this, or this." The motifs of deception of oneself and others are absolutely central in *Anna Karenina*. Exoterically, the topic is unfaithfulness, but the really fundamental theme is bad faith.

Exoterically, the novel presents a story of two marriages, one good and one bad, but what makes it such a great novel is that the author is far above any simplistic black and white, good and bad, and really deals with the ubiquity of dishonesty and inauthenticity, and with the Promethean, the Faustian, or, to be precise, the Tolstoyan struggle against them.

Exoterically, the novel contains everything: a wedding, a near death, a real death, a birth, a hunt, a horse race, legitimate and illegitimate love, and legitimate and illegitimate lack of love. Unlike lesser writers, who deal with avowedly very interesting characters but ask us in effect to take their word for it that these men are very interesting, Tolstoy immerses us compellingly in the professional experiences and interests of his characters. The sketch of Karenina working in his study, for example (Part III, Chapter XIV), is no mere virtuoso piece. It *is* a cadenza in which the author's irony is carried to dazzling heights, but it is also an acid study of inauthenticity.

When Tolstoy speaks of death—"I had forgotten—death" (413; cf. 444)—and, later, gives a detailed account of the death of Levin's brother (571-93), this is not something to which one may refer as "this moment, or this, or this," nor merely a remarkable anticipation of *The Death of Ivan Ilyitch:* it is another essential element in Tolstoy's attack on inauthenticity. What in *Anna Karenina,* a novel of about one thousand pages, is one crucial element, becomes in *The Death of Ivan Ilyitch* the device for focusing the author's central message in a short story. And confronted with this briefer treatment of the same themes, no reader is likely to miss the point and to respond with "happiness."

All the passages cited so far from *Anna Karenina* come from the first half of the book, and they could easily be multiplied without going any further. Or, turning to Part V, one could point to the many references to dread and boredom, which, in the twentieth century, are widely associated with existentialism, and which become more and more important as the novel progresses. Or one could trace overt references to self-deception through the rest of the book: "continually deceived himself with the theory . . ." (562); "this self-deception" (587); "deceived him and themselves and each other" (590); and so forth. Or one could enumerate other anticipations of existentialism, like the following brief statement which summarizes pages and pages of Jaspers on extreme situations (*Grenzsituationen*): "that grief and this joy were alike outside all the ordinary conditions of life; they were loopholes, as it were, in that ordinary life through which there came glimpses of something sublime. And in the contemplation of this sublime something the soul was exalted to inconceivable heights of which it had before had no conception, while reason lagged behind, unable to keep up with it." (831 f.) Instead, let us turn to the end of the novel.

"Now for the first time Anna turned that glaring light in which she was seeing everything on to her relations with him, which she had hitherto avoided thinking about." (887) Thus begins her final, desperate struggle for honesty. On her way to her death she thinks "that we are all created to be miserable, and that we all know it, and all invent means of deceiving each other." (892) Yet Tolstoy's irony is relentless—much more savage, cruel, and hurtful than that of Shaw, who deals with ideas or types rather than with individual human beings. Tolstoy has often been compared with Homer—by Trilling among many others—but Homer's heroes are granted a moment of truth as they die; they even see into the future. Not Anna, though numerous critics have accused the author of loving her too much—so much that it allegedly destroys the balance of the novel. Does he really love her at all? What she sees "distinctly in the piercing light" (888) is wrong; she deceives herself until the very end and, instead of recognizing the conscience that hounds her, projects attitudes into Vronsky that in fact he does not have. Like most readers, she does not understand what drives her to death, and at the very last moment, when it is too late, "she tried to get up, to drop backwards; but something huge and merciless struck her on the head and rolled her on her back."

Did Tolstoy love her as much as Shakespeare loved Cleopatra, when he lavished all the majesty and beauty he commanded on her suicide? Anna's death quite pointedly lacks the dignity with which Shakespeare allows even Macbeth to die. She is a posthumous sister of Goethe's Gretchen, squashed by the way of some Faust or Levin, a Goethe or a Tolstoy. Her death, like Gretchen's, is infinitely pathetic; in spite of her transgression she was clearly better than the society that condemned her; but what matters ultimately is neither Gretchen nor Anna but that in a world in which such cruelty abounds Faust and Levin should persist in their "darkling aspiration."

Their aspirations, however, are different. Faust's has little to do with society or honesty; his concern is pre-eminently with self-realization. Any social criticism implicit in the Gretchen tragedy is incidental. Tolstoy, on the other hand, was quite determined to attack society and bad faith, and when he found that people missed the point in *Anna Karenina* he resorted to other means. But there are passages in *Anna Karenina* that yield to nothing he wrote later, even in explicitness.

Here is a passage that comes after Anna's death. It deals with Levin. "She knew what worried her husband. It was his unbelief. Although, if she had been asked whether she supposed that in the future life, if he did not believe, he would be damned, she would have had to admit that he would be damned, his unbelief did not cause her unhappiness. And she, confessing that for an unbeliever there can be no salvation, and loving her husband's soul more than anything in the world, thought with a smile of his unbelief, and told herself that he was absurd." (912)

Tolstoy's interest in indicting bad faith does not abate with Anna's death: it is extended to Kitty's religion and to Russian patriotism. But in the end Levin's unbelief is modified without any abandonment of the quest for honesty. "He briefly went through, mentally, the whole course of his ideas during the last two years, the beginning of which was the clear confronting of death at the sight of his dear brother hopelessly ill." (926) And then his outlook is changed, but not, as some critics have said, into "the effacing of the intellect in a cloud of happy mysticism" (*Encyclopaedia*

Britannica, 11th ed.); far from it. The religious position intimated here is articulated with full force in the works reprinted in the present volume. Neither here nor there can I find any "effacing of the intellect" nor even what Trilling, at the end of his essay, calls "the energy of animal intelligence that marks Tolstoi as a novelist." What awes me is perhaps the highest, most comprehensive, and most penetrating human intelligence to be found in any great creative writer anywhere.

These remarks about *Anna Karenina* should suffice to relate *The Death of Ivan Ilyitch, How Much Land Does A Man Need?, My Religion*, and Tolstoy's reply to his excommunication, to his previous work. They show that he was not a great writer who suddenly abandoned art for tracts, and they may furnish what little explanation the writings reprinted here require. The world has been exceedingly kind to the author of *War and Peace*, but it has not taken kindly to the later Tolstoy. The attitude of most readers and critics to Tolstoy's later prose is well summarized by some of our quotations from *Anna Karenina*: "He did not want to see, and did not see. . . . He did not want to understand, and did not understand. . . . He did not allow himself to think about it, and he did not think about it. . . ."

What is true of most readers is not true of all. The exceptions include, above all, Mahatma Gandhi, whose gospel of nonviolence was flatly opposed to the most sacred traditions of his own religion. The Bhagavadgita, often called the New Testament of India, consists of Krishna's admonition of Aryuna, who wants to forswear war when his army is ready for battle; and Krishna, a god incarnate, insists that Aryuna should join the battle, and that every man should do his duty, with his mind on Krishna and the transitoriness of all the things of the world and not on the consequences of his actions. The soldier should soldier, realizing that, ultimately, this world is illusory and he who thinks he slays does not really slay. It would be a gross understatement to say that Gandhi owed more to Tolstoy than he did to Hinduism.

Among philosophers, Ludwig Wittgenstein, whose influence on British and American philosophy after World War II far exceeded that of any other thinker, had the profoundest admiration for Tolstoy; and when he inherited his father's fortune, he gave it away to live simply and austerely. But his philosophy and his academic influence do not reflect Tolstoy's impact.

Martin Heidegger, on the other hand, owes much of his influence to what he has done with Tolstoy. The central section of his main work, *Being and Time*, deals at length with death. It contains a footnote (original ed., 1927, p. 254): "L. N. Tolstoy, in his story, *The Death of Ivan Ilyitch*, has presented the phenomenon of the shattering and the collapse of this 'one dies.' " "One dies" refers to the attitude of those who admit that one dies, but who do not seriously confront the fact that they themselves will die.

In the chapter on "Death" in my *The Faith of a Heretic* I have tried to show in some detail how "Heidegger on death is for the most part an unacknowledged commentary on *The Death of Ivan Ilyitch*"; also how Tolstoy's story is far superior to Heidegger's commentary. And one of the mottos of my book comes from Tolstoy's *Reply to the Synod's Edict of Excommunication.*

This *Reply* is relevant to the misleading suggestion that *Anna Karenina* is a Christian tragedy. First of all, *Anna Karenina* is not a tragedy. Not only is it a novel in *form;* it is essentially not a tragedy that ends in a catastrophe but an epic story that continues fittingly after Anna's death to end with Levin's achievement of more insight. Secondly, it is rather odd to hold up as an example of what is possible within Christianity a man formally excommunicated, a writer whose views have not been accepted by any Christian denomination—a heretic.

Tolstoy drew his inspiration in large measure from the Gospels. His intelligence and sensitivity were of the highest order. And whether we classify him as a Christian or a heretic, his late writings remain to challenge every reader who is honestly concerned with the New Testament or, generally, with religion. We shall return to Tolstoy again and again in the following pages. Other writers one can take or leave, read and forget. To ignore Tolstoy means impoverishing one's own mind; and to read and forget him is hardly possible.

DOSTOEVSKY

Asked to name the two greatest novelists of all time, most writers would probably choose Tolstoy and Dostoevsky. They were contemporaries, Russian to the core, at home in English, French, and German literature, and deeply concerned with Christianity. But their interpretations of Christianity were as different as their temperaments and their artistic techniques.

Tolstoy thought the Christian message involved a radical criticism of society, and his conception of the gospel was social. Dostoevsky's novels, on the other hand, urge the individual to repent of his sins; to accept social injustice because, no matter how harshly we may be treated, in view of our sinfulness and guilt we deserve no better; and not to pin our faith on social reforms. This message is particularly central in his last and greatest novel, *The Brothers Karamazov.* Mitya, the victim of a miscarriage of justice, accepts his sentence willingly as a welcome penance. And his brother Ivan, though also legally innocent, considers himself no less guilty than the murderer.

Unlike *Anna Karenina* and *Resurrection* and most great novels, *The Brothers Karamazov* contains a sequence of two chapters which, though an integral part of the work, can also be read separately without doing an injustice either to this fragment or to the novel: the conversation between Ivan and Alyosha in which Ivan tells his story of the Grand Inquisitor. These chapters help to characterize the two brothers, and the views of the Grand Inquisitor are emphatically not the views of Dostoevsky: on the contrary, what is intended is an indictment of the Roman Catholic church—and probably also of such men as Jefferson and Mill and of the ideal of the pursuit of happiness.

When "The Grand Inquisitor" is read out of context, the immediately preceding chapter is generally ignored; but the story is more likely to be understood as it was meant to be by the author, if one includes the conversation that leads up to it. Moreover, Ivan's vivid sketches of the sufferings of children deserve attention in their own right, and they help to place Royce's attempt to solve the problem of suffering, reproduced later in this volume, in perspective. Oscar Wilde, too, will be found to develop some of the themes introduced here.

What makes the story of the Grand Inquisitor one of the greatest pieces of world literature is, first of all, that outside the Bible it would be hard to find another story of equal brevity that says so much so forcefully. Moreover, the story challenges some of the most confident convictions of Western Christians.

Reading the story merely as a diatribe against the Roman Catholic church and supposing that it stands or falls with its applicability to one religion is almost as foolish as supposing that the Inquisitor speaks the author's mind. What is presented to us, backed up by powerful though not conclusive arguments, is one of the most important theories of all time, for which it would be good to have a name. I shall call it *benevolent totalitarianism.*

By totalitarianism I mean a theory which holds that the government may regulate the lives of the citizens in their totality. Whether this is feasible at the moment is not essential. For political reasons or owing to technological backwardness, a totalitarian government may not actually regulate the citizens' lives in their totality: what matters is whether the government believes that it has the right to do this whenever it seems feasible.

In this sense, the governments of Hitler and Stalin were totalitarian; and their conduct explains, but does not justify, the popular assumption that totalitarianism is necessarily malignant. Ivan Karamazov submits that a man might honestly believe that, in the hands of wise rulers, totalitarianism would make men happier than any other form of government. The point is of crucial importance: what is at stake is the dogmatic and naïve self-righteousness of Western statesmen who simply take for granted their own good faith, benevolence, and virtue and the lack of all these qualities in statesmen from totalitarian countries.

Dostoevsky's point is not altogether new: the first book on political philosophy, written more than two thousand years ago—Plato's *Republic*—presents a lengthy defense of benevolent totalitarianism. Some writers balk at calling it totalitarianism, mainly because they associate the word with malignancy. Others, seeing clearly that the doctrine of the *Republic* is totalitarian, have charged Plato with malignancy. A reading of Dostoevsky's tale shows us at a glance where both camps have gone wrong.

Plato, moreover, develops his arguments over roughly three hundred pages, introducing a great wealth of other material, while the Grand Inquisitor takes less than twenty. This chapter, then, is one of the most important documents of social philosophy ever penned, and any partisan of civil liberties might well say, as John Stuart Mill did in his essay *On Liberty:* "If there are any persons who contest a received opinion, . . . let us thank them for it, open our minds to listen to them, and rejoice that there is some one to do for us what we otherwise ought, if we have any regard for either the certainty or the vitality of our convictions, to do with much greater labor for ourselves."

Still, it may not be at all clear how the tale, if it is aimed at the Vatican, could also be aimed at Mill and Jefferson; and how, if it does not stand or fall with its applicability to Catholicism, it is important for religion. Both points depend on Dostoevsky's repudiation of the pursuit of happiness.

The ideal of the greatest possible happiness for the greatest possible number—which, though this formulation is British, is nothing less than the American dream—seemed to Dostoevsky to justify benevolent totalitarianism. He thought we had to choose between Christ and this world, between freedom and happiness.

Dostoevsky might have echoed Luther's words: "Even if the government does injustice . . . yet God would have it obeyed. . . . We are to regard that which St. Peter bids us regard, namely, that its power, whether it do right or wrong, cannot harm the soul. . . . To suffer wrong destroys no one's soul, nay, it improves the soul."[1] Or this quotation, also from Luther: "There is to be no bondage because Christ has freed us all? What is all this? This would make Christian freedom fleshly! . . . Read St. Paul and see what he teaches about bondsmen. . . . A bondsman can be a Christian and have Christian freedom, even as a prisoner and a sick man can be Christians, even though they are not free. This claim aims to make all men equal and to make a worldly, external kingdom of the spiritual kingdom of Christ. And this is impossible. For a worldly kingdom cannot exist unless there is inequality among men, so that some are free and others captive."[2]

In his politics, Dostoevsky, like Luther, was a radical authoritarian

---

[1] *Treatise on Good Works* (1520), in *Werke*, Weimar ed., VI, 259; *Works*, Philadelphia ed., I, 263.

[2] Cited in Troeltsch, *Die Soziallehren der christlichen Kirchen und Gruppen* (1912), 581, note 282.

and an opponent of social reforms. His Christianity is concerned with the individual soul and its salvation; it is metaphysical, brooding, and preoccupied with guilt; it is otherworldly and content to give unto Caesar what is Caesar's. While Tolstoy wants to prepare the kingdom of God on earth, Dostoevsky seeks the kingdom only in the hearts of men. The tale of the Grand Inquisitor is meant as an indictment of all who "would make Christian freedom fleshly."

Tolstoy staked his message on his reading of the New Testament, and his interpretations and assumptions are answered to some extent by various later writers in this volume, especially Enslin and Schweitzer. Dostoevsky's bland assumption, on the other hand, that the pursuit of happiness must lead to totalitarianism, and that his Inquisitor is the nemesis of democracy, is not criticized by any of the other writers in this book and should therefore be questioned briefly at this point.

If democracy meant majority rule pure and simple, it would be compatible with totalitarianism. For democracy so understood, the men who framed the American Constitution held no brief, any more than Mill did. They were afraid of the possible tyranny of majorities and, to guard against that, devised an intricate system of checks and balances, a Constitution, and, amending that, a Bill of Rights. The whole point of the Bill of Rights is that the government may not regulate the lives of the citizens in their totality—not even if the majority should favor this. It might be objected that the Bill of Rights could be repealed. But that could be done only if the overwhelming majority of the people, and not those in one part of the country only, should insist on it over a long period of time; and in that case, of course, no framer of a constitution could prevent a revolutionary change. Any change of that sort, however, was made as difficult as possible.

What is incompatible with totalitarianism is not majority rule but belief in the overruling importance of civil liberties or human rights. You can have majority rule without civil liberties. Indeed, no country with effective guarantees of free speech and a free press is ever likely to accord its government the kind of majority endorsement which is characteristic of countries without free speech and a free press, from Hitler's Germany to Nasser's Egypt, with their 99 per cent votes for the Leader. But it may well be the case that, conversely, you cannot long protect the people's civil liberties without introducing checks and balances including popular participation.

With this in mind, two answers could be given to Dostoevsky's tale. First, human nature may be different from the Inquisitor's conception of it. Three quarters of a century after the story first appeared, the people in West Germany were happier than those in East Germany. Freedom and happiness are compatible, and loss of liberty is likely to entail a great deal of unhappiness. Suffice it here to say that this is arguable—and that there has been a disturbing lack of argument. On the whole, democrats have considered this answer to the Inquisitor to be self-evident. Reading the tale again may convince at least some readers that it is not, and that much might be gained, even internationally, by developing this answer carefully instead of merely reiterating it dogmatically.

Second, one might answer, at least partly in Dostoevsky's spirit: If a choice had to be made between freedom and happiness, we should choose freedom. But precisely for that reason I cannot agree with Dostoevsky's and Luther's authoritarian politics. I believe that freedom and happiness are compatible, but I should not base the case for freedom on this point. If a vicar of Christ or a secular Caesar or a drug discoverer found a way to give men happiness conjoined with imbecility and slavery, I should hold out for liberty.

Instead of saying that such an attitude "would make Christian freedom fleshly," one might argue that in the New Testament Jewish freedom is made otherworldly; and it is noteworthy that both Luther and Calvin associated any attempt to realize freedom in *this* world with Moses and Judaism. For quotations and discussion, see *The Faith of a Heretic*.

PIUS IX AND LEO XIII

At just about the time when Dostoevsky penned Ivan Karamazov's great attack on the Catholic church—the complete novel appeared in 1880—Pope Leo XIII issued one of the most important encyclicals of modern times, *Aeterni Patris* (1879). A revival of interest in St. Thomas Aquinas was under way even then, here and there, and the Pope decided to put the full weight of his enormous authority behind it. St. Thomas, incidentally, had supported the Inquisition with arguments, but emphatically not with the reasons of Ivan Karamazov's Grand Inquisitor; rather, to save souls from perdition.

Leo XIII became pope in 1878, and this encyclical was one of his first. It has to be understood against the background of some of the momentous proclamations made during the papacy of his predecessor; and Ivan's attack, too, may be understood more fully in this perspective.

When Giovanni Maria Mastai-Ferretti became pope in 1846 and assumed the name of Pius IX, his temporal dominion reached from Terracina, roughly halfway from Rome to Naples, in the south, to the banks of the Po river in the north. He was the ruler not only of Rome but also of Ferrara and Bologna, Urbino and Rimini, Spoleto and Civitavecchia, to name only a few of the towns in this area. When he died in 1878, his temporal power was gone, and the lands over which he ruled had become part of the new kingdom of Italy, very much against his will. But even as he lost Rome, in 1870, the Vatican Council, which he had convened—the first church council since the Council of Trent in the sixteenth century—proclaimed the pope's infallibility.

It is widely agreed that Mastai-Ferretti was a liberal when elected pope. At that time, Venetia and Lombardy were part of the Austrian empire, Tuscany was governed by a Hapsburg, the kingdom of Naples, comprising all of Italy south of the pope's state, was all but an Austrian protectorate, and Metternich, Austria's great arch-conservative statesman, used to guiding the temporal policies of the papacy, was appalled at the accession of a liberal. But the new Pope's outlook changed quickly. In March 1848, there were popular uprisings in Milan, Venice, and Rome; and Austria's troops were expelled from the first two cities. A provisional government was set up. The king of Sardinia marched into Lombardy and was hailed as the liberator of Italy. On April 8, the Sardinian army defeated the Austrians at Toito. On April 29, the Pope proclaimed his neutrality. On the following day the Sardinians won another battle, at Pastrengo. Then the tide turned: the Austrians triumphed at Vincenza and Custozza, an armistice was signed August 9, and Lombardy and Venetia were restored to Austria. Italian resentment against the Pope, however, mounted; Count de Rossi, who was trying to develop a moderately liberal policy for the Pope's government, was assassinated; a radically democratic ministry was forced on the Pope; his Swiss guard was disbanded; and his protection was entrusted to the civil militia. Disguised as an ordinary priest, the Pope fled to Gaeta, in the kingdom of Naples, in November, and appealed from there for foreign intervention. The French sent troops into Italy. At first, they were defeated by Garibaldi; but in July 1849 the French were able to announce the restoration of the pontifical dominion, and in 1850 the Pope returned to Rome, no longer a liberal. The idea of Italian unity, of course, was far from dead; the fight continued; in 1860 the Pope was deprived of most of his state, and in 1870 he lost the rest. Yet this loss of territory and temporal power was not accompanied by any corresponding loss of spiritual power and influence; and this was largely due to Pius IX, who plucked victory from defeat, vastly increasing the prestige of the papacy.

This increase is not adequately reflected in the concordats negotiated by Pius IX. One concluded with Spain in 1851 proclaimed Roman Catholicism the sole religion of the Spanish people, to the exclusion of every other creed; another, signed with Ecuador in 1862, was similar; a third, with Austria, signed in 1855, abolished all kinds of previous reforms and entrusted the supervision of schools and the censorship of literature to the Catholic clergy; and concordats were also concluded with various German states. But some of these agreements were soon revoked by the countries concerned.

The permanent importance of Pius IX is tied to his proclamation of the dogma of the immaculate conception of the Virgin Mary (1854), to the

Syllabus of Errors (1864), and to the doctrine of the pope's infallibility "when he speaks *ex cathedra*," defining "a doctrine regarding faith or morals to be held by the universal Church" (1870). These documents are offered here, along with the encyclical *Aeterni Patris*, issued by Leo XIII.

Many Catholic scholars have taken pains to point out that papal encyclicals are not necessarily infallible. Neither are they just ordinary human pronouncements. Father Thomas Pegués explained the matter in an article in *Revue Thomiste* (1904) which is quoted by Anne Fremantle in her edition of *The Papal Encyclicals in Their Historical Context* (1956): " 'The authority of the encyclicals is not at all the same as that of the solemn definitions *ex cathedra*. These demand an assent without reservations and make a formal act of faith obligatory.' He insists, however, that the authority of the encyclicals is undoubtedly great: 'It is, in a sense, sovereign. It is the teaching of the supreme pastor and teacher of the Church. Hence the faithful have a strict obligation to receive this teaching with infinite respect. A man must not be content simply to not contradict it openly . . . an internal mental assent is demanded." In sum, while a formal act of faith is not obligatory, an internal mental assent is demanded.

Etienne Gilson, widely considered the leading Thomist scholar of the twentieth century, tells us "How to Read the Encyclicals" (in *The Church Speaks to the Modern World: The Social Teachings of Leo XIII*): "When a Pope writes such a document . . . he knows very well that each and every sentence, word, noun, epithet, verb, and adverb found in his written text is going to be weighed, searched, and submitted to the most careful scrutiny by a crowd of countless readers scattered over the surface of the earth. And not only this, but the same anxious study of his pronouncements will be carried on by still many more readers, including his own successors, for generation after generation. This thought should be to us an invitation to approach these texts in a spirit of reverence and of intellectual modesty. . . . When it seems to us that an encyclical cannot possibly say what it says, the first thing to do is to make a new effort to understand exactly what it does actually say. Most of the time it will then be seen that we had missed . . . [something crucial]. . . . When one of us objects to the pretention [sic] avowed by the Popes to state, with full authority, what is true and what is false, or what is right and what is wrong, he is pitting his own personal judgment, not against the personal judgment of another man, but against the whole ordinary teaching of the Catholic Church as well as against her entire tradition. . . . The Church alone represents the point of view of a moral and spiritual authority free from all prejudices."

Not only most non-Catholics but also millions of Catholics think of papal pronouncements and of the positions of the church as more monolithic and far simpler than they generally turn out to be on close examination. In the encyclical *Aeterni Patris*, reprinted here, the reader should not overlook that the Pope qualifies his call "to restore the golden wisdom of St. Thomas" by explaining: "We say the wisdom of St. Thomas; for it is not by any means in our mind to set before this age, as a standard, those things which may have been inquired into by Scholastic Doctors with too great subtlety; or anything taught by them with too little consideration, not agreeing with the investigations of a later age; or, lastly, anything that is not probable."

The pervasiveness of this difficulty, that texts do not necessarily mean what they seem to say at first glance, is well illustrated by an issue that engendered controversy in the twentieth century. "All the principal beliefs of Catholicism are summed up in the Profession of Faith which is made by converts on their entrance into the Catholic Church and by all candidates for the priesthood before ordination. It is a fitting conclusion for this book," says John Walsh, S.J., before reprinting it at the end of *This is Catholicism* (1959). The profession comprises less than three whole pages, but is very compact and rich in content, as the following sentence may show: "I hold unswervingly that purgatory exists and that the souls there detained are aided by the intercessory prayers of the faithful; also that the saints who reign with Christ are to be venerated and invoked; that they offer prayers to God for us; and that their relics are to be venerated." The final paragraph begins: "This true Catholic faith, outside of which no one can be saved. . . ." A little earlier in the book, on page 359, we are similarly assured that "membership in the Catholic Church, the mystical body of Christ, is the solitary means of salvation. Apart from the Church, exclusive of it, independently of it, there exists absolutely no possibility of attaining heaven." But immediately after these seemingly unequivocal assurances, the question is raised, "Does this signify that all who are not actually members of the Catholic Church will be lost?" and the answer is: "Certainly not."

The difficulty is promptly explained: "One does not contradict the other. When a person . . . makes an act of perfect contrition, he must simultaneously determine, as we saw, to accomplish everything which he judges necessary to attain salvation. Now since the Catholic Church is, in fact, the sole means of salvation, a non-Catholic's resolve to do everything needful to gain heaven is, objectively considered, exactly equivalent to a resolve to belong to the Catholic Church. The two resolves automatically merge; one coincides with the other. A non-Catholic is unaware, certainly, of the identity of the two. . . . He may never have heard of the Catholic Church. Or he may . . . be quite indifferent to it. Or . . . he may be quite hostile to it and consequently would indignantly deny that his desire to please God coalesced in any way, shape, or fashion with a desire to join Catholicism. Such subjective misapprehensions on his part would not alter the objective fact, however. A sincere desire for salvation coincides necessarily with a desire to belong to the Catholic Church. . . . Strange as it may seem, therefore, a non-Catholic who sincerely yearns to do everything necessary for salvation (even when he believes that one of the requisites for salvation is to condemn Catholicism!) (Jn. 16:2) is, all unconsciously, longing to be a Catholic. Now this unconscious longing God recognizes as a substitute for belonging . . . as the equivalent of real membership. . . . The answer . . . , then, still stands: outside the Catholic Church there is no salvation."

It is not only the *Imprimatur* at the beginning of Walsh's book that assures us that this is not contrary to the doctrines of the church. When Leonard Feeney, S.J., insisted that there was literally no salvation outside the church, and that only Catholics could be saved, and he persisted, Archbishop Cushing of Boston suspended him from the priesthood in April 1949, and the Jesuits expelled him in October 1949. And when he did not follow a summons to the Vatican, he was excommunicated in February 1953.

By assembling excerpts from official pronouncements, one is quite apt to mislead the reader seriously. Even when we read entire encyclicals, we have to keep in mind that they must be studied with uncommon care, and that they have given rise to a large exegetic literature. Nor do the commentators always agree.

These cautions apply also to the Syllabus of Errors, issued in 1864. Details of interpretation may be arguable, but the documents offered here indicate at the very least the direction in which Pius IX and Leo XIII sought to influence the church of their time, and it is doubtful whether any later pope has equaled their influence.

Critics of the Roman Catholic church have called these documents symptoms of reaction. In the literal, nonpejorative sense, they certainly represent a reaction to much that is modern and the emphatic advice to ponder the attainments of a former age. But if this is called reaction, Protestant theology in the twentieth century has also been marked by reaction. If, on the other hand, the Protestant theologians are called neo-orthodox, it might be fairer to say that the Roman Catholic church spearheaded neo-orthodoxy.

There are in the twentieth century many Catholic theologians who emphatically do not consider themselves Thomists. There is a good deal of discussion, and not all of it is concerned with matters of exegesis, though most of it is. But the kind of radical re-examination of century-old traditions for which Tolstoy called has been altogether ruled out.

NIETZSCHE

With Friedrich Nietzsche we suddenly encounter an altogether different atmosphere: instead of criticizing Christendom, he attacks Christianity itself; and he does this with less inhibitions and greater passion than any major writer before him. For all that, his *Antichrist*, written in 1888 and first published in 1895, shows the influence of both Tolstoy and Dostoevsky.

Not only the *content* of the following remark (§29) but also the image of the key recalls Tolstoy's *My Religion:* " 'resist not evil'—the most profound word of the Gospels, their key in a certain sense." But this saying is not interpreted as Tolstoy interpreted it, as a social programme. On the contrary, Nietzsche's conception of Jesus is derived from Dostoevsky, of whom Nietzsche said in his *Twilight of the Idols,* completed just before *The Antichrist,* that he was "the only psychologist, by the way, from whom I have learned something." (§45) Nietzsche pictured Jesus in the image of Dostoevsky's Prince Myshkin, the hero of *The Idiot*—one of the most lovable and saintly characters of world literature, albeit deeply pathological.

Nietzsche's critique of Christianity is so detailed and complex that no brief selection can give any adequate idea of it; but one cannot for that reason omit him altogether. For he strikes a new and epoch-making note.

A detailed analysis of "Nietzsche's Repudiation of Christ" will be found in Chapter 12 of my *Nietzsche: Philosopher, Psychologist, Antichrist.* My own views of Jesus and Paul, which differ sharply from Nietzsche's, are developed in Chapter 8 of *The Faith of a Heretic.* Here it may suffice to remark that Nietzsche's conception of Jesus seems to me highly implausible, but that I should say as much of most reconstructions of Jesus' character. At least, Nietzsche's is more thought-provoking than most. But if I had to pick a single section from *The Antichrist* to give some idea of Nietzsche's importance as a critic of Christianity, I should select section 45, the last one of those reprinted here. No thoughtful reader will accept all of the points Nietzsche makes, any more than most readers will accept all of Tolstoy's and Dostoevsky's points; but here Nietzsche raises questions which are raised all too rarely.

JAMES AND *CLIFFORD*

With the possible exception of John Dewey, no American philospher is better known than William James. Many people who are interested in religion are uneasy about Dewey, who was clearly a humanist, while they like James. Unlike Dewey, he is even forgiven his pragmatism; and his *Principles of Psychology* (2 vols., 1890) and his *Varieties of Religious Experience* (1902) are often praised extravagantly. That he was a fine human being, there seems to be no doubt; but whether he was a great thinker is another question, and most philosophers would probably agree that he fell short of being first-rate.

Of his essays on religion, none has attracted more attention and discussion than "The Will to Believe." It represents an attempt to defend against the inroads of agnosticism what James later wished he might have called "the right to believe." He himself did not happen to believe in the God of Christianity but rather, as he explained in *A Pluralistic Universe*

(1909), in a "finite god"—a force for good that lacks omnipotence, omniscience, and perfection.

In the section on "Faith, evidence, and James" (§37) in my *Critique*, I have tried to show by way of a detailed analysis that "James' essay on 'The Will to Believe' is an unwitting compendium of common fallacies and a manual of self-deception." The reason for nevertheless including the essay here is that it raises some of the most interesting problems about religious beliefs, and anyone who cares to give himself an account of the demands of intellectual integrity can hardly do better than to reflect critically on James' argument.

To include the essay only in order to tear it down would not be in keeping with the spirit of this volume. But what is entirely in keeping with that spirit is to include the essay that prompted James' attack: William Kingdon Clifford's article on "The Ethics of Belief." That way, the reader gets two different views of the same problem and is led to ask himself: which, if either, of these men is right—and what do I myself think?

James' essay has often been reprinted; but though he explicitly refers to Clifford's piece, few indeed have read that; and it is not easy to find unless one has ready access to a large library. Here, for once, the two essays are offered together.

ROYCE

Josiah Royce was James' younger colleague in the Harvard Philosophy Department, and it was characteristic of James that he brought Royce to Harvard, knowing that Royce's position differed markedly from his own. Royce was an "Idealist," in the tradition of Hegel; and the butt of many of James' attacks on "Hegel" was really his friend Royce. In fact, Royce was no out-and-out Hegelian, and his interpretations of Hegel are often questionable if not clearly wrong. James criticizing "Hegel" is sometimes closer to the real Hegel than Royce was.

In his time, around the turn of the century, Royce was extremely influential as a member of the dominant school of American philosophy. While Idealism was then no longer in fashion in Germany, it was the philosophy of the age in England and the United States. But before long, a reaction set in, spearheaded by G. E. Moore's paper, "The Refutation of Idealism," published in England in 1903; and by the middle of the twentieth century hardly any English-speaking Idealists were left.

The problem of suffering is one of the most important and interesting issues of religious thought. It is powerfully presented by Ivan Karamazov in our selection from Dostoevsky. Royce's critical survey of unacceptable solutions is certainly impressive. His own attempt at a solution is typical of the manner in which many Idealists sought a holy alliance with Christianity and invites comparison with the procedure of many theologians: instead of openly repudiating Christian theism and embracing pantheism, Royce, when denying that God is separate from this world, assures us that this denial is "the immortal soul of the doctrine of the divine atonement."

Like most people, Royce did not read the Book of Job very carefully; and when he claims that "Job's problem is, upon Job's presuppositions, simply and absolutely insoluble," Royce is surely mistaken. He assumes falsely that God's justice and moral perfection are among Job's presuppositions. In fact, Job emphatically denies both, and the Lord in the end says twice that Job has "spoken of me what is right." My own views of the problem and of Job and Royce may be found in Chapter 6 of *The Faith of a Heretic:* "Suffering and the Bible."

WILDE

Oscar Wilde, famed for his wit and frivolity, lacks the stature of the men whom we encountered at the outset, though he need not fear comparison with James and Royce; but in a book dealing with religion his appearance may seem more surprising. Yet his fairy tales and poems in prose raise the question whether anyone between Tolstoy and Buber has written more memorable religious parables. And the letter reprinted here, protesting against cruelty to children in British prisons, recalls Ivan Karamazov's conversation with his brother Alyosha and may be read appropriately after Royce's "solution" of the problem of suffering—and before we come to Camus.

Most people assume that their own country is superior to all others. Great writers, who know some of the things actually done in their own country, and who are more sensitive than most people, often assume the opposite: Dostoevsky and Wilde are cases in point. In the twentieth century it has become more obvious than ever that conditions that such men considered the shame of their own countries are not exceptional but are the shame of humanity, if not part of the human condition.

The selections here made from Wilde's writings are by no means unrepresentative of his work. There is much that is closer to the material presented here than to his bright comedies; for example, the other fairy tales and poems in prose, another letter on prison reform, *The Picture of Dorian Gray*, *De Profundis*, and Wilde's most famous poem, *The Ballad of Reading Gaol.*

A GENERATION OF SCHOLARS

With one small exception, the selections considered so far belong to the late nineteenth century. In 1901 Leo Tolstoy was formally excommunicated by the Greek Orthodox church, and the first Nobel Prize for literature was given to René F. A. Sully Prudhomme. During the following years, while Tolstoy was still alive, the prize went to such men as Björnson, Mistral, Sienkiewicz, Carducci, Kipling, and Eucken. Dostoevsky, who had died earlier, did not come into his own until after World War I. James and Royce were soon eclipsed by newer philosophic schools; and while Nietzsche's ideas were widely discussed, no other philosopher at the beginning of the new century followed in his footsteps. A gap developed between careful academicians who avoided big questions and more popular but philosophically unimportant writers of inspirational literature, like Eucken.

All this does not mean that nothing of importance was written about religion during the first quarter of the twentieth century. Far from it. But the major contributions of this period were made by scholars who did not write short pieces that could be included here. In 1912, for example, Gilbert Murray, Regius Professor of Greek at Oxford, published *Four Stages of Greek Religion* (the insertion of another chapter in the second edition, in 1925, made it *Five Stages*), and Ernst Troeltsch in Germany published his monumental study of *The Social Teachings of the Christian Churches*. Both works were of great significance. Troeltsch showed in an enormous tome (two volumes in the English translation) that one could not properly speak of the social message of Christianity, or of the lack of any such message, but only of the social teachings, in the plural, of the Christian churches, again in the plural. Taking up separately the Gospels and the Epistles of the New Testament and proceeding hence historically through the Middle Ages to Luther and to Calvin and to the modern world, Troeltsch gave a painstaking and exciting account of something that turned out to be far more intricate than almost anybody, including Tolstoy, had supposed.

Troeltsch's great work is more widely respected than read, especially in the English-speaking world. In theory, it is generally accepted as a major classic; but its radical conclusions are by no means a commonplace. It is symptomatic that the title of the English version (now also available in paperback, in two Harper Torchbooks) is *The Social Teaching* [singular!] *of the Christian Churches*.

In the Gospels Troeltsch found "unlimited and unconditional individualism" and no thought whatever of "an ideal for mankind [*Menschheitsideal*]." (39) "Any program of social renovation is lacking." (48) In Paul, "the idea of predestination breaks the nerve of the idea of absolute and abstract equality"; in his Epistles Troeltsch saw "the opposite of any idea of equality based on natural law and rationality." (64) "Inequalities . . . are accepted into the basic sociological scheme of the value of personality," and what is advocated is a "type of Christian patriarchalism." (66 f.) That is only the beginning of Troeltsch's long and exceedingly well-informed and careful history. Of course, people still speak of "the message of the New Testament" and even of "the Biblical view" and "the Christian view." But since Troeltsch this is scarcely excusable.

Gilbert Murray seemingly dealt with classical antiquity only. Yet his study of the origins of Greek religion and the belief in the Olympian gods may throw light on the origins of religion and of theism in general. And occasionally he offered some overt comparisons, marked by great restraint in form, but hardly less thought-provoking for that. Speaking of some of the great philosophers and dramatists of the sixth and fifth centuries B.C., for example, Murray comments: "Indeed a metaphysician might hold that their theology is far deeper than that to which we are accustomed, since they seem not to make any particular difference between οἱ θεοί [the gods] and ὁ θεός [god] or τὸ θεῖον [the divine]. They do not instinctively suppose that the human distinctions between 'he' and 'it,' or between 'one' and 'many,' apply to the divine." (Anchor Books ed., 67) One is reminded of the story of the man who reports, in a state of shock, that he has seen God—"and she is black!"

Or consider this remark, on the next page: ". . . the religious thought of later antiquity for the most part took refuge in a sort of apotheosis of good taste, in which the great care was not to hurt other people's feelings. . . ." Even when the comparisons are not made explicitly, the discerning reader can hardly help making them for himself.

Or, another three pages later: "There is, in one sense, far more faith in some hideous miracle-working icon which sends out starving peasants to massacre Jews than in the Athena of Phidias. Yet . . . there is religion in Athena also. Athena is an ideal, an ideal and a mystery; the ideal of wisdom, of incessant labour, of almost terrifying purity, seen through the light of some mystic and spiritual devotion like, but transcending, the love of man for woman."

Toward the end of the chapter entitled "The Failure of Nerve," Murray described how the recrudescence of superstition was accompanied by the rise of theologians who tried to salvage ancient myths by giving allegorical interpretations. And in the final chapter of his little book, he related how the last of the pagans thought that all the great sages had been "trying to say the same ineffable thing; all lifting mankind towards the knowledge of God." Only the Christians and a few Cynics and, of course, the Epicureans "had committed the cardinal sin; they had denied the gods. They are sometimes lumped together as *Atheoi*. . . . The religious emotion itself becomes the thing to live for. . . . Every shrine where men have worshipped in truth of heart is thereby a house of God. The worship may be mixed up with all sorts of folly, all sorts of unedifying practice. Such things must be purged away, or, still better, must be properly understood. For the pure all things are pure; and the myths that shock the vulgar are noble allegories to the wise and reverent." But the Christians would not accept allegorical defenses of ancient myths; they rejected the ancient gods. After World War I, the Christian theologians began to embark on a similar salvage program; symbol became the war cry now, not allegory; and those who would not accept the ancient beliefs even so, were abhorred as atheists.

Besides Troeltsch and Murray, there were large numbers of other classicists and sociologists who made contributions of comparable importance; also, anthropologists who explored little-known religions, historians, hosts of Bible critics, and many, many others. It was a period of great scholarship, and some time passed before significant attempts were made to appraise the implications.

World War I shattered the complacency that had become more and more characteristic of the beginning of the century. Scholars, including theologians, felt a new urgency to relate their work to the big questions of human existence. The "Alexandrianism" which the young Nietzsche had mocked for its remoteness from life gave way to neo-orthodoxy and existentialism. But not only Gilbert Murray wondered whether this development was not essentially parallel to "the failure of nerve" which had followed upon the original Alexandrian age of scholarship.

FREUD

Sigmund Freud's thought had been formed before the war. The book which he considered his masterpiece, *The Interpretation of Dreams*, had appeared in the closing days of the nineteenth century, though the publisher had preferred to put the date of 1900 on the title page. Even if Freud had stopped writing when World War I broke out, his lasting importance would still have been assured. And like Tolstoy's, Dostoevsky's, and Nietzsche's, it is not confined to the realm of religion: like few men in any age, Freud has centrally affected man's thinking about man.

Still, it was the war that led Freud to apply his ideas to contemporary civilization. He himself emphasized often that psychoanalysis does not stand or fall with these applications and admitted that there was something personal about them. He also realized that his late books on religion were not among his best books; and *Moses and Monotheism*, though brilliantly written, may well be his worst book. Even more than his previous writings on religion, it suffers from its reliance on some nineteenth-century anthropology which Freud accepted too uncritically; and it is heartening to learn from Ernest Jones' highly instructive three-volume biography that Freud occasionally referred to his *Moses* as a historical novel.

For all its faults, *The Future of an Illusion* is a book of very great significance; and the heart of it is presented here. In these pages a man of genius deals with an extremely important subject; he attacks not merely Christendom, nor only Christianity, but religion in general; and his treatment has been highly influential.

One may perhaps wonder how applicable some of Freud's remarks are to early Buddhism, and one may note that he is thinking primarily of ancient Greece, Judaism, and Christianity. Moreover, he does not perhaps distinguish sufficiently between the causes that originally brought a belief into being and the motives that prompt those who maintain it centuries, or even thousands of years, later. But again and again Freud says beautifully and clearly what many others, coming later, have said less well at greater length. "Am I to be obliged to believe every absurdity? And if not, why just this one? There is no appeal beyond reason." Or: "Philosophers stretch the meaning of words until they retain scarcely anything of their original sense. . . ." Indeed, that whole paragraph—the penultimate one in our selection—bears pondering.

While I have criticized Freud's views in my *Critique* (§§42 and 96 ff.), and cited his own, extremely humble estimates of his books on religion in my *From Shakespeare to Existentialism* (Anchor Books ed., 327 f.), the pages here reprinted rank with the best written on religion in the twentieth century.

COHEN

Even as Royce's discussion condenses centuries of reflection on the problem of suffering into a few pages, Morris Cohen's "The Dark Side of Religion" offers in unusually compact and forceful form what critics of religion might say and have said. A psychologist of religion, James Leuba, once catalogued and classified forty-eight definitions of religion, distinguishing intellectualistic, affectivistic, and moral or practical definitions, depending on which facet of religion they emphasize especially. Cohen presses his attack on all three fronts.

To give a single example, he does not merely catalogue past clashes between religion and science, but he tries to show how religion instills and develops mental attitudes which are antithetical to those bred by scientific training. Like Nietzsche and Freud before him, he raises questions that most apologists for religion simply refuse to recognize.

ENSLIN

Another form of criticism has probably affected modern thinking about religion at least as much as any novelist, philosopher, historian, or psychologist: Bible criticism. It can be traced back to Jean Astruc, in the eighteenth century, and beyond that to Spinoza, in the seventeenth; but it did not really come into its own and gain wide influence until the latter part of the nineteenth century.

After the Bible had been read for centuries as no other book was read—as God's own revelation which was above criticism—an effort was made at long last to read the Bible critically and scientifically, like other books. Like many an overdue effort, this one, too, overshot its mark in its initial phases; and I have tried to show in detail in my *Critique*, Chapter 10, how the so-called Higher Critics, who tried to assign the verses of the Books of Moses to various supposed sources, actually read the Old Testament more mistrust-fully and destructively than any other classic; how their methods were essentially unscientific and unsound; and how they failed to examine their methods critically. But not all Bible criticism claims to reconstruct the alleged sources from which some ancient editor is then said to have patched together his book with scissors and paste. New Testament criticism has re-mained largely free of this taint, except for the assumption of many critics that material common to Matthew and Luke but not found in Mark, whose Gospel is generally considered earlier and the primary source for the two others, must be assigned to a hypothetical source called "Q" (for *Quelle*, the German word for "source").

Morton Scott Enslin has been president of both the Society for Biblical Literature and Exegesis and the American Theological Society, and his study of the New Testament, written in the nineteen-thirties, is dis-tinguished by a rare sobriety and plausibility, and free of the excesses of the late nineteenth century. He dispenses with "Q" and the hunt for hypothet-ical sources. His results, including his repudiation of the hypothetical "Q," are controversial—like almost everything in this book. But his manner is representative of Bible criticism at its best, and the reader need not doubt that he confronts a scholar of unquestionable integrity. The relevance of his discussion of the Gospels to Tolstoy's *My Religion* is surely obvious.

Aylmer Maude, who knew Tolstoy personally and translated many of his works, relates how Tolstoy himself reacted to Bible criticism in a con-versation: "They are attacking the last of the outworks, and if they carry it, and demonstrate that Christ was never born, it will be all the more evi-dent that the fortress of religion is impregnable. Take away the Church, the traditions, the Bible, and even Christ himself: the ultimate fact of man's knowledge of goodness, *i.e.* of God, directly through reason and con-science, will be as clear and certain as ever, and it will be seen that we are dealing with truths that can never perish—truths that humanity can never afford to part with."[1]

To a work like Tolstoy's *My Religion*, however, Bible criticism is cer-tainly profoundly relevant. The implications of what Tolstoy said in the

[1] Tolstoy, *On Life and Essays on Religion*, translated with an Introduction by Aylmer Maude, Oxford University Press, World's Classics, p. xv.

conversation just cited, on the other hand, lead away from reliance on exegesis and from appeal to Christ. If the appeal to "reason and conscience" is pressed, we are led from religion to philosophy, unless "reason and conscience" is nothing but a euphemism for what seems obvious to the speaker, though very different ideas may seem no less obvious to others.

We have no right to assume that, unless Christ's teachings conformed perfectly to our own personal conscience, "Christ was never born." Bible criticism opens up the disturbing possibility that there may be excellent evidence that Jesus lived—and taught what our reason and our conscience do not happen to approve.

In a short essay on "How to Read the Gospels and What is Essential in Them" Tolstoy insisted that "from what is clear we must form our idea of the drift and spirit of the whole work." We should underline, "say with a blue pencil," all that strikes us as "quite plain, clear, and comprehensible." But what is plain is perhaps what we can easily assent to, while what seems outrageous to us is not "comprehensible." If so, Tolstoy would actually be exhorting us to construe everything in such a manner that it will conform to what we especially like. This is indeed what most interpreters have always done; but this also accounts in large measure for their fateful disagreements, and in some cases for the origins of different denominations.

The modern reader who approaches the Gospels in Tolstoy's fashion is likely to let his image of Jesus be formed in very large measure by two sayings: "Let him who is without sin among you be the first to throw a stone at her" (John 8:7) and "Father, forgive them; for they know not what they do" (Luke 23:34). There may be no better way of bringing out the full significance of Bible criticism than to mention that both of these sayings are missing in most ancient manuscripts—a point duly noted not only by Enslin but also in the Revised Standard Version of the Holy Bible.

NIEMÖLLER, SCHNEIDER, AND *HAY*

Few events have been as important for the history of religion during the last century as Hitler's rise to power in Germany and his conquest of large parts of Europe. But it is exceedingly difficult to evaluate the ways in which religious people responded.

One might say that the general trend exemplified by Nietzsche, Freud, Cohen, and the Bible critics suffered an enormous setback: it was compromised by the Nazis' attack on religion. Confronted with Martin Niemöller's sermons, Enslin's arguments to the effect that the events in Scripture which the preacher cites could not have happened historically, are apt to appear academic: you cannot disprove guts. Neither, however, can a man's courage create even a small presumption that his views are true or even plausible. Scholarship cannot refute courage; neither can courage refute scholarship.

What Niemöller's heroic sermons during the weeks before his arrest by the Gestapo prove is not that neo-orthodoxy is true or that liberalism is false, but only that neo-orthodoxy, like Nazism and Communism, was capable of inspiring martyrdom. His sermons also show by way of contrast how inane most sermons are: here is preaching at its best; every time one reads "The Salt of the Earth," one's skin creeps. The man who speaks here is not a would-be professor or politician, not a public speaker who has previously announced a topical title with wide appeal, but a minister of the word of God who considers nothing more important than to let the Bible speak to us—and who never fails to let long familiar verses speak to us as if we had never heard them before.

In an important sense, religion flourished under Hitler, in spite of Hitler. Measured against the revival of religion during that period, the mid-century revival in the United States seems shallow indeed. One may well ask whether religion does not often gain intensity and depth in times of persecution, while it loses both in ages of prosperity. Certainly, many Old Testament writers thought so.

An intensity that permeates a man's whole being is always impressive; but the question of content remains. And if one pauses to reflect on Niemöller's message, one notes a striking lack of content. Transposed into a different setting where there is no persecution, his challenge evaporates and becomes trivial. Words that chilled the spine lose significance. The call to come to church and to profess allegiance to Christ and the Bible, and to obey the orders of one's church council, regardless of the consequences, is charged with meaning and daring in Berlin in 1937, but scarcely exciting in New York or London or West Berlin a quarter of a century later.

For that matter, Niemöller's message was not the same in 1937 and in 1952. He had been a U-boat commander during World War I; and after his imprisonment in a concentration camp in 1937 it was said widely that, though defiantly unwilling to accept Gestapo censorship of his sermons, he would have been willing to serve again as a submarine commander, if released. Whether these reports were true or not, about 1952 Niemöller became a Christian pacifist. And according to an interview, printed in *The Christian Century*, March 1, 1961, he made the following statements: "Military training is training for a criminal profession." "As a Christian, I cannot take a life." "No man can sacrifice any man other than himself for any higher purpose."

Still, there was no complete discontinuity between the sermons of 1937 and the pacifism of 1961: expediency and any careful reflection on the probable consequences of alternative courses of action had no place in Niemöller's outlook either in the thirties or in the sixties. In the interview he said: "If I follow Christ's way, I don't know what God will make of it.

God's creation defies the inferences of human reason." This is of a piece with the heroism of his great sermon on the salt of the earth.

To evaluate Niemöller's stand in 1937, we should ask ourselves how Tolstoy's or Dostoevsky's messages would have met Hitler's challenge, or how the Catholic Church met it. The fact that the Nazis were opposed to all of them, no less than to psychoanalysis or liberalism, does not prove that all of them were right. After all, Hitler made war on psychoanalysts, liberals, socialists, and Jews long before he openly attacked the churches—at a time, in fact, when few Protestant ministers opposed him and when Pope Pius XI, through his Secretary of State, Cardinal Eugenio Pacelli, who later succeeded him as Pope Pius XII, negotiated a concordat with Hitler which greatly enhanced Hitler's international prestige.

In a book on *The Catholic Church in the Modern World*, which bears the *Imprimatur* of Cardinal Spellman, E. E. Y. Hale says: "Ever since 1920, as nuncio first at Munich [where Hitler first tried to take over the government by force] and then at Berlin, Pacelli had striven to secure a concordat with the Weimar Republic. . . . The new concordat with Hitler's Germany, so rapidly concluded, seemed a happy augury. It secured freedom for the Church in Germany to administer its own affairs, the State retaining the right of veto over episcopal appointments and requiring an oath of loyalty to the Führer. There was to be freedom of communications with Rome, freedom for the religious orders, permission to establish Catholic theological faculties at the universities, and Catholic public primary education. . . . And although the papal Secretary of State [the future Pope Pius XII] already knew only too much about Hitler, he had also to consider that the Catholic vice-chancellor, von Papen, was pressing the negotiations, that Hindenburg was still Head of the State, and that the [Catholic] Centre party had given its support to the new government."

Hardly a Catholic or Protestant took a stand against Hitler until Hitler, in defiance of explicit promises that he had made to them, began to meddle in church affairs. At that point, Pope Pius XI as well as a few prominent Catholics inside Germany and Pastor Niemöller and the members of the Protestant Confessing Church spoke out—against Hitler's interference in their own affairs. The controversial record of the papacy and of the churches in Germany has to be considered in the perspective of the attitudes of Christians and non-Christians outside Germany and the policies of the Western governments.

In his book on *Europe and the Jews*, Malcolm Hay, a Catholic layman and a fine historian, relates something that is relevant to any charge that Christianity failed in the face of Hitler. He shows how the Western governments knew of Hitler's wholesale liquidation of Jews during World War II and actually stood a good chance of stopping it by depositing a relatively small amount of money—less than ten dollars per life—to German accounts in Switzerland, with safeguards that the Germans could not get the money until after the end of the war. But the British Foreign Office thought it would be frightfully inconvenient "if the Germans should offer to dump a million Jews on us"; and the American State Department "suppressed information about atrocities in order to prevent an outraged public opinion from forcing their hands." When the Nazis finally went ahead with their unprecedented mass murder, they had reason "to believe that their own method of dealing with the Jewish problem met with the secret approval of humanity. These fragments of a people, despised and hated everywhere for a thousand years, were not wanted by anyone." (304)

If Christians failed, it may be said, not only Christians failed. But what makes Hay's book one of the most important in the story of religion during the past hundred years is his compelling and persuasive attempt to show that Hitler's mass murders must be charged, to a very large extent, to Christianity—not just to the weaknesses of men who called themselves Christians but to the teachings of the churches and the preaching of some of the greatest saints, popes, and leaders of Protestantism.

When Hitler came to power, liberalism had lost heart and neo-orthodoxy had disengaged Christianity from culture, politics, humanity, and this world. The churches were concerned about their autonomy: the government must not interfere with their witness to Christ and the Bible. It is often supposed that liberalism cannot offer any positive program as an alternative to Communism or Nazism while Christianity, of course, can. But the Protestant churches did not meet Hitler with any program whatever—a point that comes out clearly in Niemöller's stirring sermon on the salt of the earth. The issue became simply one of courage: to bear or not to bear witness; to speak softly and be prudent or to speak loudly and let one's light shine boldly—not for any conceivable purpose, but simply because it was one's duty. When the issue was defined that way, nothing else could be expected than that a mere handful of martyrs would defy the government, without a hope in this world, while the mass of Christians would join with Hitler.

One figure symbolizes the issue even more dramatically than Niemöller: Pastor Paul Schneider. Unlike Niemöller, he is not at all famous; but like Niemöller he deserves to be.[1]

At seventeen, Schneider volunteered in World War I, was wounded and decorated for bravery, and commissioned a second lieutenant in 1918. Although he had previously planned to become a physician, he studied theology after the War; and after taking his first examination in 1922, he worked

---

[1] The following sketch is based on, or quoted from, the final section, "Paul Schneider zum Gedächtnis," of *Deutsche Kirchen-dokumente: Die Haltung der Bekennenden Kirche im Dritten Reich*, dargestellt von W. Jannasch, Evangelischer Verlag A.G., Zollikon-Zürich 1946.

for four months at a blast furnace. Later he worried whether he ought not to have stayed among the laborers. He was ordained in 1925, and took over his father's parish a year later. He married, in 1926, the daughter of a minister. They had six children.

In 1934, a little over a year after Hitler had come to power, Schneider was conducting a church funeral for a boy when someone remarked that the boy had now entered Horst Wessel's troup. Horst Wessel, a storm trooper who had been killed, was considered the Nazi martyr *par excellence*. Schneider immediately proclaimed: "Whether there is a troup of Horst Wessel in eternity, I do not know. But may the Lord God bless your departure from time and your entry into eternity. Now let us go in peace to the house of the Lord and remember the dead before God and His Holy Word." Someone shouted: "Comrade X, you have still been accepted into Horst Wessel's troup!" Schneider announced: "I protest. This is a church function, and I, as an evangelical pastor, am responsible for the pure doctrine of the Holy Scriptures." Consequently, he was imprisoned for five days.

In 1937, Schneider invoked church discipline, in accordance with the Heidelberg Catechism. For a long time, contempt and blasphemy had never occurred and church discipline had been invoked mainly when the church community took offense at the sexual conduct of people. But now "Christian parents kept their children away from church instruction and from children's services, instruction in school opened up a cleft between parish and school, a new kind of Christmas celebration emerged, and pastor and presbytery were mocked. Thus confusion invaded the parish, and intimidation and thoughtless propaganda increased it. Also, signatures were being collected to obtain [a preacher with] a different message for the community. Presbytery and pastor were unanimously determined to fight this destruction of the parish, to issue a warning, and also to invoke church discipline. The address by pastor Schneider to the parish of Womrath before the proclamation of church discipline, and a letter to those concerned show that this ecclesiastic measure of the presbytery was prompted by a sense of responsibility for men's souls; by no means was the intention to 'boycott' the three members of the parish against whom church discipline was invoked. These three members, however, reported the incident, and pastor Schneider was taken into protective custody on May 31, 1937."

In July he was released, on condition that he leave the province. He did not accept this condition and was taken to Wiesbaden, outside the province, to be set free there. The following day, he returned to preach to his parish, but then took a leave to recuperate outside the province, and instead of returning accepted a position with another parish late in August. Toward the end of September, however, his Presbytery sent him back to his old parish "that you may resume your office in God's name." Since he had left, candidates for confirmation had received no further instruction, and the young had not been confronted with Christian doctrine. The sick had not been visited, and the holy communion had been omitted twice. After explaining his decision in detail in letters to the government—including letters to the offices of the Secretary of the Interior and even of Hitler himself—Schneider returned, but was immediately arrested, October 3, 1937. On November 27, he was moved to the concentration camp at Buchenwald, and his wife was allowed one last visit.

A fellow prisoner, who survived the concentration camp, has reported Schneider's behavior during his last two years. "He tried, by means of Christian words, admonitions, requests, and active help to win his fellow prisoners for Christ. . . . It was customary . . . for the prisoners to salute the SS flag by removing their caps whenever they walked past it. This 'show of honor' Schneider refused as idolatry. . . . With this began the passion of pastor Schneider. First, he received twenty-five blows with a stick . . . and was given confinement in the dark. . . . There he professed the Christian faith to the SS, without fear. In such candor he may have had no equal in Germany. He called the devils by name: murderers, adulterers, unjust men, monsters. For this profession, which he constantly contrasted with the grace of Christ, calling for repentance, Schneider was exposed to harsh physical tortures and anxieties. The physical tortures consisted in hard blows, being hanged from the window by his backward-twisted arms . . . denial of food, prevention of sleep . . . surrounded by the screams of anxiety and suffering from nearby cells. Such times of agony alternated with relatively good times, . . . full food rations, a chance for sleep, etc. . . . When two men who had tried to escape were apprehended and murdered, Schneider called out at reveille: 'In the name of Jesus Christ I bear witness of the murder of the prisoners.' Any continuation was stifled with blows. The worst time for Schneider was probably the early summer of 1939 when he always had to remain in a half-crouching position. In the summer of 1939, presumably owing to increasing weakening of the heart, a grape sugar cure was begun with strophantin. During one of the injections, Schneider died of heart failure."

His wife received a telegram: "18 July 1939. Paul Schneider born 8-29-97 died today at 10. Corpse movable at your expense if desired. Reply within 24 hours to funeral office Weimar otherwise cremation. Camp Commander Buchenwald." The widow came in person for the body. A service was held in his old church, and the minister spoke on the verse which Schneider had selected for his confirmation; from John 18:37: "For this I was born, and for this I have come into the world, to bear witness to the truth. Every one who is of the truth hears my voice."

It is scarcely possible to read this story without being moved to the depths. Nothing can detract, however slightly, from the courage of this pastor. Neither can his martyrdom answer the criticisms of Christianity voiced by philosophers, philologists, psychologists, and others.

In the context of Schneider's life, the verse from John chills the blood. But the very next verse reads: "Pilate said to him, 'What is truth?' " And Nietzsche at his most vitriolic wrote in *The Antichrist* (§46): "The noble scorn of a Roman, confronted with an impudent abuse of the word 'truth,' has enriched the New Testament with the only saying *that has value*—one which is its criticism, even its *annihilation:* 'What is truth?'. "

Surely, one *should* respond emotionally to Schneider's fight; but not *only* emotionally. Invoking church discipline in the face of the Nazi dictatorship was an act of heroism. But we have only to picture a different situation, in which the church has the backing of the government and the people, to feel quite differently about the matter. Perhaps parents who do not like the message of a preacher have the right to keep their children away from his instruction and from children's services; perhaps it is questionable whether a new kind of Christmas celebration ought to be suppressed. And when we are told that the pastor and his presbytery were merely "prompted by a sense of responsibility for men's souls," it is well to recall that this was also true of the Salem witch hunters and the inquisitors.

The point transcends Pastor Schneider. When we read in Second Maccabees how a mother and her seven sons allowed themselves to be tortured to death rather than eat pork, we are deeply moved. But if we think of an orthodox Jewish government or rabbinate imposing traditional dietary laws by force or sanctions, that is quite another matter.

To put the point still differently: the Nazis also persecuted Communists; does the heroic martyrdom of individual Communists prove the truth of Communism? Or does the martyrdom of Nazis at Stalin's hands establish the doctrines of Nazism?

If one feels like criticizing the papacy for signing a concordat with Hitler that included a loyalty oath to Hitler on the part of the German Catholic bishops, or if one feels profoundly disappointed that most Protestant and Catholic preachers did not take a strong stand against Hitler until he began to interfere in church affairs, what should one make of the passages in the New Testament that Luther and Calvin liked to quote? Two of Luther's dicta have been discussed in connection with Dostoevsky, above. Here is another: "In the New Testament Moses counts for nothing, but there stands our Master Christ and casts us with body and possessions under the Kaiser's and worldly law when he says, 'Give to Caesar the things that are Caesar's.' "[1] And Calvin insisted that Paul had taught plainly "that spiritual liberty is perfectly compatible with civil servitude"; and he argued that "Those who domineer unjustly and tyrannically are raised up by him to punish the people for their iniquity," and "Even an individual of the worst

[1] *Werke*, Weimar ed., XVIII, 358. Cf., above all, Romans 13:1-2.

character, one most unworthy of all honor, if invested with public authority, receives that illustrious divine power" and must be obeyed and honored even "as the best of kings."[1] Schneider and Niemöller demand our admiration because they drew the line at some point so fearlessly. But did they draw it at the right point?

One way of bringing out forcefully what remains problematic about Niemöller's sermons is to follow them up with the first chapter of Malcolm Hay's book on *Europe and the Jews*. The importance of this work has already been pointed out. It might be said to be at least threefold in the present context.

First, if one finds that Hitler posed a singular challenge for Christians, hardly anyone has demonstrated so well what part of this challenge was. Then, Hay shows how the problem of the Christians' proper attitude toward Jews far antedated Hitler; how it was there from the time of the Gospels; how it has been a perennial issue. Finally, we see how a historian can affect our attitudes and thoughts about religion quite as much as a philosopher, a theologian, or a novelist.

In all three respects, the whole of Hay's book is supremely relevant. Since it is available as a Beacon paperback, it may be hoped that, after reading the first chapter, many will go on to read the entire volume.

BARTH AND BRUNNER

It was Karl Barth who at the end of World War I issued the call for neo-orthodoxy in Protestantism. Reacting against the liberal Protestantism of the preceding hundred years, which had tried to assimilate Christianity to the culture of the time and to the latest results of science and scholarship, Barth counted culture among the things that are Caesar's and associated faith in man, reason, and progress with idolatry. He took seriously the ancient doctrine of original sin and preached that there is no salvation but through Christ. The preacher of God's word should not be anxious about being up-to-date concerning the most recent human achievements; rather he should immerse himself in the word of God, which we possess in the Bible.

Der Römerbrief, Barth's commentary on Paul's Epistle to the Romans, was published in Bern, Switzerland, in 1919, and began: "Paul, as the son of his time, spoke to his contemporaries. But *much* more important than this truth is another: as a prophet and apostle of God's kingdom he speaks to all men of all times. The differences between then and now, there and here, want to be noted. But the point of noting them can only be the realization that these differences have essentially *no* significance. The historical-critical method of studying the Bible is justifiable: it indicates a preparation for understanding, and this is never superfluous. But if I had to choose be-

[1] *Institutes of the Christian Religion*, IV, 20: 1 and 25.

tween this and the old doctrine of inspiration, I should resolutely reach for
the latter: It has a greater, deeper, *more important* right, because it indicates
the work of understanding itself, and without that all preparation is worthless. . . . What was serious once is still serious today; and what is serious
today, and no mere accident or fancy, that is also immediately related to
what was serious once. Our questions are, if only we understand ourselves
right, the questions of Paul, and Paul's answers must be, if their light shines
for us, our answers."

It has become customary to explain Barth's ideas, and it is plausible to
explain his *influence*, in terms of the devastating impact of World War I,
which shook men's faith in reason, progress, and humanity. The world was
ready once again to be told about sin and salvation. It has also become a
commonplace to associate Barth with Kierkegaard. While this makes sense
as far as it goes, another perspective is perhaps equally illuminating: with
Barth, tendencies that had become prominent much earlier in the Greek
Orthodox church and in the Roman Catholic church emerged in Protestantism, too.

Still, there is one crucial difference between Karl Barth and his counter-
parts in other churches: by temperament, Barth is less of an organization
man and more of a gadfly than perhaps any other theologian. Although he
has strong reservations about Luther and occasionally stresses his own Calvinism, his prose has some of the qualities of Luther's; and I have translated
the passage just cited myself, in an attempt to bring out the virility and the
highly individual quality of Barth's style. His theological *magnum opus*
fills bulging tome upon bulging tome, and in sheer bulk invites comparison
with St. Thomas' *Summa Theologica;* but on the side he has published a
steady stream of short pieces, often, like Luther's, in pamphlet form. One
of these bears the wholly characteristic and admirable title: *Nein!* (*No!*)

That particular pamphlet was directed at Emil Brunner, another Swiss
theologian, who is widely associated with Barth—an association that makes
Barth unhappy. Barth has not founded a school, and least of all wants to be
considered a Protestant pope or the spokesman of neo-orthodoxy. More
than perhaps any other theologian, he has the temperament of a prophet as
well as a sense of humor.

To excerpt Barth's commentary on Romans or his huge *Dogmatics*
would hardly be helpful. A chapter from one of his shorter works would
hardly be much better. The exchange of letters with Emil Brunner that is
reprinted here naturally is no summary of two divergent, highly complex
theologies; but it tells us a great deal about both men and sets forth their
attitudes toward Nazism and Communism. It is taken from a collection of
Barth's "Shorter Post-War Writings 1946-52" that bears the fitting title,
Against the Stream. This phrase occurs in Barth's letter to Brunner.

PIUS XII

Karl Barth's divergent stances vis-à-vis Nazism and Communism differ deliberately from those of the Vatican, as he himself notes. The attitude of Pope Pius XII toward the Nazi government has been discussed briefly above, in connection with Niemöller's. After the War, the Pope took a far stronger stand against Communism than he had ever taken against Nazism. In 1946, for example, he excommunicated Marshal Tito, after the trial and conviction of Archbishop Aloysius Stepinac in Yugoslavia; and in 1949 he announced that any Catholic who became a Communist was automatically excommunicated. No such action had been taken against Hitler, Goebbels, and other leading Nazis who were nominal Catholics. Indeed, as noted before, as papal Secretary of State, before he became Pope Pius XII, Cardinal Pacelli had negotiated a concordat with Hitler which required Catholic priests in Germany to swear loyalty to Hitler; and this concordat went far toward making the young Nazi government internationally respectable—if only temporarily.

In 1950, Pope Pius XII defined a new dogma, reprinted here, and issued the encyclical *Humani Generis* which, among other things, proscribes existentialism. Prior to that, Gabriel Marcel had allowed himself to be called an existentialist, and the two foremost neo-Thomists had argued that St. Thomas Aquinas had been truly an existentialist. It may be argued that the point here is more one of strategy and definitions than of doctrine: certainly, Gilson and Maritain had not attributed to St. Thomas the views which the Pope found reprehensible and false in existentialism.

Section 8 of *Humani Generis* presumably refers to Barth and Brunner, and it is noteworthy that the Pope suggests that "their mutual disagreements in matters of doctrine . . . bear unwilling witness to the necessity of a living Magisterium."

MARITAIN

Jacques Maritain, like Etienne Gilson, enjoys international prestige and has won a world-wide audience for the attempt "to restore the golden wisdom of St. Thomas." His very subtle and intricate philosophy cannot be summarized in a few pages; but in a late book, *Approaches to God* (1954), he has undertaken a defense of St. Thomas' "five ways" of proving God's existence, adding a sixth way of his own. Since his sixth way has not won wide acceptance, it might be inappropriate to reproduce it here. But the five ways are still generally accepted by Catholics, though they are generally repudiated by Protestants, Jews, and infidels; and it may be of some interest how perhaps the greatest Catholic philosopher in the middle of the twentieth century defends one of them. Etienne Gilson and another highly competent Catholic historian and philosopher, Frederick Copleston, have defended the five ways, too, and Copleston says that many modern Thomists consider the third proof especially fundamental. Maritain's version of "the third way" is reprinted here. My criticism of the five ways may be found in §45 of my *Critique;* here the point is to offer Maritain's defense.

TILLICH AND BULTMANN

As we have seen, Gilbert Murray noted in his discussion of "The Failure of Nerve" during the decline of classical antiquity, how the ancient theologians tried to salvage their religious traditions: "the myths that shock the vulgar are noble allegories to the wise and reverent." In this manner, all the old beliefs and stories about Zeus and Aphrodite and the other gods could be maintained, and the cult could be justified, if only it was "properly understood."

Few Christians, if any, would quarrel with this description of pagan theology. Is it equally applicable to some modern Christian theologians? That is one of the questions one has to ask oneself when reading Paul Tillich, the most influential practitioner of symbolic interpretation.

Tillich, like Niemöller and Schneider, was born in Germany; but unlike them he was a Christian socialist, and when Hitler came to power, he accepted a professorship at Union Theological Seminary in New York, though at that time he did not yet speak English. His impressive personality and his exertions for his fellow men have helped to win him respect and admiration, but both his *Systematic Theology* and his shorter works are profoundly problematic.

Questions very similar to those raised by Tillich have been discussed in continental Europe in connection with Rudolf Bultmann's challenge to "demythologize" Christianity. Bultmann, who stayed in Germany, at the University of Marburg, has much in common with Tillich; but he speaks less of "symbols" and more of "myth." He started one of the greatest controversies in modern Protestant theology with his essay, "New Testament and Mythology: The Problem of Demythologizing the Proclamation of the New Testament." Originally published in 1941, it was reprinted in 1948 together with some of the polemical articles it provoked; and six years later this collection was issued in English as *Kerygma and Myth.* If it were not for the fact that this book was issued in paperback as a Harper Torchbook in the spring of 1961, Bultmann's long essay would have been included here; but now it is readily accessible, and it does not seem right to excerpt it, since Bultmann claims that most of his critics have misread him. Only his full statement can serve as an adequate basis for discussion of his ideas. His general outlook is similar to Tillich's, and most English and American readers will find Tillich's statement, reprinted here, far clearer.

I have offered detailed criticisms of both men in Chapter VI of my *Critique* and in the chapter on theology in *The Faith of a Heretic*. The latter deals at length with Tillich's *Dynamics of Faith*, of which the central chapter is offered here.

WISDOM

Since World War II no other philosophic movement is as influential in the English-speaking world as that associated with Ludwig Wittgenstein (1889-1951), who, though born in Austria, became a professor of philosophy at Cambridge University in England. When it spread to Oxford, this movement came to be known as ordinary language philosophy or analytic philosophy; and within a few years after Wittgenstein's death it had become much more widespread at American universities than pragmatism, not to speak of Idealism.

Most of the philosophers working in this tradition have concentrated on relatively academic problems, particularly on questions in the theory of knowledge; and some have studied linguistic uses without apparent reference to any philosophic problem whatsoever. Several have written on meta-ethics, and a few on philosophy of religion, but none of the essays on religion is as noteworthy as John Wisdom's essay "Gods," which is a minor classic.

Wisdom, unlike most of the Oxford philosophers, was personally close to Wittgenstein for a long period and, a few years after the latter's death, succeeded to his chair at Cambridge. Wisdom's style is highly original and at times exceedingly elusive. While James' "The Will to Believe" is a popular piece that does not stand up under analysis, Wisdom's "Gods" is a delicacy for thinkers, and concentrates on a crucial matter which is ignored altogether in James' essay: the question of meaning.

James had written as if one could object to religious beliefs only on the ground that there was insufficient evidence for them; and he had not even bothered to distinguish between not altogether conclusive evidence and no evidence at all. In "The Will to Believe" he failed to recognize that one might be honestly puzzled about the meaning of a religious belief—a failure that is doubly serious because careful readers are likely indeed to be thoroughly perplexed about the meaning of what he himself calls "the religious hypothesis." Now this is precisely the point on which Wisdom fastens. If you picture gods as young or old men and women who dwell on a mountain or above the clouds, it is clear what you mean, though few thoughtful men would accept your belief. But when you begin to qualify your beliefs to dissociate them from superstitions, it may become less and less clear just what you do in fact believe and, to come to the point, what it is that theists affirm and atheists deny.

Wisdom's conciliatory, if elusive, conclusion may be meant to suggest what he has occasionally affirmed more clearly in seminars and lectures: that he thinks religious beliefs, including theism, have some meaning, even though he is unsure as to what that might be. Wisdom's problem is a fitting sequel to the preceding selection.

SCHWEITZER

Albert Schweitzer is widely hailed as one of the greatest human beings of the twentieth century, and some consider him and St. Francis the two true Christians after Christ. Others, annoyed at what strikes them as sheer extravagance, have said that Schweitzer believes that all men are brothers, but that some men are older brothers; and one encounters divergent estimates of his attitude toward the African Negroes among whom he has spent most of his adult life as a medical missionary. But what is relevant in the present context is not his personality any more than that of the popes, philosophers, psychologists, and novelists considered here, but his writings on religion.

Schweitzer is one of the great New Testament scholars of the century. His work on *The Quest of the Historical Jesus* helped to undermine liberal Protestantism by showing that the popular assumption that Jesus was, in effect, a liberal Protestant, if not a Reform Jew, was highly implausible on historical grounds. Schweitzer argued carefully—and many scholars think, cogently—that Jesus had believed in the impending end of the world. As for Jesus' ethic, Schweitzer, unlike Tolstoy, considered it inapplicable and impracticable, not only today but even in Jesus' time: it was an "interim ethic" which would have been practicable only if the end of the world had really been at hand. But Jesus was in error.

In the essay reprinted here, Schweitzer tries to explain how he himself is a Christian, though he believes that Jesus' central doctrines were mistaken, and that Paul, the church fathers, the Catholic church both in the Middle Ages and in modern times, and Luther as well as Calvin were all fundamentally wrong. His answer is, in effect, that he, like Jesus, puts the idea of the kingdom of God in the center, although he does not mean by this phrase what Jesus meant by it. Indeed, he means something this-worldly which Jesus disparaged altogether.

In *The Faith of a Heretic*, I have argued at length that Schweitzer's conception of the kingdom is much closer to the Hebrew prophets than to Jesus; that he is mistaken in crediting the influence of Stoicism with ideas that are really much more indebted to the Old Testament; and that he himself might have seen this if only he had not omitted Calvinism from his account. Surely, Milton, Locke, Rousseau, Jefferson, and Woodrow Wilson did not take their inspiration from Stoicism: they quoted the Old Testament. Perhaps this point concerns not merely the history of ideas but our whole conception of Christianity and its social and moral relevance.

BUBER

Most of the men considered so far wrote as Christians; Nietzsche, as a critic of Christianity; a few of the others, without placing themselves in any particular religious tradition. With only two exceptions, even those in the last category came from a Christian background and derived their conception of religion mainly from Christianity. Only Sigmund Freud and Morris Cohen were born Jews and wrote as critics of religion generally.

In spite of the vast increase in international travel and the growing number of translations, no Muslim, Hindu, or Buddhist seems to belong in the story of "Religion from Tolstoy to Camus": the stories of these religions are still separate stories. What is even more astonishing is that though there has been no dearth of Jewish thinkers, writing in Western languages in the context of Western cultures, hardly any of them have had any appreciable influence on Christian thought. It is as if Christians had read only other Christians or critics of religion, but not champions of Islam and Hinduism, Buddhism and Judaism. Of course, many Christian writers have read in these other traditions, but apparently without receiving any decisive impulses.

Martin Buber is an exception. He has breached this barrier, possibly aided by the fact that he is not a rabbi nor a spokesman for any denomination. His *I and Thou*—a short book that appeared in 1923, the same year that saw the publication of Freud's *The Ego and the Id* (the German titles are, respectively, *Ich und Du* and *Das Ich und das Es*)—has profoundly influenced Protestant theology. Rhapsodically written, more like a poem than a philosophic treatise, the book does not lend itself to excerpting. And it is debatable whether it is really Buber's greatest work, though this opinion is held very widely.

To form some estimate of Buber's significance, it may be well to divide his works into four categories. To the first, one might assign *I and Thou*, as well as *Between Man and Man*—a collection of short works that develop some of the same themes—and his other philosophic writings. Secondly, one should note that Buber has never sought refuge in an ivory tower, and that for over half a century he has written about the problems confronting him and his fellow men, from religion to politics, from sociology to Zionism, from psychology to literature. Between them, these two categories comprise a very large body of work. But two central concerns remain: the Bible and Hasidism.

Buber's most monumental achievement in the Biblical field is his German translation of the Hebrew Scriptures, begun in collaboration with his friend, Franz Rosenzweig, continued after Rosenzweig's death in 1929, and more than three-quarters completed when Buber left Germany for Jerusalem in 1938. After World War II, Buber resumed work on his translation, revised the previously published portions for new editions, and went on to render the remaining books into German. This translation, completed in manuscript early in 1961, constitutes a milestone not only in the understanding of the Hebrew Bible but also in the art of translation. His work on the Bible has brought other fruit, too. Buber's and Rosenzweig's essays on *Die Schrift und ihre Verdeutschung* (1936, *On Scripture and Its Translation into German;* not available in English) are of immense interest for students of the Bible and for translators generally. His many books on Biblical themes deal mainly with the Old Testament, but *Two Types of Faith* includes detailed discussions of Jesus and Paul.

No other work of Buber's, however, seems as firmly assured of a lasting place in world literature as his collection of *The Tales of the Hasidim,* the climactic achievement of a lifetime. After many previous collections, the definitive German edition was issued by the Manesse Verlag in Switzerland in 1949, under the title, *Die Erzählungen der Chassidim.* An English translation in two volumes is now available in paperback (Schocken Books).

Buber's essays on Hasidism are numerous. I heartily agree with Maurice Friedman, Buber's foremost interpreter, that *The Way of Man according to the Teachings of Hasidism*—reprinted complete in this volume—"is far more than a mere interpretation or summary of Hasidic teaching. No other of Buber's works gives us so much of his own simple wisdom as this remarkable distillation."

CAMUS

Albert Camus, like some of the other men included here, was not primarily concerned with religion. His rank is subject to debate. Few philosophers think very highly of his philosophic efforts. But when he received the Nobel Prize for literature, there was relatively little of the indignation that so often meets these awards: Camus had established a place for himself.

Surely, he received the Nobel Prize in part because existentialism seemed to deserve recognition; and Sartre's politics had made him *persona non grata,* while Camus' profound humanity and sensitive conscience had made him one of the most attractive figures of modern literature. Still, that is far from the whole story; and the perspective provided by this book and summarized in its title, *Religion from Tolstoy to Camus,* may illuminate the phenomenon of Camus. What is so remarkable about Camus is, as much as anything, that he had the courage to accept the heritage of Tolstoy, when no one else had dared to stand before the world as Tolstoy's heir.

Camus lacked Tolstoy's almost superhuman gifts: that makes it doubly appropriate to speak of courage. He was not one of the world's great writers, nor even one of the most talented of the past hundred years. But he attempted great things and was motivated by a sense of obligation to humanity. His inspiration was moral, not the wish to entertain or to achieve fame. Camus' *The Plague* is the posthumous child of *The Death of Ivan Ilyitch.*

The theme is the same: the confrontation with death. Camus, like Tolstoy, attempts a parable about the human condition, an attack on the unthinking inauthenticity of most men's lives, and an appeal to conscience. *The Plague* may not be a great book by the highest standards; but it is an important book because its theme is of the utmost significance: it is a novel in the great tradition, inviting comparisons with Tolstoy and Dostoevsky. Ivan Karamazov's great plea against the suffering of children is taken up in a central section of *The Plague* (192 ff.); and though Camus' treatment is sentimental, and he suffers from juxtapositions with the two great Russian novelists, many intelligent readers prefer him to the theologians and philosophers who have written on the problem of suffering.

Confronted with the enormity of the outrages of our time, the voice of *The Plague* is a still small voice, and I find the message of Malcolm Hay, in *Europe and the Jews,* more impressive and disturbing. But it has been the voice of Camus, and not that of Hay or any other historian, that has reached the conscience of a generation.

Camus' debt to Tolstoy is great. In Tarrou's long narration (*The Plague,* 222-28), there are important echoes of Tolstoy's *Resurrection:* "The great change of heart about which I want to tell you" came about when "my father asked me to come to hear him speak in court," and Tarrou discovered that the criminal "was a living human being." His father's mouth, however, "spewed out long, turgid phrases like an endless stream of snakes. I realized he was clamoring for the prisoner's death"; indeed, he demanded "that the man should have his head cut off."

To excerpt *The Plague* would be as bad as reprinting selected passages from *Anna Karenina.* But Camus, like Tolstoy, has returned to the relevant themes elsewhere; not only in *The Rebel,* which is long and turgid, but also in *Reflections on the Guillotine,* a brief and pointed essay—and especially in the last part of these *Reflections,* which is reprinted here.

These *Reflections* are not one of Camus' major works, but the concerns around which they revolve are central in Camus' thought. Not only Tarrou's narrative abounds in parallels to the *Reflections;* the crux of *The Plague* and of *The Rebel,* too, is also the core of the shorter work: man's attitude toward the death of his fellow men. If there is one phrase in *The Plague* that crystallizes this common concern pre-eminently, it is probably the suggestion that "the most incorrigible vice" is "that of an ignorance that fancies it knows everything and therefore claims for itself the right to kill." (120 f.)

The way Camus leads up to this thought is profoundly Tolstoyan: "The evil that is in the world always comes of ignorance, and good intentions may do as much harm as malevolence, if they lack understanding. On the whole, men are more good than bad; that, however, isn't the real point. But they are more or less ignorant, and it is this that we call vice or virtue; the most incorrigible vice being that of an ignorance that fancies it knows everything and therefore claims for itself the right to kill."

Camus dissociates himself from the fashionable revival of the notion of original sin. On the last page of *The Plague* he proclaims it to be one of the central purposes and lessons of his book "that there are more things to admire in men than to despise." It is precisely for that reason that he considers it a duty to bear witness of "the injustice and outrage done them"— not by their fellow men but by the plague. Seeking a parable of the injustice and outrage inflicted on humanity in our time, Camus does not indict man's inhumanity to man; he does not at all indict man: he accuses what, if he believed in God, he would call God. But he does not believe in God.

Many people believe that disbelief in God disqualifies a man for any position of public trust, because morality seems to them to stand or fall with religion, and only theists can be humane. With his soft and engaging voice, Camus argues that "capital punishment, in fact, throughout history has always been a religious punishment," and he finds it incompatible with atheism and agnosticism. He finds humanism more humane than theism.

Both *The Stranger* and *The Fall* end with powerful attacks on Christianity. In the former work, "the stranger" speaks directly to a priest and tells him what he thinks of him and his religion. In *The Fall*, the outlook of the believers in original sin who make a point of their own guiltiness is indicted more subtly but nonetheless surely. Indeed, Camus' critique of this particular form of inhumanity is the heart of *The Fall*.

In 1961, a year after Camus' death, some shorter pieces that he himself had selected from the three volumes of his *Actuelles* were published in the United States under the title, *Resistance, Rebellion, and Death*. One of these pieces contains Camus' reflections on "The Unbeliever and Christians." Here Camus says: "What the world expects of Christians is that Christians should speak out, loud and clear. . . ." He gives expression to his disappointment that Christianity has failed in our time in this respect; he explains that he did not hear it speak out at all, but that he was referred by others to papal encyclicals; and he voices his irritation at the form of the encyclical, which does not strike him as sufficiently forthright. "The grouping we need is a grouping of men resolved to speak out clearly and to pay up personally. When a Spanish bishop blesses political executions . . . he is a dog." Camus goes on to say that Christianity may "insist on losing once and for all the virtue of revolt and indignation. . . . In that case Christians will live and Christianity will die."

ANY MORAL?

Any claim that the selections offered here point clearly to some definite conclusion would amount to an admission that they had been tailored. For the development of religion during the past hundred years, or four thousand years, cannot rid us of the onus of making our own choices. This was one of Kierkegaard's great insights: those who believe that history, development, and survival show us what, as a matter of fact, is superior, deceive themselves. What Kierkegaard failed to appreciate is that those who have studied history, read widely, and reflected on a variety of views, are in a far better position than other men to make an informed, intelligent, and responsible choice.

If a demon came to me and offered me, without exacting any price, that all of mankind might accept *my* faith, my views, my standards, I should not even be tempted. Demon, I might say, I have no wish for mankind to conform to any single faith or set of views or standards; but if you are intent on granting me such a great favor, make men's disagreements more responsible and more humane. Cure their brutal want of intellectual imagination; give them more curiosity about the feelings, thoughts, and sufferings of their fellow men. Increase their humbition (the rare fusion of ambition with humility and humor) and their courage, love, and honesty. Then, instead of accepting my views, they will point out my mistakes to me, while also learning from me about some of their errors, and we shall all become better men.

Suppose the demon tempted me and asked: But what is *your* conclusion? and my begging off and pointing out that I had developed my conclusions elsewhere did not satisfy him. Suppose he persisted: Your conclusions may provoke your readers to develop their own answers in reply to yours; if you refuse to point a moral, most of them will beg off, too, and think less. In that spirit one might after all venture a suggestion.

With extremely few exceptions, religion is most moving in the form of stories—stories that challenge the way we live. That is true not only of the Old and New Testaments but also of Tolstoy and Buber. Religion should not be discussed solely on the basis of the writings of the theologians: the best religious stories are so much better than the best the theologians have to offer. But what happens when one concentrates on religious stories? They can be read as a species of literature, along with the plays of Shakespeare and Sophocles: not as mere entertainment but as a source of profound experiences that help, or can help, to make us more humane. Most religious *beliefs* I should class with ritual: at best, beautiful; more often, superstitious. I can imagine Isaiah returning today and proclaiming (changing but a few words in Isaiah 1):

> What to me is the multitude of your tracts?
>   says the Lord;
> I have had enough of theological speculations
>   and fat tomes;
> I do not delight in allegories, symbols,
>   or proofs.
>
> When you come to appear before me,
>   who requires of you
>   this crowding of my churches?
> Bring no more vain prayers;
>   sermons are an abomination to me.
> Christmas and Easter and sabbaths—
>   I cannot endure iniquity and solemn assembly.
> Your Christmases and your appointed feasts
>   my soul hates;
> they have become a burden to me,
>   I am weary of bearing them.
> When you recount your beliefs,
>   I will hide my eyes from you;
> even though you make many prayers,
>   I will not listen;
>   your hands are full of blood.
>
> Wash yourselves; make yourselves clean;
>   remove the evil of your doings
>   from before my eyes;
> cease to do evil,
>   learn to do good;
> seek justice,
>   correct oppression;
> defend the fatherless,
>   plead for the widow.

There is much talk of a revival of religion. But this prophetic note is conspicuously absent. Attendance at services has gone up, no less than in Isaiah's day. One cannot imagine that he or Amos, Kierkegaard or Tolstoy would have liked twentieth-century religion any better than the religion they attacked with so much passion.

Schweitzer has at least come close to sounding the prophetic note; but he has failed in at least two ways. First, his own scholarship, his very honesty, has undermined his challenge: for he has shown that the prophetic concern was abandoned by Jesus, and that Jesus' ethic, predicated on his false belief in the impending end of the world, was really impracticable. in his own time and cannot be our standard now. Schweitzer's ethic is, on his own showing, neither Jesus' nor Paul's, nor that of the Catholic church, nor that of Luther. A Christian can consistently repudiate it, and a non-Christian accept it.

Secondly, Schweitzer's noble example is not strikingly relevant for most of us. One wonders whether there was really more to be done in Africa, where he went, than in Germany, which he left. The point is not to accuse him: few men have done as much as he. Still, his example has given little guidance to those who wrestled with the problems of the Weimar Republic and Hitler Germany, of Communist occupation and war and peace. He got away from these problems and did not deal with them, while Camus, for example, has at least tried to deal with them. Indeed, in 1960, if not before, it became painfully obvious that there had been enormous and alarmingly acute problems in Africa; but for all his nobility, Albert Schweitzer does not seem to have contributed to their solution though he lived in their midst and commanded a singularly wide hearing.

The story of religion from Tolstoy to Camus is to a large extent the story of a manifold refusal to face the responsibilities Tolstoy faced. He asked at least a few of the right questions, though subsequent scholarship and reflection have made his answers doubtful. But much of the most renowned religious literature since his time is a form of escape literature. Camus is no Tolstoy, but his fame has filled a vacuum left by the retreat of religion.

A volume this size could have been filled with social preaching. But would that have given a fairer picture of religion during the period from Tolstoy to Camus? One could also have included William Jennings Bryan, Norman Vincent Peale, and Billy Graham; Protestants and Catholics who blessed Hitler and collaborated; fundamentalists and anthropologists; and many more critics of religion. The picture given in these pages is prompted not by ill will, but by concern.

To speak of religion without disturbing men is to be a false prophet. To deal at length with the history of the past hundred years without disturbing men is also to be a false prophet. In a book on *Religion from Tolstoy to Camus* one must beware doubly of crying peace, peace, when there is no peace.

Leo Tolstoy was born at Yasnaya Polyana, Russia, in 1828. *War and Peace* (1864-69) and *Anna Karenina* (1873-76) are his two most celebrated and ambitious works and certain of inclusion in almost any list of the greatest novels of all time. While writing the latter, Tolstoy became more and more concerned with religion, and during the second half of his life he devoted himself almost wholly to writing on moral and religious subjects. His later works include essays, plays, stories, and another great novel, *Resurrection* (1899). In 1901, the Orthodox church excommunicated him. He died in 1910 at Astapovo, Russia.

Four of his works follow. *My Religion* was completed January 22, 1884. The book has also been translated under the title, *What I Believe*. It contains twelve chapters; but the last nine are omitted here.

The Death of Ivan Ilyitch first appeared in 1886; *How Much Land Does A Man Need?* in 1885; his *Reply to the Synod's Edict of Excommunication*, in 1901. All three are offered here complete.

My Religion

I have lived in the world fifty-five years, and after the fourteen or fifteen years of my childhood, for thirty-five years of my life I was, in the proper acceptation of the word, a nihilist,—not a socialist and revolutionist, as is generally understood by that word, but a nihilist in the sense of one who believed in nothing. Five years ago I came to believe in the doctrine of Christ, and my whole life underwent a sudden transformation. What I had once wished for I wished for no longer. What had once appeared to me good now became evil, and the evil of the past I beheld as good.

My condition was like that of a man who goes forth on some errand, and suddenly on the way decides that the matter is of no importance, and returns home. What was at first on his right hand is now on his left, and what was at his left hand is now on his right; his former desire to be as far as possible from home has changed into a desire to be as near to it as possible. The direction of my life and my desires were completely changed; good and evil had changed places. All this resulted from the fact that I understood the doctrine of Christ in a different way from that in which I had understood it before.

I do not care to expound the doctrine of Christ; I wish only to tell how it was that I came to understand what in this doctrine is most simple, clear, evident, indisputable, and appeals most to all men, and how this understanding refreshed my soul and gave me happiness and peace.

I do not care to expound the doctrine of Christ; I should wish only one thing: to do away with all exposition.

All the Christian Churches have always maintained that all men, however unequal in education and intellect,—the wise and the foolish,—are equal before God; that divine truth is accessible to every one. Christ has even declared it to be the will of God that what is concealed from the wise shall be revealed to the simple.

Not every one is able to understand the mysteries of dogmatics, homiletics, patristics, liturgics, hermeneutics, apologetics; but every one is able and ought to understand what Christ said to the millions of simple and ignorant people who have lived, and who are living to-day. Now, the things that Christ said to all these simple people who could not avail themselves of the comments of Paul, of Clement, of Chrysostom, and of others, are just what I did not understand, and which, now that I have come to understand them, I wish to make plain to all.

The thief on the cross believed in Christ, and was saved. Would it have been bad or injurious to any one if the thief had not died on the cross, but had descended from it, and told all men how he believed in Christ?

Like the thief on the cross, I believed in the doctrine of Christ, and was saved. This is not a vain comparison, but a most accurate expression of my spiritual condition of horror and despair in the presence of life and death, in which I found myself formerly, and of that condition of happiness and peace in which I find myself now.

Like the thief, I knew that my past and present life was vile; I saw that the majority of men about me lived in the same way. I knew, like the thief, that I was wretched and suffering, that all those about me suffered and were wretched; and I saw before me no escape from this condition but in death. As the thief was nailed to his cross, so was I nailed to this life of suffering and evil by an incomprehensible power. And as the thief saw before him, after the senseless and evil sufferings of life, the horrible shadows of death, so did I behold the same prospect.

In all this I was absolutely like the thief. But there was a difference in our conditions; he was about to die, and I was still alive. The thief might believe that his salvation would be beyond the grave, while I had not only that before me, but also life this side the grave. I understood nothing of this life, it seemed to me frightful; and then suddenly I heard the words of Christ, and understood them; life and death ceased to seem evil, and instead of despair I tasted the joy and happiness that death could not take away.

Can it be harmful to any one, then, if I tell how this came about?

CHAPTER I

I have written two large works explaining why I did not understand the doctrine of Christ, and why it became clear to me. "A Criticism of Dogmatic Theology" and a new translation of the four Gospels, followed by a Concordance. In these writings I seek methodically, step by step, to disentangle everything that conceals the truth from men; I translate the four Gospels anew, verse by verse, and I bring them together in a new concordance.

This work has lasted more than five years. Each year, each month, I discover new explanations and corroborations of the fundamental idea; I correct the errors which have crept in through haste and impulse, and I put the last touches to what I have already written. My life, of which only a small portion is before me, will doubtless end before I have finished my work; but I am convinced that the work will be of great service; so I shall do all that I can as long as I live.

Such was my prolonged outward work on theology and the Gospels, but my inward work, that which I propose to tell about in these pages, was of a very different nature. It was not a methodical exposition of theology and the text of the Gospels; it was an instantaneous removal of all that had hidden the meaning of the teaching, and an instantaneous illumination with the light of Truth.

It was an experience similar to that which might happen to a man who, following an erroneous model, should try to find the meaning of a heap of intermingled fragments, and should suddenly, by means of one large fragment, come to the conclusion that it was an entirely different statue from what he had supposed it to be; then beginning to fashion it anew, instead of the former incoherent mass of pieces, he would find, as he observed the outlines of each fragment, that all fitted well together, and formed one consistent whole, and he would be amazed at the confirmation of his thought.

This is exactly what happened to me, and this is what I wish to relate. I wish to tell how I found the key to the true meaning of the doctrine of Christ, which revealed to me the truth clearly and convincingly, so that doubt was out of the question. The discovery came about in this way:—

Almost from the first period of my childhood, when I began to read the New Testament, I was touched and stirred most of all by that portion of the doctrine of Christ which inculcates love, humility, self-denial, and the duty of returning good for evil. This, to me, has always been the substance of Christianity; it was what I loved in it with all my heart, it was that in the name of which, after despair and disbelief, caused me to accept as true the meaning found in the Christian life by the working people, and in the name of which I submitted myself to those doctrines professed by these same working people—in other words, the Orthodox Church.

But in making my submission to the Church, I soon saw that I should not find in its creed the confirmation, the explanation of those principles of Christianity which seemed to me essential; I observed that the essence of Christianity, dear though it was to me, did not constitute the chief element in the doctrine of the Church. I observed that what seemed to me essential in Christ's teaching was not recognized by the Church as most important. Something else was regarded by the Church as most important. At first I did not appreciate the significance of this peculiarity of the Church teaching. "Well now,"—I thought—"the Church sees in Christianity, aside from its inner meaning of love, humility, and self-denial, an outer, dogmatic meaning. This meaning is strange and even repulsive to me, but it is not in itself pernicious."

But the longer I continued to live in submission to the doctrine of the Church, the more clearly I saw this particular point was not so unimportant as it had seemed to me at first. I was driven from the Church by the strangeness of its dogmas, and the approval and the support which it gave to persecutions, to the death penalty, to wars, and by the intolerance common to all sects; but my faith was chiefly shattered by the indifference of the Church to what seemed to me essential in the teachings of Jesus, and by its avidity for what seemed to me not essential. I felt that something was wrong; but I could not discover what was wrong. I could not discover, because the doctrine of the Church did not deny, what seemed to me essential in the doctrine of Christ; it fully recognized it, yet recognized it in such a way that what was chief in the teaching of Christ was not given the first place. I could not blame the Church because she denied the essence of the doctrine of Jesus, but because she recognized it in a way which did not satisfy me. The Church did not give me what I expected from her.

I had passed from nihilism to the Church simply because I felt it to be impossible to live without religion, without a knowledge of good and evil beyond the animal instincts. I hoped to find this knowledge in Christianity; but Christianity, as it then presented itself to me, was only a very indeterminate spiritual tendency, from which it was impossible to deduce any clear and obligatory principles of life. For these rules I turned to the Church. The Church offered me certain rules, but they not only did not attract me to the Christian dispensation now so dear to me, but rather repelled me from it. I could not follow the Church. A life based on Christian truth was precious and indispensable to me, and the Church offered me rules completely at variance with the truth I loved. The rules of the Church touching belief in dogmas, the observance of the sacrament, fasts, prayers, were not necessary to me, and did not seem to be based on Christian truth. Moreover, the rules of the Church weakened and sometimes destroyed the desire for Christian truth which alone gave meaning to my life.

I was troubled most by the fact that all human evil, the habit of judging private persons, of judging whole nations, of judging other religions, and the wars and massacres that were the consequence of such judgments, all went on with the approbation of the Church. Christ's teaching—judge not, be humble, forgive offenses, deny self, love,—this doctrine was extolled by the Church in words, but at the same time the Church approved what was incompatible with the doctrine. Was it possible that Christ's teaching admitted of such contradiction? I could not believe so.

Moreover, it always seemed to me astonishing that, as far as I knew the Gospels, the passages on which the Church based affirmation of its dogmas were those that were most obscure, while the passages from which came the fulfilment of its teaching were the most clear and precise. And yet the dogmas and the obligations depending on them were definitely formulated by the Church, while the recommendation to obey the moral law was put in the most obscure, vague, and mystical terms. Was this the intention of Jesus in teaching His doctrine? A resolution of my doubts I could find only in the Gospels, and I read them, and reread them.

Of everything in the Gospels, the Sermon on the Mount always had for me an exceptional importance. I now read it more frequently than ever. Nowhere else does Christ speak with so great solemnity as in these passages, nowhere else does He give so many clear and comprehensible moral laws, appealing to every man's heart; nowhere else does He address Himself to a larger multitude of the common people. If there are any clear and precise Christian principles, one ought to find them here. I therefore sought the solution of my doubts in these three[1] chapters of Matthew. I read the Sermon on the Mount many, many times, and I always experienced the same feelings of enthusiasm and emotion, as I read the verses that exhort the hearer to turn the other cheek, to give up his cloak, to be at peace with all men, to love his enemies,—but each time with the same disappointment. The divine words—addressed to all men—were not clear. They exhorted to an absolute renunciation of everything, such as entirely stifled life, as I understood it; to renounce everything, therefore, could not, it seemed to me, be an absolute condition of salvation. But the moment this ceased to be an absolute condition, clearness and precision were at an end.

I read not only the Sermon on the Mount; I read all the Gospels, and all the theological commentaries on them. I was not satisfied with the declarations of the theologians that the Sermon on the Mount was only an indication of the degree of perfection to which man should aspire; but that fallen man, weighed down by sin, could not reach such an ideal; and that the salvation of humanity was in faith and prayer and grace.

I could not admit the truth of these propositions, because it seemed to me strange that Christ, knowing beforehand that it was impossible for man, with his own powers, to carry his teaching into practice, should propound

[1] 5, 6, and 7.

rules so clear and admirable, addressed to the understanding of every one. But as I read these maxims it always seemed to me that they applied directly to me, that their fulfilment was demanded of me. As I read these maxims I was filled with the joyous assurance that I might that very hour, that very moment, begin to practice them. I desired to do so, I tried to do so, but as soon as I began to enter upon the struggle I could not help remembering the teaching of the Church—*Man is weak, and to this he cannot attain*—and my strength failed. I was told, "You must believe and pray"; but I was conscious that I had small faith, and so I could not pray. I was told, "You must pray, and God will give you faith; this faith will inspire prayer, which in turn will invoke faith that will inspire more prayer, and so on, indefinitely."

But reason and experience alike convinced me that such methods were useless. It seemed to me that the only true way was for me to try to follow the teaching of Christ.

And so, after all this fruitless search, study of all that had been written for and against the divinity of this doctrine, after all this doubt and suffering, I remained alone with my heart and with the mysterious book before me. I could not give to it the meanings that others gave, neither could I discover what I sought nor could I get away from it. Only after I had gone through alike all the interpretations of the wise critics and all the interpretations of the wise theologians and had rejected them all according to the words of Jesus, "*Except ye . . . become as little children, ye shall not enter into the kingdom of heaven*"[1]—I suddenly understood what I had not understood before. I understood, not because I made any artificial combination of texts, or any profound and ingenious misinterpretations; on the contrary, I understood everything because I put all commentaries out of my mind. The passage that gave me the key to the whole was from the fifth chapter of Matthew, verses thirty-eight and thirty-nine:—

"*It has been said unto you, An eye for an eye, and a tooth for a tooth: But I say unto you, That you resist not evil.*"

Suddenly, for the first time, I understood the exact and simple meaning of those words; I understood that Jesus said exactly what he said. Immediately—not that I saw anything new; only the veil that had hidden the truth from me fell away, and the truth was revealed in all its significance.

"*It has been said unto you, An eye for an eye, and a tooth for a tooth: But I say unto you, That you resist not evil.*"

These words suddenly appeared to me absolutely new, as if I had never read them before. Always before, when I had read this passage, I had, singularly enough, allowed certain words to escape me, "*But I say unto you, that you resist not evil.*" To me it had always been as if the words just quoted had never existed, or had never possessed a definite meaning.

Later on, as I talked with many Christians familiar with the Gospel, I

[1] Matt. 18:3.

noticed frequently the same blindness with regard to these words. No one remembered them, and often, in speaking of this passage, Christians took up the Gospel to see for themselves if the words were really there. Through a similar neglect of these words I had failed to understand the words that follow:—

"But whosoever shall smite thee on thy right cheek, turn to him the other also," etc.[1]

Always these words had seemed to me to demand long-suffering and privation contrary to human nature. These words touched me; I felt that it would be noble to follow them, but I also felt that I should never have the strength to put them into practice, only to put them into practice so as to suffer. I said to myself, "If I turn the other cheek, I shall get another blow; if I give, all that I have will be taken away. Life would be an impossibility. Since life is given to me, why should I deprive myself of it? Christ cannot demand that." Thus I reasoned, persuaded that Christ in these words exalted suffering and deprivation, and in exalting them, made use of exaggerated terms lacking in clearness and precision; but when I understood the words *"Resist not evil,"* it became clear to me that Jesus did not exaggerate, that he did not demand suffering for suffering, but that he said with great clearness and precision exactly what he wished to say.

He said *"Resist not evil,* and if you do so you will know beforehand that you may meet with those who, when they have struck you on one cheek and met with no resistance, will strike you on the other; who, having taken away your coat, will take away your cloak also; who, having profited by your labor, will force you to labor still more without reward. And yet, though all this should happen to you, *'Resist not evil';* do good to them that injure you."

When I understood these words as they were said, all that had been obscure became clear to me, and what had seemed exaggerated I saw to be perfectly reasonable. For the first time I saw that the center of gravity of the whole idea lay in the words *"Resist not evil";* and that what followed was only a development of this command; I saw that Jesus did not exhort us to turn the other cheek and give up the cloak that we might endure suffering, but that his exhortation was, *"Resist not evil,"* and that he afterward declared suffering to be the possible consequence of the practice of this maxim.

Exactly as a father who is sending his son on a far journey does not command him to pass his nights without shelter, to go without food, to expose himself to rain and cold when he says to him, "Go thy way, and tarry not, even though thou should'st be wet or cold," so Jesus does not say, "Turn the other cheek and suffer." He says, *"Resist not evil";* no matter what happens, *"Resist not evil."*

[1] Matt. 5:39, *et seq.*

These words, *"Resist not evil or the evil man,"* understood in their direct significance, were to me truly the key that opened all the rest. And I began to be astonished that I could have miscomprehended words so clear and precise.

"It has been said unto you, An eye for an eye, and a tooth for a tooth: but I say unto you, That you resist not evil or the evil man."

Whatever injury the evil-disposed may inflict upon you, bear it, give all that you have, but resist not evil or the evil one. Could anything be more clear, more definite, more intelligible than that? I had only to grasp the simple and exact meaning of these words, just as they were spoken, when the whole teaching of Christ, not only as set forth in the Sermon on the Mount, but in the entire Gospels, became clear to me; what had seemed contradictory was now in harmony; above all, what had seemed superfluous was now indispensable. Each portion fell into harmonious unison and filled its proper part, like the fragments of a broken statue when put together as they should be. In the Sermon on the Mount, as well as throughout the whole Gospel, I found everywhere affirmation of the same doctrine, *"Resist not evil."*

In the Sermon on the Mount, as well as in all other places, Christ presents Himself to His disciples, in other words, to those that observe the rule of non-resistance to evil, as turning the other cheek, giving up their cloaks, persecuted, used despitefully, and in want. Elsewhere, many times Christ says that he who does not take up his cross, who does not renounce worldly advantage, he who is not ready to bear all the consequences of the commandment, *"Resist not evil,"* cannot become His disciple.

To His disciples Jesus says, Choose to be poor; be ready to bear persecution, suffering, and death, without resistance to evil.

He himself was ready to bear suffering and death rather than resist evil, and He reproved Peter for wishing to avenge Him, and He died forbidding His followers to resist, nor did He make any modification in His doctrine. All His early disciples observed this rule, and passed their lives in poverty and persecution, and never rendered evil for evil.

Christ must have said what He said. We may declare the universal practice of such a rule is very difficult; we may deny that he who follows it will find happiness; we may say with the unbelievers that it is stupid, that Christ was a dreamer, an idealist who propounded impracticable maxims which His disciples followed out of sheer stupidity; but it is impossible not to admit that Christ expressed in a manner at once clear and precise what He wished to say; that is, that according to His doctrine a man must not resist evil, and, consequently, that whoever adopts His doctrine cannot resist evil. And yet neither believers nor unbelievers will admit this simple and clear interpretation of Christ's words.

CHAPTER II

When I understood that the words *"Resist not evil,"* meant *resist not evil*, my whole former conception of Christ's teaching suddenly changed; and I was horrified, not that I had failed to understand it before, but that I had misunderstood it so strangely. I knew, as we all know, that the true significance of the Christian doctrine was comprised in the injunction to love one's neighbor. When we say, *"Turn the other cheek," "Love your enemies,"* we express the very essence of Christianity. I knew all that from my childhood; but why had I failed to understand aright these simple words? Why had I always sought for some ulterior meaning? *"Resist not evil"* means never resist, never oppose violence; or, in other words, never do anything contrary to the law of love. If any one takes advantage of this disposition and affronts you, bear the affront, and do not, above all, have recourse to violence. Christ said this in words so clear and simple that it would be impossible to express the idea more clearly. How was it, then, that believing or trying to believe that He who said this was God, I still maintained that it is beyond my power to obey them? If my master says to me, "Go; cut some wood," and I reply, "I cannot do this: it is beyond my strength," I say one of two things: either I do not believe what my master says, or I do not wish to do what my master commands. Should I, without having made the slightest effort of my own to obey, then say of God's commandment that I could not obey it without the aid of a supernatural power? Should I say this of a commandment which He gave us to obey, concerning which He said that whoever obeyed it and taught it should be called great, concerning which He declared that only those that obey it shall have life, which He Himself obeyed, and which He expressed so clearly and simply that it leaves no room for doubt as to its meaning!

God descended to earth to save mankind; salvation was secured by the second person of the Trinity, God-the-Son, who suffered for men, thereby redeeming them from sin, and gave them the Church as the shrine for the transmission of grace to all believers; but aside from this, Person God-the-Son gave to men a doctrine and the example of a life for their salvation. How, then, could I say that the rules of life formulated by Him so clearly and simply for every one—were so difficult to obey that it was impossible to obey them without supernatural aid? He not only did not say, but He distinctly declared, that those that did not obey could not enter into the kingdom of God. Nowhere did He say that obedience would be difficult; on the contrary, He said, *"My yoke is easy and my burden is light."*[1] And John, His evangelist, says, *"His commandments are not grievous."*[2] Since God laid down His command and defined so accurately the conditions of its fulfilment and obedience to it to be easy, and Himself practised it in

[1] Matt. 11:30. [2] I John 5:3.

human form, as did also His disciples, how could I say it was hard or impossible to obey without supernatural aid?

If a man should bend all the energies of his mind to overthrow any law, what could this man say of greater force than that the law was essentially impracticable, and that the maker of the law knew that it was impracticable, and that to obey it required supernatural aid.

Yet that is exactly what I had been thinking of the command, *"Resist not evil."* I endeavored to find out how and when I got the strange idea that Christ's law was divine, but could not be obeyed; and as I reviewed my past history, I perceived that the idea had not been communicated to me in all its crudeness,—it would then have been revolting to me,—but that I had drunk it in with my mother's milk insensibly from earliest childhood, and all my after life had only confirmed me in this strange error.

From my childhood I had been taught that Christ was God, and that His doctrine was divine, but at the same time, I was taught to respect the institutions that protected me from violence and evil, and to regard them as sacred. I was taught to resist evil; I was inspired with the idea that it was humiliating to submit to evil, and that resistance to it was praiseworthy. I was taught to judge, and to inflict punishment. Then I was taught the soldier's trade, that is, to resist evil by homicide; the army to which I belonged was called "The Christophile Army,"[1] and it was sent forth with a Christian benediction. Moreover, from infancy to manhood I learned to venerate what was in direct contradiction to Christ's law,—to meet an aggressor with his own weapons, to avenge myself by violence for all offenses against my person, my family, or my people. Not only was I not blamed for this, but I was led to regard it as fine, and not contrary to Christ's law.

All that surrounded me, my comfort, my personal security, and that of my family and my property, depended then on a law which Christ repudiated,—the law of "a tooth for a tooth."

My Church instructors taught me that Christ's teaching was divine, but, because of human weakness, impossible of practice, and that the grace of Christ alone could aid us to follow its precepts. My secular teachers and the whole organization of life agreed in calling Christ's teaching impracticable and visionary, and by words and deeds taught what was opposed to it. I was so thoroughly possessed with this idea of the impracticability of the divine doctrine, it had gradually become such a habit with me, the idea conformed so well with my desires, that I had never noticed the contradiction in which I had become involved. I did not see how impossible it was to confess Christ as God, the basis of whose teaching is the law of the non-resistance of evil, and at the same time deliberately to assist in the organization of property, of tribunals, of the government, of the army; to arrange my life in a manner

---

[1] *Khristoliubivoye voïnstvo.*

entirely contrary to the doctrine of Jesus, and at the same time to pray to this same Christ to help us to obey His commands, to forgive our sins, and to aid us that we resist not evil. It did not enter my head, clear as it is to me now, how much more simple it would be to arrange and organize life conformably to Christ's law, and then to pray for tribunals, and massacres, and wars, if these things are so indispensable to our happiness.

Thus I came to understand how my error arose. It arose from my confessing Christ in words and rejecting Him in reality.

The position concerning the resistance of evil is a position which unites the whole teaching into one whole, nor only because it is not a mere verbal affirmation; it is a rule the practice of which is obligatory, since it is a law.

It is exactly like a key which opens everything, but only when the key is thrust into the lock. When we regard it as a verbal affirmation impossible of performance without supernatural aid, it amounts to the nullification of the entire doctrine. Why should not a doctrine seem impracticable, when we have suppressed its fundamental proposition? Unbelievers look on it as totally absurd—they cannot look on it in any other way. To set up an engine, to heat the boiler, to start it, but not to attach the belt—that is what is done with Christ's teaching when it is taught that one may be a Christian without observing the commandment, *"Resist not evil."*

Not long ago I was reading the fifth chapter of Matthew with a Hebrew rabbi. At nearly every verse the rabbi said, "That is in the Bible," or "That is in the Talmud," and he showed me in the Bible and in the Talmud sentences very like the declarations of the Sermon on the Mount. But when we reached the verse about non-resistance of evil the rabbi did not say, "This also is in the Talmud," but he asked me, with a cynical smile, "Do the Christians obey this command? Do they turn the other cheek?"

I had nothing to say in reply, especially as at that particular time Christians not only were not turning the other cheek, but were smiting the Jews on both cheeks. But I was interested to know if there were anything similar in the Bible or in the Talmud, and I asked him about it.

"No," he replied, "there is nothing like it; but tell me, do the Christians obey this law?"

By this question he told me that the presence in the Christian doctrine of a commandment which no one observed, and which Christians themselves regarded as impracticable, is simply an avowal of the foolishness and nullity of that law. I could say nothing in reply to the rabbi.

Now that I understand the exact meaning of the doctrine, I see clearly the strangely contradictory position in which I was placed. Having recognized Christ as God, and His doctrine as divine, and having at the same time organized my life wholly contrary to that doctrine, what remained for me but to regard the doctrine as impracticable? In words I had recognized Christ's teaching as sacred; in actions I had professed a doctrine not at all

Christian, and I had recognized and reverenced the unchristian customs which hampered my life on every side.

The Old Testament, throughout, teaches that misfortunes came upon the people of Judaea because they believed in false gods, and not in the true God. Samuel, in the eighth and twelfth chapters of the first book, accuses the people of adding to their other apostasies a new one: in place of God, who was their King, they had raised up a man for a king, who, they thought, would deliver them. "*Turn not aside after* tohu, *after vain things,*" Samuel says to the people; "*turn not aside after vain things, which cannot profit nor deliver; for they are* tohu, *are vain.*" "*Fear Jehovah and serve him. . . . But if ye shall still do wickedly, ye shall be consumed, both ye and your king.*"[1]

And so with me, faith in *tohu,* in vain things, in empty idols, had concealed the truth from me. Across the path which led to the truth, *tohu,* the idol of vain things, rose before me, cutting off the light, and I had not the strength to beat it down.

One day I was walking (in Moscow) in the Borovitskiya Gates. At the gates an old lame beggar was sitting, with a dirty cloth wrapped about his ears. I was just taking out my purse to give him something. At the same moment down from the Kremlin ran a gallant ruddy-faced young soldier, a grenadier in the crown tulup. The beggar, on perceiving the soldier, arose in fear, and ran with all his might toward the Alexandrovsky Park. The grenadier chased him for a time, but not overtaking him, stopped and began to curse the poor wretch because he had established himself under the gateway contrary to regulations. I waited for the soldier. When he approached me, I asked him if he knew how to read.

"Yes; why do you ask?"

"Have you read the New Testament?"

"I have."

"And do you remember the words, 'If thine enemy hunger, feed him'. . . . ?"

I repeated the passage. He remembered it, and heard me to the end, and I saw that he was uneasy. Two passers-by stopped and listened. The grenadier seemed to be troubled that he should be condemned for doing his duty in driving persons away as he was ordered to drive them away. He was confused, and evidently sought for an excuse. Suddenly a light flashed in his intelligent dark eyes; he looked at me over his shoulder, as if he were about to move away.

"And have you read the military regulation?" he asked.

I said that I had not read it.

"Then don't speak to me," said the grenadier, with a triumphant wag of the head, and buttoning up his tulup he marched gallantly away to his post.

[1] I Sam. 12:21, 24, 25.

He was the only man that I ever met who had solved, with an inflexible logic, the question which eternally confronted me in social relations, and which rises continually before every man who calls himself a Christian.

We are wrong when we say that the Christian doctrine is concerned only with the salvation of the individual, and has nothing to do with questions of State. Such an assertion is simply a bold and proofless affirmation of a most manifest untruth, which, when we examine it seriously, falls of itself to the ground. It is well, I said to myself; I will not resist evil; I will turn the other cheek in private life; but if the enemy comes, or here is an oppressed nation, and I am called upon to do my part in the struggle against evil men, to go forth and kill them, I must decide the question, to serve God or *tohu*, to go to war or not to go. I am a peasant; I am appointed starshina of a village, a judge, a juryman; I am obliged to take the oath of office, to judge, to condemn. What ought I to do? Again I must choose between God's law and the human law. I am a monk, I live in a monastery; the neighboring peasants trespass on our pasturage, and I am appointed to take part in the struggle with the evil doers, to plead for justice against the muzhiks. Again I must choose. No man can escape the decision of this question.

I do not speak of those, the largest part of whose activity is spent in resisting evil: military men, judges, governors. No one is so obscure as not to be obliged to choose between God's service, the fulfilment of His commandments, and the service of *tohu*, in his relation to the State. My personal existence is entangled with that of the State, but the State exacts from me an unchristian activity directly contrary to Christ's commands. Now, with general military conscription and the part that every man, in his quality as juror, must take in judicial affairs, this dilemma arises before every one with remarkable definiteness. Every man is forced to take up murderous weapons —the gun, the sword; and even if he does not get as far as murder, his carbine must be loaded, and his sword keen of edge; that is, he must be ready for murder. Every citizen is forced into the service of the courts to take part in meting out judgment and sentence; that is, to deny Christ's command regarding non-resistance of evil, in acts as well as in words.

Mankind to-day faces the grenadier's problem: the gospel or military regulations, divine law or human law, exactly as Samuel faced it. Christ Himself faced it, and so did His disciples; and those that would be Christians now face it; and I also faced it.

Christ's law, with its doctrine of love, humility, and self-denial, had always long before touched my heart and attracted me ·to it. But everywhere, in history, in the events that were going on about me, in my individual life, I saw a contrary law revolting to my heart, my conscience, and my reason, and encouraging to my animal instincts. I felt that if I adopted Christ's law, I should be alone; I might be unhappy; I was likely to be persecuted and afflicted as Christ had said. But if I adopted the human law, every one would approve; I should be in peace and safety, with all the capabilities of intellect at my command to put my conscience at ease. As Christ said, I should laugh and be glad. I felt this, and so I did not analyze the meaning of Christ's law, but sought to understand it in such a way that it might not interfere with my life as an animal. But it was impossible to understand it in that way, and so I did not understand it at all.

Through this lack of understanding, I reached a degree of blindness which now astounds me. As an instance in point, I will adduce my former understanding of these words,—

"Judge not, that ye be not judged."[1]

"Judge not, and ye shall not be judged; condemn not, and ye shall not be condemned."[2]

The courts in which I served, and which insured the safety of my property and my person, seemed to be institutions so indubitably sacred and so entirely in accord with the divine law, it had never entered into my head that the words I have quoted could have any other meaning than an injunction not to speak ill of one's neighbor. It never entered into my head that Christ spoke in these words of the court of the zemstvo, of the criminal tribunal, of the circuit court, and all the senates and departments. Only when I understood the true meaning of the words, *"Resist not evil,"* did the question arise as to Christ's relation to all these courts and departments; and when I understood that Christ would renounce them, I asked myself, "Is not this the real meaning: Not only do not judge your neighbor, do not speak ill of him; but do not judge him in the courts, do not judge him in any of the tribunals that you have instituted?"

Now in Luke (vi. 37-49) these words follow immediately the doctrine that exhorts us to resist not evil and to render for evil, good. And after the injunction, *"Be ye therefore merciful, as your Father also is merciful,"* it says, *"Judge not, and ye shall not be judged; condemn not, and ye shall not be condemned."*

"Judge not"; I asked myself, "does not this mean, Institute no tribunals, for the judgment of your neighbor?" I had only to put this question boldly, when heart and reason united in an affirmative reply.

I know how surprising at first such an understanding of these words must be. It also surprised me. In order to show how far I was before from the true interpretation, I shall confess a shameful pleasantry. Even after I had become a believer, and was reading the New Testament as a divine book, on meeting such of my friends as were judges or attorneys, I was in the habit of saying, "And you still judge, although it is said, 'Judge not, and

[1] Matt. 7:1.   [2] Luke 6:37.

ye shall not be judged'?" I was so sure that these words could have no other meaning than a condemnation of evil speaking that I did not comprehend the horrible blasphemy I thus committed. I was so thoroughly convinced that these words did not mean what they did mean, that I quoted them in their true sense in the form of a pleasantry.

I shall relate in detail how it was that all doubt with regard to the true meaning of these words was effaced from my mind, and how I saw their purport to be that Christ denounced the institution of all human tribunals of whatever sort; that he meant to say so, and could not have expressed himself otherwise.

When I understood the command, *"Resist not evil,"* in its proper sense, the first thing that occurred to me was that human tribunals, instead of conforming to this law, were directly opposed to it, and indeed to the entire doctrine; and therefore that if Christ had thought of tribunals at all, He would have condemned them.

Christ said, *"Resist not evil."* The aim of tribunals is to resist evil. Christ exhorted us to *return good for evil;* tribunals return evil for evil. Christ said, Make no distinction between the good and the evil; tribunals do nothing else. Christ said, *Forgive; forgive not once or seven times,* but without limit; *love your enemies, do good to them that hate you,*—but tribunals do not forgive, they punish; they return not good but evil to those whom they regard as the enemies of society. It would seem, then, that Christ denounced judicial institutions.

But perhaps, said I to myself, Christ never had anything to do with courts of justice, and so did not think of them. But I saw that such a theory was not tenable. Jesus, from His childhood to His death, was concerned with the tribunals of Herod, of the Sanhedrin, and of the High Priests. I saw that Jesus must really have spoken many times of the courts of justice as of an evil. He told His disciples that they would be dragged before the judges, and He Himself told them how to behave in court. He said of Himself that He should be condemned by a tribunal, and He showed what the attitude toward judges ought to be. Christ then must have had in mind the judicial institutions that condemned Him and His disciples; that have condemned and continue to condemn millions of men.

Christ saw the wrong, and pointed it out. When the sentence against the woman taken in adultery was about to be carried into execution, He absolutely repudiated the judgment, and demonstrated that man could not be the judge, since man himself was guilty. And this idea He propounded many times, as where it is declared that the man with a beam in his eye cannot see the mote in another's eye, or that the blind cannot lead the blind. He even pointed out the consequences of such misconceptions,—the disciple would be the same as his Master.

But, perhaps, after having said this in regard to the judgment of the woman taken in adultery, and illustrated the general weakness of humanity by the parable of the beam; perhaps, after all, Christ would admit of an appeal to the justice of men where it was necessary for protection against evil men; but I soon saw that this is inadmissible. In the Sermon on the Mount, he says, addressing the multitude,—

"And if any man will sue thee at the law, and take away thy coat, let him have thy cloak also."[1]

Of course He forbids all men to go to law.

Once more, perhaps, Christ spoke only of the personal bearing which a man should have when brought before judicial institutions, and did not condemn justice, but admitted the necessity in a Christian society of individuals who judge others in properly constituted forms. But I saw that this view also is inadmissible. In the Lord's prayer all men, without exception, are commanded to forgive others, that their own trespasses may be forgiven. This thought Christ often expresses. He who brings his gift to the altar with prayer must first forgive all men. How, then, can a man judge and condemn when his religion commands him to forgive all trespasses without limit? So I saw that according to Christ's teaching no Christian judge could pass sentence of condemnation.

But might not the relation between the words *"Judge not, and ye shall not be judged"* and the preceding or subsequent passages permit us to conclude that Christ, in saying, *"Judge not,"* had no reference to human tribunals? No; this could not be so: on the contrary, it is clear from the relation of the phrases that in saying *"Judge not,"* Christ did actually speak of judicial institutions. According to Matthew and Luke, before saying *"Judge not, condemn not,"* He said, *"Resist not evil; endure evil; do good to all men."* And prior to this, as Matthew tells us, He repeated the ancient criminal law of the Jews, *"An eye for an eye, and a tooth for a tooth."* Then, after this reference to the old criminal law, He added, *"But I say unto you, That ye resist not evil";* and, after that, *"Judge not."* Jesus did, then, refer directly to human criminal law, and repudiated it in the words, *"Judge not."*

Moreover, according to Luke, He not only said, *"Judge not,"* but also, *"Condemn not."* He had some purpose in adding this almost synonymous word; the addition of this word can have only one object: it shows clearly what meaning should be attributed to the other.

If He had wished to say "Judge not your neighbor," He would have said "neighbor"; but He added the words which are translated *"Condemn not,"* and then completed the sentence, *"And ye shall not be condemned; forgive, and ye shall be forgiven."*

But some may still insist that Christ, in expressing Himself in this way,

[1] Matt. 5:40.

did not refer at all to the tribunals, and that I have read my own thoughts into words of His that have a different significance. I will ask how Christ's first disciples, the apostles, regarded courts of justice,—whether they recognized and approved of them. The apostle James says:—[1]

"Speak not evil one of another, brethren. He that speaketh evil of his brother, and judgeth his brother, speaketh evil of the law, and judgeth the law: but if thou judge the law, thou art not a doer of the law, but a judge. There is one lawgiver, who is able to save and to destroy: who art thou that judgest another?"

The word translated "speak evil" is the verb καταλαλέω. It may be seen, without consulting a lexicon, that this word ought to mean "to speak against, to accuse"; and this is its true meaning, as any one may find out for himself by opening a lexicon. In the translation we read, *"He that speaketh evil of his brother, . . . speaketh evil of the law."* Why so? is the question that involuntarily arises. I may speak evil of my brother, but I do not thereby speak evil of the law; but if I *accuse* my brother, if I bring him to court, it is plain that I thereby accuse Christ's law; in other words, I consider Christ's law inadequate: I accuse and judge the law. It is clear, then, that I do not practise His law, but that I make myself a judge of the law. The judge, says Christ, is he who can save. How then shall I, who cannot save, become a judge and punish?

The entire passage refers to human justice, and repudiates it. The whole epistle is permeated with the same idea. In the second chapter we read:—

"(1) My brethren, faith in our Lord Jesus Christ the glorified should be without respect of persons.

"(2) For if there come into your synagogue a man with a gold ring, in rich apparel, and there come in also a poor man in vile raiment (3) and you have respect to him that wears the rich apparel and you say to him: 'It is seemly for you to sit here,' and you say to the poor man: 'You stand there or sit here under my foot-stool'; (4) are you not then partial among yourselves, and are you not become judges with evil thoughts?

"(5) Hearken, my beloved brethren, has not God chosen the poor of this world to be rich in faith and heirs of the kingdom which He promised to those that love Him? (6) But you despised the poor! Do not the rich oppress you, and do they not draw you before the judgment-seat? (7) Do they not dishonor the worthy name by which you are called?

"(8) If you fulfil the royal law according to the Scripture,—Thou shalt love thy neighbor as thyself,[2]—you do well. (9) But if you have respect to persons, you commit sin, and are convicted as transgressors before the law. (10) For whosoever shall keep the whole law and offend in one point, he is guilty in all. (11) For he that said, 'Do not commit adultery' said also 'Do

---

[1] Jas. 4:11, 12.   [2] Lev. 19:18.

not kill.' Now if thou commit no adultery, yet if thou kill, thou art become a transgressor of the law.[1]

"(12) *So speak and so do as men that shall be judged by the law of liberty.*

"(13) *For he shall have judgment without mercy, that hath shewed no mercy; and mercy shall triumph over judgment.*"[2]

(The last phrase, "*mercy shall triumph over judgment,*" has been frequently translated "*mercy is exalted above judgment,*" and cited thus in the sense that there can be such a thing as Christian judgment, but that it ought to be merciful.)

James exhorts his brethren to have no respect of persons. If you διασκρίβιτε—have respect of the condition of persons,—you discriminate; you are like the untrustworthy judges of the tribunals. You regard the beggar as worse, while on the contrary the rich man is worse. He oppresses you and draws you before the judgment-seats. If you live according to the law of love for your neighbor, according to the law of mercy (which James calls "*the law of liberty,*" to distinguish it from all others)—if you live according to this law, it is well. But if you have respect of persons, if you make discriminations among men, you transgress the law of mercy. Then, doubtless thinking of the case of the woman taken in adultery, who was brought before Jesus, about to be stoned to death according to the law, or thinking of the crime of adultery in general, James says that he who inflicts death on the adulterous woman would himself be guilty of murder, and thereby transgress the eternal law; for the eternal law forbids both adultery and murder. He says:—

"*So speak ye, and so do, as they that shall be judged by the law of liberty. For he shall have judgment without mercy, that hath shewed no mercy; and therefore mercy blots out judgment.*"[3]

Could the idea be expressed in terms more clear and precise? All discrimination among men is forbidden, as well as any judgment that shall classify persons as good or bad; human judgment is declared to be inevitably defective, and such judgment is denounced as criminal when it condemns for crime; judgment is blotted out by the law of God, the law of mercy.

I open the epistles of the Apostle Paul, who had been a victim of tribunals, and in the first chapter of Romans I read the admonitions of the apostle for the vices and errors of those to whom his words are addressed; among other matters he speaks of courts of justice:—

"*Who, knowing the righteous judgment of God, that they which commit such things are worthy of death, not only do the same, but have pleasure in them that do them.*"[4]

"*Therefore thou art inexcusable, O man, whosoever thou art that judg-*

---

[1] Deut. 22:22; Lev. 18:17-25.
[2] Jas. 2:13. (Count Tolstoy's rendering.)
[3] Jas. 2:12, 13.
[4] Rom. 1:32.

est another: for wherein thou judgest another, thou condemnest thyself; for thou that judgest another doest the same things.

"But we know that the judgment of God against those that do such things is righteous.

"And thinkest thou, O man, to escape the judgment of God, when thou judgest those that do such things, and yet doest them thyself?

"Or despisest thou the riches of His goodness and forbearance and long-suffering: not knowing that the goodness of God leadeth thee to repentance?"[1]

The Apostle Paul says that they who know the righteous judgment of God, themselves act unjustly and teach others to do the same, and therefore it is impossible to absolve a man who judges.

Such an opinion regarding tribunals I find in the epistles of the apostles, and we know that human justice was among the trials and sufferings that they endured with resignation to the will of God. When we think of the situation of the early Christians, in the midst of heathen, we can easily understand that it could never have occurred to the Christians persecuted by human tribunals to defend human tribunals. Only on occasion could they touch upon this evil, denying that on which it is based, and thus they did. The apostles speak of this evil.

I consulted with the early Fathers of the Church, and found that they all invariably had distinct teaching which distinguishes them from all others—in this respect, that they laid no obligation on any one, they did not judge[2] or condemn any one, and that they endured the tortures inflicted by human justice. The martyrs, by their acts, declared themselves to be of the same mind. I saw that Christianity before Constantine regarded tribunals only as an evil which was to be endured with patience; but it never could have occurred to any early Christian that a Christian could take part in the administration of the courts of justice.

I saw that Christ's words, *"Judge not, condemn not,"* were understood by His first disciples exactly as I understood them now, in their direct and literal meaning: judge not in courts of justice; take no part in them.

All this seemed absolutely to corroborate my conviction that the words, *"Judge not, condemn not,"* referred to the justice of tribunals. Yet the meaning, "Speak not evil of your neighbor," is so firmly established, and courts of justice flaunt their decrees with so much assurance and audacity in all Christian countries, with the support even of the Church, that for a long time still I doubted the correctness of my interpretation.

"If men have understood the words in this way," I said to myself, "and have instituted Christian tribunals, they must certainly have some reason for so doing; there must be a good reason for regarding these words as a

[1] Rom. 2:1-4.   [2] Athenagoras, Origen.

denunciation of evil speaking, and there must be a basis of some sort for the institution of Christian tribunals."

I turned to the Church commentaries. In all, from the fifth century onward, I found the invariable interpretation to be, "Accuse not your neighbor"; that is, avoid evil speaking. As the words came to be understood exclusively in this sense, a difficulty arose,—How to refrain from judgment? It is impossible not to condemn evil; and so all the commentators discussed the question, What is blamable, and what is not blamable? Some, such as Chrysostom and Theophylact, said that, as far as servants of the Church were concerned, the phrase could not be construed as a prohibition of judgment, since the apostles themselves judged men. Others said that Christ doubtless referred to the Jews, who accused their neighbors of shortcomings, and were themselves guilty of great sins.

Nowhere a word about human institutions, about tribunals, to show how they were affected by the warning, *"Judge not."* Did Jesus sanction courts of justice, or did he not?

To this natural question I found no reply—as if it was evident that from the moment a Christian took his seat on the judge's bench he might not only judge his neighbor, but condemn him to death.

I turned to other writers, Greek, Catholic, Protestant,—to the Tübingen school, to the historical school. All, even the most liberal commentators, interpreted the words in question as an injunction against evil speaking.

But why, contrary to the spirit of the whole doctrine of Christ, are these words interpreted in such a narrow way as to exclude courts of justice from the injunction, *"Judge not"?* Why is it supposed that Christ, in forbidding as an offense the judgment of a neighbor which may involuntarily slip from the tongue, did not forbid, did not even consider, the more deliberate judgment that results in punishment inflicted upon the condemned? To this there is no response; not even an allusion to the least possibility that the words "to judge" could be used as referring to a court of justice, to the tribunals from whose punishments millions have suffered.

Moreover, when the words, *"Judge not, condemn not,"* are under discussion, the cruelty of judging in courts of justice is passed over in silence, or else commended. The commentators and theologians all declare that in Christian countries tribunals are necessary, and are not contrary to the law of Christ.

Realizing this, I began to doubt the sincerity of the commentators, and I did what I should have done in the first place; I turned to the translation of the words rendered "to judge" and "to condemn." In the original these words are κρίνω and καταδικάζω. The defective translation in the Epistle of James of the word καταλαλέω which is rendered "to speak evil," strengthened my doubts as to the correct translation of the others. When I looked through different versions of the Gospels, I found καταδικάζω rendered in the Vulgate by *condemnare*, "to condemn"; in the French it is the same; in the Slavonian the rendering is *asuzhdaïte*, "condemn." Luther has *verdammen*, "to curse."

The divergency of these renderings increased my doubts, and I propounded to myself this question: What is and what must be the meaning of the Greek word κρίνω, as used by the two evangelists, and of καταδικάζω, as used by Luke, who, scholars tell us, wrote very correct Greek.

How would these words be translated by a man who knew nothing of the evangelical creed and its commentators, and who had before him only this sentence?

I consulted the general lexicon, and found that the word κρίνω has several different meanings, the one most used being "to condemn in a court of justice," and even "to condemn to death," but in no instance does it signify "to speak evil." I consulted a lexicon of New Testament Greek, and found that it was often used in the sense "to condemn in a court of justice," sometimes in the sense "to choose," never as meaning "to speak evil." And so I inferred that the word κρίνω might be translated in different ways, but that the rendering "to speak evil" was the most forced and far-fetched.

I looked for the word καταδικάζω, which follows κρίνω, evidently to define more closely the sense in which the first word is understood by the writer. I looked for καταδικάζω in the general lexicon, and found that it never had any other signification than "to condemn in judgment," or "to judge worthy of death." I examined the contents and found that the word was used four times in the New Testament, each time in the sense "to condemn under sentence, to judge worthy of death." In James (v. 6) we read, *"Ye have condemned and killed the just."* The word rendered "condemned" is this same καταδικάζω, and is used with reference to Christ, who was judged. The word is never used in any other sense in the New Testament or in any other writing in the Greek language.

What, then, are we to say to all this? To what degree is my conclusion lame? Are not all of us who live in our circle, whenever we consider the fate of humanity, filled with horror at the sufferings and the evil inflicted on mankind by the enforcement of criminal codes,—a scourge to those who condemn as well as to the condemned,—from the slaughters of Genghis Khan to those of the French Revolution and the executions of our own times? He would indeed be without compassion who could refrain from feeling horror and repulsion, not only at the sight of human beings thus treated by their kind, but at the simple recital of death inflicted by the knout, the guillotine, or the gibbet.

The Gospel, every word of which we regard as sacred, declares distinctly and without equivocation: "You have a criminal law, a tooth for a tooth;

but I give you a new law, That you resist not evil. Obey this law; render not evil for evil, but do good to every one, forgive every one, under all circumstances."

Further on comes the injunction, *"Judge not";* and that these words might not be misunderstood, Christ added, *"Condemn not;* condemn not to punishment."

My heart said clearly, distinctly, "Punish not with death," "Punish not with death," said Science; "the more you kill, the more evil increases." Reason said, "Punish not with death; evil cannot suppress evil." The Word of God, in which I believed, said the same thing. And when, in reading the doctrine, I came to the words, *"Condemn not, and ye shall not be condemned; forgive, and ye shall be forgiven,"* I confessed that this was God's Word, and I declared that it meant that I was not to indulge in gossip and evil speaking, and yet I continued to regard tribunals as a Christian institution, and myself as a Christian judge!

I was overwhelmed with horror at the grossness of the error into which I had fallen.

The Death of Ivan Ilyitch

CHAPTER I

*I*n the great building of the law-courts, while the proceedings in the Mielvinsky suit were at a standstill, the members of the board and the prokuror met in Ivan Yegorovitch Shebek's private room, and the conversation turned on the famous Krasovsky suit. Feodor Vasilyevitch talked himself into a passion in pointing out the men's innocence; Ivan Yegorovitch maintained his side; but Piotr Ivanovitch, who had not entered into the discussion at first, took no part in it even now, and was glancing over the *Vyedomosti*, which had just been handed to him.

"Gentlemen!" said he, "Ivan Ilyitch is dead!"

"Is it possible?"

"Here! read for yourself," said he to Feodor Vasilyevitch, handing him the paper, which had still retained its odor of freshness.

Heavy black lines inclosed these printed words:—

"Praskovia Feodorovna Golovina, with heartfelt sorrow, announces to relatives and friends the death of her beloved husband, Ivan Ilyitch Golovin, member of the Court of Appeal,[1] *who departed this life on the 16th Febru-*

[1] *Sudyebnaya Palata.*

ary, 1882. The funeral will take place on Friday, at one o'clock in the afternoon."

Ivan Ilyitch had been the colleague of the gentlemen there assembled, and all liked him. He had been ill for several weeks, and it was said that his case was incurable. His place was kept vacant for him; but it had been decided that, in case of his death, Alekseyef might be assigned to his place, while either Vinnikof or Schtabel would take Alekseyef's place. And so, on hearing of Ivan Ilyitch's death, the first thought of each of the gentlemen gathered in that room was in regard to the changes and promotions which this death might bring about among the members of the council and their acquaintances.

"Now, surely, I shall get either Schtabel's or Vinnikof's place," was Feodor Vasilyevitch's thought. "It has been promised me for a long time; and this promotion will mean an increase in my salary of eight hundred rubles, besides allowances."

"I must propose right away to have my brother-in-law transferred from Kaluga," thought Piotr Ivanovitch. "My wife will be very glad. Then it will be impossible for her to say that I have never done anything for her relations."

"I have been thinking that he wouldn't get up again," said Piotr Ivanovitch aloud. "It is too bad."

"But what was really the matter with him?"

"The doctors could not determine. That is to say, they determined it, but each in his own way. When I saw him the last time, it seemed to me that he was getting better."

"But I haven't been to see him since the Christmas holidays. I kept meaning to go."

"Did he have any property?"

"His wife had a very little, I think. But a mere pittance."

"Well, we must go to see her. They live a frightful distance off."

"That is, from you. Everything is far from you!"

"Now, see here! He can't forgive me because I live on the other side of the river," said Piotr Ivanovitch to Shebek, with a smile.

And then they talked about the long distances in cities, till the recess was over.

Over and above the considerations caused by the death of this man, in regard to the mutations and possible changes in the court that might result from it, the very fact of the death of an intimate friend aroused as usual in all who heard about it a feeling of pleasure that "it was he, and not I, who was dead."

Each one said to himself, or felt:—

"Well, he is dead, and I am not."

The intimate acquaintances, the so-called friends, of Ivan Ilyitch could not help having these thoughts, and also felt that now it was incumbent on them to fulfil the very melancholy obligation of propriety, in going to the funeral and paying a visit of condolence to the widow.

Feodor Vasilyevitch and Piotr Ivanovitch had been more intimate with him than the others.

Piotr Ivanovitch had been his fellow in the law-school, and had felt under obligations to Ivan Ilyitch.

Having, at dinner-time, informed his wife of Ivan Ilyitch's death, and his reflections as to the possibility of his brother-in-law's transfer into their circle, Piotr Ivanovitch, not stopping to rest, put on his dress-coat, and drove off to Ivan Ilyitch's.

At the door of Ivan Ilyitch's residence stood a carriage and two izvoshchiks. At the foot of the stairs, in the hallway by the hat-rack, pushed back against the wall, was the brocaded coffin-cover, with tassels and lace full of purified powdered camphor. Two ladies in black were taking off their shubkas. One whom he knew was Ivan Ilyitch's sister; the other lady he did not know. Piotr Ivanovitch's colleague, Schwartz, was just coming down-stairs; and, as he recognized the newcomer, he stopped on the upper step, and winked at him as much as to say:—

"Ivan Ilyitch was a bad manager; you and I understand a thing or two."

Schwartz's face, with its English side-whiskers, and his spare figure under his dress-coat, had, as always, an elegant solemnity; and this solemnity, which was forever contradicted by Schwartz's jovial nature, here had a peculiar piquancy, so Piotr Ivanovitch thought.

Piotr Ivanovitch gave precedence to the ladies, and slowly followed them up-stairs. Schwartz did not make any move to descend, but waited at the landing. Piotr Ivanovitch understood his motive; without doubt, he wanted to make an appointment for playing cards that evening. The ladies mounted the stairs to the widow's room; and Schwartz, with lips gravely compressed and firm, and with mischievous eyes, indicated to Piotr Ivanovitch, by the motion of his brows, the room at the right, where the dead man was.

Piotr Ivanovitch entered, having that feeling of uncertainty, ever present under such circumstances, as to what would be the proper thing to do. But he knew that in such circumstances the sign of the cross never came amiss. As to whether he ought to make a salutation or not, he was not quite sure; and he therefore took a middle course. As he went into the room, he began to cross himself, and, at the same time, he made an almost imperceptible inclination. As far as he was permitted by the motion of his hands and head, he took in the appearance of the room. Two young men, apparently nephews,—one, a scholar at the gymnasium,—were just leaving the room, making the sign of the cross. An old woman was standing motionless; and a lady, with strangely arched eyebrows, was saying something to

her in a whisper. A hearty-looking, energetic sacristan[1] in a frock was reading something in a loud voice, with an expression which forbade all objection. The muzhik, Gerasim, who acted as butler, was sprinkling something
on the floor, passing slowly in front of Piotr Ivanovitch. As he saw this,
Piotr Ivanovitch immediately became cognizant of a slight odor of de-
composition.

Piotr Ivanovitch, at his last call on Ivan Ilyitch, had seen this muzhik in
the library. He was performing the duties of nurse, and Ivan Ilyitch was
extremely fond of him.

Piotr Ivanovitch kept crossing himself, and bowing impartially toward
the corpse, the sacristan, and the ikons that stood on a table in the corner.
Then, when it seemed to him that he had already continued too long making
signs of the cross with his hand, he stopped short, and began to gaze at
the dead man.

The dead man lay in the drapery of the coffin, as dead men always
lie, a perfectly lifeless weight, absolutely unconscious, with stiffened limbs,
with head forever at rest on the pillow; and showing, as all corpses show,
a brow like yellow wax, with spots on the sunken temples, and a nose so
prominent as almost to press down on the upper lip.

He had greatly changed, and was far more emaciated than when Piotr
Ivanovitch had last seen him; but, as in the case of all the dead, his face
was more beautiful, especially more dignified, than it had been when he
was alive. On his face was an expression signifying that what was necessary
to do, that had been done, and had been done in due form. Besides this,
there was in his expression a reproach or warning to the living. This warning seemed ill-judged to Piotr Ivanovitch, or at least was not applicable to
him. There was something displeasing in it; and therefore Piotr Ivanovitch
again crossed himself hastily, and, it seemed to him, too hastily for proper
decorum, turned around and went to the door.

Schwartz was waiting for him in the next room, standing with legs wide
apart, and with both hands behind his back twirling his "cylinder" hat. Piotr
Ivanovitch was cheered by the first glance at Schwartz's jovial, tidy, elegant
figure. Piotr Ivanovitch comprehended that Schwartz was superior to these
things, and did not give way to these harassing impressions. His appearance alone said:—

The incident of Ivan Ilyitch's funeral cannot serve as a sufficient reason
for breaking into the order of exercises of the session; that is to say, nothing
shall hinder us this very evening from opening and shuffling a pack of
cards while the servant is putting down four fresh candles; in general, there
is no occasion to presuppose that this incident can prevent us from having a
good time this evening, as well as any other.

He even said this in a whisper to Piotr Ivanovitch as he joined him,

[1] *Diachok.*

and proposed that they meet for a game at Feodor Vasilyevitch's. But evidently it was not Piotr Ivanovitch's fate to play cards that evening.

Praskovia Feodorovna, a short woman, and stout in spite of all her efforts to the contrary,—for her figure grew constantly wider and wider from her shoulders down,—dressed all in black, with lace on her head, and with the same extraordinarily arched eyebrows as the lady who had been standing by the coffin, came out from her rooms with other ladies; and as she preceded them through the door of the death-chamber, she said:—

"Mass will take place immediately. Please come in."

Schwartz, making a slight, indefinite bow, stood still, evidently undecided whether to accept or to decline this invitation. Praskovia Feodorvna, as soon as she recognized Piotr Ivanovitch, sighed, came quite close to him, took him by the hand, and said:—

"I know that you were a true friend of Ivan Ilyitch's." And she fixed her eyes on him, awaiting his action to respond to her words.

Piotr Ivanovitch knew that, just as in the other case it had been incumbent upon him to make the sign of the cross, so here he must press her hand, sigh, and say, "Why, certainly." And so he did. And having done so, he realized that the desired result was obtained,—that he was touched, and she was touched.

"Come," said the widow; "before it begins, I must have a talk with you. Give me your arm."

Piotr Ivanovitch offered her his arm; and they walked along to the inner rooms, passing by Schwartz, who winked compassionately at Piotr Ivanovitch.

His jovial glance said:—

"It's all up with your game of *vint;* but don't be concerned, we'll find another partner. We'll cut in when you have finished."

Piotr Ivanovitch sighed still more deeply and grievously, and Praskovia Feodorovna pressed his arm gratefully.

When they entered her drawing-room, which had hangings of rose-colored cretonne, and was dimly lighted by a lamp, they sat down near a table,—she on a divan, but Piotr Ivanovitch on a low ottoman,[1] the springs of which were out of order, and yielded unevenly under his weight.

Praskovia Feodorovna wanted to suggest to him to take another chair; but to make such a suggestion seemed out of place in her situation, and she gave it up. As he sat down on the ottoman, Piotr Ivanovitch remembered how, when Ivan Ilyitch was decorating that drawing-room, he had asked his opinion about this very same rose-colored cretonne, with its green leaves.

As the widow passed by the table in going to the divan,—the whole room was crowded with ornaments and furniture,—she caught the black

[1] *Puff.*

lace of her black mantilla on the woodwork. Piotr Ivanovitch got up, in order to detach it; and the ottoman, freed from his weight, began to shake and jostle him. The widow herself was busy disengaging her lace; and Piotr Ivanovitch sat down again, flattening out the ottoman which had rebelled under him. But still the widow could not get free, and Piotr Ivanovitch again arose; and again the ottoman rebelled, and even creaked.

When all this was arranged, she took out a clean cambric handkerchief, and began to weep. The episode with the lace and the struggle with the ottoman had thrown a chill over Piotr Ivanovitch, and he sat with a frown. This awkward situation was interrupted by Sokolof, Ivan Ilyitch's butler, with the announcement that the lot in the graveyard, which Praskovia Feodorovna had selected, would cost two hundred rubles. She ceased to weep, and, with the air of a martyr, looked at Piotr Ivanovitch, saying in French that it was very trying for her. Piotr Ivanovitch made a silent gesture, signifying his undoubted belief that this was inevitable.

"Smoke, I beg of you!" she said with a voice expressive of magnanimity as well as melancholy. And she discussed with Sokolof the price of the lot.

As Piotr Ivanovitch began to smoke, he overheard how she very circumstantially inquired into the various prices of land, and finally determined on the one which it suited her to purchase. When she had settled upon the lot, she also gave her orders in regard to the singers. Sokolof withdrew.

"I attend to everything myself," she said to Piotr Ivanovitch, moving to one side the albums that lay on the table; and then, noticing that the ashes were about to fall on the table, she hastened to hand Piotr Ivanovitch an ash-tray, and continued:—

"It would be hypocritical for me to declare that grief prevents me from attending to practical affairs. On the contrary, though it cannot console me, yet it may divert my mind from my troubles."

Again she took out her handkerchief, as if preparing to weep; and suddenly, apparently making an effort over herself, she shook herself, and began to speak calmly:—

"At all events, I have some business with you."

Piotr Ivanovitch bowed, not giving the springs of the ottoman a chance to rise up against him, since only the moment before they had been misbehaving under him.

"During the last days, his sufferings were terrible."

"He suffered very much?" asked Piotr Ivanovitch.

"Oh! terribly! For hours before he died he did not cease to shriek. For three days and nights he shrieked all the time. It was unendurable. I cannot understand how I stood it. You could hear him through three doors! Akh! how I suffered!"

"And was he in his senses?" asked Piotr Ivanovitch.

"Yes," she said in a whisper, "to the last moment. He bade us farewell a quarter of an hour before he died, and even asked us to send Volodya out."

The thought of the sufferings of a man whom he had known so intimately, first as a jolly child and schoolboy, and then in adult life as his colleague, suddenly filled Piotr Ivanovitch with terror in spite of the unpleasant sense of this woman's hypocrisy and his own. Once more he saw that forehead, that nose nipping on the lip, and he felt frightened for himself.

"Three days and nights of horrible sufferings and death! Perhaps this may happen to me also, immediately, at any moment," he said to himself. And for an instant he felt panic-stricken. But immediately, though he himself knew not how, there came to his aid the common idea that this had happened to Ivan Ilyitch, and not to him, and therefore such a thing had no business to happen to him, and could not be possible; that, in thinking so, he had fallen into a melancholy frame of mind, which was a foolish thing to do, as was evident by Schwartz's face.

In the course of these reflections, Piotr Ivanovitch became calm, and began with interest to ask for the details of Ivan Ilyitch's decease, as if death were some accident peculiar to Ivan Ilyitch alone, and absolutely remote from himself.

After speaking at greater or less length of the details of the truly terrible physical sufferings endured by Ivan Ilyitch,—Piotr Ivanovitch listened to these details simply because Praskovia Feodorovna's nerves had been affected by her husband's sufferings,—the widow evidently felt that it was time to come to the point.

"Oh! Piotr Ivanovitch! how painful! how horribly painful! how horribly painful!" and again the tears began to flow.

Piotr Ivanovitch sighed, and waited till she had blown her nose. When she had blown her nose, he said:—

"Believe me. . . ."

And again the springs of her speech were unloosed, and she explained what was apparently her chief object in seeing him: this matter concerned the problem of how she should make her husband's death secure her funds from the treasury.

She pretended to ask Piotr Ivanovitch's advice about a pension; but he clearly saw that she had already mastered the minutest points, even those that he himself knew not, in the process of extracting from the treasury the greatest possible amount in case of death. But what she wanted to find out, was whether it were not possible to become the recipient of still more money.

Piotr Ivanovitch endeavored to devise some means to this effect; but, having pondered a little, and out of politeness condemned our government for its niggardliness, he said that it seemed to him impossible to obtain more. Then she sighed, and evidently began to devise some means of getting rid of her visitor. He understood, put out his cigarette, arose, pressed her hand, and passed into the anteroom.

In the dining-room, where stood the clock that Ivan Ilyitch had taken such delight in, when he purchased it at a bric-à-brac shop, Piotr Ivanovitch met the priest and a few more acquaintances who had come to the funeral; and he recognized Ivan Ilyitch's daughter, a pretty young lady, whom he knew. She was all in black. Her very slender figure seemed more slender than usual. She looked melancholy, determined, almost irritated. She bowed to Piotr Ivanovitch as if he were in some way to blame. Behind the daughter, with the same melancholy look, stood a rich young man, a magistrate[1] of Piotr Ivanovitch's acquaintance, who, as he heard, was her betrothed. He bowed to them disconsolately, and was about to pass into the death-chamber, when he saw coming up the stairs the slender form of Ivan Ilyitch's son,—a gymnasium student, and a striking image of Ivan Ilyitch. It was the same little Ivan Ilyitch whom Piotr Ivanovitch remembered at the law-school. His eyes were wet with tears, and had the faded appearance common to unwealthy boys of thirteen or fourteen. The boy, as soon as he saw Piotr Ivanovitch, scowled rudely and bashfully. Piotr Ivanovitch nodded at him, and entered the death-chamber.

The mass had begun; there were candles, groans, incense, tears, and sobs. Piotr Ivanovitch stood looking gloomily down at his feet. He did not once glance at the corpse, and to the end did not yield to the softening influences; and he was one of the first to leave. There was no one in the anteroom. Gerasim, the butler,[2] rushed from the dead man's late room, tossed about all the fur garments with his strong hands, in order to find Piotr Ivanovitch's shuba, and handed it to him.

"Well, brother Gerasim," said Piotr Ivanovitch, so as to say something, "it's too bad, isn't it?"

"God's will. We shall all be there," said Gerasim, showing his close, white, peasant's teeth; and, like a man earnestly engaged in some great work, he opened the door with alacrity, called the coachman, helped Piotr Ivanovitch into the carriage, and then hastened back up the front steps, as if he were eager to find something else to do.

It was particularly agreeable to Piotr Ivanovitch to breathe the fresh air, after the odor of the incense, of the dead body, and carbolic acid.

"Where shall I drive to?" asked the coachman.

"It's not too late. I'll go to Feodor Vasilyevitch's, after all."

And Piotr Ivanovitch drove off. And, in fact, he found them just finishing the first rubber, so that it was convenient for him to cut in.

---

[1] *Sudyebnui slyedovatyel.*   [2] *Bufetnui muzhik.*

CHAPTER II

The past history of Ivan Ilyitch's life was most simple and uneventful, and yet most terrible.

Ivan Ilyitch died at the age of forty-five, a member of the Court of Justice. He was the son of a functionary who had followed, in various ministries and departments at Petersburg, a career such as brings men into a position from which, on account of their long service and their rank, they are never turned adrift, even though it is plainly manifest that their actual usefulness is at an end; and consequently they obtain imaginary, fictitious places, and from six to ten thousand that are not fictitious, on which they live till a good old age.

Such had been Ilya Yefimovitch Golovin, privy councilor, a useless member of various useless commissions.

He had three sons; Ivan Ilyitch was the second. The eldest had followed the same career as his father's, but in a different ministry, and was already nearing that period of his service in which inertia carries a man into emoluments. The third son had been a failure. He had completely gone to pieces in several positions, and he was now connected with railways; and his father and his brothers and especially their wives not only disliked to meet him, but, except when it was absolutely necessary, even forgot that he existed.

A sister was married to Baron Gref, who, like his father-in-law, was a Petersburg chinovnik. Ivan Ilyitch had been *le phénix de la famille*, as they used to say. He was neither so chilling and formal as the eldest brother, nor so unpromising as the youngest. He was the mean between them,—an intelligent, lively, agreeable, and polished man. He had studied at the law-school with his younger brother, who did not graduate but was expelled from the fifth class; Ivan Ilyitch, however, finished his course creditably. At the law-school he showed the same characteristics by which he was afterward distinguished all his life: he was capable, good-natured even to gayety, and sociable, but strictly fulfilling all that he considered to be his duty; duty, in his opinion, was all that is considered to be such by men in the highest station. He was not one to curry favor, either as a boy, or afterward in manhood; but from his earliest years he had been attracted by men in the highest station in society, just as a fly is by the light;[1] he adopted their ways, their views of life, and entered into relations of friendship with them. All the passions of childhood and youth had passed away, not leaving serious traces. He had yielded to sensuality and vanity, and toward the last of his life, to the higher forms of liberalism, but all within certain limits which his nature faithfully prescribed for him.

While at the law-school, he had done some things which hitherto had

[1] In Russian, the word for *light* and *society* is the same.

seemed to him very shameful, and which while he was engaged in them aroused in him deep scorn for himself. But afterward, finding that these things were also done by men of high position, and were not considered by them disgraceful, he came to regard them, not indeed as worthy, but as something to put entirely out of his mind, and he was not in the least troubled by the recollection of them.

When Ivan Ilyitch had graduated from the law-school with the tenth rank,[1] and received from his father some money for his uniform, he ordered a suit of Scharmer, added to his trinkets the little medal with the legend *respice finem*, bade the prince and principal farewell, ate a dinner with his classmates at Donon's, and, furnished with new and stylish trunk, linen, uniform, razors, and toilet articles, and a plaid, ordered or bought at the very best shops, he departed for the province, as chinovnik and private secretary to the governor—a place which his father procured for him.

In the province, Ivan Ilyitch at once got himself into the same sort of easy and agreeable position as his position in the law-school had been. He attended to his duties, pressed forward in his career, and at the same time enjoyed life in a cheerful and circumspect manner. From time to time, delegated by his chief, he visited the districts, bore himself with dignity toward both his superiors and subordinates, and, without overweening conceit, fulfilled with punctuality and incorruptible integrity the duties imposed upon him, preëminently in the affair of the dissenters.[2]

Notwithstanding his youth, and his tendency to be gay and easy-going, he was, in matters of State, thoroughly discreet, and carried his official reserve even to sternness. But in society he was often merry and witty, and always good-natured, polite, and *bon enfant*, as he was called by his chief and his chief's wife, at whose house he was intimate.

While he was in the province, he had maintained relations with one of those ladies who are ready to fling themselves into the arms of an elegant young lawyer. There was also a dressmaker; and there were occasional sprees with visiting flügel-adjutants, and visits to some out-of-the-way street after supper; he had also the favor of his chief and even of his chief's wife, but everything of this sort was attended with such a high tone of good-breeding that it could not be qualified by hard names; it all squared with the rubric of the French expression, *Il faut que jeunesse se passe*.[3]

---

[1] That is, as *Kollyezhski Sekretar*, corresponding to *Shtaps-Kapitan* in the army; the next rank in the *chin* would be titular councilor,—*Titulyarnui Sovyetnik*,—which confers personal nobility.

[2] The first body of *raskolniks*, or dissenters, called the "Old Believers," arose in the time of the Patriarch Nikon, who, in 1654, revised the Scriptures. A quarrel as to the number of fingers to be used in giving the blessing, and the manner of spelling Jesus, seems to have been the chief cause of the *raskol*, or schism. The Greek Church has now to contend with a host of different forms of dissent.—ED.

[3] "A man must sow his wild oats."

All was done with clean hands, with clean linen, with French words, and, above all, in company with the very highest society, and therefore with the approbation of those high in rank.

In this way Ivan Ilyitch served five years, and a change was instituted in the service. The new tribunals were established; new men were needed.

And Ivan Ilyitch was chosen as one of the new men.

He was offered the position of examining magistrate;[1] and accepted it, notwithstanding the fact that this place was in another government, and that he would be obliged to give up the connections he had formed, and form new ones.

Ivan Ilyitch's friends saw him off. They were photographed in a group, they presented him a silver cigarette case, and he departed for his new post.

As an examining magistrate, Ivan Ilyitch was just as *comme il faut*, just as circumspect, and careful to sunder the obligations of his office from his private life, and as successful in winning universal consideration, as when he was a chinovnik with special functions. The office of magistrate itself was vastly more interesting and attractive to Ivan Ilyitch than his former position had been.

To be sure, it used to be agreeable to him, in his former position, to pass with free and easy gait, in his Scharmer-made uniform, in front of trembling petitioners and petty officials, waiting for an interview, and envying him, as he went without hesitation into his chief's private room, and sat down with him to drink a cup of tea, and smoke a cigarette; but the men who had been directly dependent on his pleasure were few,—merely police captains and dissenters,[2] if he were sent out with special instructions. And he liked to meet these men, dependent on him, not only politely, but even on terms of comradeship; he liked to make them feel that he, who had the power to crush them, treated them simply, and like friends. Such men at that time were few.

But now, as examining magistrate, Ivan Ilyitch felt that all, all without exception, even men of importance, of distinction, all were in his hands, and that all he had to do was to write such and such words on a piece of paper with a heading, and this important, distinguished man would be brought to him in the capacity of accused or witness, and, unless he wished to ask him to sit down, he would have to stand in his presence, and submit to his questions. Ivan Ilyitch never took undue advantage of this power; on the contrary, he tried to temper the expression of it. But the consciousness of this power, and the possibility of tempering it, furnished for him the chief interest and attractiveness of his new office.

In the office itself, especially in investigations, Ivan Ilyitch was very quick to master the process of eliminating all circumstances extraneous to the

---

[1] *Sudyebnui Slyedovatyel;* see Anatole Leroy Beaulieu's "L'Empire des Tsars," vol. ii.
[2] *Ispravniks* and *raskolniks.*

case, and of disentangling the most complicated details in such a manner that the case would be presented on paper only in its essentials, and absolutely shorn of his own personal opinion, and, last and not least, that every necessary formality would be fulfilled. This was a new mode of doing things. And he was one of the first to be engaged in putting into operation the code of 1864.

When he took up his residence in the new city, as examining magistrate, Ivan Ilyitch made new acquaintances and ties; he put himself on a new footing, and adopted a somewhat different tone. He held himself rather aloof from the provincial authorities, and took up with a better circle among the judges and wealthy nobles living in the city; and he adopted a tone of easy-going criticism of the government, together with a moderate form of liberalism and "civilized citizenship." At the same time, though Ivan Ilyitch in no wise diminished the elegance of his toilet, yet he ceased to shave his chin, and allowed his beard to grow as it would.

Ivan Ilyitch's life in the new city also passed very agreeably. The society which *fronded* against the government was good and friendly; his salary was larger than before; and, while he had no less zest in life, he had the additional pleasure of playing whist, a game in which, as he enjoyed playing cards, he quickly learned to excel, so that he was always on the winning side.

After two years of service in the new city Ivan Ilyitch met the lady who. became his wife. Praskovia Feodorovna Mikhel was the most fascinating, witty, brilliant young girl in the circle where Ivan Ilyitch moved. In the multitude of other recreations, and as a solace from the labors of his office, Ivan Ilyitch established sportive, easy-going relations with Praskovia Feodorovna.

At the time when Ivan Ilyitch was a chinovnik with special functions, he had been a passionate lover of dancing; but now that he was examining magistrate, he danced only as an occasional exception. He now danced with the idea that, "though I am an advocate of the new order of things, and belong to the fifth class, still, as far as the question of dancing goes, I can at least show that in this respect I am better than the rest."

Thus, it frequently happened that, toward the end of a party, he danced with Praskovia Feodorovna; and it was principally at the time of these dances, that he made the conquest of Praskovia Feodorovna. She fell in love with him. Ivan Ilyitch had no clearly decided intention of getting married; but when the girl fell in love with him, he asked himself this question: "In fact, why should I not get married?" said he to himself.

The young lady, Praskovia Feodorovna, came of a good family belonging to the nobility,[1] far from ill-favored, had a small fortune. Ivan Ilyitch might have aspired to a more brilliant match, but this was an excellent one.

[1] *Dvorianstvo.*

Ivan Ilyitch had his salary; she, he hoped, would have as much more. She was of good family; she was sweet, pretty, and a thoroughly well-bred woman. To say that Ivan Ilyitch got married because he was in love with his betrothed, and found in her sympathy with his views of life, would be just as incorrect as to say that he got married because the men of his set approved of the match.

Ivan Ilyitch took a wife for two reasons: he gave himself a pleasure in taking such a wife; and, at the same time, the people of the highest rank considered such an act proper.

And so Ivan Ilyitch got married.

The wedding ceremony itself, and the first few days of their married life with its connubial caresses, their new furniture, their new plate, their new linen, everything, even the prospects of an increasing family, were all that could be desired. So that Ivan Ilyitch began to think that marriage not only was not going to disturb his easy-going, pleasant, gay, and always respectable life, so approved by society, and which Ivan Ilyitch considered a perfectly natural characteristic of life in general, but was also going to add to it. But from the first months of his wife's pregnancy, there appeared something new, unexpected, disagreeable, hard, and trying, which he could not have foreseen, and from which it was impossible to escape.

His wife, without any motive, as it seemed to Ivan Ilyitch, *de gaité de coeur*, as he said to himself, began to interfere with the pleasant and decent current of his life; without any cause she grew jealous of him, demanded attentions from him, found fault with everything, and caused him disagreeable and stormy scenes.

At first Ivan Ilyitch hoped to free himself from this unpleasant state of things by the same easy-going and respectable acceptation of life which had helped him in days gone by. He tried to ignore his wife's disposition, and continued to live as before in an easy and pleasant way. He invited his friends, he gave card-parties, he attempted to make his visits to the club or to friends; but his wife began one time to abuse him with rough and energetic language, and continued persistently to scold him each time that he failed to fulfil her demands, having evidently made up her mind not to cease berating him until he was completely subjected to her authority,— in other words, until he would stay at home, and be just as deeply in the dumps as she herself,—a thing which Ivan Ilyitch dreaded above all.

He learned that married life, at least as far as his wife was concerned, did not always add to the pleasantness and decency of existence, but, on the contrary, disturbed it, and that, therefore, it was necessary to protect himself from such interference. And Ivan Ilyitch tried to devise means to this end. His official duties were the only thing that had an imposing effect upon Praskovia Feodorovna; and Ivan Ilyitch, by means of his office, and the duties arising from it, began the struggle with his wife, for the defense of his independent life.

When the child was born, and in consequence of the various attempts and failures to have it properly nursed, and the illnesses, real and imaginary, of both mother and child, wherein Ivan Ilyitch's sympathy was demanded, but which were absolutely foreign to him, the necessity for him to secure a life outside of his family became still more imperative.

According as his wife grew more irritable and exacting, so Ivan Ilyitch transferred the center of his life's burdens more and more into his office. He began to love his office more and more, and became more ambitious than he had ever been.

Very soon, not longer than a year after his marriage, Ivan Ilyitch came to the conclusion that married life, while affording certain advantages, was in reality a very complicated and burdensome thing, in relation to which, if one would fufil his duty, that is, live respectably and with the approbation of society, one must work out a certain system, just as in public office.

And such a system Ivan Ilyitch secured in his matrimonial life. He demanded of family life only such conveniences in the way of home dinners, a housekeeper, a bed, as it could furnish him, and, above all, that respectability in external forms which was in accordance with the opinions of society. As for the rest, he was anxious for pleasant amenities; and if he found them, he was very grateful. On the other hand, if he met with opposition and complaint, then he immediately took refuge in the far-off world of his official duties, which alone offered him delight.

Ivan Ilyitch was regarded as an excellent magistrate, and at the end of three years he was appointed deputy-prokuror. His new functions, their importance, the power vested in him of arresting and imprisoning any one, the publicity of his speeches, his success obtained in this field,—all this still more attached him to the service.

Children came; his wife kept growing more irritable and ill-tempered; but the relations which Ivan Ilyitch maintained toward family life made him almost proof against her temper.

After seven years of service in one city, Ivan Ilyitch was promoted to the office of prokuror in another government. They moved; they had not much money, and the place where they went did not suit his wife. Although his salary was larger than before, yet living was more expensive; moreover, two of their children died; and thus family life became still more distasteful to Ivan Ilyitch.

Praskovia Feodorovna blamed her husband for all the misfortunes that came on them in their new place of abode. Most of the subjects of conversation between husband and wife, especially the education of their children, led to questions which were productive of quarrels, so that quarrels were always ready to break out. Only at rare intervals came those periods of affection which distinguish married life, but they were not of long duration. These were little islands in which they rested for a time; but then again they pushed out into the sea of secret animosity, which expressed itself by driving them farther and farther apart.

This alienation might have irritated Ivan Ilyitch, if he had not considered that it was inevitable; but he now began to look on this situation not merely as normal, but even as the goal of his activity in the family. This goal consisted in withdrawing as far as possible from these unpleasantnesses, or of giving them a character of innocence and respectability; and he attained this end by spending less and less time with his family; but when he was to do so, then he endeavored to guarantee his position by the presence of strangers.

But Ivan Ilyitch's chief resource was his office. In the world of his duties was concentrated all his interest in life. And this interest wholly absorbed him. The consciousness of his power of ruining any one whom he might wish to ruin; the importance of his position manifested outwardly when he came into court or met his subordinates; his success with superiors and subordinates; and, above all, his skill in the conduct of affairs,—and he was perfectly conscious of it,—all this delighted him, and, together with conversations with his colleagues, dinners and whist, filled all his life. Thus, for the most part, Ivan Ilyitch's life continued to flow in its even tenor as he considered that it ought to flow,—pleasantly and respectably.

Thus he lived seven years longer. His eldest daughter was already sixteen years old; still another little child had died; and there remained a lad, the one who was in school, the object of their wrangling. Ivan Ilyitch wanted to send him to the law-school; but Praskovia, out of spite toward him, selected the gymnasium. The daughter studied at home, and made good progress; the lad also was not at all backward in his studies.

CHAPTER III

Thus seventeen years of Ivan Ilyitch's life passed since the time of his marriage. He was already an old prokuror, having declined several transfers in the hope of a still more desirable place, when there occurred unexpectedly an unpleasant turn of affairs which was quite disturbing to his peaceful life.

Ivan Ilyitch had been hoping for the position of president[1] in a university city; but Hoppe got in ahead of him, and obtained the place. Ivan Ilyitch became irritated, began to make recriminations, got into a quarrel with him and his next superior; signs of coolness were manifested toward him, and in the subsequent appointments he was passed over.

This was in 1880. This year was the most trying of Ivan Ilyitch's life.

[1] *Predsyedatyel.*

It happened, on the one hand, that his salary did not suffice for his expenses; on the other, that he was forgotten by all, and that what seemed to him a great, an atrocious, injustice toward himself was regarded by others as a perfectly natural thing. Even his father did not think it his duty to come to his aid. He felt that he was abandoned by all his friends, who considered that his position, worth thirty-five hundred rubles a year, was very normal and even fortunate. He alone knew that with the consciousness of the injustice which had been done him, and with his wife's everlasting rasping, and with the debts which began to accumulate, now that he lived beyond his means—he alone knew that his situation was far from normal.

The summer of that year, in order to lighten his expenses, he took leave of absence, and went with his wife to spend the summer at the country place belonging to Praskovia Feodorovna's brother.

In the country, relieved of his official duties, Ivan Ilyitch for the first time felt not only irksomeness, but insupportable anguish; and he made up his mind that it was impossible to live in such a way, and that he must take immediate and decisive steps, no matter what they were.

After a long, sleepless night, which he spent walking up and down the terrace, Ivan Ilyitch decided to go to Petersburg, to bestir himself and to get transferred into another ministry so as to punish *them* who had not known how to appreciate him.

On the next day, notwithstanding all the protests of his wife and brother-in-law, he started for Petersburg.

He wanted only one thing,—to obtain a place worth five thousand a year. He would not stipulate for any special ministry, any special direction, any form of activity. All that he needed was a place,—a place with a salary of five thousand, in the administration, in the banks, on the railways, in the institutions of the Empress Maria, even in the customs service; but the sole condition was the five thousand salary, the sole condition to be relieved from the ministry where they did not know how to appreciate him.

And lo! this trip of Ivan Ilyitch's met with astonishing, unexpected success. At Kursk an acquaintance of his, F. S. Ilyin, came into the first-class carriage, and informed him of a telegram just received by the governor of Kursk to the effect that a change was about to be made in the ministry: in Piotr Ivanovitch's place would be appointed Ivan Semyonovitch.

This probable change, over and above its significance for Russia, had a special significance for Ivan Ilyitch, from the fact that by bringing up a new official, Piotr Petrovitch, and probably his friend Zakhar Ivanovitch, it was in the highest degree favorable for Ivan Ilyitch. Zakhar Ivanovitch was a colleague and friend of Ivan Ilyitch.

In Moscow the tidings were confirmed. And when he reached Petersburg, Ivan Ilyitch sought out Zakhar Ivanovitch, and obtained the promise of a sure position in his old ministry,—that of justice.

At the end of a week he telegraphed his wife:—

"*Zakhar, in Miller's place; in the first report shall be appointed.*"

Ivan Ilyitch, thanks to this change of administration, suddenly obtained in his old ministry such an appointment as put him two grades above his colleagues,—five thousand salary, and thirty-five hundred for traveling expenses.

All his grievances against his former rivals and against the whole ministry were forgotten, and Ivan Ilyitch was entirely happy.

Ivan Ilyitch returned to the country, jocund, contented, as he had not been for a long time. Praskovia Feodorovna also brightened up, and peace was reëstablished between them. Ivan Ilyitch related how he was honored by every one in Petersburg; how all those who had been his enemies were covered with shame and now fawned on him; how they envied him his position, and especially how dearly every one in Petersburg loved him.

Praskovia Feodorovna listened to this, and made believe that she believed it, and did not contradict him in anything, but only made plans for the arrangement of their new life in the city where they were going. And Ivan Ilyitch had the joy of seeing that these plans were his plans, that they coincided, and that his life, interrupted though it had been, was now about to regain its own character of festive pleasure and decency.

Ivan Ilyitch went back for a short visit only. On the 22d of September he was obliged to assume his duties; and, moreover, he needed time to get established in his new place, to transport all his possessions from the province, to buy new things, to give orders for still more,—in a word, to install himself as it seemed proper to his mind, and pretty nearly as it seemed proper to Praskovia Feodorovna's ideas.

And now, when all was ordered so happily, and when he and his wife were in accord, and, above all, lived together but a small portion of the time, they became better friends than they had been since the first years of their married life.

Ivan Ilyitch at first thought of taking his family with him immediately; but the insistence of his sister- and brother-in-law, who suddenly manifested an extraordinary friendliness and brotherly love for Ivan Ilyitch and his family, induced him to depart alone.

Ivan Ilyitch took his departure; and his jocund frame of mind, arising from his success and his reconciliation with his wife, the one consequent upon the other, did not for a moment leave him.

He found admirable apartments, exactly coinciding with the dreams of husband and wife,—spacious, lofty reception-rooms in the old style; a convenient, grandiose library; rooms for his wife and daughter; study-room for his son,—all as if expressly designed for them. Ivan Ilyitch himself took charge of the arrangements. He selected the wall-papers; he bought the furniture, mostly antique, to which he attributed a specially *comme-il-faut* style;[1] hangings and all took form, and took form and approached that ideal which he had established in his conception.

When his arrangements were half completed, they surpassed his expectations. He perceived what a *comme-il-faut*, exquisite, and far from commonplace character all would have when completed. When he lay down to sleep, he imagined his "hall" as it would be. As he looked about his drawing-room, still unfinished, he already saw the fireplace, the screen, the little *étagère*, and those easy-chairs scattered here and there, those plates and saucers on the walls, and the bronzes, just as they would be when all was in place.

He was delighted with the thought of how he should astonish Pasha and Lizanka, who also had such good taste in these things. "They would never look for this. Especially that he would have the thought of going and buying, at such a low price, these old things that gave the whole an extraordinary character of gentility."

In his letters he purposely represented everything worse than it really was—so as to surprise them. All this so occupied him, that even his new duties, much as he enjoyed them, were not so absorbing as he expected. Even while court was in session, he had his moments of abstraction; he was cogitating as to what sort of cornices he should have for his curtains,— straight or matched. He was so interested in this, that often he himself took hold, rearranged the furniture, and even rehung the curtains himself.

One time, when he was climbing on a pair of steps, so as to explain to a dull-minded upholsterer how he wished a drapery to be arranged, he slipped and fell; but, being a strong, dexterous man, he saved himself. He only hit his side on the edge of the frame. He received a bruise, but it quickly passed away. Ivan Ilyitch all this time felt perfectly happy and well. He wrote, "I feel as if I were fifteen years younger."

He expected to finish in September, but circumstances delayed it till the middle of October. But it was all admirable; not only he himself said so, but all who saw it said the same.

In reality, it was exactly what is customary among those people who are not very rich, but who like to ape the rich, and therefore only resemble one another,—silken fabrics, mahogany, flowers, carpets, and bronzes, dark and shining, all that which all people of a certain class affect, so as to be comparable to all people of a certain class. And in his case, there was a greater resemblance, so that it was impossible to single out anything for attention; but still, this to him was something extraordinary.

When he met his family at the railway station, he took them to their apartments, freshly put in order for them; and the lackey, in a white necktie, opened the door into the vestibule, ornamented with flowers; and then they

[1] *Komilfotny stil.*

went into the parlor, the library, and ohed and ahed with delight; and he was very happy; he showed them everything, drank in their praises, and shone with satisfaction. On that very evening at tea, when Praskovia Feodorovna asked him, among other things, how he fell, he laughed, and illustrated in pantomime how he went head over heels, and scared the upholsterer.

"I'm not a gymnast for nothing. Another man would have been killed, but I just struck myself here a little; when you touch it, it hurts; but it's already wearing off—it's a mere bruise."

And they began to live in the new domicile, in which, as always, after one has become fairly established, it was discovered that there was just one room too few; and with their new means, which, as always, lacked a little of being sufficient; about five hundred rubles additional, and it would have been well.

All went extraordinarily well at first, while still their arrangements were not wholly regulated, and there was still much to do,—buying this thing, giving orders for that, rearranging, mending. Although there were occasional disagreements between husband and wife, yet both were so satisfied, and they had so many occupations, that no serious quarrel resulted. Still, when there was nothing left to arrange, they became a trifle bored, and felt that something was lacking; but now they began to form new acquaintances, new habits, and their lives became full.

Ivan Ilyitch spent the morning at court, but returned home to dinner; and at first he was in excellent humor, although sometimes he was a little vexed by something or other in the household management.

Any kind of spot on the table-cloth, on the draperies, any break in the curtain-cords, irritated him. He had taken so much pains in getting things in order, that any kind of harm befalling was painful to him.

But, on the whole, Ivan Ilyitch's life ran on, as in his opinion life ought to run, smoothly, pleasantly, and decently.

He rose at nine o'clock, drank his coffee, read the paper, then donned his uniform, and went down to court. There he instantly got himself into the harness to which he had been so long accustomed,—petitioners, inquiries at the chancery, the chancery itself, sessions public and administrative. In all this, it was necessary to devise means to exclude all those external concerns of life which forever tend to trespass on the accuracy of conducting official duties; it was necessary that he should tolerate no relations with people except on an official basis; and the cause for such relations must be official, and the relations themselves must be only official.

For example, a man comes, and wants to know something or other. Ivan Ilyitch, as a man apart from his office, cannot have any relations with this man; but if the relationship of this man to the magistrate is such that it can be expressed on letter-head paper, then, within the limits of these relations, Ivan Ilyitch would do all, absolutely all, in his power, and at the same time preserve the semblance of affable, philanthropical relations,—in other words, of politeness. The point where his official life and his private life joined was very strictly drawn. Ivan Ilyitch had a high degree of skill in separating the official side from the other without confounding them; and his long practice and talent gave him such *finesse*, that he sometimes, as a virtuoso, allowed himself, by way of a jest, to confound the humanitarian and his official relations.

This act in Ivan Ilyitch's case was played, not only smoothly, pleasantly, and decently, but also in a virtuoso manner. During the intervals, he smoked, drank tea, talked a little about politics, a little about affairs in general, a little about cards, and more than all about appointments; and when weary, but still conscious of his virtuosity, as of one who has well played his part, like one of the first violins of an orchestra, he went home.

At home the mother and daughter had been receiving or making calls; the son was at the gymnasium, preparing his lessons with tutors; and he learned accurately whatever was taught him in the gymnasium. All was excellent.

After dinner, unless he had guests, Ivan Ilyitch sometimes read some book which was much talked about; and during the evening he sat down to his work,—that is, read papers, consulted the laws, compared depositions and applied the law to them.

This was neither tedious nor inspiriting. It was tedious when he had the chance to play *vint;* but if there was no *vint*, then it was far better than to sit alone or with his wife.

Very delightful to Ivan Ilyitch were the little dinners to which he invited ladies and gentlemen holding high positions in society; and such entertainments were like the entertainments of people of the same class, just as his drawing-room was like all drawing-rooms.

One evening they even had a party; they danced, and Ivan Ilyitch felt gay, and all was good; only a great quarrel arose between husband and wife about the patties and sweetmeats. Praskovia Feodorovna had her ideas about them; but Ivan Ilyitch insisted on buying them all of an expensive confectioner, and he got a great quantity of patties; and the quarrel was because there was an extra quantity, and the confectioner's bill amounted to forty-five rubles.

The quarrel was sharp and disagreeable, inasmuch as Praskovia Feodorovna called him "Fool! Pig-head!"

And he, putting his hands to his head in his vexation, muttered something about divorce.

But the party itself was gay. The very best society were present; and Ivan Ilyitch danced with the Princess Trufonova, the sister of the well-known founder of the society called *"Unesi tui mayo gore."*[1]

[1] "Take away my sorrow."

Ivan Ilyitch's official pleasures were the pleasures of self-love; his pleasures in society were pleasures of vanity; but his real pleasures were the pleasures of playing *vint*. He confessed that, after all, after any disagreeable event befalling his life, the pleasure which, like a candle, glowed brighter than all others, was that of sitting down—four good players, and partners who did not shout—to a game of *vint*—and always four, for it is very bad form to have any one cut in, even though you say, "I like it very much"—and have a reasonable, serious game—when the cards run well,—and then to eat a little supper, and drink a glass of wine. And Ivan Ilyitch used to go to sleep, especially after a game of *vint*, when he had won a little something—a large sum is disagreeable—and feel particularly happy in his mind.

Thus they lived. The circle of their friends consisted of the very best society; men of high position visited them, and young men came.

As far as their views upon the circle of their acquaintance were concerned, husband, wife, and daughter were perfectly unanimous. And tacitly they each in the same way pushed aside, and rid themselves of, certain friends and relatives,—the undesirable kind, who came fawning around them in their drawing-room decorated with Japanese plates on the wall. Very soon these undesirable friends ceased to flutter around them, and the Golovins had only the very best society.

Young men were attracted to Lizanka; and the examining magistrate, Petrishchef, the son of Dmitri Ivanovitch Petrishchef, and the sole heir to his wealth, began to flutter around Liza so assiduously, that Ivan Ilyitch already asked Praskovia Feodorovna whether it would not be a good plan to take them on a troïka-ride together, or arrange some private theatricals.

Thus they lived. And thus all went along in its even course, and all was very good.

CHAPTER IV

All were well. It was impossible to see any symptom of ill-health in the fact that Ivan Ilyitch sometimes spoke of a strange taste in his mouth and an uneasiness in the left side of his abdomen.

But it happened that this unpleasant feeling kept increasing; it did not as yet become a pain, but he was all the time conscious of a dull weight in his side, and of an irritable temper. This irritability, constantly increasing and increasing, began to disturb the pleasant, easy-going, decent life that had been characteristic of the Golovin family. The husband and wife began to quarrel more and more frequently; and before long their easy, pleasant relations were broken up, and even the decency was maintained under difficulties.

Scenes once more became very frequent. Once more, but quite infrequently, the little islands appeared, on which husband and wife could meet without an explosion. And Praskovia Feodorovna now said, with some justification, that her husband had a very trying disposition. With her peculiar tendency to exaggeration, she declared that he had always had such a horrible disposition, that nothing but her good nature had enabled her to endure it for twenty years.

It was indeed true that now he was the one that began the quarrels. His querulousness began always before dinner, and often, indeed, just as they sat down to eat the soup. Sometimes he noticed that a dish was chipped; sometimes the food did not suit him; now his son rested his elbows on the table; now it was the way his daughter dressed her hair. And he blamed Praskovia Feodorovna for everything. At first Praskovia Feodorovna answered him back, and said disagreeable things to him; but twice, during dinner-time, he broke out into such a fury that she perceived this to be an unhealthy state, which proceeded from the assimilation of his food; and she held her peace; she did not reply, and merely hastened to finish dinner.

Praskovia Feodoronva regarded her meekness as a great merit. As she had made up her mind that her husband had a horrible disposition, and was making her life wretched, she began to pity herself. And the more she pitied herself, the more she detested her husband. She began to wish that he would die; but she could not wish it, because then they would not have his salary any more. And this actually exasperated her still more against him. She regarded herself as terribly unhappy, from the very fact that his death could not relieve her; and she grew bitter, but concealed it; and this concealed bitterness strengthened her hatred of him.

After one scene in which Ivan Ilyitch was particularly injust, and which he afterward explained on the ground of his irritability being the result of not being well, she told him that, if he was ill, then he ought to take some medicine; and she begged him to go to a famous physician.

He went. Everything was as he expected: everything was done according to the usual way,—the delay; and the pompous, *doctorial* air of importance, so familiar to him, the same as he himself assumed in court; and the tapping and the auscultation; and the leading questions requiring answers predetermined, and apparently not heard; and the look of superlative wisdom which seemed to say, "You, now, just trust yourself to us, and we will do everything; we understand without fail how to manage; everything is done in the same way for any man."

Everything was just exactly as in court. The airs he put on in court for the benefit of those brought before him, the same were assumed by the famous doctor for his benefit.

The doctor said, "Such and such a thing shows that you have such and such a thing in you; but if this is not confirmed according to the investigations of such and such a man, then you must suppose such and such a thing. Now, if we suppose such and such a thing, then"—and so on.

For Ivan Ilyitch, only one question was momentous: Was his case dangerous, or not? But the doctor ignored this inconvenient question. From a doctor's point of view, this question was idle, and deserved no consideration; the only thing to do was to weigh probabilities,—floating kidney, chronic catarrh, appendicitis.[1]

It was not a question about Ivan Ilyitch's life, but there was doubt whether it was floating kidney, or appendicitis; and this doubt the doctor, in Ivan Ilyitch's presence, settled in the most brilliant manner in favor of the appendix, making a reserve in case an analysis of the urine should give new results, and then the case would have to be examined anew.

All this was exactly what Ivan Ilyitch himself had done a thousand times in the same brilliant manner for the benefit of the prisoner at the bar. Thus, even more brilliantly, the doctor made his *résumé*, and with an air of still more joyful triumph gazed down from over his spectacles on the prisoner at the bar. From the doctor's *résumé*, Ivan Ilyitch came to the conclusion that, as far as he was concerned, it was bad; but as far as the doctor, and perhaps the rest of the world, was concerned, it made no difference; but for him it was bad!

And this conclusion struck Ivan Ilyitch with a painful shock, causing in him a feeling of painful pity for himself, and of painful wrath against this physician who showed such indifference to such a vital question.

But he said nothing; then he got up, laid some money on the table, and, with a sigh, said:—

"Probably we sick men often ask you foolish questions," said he; "but, in general, is this trouble serious, or not?"

The doctor gave him a severe glance with one eye, through the spectacles, as if to say:—

"Prisoner at the bar, if you do not confine yourself to the limits of the questions already put to you, I shall be constrained to take measures for having you put out of the audience-chamber."

"I have already told you what I considered necessary and suitable," said the doctor; "a further examination will complete the diagnosis"; and the doctor bowed him out.

Ivan Ilyitch went out slowly, lugubriously took his seat in his sledge, and drove home. All the way he kept repeating what the doctor had said, endeavoring to translate all those involved scientific phrases into simple

---

[1] Russian, "Disease of the blind intestine." "The anatomy is so made sometimes that the kidney on each side may be so loose that it is said to be 'floating' or, more rarely, 'wandering.' In three thousand post-mortem examinations, I have seen some three such cases. The kidney, so loose in its position sometimes, by getting in the wrong place disturbs the anatomy elsewhere; and the surgeon cuts down upon it, and fastens it in its proper place. The spleen is very variable in its size, but does not wander. The blind intestine is the 'head' of the large gut just below where the small gut enters it."—Dr. F. FERGUSON *in note to Translator*

language, and find in them an answer to the question, "Is it a serious, very serious, case for me, or is it a mere nothing?"

And it seemed to him that the sense of all the doctor's words indicated a very serious case. The aspect of everything in the streets was gloomy. The izvoshchiks were gloomy; gloomy the houses, the pedestrians; the shops were gloomy. This pain, this obscure, dull pain, which did not leave him for a second, seemed to him, when taken in connection with the doctor's ambiguous remarks, to gather a new and more serious significance. Ivan Ilyitch, with a new sense of depression, now took heed of it.

He reached home, and began to tell his wife. His wife listened, but while he was in the midst of his account, his daughter came in with her hat on; she was ready to go out with her mother. She sat down with evident disrelish to listen to this wearisome tale, but she was not detained long; her mother did not hear him out.

"Well," said she, "I am very glad, for now you will be careful, and take your medicine properly. Give me the prescription, and I will send Gerasim to the apothecary's."

And she went to get dressed.

He could not get a long breath all the time that she was in the room, and he sighed heavily when she went out.

"Well," said he, "perhaps it's a mere nothing, after all." . . .

He began to take his medicine, and to follow the doctor's prescriptions, which were somewhat modified after the urine had been analyzed. But just here it so happened exactly that in this analysis, and in what ought to have followed it, there was some confusion. It was impossible to trace it back to the doctor, but the result was that what the doctor said to him did not take place. Either he had forgotten or neglected or concealed something from him.

But Ivan Ilyitch nevertheless began faithfully to follow the doctor's prescriptions, and in this way at first he found consolation.

Ivan Ilyitch's principal occupation, after he went to consult the doctor, consisted in carefully carrying out the doctor's prescription in regard to hygiene, and taking his medicine, and watching the symptoms of his malady, all the functions of his organism. Ivan Ilyitch became chiefly interested in human disease and human health. When people spoke in his presence of those who were sick, of those who had died, of those who were recuperating, especially from diseases like his own, he would listen, endeavoring to hide his agitation, would ask questions, and make comparisons with his own ailment.

The pain did not diminish, but Ivan Ilyitch compelled himself to feign that he was getting better. And he was able to deceive himself as long as there was nothing to irritate him. But the moment that he had any disagreeable scene with his wife, any failure at court, a bad hand at *vint*, then he instantly felt the full force of his malady; formerly he endured these reverses, hopefully saying to himself:—

"Now I shall straighten out this wretched business, shall conquer, shall attain success, win the next hand."

But now every little failure cut him down, and plunged him in despair. He said to himself:—

"Here I was just beginning to get a little better, and the medicine was already helping me, and here this cursed bad luck or this unpleasantness . . ."

And he would break out against his bad luck, or against the people that brought him unpleasantness, and were killing him; and he realized how this fit of anger was killing him, but he could not control it.

It would seem that it must be clear to him that these fits of anger against circumstances and people made his malady worse, and that, therefore, he ought not to notice disagreeable trifles; but he reasoned in precisely the opposite way: he said that he needed quiet; he was on the watch for everything which disturbed this quiet, and at every least disturbance his irritation broke out.

His condition was rendered worse by the fact that he read medical works, and consulted doctors. The progress of his disease was so gradual that he was able to deceive himself by comparing one evening with the next; there was little difference. But when he consulted the doctors, then it seemed to him that it was growing worse, and very rapidly also. And notwithstanding that he constantly consulted doctors.

During this month he went to another celebrity; the second celebrity said pretty much the same as the first had said, but he asked questions in a different way. And the consultation with this celebrity redoubled Ivan Ilyitch's doubt and fear.

A friend of a friend of his—a very good doctor—gave an absolutely different definition of his malady; and, notwithstanding the fact that he predicted recovery, his questions and hypotheses still further confused Ivan Ilyitch, and increased his doubts.

A homeopathist defined his disease in a still different manner, and gave him some pellets; and Ivan Ilyitch, without being suspected by any one, took them for a week. But at the end of the week, not perceiving that any relief came of them, and losing faith, not only in this, but in his former methods of treatment, he fell into still greater melancholy.

One time a lady of his acquaintance was telling him about cures effected by means of ikons. Ivan Ilyitch surprised himself by listening attentively, and believing in the reality of the fact. This circumstance frightened him.

"Is it possible that I have reached such a degree of mental weakness?" he asked himself. "Nonsense! All rubbish! One must not give way to mere fancies. Now I'm going to select one physician, and rigorously follow his advice. That's what I will do. That's the end of it. I will not bother my brain, and till summer I will strictly carry out his prescription; and then the result will be seen. Now for an end to these hesitations." . . .

It was easy to say this, but impossible to carry it out. The pain in his side kept troubling him, kept growing if anything worse, became incessant; the taste in his mouth became always more and more peculiar; it seemed to him that his breath was disagreeable, and that he was all the time losing his appetite and strength.

It was impossible to deceive himself; something terrible, novel, and significant, more significant than anything which had ever happened before to Ivan Ilyitch, was taking place in him. And he alone was conscious of it; those who surrounded him did not comprehend it, or did not wish to comprehend it, and thought that everything in the world was going on as before.

This more than aught else pained Ivan Ilyitch. His family,—especially his wife and daughter, who were in the very white-heat of social pleasures, —he saw, did not comprehend at all, were vexed with him because he was gloomy and exacting, as if he were to blame for it. Even though they tried to hide it, he saw that he was in their way, but that his wife had definitely made up her mind in regard to his trouble, and stuck to it, no matter what he might say or do.

This mental attitude was expressed in some such way as this:—

"You know," she would say to an acquaintance, "Ivan Ilyitch, like all easy-going men, can't carry out the doctor's prescriptions strictly. One day he will take his drops, and eat what is ordered for him, and go to bed in good season; then all of a sudden, if I don't look out, he will forget to take his medicine, will eat sturgeon,—though it is forbidden,—yes, and sit up at *vint* till one o'clock."

"Well, now, when?" asks Ivan Ilyitch, with asperity. "Just once at Piotr Ivanovitch's."

"And last evening with Shebek."

"All right,—I could not sleep from pain." . . .

"Yes, not matter what it comes from; only you will never get over it in this way, and will keep on tormenting us."

Paskovia Feodorovna's settled conviction in regard to his ailment,—and she impressed it on every one, and on Ivan Ilyitch himself,—was that he was to blame for it, and that his whole illness was a new affliction which he was causing his wife. Ivan Ilyitch felt that this was involuntary on her part, but it was not on that account any easier for him to bear it.

In court Ivan Ilyitch noticed, or thought he noticed, the same strange behavior toward him; now it seemed to him that he was regarded as a man who was soon to give up his place; again, his friends would suddenly begin to rally him about his low spirits, as if this horrible, strange, and unheard-of something that was breeding in him and ceaselessly sucking up his vitality, and irresistibly dragging him away, were a pleasant subject for raillery! Schwartz especially irritated him with his jocularity, his lively ways, and his *comme-il-faut-ness*, reminding Ivan Ilyitch of himself as he had been ten years before.

Friends came in to have a game of cards. They sat down, they dealt, new cards were shuffled, diamonds were thrown on diamonds,—seven of them. His partner said, "No trumps," and held up two diamonds. What more could be desired? It ought to have been a gay proud moment,—a clean sweep.[1]

And suddenly Ivan Ilyitch was conscious of that living pain, of that taste in his mouth, and it seemed to him barbarous that he should be able thus to rejoice in his hand. He looked at Mikhaïl Mikhaïlovitch, his partner, as he rapped the table with his big red hand, and courteously and condescendingly refrained from gathering up the tricks, but pushed them over to Ivan Ilyitch that he might have the pleasure of counting them, without inconveniencing himself, without putting his hand out.

"What! does he think that I am so weak that I can't put my hand out?" said Ivan Ilyitch to himself; then he forgot what were trumps; trumped his partner's trick, and lost the sweep by three points. And what was more terrible than all was that he saw how Mikhaïl Mikhaïlovitch suffers, and yet to him it was a matter of indifference. And it was terrible to think why it was a matter of indifference to him.

All could see that it was hard for him, and they said to him:—

"We can stop playing if you are tired. You rest awhile." . . .

Rest? No, he was not tired at all; they would finish the rubber. All were gloomy and taciturn. Ivan Ilyitch felt that he was the cause of their gloominess, and he could not enliven it. They had supper, and then went home; and Ivan Ilyitch was left alone, with the consciousness that his life is poisoned for him, and that he is poisoning the lives of others, and that this poison is not growing weaker, but is always working its way deeper and deeper into his being.

And with this consciousness, sometimes also with physical pain, sometimes with terror, he would have to go to bed, and frequently not sleep from anguish the greater part of the night. And in the morning he would have to get up again and dress and go to court and speak, write, and, unless he went out to ride, stay at home for those twenty-four hours, each one of which was a torture. And he had to live thus on the edge of destruction—alone, without any one to understand him and pity him.

[1] *Shlem*, English "slam."

CHAPTER V

Thus passed one month and two.

Before New Year's his brother-in-law came to their city, and stopped at their house. Praskovia Feodorovna had gone out shopping. Ivan Ilyitch was in court. When he came home, and went into his library, he found his brother-in-law there, a healthy, sanguine man, engaged in opening his trunk. He raised his head as he heard Ivan Ilyitch's steps, and looked at him a moment in silence. This look revealed all to Ivan Ilyitch. His brother-in-law opened his mouth to exclaim at him, and refrained. This motion confirmed everything.

"What? Have I changed?"

"Yes . . . there is a change."

And whenever afterward Ivan Ilyitch tried to bring the conversation round to the subject of his external appearance, his brother-in-law avoided it. Praskovia Feodorovna came in and his brother-in-law went to her room. Ivan Ilyitch locked the door, and began to look at himself in the glass, first front face, then his profile. He took his portrait painted with his wife, and compared it with what he saw in the mirror. The change was portentous. Then he bared his arm to the elbow, looked at it, pulled down his sleeve, sat down on the otomanka, and it became darker than night.

"It must not . . . . it must not be!" said he to himself; jumped up, went to the table, unfolded a document, began to read it, but could not. He opened the door, went out into the "hall." The drawing-room door was shut. He tiptoed up to it, and began to listen.

"No, you exaggerate," Praskovia Feodorovna was saying.

"How do I exaggerate? Isn't it plain to you? He's a dead man. Look at his eyes, no light in them. . . . But what's the matter with him?"

"No one knows. Nikolayef"—that was another doctor—"says one thing, but I don't know about it. Leshchititsky"—that was the famous doctor—"says the opposite." . . .

Ivan Ilyitch turned away, went to his room, lay down, and began to think: "Kidney—a floating kidney!"

He recalled all that the doctors had told him,—how it was torn away, and how it was loose. And by an effort of his imagination he endeavored to catch this kidney, to stop it, to fasten it. "It is such a small thing to do," it seemed to him.

"No; I will make another visit to Piotr Ivanovitch."

This was the friend whose friend was a doctor.

He rang, ordered the horse to be harnessed, and got ready to go out.

"Where are you going, *Jean?*" asked his wife, with a peculiarly gloomy and unusually gentle expression.

This unusually gentle expression angered him. He looked at her grimly. "I have got to go to Piotr Ivanovitch's."

He went to the friend whose friend was a doctor. They went together to this doctor's. He found him and had a long talk with him.

As he examined the anatomical and physiological details of what, according to the doctor, was taking place in him, he comprehended it perfectly.

There was one more trifle—the least bit of a trifle in the vermiform appendix. All that could be put to rights. Strengthen the force of one organ, weaken the activity of another—assimilation ensues, and all is set to rights.

He was a little late to dinner. He ate heartily, he talked gayly, but for a long time he was not able to make up his mind to go to work.

At last he went to his library, and immediately sat down to his labors. He read his documents, and labored over them; but he did not get rid of the consciousness that he had before him an important, private duty, which he must carry out to a conclusion.

When he had finished with his documents, he remembered that this private duty was the thought about the vermiform appendix. But he did not give in to it; he went to the drawing-room to tea. They had callers; there was conversation, there was playing on the pianoforte, and singing; the examining magistrate, the desirable match for their daughter, was there. Ivan Ilyitch spent the evening, as Praskovia Feodorovna observed, more cheerfully than usual; but he did not for a moment forget that he had before him those important thoughts about the vermiform appendix.

At eleven o'clock he bade his friends good-night, and retired to his own room. Since his illness began, he had slept alone in a little room off the library. He went to it, undressed, and took a romance of Zola's; but he did not read it; he thought. And in his imagination the longed-for cure of the vermiform appendix took place. Assimilation, secretion, were stimulated; regulated activity was established.

"Yes, it is just exactly so," said he to himself. "It is only necessary to help nature."

He remembered his medicine, got up, took it, lay on his back, waiting for the medicine to have its beneficent effect, and gradually ease his pain.

"Only take it regularly, and avoid unhealthy influences; even now I feel a little better, considerably better."

He began to punch his side; it was not painful to the touch.

"No, I don't feel it . . . already I feel considerably better."

He blew out the candle, and lay on his side. . . . "The vermiform appendix becomes regulated, is absorbed . . ."

And suddenly he began to feel the old, well-known, dull, lingering pain, stubborn, silent, serious; in his mouth the same well-known taste. His heart sank within him; his brain was in a whirl.

"My God! my God!" he cried, "again, again! and it will never cease!"

And suddenly the trouble presented itself to him absolutely in another guise.

"The vermiform appendix! the kidney!" he said to himself. "The trouble lies, not in the blind intestine, not in the kidney . . . but in life . . . and death! Yes, once there was life; but now it is passing away, passing away, and I cannot hold it back. Yes. Why deceive one's self? Is it not evident to every one, except myself, that I am going to die? and it is only a question of weeks, of days . . . maybe instantly. It was light, but now darkness . . . Now I was here, but then I shall be there! Where?"

A chill ran over him, his breathing ceased. He heard only the thumping of his heart.

"I shall not be, but what will be? There will be nothing. Then, where shall I be when I am no more? Will that be death? No, I will not have it!"

He leaped up, wished to light the candle, fumbled about with trembling hands, knocked the candle and candlestick to the floor, and again fell back on the pillow.

"Wherefore? It is all the same," he said to himself, gazing into the darkness with wide-open eyes.

"Death! Yes, death! And *they* know nothing about it, and wish to know nothing about it; and they do not pity me. They are playing."—He heard through the door the distant sound of voices and *ritornelles.*—"To them it is all the same . . . and they also will die. Little fools! I first, and they after me. It will be their turn also. But they are enjoying themselves! Cattle!"

Anger choked him, and he felt an insupportably heavy burden of anguish.

"It cannot be that all men have been exposed to this horrible terror."

He lifted himself once more.

"No, it is not so at all. I must calm myself; I must think it all over from the beginning."

And here he began to reflect:—

"Yes, the beginning of the trouble. I hit my side, and I was just the same as before, one day and the next, only a little ache, then more severe, then the doctor, then low spirits, anxiety, the doctor again. And I am all the time coming nearer and nearer to the abyss. Less strength. Nearer, nearer! And how wasted I am! I have no light in my eyes. And death . . . and I thinking about the intestine! I am thinking only how to cure my intestine; but this is death!—Is it really death?"

Again fear fell on him. He panted, bent over, tried to find the matches, hit his elbow against the table. It hindered him, and hurt him; he lost his patience, pushed angrily against it with more violence, and tipped it over. And in despair, all out of breath, he fell back, expecting death instantly.

At this time the visitors were going. Praskovia Feodorovna was showing them out. She heard the table fall, and came in.

"What is the matter?"

"Nothing . . . I unintentionally knocked it over."

She went out, and brought in a candle. He was lying, breathing heavily, and quickly, like a man who has just run a verst; his eyes were staring at her.

"What is it, *Jean?*"

"No-o-thing. I . . . knock-ed . . . over. . . . Why say anything? she will not understand," he thought.

She did not in the least understand. She picked up the table, lighted the candle for him, and hurried out. She had to say good-night to her company.

When she came back, he was still lying on his back, looking up.

"What is the matter? Are you worse?"

"Yes."

She shook her head, and sat down.

"Do you know, *Jean,* I think we had better send for Leshchititsky? don't you?"

That meant, send for the celebrated doctor, and not mind the expense. He smiled bitterly, and said:—

"No."

She sat a moment, then came to him, and kissed him on the forehead.

He abhorred her, with all the strength of his soul, at that moment when she kissed him; and he had to restrain himself from pushing her away.

"Good-night![1] God give you pleasant sleep!"

"Yes."

CHAPTER VI

Ivan Ilyitch saw that he was going to die, and he was in perpetual despair.

In the depths of his soul, he knew that he was going to die; but he not only failed to get used to the thought, but also simply did not comprehend it, could not comprehend it.

This form of syllogism, which he had studied in Kiziveter's "Logic,"— "Kaï[2] is a man, men are mortal, therefore Kaï is mortal,"—had seemed to him all his life true only in its application to Kaï, but never to himself. It was Kaï as man, as man in general, and in this respect it was perfectly correct; but he was not Kaï, and not man in general, and he had always been an entity absolutely, absolutely distinct from all others; he had been Vanya

[1] *Proshchaï.*
[2] The typical being in logic, like our A. *Kaï* means "word."

with mamma and papa, with Mitya and Volodya,[1] with his playthings, the coachman, with the nurse; then with Katenka, with all the joys, sorrows, enthusiasms of childhood, boyhood, youth.

Was it Kaï who smelt the odor of the little striped leather ball that Vanya had loved so dearly? Was it Kaï who had kissed his mother's hand? and was it for Kaï that the silken folds of his mother's dress had rustled so pleasantly? Was it he who made a conspiracy for the tarts at the law-school? Was it Kaï who had been so deeply in love? Was it Kaï who had such ability in conducting the sessions?

"And Kaï is certainly mortal, and it is proper that he should die; but for me, Vanya, Ivan Ilyitch, with all my feelings, my thoughts,—for me, that is another thing, and it cannot be that I must take my turn and die. That would be too horrible."

This was the way that he felt about it:—

"If I were going to die, like Kaï, then, surely, I should have known it; some internal voice would have told me; but nothing of the sort happened in me, and I myself, and my friends, all of us, have perceived that it was absolutely different in our case from what it was with Kaï. But now how is it?" he said to himself. "It cannot be, it cannot be, but it is! How is this? How understand it?"

And he could not understand it; and he endeavored to put away this thought as false, unjust, unwholesome, and to supplant it with other thoughts true and wholesome. But this thought, not merely as a thought, but, as it were, a reality, kept recurring and taking form before him.

And he summoned in place of this thought other thoughts, one after the other, in the hope of finding succor in them. He strove to return to his former course of reasoning, which hid from him of old the thought of death. But, strangely enough, all that which formerly hid, concealed, destroyed the image of death, was now incapable of producing that effect.

Ivan Ilyitch came to spend the larger part of his time in these attempts to restore the former current of feeling which put death out of sight. Sometimes he said to himself:—

"I will take up my duties again; they certainly kept me alive."

And he went to court, driving away every sort of doubt. He joined his colleagues in conversation, and sat down, according to his old habit, pensively looking with dreamy eyes on the throng, and resting his two emaciated hands on the arms of his oak chair, leaning over, just as usual, toward his colleague, running through the brief, whispering his comments; and then, suddenly lifting his eyes, and sitting straight, he pronounced the well-known words, and began business.

But suddenly, right in the midst of it, the pain in his side, entirely disregarding the time of public business, began its simultaneous business. Ivan

[1] Diminutions respectively of Ivan, Dmitri, and Vladimir.

Ilyitch perceived it, tried to turn his thoughts from it; but it took its course, and DEATH[1] came up and stood directly before him, and gazed at him: and he was stupefied; the fire died out in his eyes, and he began once more to ask himself:—

"Is there nothing true save IT?"

And his colleagues and subordinates saw with surprise and concern that he, this brilliant, keen judge, was confused, was making mistakes.

He shook himself, tried to collect his thoughts, and in a way conducted the session till it adjourned, and then returned home with the melancholy consciousness that he no longer had the ability, as of old, to separate between his judicial acts and what he wished to put out of his thoughts; that even in the midst of his judicial acts, he could not deliver himself from IT. And what was worse than all, was the fact that IT distracted his attention, not to make him do anything, but only to make him look at IT, straight in the eye,—look at IT, and, though doing nothing, suffer beyond words.

And, while attempting to escape from this state of things, Ivan Ilyitch sought relief, sought other shelter; and other aids came along, and for a short time seemed to help him; but immediately they not so much failed, as grew transparent, as if IT became visible through all, and nothing could hide it.

It happened in this latter part of the time that he went into the drawing-room which he had decorated,—that very drawing-room where he had met with the fall, for which he—as he had to think with bitterness and scorn—for the decoration of which he had sacrificed his life; because he knew that his malady began with that bruise: he went in, and saw that on the varnished table was a scratch, cut by something. He sought for the cause of it, and found it in the bronze decoration of an album, which was turned up at the edge. He took the precious album, lovingly filled by him, and broke out in a passion against the carelessness of his daughter and her friends, who destroyed things so, who dog-eared photographs. He put this carefully to rights, and bent back the ornament.

Then the idea occurred to him to transfer this *établissement*,[2] albums and all, to the other corner, where the flowers were. He summoned a servant. Either his wife or his daughter came to his help; they did not agree with him; they argued against the change: he argued, he lost his temper; but everything was good, because he did not think about IT, IT did not appear.

But here, as he himself was beginning to shift the things, his wife said:—

"Hold on! the men will attend to that; you will strain yourself again."

And suddenly IT gleamed through the shelter; he saw IT. IT gleamed; he was already hoping that IT had disappeared, but involuntarily he watched for the pain in his side—there it was, all the time, always making its

---

[1] *Ona*, "she"; that is, death, or the thought of death.
[2] In French in the original.

advance; and he could not forget it, and IT clearly gazed at him from among the flowers. What was the purpose of it all?

"And it is true that here I have lost my life on that curtain as in a charge! It is possible? How horrible and how ridiculous! It cannot be! It cannot be! but it is."

He went back to his library, went to bed, and found himself again alone with IT. Face to face with IT. But to do anything with IT—impossible! Only to look at IT, and grow chill!

CHAPTER VII

How it came about in the third month of Ivan Ilyitch's illness, it was impossible to say, because it came about step by step, imperceptibly; but it came about that his wife and daughter, and his son and the servants, and his acquaintances and the doctors, and chiefly he himself, knew that all the interest felt in him by others was concentrated in this one thing,—how soon he would vacate his place, would free the living from the constraint caused by his presence, and be himself freed from his sufferings.

He slept less and less; they gave him opium, and began to try hypodermic injections of morphine. But this did not relieve him. The dull distress which he experienced in his half-drowsy condition at first merely afforded the relief of change; but soon it came back as severe as ever, or even more intense than open pain.

They prepared for him special dishes, according to the direction of the physicians; but these dishes became ever more and more tasteless, more and more repugnant to him.

Special arrangements also had been made, so that he might perform the wants of nature; and each time it became more trying for him. The torture came from the uncleanliness, the indecency, of it, and the ill odor, from the knowledge that he required the assistance of another.

But from this very same disagreeable circumstance Ivan Ilyitch drew a consolation. His butler, the muzhik Gerasim, always came to set things to rights.

Gerasim was a clean, ruddy young muzhik, who had grown stout in waiting on the table in the city houses. He was always festive, always serene. From the very first, the sight of this man, always so neatly attired in his Russian costume, engaged in this repulsive task, made Ivan Ilyitch ashamed.

One time, after he had got up and was feeling too weak to lift his pantaloons, he threw himself into an easy-chair and was contemplating with horror his bare thighs with their strangely flabby muscles standing out.

Gerasim came in with light, buoyant steps, in thick boots, diffusing an agreeable odor of tar from his boots, and the freshness of the winter air. He wore a clean hempen apron and a clean cotton shirt, with the cuffs rolled up on his bare, strong young arms; and, not looking at Ivan Ilyitch, evidently curbing the joy in life which shone in his face, so as not to offend the sick man, he began to do his work.

"Gerasim," said Ivan Ilyitch, in a weak voice.

Gerasim started, evidently fearing that he had failed in some duty, and turned toward the sick man his fresh, good, simple young face, on which the beard was only just beginning to sprout.

"What can I do for you?"

"This, I am thinking, is disagreeable to you. Forgive me. I cannot help it."

"Do not mention it."[1] And Gerasim's eyes shone, and he showed his white young teeth. "Why should I not do you this service? It is for a sick man."

And with expert, strong hands, he fulfilled his wonted task and went out with light steps. After five minutes he returned, still walking with light steps. He had made everything clean and sweet.

Ivan Ilyitch was still sitting in his arm-chair.

"Gerasim," he said, "be good enough to assist me. Come here."

Gerasim went to him.

"Lift me up. It is hard for me alone, and I sent Dmitri away."

Gerasim went to him. In just the same way as he walked, he lifted him with his strong arm, deftly, gently, and held him. With his other hand he adjusted his clothing, and then was about to let him sit down. But Ivan Ilyitch requested him to help him to the divan. Gerasim, without effort, and exercising no sensible pressure, supported him, almost carrying him, to the divan, and set him down.

"Thank you. How easily, how well, you do it all!"

Gerasim again smiled, and was about to go. But Ivan Ilyitch felt so good with him, that he wanted him to stay.

"Wait! Please bring me that chair . . . no; that one there. Put it under my feet. It is easier for me when my feet are raised."

Gerasim brought the chair, put it down noiselessly, arranged so that it sat even on the floor, and put Ivan Ilyitch's legs on the chair. It seemed to Ivan Ilyitch that he felt more comfortable while Gerasim was holding up his legs.

"It is better when my legs are up," said Ivan Ilyitch. "Bring me that cushion."

Gerasim did this. Again he lifted his legs, and arranged it all. Again Ivan Ilyitch felt better while Gerasim was holding his legs. When he put them down, he felt worse.

"Gerasim," said he, "are you busy just now?"

[1] *Pomilúite-s.*

"Not at all,"[1] said Gerasim, having learned of city people how to speak with gentlefolk.

"What more have you to do?"

"What more have I to do? Everything has been done, except splitting wood against to-morrow."

"Then, hold my legs a little higher, can you?"

"Why not? Of course I can!"

Gerasim lifted his legs higher, and it seemed to Ivan Ilyitch that in this position he felt no pain at all.

"But how about the wood?"

"Don't be worried about that. We shall have time enough."

Ivan Ilyitch bade Gerasim to sit down and hold his legs, and he talked with him. And, strangely enough, it seemed to him that he felt better while Gerasim was holding his legs.

From that time forth Ivan Ilyitch would sometimes call Gerasim, and make him hold his legs on his shoulders, and he liked to talk with him. Gerasim did this easily, willingly, simply, and with a goodness of heart which touched Ivan Ilyitch. In all other people, good health, strength, and vigorous life affronted Ivan Ilyitch; but Gerasim's strength and vigorous life did not affront Ivan Ilyitch, but calmed him.

Ivan Ilyitch's chief torment was a lie,—the lie somehow accepted by every one, that he was only sick, but not dying, and that he needed only to be calm, and trust to the doctors, and then somehow he would come out all right. But *he* knew that, whatever was done, nothing would come of it, except still more excruciating anguish and death. And this lie tormented him; it tormented him that they were unwilling to acknowledge what all knew as well as he knew, but preferred to lie to him about his terrible situation, and made him also a party to this lie. This lie, this lie, it clung to him, even to the very evening of his death; this lie, tending to reduce the strange, solemn act of his death to the same level as visits, curtains, sturgeon for dinner—it was horribly painful for Ivan Ilyitch. And strange! many times, when they were playing this farce for his benefit, he was within a hair's-breadth of shouting at them:—

"Stop your foolish lies! you know as well as I know that I am dying, and so at least stop lying."

But he never had the spirit to do this. The strange, terrible act of his dissolution, he saw, was reduced by all who surrounded him to the grade of an accidental unpleasantness, often unseemly—when he was treated as a man who should come into the drawing-room and diffuse about him a bad odor —and contrary to those principles of "propriety" which he had served all his life. He saw that no one pitied him, because no one was willing even to appreciate his situation. Only Gerasim appreciated his situation, and pitied

[1] *Nikak-nyet-s.*

him. And, therefore, Ivan Ilyitch was contented only when Gerasim was with him.

He was contented when Gerasim for whole nights at a time held his legs, and did not care to go to sleep, saying:—

"Don't you trouble yourself, Ivan Ilyitch; I shall get sleep enough."

Or when suddenly, using *thou* instead of *you*, he would add:—

"If thou wert not sick . . . but since thou art, why not serve thee?"

Gerasim alone did not lie: in every way it was evident that he alone comprehended what the trouble was, and thought it unnecessary to hide it, and simply pitied his sick barin, who was wasting away. He even said directly when Ivan Ilyitch wanted to send him off to bed:—

"We shall all die. Then, why should I not serve you?" he said, meaning by this that he was not troubled by his extra work, for precisely the reason that he was doing it for a dying man, and he hoped that, when his time came, some one would undertake the same service for him.

Besides this lie, or in consequence of it, Ivan Ilyitch felt the greatest torment from the fact that no one pitied him as he longed for them to pity him. At some moments after long agonies he yearned more than all—although he would have been the last to confess it—he yearned for some one to pity him as a sick child is pitied. He longed to be caressed, to be kissed, to be wept for, as a child is caressed and comforted. He knew that he was a magistrate of importance, that his beard was turning gray, and that hence it was impossible; but nevertheless he longed for it. And in his relations with Gerasim there was something that approached this. And, therefore, his relations with Gerasim comforted him.

Ivan Ilyitch would have liked to weep, would have liked to be caressed, and have tears shed for him; and here came his colleague, the member Shebek, and, instead of weeping and being caressed, Ivan Ilyitch puts on a serious, stern, melancholy expression of countenance, and with all his energy speaks his opinions concerning the significance of a judgment of cassation, and obstinately stands up for it.

This lie surrounding him, and existing in him, more than all else poisoned Ivan Ilyitch's last days.

CHAPTER VIII

It was morning.

It was morning merely because Gerasim had gone, and Piotr, the lackey, had come. He put out the candles, opened one curtain, and began noiselessly to put things to rights. Whether it were morning, whether it were evening, Friday or Sunday, all was a matter of indifference to him, all was one and the same thing. The agonizing, shooting pain, never for an instant appeased; the consciousness of a life hopelessly wasting away, but not yet departed; the same terrible, cursed death coming nearer and nearer, the one reality, and always the same lie,—what matter, then, here, of days, weeks, and hours of the day?

"Will you not have me bring the tea?"

"He must follow form, and that requires masters to take tea in the morning," he thought; and he said merely:—

"No."

"Wouldn't you like to go over to the divan?"

"He has to put the room in order, and I hinder him; I am uncleanness, disorder!" he thought to himself, and said merely:—

"No; leave me!"

The lackey still bustled about a little. Ivan Ilyitch put out his hand. Piotr officiously hastened to him:—

"What do you wish?"

"My watch."

Piotr got the watch, which lay near by, and gave it to him.

"Half-past eight. They aren't up yet?"

"No one at all. Vasili Ivanovitch"—that was his son—"has gone to school, and Praskovia Feodorovna gave orders to wake her up if you asked for her. Do you wish it?"

"No, it is not necessary.—Shall I not try the tea?" he asked himself. "Yes . . . tea . . . bring me some."

Piotr started to go out. Ivan Ilyitch felt terror-stricken at being left alone. "How can I keep him? Yes, my medicine. Piotr, give me my medicine.—Why not? perhaps the medicine may help me yet."

He took the spoon, sipped it.

"No, there is no help. All this is nonsense and delusion," he said, as he immediately felt the familiar, mawkish, hopeless taste.

"No, I cannot have any faith in it. But this pain, . . . why this pain? Would that it might cease for a minute!"

And he began to groan. Piotr came back.

"Nothing . . . go! Bring the tea."

Piotr went out. Ivan Ilyitch, left alone, began to groan, not so much from the pain, although it was horrible, as from mental anguish.

"Always the same thing, and the same thing; all these endless days and nights. Would it might come very soon! What very soon? Death, blackness? No, no! Anything rather than death!"

When Piotr came back with the tea on a tray, Ivan Ilyitch stared long at him in bewilderment, not comprehending who he was, what he was. Piotr was abashed at his gaze; and when Piotr showed his confusion, Ivan Ilyitch came to himself.

"Oh, yes," said he, "the tea; very well, set it down. Only help me to wash, and to put on a clean shirt."

And Ivan Ilyitch began to perform his toilet. With resting spells he washed his hands and face, cleaned his teeth, began to comb his hair, and looked into the mirror. It seemed frightful, perfectly frightful, to him, to see how his hair lay flat upon his pale brow.

While he was changing his shirt, he knew that it would be still more frightful if he gazed at his body; and so he did not look at himself. But now it was done. He put on his khalat, wrapped himself in his plaid, and sat down in his easy-chair to take his tea. For a single moment he felt refreshed; but as soon as he began to drink the tea, again that same taste, that same pain. He compelled himself to drink it all, and lay down, stretching out his legs. He lay down, and let Piotr go.

Always the same thing. Now a drop of hope gleaming, then a sea of despair rising up, and always pain, always melancholy, and always the same monotony. It was terribly melancholy to the lonely man; he longed to call in some one, but he knew in advance that it is still worse when others are present.

"Even morphine again . . . to get a little sleep! . . . I will tell him, tell the doctor, to find something else. It is impossible, impossible so."

One hour, two hours, would pass in this way. But there! the bell in the corridor. Perhaps it is the doctor. Exactly: it is the doctor, fresh, hearty, portly, jovial, with an expression as if he said, "You may feel apprehension of something or other, but we will immediately straighten things out for you."

The doctor knows that this expression is not appropriate here; but he has already put it on once for all, and he cannot rid himself of it—like a man who has put on his dress-coat in the morning, and gone to make calls.

The doctor rubs his hands with an air of hearty assurance.

"I am cold. A healthy frost. Let me get warm a little," says he, with just the expression that signifies that all he needs is to wait until he gets warmed a little, and, when he is warmed, then he will straighten things out.

"Well, now, how goes it?"

Ivan Ilyitch feels that the doctor wants to say, "How go your little affairs?" but that he feels that it is impossible to say so; and he says, "What sort of a night did you have?"

Ivan Ilyitch would look at the doctor with an expression which seemed to ask the question, "Are you never ashamed of lying?"

But the doctor has no desire to understand his question.

And Ivan Ilyitch *says:*—

"It was just horrible! The pain does not cease, does not disappear. If you could only give me something for it!"

"That is always the way with you sick folks! Well, now, it seems to me I am warm enough; even the most particular Praskovia Feodorovna would not find anything to take exception to in my temperature. Well, now, how are you really?"

And the doctor shakes hands with him.

And, laying aside his former jocularity, the doctor begins with serious mien to examine the sick man, his pulse and temperature, and he renews the tappings and the auscultation.

Ivan Ilyitch knew for a certainty, and beyond peradventure, that all this was nonsense and foolish deception; but when the doctor, on his knees, leaned over toward him, applying his ear, now higher up, now lower down, and with most sapient mien performed various gymnastic evolutions on him, Ivan Ilyitch succumbed to him, as once he succumbed to the discourses of the lawyers, even when he knew perfectly well that they were deceiving him, and why they were deceiving him.

The doctor, still on his knees on the divan, was still performing the auscultation, when at the door were heard the rustle of Praskovia Feodorovna's silk dress, and her words of blame to Piotr because he had not informed her of the doctor's visit.

She came in, kissed her husband, and immediately began to explain that she had been up a long time; and only through a misunderstanding she had not been there when the doctor came.

Ivan Ilyitch looked at her, observed her from head to foot, and felt a secret indignation at her fairness and her plumpness, and the cleanliness of her hands, her neck, her glossy hair, and the brilliancy of her eyes, brimming with life. He hated her with all the strength of his soul, and her touch made him suffer an actual paroxysm of hatred of her.

Her attitude toward him and his malady was the same as before. Just as the doctor had formulated his treatment of his patient and could not change it, so she had formulated her treatment of him, making him feel that he was not doing what he ought to do, and was himself to blame; and she liked to reproach him for this, and she could not change her attitude toward him.

"Now, just see! he does not heed, he does not take his medicine regularly; and, above all, he lies in a position that is surely bad for him—his feet up."

She related how he made Gerasim hold his legs.

The doctor listened with a disdainfully good-natured smile, as much as to say:—

"What is to be done about it, pray? These sick folks are always conceiving some such foolishness. But you must let it go."

When the examination was over, the doctor looked at his watch; and then Praskovia Feodorovna declared to Ivan Ilyitch that, whether he was willing or not, she was going that very day to call in the celebrated doctor to come and have an examination and consultation with Mikhaïl Danilovitch—that was the name of their ordinary doctor.

"Now, don't oppose it, please. I am doing this for my own self," she said ironically, giving him to understand that she did it all for him, and only on this account did not allow him the right to oppose her.

He said nothing, and frowned. He felt that this life surrounding him was so complicated that it was now hard to escape from it.

She did all this for him, only in her own interest; and she said that she was doing it for him, while she was in reality doing it for herself, as some incredible thing, so that he was forced to take it in its opposite sense.

The celebrated doctor, in fact, came about half-past eleven. Once more they had auscultations; and learned discussions took place before him, or in the next room, about his kidney, about the blind intestine, and questions and answers in such a learned form that again the place of the real question of life and death, which now alone faced him, was driven away by the question of the kidney and the blind intestine, which were not acting as became them, and on which Mikhaïl Danilovitch and the celebrity were to fall instantly and compel to attend to their duties.

The famous doctor took leave with a serious but not hopeless expression. And in reply to the timid question which Ivan Ilyitch's eyes, shining with fear and hope, asked of him, whether there was a possibility of his getting well, it replied that it could not vouch for it, but there was a possibility.

The look of hope with which Ivan Ilyitch followed the doctor was so pathetic that Praskovia Feodorovna, seeing it, even wept, as she went out of the library door in order to give the celebrated doctor his honorarium.

The raising of his spirits, caused by the doctor's hopefulness, was but temporary. Again the same room, the same pictures, curtains, wall-paper, vials, and his aching, pain-broken body. And Ivan Ilyitch began to groan. They gave him a subcutaneous injection, and he fell asleep.

When he woke up it was beginning to grow dusky. They brought him his dinner. He forced himself to eat a little *bouillon*. And again the same monotony, and again the advancing night.

About seven o'clock, after dinner, Praskovia Feodorovna came into his room, dressed as for a party, with her exuberant bosom swelling in her stays, and with traces of powder on her face. She had already that morning told him that they were going to the theater. Sarah Bernhardt had come to town, and they had a box which he had insisted on their taking.

Now he had forgotten about that, and her toilet offended him. But he concealed his vexation when he recollected that he himself had insisted on their taking a box, and going, on the ground that it would be an instructive, esthetic enjoyment for the children.

Praskovia Feodorovna came in self-satisfied, but, as it were, feeling a little to blame. She sat down, asked after his health, as he saw, only for the sake of asking, and not so as to learn, knowing that there was nothing to learn, and began to say what was incumbent on her to say,—that she would not have gone for anything, but that they had taken the box; and that Elen and her daughter and Petrishchef—the examining magistrate, her daughter's betrothed—were going, and it was impossible to let them go alone, but that it would have been more agreeable to her to stay at home with him. Only he should be sure to follow the doctor's prescriptions in her absence.

"Yes—and Feodor Petrovitch"—the betrothed—"wanted to come in. May he? And Liza!"

"Let them come."

The daughter came in, in evening dress, with her fair young body,—her body that made his anguish more keen. But she paraded it before him, strong, healthy, evidently in love, and irritated against the disease, the suffering, and death which stood in the way of her happiness.

Feodor Petrovitch also entered, in his dress-coat, with curly hair *à la Capoul*, with long, sinewy neck tightly incased in a white standing collar, with a huge white bosom, and his long, muscular legs in tight black trousers, with a white glove on one hand, and with an opera hat.[1]

Immediately behind him, almost unnoticed, came the gymnasium scholar, in his new uniform, poor little fellow, with gloves on, and with that terrible blue circle under the eyes, the meaning of which Ivan Ilyitch understood.

He always felt a pity for his son. And terrible was his timid and compassionate glance. With the exception of Gerasim, Vasya alone, it seemed to Ivan Ilyitch, understood and pitied him.

All sat down; again they asked after his health. Silence ensued. Liza asked her mother if she had the opera-glasses. A dispute arose between mother and daughter as to who had mislaid them. It was a disagreeable episode.

Feodor Petrovitch asked Ivan Ilyitch if he had seen Sarah Bernhardt. Ivan Ilyitch did not at first understand his question, but in a moment he said:—

"No . . . why, have you seen her yet?"

"Yes, in 'Adrienne Lecouvreur.' "

Praskovia Feodorovna said that she was especially good in that. The daughter disagreed with her. A conversation arose about the grace and realism of her acting,—the same conversation, which is always and forever one and the same thing.

In the midst of the conversation, Feodor Petrovitch glanced at Ivan Ilyitch, and grew silent. The others glanced at him, and grew silent. Ivan Ilyitch was looking straight ahead with gleaming eyes, evidently indignant at them. Some one had to extricate them from their embarrassment, but there seemed to be no way out of it. No one spoke; and a panic seized them all, lest suddenly this ceremonial lie should somehow be shattered, and the absolute truth become manifest to all.

[1] *Klak*, from French *claque*.

Liza was the first to speak. She broke the silence. She wished to hide what all felt, but she betrayed it.

"One thing is certain,—*if we are going*, it is time," she said, glancing at her watch, her father's gift; and giving the young man a sign, scarcely perceptible, and yet understood by him, she smiled, and arose in her rustling dress.

All arose, said good-by, and went.

When they had gone, Ivan Ilyitch thought that he felt easier: the lying was at an end; it had gone with them; but the pain remained. Always this same pain, always this same terror, made it hard as hard could be. There was no easing of it. It grew ever worse, always worse.

Again minute after minute dragged by, hour after hour, forever the same monotony, and forever endless, and forever more terrible—the inevitable end.

"Yes, send me Gerasim," was his reply to Piotr's question.

CHAPTER IX

Late at night his wife returned. She came in on her tiptoes, but he heard her; he opened his eyes, and quickly closed them again. She wanted to send Gerasim away, and sit with him herself. He opened his eyes, and said:—

"No, go away."

"You suffer very much."

"It makes no difference."

"Take some opium."

He consented, and drank it. She went.

Until three o'clock he was in a painful sleep. It seemed to him that they were forcing him cruelly into a narrow sack, black and deep; and they kept crowding him down, but could not force him in. And this performance, horrible for him, was accompanied with anguish. And he was afraid, and yet wished to get in, and struggled against it, and yet tried to help.

And here suddenly he broke through, and fell . . . and awoke.

There was Gerasim still sitting at his feet on the bed, dozing peacefully, patiently.

But he was lying there with his emaciated legs in stockings resting on his shoulders, the same candle with its shade, and the same never ending pain.

"Go away, Gerasim," he whispered.

"It's nothing; I will sit here a little while."

"No, go away."

He took down his legs, lay on his side on his arm, and began to pity himself. He waited only until Gerasim had gone into the next room, and then he no longer tried to control himself, but wept like a child. He wept over his helplessness, over his terrible loneliness, over the cruelty of men, over the cruelty of God, over the absence of God.

"Why hast Thou done this? Why didst Thou place me here? Why, why dost Thou torture me so horribly?"

He expected no reply; and he wept because there was none, and could be none. The pain seized him again; but he did not stir, did not call. He said to himself:—

"There, now, again, now strike! But why? What have I done to Thee? Why is it?"

Then he became silent; ceased not only to weep, ceased to breathe, and became all attention: as it were, he heard, not a voice speaking with sounds, but the voice of his soul, the tide of his thoughts, arising in him.

"What dost thou need?" was the first clear concept possible to be expressed in words which he heard.

" 'What dost thou need? What dost thou need?' " he said to himself. "What? Freedom from suffering. To live," he replied.

And again he gave his attention, with such effort that already he did not even notice his pain.

"To live? how live?" asked the voice of his soul.

"Yes, to live as I used to live—well, pleasantly."

"How didst thou live before when thou didst live well and pleasantly?" asked the voice.

And he began to call up in his imagination the best moments of his pleasant life. But, strangely enough, all these best moments of his pleasant life seemed to him absolutely different from what they had seemed then,—all, except the earliest remembrances of his childhood. There, in childhood, was something really pleasant, which would give new zest to life if it were to return. But the person who had enjoyed that pleasant existence was no more; it was as if it were the remembrance of some one else.

As soon as the period began which had produced the present *he*, Ivan Ilyitch, all the pleasures which seemed such then, now in his eyes dwindled away, and changed into something of no account, and even disgusting.

And the farther he departed from infancy, and the nearer he came to the present, so much the more unimportant and dubious were the pleasures.

This began in the law-school. There was still something even then which was truly good; then there was gayety, there was friendship, there were hopes. But in the upper classes these good moments became rarer.

Then, in the time of his first service at the governor's, again appeared good moments; these were the recollections of love for a woman. Then all this became confused, and the happy time grew less. The nearer he came to the present, the worse it grew, and still worse and worse it grew.

"My marriage . . . so unexpected, and disillusionment and my wife's breath, and sensuality, hypocrisy! And this dead service, and these labors for money; and thus one year, and two, and ten, and twenty,—and always the same thing. And the longer it went, the more dead it became.

"It is as if all the time I were going down the mountain, while thinking that I was climbing it. So it was. According to public opinion, I was climbing the mountain; and all the time my life was gliding away from under my feet . . . And here it is already . . . die!

"What is this? Why? It cannot be! It cannot be that life has been so irrational, so disgusting. But even if it is so disgusting and irrational, still, why die, and die in such agony? There is no reason.

"Can it be that I did not live as I ought?" suddenly came into his head. "But how can that be, when I have done all that it was my duty to do?" he asked himself. And immediately he put away this sole explanation of the enigma of life and death as something absolutely impossible.

"What dost thou wish now?—To live? To live how? To live as thou livest in court when the usher[1] proclaims, 'The court is coming! the court is coming'?[2]

"The court is coming—the court," he repeated to himself. "Here it is, the court. Yes; but I am not guilty," he cried with indignation. "What for?"

And he ceased to weep; and, turning his face to the wall, he began to think about that one thing, and that alone. "Why, wherefore, all this horror?"

But, in spite of all his thoughts, he received no answer. And when the thought occurred to him, as it had often occurred to him, that all this came from the fact that he had not lived as he should, he instantly remembered all the correctness of his life, and he drove away this strange thought.

CHAPTER X

Thus two weeks longer passed. Ivan Ilyitch no longer got up from the divan. He did not wish to lie in bed, and he lay on the divan. And, lying almost all the time with his face to the wall, he still suffered in solitude the same inexplicable sufferings, and still thought in solitude the same inexplicable thought.

"What is this? Is it true that this is death?"

And an inward voice responded:—

"Yes, it is true."

"Why these torments?"

And the voice responded:—

"But it is so. There is no why."

Farther and beyond this, there was nothing.

[1] *Sudyebnui pristaf.*
[2] *Sud idyot,*—a preliminary proclamation, like our *oyes.*

From the very beginning of his malady, from the time when Ivan Ilyitch for the first time went to the doctor, his life was divided into two conflicting tendencies, alternately succeeding each other. Now it was despair, and the expectation of an incomprehensible and frightful death; now it was hope, and the observation of the functional activity of his body, so full of interest for him. Now before his eyes was the kidney, or the intestine, which, for the time being, failed to fulfil its duty. Then it was that incomprehensible, horrible death, from which it was impossible for any one to escape.

These two mental states, from the very beginning of his illness, kept alternating with one another. But the farther the illness progressed, the more dubious and fantastical became his ideas about the kidney, and the more real his consciousness of approaching death.

He had but to call to mind what he had been three months before, and what he was now, to call to mind with what regularity he had been descending the mountain; and that was sufficient for all possibility of hope to be dispelled.

During the last period of this solitude through which he was passing, as he lay with his face turned to the back of the divan,—a solitude amid a populous city, and amid his numerous circle of friends and family,—a solitude deeper than which could not be found anywhere, either in the depths of the sea, or in the earth,—during the last period of this terrible solitude, Ivan Ilyitch lived only by imagination in the past.

One after another, the pictures of his past life arose before him. They always began with the time nearest to the present, and went back to the very remotest,—to his childhood, and there they rested.

If Ivan Ilyitch remembered the stewed prunes which they had given him to eat that very day, then he remembered the raw, puckery French prunes of his childhood, their peculiar taste, and the abundant flow of saliva caused by the stone. And in connection with these recollections of taste, started a whole series of recollections of that time,—his nurse, his brother, his toys.

"I must not think about these things; it is too painful," said Ivan Ilyitch to himself. And again he transported himself to the present,—the button on the back of the divan, and the wrinkles of the morocco. "Morocco is costly, not durable. There was a quarrel about it. But there was some other morocco, and some other quarrel, when we tore father's portfolio and got punished, and mamma brought us some tarts."[1]

And again his thoughts reverted to childhood; and again it was painful to Ivan Ilyitch, and he tried to avoid it, and think of something else.

And again, together with this current of recollections, there passed through his mind another current of recollections about the progress and rise

[1] *Pirozhki.*

of his disease. Here, also, according as he went back, there was more and more of life. There was more, also, of excellence in life, and more of life itself. And the two were confounded.

"Just as this agony goes from worse to worse, so also all my life has gone from worse to worse," he thought. "One shining point, there back in the distance, at the beginning of life; and then all growing blacker and blacker, swifter and swifter, in inverse proportion to the square of the distance from death," thought Ivan Ilyitch.

And the comparison of a stone falling with accelerating rapidity occurred to his mind. Life, a series of increasing tortures, always speeding swifter and swifter to the end,—the most horrible torture.

"I am falling." . . . .

He shuddered, he tossed, he wished to resist it. But he already knew that it was impossible to resist; and again, with eyes weary of looking, but still not able to resist looking at what was before him, he stared at the back of the divan, and waited, waited for this frightful fall, shock, and destruction.

"It is impossible to resist," he said to himself. "But can I not know the wherefore of it? Even that is impossible. It might be explained by saying that I had not lived as I ought. But it is impossible to acknowledge that," he said to himself, recollecting all the legality, the uprightness, the propriety of his life.

"It is impossible to admit that," he said to himself, with a smile on his lips, as if some one were to see that smile of his, and be deceived by it.

"No explanation! torture, death . . . why?"

CHAPTER XI

Thus passed two weeks. In these weeks, there occurred an event desired by Ivan Ilyitch and his wife. Petrishchef made a formal proposal. This took place in the evening. On the next day, Praskovia Feodorovna went to her husband, meditating in what way to explain to him Feodor Petrovitch's proposition; but that very same night, a change for the worse had taken place in Ivan Ilyitch's condition. Praskovia Feodorovna found him on the same divan, but in a new position. He was lying on his back; he was groaning, and looking straight up with a fixed stare.

She began to speak about medicines. He turned his eyes on her. She did not finish saying what she had begun, so great was the hatred against her expressed in that look.

"For Christ's sake, let me die in peace!" said he.

She was about to go out; but just at this instant the daughter came in, and came near to wish him good-morning. He looked at his daughter as he had looked at his wife, and, in reply to her questions about his health, told her dryly that he would quickly relieve them all of his presence. Neither mother nor daughter said anything more; but they sat for a few moments longer, and then went out.

"What are we to blame for?" said Liza to her mother. "As if we had made him so! I am sorry for papa, but why should he torment us?"

At the usual time the doctor came. Ivan Ilyitch answered "yes," "no," not taking his angry eyes from him; and at last he said:—

"Now see here, you know that you don't help any, so leave me!"

"We can appease your sufferings," said the doctor.

"You cannot even do that; leave me!"

The doctor went into the drawing-room, and advised Praskovia Feodorovna that it was very serious, and that there was only one means—opium—of appeasing his sufferings, which must be terrible.

The doctor said that his physical sufferings were terrible, and this was true; but more terrible than his physical sufferings were his moral sufferings, and in this was his chief torment.

His moral sufferings consisted in the fact that that very night, as he looked at Gerasim's sleepy, good-natured face, with its high cheek-bones, it had suddenly come into his head:—

"But how is it if in reality my whole life, my conscious life, has been wrong?"

It came into his head that what had shortly before presented itself to him as an absolute impossibility—that he had not lived his life as he ought—might be true. It came into his head that the scarcely recognizable desires to struggle against what men highest in position considered good,—desires scarcely recognizable, which he had immediately banished,—might be true, and all the rest might be wrong. And his service, and his course of life, and his family, and these interests of society and office—all this might be wrong.

He endeavored to defend all this before himself. And suddenly he realized all the weakness of what he was defending. And there was nothing to defend.

"But if this is so," he said to himself, "and I am departing from life with the consciousness that I have wasted all that was given me, and that it is impossible to rectify it, what then?"

He lay flat on his back, and began entirely anew to examine his whole life.

When in the morning he saw the lackey, then his wife, then his daughter, then the doctor, each one of their motions, each one of their words, confirmed for him the terrible truth which had been disclosed to him that night. He saw in them himself, all that for which he had lived; and he saw clearly that all this was wrong, all this was a terrible, monstrous lie, concealing both life and death.

This consciousness increased his physical sufferings, added tenfold to them. He groaned and tossed, and threw off the clothes. It seemed to him that they choked him, and loaded him down.

And that was why he detested them.

They gave him a great dose of opium; he became unconscious, but at dinner-time the same thing began again. He drove them from him, and threw himself from place to place.

His wife came to him, and said:—

"*Jean*, darling,[1] do this for me (*for me!*). It cannot do any harm, and sometimes it helps. Why, it is a mere nothing. And often well people try it."

He opened his eyes wide.

"What? Take the sacrament? Why? It's not necessary. But, however . . . ."

She burst into tears.

"Will you, my dear? I will get our priest. He is so sweet!"

"Excellent! very good," he continued.

When the priest came, and confessed him, he became calmer, felt, as it were, an alleviation of his doubts, and consequently of his sufferings; and there came a moment of hope. He again began to think about the blind intestine and the possibility of curing it. He took the sacrament with tears in his eyes.

When they put him to bed after the sacrament, he felt comfortable for the moment, and once more hope of life appeared. He began to think of the operation which they had proposed.

"I want to live, to live," he said to himself.

His wife came to congratulate him. She said the customary words, and added:—

"You feel better, don't you?"

Without looking at her, he said:—

"Yes."

Her hope, her temperament, the expression of her face, the sound of her voice, all said to him one thing:—

"Wrong! all that for which thou hast lived, and thou livest, is falsehood, deception, hiding from thee life and death."

And as soon as he expressed this thought, his exasperation returned, and, together with his exasperation, the physical, tormenting agony; and, with the agony, the consciousness of inevitable death close at hand. Something new took place; a screw seemed to turn in him, twinging pain to show through him, and his breathing was constricted.

The expression of his face, when he said "yes," was terrible. After he had said that "yes," he looked straight into her face, and then, with extraordinary quickness for one so weak, he threw himself on his face and cried:—

"Go away! go away! leave me!"

[1] *Galubchik;* literally, little pigeon.

CHAPTER XII

From that moment began that shriek that did not cease for three days, and was so terrible that, when it was heard two rooms away, it was impossible to hear it without terror. At the moment that he answered his wife, he felt that he was lost, and there was no return, that the end had come, absolutely the end, and the question was not settled, but remained a question.

"U! uu! u!" he cried in varying intonations. He began to shriek, "*N'ye khotchu*—I won't"; and thus he kept up the cry on the letter *u*.

Three whole days, during which for him there was no time, he struggled in that black sack into which an invisible, invincible power was thrusting him. He fought as one condemned to death fights in the hands of the hangman, knowing that he cannot save himself, and at every moment he felt that, notwithstanding all the violence of his struggle, he was nearer and nearer to that which terrified him. He felt that his suffering consisted, both in the fact that he was being thrust into that black hole, and still more that he could not make his way through into it. What hindered him from making his way through was the confession that his life had been good. This justification of his life caught him, and did not let him advance, and more than all else tormented him.

Suddenly some force knocked him in the breast, in the side, still more forcibly compressed his breath; he was hurled through the hole, and there at the bottom of the hole some light seemed to shine on him. It happened to him as it sometimes does on a railway carriage when you think that you are going forward, but are really going backward, and suddenly recognize the true direction.

"Yes, all was wrong," he said to himself; "but that is nothing. I might, I might have done right. What is right?" he asked himself, and suddenly stopped.

This was at the end of the third day, two hours before his death. At this very same time the little student noiselessly stole into his father's room, and approached his bed. The moribund was continually shrieking desperately, and tossing his arms. His hand struck upon the little student's head. The little student seized it, pressed it to his lips, and burst into tears.

It was at this very same time that Ivan Ilyitch fell through, saw the light, and it was revealed to him that his life had not been as it ought, but that still it was possible to repair it. He was just asking himself, "What is right?" and stopped to listen.

Then he felt that some one was kissing his hand. He opened his eyes, and looked at his son. He felt sorry for him. His wife came to him. He looked at her. With open mouth, and with her nose and cheeks wet with tears, with an expression of despair, she was looking at him. He felt sorry for her.

"Yes, I am a torment to them," he thought. "I am sorry for them, but they will be better off when I am dead."

He wanted to express this, but he had not the strength to say it.

"However, why should I say it? I must do it."

He pointed out his son to his wife by a glance, and said:—

"Take him away . . . I am sorry . . . and for thee."

He wanted to say also, "*Prosti*—Forgive," but he said, "*Propusti*—Let it pass"; and, not having the strength to correct himself, he waved his hand, knowing that he would comprehend who had the right.

And suddenly it became clear to him that what oppressed him, and was hidden from him, suddenly was lighted up for him all at once, and on two sides, on ten sides, on all sides.

He felt sorry for them; he felt that he must do something to make it less painful for them. To free them, and free himself, from these torments, "How good and how simple!" he thought.

"But the pain," he asked himself, "where is it?—Here, now, where art thou, pain?"

He began to listen.

"Yes, here it is! Well, then, do your worst, pain!"

"And death? where is it?"

He tried to find his former customary fear of death, and could not.

"Where is death? What is it?"

There was no fear, because there was no death.

In place of death was light!

"Here is something like!" he suddenly said aloud. "What joy!"

For him all this passed in a single instant, and the significance of this instant did not change.

For those who stood by his side, his death-agony was prolonged two hours more. In his breast something bubbled up, his emaciated body shuddered. Then more and more rarely came the bubbling and the rattling.

"It is all over," said some one above him.

He heard these words, and repeated them in his soul.

"It is over! death!" he said to himself. "It does not exist more."

He drew in one more breath, stopped in the midst of it, stretched himself, and died.

How Much Land Does a Man Need?

I

A woman came from the city, to visit her younger sister in the country. The elder was a city merchant's wife; the younger, a country muzhik's. The two sisters drank tea together and talked. The older sister began to boast—to praise up her life in the city; how she lived roomily and elegantly, and went out, and how she dressed her children, and what rich things she had to eat and drink, and how she went to drive, and to walk, and to the theater.

The younger sister felt affronted, and began to depreciate the life of a merchant, and to set forth the advantages of her own,—that of the peasant.

"I wouldn't exchange my life for yours," says she. "Granted that we live coarsely, still we don't know what fear is. You live more elegantly; but you have to sell a great deal, else you find yourselves entirely sold. And the proverb runs, 'Loss is Gain's bigger brother.' It also happens, to-day you're rich, but to-morrow you're a beggar.[1] But our muzhiks' affairs are more reliable; the muzhik's life is meager, but long; we may not be rich, but we have enough."

The elder sister began to say:—

"Enough,—I should think so! So do pigs and calves! No fine dresses, no good society. How your goodman[2] works! how you live in the dunghill! and so you will die and it will be the same thing with your children."

"Indeed," said the younger, "our affairs are all right. We live well. We truckle to no one, we stand in fear of no one. But you in the city all live in the midst of temptations: to-day it's all right; but to-morrow up comes some improper person, I fear, to tempt you, and tempts your khozyaïn either to cards, or to wine, or to women. And everything goes to ruin. Isn't it so?"

Pakhom, the "goodman," was listening on the oven, as the women discussed.

"That's true," says he, "the veritable truth. As we peasants[3] from childhood turn up mother earth,[4] so folly stays in our head, and does not depart. Our one trouble is,—so little land. If I only had as much land as I wanted, I shouldn't be afraid of any one—even of the Devil."

The women drank up their tea, talked some more about dresses, put away the dishes, and went to bed.

But the Devil was sitting behind the oven; he heard everything. He was

---

[1] Literally, find thyself under the windows.
[2] *Khozyaïn.*

[3] *Nash brat;* literally, our brother.
[4] *Zemlya-matushka.*

delighted because the peasant woman had induced her husband to boast with her; he had boasted that, if he had land enough, the Devil could not get him!

"All right," he thinks; "you and I'll have to fight it out. I will give you a lot of land. I'll get you through the land."

II

Next the muzhiks lived a lady.[1] She had one hundred and twenty desyatins[2] of land. And she had always lived peaceably with the muzhiks, never taking any advantage of them. But a retired soldier engaged himself as her overseer, and he began to vex the muzhiks with fines. No matter how careful Pakhom was, either his horse would trample down the oats, or his cow would wander into the garden, or his calves would get into the meadows; there was a fine for everything.

Pakhom paid the fines, and scolded and beat the domestics. And during the summer Pakhom fell into many a sin on account of this overseer. And still he was glad that he had cattle in his dvor; though fodder was scarce, he was in no apprehension.

During the winter, the rumor spread that the lady was going to sell her land, and that a dvornik from the highway had made arrangements to buy it.

The muzhiks heard it, and groaned.

"Now," think they, "the land will belong to the dvornik; he will make us pay worse fines than the lady did. It is impossible for us to live without this land. All of us around here live on it."

The peasants went to the lady in a body and began to beg her not to sell the land to the dvornik, but to let them have it. They promised to pay a higher price.

The lady agreed. The muzhiks tried to arrange, as a mir, to buy all the land. Once, twice, they collected in meeting, but there was a hitch in affairs. The evil one put them at variance; they were utterly unable to come to any agreement.

And the muzhiks determined to purchase the land individually, according to the ability of each. And the lady agreed to this also.

Pakhom heard that a neighbor had bought twenty desyatins[3] from the lady, and that she had given him a year in which to pay her half of the money. Pakhom was envious.

"They will buy all the land," he said to himself, "and I shall be behind them." He began to reason with his wife.

"The people are buying it up," said he. "We must buy ten desyatins too.

---

[1] Baruinka, diminutive of *baruinya*, gracious lady.
[2] Three hundred and twenty-four acres.
[3] Fifty-four acres.

Otherwise it will be impossible to live; the overseer was eating us up with fines."

They planned how to buy it. They had laid up a hundred rubles; then they sold a colt and half their bees; and they put their son out as a laborer, and they got some more from their brother-in-law; and thus they collected half of the money.

Pakhom gathered up the money, selected fifteen desyatins of land with forest on it, and went to the lady to make the purchase. He negotiated for fifteen desyatins, struck a bargain, and paid down the earnest-money. They went to the city, ratified the purchase; he paid down half of the money; the remainder he bound himself to pay in two years.

And Pakhom now had his land. Pakhom took seed, and sowed the land that he had bought. In a single year he paid up the debt to the lady and to his brother-in-law. And Pakhom became a proprietor.[1] He plowed all his land, and sowed it; he made hay on his own land; he cut stakes on his own land; and on his own land he pastured cattle. Pakhom would ride out over his wide fields to plow, or he would take note of his crops, or gaze at his meadows. And yet he was not happy. The grass seemed to him to be wasted, and the flowers flowering in it seemed entirely different. Formerly he used to ride over this land,—the land as land; but now the land began to be absolutely peculiar.

III

Thus Pakhom lived, and enjoyed himself. Everything would have been good, only the muzhiks began to trespass on his grain and meadows. He begged them to refrain, but they would not stop it. Now the cowboys let the cows into the meadow; now the horses escaped from the night-guard into his corn-field.

And Pakhom drove them out, and forgave it, and never went to law; then he got tired of it, and complained to the volost-court.[2] And though he knew that the muzhiks did it from carelessness, and not from malice, he said to himself:—

"It is impossible to overlook it, otherwise they'll always be pasturing their cattle there. We must teach them a lesson."

He thus taught them in court once; he taught them twice: first one was fined, then another. The muzhiks, Pakhom's neighbors, began to harbor spite against him. Once more they began to trespass, and this time on purpose. Some one got into his woodland by night. They cut down a dozen of his lindens for basts. Pakhom went to his grove, saw what had been done, and turned pale. Some one had been there; the linden branches lay scattered

---

[1] *Pomyeshchick.*
[2] The *volost* is a district including several villages.

about, the stumps stood out. The whole clump had been cut down to the very last; the rascal had cleaned it all out; only one was left standing.

Pakhom fell into a rage. "Akh!" said he to himself, "if I only knew who did that, I would give him a kneading."

He thought and he thought, "Who could it be?"

"No one more likely," said he to himself, "than Semka."[1]

He went to search through Semka's dvor; he found nothing; they only exchanged some quarrelsome words. And Pakhom felt still more certain that Semyon had done it. He entered a complaint against him. They took it into court and had a long trial. The muzhik was acquitted, for there was no proof against him. Pakhom was still more affronted; he got incensed at the starshina and at the judges.

"You," said he, "are on the side of a pack of thieves. If you were decent men, you wouldn't acquit thieves."

Pakhom quarreled both with the judges and with his neighbors. They began even to threaten him with the "red rooster."[2] Pakhom had come to live on a broader scale on his farm, but with more constraint in the commune.

And about this time the rumor spread that the people were going to new places. And Pakhom said to himself:—

"There is no reason for *me* to go from my land; but if any of our neighbors should go, it would give us more room. I would take their land for myself; I would get it around here: life would be much better, for now it is too confined."

One time Pakhom was sitting at home; a wandering muzhik came along. They let the muzhik have a night's lodging; they gave him something to eat; they entered into conversation with him:—

"Whither, please, is God taking you?"

The muzhik said that he was on his way from down the Volga, where he had been at work. The muzhik related, a word at a time, how the people had gone colonizing there. He related how they had settled there, made a community, and given each *soul* ten desyatins of land. "But the land is such," said he, "that they sowed rye. Such stalks—the horses never saw the like—so thick! five handfuls made a sheaf. One muzhik," said he, "was perfectly poor,—came with his hands alone,—and now he has six horses and two cows."

Pakhom's heart burned within him; he said to himself: "Why remain here in straitened circumstances, when it is possible to live well? I will sell my house and land here; then, with the money I get, I will start anew, and have a complete establishment. But here in these narrow quarters—it's a sin. Only I must find out all about it for myself."

[1] Semka, diminutive of Semyon, Simeon.
[2] The picturesque Russian metaphor for a conflagration.

He planned to be gone all summer, and started. From Samara he sailed down the Volga in a steamboat, then he went on foot four hundred versts. He reached the place. It was just so. The muzhiks were living on a generous scale,[1] on farms of ten desyatins each, and they were glad to have accessions to their community. "And any one who has a little money can buy for three rubles as much of the very best land as he wishes, besides his allotment. You can buy just as much as you wish."

Pakhom made a thorough study of it; in the autumn he returned home, and proceeded to sell out everything. He sold his land to advantage, sold his dvor, sold all his cattle, withdrew his name from the community, waited till spring, and moved with his family to the new place.

IV

Pakhom came with his family to the new place, and enrolled himself in a large village. He treated the elders to vodka, arranged all the papers. Pakhom was accepted; he was allotted, as for five persons, fifty desyatins[2] of the land, to be located in different fields, besides the pasturage. Pakhom settled down. He got cattle. He had three times as much land as he had had before, and the land was fertile. Life was tenfold better than what it had been in the old time; he had all the arable land and fodder that he needed. He could keep as many cattle as he liked.

At first, while he was getting settled, and putting his house in order, Pakhom was well pleased; but after he began to feel at home, even this farm seemed to him rather narrow quarters.

The first year Pakhom sowed wheat on his allotment; it came up well. He was anxious to sow wheat; but his allotment seemed to him altogether too small for his ambition.

Wheat is sowed there on grass or fallow land. They sow it one year, two years, and let it lie fallow till the feather-grass comes up again. There are many rival claimants for such land and there's not nearly enough to go round.

Quarrels also arose on account of this; one was richer than another: they all wanted to sow, but the poorer ones had to resort to merchants for loans.

Pakhom was desirous of sowing as much as possible. The next year he went to a merchant and hired land for a year. He sowed more; it came up well, but he had to go a long way from the village, not less than fifteen versts. He saw how muzhik-merchants in the vicinity lived in fine houses, and got rich.

"That's the thing," said Pakhom to himself. "If only I could buy the land, then I would have a fine house. It would all be in one piece."

[1] *Prostorno,* roomily.
[2] One hundred and thirty-five acres.

And Pakhom began to cogitate how he might get a perpetual title.

Thus Pakhom lived three years. He hired land and sowed more wheat. The years were good, and the wheat grew well, and extra money was laid away.

As life passed, it became every year irksome to Pakhom to buy land with the men, to waste time over it; where the land is pretty good, the muzhiks instantly fly to it and divide it all up. He was always too late to buy cheap, and he had nothing to sow on.

But in the third year, he bought, on shares with a merchant, a pasturage of the muzhiks; and they had already plowed it. The muzhiks had been at law about it, and so the work was lost. "If I owned the land," he thinks, "I should not truckle to any one; and it would not be a sin."

And Pakhom began to inquire where he might buy land in perpetuity. And he struck upon a muzhik. The muzhik had five hundred desyatins[1] for sale; and, as he was anxious to get rid of it, he would sell at a bargain.

Pakhom began to dicker with him. He argued and argued, and finally the muzhik agreed to sell for fifteen hundred rubles, half the money on mortgage. They had already come to an agreement, when a peddler happened along, and asked Pakhom to let him have a little something to eat.

While they were drinking a cup of tea, they entered into conversation. The peddler related how he was on his way from the distant Bashkirs.

"There," said he, "I bought of the Bashkirs fifteen hundred desyatins of land; and I had to pay only a thousand rubles."

Pakhom began to ask questions. The peddler told his story.

"All I did," said he, "was to satisfy the old men. I distributed some khalats and carpets, worth a hundred rubles, besides a chest of tea; and I gave a little wine to those who drank. And I got it for twenty kopeks a desyatin."—He exhibited the title-deed.—"The land," says he, "is by a little river, and the steppe is all covered with grass."

Pakhom went on asking more questions,—How he managed it, and who?

"The land," said the merchant, "you wouldn't go round it in a year,—it's all Bashkirian. And the people are as stupid as rams. You could almost get it for nothing."

"Well," said Pakhom to himself, "why should I spend my thousand rubles for five hundred desyatins, and hang a burden of debt around my neck besides? But there, how much I could get for a thousand rubles!"

v

Pakhom asked how he went; and, as soon as he said good-by to the peddler, he determined to go. He left his house in his wife's care, took his man, and started. When they reached the city, he bought a chest of tea, gifts, wine,

---

[1] Thirteen hundred and fifty acres.

just as the merchant said. They traveled and traveled; they traveled five hundred versts.[1] On the seventh day they came to the range of the wandering Bashkirs. It was all just as the merchant had said. They all live in the steppe, along a little river, in felt-covered kibitkas. They themselves do not plow and they eat no bread. And their cattle graze along the steppe, and their horses are in droves. Behind the kibitkas the colts are tied, and twice a day they bring the mares to them. They milk the mares, and make kumys out of the milk. The women churn the mares' milk, and make cheese; and all the muzhiks can do is to drink kumys and tea, to eat mutton, and play on their dudkas.[2] All are polite and jolly; they keep festival all summer. The people are very dark, and cannot speak Russian, but are affable.

As soon as the Bashkirs saw Pakhom, they came forth from their kibitkas; they surrounded their guest. The interpreter made his acquaintance. Pakhom told him that he had come to see about land. The Bashkirs were delighted, took him to a fine kibitka, spread rugs down, gave him a down-cushion to sit on, sat round him, and proceeded to treat him to tea and kumys. They slaughtered a ram, and gave him mutton.

Pakhom fetched from his tarantas his gifts, and began to distribute them among the Bashkirs.

Pakhom gave the Bashkirs his gifts, and divided the tea. The Bashkirs were overjoyed. They jabbered and jabbered together, and then commanded the interpreter to speak.

"They bid me tell you," says the interpreter, "that they have taken a fancy to you; and that we have a custom of doing everything possible to gratify a guest, and repay him for his gifts. You have given us gifts. Now tell what you wish from among our possessions, in order that we may give it to you."

"Above all else that you have," says Pakhom, "I would like some of your land. In my country," says he, "there is a scarcity of land. The land is cultivated to death. But you have much land, and good land. I never saw the like."

The interpreter translated for him. The Bashkirs talked and talked. Pakhom could not understand what they were saying; but he saw that they were good-natured, that they were talking at the top of their voices and laughing. Then they relapsed into silence, looked at Pakhom; and the interpreter said:—

"They bid me tell you that, in return for your kindness, they are happy to give you as much land as you wish. Only show us your hand—it shall be yours."

They were still talking, and began to dispute angrily. And Pakhom asked what they were quarreling about.

[1] Three hundred and thirty miles.   [2] Reed-pipes.

And the interpreter replied:—

"Some say that they ought to ask the head man about the land, and that without his consent it is impossible. And others say that it can be done without the head man."

V I

The Bashkirs were quarreling; suddenly a man came in a foxskin shapka.

They grew silent, and all stood up. And the interpreter said:—

"This is the head man himself."

Instantly Pakhom got out his best khalat, and gave it to the head man, together with five pounds of tea.

The head man accepted it, and sat down in the chief place. And immediately the Bashkirs began to tell him all about it.

The head man listened and listened; nodded his head, in sign of silence for all, and began to speak to Pakhom in Russian.

"Well," said he, "it can be done. Take it wherever you please. There is plenty of land."

"I shall get as much as I want," said Pakhom to himself. "I must secure it immediately, else they'll say it's mine, and then take it away."

"I thank you," says he, "for your kind words. I have seen that you have much land, and I need not very much. Only you must let me know what shall be mine. As soon as possible you must have it measured off and secured to me. God disposes of life and death. You good people make the grant, but the time may come when your children will take it away."

"You are right," says the head man; "it must be secured to you."

Pakhom began to speak:—

"I have heard that a merchant was here with you. You also gave him land, and struck a bargain. I should like to do the same."

The head man understood perfectly.

"This can all be done," says he. "We have a clerk; and we will go to the city, and will all put on our seals."

"And the price will be how much?" asked Pakhom.

"We have one price: one thousand rubles a day."

Pakhom did not understand. "What is this measure, the day? How many desyatins are there in it?"

"We can't reckon it," says he. "But we sell it by the day: all that you can go round in a day—that is yours; and the price of a day is one thousand rubles."

Pakhom was astonished.

"Look here," said he. "What I can go round in a day is a good deal of land!"

The head man laughed.

"It's all yours," said he. "Only one stipulation: if you don't come back within the day to the place from which you started, your money is lost."

"But how," says Pakhom, "can I mark where I am going?"

"Well, we'll stand on the place where it pleases you; we will be standing there; and you shall go and draw the circle, and take with you a hoe, and make a mark wherever you please; at the angle dig a little hole, put some turf in it; and we will go over it, from hole to hole, with the plow. Make your circle as large as you like, only at sunset you must be back at that place from which you set out. All that you encircle is yours."

Pakhom was delighted. They agreed to go out early. They talked it over, drank still more kumys, ate the mutton, and drank some more tea. It approached night-fall. They arranged for Pakhom to sleep in a down-bed, and the Bashkirs went off. They agreed to come together at early dawn the next day, and to go out at sunrise.

VII

Pakhom lay in his down-bed; and there he could not sleep, all on account of thinking of his land.

"I will get hold of a great tract," said he to himself. "I can go over fifty versts in one day. A day now is worth a year. There'll be a good bit of land in a circle of fifty versts. I will sell off the worst parts, or let it to the muzhiks; and I will pick out what I like, and I will settle on it. I will have a two-ox plow, and I will take two men as laborers. I will cultivate fifty desyatins, and I will pasture my cattle on the rest."

Pakhom did not get a wink of sleep all night. Just before dawn he dropped into a doze. He just dropped into a doze and had a dream. He seemed to see himself lying in this very same kibitka, and listening to somebody cackling outside. And it seemed to him that he wanted to see who was laughing; and he got up and went out of the kibitka, and lo! that very same head man of the Bashkirs was sitting in front of the kibitka, and was holding his sides, and roaring and cackling about something.

He went up to him and asked:—

"What are you laughing at?"

And then it seemed to him that it was no longer the head man of the Bashkirs, but the peddler who had come to him and told him about the land.

And as soon as he saw that it was the peddler, he asked:—

"Have you been here long?"

And then it was no longer the peddler, but that muzhik who had come down the Volga so long ago.

And Pakhom saw that it was not the muzhik either, but the Devil himself, with horns and hoofs, sitting and laughing; and before him was lying a man barefooted, in shirt and drawers. And Pakhom looked more attentively to find out who the man was.

And he saw that the dead man was none other than—himself! Pakhom was frightened, and woke up.

He woke up.

"What was I dreaming about?" he asked himself. He looked around, he peered out of the closed door: it was already getting light, day was beginning to dawn.

"The people must be getting up," he thinks; "it's time to start."

Pakhom arose, aroused his man in the tarantas, told him to harness up, and then went to arouse the Bashkirs.

"Time," says he, "to go out on the steppe, to measure it off."

The Bashkirs got up, all collected; and the head man came forth. The Bashkirs again began by drinking kumys; they wished Pakhom to treat them to tea, but he was not inclined to delay.

"If we go . . . . it is time to go now," said he.

VIII

The Bashkirs made ready; some got on horseback, some climbed into carts; they started. And Pakhom rode with his man in their tarantas, and took with him a hoe. They rode out into the steppe; the dawn was beginning. They reached a mound—*shikhan* in Bashkirian. They descended from their carts, dismounted from their horses, collected in a crowd. The chief man came to Pakhom, and pointed with his hand.

"Here," says he, "all is ours, as far as you can see. Take what you desire."

Pakhom's eyes burned. The whole region was grassy, flat as the palm of your hand, black as a pot; and where there was a hollow, it was filled with grass as high as one's breast.

The chief man took off his foxskin cap, and laid it on the ground.

"Here," says he, "is the spot. Start from here, come back here. All that you go round shall be yours."

Pakhom took out his money, laid it in the cap; took off his kaftan, stood in his blouse[1] alone; girded himself around the belly with his sash, pulled it tighter; hung round his neck a little bag with bread, put a little flask with water into his belt, tightened his leg-wrappers, took the hoe from his man, and got ready to start.

He pondered and pondered on which side to take it; it was good everywhere.

He said to himself:—

"It's all one; I will go toward the sunrise."

[1] *Poddyovka,* a sort of half kaftan.

He faced toward the east and paced back and forth, waiting till the sun should show above the horizon.

He said to himself, "I will not lose any time. It's cool, and easier to walk."

As soon as the sunlight gushed out over the horizon, he threw his hoe over his shoulder, and started out on the steppe.

Pakhom proceeded neither slow nor fast. He went about a verst;[1] he halted and he dug a little pit and piled the turf in it, so that it might attract attention.

He went farther. As he went on, he quickened his pace. As he kept going on, he dug other little pits.

Pakhom looked around. The shikhan was still in sight in the sun, and the people were standing on it; the tires on the tarantas wheels glistened. Pakhom conjectured that he has been five versts. He began to get warm; he took off his blouse, threw it over his shoulder, and went on. It grew hot. He looked at the sun.[2] It was already breakfast-time.

"One stage over," thinks Pakhom, "and four of them make a day; it's too early as yet to turn round. Only let me take off my boots."

He sat down and took off his boots, put them in his belt, and went on. It was easy walking. He said to himself, "Let me go five versts farther, then I will swing round to the left. This place is very good; it's a pity to give it up."

The farther he went, the better it became. He still went straight ahead. He looked round—the shikhan was now scarcely visible; and the people, like little ants, made a black spot on it; and something barely glistened.

"Well," said Pakhom, "I have enough in this direction; I must be turning round. I am sweaty enough. I should like a drink."

He halted, dug a pit, filled it with turf, unfastened his flask, took a drink, and turned sharply to the left. He went and went—the grass was deep, and it was hot.

Pakhom began to feel weary; he looked at the sun and saw that it was dinner-time.

"Well," said he, "I must have a rest."

Pakhom halted. He sat down and ate his bread and water, but did not try to lie down. He said to himself:—

"If I lie down, I may fall asleep."

He sat a little while; then he started on again; he found it easy walking; his strength was renewed by his meal, but now it was growing very hot—yes, and the sun began to decline; but still he kept going. He said:—

"Endure it for an hour, and you have an age to live."

He still went on a long distance in this direction. He kept intending to

---

[1] Thirty-five hundred feet. [2] Russian, *solnuishko*, little sun.

turn to the left, but lo! it was a low land and a moist soil. I was a pity to throw it away! He said to himself:—

"This day has been a good one."

He still continued straight on. He took in the low land—dug his pit on the farther side of the low land, the hollow, and then turned the second corner.

Pakhom gazed back in the direction of the shikhan. The heat had caused a haziness, there was a quivering in the atmosphere, and through the haziness the people on the shikhan could scarcely be seen.

"Well," said Pakhom, "I have taken long sides—I must make this one shorter."

He started on the third side—he tried to hasten his pace. He looked at the sun—it was already far down the west, and on the third side he had only gone two versts; and back to the starting-point, there were fifteen versts.

"No," he said, "even though the tract should be uneven I must hurry back in a straight line. It wouldn't do to take too much; even as it is, I have already a good deal of land."

Pakhom dug his little pit in all haste, and headed straight for the shikhan.

IX

Pakhom went straight toward the shikhan, and now it began to be heavy work for him. He was bathed in sweat; and his bare legs were cut and torn, and began to fail under him. He felt a desire to rest, but it was impossible; he could not stop till sunset. The sun did not delay, but was sinking lower and lower.

"Akh!" he says to himself, "can I have made a blunder? can I have taken too much? why don't you hurry along faster?"

He gazed at the shikhan—it gleamed in the sun; it was still a long distance to the place, and the sun was now not far from the horizon.

Still Pakhom hurried on; it was hard for him, but he kept quickening his pace, quickening his pace. He walked and walked—it was still always far away. He took to the double-quick. He threw away his blouse, his boots, his flask. He threw away his cap, but he clung to his hoe and helped himself along with it.

"Akh!" he said to himself, "I was too greedy; I have ruined the whole business; I shall not get there before sunset."

And his breath began to fail him all the worse because of his apprehension. Pakhom ran—his shirt and drawers clung to his body by reason of sweat—his mouth was parched. In his breast a pair of blacksmith's bellows, as it were, were working; and in his heart a mill was beating; and his legs were almost breaking down under him.

It became painful for Pakhom. He said to himself:—

"Suppose I should die from the strain?"

He was afraid of dropping dead, and yet he could not stop.

"If after running, I were to stop now, they would call me a fool."

He ran and ran. He was now getting near, and he could hear the Bashkirs shouting—screaming at him; and their screams made his heart pain him more than ever.

Pakhom ran on with the last of his strength, and the sun was still hovering on the horizon's edge; it went into the haze; there was a great glow, red as blood. Now—now it was setting! The sun had nearly set, but now Pakhom was not far from the place. He could see it; and the people on the shikhan gesticulating to him, urging him on. He saw the foxskin cap on the ground, he could even see the money in it. And he saw the head man sitting on the ground, holding his belly with his hands. And Pakhom remembered his dream.

"Much land," he said to himself, "but perhaps God has not willed me to live on it. Okh! I have ruined myself," he thinks. "I shall not get it."

Pakhom looked at the sun, but the sun had gone down under the earth; its body was already hidden, and its last segment had disappeared under the horizon.

Pakhom exerted his last energies, threw himself forward with his body; his legs just kept him from falling.

Just as Pakhom reached the shikhan, it suddenly grew dark. He saw that the sun had gone. Pakhom groaned.

"I have lost my labor," thinks he. He was just about to stop; but as he still heard the Bashkirs all screaming, he remembered that he was below them, and therefore the sun seemed to have set, although it had not set to those on top of the shikhan. Pakhom took a breath and ran up the shikhan. It was still light on the mound. Pakhom ran, and there was the cap. In front of the cap sat the head man, laughing and holding his sides.

Pakhom remembered his dream, groaned "Akh!" his legs gave way under him, and he fell forward, reaching out his arms toward the cap.

"Aï! brave lad!" shouted the head man. "You have got a good piece of land."

Pakhom's man ran to him, attempted to help him to his feet; but from his mouth poured a stream of blood, and he lay dead.

The Bashkirs clucked with their tongues, expressing their sorrow.

Pakhom's man took the hoe, dug a grave for him, made it just long enough, from head to foot,—three arshins,[1]—and buried him.

---

[1] About seven feet.

A Reply to the Synod's Edict of Excommunication, and to Letters Received by Me Concerning It

"He who begins by loving Christianity better than truth, will proceed by loving his own sect or church better than Christianity, and end in loving himself better than all."—
COLERIDGE.

At first I did not wish to reply to the Synod's Edict about me, but it has called forth very many letters in which correspondents unknown to me write—some of them scolding me for rejecting things I never rejected, others exhorting me to believe in things I have always believed in, others again expressing an agreement with me which probably does not really exist and a sympathy to which I am hardly entitled. So I have decided to reply both to the Edict itself—indicating what is unjust in it—and to the communications of my unknown correspondents.

The Edict of the Synod has in general many defects. It is either illegal or else intentionally equivocal; it is arbitrary, unfounded, untruthful, and is also libellous, and incites to evil feelings and deeds.

It is illegal or intentionally equivocal; for if it is intended as an Excommunication from the Church, it fails to conform to the Church regulations subject to which Excommunications can be pronounced; while if it is merely an announcement of the fact that one who does not believe in the Church and its dogmas does not belong to the Church—that is self-evident, and the announcement can have no purpose other than to pass for an Excommunication without really being one, as in fact happened, for that is how the Edict has been understood.

It is arbitrary, for it accuses me alone of disbelief in all the points enumerated in the Edict; whereas many, in fact almost all educated people, share that disbelief and have constantly expressed and still express it both in conversations, in lectures, in pamphlets, and in books.

It is unfounded because it gives as a chief cause of its publication the great circulation of the false teaching wherewith I pervert the people—whereas I am well assured that hardly a hundred people can be found who share my views, and the circulation of my writings on religion, thanks to the Censor, is so insignificant that the majority of those who have read the Synod's Edict have not the least notion of what I may have written about religion—as is shown by the letters I have received.

It contains an obvious falsehood, for it says that efforts have been made by the Church to show me my errors but that these efforts have been unsuccessful. Nothing of the kind ever took place.

It constitutes what in legal terminology is called a libel, for it contains assertions known to be false and tending to my hurt.

It is, finally, an incentive to evil feelings and deeds, for as was to be expected it evoked in unenlightened and unreasoning people anger and hatred against me, culminating in threats of murder expressed in letters I received. One writes: "Now thou hast been anathematized, and after death wilt go to everlasting torments and wilt perish like a dog ... anathema upon thee, old devil ... be damned." Another blames the Government for not having as yet shut me up in a monastery, and fills his letter with abuse. A third writes: "If the Government does not get rid of you, we will ourselves make you shut your mouth," and the letter ends with curses. "May you be destroyed—you blackguard!" writes a fourth, "I shall find means to do it ..." and then follows indecent abuse. After the publication of the Synod's Edict I also noticed indications of anger of this kind in some of the people I met. On the very day (February 25) when the Edict was made public, while crossing a public square I heard the words: "See! there goes the devil in human form," and had the crowd been composed of other elements I should very likely have been beaten to death, as happened some years ago to a man at the Panteléymon Chapel.

So that altogether the Synod's Edict is very bad, and the statement at the end that those who sign it pray that I may become such as they are does not make it any better.

That relates to the Edict as a whole; as to details, it is wrong in the following particulars. It is said in the Edict: "A writer well known to the world, Russian by birth, Orthodox by baptism and education—Count Tolstoy—under the seduction of his intellectual pride has insolently risen against the Lord and against his Christ and against his holy heritage, and has publicly, in the sight of all men, renounced the Orthodox Mother Church which has reared him and educated him."

That I have renounced the Church which calls itself Orthodox is perfectly correct.

But I renounced it not because I had risen against the Lord, but on the contrary only because with all the strength of my soul I wished to serve him. Before renouncing the Church, and fellowship with the people which was inexpressibly dear to me, I—having seen some reasons to doubt the Church's integrity—devoted several years to the investigation of its theoretic and practical teachings. For the theory, I read all I could about Church doctrine and studied and critically analysed dogmatic theology; while as to practice, for more than a year I followed strictly all the injunctions of the Church observing all the fasts and all the services. And I became convinced that Church doctrine is theoretically a crafty and harmful lie, and practically a collection of the grossest superstitions and sorcery, which completely conceals the whole meaning of Christ's teaching.[1]

And I really repudiated the Church, ceased to observe its ceremonies, and wrote a will instructing those near me that when I die they should not allow any servants of the Church to have access to me, but should put away my dead body as quickly as possible without having any incantations or prayers over it, just as one puts away any objectionable and useless object that it may not be an inconvenience to the living.

As to the statements made about me, that I devote the "literary activity and the talent given to him by God, to disseminating among the people teachings contrary to Christ and to the Church," and that, "in his works and in letters issued by him and by his disciples in great quantities over the whole world, but particularly within the limits of our dear fatherland, he preaches with the zeal of a fanatic the overthrow of all the dogmas of the Orthodox Church and the very essence of the Christian faith"—this is not true. I never troubled myself about the propagation of my teaching. It is true that for myself I have expressed in writings my understanding of Christ's teaching and have not hidden these works from those who wished to become acquainted with them, but I never published them myself. Only when they have asked me about it have I told people how I understand Christ's teaching. To those that asked, I said what I thought and (when I had them) gave them my books.

Then it is said that "he denies God worshipped in the Holy Trinity, the Creator and Protector of the universe; denies our Lord Jesus Christ, God-man, Redeemer and Saviour of the world, who suffered for us men and for our salvation and was raised from the dead; denies the immaculate conception of the Lord Christ as man, and the virginity before his birth and after his birth of the Most Pure Mother of God." That I deny the incomprehensible Trinity; the fable, which is altogether meaningless in our time, of the fall of the first man; the blasphemous story of a God born of a virgin to redeem the human race—is perfectly true. But God, a Spirit; God, love; the only God—the Source of all—I not only do not deny, but I attribute real existence to God alone and I see the whole meaning of life only in fulfilling His will, which is expressed in the Christian teaching.

It is also said: "He does not acknowledge a life and retribution beyond

---

[1] One need only read the Prayer-Book and follow the ritual which is continually performed by the Orthodox priests and is considered a Christian worship of God, to see that all these ceremonies are nothing but different kinds of sorcery adapted to all the incidents of life. That a child in case of death should go to Paradise, one has to know how to oil him and how to immerse him while pronouncing certain words; in order that a mother may cease to be unclean after child-birth, certain incantations have to be pronounced; to be successful in one's affairs, to live comfortably in a new house, that corn may grow well, that a drought may cease, to recover from sickness, to ease the condition in the next world of one who is dying,—for all these and a thousand other incidents there are certain incantations which are pronounced by a priest at a certain place, for a certain consideration.—L. T.

the grave." If one is to understand, by life beyond the grave, the Second Advent, a hell with eternal torments, devils, and a Paradise of perpetual happiness—it is perfectly true that I do not acknowledge such a life beyond the grave; but eternal life and retribution here and everywhere, now and for ever, I acknowledge to such an extent that, standing now at my age on the verge of my grave, I often have to make an effort to restrain myself from desiring the death of this body—that is, birth to a new life; and I believe every good action increases the true welfare of my eternal life and every evil action decreases it.

It is also stated that I reject all the Sacraments. That is quite true. I consider all the Sacraments to be coarse, degrading sorcery, incompatible with the idea of God or with the Christian teaching, and also as infringements of very plain injunctions in the Gospels. In the Baptism of Infants I see a palpable perversion of the whole meaning which might be attached to the baptism of adults who consciously accepted Christianity; in the performance of the Sacrament of Marriage over those who are known to have had other sexual unions, in the permission of divorce, and in the consecration of the marriages of divorced people, I see a direct infringement both of the meaning and of the words of the Gospel teaching.

In the periodical absolution of sins at Confession I see a harmful deception which only encourages immorality and causes men not to fear to sin.

Both in Extreme Unction and in Anointing I see methods of gross sorcery—as in the worship of icons and relics, and as in all the rites, prayers, and exorcisms which fill the Prayer-Book. In the Sacrament I see a deification of the flesh and a perversion of Christian teaching. In Ordination I see (besides an obvious preparation for deception) a direct infringement of the words of Jesus, which plainly forbid anyone to be called teacher, father, or master.[1]

It is stated finally, as the last and greatest of my sins, that "reviling the most sacred objects of the faith of the Orthodox people, he has not shrunk from subjecting to derision the greatest of Sacraments, the Holy Eucharist."[2] That I did not shrink from describing simply and objectively what the priest does when preparing this so-called Sacrament is perfectly true; but that this so-called Sacrament is anything holy, and that it is blasphemy to describe it simply, just as it is performed, is quite untrue. Blasphemy does not consist in calling a partition a partition, and not an iconostasis,[3] and a cup a cup, and not a chalice, &c.; but it is a most terrible,

---

[1] "But be not ye called Rabbi: for one is your Master, and all ye are brethren. And call no man your father upon the earth: for one is your Father, which is in heaven. Neither be ye called masters: for one is your Master, even Christ."—Matt. 23:8-10.

[2] See chapter 39, book i, of *Resurrection;* but see also, as a probable provocative of Tolstoy's Excommunication, the description of the Head of the Holy Synod in chapter 27, book ii, of that work.—A. M. [Aylmer Maude, the translator.]

[3] The iconostasis in Russo-Greek churches corresponds somewhat both to the Western altar-rails and to a rood-screen.—A. M.

continual, and revolting blasphemy that men (using all possible means of deception and hypnotization) should assure children and simple-minded folk that if bits of bread are cut up in a particular manner while certain words are pronounced over them, and if they are put into wine,[1] God will enter into those bits of bread, and any living person named by the priest when he takes out one of these sops will be healthy, and any dead person named by the priest when he takes out one of these sops will be better off in the other world on that account, and that into the man who eats such a sop God himself will enter.

Surely that is terrible!

They undertake to teach us to understand the personality of Christ, but his teaching—which destroys evil in the world and blesses men so simply, easily, and undoubtedly, if only they do not pervert it—is all hidden, is all transformed into a gross sorcery of washings, smearing with oil, gestures, exorcisms, eating of bits of bread, &c., so that of the true teaching nothing remains. And if at any time some one tries to remind men that Christ's teaching consists not in this sorcery, not in public prayer, liturgies, candles, and icons, but in loving one another, in not returning evil for evil, in not judging or killing one another—the anger of those to whom deception is profitable is aroused, and with incomprehensible audacity they publicly declare in churches, and print in books, newspapers and catechisms, that Jesus never forbade oaths (swearing allegiance or swearing in court of law), never forbade murder (executions and wars), and that the teaching of non-resistance to evil has with Satanic ingenuity been invented by the enemies of Christ.[2]

What is most terrible is that people to whom it is profitable not only deceive adults, but (having power to do so) deceive children also—those very children concerning whom Jesus pronounced woe on him who deceives them. It is terrible that these people for their own petty advantage do such fearful evil, hiding from men the truth Jesus revealed, and that gives blessing a thousandfold greater than the gains these men obtain for themselves. They behave like a robber who kills a whole family of five or six people to carry off an old coat and ten-pence in money. They would willingly have given him all their clothes and all their money not to be killed, but he could not act otherwise.

So it is with the religious deceivers. It would be worth while keeping them ten times better and letting them live in the greatest luxury, if only they would refrain from ruining men by their deceptions. But they cannot act differently. That is what is awful. And therefore we not only may, but

---

[1] In the Greek Church the priest mixes the sacramental bread with the wine before administering it to the communicant. The reader will note in this article allusions to several practices (baptism by immersion, unction, &c.) which do not exist in the Church of England, or are differently carried out.—A. M.

[2] Speech by Ambrosius, Bishop of Khàrkov.—L. T.

should, unmask their deceptions. If there be a sacred thing, it is surely not what they call Sacraments, but just this very duty of unmasking their religious deceptions when one detects them.

When a Tchouvásh smears his idol with sour cream or beats it, I can refrain from insulting his faith and can pass it by with equanimity, for he does these things in the name of a superstition of his own, foreign to me, and he does not interfere with what to me is holy. But I cannot endure it passively when with their barbarous superstitions, men (however numerous, however ancient their superstitions, and however powerful they may be) preach gross sorcery in the name of the God by whom I live, and of that teaching of Christ's which has given life to me and is capable of giving life to all men.

And if I call what they are doing by its name, I only do my duty and what I cannot refrain from doing because I believe in God and in the Christian teaching. If they call the exposure of their imposture "blasphemy," that only shows the strength of their deception, and should increase the efforts to destroy this deception, made by those who believe in God and in Christ's teaching, and who see that this deception hides the true God from men's sight.

They should say of Christ—who drove bulls and sheep and dealers from the temple—that he blasphemed. Were he to come now and see what is done in his name in church, he would surely with yet greater and most just anger throw out all these horrible altar-cloths,[1] lances, crosses, cups and candles and icons and all the things wherewith the priests—carrying on their sorcery—hide God and his truth from mankind.

So that is what is true and what is untrue in the Synod's Edict about me. I certainly do not believe in what they say they believe in. But I believe in what they wish to persuade people that I disbelieve in.

I believe in this: I believe in God, whom I understand as Spirit, as Love, as the Source of all. I believe that he is in me and I in him. I believe that the will of God is most clearly and intelligibly expressed in the teaching of the man Jesus, whom to consider as God and pray to, I esteem the greatest blasphemy. I believe that man's true welfare lies in fulfilling God's will, and his will is that men should love one another and should consequently do to others as they wish others to do to them—of which it is said in the Gospels that in this is the law and the prophets. I believe therefore that the meaning of the life of every man is to be found only in increasing the love that is in him; that this increase of love leads man, even in this life, to ever greater and greater blessedness, and after death gives him the more blessedness the more love he has, and helps more than anything else towards the establishment of

---

[1] The altar-cloths referred to are those containing fragments of holy relics, on which alone mass can be celebrated. The "lances" are diminutive ones with which the priest cuts bits out of the holy bread, in remembrance of the lance that pierced Christ's side.—A. M.

the Kingdom of God on earth: that is, to the establishment of an order of life in which the discord, deception, and violence that now rule will be replaced by free accord, by truth, and by the brotherly love of one for another. I believe that to obtain progress in love there is only one means: prayer—not public prayer in churches, plainly forbidden by Jesus,[1] but private prayer, like the sample give us by Jesus, consisting of the renewing and strengthening in our own consciousness of the meaning of our life and of our complete dependence on the will of God.

Whether or not these beliefs of mine offend, grieve, or prove a stumbling-block to anyone, or hinder anything, or give displeasure to anybody, I can as little change them as I can change my body. I must myself live my own life and I must myself alone meet death (and that very soon), and therefore I cannot believe otherwise than as I—preparing to go to that God from whom I came—do believe. I do not believe my faith to be the one indubitable truth for all time, but I see no other that is plainer, clearer, or answers better to all the demands of my reason and my heart; should I find such a one I shall at once accept it, for God requires nothing but the truth. But I can no more return to that from which with such suffering I have escaped, than a flying bird can re-enter the eggshell from which it has emerged.

"He who begins by loving Christianity better than Truth, will proceed by loving his own sect or Church better than Christianity, and end in loving himself (his own peace) better than all," said Coleridge.

I travelled the contrary way. I began by loving my Orthodox faith more than my peace, then I loved Christianity more than my Church, and now I love truth more than anything in the world. And up to now truth for me corresponds with Christianity as I understand it. And I hold to this Christianity, and to the degree in which I hold to it I live peacefully and happily, and peacefully and happily approach death.

[April 4, o.s., 1901.]

[1] "And when thou prayest, thou shall not be as the hypocrites are: for they love to pray standing in the synagogues and in the corners of the streets, that they may be seen of men. Verily I say unto you, They have their reward. But thou, when thou prayest, enter into thy closet, and when thou hast shut thy door, pray to thy Father which is in secret; and thy Father which seeth in secret shall reward thee openly. But when ye pray, use not vain repetitions, as the heathen do: for they think that they shall be heard for their much speaking. Be not therefore like unto them: for your Father knoweth what things ye have need of, before ye ask him. After this manner therefore pray ye: Our Father," &c.—Matt. 6:5-13.

Fyodor Mikhailovich Dostoevsky was born in Moscow in 1821, the year Napoleon died, seven years before Tolstoy was born. His five greatest works are probably *Notes from Underground* (1864), *Crime and Punishment* (1867), *The Idiot* (1868), *The Possessed* (1871), and *The Brothers Karamazov* (1879-80). He died in 1881.

His little-known journalism may be bigoted; but in his novels, his political and religious ideas are tempered by his uncanny understanding of human beings: like few writers of any age, he makes his readers more humane by forcing them to sympathize with all kinds of men and women whom in real life one might pass by with contempt, void of understanding.

He not only fathoms his characters, he lets them think their own thoughts and feel their own feelings. The most interesting things Dostoevsky ever wrote about religion appear in *The Brothers Karamazov*, in the mouth of Ivan Karamazov, in two successive chapters in which Ivan converses with his brother Alyosha. This long conversation is reprinted in the following pages. Dostoevsky does not share Ivan's outlook and Ivan does not accept the views he attributes to the Grand Inquisitor in his tale. Least of all does Dostoevsky agree with the Inquisitor. Yet Ivan's doubts and the Grand Inquisitor's speech have profoundly impressed generations of readers.

Rebellion

"*Y*ou see, I am fond of collecting certain facts, and, would you believe, I even copy anecdotes of a certain sort from newspapers and books, and I've already got a fine collection. The Turks, of course, have gone into it, but they are foreigners. I have specimens from home that are even better than the Turks. You know we prefer beating—rods and scourges—that's our national institution. Nailing ears is unthinkable for us, for we are, after all, Europeans. But the rod and the scourge we have always with us and they cannot be taken from us. Abroad now they scarcely do any beating. Manners are more humane, or laws have been passed, so that they don't dare to flog men now. But they make up for it in another way just as national as ours. And so national that it would be practically impossible among us, though I believe we are being inoculated with it, since the religious movement began in our aristocracy. I have a charming pamphlet, translated from the French, describing how, quite recently, five years ago, a murderer, Richard, was executed—a young man, I believe, of three and twenty, who repented and was converted to the Christian faith at the very scaffold. This

Richard was an illegitimate child who was given as a child of six by his parents to some shepherds on the Swiss mountains. They brought him up to work for them. He grew up like a little wild beast among them. The shepherds taught him nothing, and scarcely fed or clothed him, but sent him out at seven to herd the flock in cold and wet, and no one hesitated or scrupled to treat him so. Quite the contrary, they thought they had every right, for Richard had been given to them as a chattel, and they did not even see the necessity of feeding him. Richard himself describes how in those years, like the Prodigal Son in the Gospel, he longed to eat of the mash given to the pigs, which were fattened for sale. But they wouldn't even give him that, and beat him when he stole from the pigs. And that was how he spent all his childhood and his youth, till he grew up and was strong enough to go away and be a thief. The savage began to earn his living as a day labourer in Geneva. He drank what he earned, he lived like a brute, and finished by killing and robbing an old man. He was caught, tried, and condemned to death. They are not sentimentalists there. And in prison he was immediately surrounded by pastors, members of Christian brotherhoods, philanthropic ladies, and the like. They taught him to read and write in prison, and expounded the Gospel to him. They exhorted him, worked upon him, drummed at him incessantly, till at last he solemnly confessed his crime. He was converted. He wrote to the court himself that he was a monster, but that in the end God had vouchsafed him light and shown grace. All Geneva was in excitement about him—all philanthropic and religious Geneva. All the aristocratic and well-bred society of the town rushed to the prison, kissed Richard and embraced him; 'You are our brother, you have found grace.' And Richard does nothing but weep with emotion, 'Yes, I've found grace! All my youth and childhood I was glad of pigs' food, but now even I have found grace. I am dying in the Lord.' 'Yes, Richard, die in the Lord; you have shed blood and must die. Though it's not your fault that you knew not the Lord, when you coveted the pigs' food and were beaten for stealing it (which was very wrong of you, for stealing is forbidden); but you've shed blood and you must die.' And on the last day, Richard, perfectly limp, did nothing but cry and repeat every minute: 'This is my happiest day. I am going to the Lord.' 'Yes,' cry the pastors and the judges and philanthropic ladies. 'This is the happiest day of your life, for you are going to the Lord!' They all walk or drive to the scaffold in procession behind the prison van. At the scaffold they call to Richard: 'Die, brother, die in the Lord, for even thou hast found grace!' And so, covered with his brothers' kisses, Richard is dragged on to the scaffold, and led to the guillotine. And they chopped off his head in brotherly fashion, because he had found grace. Yes, that's characteristic. That pamphlet is translated into Russian by some Russian philanthropists of aristocratic rank and evangelical aspirations, and has been distributed gratis for the enlightenment of the people. The case of

Richard is interesting because it's national. Though to us it's absurd to cut off a man's head, because he has become our brother and has found grace, yet we have our own speciality, which is all but worse. Our historical pastime is the direct satisfaction of inflicting pain. There are lines in Nekrassov describing how a peasant lashes a horse on the eyes, 'on its meek eyes,' every one must have seen it. It's peculiarly Russian. He describes how a feeble little nag had foundered under too heavy a load and cannot move. The peasant beats it, savagely, beats it at last not knowing what he is doing in the intoxication of cruelty, thrashes it mercilessly over and over again. 'However weak you are, you must pull, if you die for it.' The nag strains, and then he begins lashing the poor defenceless creature on its weeping, on its 'meek eyes.' The frantic beast tugs and draws the load, trembling all over, gasping for breath, moving sideways, with a sort of unnatural spasmodic action—it's awful in Nekrassov. But that's only a horse, and God has given horses to be beaten. So the Tatars have taught us, and they left us the knout as a remembrance of it. But men, too, can be beaten. A well-educated, cultured gentleman and his wife beat their own child with a birch-rod, a girl of seven. I have an exact account of it. The papa was glad that the birch was covered with twigs. 'It stings more,' said he, and so he began stinging his daughter. I know for a fact there are people who at every blow are worked up to sensuality, to literal sensuality, which increases progressively at every blow they inflict. They beat for a minute, for five minutes, for ten minutes, more often and more savagely. The child screams. At last the child cannot scream, it gasps, 'Daddy! daddy!' By some diabolical unseemly chance the case was brought into court. A counsel is engaged. The Russian people have long called a barrister 'a conscience for hire.' The counsel protests in his client's defence. 'It's such a simple thing,' he says, 'an every-day domestic event. A father corrects his child. To our shame be it said, it is brought into court.' The jury, convinced by him, give a favourable verdict. The public roars with delight that the torturer is acquitted. Ah, pity I wasn't there. I would have proposed to raise a subscription in his honour! . . . Charming pictures.

"But I've still better things about children. I've collected a great, great deal about Russian children, Alyosha. There was a little girl of five who was hated by her father and mother, 'most worthy and respectable people, a good education and breeding.' You see, I must repeat again, it is a peculiar characteristic of many people, this love of torturing children, and children only. To all other types of humanity these torturers behave mildly and benevolently, like cultivated and humane Europeans; but they are very fond of tormenting children, even fond of children themselves in that sense. It's just their defencelessness that tempts the tormentor, just the angelic confidence of the child who has no refuge and no appeal, that sets his vile blood on fire. In every man, of course, a demon lies hidden—the demon of rage, the demon of lustful heat at the screams of the tortured victim, the demon of lawlessness let off the chain, the demon of diseases that follow on vice, gout, kidney disease, and so on.

"This poor child of five was subjected to every possible torture by those cultivated parents. They beat her, thrashed her, kicked her for no reason till her body was one bruise. Then, they went to greater refinements of cruelty—shut her up all night in the cold and frost in a privy, and because she didn't ask to be taken up at night (as though a child of five sleeping its angelic, sound sleep could be trained to wake and ask), they smeared her face and filled her mouth with excrement, and it was her mother, her mother did this. And that mother could sleep, hearing the poor child's groans! Can you understand why a little creature, who can't even understand what's done to her, should beat her little aching heart with her tiny fist in the dark and the cold, and weep her meek unresentful tears to dear, kind God to protect her? Do you understand that, friend and brother, you pious and humble novice? Do you understand why this infamy must be and is permitted? Without it, I am told, man could not have existed on earth, for he could not have known good and evil. Why should he know that diabolical good and evil when it costs so much? Why, the whole world of knowledge is not worth that child's prayer to 'dear, kind God'! I say nothing of the sufferings of grown-up people, they have eaten the apple, damn them, and the devil take them all! But these little ones! I am making you suffer, Alyosha, you are not yourself. I'll leave off if you like."

"Never mind. I want to suffer too," muttered Alyosha.

"One picture, only one more, because it's so curious, so characteristic, and I have only just read it in some collection of Russian antiquities. I've forgotten the name. I must look it up. It was in the darkest days of serfdom at the beginning of the century, and long live the Liberator of the People! There was in those days a general of aristocratic connections, the owner of great estates, one of those men—somewhat exceptional, I believe, even then— who, retiring from the service into a life of leisure, are convinced that they've earned absolute power over the lives of their subjects. There were such men then. So our general, settled on his property of two thousand souls, lives in pomp, and domineers over his poor neighbours as though they were dependents and buffoons. He has kennels and hundreds of hounds and nearly a hundred dog-boys—all mounted, and in uniform. One day a serf boy, a little child of eight, threw a stone in play and hurt the paw of the general's favourite hound. 'Why is my favourite dog lame?' He is told that the boy threw a stone that hurt the dog's paw. 'So you did it.' The general looked the child up and down. 'Take him.' He was taken—taken from his mother and kept shut up all night. Early that morning the general comes out on horseback, with the hounds, his dependents, dog-boys, and hunts-men, all mounted around him in full hunting parade. The servants are summoned for their edification, and in front of them all stands the mother of the child. The child is brought from the lock-up. It's a gloomy cold, foggy autumn day, a capital day for hunting. The general orders the child to be undressed; the child is stripped naked. He shivers, numb with terror, not daring to cry . . . . 'Make him run,' commands the general. 'Run! run!' shout the dog-boys. The boy runs . . . . 'At him!' yells the general, and he sets the whole pack of hounds on the child. The hounds catch him, and tear him to pieces before his mother's eyes! . . . I believe the general was afterwards declared incapable of administering his estates. Well—what did he deserve? To be shot? To be shot for the satisfaction of our moral feelings? Speak, Alyosha!"

"To be shot," murmured Alyosha, lifting his eyes to Ivan with a pale, twisted smile.

"Bravo!" cried Ivan delighted. "If even you say so . . . . You're a pretty monk! So there is a little devil sitting in your heart, Alyosha Karamazov!"

"What I said was absurd, but——"

"That's just the point that 'but'!" cried Ivan. "Let me tell you, novice, that the absurd is only too necessary on earth. The world stands on absurdities, and perhaps nothing would have come to pass in it without them. We know what we know!"

"What do you know?"

"I understand nothing," Ivan went on, as though in delirium. "I don't want to understand anything now. I want to stick to the fact. I made up my mind long ago not to understand. If I try to understand anything, I shall be false to the fact and I have determined to stick to the fact."

"Why are you trying me?" Alyosha cried, with sudden distress. "Will you say what you mean at last?"

"Of course, I will; that's what I've been leading up to. You are dear to me, I don't want to let you go, and I won't give you up to your Zossima."

Ivan for a minute was silent, his face became all at once very sad.

"Listen! I took the case of children only to make my case clearer. Of the other tears of humanity with which the earth is soaked from its crust to its center, I will say nothing. I have narrowed my subject on purpose. I am a bug, and I recognise in all humility that I cannot understand why the world is arranged as it is. Men are themselves to blame, I suppose; they were given paradise, they wanted freedom, and stole fire from heaven, though they knew they would become unhappy, so there is no need to pity them. With my pitiful, earthly, Euclidian understanding, all I know is that there is suffering and that there are none guilty; that cause follows effect, simply and directly; that everything flows and finds its level—but that's only Euclidian nonsense, I know that, and I can't consent to live by it! What comfort is it to me that there are none guilty and that cause follows effect simply and directly, and that I know it—I must have justice, or I will destroy myself. And not justice in some remote infinite time and space, but here on earth, and that I could see myself. I have believed in it. I want to see it, and if I am dead by then, let me rise again, for if it all happens without me, it will be too unfair. Surely I haven't suffered, simply that I, my crimes and my sufferings, may manure the soil of the future harmony for somebody else. I want to see with my own eyes the hind lie down with the lion and the victim rise up and embrace his murderer. I want to be there when every one suddenly understands what it has all been for. All the religions of the world are built on this longing, and I am a believer. But then there are the children, and what am I to do about them? That's a question I can't answer. For the hundredth time I repeat, there are numbers of questions, but I've only taken the children, because in their case what I mean is so unanswerably clear. Listen! If all must suffer to pay for the eternal harmony, what have children to do with it, tell me, please? It's beyond all comprehension why they should suffer, and why they should pray for the harmony. Why should they, too, furnish material to enrich the soil for the harmony of the future? I understand solidarity in sin among men. I understand solidarity in retribution, too; but there can be no such solidarity with children. And if it is really true that they must share responsibility for all their fathers' crimes, such a truth is not of this world and is beyond my comprehension. Some jester will say, perhaps, that the child would have grown up and have sinned, but you see he didn't grow up, he was torn to pieces by the dogs, at eight years old. Oh, Alyosha, I am not blaspheming! I understand, of course, what an upheaval of the universe it will be, when everything in heaven and earth blends in one hymn of praise and everything that lives and has lived cries aloud: 'Thou art just, O Lord, for Thy ways are revealed.' When the mother embraces the fiend who threw her child to the dogs, and all three cry aloud with tears, 'Thou art just, O Lord!' then, of course, the crown of knowledge will be reached and all will be made clear. But what pulls me up here is that I can't accept that harmony. And while I am on earth, I make haste to take my own measures. You see, Alyosha, perhaps it really may happen that if I live to that moment, or rise again to see it, I, too, perhaps, may cry aloud with the rest, looking at the mother embracing the child's torturer, 'Thou art just, O Lord!' but I don't want to cry aloud then. While there is still time, I hasten to protect myself and so I renounce the higher harmony altogether. It's not worth the tears of that one tortured child who beat itself on the breast with its little fist and prayed in its stinking outhouse, with its unexpiated tears to 'dear, kind God'! It's not worth it, because those tears are unatoned for. They must be atoned for, or there can be no harmony. But how? How are you going to atone for them? Is it possible? By their being avenged? But what do I care for avenging them? What do I care for a hell for oppressors? What good can hell do, since those children have already been tortured? And what becomes of harmony, if there is hell? I want to forgive. I want to embrace. I don't want more suffering. And if the sufferings of children go to swell the sum of sufferings which was necessary to pay for truth, then I protest that the truth is not worth such a price. I don't want the mother to embrace the oppressor who threw her son to the dogs! She dare not forgive him! Let her forgive him for herself, if she will, let her forgive the torturer for the immeasurable suffering of her mother's heart. But the sufferings of her tortured child she has no right to forgive; she dare not forgive the torturer, even if the child were to forgive him! And if that is so, if they dare not forgive, what becomes of harmony? Is there in the whole world a being who would have the right to forgive and could forgive? I don't want harmony. From love for humanity I don't want it. I would rather be left with the unavenged suffering. I would rather remain with my unavenged suffering and unsatisfied indignation, *even if I were wrong*. Besides, too high a price is asked for harmony; it's beyond our means to pay so much to enter on it. And so I hasten to give back my entrance ticket, and if I am an honest man I am bound to give it back as soon as possible. And that I am doing. It's not God that I don't accept, Alyosha, only I most respectfully return Him the ticket."

"That's rebellion," murmured Alyosha, looking down.

"Rebellion? I am sorry you call it that," said Ivan earnestly. "One can hardly live in rebellion, and I want to live. Tell me yourself, I challenge you—answer. Imagine that you are creating a fabric of human destiny with the object of making men happy in the end, giving them peace and rest at last, but that it was essential and inevitable to torture to death only one tiny creature—that baby beating its breast with its fist, for instance—and to found that edifice on its unavenged tears, would you consent to be the architect on those conditions? Tell me, and tell the truth."

"No, I wouldn't consent," said Alyosha softly.

"And can you admit the idea that men for whom you are building it would agree to accept their happiness on the foundation of the unexpiated blood of a little victim? And accepting it would remain happy for ever?"

"No, I can't admit it. Brother," said Alyosha suddenly, with flashing eyes, "you said just now, is there a being in the whole world who would have the right to forgive and could forgive? But there is a Being and He can forgive everything, all and for all, because He gave His innocent blood for all and everything. You have forgotten Him, and on Him is built the edifice, and it is to Him they cry aloud, 'Thou art just, O Lord, for Thy ways are revealed!' "

"Ah! the One without sin and His blood! No, I have not forgotten Him; on the contrary I've been wondering all the time how it was you did not bring Him in before, for usually all arguments on your side put Him in the foreground. Do you know, Alyosha—don't laugh! I made a poem about a year ago. If you can waste another ten minutes on me, I'll tell it to you."

"You wrote a poem?"

"Oh, no, I didn't write it," laughed Ivan, "and I've never written two lines of poetry in my life. But I made up this poem in prose and I remembered it. I was carried away when I made it up. You will be my first reader—that is, listener. Why should an author forego even one listener?" smiled Ivan. "Shall I tell it to you?"

"I am all attention," said Alyosha.

"My poem is called 'The Grand Inquisitor'; it's a ridiculous thing, but I want to tell it to you."

The Grand Inquisitor

"*E*ven this must have a preface—that is, a literary preface," laughed Ivan, "and I am a poor hand at making one. You see, my action takes place in the sixteenth century, and at that time, as you probably learnt at school, it was customary in poetry to bring down heavenly powers on earth. Not to speak of Dante, in France, clerks, as well as the monks in the monasteries, used to give regular performances in which the Madonna, the saints, the angels, Christ, and God Himself were brought on the stage. In those days it was done in all simplicity. In Victor Hugo's 'Notre Dame de Paris' an edifying and gratuitous spectacle was provided for the people in the Hotel de Ville of Paris in the reign of Louis XI in honour of the birth of the dauphin. It was called *Le bon jugement de la très sainte et gracieuse Vierge Marie*, and she appears herself on the stage and pronounces her *bon jugement*. Similar plays, chiefly from the Old Testament, were occasionally performed in Moscow too, up to the times of Peter the Great. But besides plays there were all sorts of legends and ballads scattered about the world, in which the saints and angels and all the powers of Heaven took part when required. In our monasteries the monks busied themselves in translating, copying, and even composing such poems—and even under the Tatars. There is, for instance, one such poem (of course, from the Greek), 'The Wanderings of Our Lady through Hell,' with descriptions as bold as Dante's. Our Lady visits Hell, and the Archangel Michael leads her through the torments. She sees the sinners and their punishment. There she sees among others one noteworthy set of sinners in a burning lake; some of them sink to the bottom of the lake so that they can't swim out, and 'these God forgets'—an expression of extraordinary depth and force. And so Our Lady, shocked and weeping, falls before the throne of God and begs for mercy for all in Hell—for all she has seen there, indiscriminately. Her conversation with God is immensely interesting. She beseeches Him, she will not desist, and when God points to the hands and feet of her Son, nailed to the Cross, and asks, 'How can I forgive His tormentors?' she bids all the saints, all the martyrs, all the angels and archangels to fall down with her and pray for mercy on all without distinction. It ends by her winning from God a respite of suffering every year from Good Friday till Trinity day, and the sinners at once raise a cry of thankfulness from Hell, chanting, 'Thou art just, O Lord, in this judgment.' Well, my poem would have been of that kind if it had appeared at that time. He comes on the scene in my poem, but He says nothing, only appears and passes on. Fifteen centuries have passed since He promised to come in His glory, fifteen centuries since His prophet wrote, 'Behold, I come quickly'; 'Of that day and that hour knoweth no man, neither the Son, but the Father,' as He Himself predicted on earth. But humanity awaits him with the same faith and with the same love. Oh, with greater faith, for it is fifteen centuries since man has ceased to see signs from Heaven.

> No signs from Heaven come to-day
> To add to what the heart doth say.

There was nothing left but faith in what the heart doth say. It is true there were many miracles in those days. There were saints who performed miraculous cures; some holy people, according to their biographies, were visited by the Queen of Heaven herself. But the devil did not slumber, and doubts were already arising among men of the truth of these miracles. And just then there appeared in the north of Germany a terrible new heresy. 'A huge star like to a torch' (that is, to a church) 'fell on the sources of the waters and they became bitter.' These heretics began blasphemously denying miracles. But those who remained faithful were all the more ardent in their faith. The tears of humanity rose up to Him as before, awaited His coming, loved Him, hoped for Him, yearned to suffer and die for Him as before. And so many ages mankind had prayed with faith and fervour, 'O Lord our God, hasten Thy coming,' so many ages called upon Him, that in His infinite mercy He deigned to come down to His servants. Before that day He had come down, He had visited some holy men, martyrs and hermits, as is written in their 'Lives.' Among us, Tyutchev, with absolute faith in the truth of his words, bore witness that

> Bearing the Cross, in slavish dress,
> Weary and worn, the Heavenly King
> Our mother, Russia, came to bless,
> And through our land went wandering.

And that certainly was so, I assure you.

"And behold, He deigned to appear for a moment to the people, to the tortured, suffering people, sunk in iniquity, but loving Him like children.

My story is laid in Spain, in Seville, in the most terrible time of the Inquisition, when fires were lighted every day to the glory of God, and 'in the splendid *auto da fé* the wicked heretics were burnt.' Oh, of course, this was not the coming in which He will appear according to His promise at the end of time in all His heavenly glory, and which will be sudden 'as lightning flashing from east to west.' No, He visited His children only for a moment, and there where the flames were crackling round the heretics. In His infinite mercy He came once more among men in that human shape in which He walked among men for three years fifteen centuries ago. He came down to the 'hot pavement' of the southern town in which on the day before almost a hundred heretics had, *ad majorem gloriam Dei*, been burnt by the cardinal, the Grand Inquisitor, in a magnificent *auto da fé*, in the presence of the king, the court, the knights, the cardinals, the most charming ladies of the court, and the whole population of Seville.

"He came softly, unobserved, and yet, strange to say, every one recognised Him. That might be one of the best passages in the poem. I mean, why they recognised Him. The people are irresistibly drawn to Him, they surround Him, they flock about Him, follow Him. He moves silently in their midst with a gentle smile of infinite compassion. The sun of love burns in His heart, light and power shine from His eyes, and their radiance, shed on the people, stirs their hearts with responsive love. He holds out His hands to them, blesses them, and a healing virtue comes from contact with Him, even with His garments. An old man in the crowd, blind from childhood, cries out, 'O Lord, heal me and I shall see Thee!' and, as it were, scales fall from his eyes and the blind man sees Him. The crowd weeps and kisses the earth under His feet. Children throw flowers before Him, sing, and cry hosannah. 'It is He—it is He!' all repeat. 'It must be He, it can be no one but Him!' He stops at the steps of the Seville cathedral at the moment when the weeping mourners are bringing in a little open white coffin. In it lies a child of seven, the only daughter of a prominent citizen. The dead child lies hidden in flowers. 'He will raise your child,' the crowd shouts to the weeping mother. The priest, coming to meet the coffin, looks perplexed, and frowns, but the mother of the dead child throws herself at His feet with a wail. 'If it is Thou, raise my child!' she cries, holding out her hands to Him. The procession halts, the coffin is laid on the steps at His feet. He looks with compassion, and His lips once more softly pronounce, 'Maiden, arise!' and the maiden arises. The little girl sits up in the coffin and looks around, smiling with wide-open wondering eyes, holding a bunch of white roses they had put in her hand.

"There are cries, sobs, confusion among the people, and at that moment the cardinal himself, the Grant Inquisitor, passes by the cathedral. He is an old man, almost ninety, tall and erect, with a withered face and sunken eyes, in which there is still a gleam of light. He is not dressed in his gorgeous cardinal's robes, as he was the day before, when he was burning the enemies of the Roman Church—at that moment he was wearing his coarse, old, monk's cassock. At a distance behind him come his gloomy assistants and slaves and the 'holy guard.' He stops at the sight of the crowd and watches it from a distance. He sees everything; he sees them set the coffin down at His feet, sees the child rise up, and his face darkens. He knits his thick grey brows and his eyes gleam with a sinister fire. He holds out his finger and bids the guards take Him. And such is his power, so completely are the people cowed into submission and trembling obedience to him, that the crowd immediately make way for the guards, and in the midst of deathlike silence they lay hands on Him and lead Him away. The crowd instantly bows down to the earth, like one man, before the old inquisitor. He blesses the people in silence and passes on. The guards lead their prisoner to the close, gloomy vaulted prison in the ancient palace of the Holy Inquisition and shut Him in it. The day passes and is followed by the dark, burning 'breathless' night of Seville. The air is 'fragrant with laurel and lemon.' In the pitch darkness the iron door of the prison is suddenly opened and the Grand Inquisitor himself comes in with a light in his hand. He is alone; the door is closed at once behind him. He stands in the doorway and for a minute or two gazes into His face. At last he goes up slowly, sets the light on the table and speaks.

" 'Is it Thou? Thou?' but receiving no answer, he adds at once, 'Don't answer, be silent. What canst Thou say, indeed? I know too well what Thou wouldst say. And Thou hast no right to add anything to what Thou hadst said of old. Why, then, art Thou come to hinder us? For Thou hast come to hinder us, and Thou knowest that. But dost Thou know what will be to-morrow? I know not who Thou art and care not to know whether it is Thou or only a semblance of Him, but to-morrow I shall condemn Thee and burn Thee at the stake as the worst of heretics. And the very people who have to-day kissed Thy feet, to-morrow at the faintest sign from me will rush to heap up the embers of Thy fire. Knowest Thou that? Yes, maybe Thou knowest it,' he added with thoughtful penetration, never for a moment taking his eyes off the Prisoner."

"I don't quite understand, Ivan. What does it mean?" Alyosha, who had been listening in silence, said with a smile. "Is it simply a wild fantasy, or a mistake on the part of the old man—some impossible *quiproquo*?"

"Take it as the last," said Ivan, laughing, "if you are so corrupted by modern realism and can't stand anything fantastic. If you like it to be a case of mistaken identity, let it be so. It is true," he went on, laughing, "the old man was ninety, and he might well be crazy over his set idea. He might have been struck by the appearance of the prisoner. It might, in fact, be simply his ravings, the delusion of an old man of ninety, over-excited by the *auto da fé* of a hundred heretics the day before. But does it matter to us after all whether it was a mistake of identity or a wild fantasy? All that matters is that the old man should speak out, should speak openly of what he has thought in silence for ninety years."

"And the Prisoner too is silent? Does He look at him and not say a word?"

"That's inevitable in any case," Ivan laughed again. "The old man has told Him He hasn't the right to add anything to what He has said of old. One may say it is the most fundamental feature of Roman Catholicism, in my opinion at least. 'All has been given by Thee to the Pope,' they say, 'and all, therefore, is still in the Pope's hands, and there is no need for Thee to come now at all. Thou must not meddle for the time, at least.' That's how they speak and write too—the Jesuits, at any rate. I have read it myself in the works of their theologians. 'Hast Thou the right to reveal to us one of the mysteries of that world from which Thou hast come?' my old man asks Him, and answers the question for Him. 'No, Thou hast not; that Thou mayest not add to what has been said of old and mayest not take from men the freedom which Thou didst exalt when Thou wast on earth. Whatsoever Thou revealest anew will encroach on men's freedom of faith; for it will be manifest as a miracle, and the freedom of their faith was dearer to Thee than anything in those days fifteen hundred years ago. Didst Thou not often say then, "I will make you free"? But now Thou hast seen these "free" men,' the old man adds suddenly, with a pensive smile. 'Yes, we've paid dearly for it,' he goes on, looking sternly at Him, 'but at last we have completed that work in Thy name. For fifteen centuries we have been wrestling with Thy freedom, but now it is ended and over for good. Dost Thou not believe that it's over for good? Thou lookest meekly at me and deignest not even to be wroth with me. But let me tell Thee that now, today, people are more persuaded than ever that they have perfect freedom, yet they have brought their freedom to us and laid it humbly at our feet. But that has been our doing. Was this what Thou didst? Was this Thy freedom?'"

"I don't understand again," Alyosha broke in. "Is he ironical, is he jesting?"

"Not a bit of it! He claims it as a merit for himself and his Church that at last they have vanquished freedom and have done so to make men happy. 'For now' (he is speaking of the Inquisition, of course) 'for the first time it has become possible to think of the happiness of men. Man was created a rebel; and how can rebels be happy? Thou wast warned,' he says to Him. 'Thou hast had no lack of admonitions and warnings, but Thou didst not listen to those warnings; Thou didst reject the only way by which men might be made happy. But fortunately, departing Thou didst hand on the work to us. Thou hast promised, Thou hast established by Thy word, Thou hast given to us the right to bind and to unbind, and now, of course, Thou canst not think of taking it away. Why, then, hast Thou come to hinder us?'"

"And what's the meaning of 'no lack of admonitions and warnings'?" asked Alyosha.

"Why, that's the chief part of what the old man must say."

" 'The wise and dread spirit, the spirit of self-destruction and non-existence,' the old man goes on, 'the great spirit talked with Thee in the wilderness, and we are told in the books that he "tempted" Thee. Is that so? And could anything truer be said than what he revealed to Thee in three questions and what Thou didst reject, and what in the books is called "the temptation"? And yet if there has ever been on earth a real stupendous miracle, it took place on that day, on the day of the three temptations. The statement of those three questions was itself the miracle. If it were possible to imagine simply for the sake of argument that those three questions of the dread spirit had perished utterly from the books, and that we had to restore them and to invent them anew, and to do so had gathered together all the wise men of the earth—rulers, chief priests, learned men, philosophers, poets—and had set them the task to invent three questions, such as would not only fit the occasion, but express in three words, three human phrases, the whole future history of the world and of humanity—dost Thou believe that all the wisdom of the earth united could have invented anything in depth and force equal to the three questions which were actually put to Thee then by the wise and mighty spirit in the wilderness? From those questions alone, from the miracle of their statement, we can see that we have here to do not with the fleeting human intelligence, but with the absolute and eternal. For in those three questions the whole subsequent history of mankind is, as it were, brought together into one whole, and foretold, and in them are united all the unsolved historical contradictions of human nature. At the time it could not be so clear, since the future was unknown; but now that fifteen hundred years have passed, we see that everything in those three questions was so justly divined and foretold, and has been so truly fulfilled, that nothing can be added to them or taken from them.

" 'Judge Thyself who was right—Thou or he who questioned Thee then? Remember the first question; its meaning, in other words, was this: "Thou wouldst go into the world, and art going with empty hands, with some promise of freedom which men in their simplicity and their natural unruliness cannot even understand, which they fear and dread—for nothing has ever been more insupportable for a man and a human society than freedom. But seest Thou these stones in this parched and barren wilderness? Turn them into bread, and mankind will run after Thee like a flock of sheep, grateful and obedient, though for ever trembling, lest Thou withdraw Thy hand and deny them Thy bread." But Thou wouldst not deprive man of freedom and didst reject the offer, thinking, what is that freedom worth, if obedience is bought with bread? Thou didst reply that man lives not by bread alone. But dost Thou know that for the sake of that earthly bread the spirit of the earth will rise up against Thee and will strive with Thee and overcome Thee, and all will follow him, crying, "Who can compare with this beast? He has given us fire from heaven!" Dost Thou know that the ages will pass, and humanity will proclaim by the lips of their sages that there is no crime, and therefore no sin; there is only hunger? "Feed men, and then ask of them virtue!" that's what they'll write on the banner, which they will raise against Thee, and with which they will destroy Thy temple. Where Thy temple stood will rise a new building; the terrible tower of Babel will be built again, and though, like the one of old, it will not be finished, yet Thou mightest have prevented that new tower and have cut short the sufferings of men for a thousand years; for they will come back to us after a thousand years of agony with their tower. They will seek us again, hidden underground in the catacombs, for we shall be again persecuted and tortured. They will find us and cry to us, "Feed us, for those who have promised us fire from heaven haven't given it!" And then we shall finish building their tower, for he finishes the building who feeds them. And we alone shall feed them in Thy name, declaring falsely that it is in Thy name. Oh, never, never can they feed themselves without us! No science will give them bread so long as they remain free. In the end they will lay their freedom at our feet, and say to us, "Make us your slaves, but feed us." They will understand themselves, at last, that freedom and bread enough for all are inconceivable together, for never, never will they be able to share between them! They will be convinced, too, that they can never be free, for they are weak, vicious, worthless and rebellious. Thou didst promise them the bread of Heaven, but, I repeat again, can it compare with earthly bread in the eyes of the weak, ever sinful and ignoble race of man? And if for the sake of the bread of Heaven thousands and tens of thousands shall follow Thee, what is to become of the millions and tens of thousands of millions of creatures who will not have the strength to forego the earthly bread for the sake of the heavenly? Or dost Thou care only for the tens of thousands of the great and strong, while the millions, numerous as the sands of the sea, who are weak but love Thee, must exist only for the sake of the great and strong? No, we care for the weak too. They are sinful and rebellious, but in the end they too will become obedient. They will marvel at us and look on us as gods, because we are ready to endure the freedom which they have found so dreadful and to rule over them—so awful it will seem to them to be free. But we shall tell them that we are Thy servants and rule them in Thy name. We shall deceive them again, for we will not let Thee come to us again. That deception will be our suffering, for we shall be forced to lie.

"'This is the significance of the first question in the wilderness, and this is what Thou hast rejected for the sake of that freedom which Thou hast exalted above everything. Yet in this question lies hid the great secret of this world. Choosing "bread," Thou wouldst have satisfied the universal and everlasting craving of humanity—to find some one to worship. So long as man remains free he strives for nothing so incessantly and so painfully as to find some one to worship. But man seeks to worship what is established beyond dispute, so that all men would agree at once to worship it. For these pitiful creatures are concerned not only to find what one or the other can worship, but to find something that all would believe in and worship; what is essential is that all may be *together* in it. This craving for *community* of worship is the chief misery of every man individually and of all humanity from the beginning of time. For the sake of common worship they've slain each other with the sword. They have set up gods and challenged one another, "Put away your gods and come and worship ours, or we will kill you and your gods!" And so it will be to the end of the world, even when gods disappear from the earth; they will fall down before idols just the same. Thou didst know, Thou couldst not but have known, this fundamental secret of human nature, but Thou didst reject the one infallible banner which was offered Thee to make all men bow down to Thee alone—the banner of earthly bread; and Thou hast rejected it for the sake of freedom and the bread of Heaven. Behold what Thou didst further. And all again in the name of freedom! I tell Thee that man is tormented by no greater anxiety than to find some one quickly to whom he can hand over that gift of freedom with which the ill-fated creature is born. But only one who can appease their conscience can take over their freedom. In bread there was offered Thee an invincible banner; give bread, and man will worship Thee, for nothing is more certain than bread. But if some one else gains possession of his conscience—oh! then he will cast away Thy bread and follow after him who has ensnared his conscience. In that Thou wast right. For the secret of man's being is not only to live but to have something to live for. Without a stable conception of the object of life, man would not consent to go on living, and would rather destroy himself than remain on earth, though he had bread in abundance. That is true. But what happened? Instead of taking men's freedom from them, Thou didst make it greater than ever! Didst Thou forget that man prefers peace, and even death, to freedom of choice in the knowledge of good and evil? Nothing is more seductive for man than his freedom of conscience, but nothing is a greater cause of suffering. And behold, instead of giving a firm foundation for setting the conscience of man at rest for ever, Thou didst choose all that is exceptional, vague and enigmatic; Thou didst choose what was utterly beyond the strength of men, acting as though Thou didst not love them at all—Thou who didst come to give Thy life for them! Instead of taking possession of men's freedom, Thou didst increase it, and burdened the spiritual kingdom of mankind with its sufferings for ever. Thou didst desire man's free love, that he should follow Thee freely, enticed and taken captive by Thee. In place of the rigid ancient law, man must hereafter with free heart decide for himself what is good and what is evil, having only Thy image before him as his guide. But didst Thou not know he would at last reject even Thy image and Thy truth, if he is weighed down with the fearful burden of free choice? They will cry aloud at last that the truth is not in Thee, for they could not have been left in greater confusion and suffering than Thou hast caused, laying upon them so many cares and unanswerable problems.

" 'So that, in truth, Thou didst Thyself lay the foundation for the destruction of Thy kingdom, and no one is more to blame for it. Yet what was offered Thee? There are three powers, three powers alone, able to conquer and to hold captive for ever the conscience of these impotent rebels for their happiness—those forces are miracle, mystery and authority. Thou hast rejected all three and hast set the example for doing so. When the wise and dread spirit set Thee on the pinnacle of the temple and said to Thee, 'If Thou wouldst know whether Thou art the Son of God then cast Thyself down, for it is written: the angels shall hold him up lest he fall and bruise himself, and Thou shalt know then whether Thou art the Son of God and shalt prove then how great is Thy faith in Thy Father.' But Thou didst refuse and wouldst not cast Thyself down. Oh! of course, Thou didst proudly and well, like God; but the weak, unruly race of men, are they gods? Oh, Thou didst know then that in taking one step, in making one movement to cast Thyself down, Thou wouldst be tempting God and have lost all Thy faith in Him, and wouldst have been dashed to pieces against that earth which Thou didst come to save. And the wise spirit that tempted Thee would have rejoiced. But I ask again, are there many like Thee? And couldst Thou believe for one moment that men, too, could face such a temptation? Is the nature of men such, that they can reject miracle, and at the great moments of their life, the moments of their deepest, most agonising spiritual difficulties, cling only to the free verdict of the heart? Oh, Thou didst know that Thy deed would be recorded in books, would be handed down to remote times and the utmost ends of the earth, and Thou didst hope that man, following Thee, would cling to God and not ask for a miracle. But Thou didst not know that when man rejects miracle he rejects God too; for man seeks not so much God as the miraculous. And as man cannot bear to be without the miraculous, he will create new miracles of his own for himself, and will worship deeds of sorcery and witchcraft, though he might be a hundred times over a rebel, heretic and infidel. Thou didst not come down from the Cross when they shouted to Thee, mocking and reviling Thee, "Come down from the cross and we will believe that Thou art He." Thou didst not come down, for again Thou wouldst not enslave man by a miracle, and didst crave faith given freely, not based on miracle. Thou didst crave for free love and not the base raptures of the slave before the might that has overawed him forever. But Thou didst think too highly

but
he
did.

of men therein, for they are slaves, of course, though rebellious by nature. Look round and judge; fifteen centuries have passed, look upon them. Whom hast Thou raised up to Thyself? I swear, man is weaker and baser by nature than Thou hast believed him! Can he, can he do what Thou didst? By showing him so much respect, Thou didst, as it were, cease to feel for him, for Thou didst ask far too much from him—Thou who hast loved him more than Thyself! Respecting him less, Thou wouldst have asked less of him. That would have been more like love, for his burden would have been lighter. He is weak and vile. What though he is everywhere now rebelling against our power, and proud of his rebellion? It is the pride of a child and a schoolboy. They are little children rioting and barring out the teacher at school. But their childish delight will end; it will cost them dear. They will cast down temples and drench the earth with blood. But they will see at last, the foolish children, that, though they are rebels, they are impotent rebels, unable to keep up their own rebellion. Bathed in their foolish tears, they will recognise at last that He who created them rebels must have meant to mock at them. They will say this in despair, and their utterance will be a blasphemy which will make them more unhappy still, for man's nature cannot bear blasphemy, and in the end always avenges it on itself. And so unrest, confusion and unhappiness—that is the present lot of man after Thou didst bear so much for their freedom! Thy great prophet tells in vision and in image, that he saw all those who took part in the first resurrection and that there were of each tribe twelve thousand. But if there were so many of them, they must have been not men but gods. They had borne Thy cross, they had endured scores of years in the barren, hungry wilderness, living upon locusts and roots—and Thou mayest indeed point with pride at those children of freedom, of free love, of free and splendid sacrifice for Thy name. But remember that they were only some thousands; and what of the rest? And how are the other weak ones to blame, because they could not endure what the strong have endured? How is the weak soul to blame that it is unable to receive such terrible gifts? Canst Thou have simply come to the elect and for the elect? But if so, it is a mystery and we cannot understand it. And if it is a mystery, we too have a right to preach a mystery, and to teach them that it's not the free judgment of their hearts, not love that matters, but a mystery which they must follow blindly, even against their conscience. So we have done. We have corrected Thy work and have founded it upon *miracle, mystery* and *authority*. And men rejoiced that they were again led like sheep, and that the terrible gift that had brought them such suffering, was, at last, lifted from their hearts. Were we right teaching them this? Speak! Did we not love mankind, so meekly acknowledging their feebleness, lovingly lightening their burden, and permitting their weak nature even sin with our sanction? Why hast Thou come now to hinder us? And why dost Thou look silently and searchingly at me with Thy mild eyes? Be angry. I don't want Thy love, for I love Thee not. And what use is it for me to hide anything from Thee? Don't I know to Whom I am speaking? All that I can say is known to Thee already. And is it for me to conceal from Thee our mystery? Perhaps it is Thy will to hear it from my lips. Listen, then. We are not working with Thee, but with *him*—that is our mystery. It's long—eight centuries—since we have been on *his* side and not on Thine. Just eight centuries ago, we took from him what Thou didst reject with scorn, that last gift he offered Thee, showing Thee all the kingdoms of the earth. We took from him Rome and the sword of Caesar, and proclaimed ourselves sole rulers of the earth, though hitherto we have not been able to complete our work. But whose fault is that? Oh, the work is only beginning, but it has begun. It has long to await completion and the earth has yet much to suffer, but we shall triumph and shall be Caesars, and then we shall plan the universal happiness of man. But Thou mightest have taken even then the sword of Caesar. Why didst Thou reject that last gift? Hadst Thou accepted that last counsel of the mighty spirit, Thou wouldst have accomplished all that man seeks on earth—that is, some one to worship, some one to keep his conscience, and some means of uniting all in one unanimous and harmonious ant-heap, for the craving for universal unity is the third and last anguish of men. Mankind as a whole has always striven to organise a universal state. There have been many great nations with great histories, but the more highly they were developed the more unhappy they were, for they felt more acutely than other people the craving for worldwide union. The great conquerors, Timours and Ghenghis-Kahns, whirled like hurricanes over the face of the earth striving to subdue its people, and they too were but the unconscious expression of the same craving for universal unity. Hadst Thou taken the world and Caesar's purple, Thou wouldst have founded the universal state and have given universal peace. For who can rule men if not he who holds their conscience and their bread in his hands? We have taken the sword of Caesar, and in taking it, of course, have rejected Thee and followed *him*. Oh, ages are yet to come of the confusion of free thought, of their science and cannibalism. For having begun to build their tower of Babel without us, they will end, of course, with cannibalism. But then the beast will crawl to us and lick our feet and spatter them with tears of blood. And we shall sit upon the beast and raise the cup, and on it will be written, "Mystery." But then, and only then, the reign of peace and happiness will come for men. Thou art proud of Thine elect, but Thou hast only the elect, while we give rest to all. And besides, how many of those elect, those mighty ones who could become elect, have grown weary waiting for Thee, and have transferred and will transfer the powers of their spirit and the warmth of their heart to the other camp, and end by raising their *free* banner against Thee. Thou didst Thyself lift up that banner. But with us all will be happy and will no more rebel nor destroy one another as under Thy freedom. Oh, we shall persuade them that they will only become free whey they renounce their freedom to us and submit to us. And shall we be right or shall we be lying? They will be convinced that we are right, for they will remember the horrors of slavery and confusion to which Thy freedom brought them. Freedom, free thought and science, will lead them into such straits and will bring them face to face with such marvels and insoluble mysteries, that some of them, the fierce and rebellious, will destroy themselves, others, rebellious but weak, will destroy one another, while the rest, weak and unhappy, will crawl fawning to our feet and whine to us: "Yes, you were right, you alone possess His mystery, and we come back to you, save us from ourselves!"

" 'Receiving bread from us, they will see clearly that we take the bread made by their hands from them, to give it to them, without any miracle. They will see that we do not change the stones to bread, but in truth they will be more thankful for taking it from our hands than for the bread itself! For they will remember only too well that in old days, without our help, even the bread they made turned to stones in their hands, while since they have come back to us, the very stones have turned to bread in their hands. Too, too well they know the value of complete submission! And until men know that, they will be unhappy. Who is most to blame for their not knowing it, speak? Who scattered the flock and sent it astray on unknown paths? But the flock will come together again and will submit once more, and then it will be once for all. Then we shall give them the quiet humble happiness of weak creatures such as they are by nature. Oh, we shall persuade them at last not to be proud, for Thou didst lift them up and thereby taught them to be proud. We shall show them that they are weak, that they are only pitiful children, but that childlike happiness is the sweetest of all. They will become timid and will look to us and huddle close to us in fear, as chicks to the hen. They will marvel at us and will be awe-stricken before us, and will be proud at our being so powerful and clever, that we have been able to subdue such a turbulent flock of thousands of millions. They will tremble impotently before our wrath, their minds will grow fearful, they will be quick to shed tears like women and children, but they will be just as ready at a sign from us to pass to laughter and rejoicing, to happy mirth and childish song. Yes, we shall set them to work, but in their leisure hours we shall make their life like a child's game, with children's songs and innocent dance. Oh, we shall allow them even sin, they are weak and helpless, and they will love us like children because we allow them to sin. We shall tell them that every sin will be expiated, if it is done with our permission, that we allow them to sin because we love them, and the punishment for these sins we take upon ourselves. And we shall take it upon ourselves, and they will adore us as their saviours who have taken on themselves their sins before God. And they will have no secrets from us. We shall allow or forbid them to live with their wives and mistresses, to have or not to have children—according to whether they have been obedient or disobedient—and they will submit to us gladly and cheerfully. The most painful secrets of their conscience, all, all they will bring to us, and we shall have an answer for all. And they will be glad to believe our answer, for it will save them from the great anxiety and terrible agony they endure at present in making a free decision for themselves. And all will be happy, all the millions of creatures except the hundred thousand who rule over them. For only we, we who guard the mystery, shall be unhappy. There will be thousands of millions of happy babes, and a hundred thousand sufferers who have taken upon themselves the curse of the knowledge of good and evil. Peacefully they will die, peacefully they will expire in Thy name, and beyond the grave they will find nothing but death. But we shall keep the secret, and for their happiness we shall allure them with the reward of heaven and eternity. Though if there were anything in the other world, it certainly would not be for such as they. It is prophesied that Thou wilt come again in victory, Thou wilt come with Thy chosen, the proud and strong, but we will say that they have only saved themselves, but we have saved all. We are told that the harlot who sits upon the beast, and holds in her hands the *mystery*, shall be put to shame, that the weak will rise up again, and will rend her royal purple and will strip naked her loathsome body. But then I will stand up and point out to Thee the thousand millions of happy children who have known no sin. And we who have taken their sins upon us for their happiness will stand up before Thee and say: "Judge us if Thou canst and darest." Know that I fear Thee not. Know that I too have been in the wilderness, I too have lived on roots and locusts, I too prized the freedom with which Thou hast blessed men, and I too was striving to stand among Thy elect, among the strong and powerful, thirsting "to make up the number." But I awakened and would not serve madness. I turned back and joined the ranks of those *who have corrected Thy work*. I left the proud and went back to the humble, for the happiness of the humble. What I say to Thee will come to pass, and our dominion will be built up. I repeat, to-morrow Thou shalt see that obedient flock who at a sign from me will hasten to heap up the hot cinders about the pile on which I shall burn Thee for coming to hinder us. For if any one has ever deserved our fires, it is Thou. To-morrow I shall burn Thee. **Dixi.**' "

Ivan stopped. He was carried away as he talked and spoke with excitement; when he had finished, he suddenly smiled.

Alyosha had listened in silence; towards the end he was greatly moved and seemed several times on the point of interrupting, but restrained himself. Now his words came with a rush.

"But . . . that's absurd!" he cried, flushing. "Your poem is in praise of

Jesus, not in blame of Him—as you meant it to be. And who will believe you about freedom? Is that the way to understand it? That's not the idea of it in the Orthodox Church . . . That's Rome, and not even the whole of Rome, it's false—those are the worst of the Catholics, the Inquisitors, the Jesuits! . . . And there could not be such a fantastic creature as your Inquisitor. What are these sins of mankind they take on themselves? Who are these keepers of the mystery who have taken some curse upon themselves for the happiness of mankind? When have they been seen? We know the Jesuits, they are spoken ill of, but surely they are not what you describe? They are not that at all, not at all. . . . They are simply the Romish army for the earthly sovereignty of the world in the future, with the Pontiff of Rome for Emperor . . . that's their ideal, but there's no sort of mystery or lofty melancholy about it. . . . It's simple lust of power, of filthy earthly gain, of domination—something like a universal serfdom with them as masters—that's all they stand for. They don't even believe in God perhaps. Your suffering inquisitor is a mere fantasy."

"Stay, stay," laughed Ivan, "how hot you are! A fantasy you say, let it be so! Of course it's a fantasy. But allow me to say: do you really think that the Roman Catholic movement of the last centuries is actually nothing but the lust of power, of filthy earthly gain? Is that Father Païssy's teaching?"

"No, no, on the contrary, Father Païssy did once say something rather the same as you . . . but of course it's not the same, not a bit the same," Alyosha hastily corrected himself.

"A precious admission, in spite of your 'not a bit the same.' I ask you why your Jesuits and Inquisitors have united simply for vile material gain? Why can there not be among them one martyr oppressed by great sorrow and loving humanity? You see, only suppose that there was one such man among all those who desire nothing but filthy material gain—if there's only one like my old inquisitor, who had himself eaten roots in the desert and made frenzied efforts to subdue his flesh to make himself free and perfect. But yet all his life he loved humanity, and suddenly his eyes were opened, and he saw that it is no great moral blessedness to attain perfection and freedom, if at the same time one gains the conviction that millions of God's creatures have been created as a mockery, that they will never be capable of using their freedom, that these poor rebels can never turn into giants to complete the tower, that it was not for such geese that the great idealist dreamt his dream of harmony. Seeing all that he turned back and joined—the clever people. Surely that could have happened?"

"Joined whom, what clever people?" cried Alyosha, completely carried away. "They have no such great cleverness and no mysteries and secrets. . . . Perhaps nothing but Atheism, that's all their secret. Your inquisitor does not believe in God, that's his secret!"

"What if it is so! At last you have guessed it. It's perfectly true that that's the whole secret, but isn't that suffering, at least for a man like that, who has wasted his whole life in the desert and yet could not shake off his incurable love of humanity? In his old age he reached the clear conviction that nothing but the advice of the great dread spirit could build up any tolerable sort of life for the feeble, unruly, 'incomplete, empirical creatures created in jest.' And so, convinced of this, he sees that he must follow the counsel of the wise spirit, the dread spirit of death and destruction, and therefore accept lying and deception, and lead men consciously to death and destruction, and yet deceive them all the way so that they may not notice where they are being led, that the poor blind creatures may at least on the way think themselves happy. And note, the deception is in the name of Him in Whose ideal the old man had so fervently believed all his life long. Is not that tragic? And if only one such stood at the head of the whole army 'filled with the lust of power only for the sake of filthy gain'—would not one such be enough to make a tragedy? More than that, one such standing at the head is enough to create the actual leading idea of the Roman Church with all its armies and Jesuits, its highest idea. I tell you frankly that I firmly believe that there has always been such a man among those who stood at the head of the movement. Who knows, there may have been some such even among the Roman Popes. Who knows, perhaps the spirit of that accursed old man who loves mankind so obstinately in his own way, is to be found even now in a whole multitude of such old men, existing not by chance but by agreement, as a secret league formed long ago for the guarding of the mystery, to guard it from the weak and the unhappy, so as to make them happy. No doubt it is so, and so it must be indeed. I fancy that even among the Masons there's something of the same mystery at the bottom, and that that's why the Catholics so detest the Masons as their rivals breaking up the unity of the idea, while it is so essential that there should be one flock and one shepherd. . . . But from the way I defend my idea I might be an author impatient of your criticism. Enough of it."

"You are perhaps a Mason yourself!" broke suddenly from Alyosha. "You don't believe in God," he added, speaking this time very sorrowfully. He fancied besides that his brother was looking at him ironically. "How does your poem end?" he asked, suddenly looking down. "Or was it the end?"

"I meant to end it like this. When the Inquisitor ceased speaking he waited some time for his Prisoner to answer him. His silence weighed down upon him. He saw that the Prisoner had listened intently all the time, looking gently in his face and evidently not wishing to reply. The old man longed for Him to say something, however bitter and terrible. But He suddenly approached the old man in silence and softly kissed him on his bloodless aged lips. That was all his answer. The old man shuddered. His lips moved. He went to the door, opened it, and said to Him: 'Go, and come no more . . . come not at all, never, never!' And he let Him out into the dark alleys of the town. The Prisoner went away."

"And the old man?"

"The kiss glows in his heart, but the old man adheres to his idea."

"And you with him, you too?" cried Alyosha, mournfully.

Ivan laughed.

"Why, it's all nonsense, Alyosha. It's only a senseless poem of a senseless student, who could never write two lines of verse. Why do you take it so seriously? Surely you don't suppose I am going straight off to the Jesuits, to join the men who are correcting His work? Good Lord, it's no business of mine. I told you, all I want is to live on to thirty, and then . . . dash the cup to the ground!"

"But the little sticky leaves, and the precious tombs, and the blue sky, and the woman you love! How will you live, how will you love them?" Alyosha cried sorrowfully. "With such a hell in your heart and your head, how can you? No, that's just what you are going away for, to join them . . . if not, you will kill yourself, you can't endure it!"

"There is a strength to endure everything," Ivan said with a cold smile.

"What strength?"

"The strength of the Karamazov—the strength of the Karamazov baseness."

"To sink into debauchery, to stifle your soul with corruption, yes?"

"Possibly even that . . . only perhaps till I am thirty I shall escape it, and then."

"How will you escape it? By what will you escape it? That's impossible with your ideas."

"In the Karamazov way, again."

" 'Everything is lawful,' you mean? Everything is lawful, is that it?"

Ivan scowled, and all at once turned strangely pale.

"Ah, you've caught up yesterday's phrase, which so offended Miüsov—and which Dmitri pounced upon so naïvely and paraphrased!" he smiled queerly. "Yes, if you like, 'everything is lawful' since the word has been said. I won't deny it. And Mitya's version isn't bad."

Alyosha looked at him in silence.

"I thought that going away from here I have you at least," Ivan said suddenly, with unexpected feeling; "but now I see that there is no place for me even in your heart, my dear hermit. The formula, 'all is lawful,' I won't renounce—will you renounce me for that, yes?"

Alyosha got up, went to him and softly kissed him on the lips.

"That's plagiarism," cried Ivan, highly delighted. "You stole that from my poem. Thank you though. Get up, Alyosha, it's time we were going, both of us."

Giovanni Maria Mastai-Ferretti was born at Sinigaglia, Italy, in 1792, the son of a count. He was ordained priest in 1819, became archbishop of Spoleto in 1830, and was created a cardinal in 1840. On the death of Gregory XVI, in 1846, he was elected pope and assumed the name of Pius IX.

During the thirty-two years of his papacy, Italy achieved unification, and the pope lost his very considerable temporal dominion, which in 1846 comprised a large part of continental Italy. Pius IX, however, refused to accept the idea that the power of the papacy might be approaching an end; and the documents that follow reflect his indomitable and militant spirit.

The dogma of the immaculate conception of the Virgin Mary was proclaimed on December 8, 1854, in the papal bull, *Ineffabilis Deus*. The Syllabus of Errors and the encyclical *Quanta Cura* were issued on December 8, 1864, along with a letter, also reprinted here, from the papal Secretary of State. The dogma of papal infallibility was published in the third session of the Vatican Council, April 24, 1870.

Pope Pius IX died in 1878, and Leo XIII succeeded him.

The Dogma of the Immaculate Conception

*W*e declare, pronounce, and define that the doctrine which holds that the most blessed Virgin Mary, in the first instant of her conception, by a singular grace and privilege granted by almighty God, in view of the merits of Jesus Christ, the Saviour of the human race, was preserved free from all stain of original sin, is a doctrine revealed by God and therefore to be believed firmly and constantly by all the faithful.

The Encyclical Quanta Cura *(in part)*

*F*or you know well, Venerable Brethren, that at this time there are found not a few who, applying to civil intercourse the impious and absurd principles of what they call *Naturalism*, dare teach "that the best form of Society, and the exigencies of civil progress, absolutely require human society to be constituted and governed without any regard whatsoever to Religion, as if this [Religion] did not even exist, or at least without making any distinction between true and false religions." Contrary to the teachings of the Holy Scriptures, of the Church, and of the Holy Fathers, these persons do not hesitate to assert, that "the best condition of human society is that wherein no duty is recognized by the Government of correcting, by enacted penalties, the violators of the Catholic Religion, except when the maintenance of the public peace requires it." From this totally false notion of social government, they fear not to uphold that erroneous opinion most pernicious to the Catholic Church, and to the salvation of souls, which was called by Our Predecessor, Gregory XVI (lately quoted) the insanity [*deliramentum*] (Encycl. 13 August, 1832): namely, "that the liberty of conscience and of worship is the peculiar (or inalienable) right of every man, which should be proclaimed by law, and that citizens have the right to all kinds of liberty, to be restrained by no law, whether ecclesiastical or civil, by which they may be enabled to manifest openly and publicly their ideas, by word of mouth, through the press, or by any other means." But whilst these men make these rash assertions, they do not reflect, or consider, that they preach the liberty of perdition (St. Augustine, Epistle 105, al. 166), and that, "if it is always free to human arguments to discuss, men will never be wanting who will dare to resist the truth, and to rely upon the loquacity of human wisdom, when we know from the command of Our Lord Jesus Christ, how faith and Christian wisdom ought to avoid this most mischievous vanity." (St. Leo, Epistle 164, al. 133, sec 2, Boll. ed.)

Letter from the Papal Secretary of State, which accompanied the *Syllabus of Errors*:

Our most Holy Father, Pius IX, Sovereign Pontiff, being profoundly anxious for the salvation of souls and concerned with sound doctrine, has never, since the beginning of his pontificate, ceased to proscribe and condemn the chief errors and false doctrines of our most unhappy age, by his published Encyclicals, by his Consistorial Allocutions and other Apostolic Letters. But, as it may happen that all the pontifical acts do not reach each one of the ordinaries, the same Sovereign Pontiff has willed that a Syllabus of the same errors be compiled, to be sent to all the Bishops of the Catholic world, in order that these same Bishops may have before their eyes all the errors and pernicious doctrines which he has reprobated and condemned.

He has consequently charged me with the duty of seeing to it that this Syllabus, having been printed, should be sent to your most reverend excellencies on this occasion and at this time, in which the Sovereign Pontiff, because of his great concern for the welfare and the good of the Christian Church and of the whole flock which has been divinely committed to him by the Lord, has thought it expedient to write another encyclical letter to all the Catholic Bishops. Thus fulfilling, as is my duty, with all the zeal and respect that is their due, the orders of this same Sovereign Pontiff, I hasten to send to your excellencies this syllabus with these letters.

The Syllabus of Errors

Syllabus of the principal errors of our time, which are censured in the consistorial Allocutions, Encyclical and other Apostolic Letters of our Most Holy Lord, Pope Pius IX.

I. PANTHEISM, NATURALISM AND ABSOLUTE RATIONALISM

1. There exists no Supreme, all-wise, all-provident Divine Being, distinct from the universe, and God is identical with the nature of things, and is, therefore, subject to changes. In effect, God is produced in man and in the world, and all things are God and have the very substance of God, and God is one and the same thing with the world, and, therefore, spirit with matter, necessity with liberty, good with evil, justice with injustice.—*Allocution "Maxima quidem," June 9, 1862.*

2. All action of God upon man and the world is to be denied.—*Ibid.*

3. Human reason, without any reference whatsoever to God, is the sole arbiter of truth and falsehood, and of good and evil; it is law to itself, and suffices, by its natural force, to secure the welfare of men and of nations.—*Ibid.*

4. All the truths of religion proceed from the innate strength of human reason; hence reason is the ultimate standard by which man can and ought to arrive at the knowledge of all truths of every kind.—*Ibid. and Encyclical "Qui pluribus," Nov. 9, 1846,* etc.

5. Divine revelation is imperfect, and therefore subject to a continual and indefinite progress, corresponding with the advancement of human reason.—*Ibid.*

6. The faith of Christ is in opposition to human reason, and divine revelation not only is not useful, but is even hurtful to the perfection of man.—*Ibid.*

7. The prophecies and miracles set forth and recorded in the Sacred Scriptures are the fiction of poets, and the mysteries of the Christian faith the result of philosophical investigations. In the books of the Old and the New Testament there are contained mythical inventions, and Jesus Christ is Himself a myth.—*Ibid.*

II. MODERATE RATIONALISM

8. As human reason is placed on a level with religion itself, so theological must be treated in the same manner as philosophical sciences.—*Allocution "Singulari quadam," Dec. 9, 1854.*

9. All the dogmas of the Christian religion are indiscriminately the object of natural science or philosophy; and human reason, enlightened solely in an historical way, is able, by its own natural strength and principles, to attain to the true science of even the most abstruse dogmas; provided only that such dogmas be proposed to reason itself as its object.—*Letters to the Archbishop of Munich, "Gravissimas inter," Dec. 11, 1862, and "Tuas libenter," Dec. 21, 1863.*

10. As the philosopher is one thing, and philosophy another, so it is the right and duty of the philosopher to subject himself to the authority which he shall have proved to be true; but philosophy neither can nor ought to submit to any such authority—*Ibid. Dec. 11, 1862.*

11. The Church not only ought never to pass judgment on philosophy, but ought to tolerate the errors of philosophy, leaving it to correct itself. —*Ibid., Dec. 21, 1863.*

12. The decrees of the Apostolic See and of the Roman congregations impede the true progress of science.—*Ibid.*

13. The method and principles by which the old scholastic doctors cultivated theology are no longer suitable to the demands of our times and to the progress of the sciences.—*Ibid.*

14. Philosophy is to be treated without taking any account of supernatural revelation.—*Ibid.*

N.B. To the rationalistic system belong in great part the errors of Anthony Günther, condemned in the letter to the Cardinal Archbishop of Cologne, "Eximiam tuam," June 15, 1857, and in that to the Bishop of Breslau, "Dolore haud mediocri," April 30, 1860.

III. INDIFFERENTISM. LATITUDINARIANISM

15. Every man is free to embrace and profess that religion which, guided by the light of reason, he shall consider true.— *Allocution "Maxima quidem," June 9, 1862; Damnatio "Multiplices inter," June 10, 1851.*

16. Man may, in the observance of any religion whatever, find the way of eternal salvation, and arrive at eternal salvation.—*Encyclical "Qui pluribus," Nov. 9, 1846.*

17. Good hope at least is to be entertained of the eternal salvation of all those who are not at all in the true Church of Christ.—*Encyclical "Quanto conficiamur," Aug. 10, 1863, etc.*

18. Protestantism is nothing more than another form of the same true

Christian religion, in which form it is given to please God equally as in the Catholic Church.—*Encyclical "Noscitis," Dec. 8, 1849.*

IV. SOCIALISM, COMMUNISM, SECRET SOCIETIES, BIBLICAL SOCIETIES, CLERICO-LIBERAL SOCIETIES

Pests of this kind are frequently reprobated in the severest terms in the Encyclical "Qui pluribus," Nov. 9, 1846, Allocution "Quibus quantisque," April 20, 1849, Encyclical "Noscitis et nobiscum," Dec. 8, 1849, Allocution "Singulari quadam," Dec. 9, 1854, Encyclical "Quanto conficiamur," Aug. 10, 1863.

V. ERRORS CONCERNING THE CHURCH AND HER RIGHTS

19. The Church is not a true and perfect society, entirely free; nor is she endowed with proper and perpetual rights of her own, conferred upon her by her Divine Founder; but it appertains to the civil power to define what are the rights of the Church, and the limits within which she may exercise those rights.—*Allocution "Singulari quadam," Dec. 9, 1854,* etc.

20. The ecclesiastical power ought not to exercise its authority without the permission and assent of the civil government.—*Allocution "Meminit unusquisque," Sept 30, 1861.*

21. The Church has not the power of defining dogmatically that the religion of the Catholic Church is the only true religion.—*Damnatio "Multiplices inter," June 10, 1851.*

22. The obligation by which Catholic teachers and authors are strictly bound is confined to those things only which are proposed to universal belief as dogmas of faith by the infallible judgment of the Church.—*Letter to the Archbishop of Munich, "Tuas libenter," Dec. 21, 1863.*

23. Roman pontiffs and ecumenical councils have wandered outside the limits of their powers, have usurped the rights of princes, and have even erred in defining matters of faith and morals.—*Damnatio "Multiplices inter," June 10, 1851.*

24. The Church has not the power of using force, nor has she any temporal power, direct or indirect.—*Apostolic Letter "Ad Apostolicae," Aug. 22, 1851.*

25. Besides the power inherent in the episcopate, other temporal power has been attributed to it by the civil authority, granted either explicitly or tacitly, which on that account is revocable by the civil authority whenever it thinks fit.—*Ibid.*

26. The Church has no innate and legitimate right of acquiring and possessing property.—*Allocution "Nunquam fore," Dec. 15, 1856; Encyclical "Incredibili," Sept. 7, 1863.*

27. The sacred ministers of the Church and the Roman pontiff are to

be absolutely excluded from every charge and dominion over temporal affairs.— *Allocution "Maxima quidem," June 9, 1862.*

28. It is not lawful for bishops to publish even letters Apostolic without the permission of Government.— *Allocution "Nunquam fore," Dec. 15, 1856.*

29. Favours granted by the Roman pontiff ought to be considered null, unless they have been sought for through the civil government.—*Ibid.*

30. The immunity of the Church and of ecclesiastical persons derived its origin from civil law.— *Damnatio "Multiplices inter," June 10, 1851.*

31. The ecclesiastical forum or tribunal for the temporal causes, whether civil or criminal, of clerics, ought by all means to be abolished, even without consulting and against the protest of the Holy See.—*Allocution "Nunquam fore," Dec. 15, 1856; Allocution "Acerbissimum," Sept. 27, 1852.*

32. The personal immunity by which clerics are exonerated from military conscription and service in the army may be abolished without violation either of natural right or equity. Its abolition is called for by civil progress, especially in a society framed on the model of a liberal government.— *Letter to the Bishop of Monreale "Singularis nobisque," Sept. 29, 1864.*

33. It does not appertain exclusively to the power of ecclesiastical jurisdiction by right, proper and innate, to direct the teaching of theological questions.—*Letter to the Archbishop of Munich, "Tuas libenter," Dec. 21, 1863.*

34. The teaching of those who compare the Sovereign Pontiff to a prince, free and acting in the universal Church, is a doctrine which prevailed in the Middle Ages.—*Apostolic Letter "Ad Apostolicae," Aug. 22, 1851.*

35. There is nothing to prevent the decree of a general council, or the act of all peoples, from transferring the supreme pontificate from the bishop and city of Rome to another bishop and another city.—*Ibid.*

36. The definition of a national council does not admit of any subsequent discussion, and the civil authority can assume this principle as the basis of its acts.—*Ibid.*

37. National churches, withdrawn from the authority of the Roman pontiff and altogether separated, can be established.—*Allocution "Multis gravibusque," Dec. 17, 1860.*

38. The Roman pontiffs have, by their too arbitrary conduct, contributed to the division of the Church into Eastern and Western.—*Apostolic Letter "Ad Apostolicae," Aug. 22, 1851.*

VI. ERRORS ABOUT CIVIL SOCIETY, CONSIDERED BOTH IN ITSELF AND IN ITS RELATION TO THE CHURCH

39. The State, as being the origin and source of all rights, is endowed with a certain right not circumscribed by any limits.—*Allocution "Maxima quidem," June 9, 1862.*

40. The teaching of the Catholic Church is hostile to the well-being and interests of society.—*Encyclical "Qui pluribus," Nov. 9, 1846; Allocution "Quibus quantisque," April 20, 1849.*

41. The civil government, even when in the hands of an infidel sovereign, has a right to an indirect negative power over religious affairs. It therefore possesses not only the right called that of *exsequatur*, but also that of appeal, called *appellatio ab abusu.—Apostolic Letter "Ad Apostolicae," Aug. 22, 1851.*

42. In the case of conflicting laws enacted by the two powers, the civil law prevails.—*Ibid.*

43. The secular power has authority to rescind, declare and render null, solemn conventions, commonly called concordats, entered into with the Apostolic See, regarding the use of rights appertaining to ecclesiastical immunity, without the consent of the Apostolic See, and even in spite of its protest.—*Allocution "Multis gravibusque," Dec. 17, 1860; Allocution "In consistoriali," Nov. 1, 1850.*

44. The civil authority may interfere in matters relating to religion, morality and spiritual government: hence, it can pass judgment on the instructions issued for the guidance of consciences, conformably with their mission, by the pastors of the Church. Further, it has the right to make enactments regarding the administration of the divine sacraments, and the dispositions necessary for receiving them.—*Allocutions "In consistoriali," Nov. 1, 1850, and "Maxima quidem," June 9, 1862.*

45. The entire government of public schools in which the youth of a Christian state is educated, except (to a certain extent) in the case of episcopal seminaries, may and ought to appertain to the civil power, and belong to it so far that no other authority whatsoever shall be recognized as having any right to interfere in the discipline of the schools, the arrangement of the studies, the conferring of degrees, in the choice or approval of the teachers. —*Allocutions "Quibus luctuosissimis," Sept. 5, 1851, and "In consistoriali," Nov. 1, 1850.*

46. Moreover, even in ecclesiastical seminaries, the method of studies to be adopted is subject to the civil authority.—*Allocution "Nunquam fore," Dec. 15, 1856.*

47. The best theory of civil society requires that popular schools open to children of every class of the people, and, generally, all public institutes intended for instruction in letters and philosophical sciences and for carrying on the education of youth, should be freed from all ecclesiastical authority, control and interference, and should be fully subjected to the civil and political power at the pleasure of the rulers, and according to the standard of the prevalent opinions of the age.—*Epistle to the Archbishop of Freiburg, "Cum non sine," July 14, 1864.*

48. Catholics may approve of the system of educating youth unconnected

with Catholic faith and the power of the Church, and which regards the knowledge of merely natural things, and only, or at least primarily, the ends of earthly social life.—*Ibid.*

49. The civil power may prevent the prelates of the Church and the faithful from communicating freely and mutually with the Roman pontiff.— *Allocution "Maxima quidem," June 9, 1862.*

50. Lay authority possesses of itself the right of presenting bishops, and may require of them to undertake the administration of the diocese before they receive canonical institution, and the Letters Apostolic from the Holy See.—*Allocution "Numquam fore," Dec. 15, 1856.*

51. And, further, the lay government has the right of deposing bishops from their pastoral functions, and is not bound to obey the Roman pontiff in those things which relate to the institution of bishoprics and the appointment of bishops.—*Allocution "Acerbissimum," Sept. 27, 1852; Damnatio "Multiplices inter," June 10, 1851.*

52. Government can, by its own right, alter the age prescribed by the Church for the religious profession of women and men; and may require of all religious orders to admit no person to take solemn vows without its permission.—*Allocution "Nunquam fore," Dec. 15, 1856.*

53. The laws enacted for the protection of religious orders and regarding their rights and duties ought to be abolished; nay, more, civil Government may lend its assistance to all who desire to renounce the obligation which they have undertaken of a religious life, and to break their vows. Government may also suppress the said religious orders, as likewise collegiate churches and simple benefices, even those of advowson, and subject their property and revenues to the administration and pleasure of the civil power. —*Allocutions "Acerbissimum," Sept. 27, 1852; "Probe memineritis," Jan. 22, 1855; "Cum saepe," July 26, 1855.*

54. Kings and princes are not only exempt from the jurisdiction of the Church, but are superior to the Church in deciding questions of jurisdiction. —*Damnatio "Multiplices inter," June 10, 1851.*

55. The Church ought to be separated from the State, and the State from the Church.—*Allocution "Acerbissimum," Sept. 27, 1852.*

VII. ERRORS CONCERNING NATURAL AND CHRISTIAN ETHICS

56. Moral laws do not stand in need of the divine sanction, and it is not at all necessary that human laws should be made conformable to the laws of nature, and receive their power of binding from God.—*Allocution "Maxima quidem," June 9, 1862.*

57. The science of philosophical things and morals and also civil laws may and ought to keep aloof from divine and ecclesiastical authority.—*Ibid.*

58. No other forces are to be recognized except those which reside in matter, and all the rectitude and excellence of morality ought to be placed in the accumulation and increase of riches by every possible means, and the gratification of pleasure.—*Ibid.; Encyclical "Quanto conficiamur," Aug. 10, 1863.*

59. Right consists in the material fact. All human duties are an empty word, and all human facts have the force of right.—*Allocution "Maxima quidem," June 9, 1862.*

60. Authority is nothing else but numbers and the sum total of material forces.—*Ibid.*

61. The injustice of an act when successful inflicts no injury on the sanctity of right.—*Allocution "Jamdudum cernimus," March 18, 1861.*

62. The principle of non-intervention, as it is called, ought to be proclaimed and observed.—*Allocution "Novos et ante," Sept. 28, 1860.*

63. It is lawful to refuse obedience to legitimate princes, and even to rebel against them.—*Encyclical "Qui pluribus," Nov. 9, 1864; Allocution "Quibusque vestrum," Oct. 4, 1847; "Noscitis et Nobiscum," Dec. 8, 1849; Letter Apostolic "Cum Catholica."*

64. The violation of any solemn oath, as well as any wicked and flagitious action repugnant to the eternal law, is not blamable but is altogether lawful and worthy of the highest praise when done through love of country. —*Allocution "Quibus quantisque," April 20, 1849.*

VIII. ERRORS CONCERNING CHRISTIAN MARRIAGE

65. The doctrine that Christ has raised marriage to the dignity of a sacrament cannot be at all tolerated.—*Apostolic Letter "Ad Apostolicae," Aug. 22, 1851.*

66. The Sacrament of Marriage is only a something accessory to the contract and separate from it, and the sacrament itself consists in the nuptial benediction alone.—*Ibid.*

67. By the law of nature, the marriage tie is not indissoluble, and in many cases divorce properly so called may be decreed by the civil authority.— *Ibid.; Allocution "Acerbissimum," Sept. 27, 1852.*

68. The Church has not the power of establishing diriment impediments of marriage, but such a power belongs to the civil authority by which existing impediments are to be removed.—*Damnatio "Multiplices inter," June 10, 1851.*

69. In the dark ages the Church began to establish diriment impediments, not by her own right, but by using a power borrowed from the State.— *Apostolic Letter "Ad Apostolicae," Aug. 22, 1851.*

70. The canons of the Council of Trent, which anathematize those who

dare to deny to the Church the right of establishing diriment impediments, either are not dogmatic, or must be understood as referring to such borrowed power.—*Ibid.*

71. The form of solemnizing marriage prescribed by the Council of Trent, under pain of nullity, does not bind in cases where the civil law lays down another form, and declares that when this new form is used the marriage shall be valid.—*Ibid.*

72. Boniface VIII was the first who declared that the vow of chastity taken at ordination renders marriage void.—*Ibid.*

73. In force of a merely civil contract there may exist between Christians a real marriage, and it is false to say either that the marriage contract between Christians is always a sacrament, or that there is no contract if the sacrament be excluded.—*Ibid.; Letter to the King of Sardinia, Sept. 9, 1852; Allocutions "Acerbissimum," Sept. 27, 1852; "Multis gravibusque," Dec. 17, 1860.*

74. Matrimonial causes and espousals belong by their nature to civil tribunals.—*Encyclical "Qui pluribus," Nov. 9, 1846; Damnatio "Multiplices inter," June 10, 1851; "Ad Apostolicae," Aug. 22, 1851; Allocution "Acerbissimum," Sept. 27, 1852.*

N.B.—To the preceding questions may be referred two other errors regarding the celibacy of priests and the preference due to the state of marriage over that of virginity. These have been stigmatized: the first in the Encyclical "Qui pluribus," Nov. 9, 1846; the second, in the Letter Apostolic "Multiplices inter," June 10, 1851.

IX. ERRORS REGARDING THE CIVIL POWER OF THE SOVEREIGN PONTIFF

75. The children of the Christian and Catholic Church are divided amongst themselves about the compatibility of the temporal with the spiritual power.—*"Ad Apostolicae," Aug. 22, 1851.*

76. The abolition of the temporal power of which the Apostolic See is possessed would contribute in the greatest degree to the liberty and prosperity of the Church.—*Allocutions "Quibus quantisque," April 20, 1849; "Si semper antea," May 20, 1850.*

N.B.—Besides these errors, explicitly censured, very many others are implicitly condemned by the doctrine propounded and established, which all Catholics are bound most firmly to hold touching the temporal sovereignty of the Roman pontiff. This doctrine is clearly stated in the Allocutions "Quibus quantisque," April 20, 1849, and "Si semper antea," May 20, 1850; Letter Apostolic, "Cum Catholica ecclesia," March 26, 1860; Allocutions, "Noves et antea," Sept. 28, 1860; "Jamdudum cernimus," March 18, 1861; "Maxima quidem," June 9, 1862.

X. ERRORS HAVING REFERENCE TO MODERN LIBERALISM

77. In the present day it is no longer expedient that the Catholic religion should be held as the only religion of the State, to the exclusion of all other forms of worship.—*Allocution "Nemo vestrum," July 26, 1855.*

78. Hence it has been wisely decided by law, in some Catholic countries, that persons coming to reside therein shall enjoy the public exercise of their own peculiar worship.—*Allocution "Acerbissimum," Sept. 27, 1852.*

79. Moreover, it is false that the civil liberty of every form of worship, and the full power, given to all, of overtly and publicly manifesting any opinions whatsoever and thoughts, conduce more easily to corrupt the morals and minds of the people, and to propagate the pest of indifferentism.—*Allocution "Nunquam fore," Dec. 15, 1856.*

80. The Roman Pontiff can, and ought to, reconcile himself, and come to terms with progress, liberalism and modern civilization.—*Allocution "Jamdudum cernimus," March 18, 1861.*

The Dogma of Papal Infallibility

CONCERNING THE INFALLIBLE TEACHING OF THE ROMAN PONTIFF

*M*oreover, that the supreme power of teaching is also included in the Apostolic primacy, which the Roman Pontiff, as the successor of Peter, Prince of the Apostles, possesses over the whole Church, this Holy See has always held, the perpetual practice of the Church confirms, and oecumenical Councils also have declared, especially those in which the East with the West met in the union of faith and charity. For the Fathers of the Fourth Council of Constantinople, following in the footsteps of their predecessors, gave forth this solemn profession: The first condition of salvation is to keep the rule of the true faith. And because the sentence of our Lord Jesus Christ can not be passed by, who said: "Thou art Peter, and upon this rock I will build my Church,"[1] these things which have been said are approved by events, because in the Apostolic See the Catholic religion and her holy and well-known doctrine has always been kept undefiled. Desiring, therefore, not to be in the least degree separated from the faith and doctrine of that See, we hope that we may deserve to be in the one communion, which the Apostolic See preaches, in which is the entire and true solidity of the Chris-

[1] Matt. 16:18.

tian religion.[1] And, with the approval of the Second Council of Lyons, the Greeks professed that the holy Roman Church enjoys supreme and full primacy and pre-eminence over the whole Catholic Church, which it truly and humbly acknowledges that it has received with the plentitude of power from our Lord himself in the person of blessed Peter, Prince or Head of the Apostles, whose successor the Roman Pontiff is; and as the Apostolic See is bound before all others to defend the truth of faith, so also, if any questions regarding faith shall arise, they must be defined by its judgment.[2] Finally, the Council of Florence defined:[3] That the Roman Pontiff is the true vicar of Christ, and the head of the whole Church, and the father and teacher of all Christians; and that to him in blessed Peter was delivered by our Lord Jesus Christ the full power of feeding, ruling, and governing the whole church.[4]

To satisfy this pastoral duty, our predecessors ever made unwearied efforts that the salutary doctrine of Christ might be propagated among all the nations of the earth, and with equal care watched that it might be preserved genuine and pure where it had been received. Therefore the Bishops of the whole world, now singly, now assembled in Synod, following the long-established custom of churches,[5] and the form of the ancient rule,[6] sent word to this Apostolic See of those dangers especially which sprang up in matters of faith, that there the losses of faith might be most effectually repaired where the faith can not fail.[7] And the Roman Pontiffs, according to the exigencies of times and circumstances, sometimes assembling oecumenical Councils, or asking for the mind of the Church scattered throughout the world, sometimes by particular Synods, sometimes using other helps which Divine Providence supplied, defined as to be held those things which with the help of God they had recognized as conformable with the sacred Scriptures and Apostolic tradition. For the Holy Spirit was not promised to the successors of Peter, that by his revelation they might make known new doctrine; but that by his assistance they might inviolably keep and faithfully expound the revelation or deposit of faith delivered through the Apostles. And, indeed, all the venerable Fathers have embraced, and the holy orthodox doctors have venerated and followed, their Apostolic doc-

---

[1] From the Formula of St. Hormisdas, subscribed by the Fathers of the Eighth General Council (Fourth of Constantinople), A.D. 869 (Labbe's Councils, Vol. V, pp. 583, 622).

[2] From the Acts of the Fourteenth General Council (Second of Lyons), A.D. 1274 (Labbe, Vol. XIV, p. 512).

[3] From the Acts of the Seventeenth General Council of Florence, A.D. 1438 (Labbe, Vol. XVIII, p. 526).

[4] John 21:15-17.

[5] From a letter of St. Cyril of Alexandria to Pope St. Celestine I, A.D. 422 (Vol. VI, Pt. II, p. 36, Paris ed. of 1638).

[6] From a Rescript of St. Innocent I to the Council of Milevis, A.D. 402 (Labbe, Vol. III, p. 47).

[7] From a letter of St. Bernard to Pope Innocent II, A.D. 1130 (Epist. 191, Vol. IV, p. 433, Paris ed. of 1742).

trine; knowing most fully that this See of holy Peter remains ever free from all blemish of error according to the divine promise of the Lord our Saviour made to the Prince of his disciples: "I have prayed for thee that thy faith fail not, and, when thou art converted, confirm thy brethren."[1]

This gift, then, of truth and never-failing faith was conferred by heaven upon Peter and his successors in this chair, that they might perform their high office for the salvation of all; that the whole flock of Christ, kept away by them from the poisonous food of error, might be nourished with the pasture of heavenly doctrine; that the occasion of schism being removed, the whole Church might be kept one, and, resting on its foundation, might stand firm against the gates of hell.

But since in this very age, in which the salutary efficacy of the Apostolic office is most of all required, not a few are found who take away from its authority, we judge it altogether necessary solemnly to assert the prerogative which the only-begotten Son of God vouchsafed to join with the supreme pastoral office.

Therefore faithfully adhering to the tradition received from the beginning of the Christian faith, for the glory of God our Saviour, the exaltation of the Catholic religion, and the salvation of Christian people, the sacred Council approving, we teach and define that it is a dogma divinely revealed: that the Roman Pontiff, when he speaks *ex cathedra*, that is, when in discharge of the office of pastor and doctor of all Christians, by virtue of his supreme Apostolic authority, he defines a doctrine regarding faith or morals to be held by the universal Church, by the divine assistance promised to him in blessed Peter, is possessed of that infallibility with which the divine Redeemer willed that his Church should be endowed for defining doctrine regarding faith or morals; and that therefore such definitions of the Roman Pontiff are irreformable[2] of themselves, and not from the consent of the Church.

But if any one—which may God avert—presume to contradict this our definition: let him be anathema.

Given at Rome in public Session solemnly held in the Vatican Basilica in the year of our Lord one thousand eight hundred and seventy, on the eighteenth day of July, in the twenty-fifth year of our Pontificate.

[1] Luke 22:32. See also the Acts of the Sixth General Council, A.D. 680 (Labbe, Vol. VII, p. 659).

[2] That is, in the words used by Pope Nicholas I, note 13, and in the Synod of Quedlinburg, A.D. 1085, "It is allowed to none to revise its judgment, and to sit in judgment upon what it has judged" (Labbe, Vol. XII, p. 679).

Gioacchino Vincenzo Raffaele Luigi Pecci was born at Carpineto in 1810. He received a doctorate of theology in 1832, and was ordained priest, December 31, 1837. He became bishop of Perugia and, in 1853, was created a cardinal. In 1860 he issued a pastoral letter on the necessity of the temporal power of the pope; but in September of that year, the pope lost Perugia and the whole of Umbria. In 1872, Cardinal Pecci established an *Accademia di S. Tommaso*. In 1877, Pope Pius IX appointed him *camerlengo*, and the cardinal moved to Rome. A year later, Pius IX died, and Cardinal Pecci succeeded to the papacy, assuming the name of Leo XIII. He was pope for a quarter of a century, and died in 1903.

His encyclical *Aeterni Patris* (1879), reprinted here, has profoundly influenced Catholic philosophy. Several of his other encyclicals dealt with social problems and are readily accessible in a paperback volume: *The Church Speaks to the Modern World: The Social Teachings of Leo XIII*, edited, annotated and with an introduction by Etienne Gilson (Doubleday Image Books, 1954).

The Encyclical Aeterni Patris

TO HIS VENERABLE BRETHREN, ALL THE PATRIARCHS, PRIMATES, ARCHBISHOPS, AND BISHOPS OF THE CATHOLIC WORLD, IN FAVOUR AND COMMUNION WITH THE APOSTOLIC SEE,

POPE LEO XIII.

VENERABLE BRETHREN,
Health and Apostolic Benediction.

The Only-begotten Son of the Eternal Father appeared on earth to bring salvation and the light of the wisdom of God to the human race. As He was ascending to Heaven He bestowed on the world a blessing, truly great and wondrous, when, commanding His Apostles to "go and teach all nations,"[1] He left a Church, founded by Himself, as the universal and supreme mistress of all people. Man, whom the truth had set free, was to be kept safe by the truth. Indeed, the fruits of heavenly doctrine, by which salvation was gained for man, could not have endured for long unless Christ our Lord had set up a perpetual teaching authority (*magisterium*) for the

---

[1] Matt. 28:19.

instruction of souls in the faith. This Church, then, not only built on the promises of its Divine Author, but following in His love, has kept His commands. She has always looked to one end, and desired it with great desire; that is, to teach the true religion and wage ceaseless war with error. For this there have been the watchful labours of Bishops, each in his own place; and for this Councils have made laws and decrees. More than all, for this there has been the daily anxiety of the Roman Pontiffs. They are the successors of Blessed Peter, the Prince of the Apostles, in his Primacy, and therefore it is their right and their duty to teach the brethren, and confirm them in the faith.

Now, the Apostle warns us that the faithful of Christ are often deceived in mind "by philosophy and vain deceit,"[1] and that thus the sincerity of faith is corrupted in men. For this reason the Supreme Pastors of the Church have always held that it is part of their office to advance, with all their power, knowledge truly so called; but at the same time to watch with the greatest care that all human learning shall be imparted according to the rule of the Catholic faith. Especially is this true of "philosophy," on which the right treatment of other sciences depends in great measure. We Ourselves spoke to you shortly of this, among other things, Venerable Brothers, when first We addressed you all by an Encyclical Letter. Now, by the importance of this matter, and by the state of the times, We are forced again to write to you, that you may so organize the course of philosophical studies as to insure their perfect correspondence with the gift of Faith, and also their agreement with the dignity of human knowledge.

If anyone look carefully at the bitterness of our times, and if, further, he consider earnestly the cause of those things that are done in public and in private, he will discover with certainty the fruitful root of the evils which are now overwhelming us, and of the evils which we greatly fear. The cause he will find to consist in this—evil teaching about things, human and divine, has come forth from the schools of philosophers; it has crept into all the orders of the State; and it has been received with the common applause of very many. Now, it has been implanted in man by Nature to follow reason as the guide of his actions, and therefore, if the understanding go wrong in anything, the will easily follows. Hence it comes about that wicked opinions in the understanding, flow into human actions and make them bad. On the other hand, if the mind of man be healthy, and strongly grounded in solid and true principles, it will assuredly be the source of great blessings, both as regards the good of individuals and as regards the common weal.

We do not, indeed, attribute to human philosophy such force and authority as to judge it sufficient for the utter shutting out and uprooting of all errors. When the Christian religion was first established by the wondrous

[1] Col. 2:8.

light of Faith shed abroad, "not in the persuasive words of human wisdom,[1] but in showing of the Spirit and power," the whole world was restored to its primeval dignity. So also now, chiefly from the almighty power and help of God, we may hope that the darkness of error will be taken away from the minds of men, and that they will repent. But we must not despise or undervalue those natural helps which are given to man by the kindness and wisdom of God, Who strongly and sweetly orders all things; and it stands to reason that a right use of philosophy is the greatest of these helps. For God did not give the light of reason in vain to the soul of man, nor does the superadded light of Faith quench, or even lessen, the strength of the understanding. Its effect is far from this. It perfects the understanding, gives it new strength, and makes it fit for greater works. The very nature of the providence of God Himself, therefore, makes it needful for us to seek a safeguard in human knowledge when we strive to bring back the people to Faith and salvation. The records of antiquity bear witness that this method, both probable and wise, was used habitually by the most illustrious Fathers of the Church. They, in truth, were wont to give to reason offices neither few nor small; and these the great Augustine has summed up very shortly: "Attributing to this science . . . that by which the life-giving Faith . . . is begotten, nourished, guarded, and strengthened."

In the first place, then, if philosophy be rightly and wisely used, it is able in a certain measure to pave and to guard the road to the true Faith; and is able, also, to prepare the minds of its followers in a fitting way for the receiving of revelation. Hence it has not untruly been called by the ancients "an education leading to the Christian Faith," "a prelude and help of Christianity," "a schoolmaster for the Gospel."

In truth, the loving-kindness of God, with regard to the things concerning Himself, has not only made known by the light of Faith many truths beyond the reach of the human understanding, but has also revealed some which are not altogether beyond the power of reason to find out. Such truths, when the authority of God is thus added, become known to all both at once and without any mixture of error. This being so, certain truths, either divinely revealed to us for our belief, or bound up closely with the doctrine of the Faith, were known to wise men among the Gentiles, who were guided only by the light of natural reason. By fitting arguments they vindicated and demonstrated these truths. St. Paul says: "The invisible things of Him, from the creation of the world, are clearly seen, being understood by the things that are made; His eternal power also and divinity." Again: "The Gentiles, who have not the law," nevertheless "show the work of the law written in their hearts."

It is opportune, therefore, in a high degree to use, for the good and the advantage of revealed truth, these other truths that were known even to

[1] I Cor. 2:4.

wise heathens; for thus human wisdom, and the very testimony of the adversaries, give their witness to the Catholic Faith. Further, it is plain that this way of treating the question is not a thing newly devised, but an ancient way very much used by the holy Fathers of the Church. Moreover, these venerable witnesses and guardians of holy traditions see a kind of form of this, and almost a type of it, in one action of the Hebrews; who, as they were going out of Egypt, were commanded to take with them vessels of silver and of gold, with precious garments of the Egyptians. This was done that, by a use suddenly changed, the riches which had ministered to superstition and to rites of ignominy might be dedicated to the service of the true God. Gregory of Neocaesaraea praises Origen for this very reason, that, skilfully gathering together much of the teaching of the Gentiles for the defence of Christian wisdom, and for the destruction of superstition, he used these things as weapons taken from the enemy, and with wondrous power hurled them back. Both Gregory Nazianzen and Gregory of Nyssa approve and praise this manner of teaching in Basil the Great. So also Jerome greatly commends the same thing in Quadratus, a disciple of the Apostles; in Aristides, in Justin, in Irenaeus, and in very many others. Augustine also says: "Do we not see how Cyprian, that doctor of great sweetness and that martyr of great blessedness, was laden with gold and silver and raiment when he went forth from Egypt? Was it not so with Lactantius, with Victorinus, Optatus, and Hilary? Not to speak of the living, was it not so with countless Greeks?" If, then, natural reason produced so rich a crop of learning as this before it was fertilized by the power and working of Christ, much more abundant will be its harvests now, when the grace of the Saviour renews and increases the inborn powers of the mind of man. Is there, indeed, anyone who does not see that a plain and easy road is opened to the Faith by philosophy such as this?

The usefulness, however, which springs from such a way of studying philosophy is not confined within these limits; for in truth severe reproof is given, in the words of the wisdom of God, to the foolishness of those men who, "by these good things that are seen, could not understand Him that is; neither, by attending to the works, have acknowledged (Him) who was the workman."

In the first place, then, this great and glorious fruit is gathered from human reason—namely, that it demonstrates the existence of God: "By the greatness of the beauty and of the creature the Creator of them may be seen, so as to be known thereby."

In the next place, reason shows that God, in a way belonging only to Himself, excels by the sum of all perfections—that is, by an infinite wisdom, from which nothing can be hidden; and also by a supreme justice which no affection of evil can touch. Hence reason proves that God is not only true, but the very Truth itself, which cannot deceive or be deceived. Further, it is a clear consequence from this that the human reason obtains for the word of God full belief and authority.

In like manner reason declares that the evangelical doctrine has shone as the light from its very beginning, by signs and miracles which are infallible proofs of infallible truth; and that therefore they who receive the Faith by the Gospel do not act rashly, as if they had "followed cunningly devised fables," but, by an obedience that is altogether reasonable, submit their understanding and their judgment to the authority of God.

Further, not less than these things in value is it that reason clearly shows us the truth about the Church instituted by Christ. That Church, as the Vatican Synod decreed—"because of the wonderful way in which it spreads; because of its great holiness and inexhaustible fruitfulness in all places; because of its Catholic unity and invincible stability—is in itself a great and perpetual motive of credibility, and an unanswerable argument for its own Divine legation."

The foundations, then, having been laid in the most solid way, there is needed, further, a use of philosophy, both perpetual and manifold, in order that Sacred Theology may assume and put on the nature, habit, and character of true science. For in this noblest kind of learning it is above everything necessary that the parts of heavenly doctrine, being many and different, should be gathered together, as it were, into one body. Thus they are united by a union of harmony among themselves, all the parts being fittingly arranged, and derived from their own proper principles. Lastly, all of these parts, and each of them, must be strengthened by unanswerable arguments suited to each case.

Nor must we pass by in silence, or reckon of little account, that fuller knowledge of our brief, and, as far as may be, that clearer understanding of the mysteries of the faith which Augustine and other Fathers praised, and laboured to attain, and which the Vatican Synod itself decreed to be very fruitful. Such knowledge and understanding are certainly acquired more fully and more easily by those who, to integrity of life and study of the faith, join a mind that has been disciplined by philosophical culture. Specially is this so since the same Vatican Synod teaches that we ought to seek for understanding of holy dogmas of that kind "both from the analogy of the things which naturally are known, and also from the way in which the mysteries themselves are related to one another, and also to the last end of man."

Lastly, it pertains to philosophical discipline to guard with religious care all truths that come to us by Divine tradition, and to resist those who dare to attack them. Now, as regards this point, the praise of philosophy is great, in that it is reckoned a bulwark of the faith, and as a strong defence of religion. "The doctrine of our Saviour," as Clement of Alexandria bears witness, "is indeed perfect in itself, and has need of nothing, forasmuch as it is the power and the wisdom of God. But Greek philosophy, though it does not by its approach make the truth more powerful, has yet been called a fit hedge and ditch for the vineyard, because it weakens the arguments of sophists against the truth, and wards off the crafty tricks of those by whom the truth is attacked."

In fact, as the enemies of the Catholic name borrow their warlike preparations from philosophic method, when they begin their attacks on religion, so the defenders of the science of God borrow many weapons from the stores of philosophy, by which to defend the dogmas of revelation. Again, we must count it no small victory for the Christian Faith, that human reason powerfully and promptly wards off those very weapons of the enemy which have been got together by the skill of the same human reason for purposes of harm. St. Jerome, writing to Magnus, shows how the Apostle of the Gentiles himself adopted this kind of argument. "Paul, the leader of the Christian army and the unanswered speaker, pleading a cause for Christ, turns skilfully even a chance inscription into an argument for the faith. From the true David he had learnt indeed how to pluck the weapon from the hands of his enemies, and how to cut off the head of Goliath in his greatest pride with his own sword."

Nay, more; the Church herself not only advises Christian teachers, but commands them to draw this safeguard from philosophy. For the fifth Lateran Council decreed that "every assertion contrary to the truth of enlightened faith is altogether false, because the truth cannot possibly contradict the truth": and then it commands doctors of philosophy to apply themselves studiously to the refutation of fallacious arguments; for St. Augustine says: "If any reason be given against the authority of the Holy Scriptures, then, however subtle it may be, it deceives by its likeness to the truth; for true it cannot possibly be."

But if philosophy has to be found equal to the work of bringing forth such precious fruits as We have mentioned, it must, above everything, take care never to wander from the path trodden by the venerable antiquity of the Fathers, and approved in the Vatican Synod by the solemn suffrage of authority. It is plainly seen that we must accept many truths in the supernatural order which far surpass the power of any intellect. The human reason, therefore, conscious of its own weakness, must not dare to handle things greater than itself; nor to deny these truths. Again, it must not measure them by its own strength, or interpret them at its own will. Rather let it receive them in the fulness and humility of Faith; reckoning this its greatest honour, that by the goodness of God it is allowed as a handmaid and servant to be busied about heavenly doctrines, and in a certain measure to reach them.

In those heads of doctrine, however, which the human understanding naturally can take in, it is clearly just that philosophy should use its own method, its own principles, and its own arguments: yet not so as to seem to draw itself away with audacity from the authority of God. So, also, when it is plain that things known to us by revelation are most certainly true, and that the arguments brought against the Faith are not in accord with right reason, the Catholic philosopher should bear in mind that he will violate the rights both of Faith and reason, if he embrace any conclusion which he understands to be contrary to revealed doctrine.

We know indeed that there are to be found men who, exalting too highly the powers of human nature, contend that the understanding of man falls from its native dignity when it becomes subject to Divine authority, and that being thus bound, as it were, in a yoke of slavery, it is greatly retarded and hindered from reaching the heights of truth and excellence. Such teaching as that is full of error and falsehood. The end of it is that men, in the height of folly and sinful thanklessness, reject all higher truths. They deliberately cast away the Divine blessings of faith, from which the streams of all good flow, even to civil society. Now, the mind of man is shut up and held in certain bounds, and narrow enough those boundaries are. The consequence is that it falls into many mistakes and is ignorant of many things. On the other hand, the Christian Faith, resting as it does on the authority of God, is the certain teacher of truth. He who follows this guidance is neither entangled in the nets of error nor tossed about on the waves of doubt. Hence the best philosophers are they who join philosophical study with the obedience of the Christian Faith. Then the brightness of Christian truths falls on the mind, and by that brightness the understanding itself is helped. This takes nothing from the dignity of the reason; nay, rather, it adds to the reason a great deal of grandeur and subtlety and strength.

Worthily and most fruitfully do we use the keenness of the understanding when we set ourselves to refute opinions against the Faith, and to prove those things which agree with it. For in disproving errors we ascertain their causes, and then show the falsity of the arguments by which they are bolstered up; while in proving truths we use the force of the reasons by which they are demonstrated with certainty, and by which all prudent men are persuaded. If, then, anyone deny that the riches of the mind are increased and its powers extended by studies and arguments such as these, he must of necessity contend absurdly that the discrimination of truth and falsehood does not in any way help towards intellectual advancement. Rightly, therefore, does the Vatican Synod mention in the following words the great benefits which are received by Faith from reason: "Faith frees the reason from error, and guards it, and instructs it with a manifold knowledge." If, then, man were wise, he would not blame Faith as being hostile to reason and natural truths. Rather he would give hearty thanks to God and rejoice greatly that, among so many causes of ignorance and in the midst of such floods of error, the most holy Faith shines brightly on him; for, like a friendly star, that Faith points out to him the harbour of truth, so that he can have no fear of going out of his course.

If, then, Venerable Brothers, you look back at the history of philosophy, you will see that all the words which We have spoken are approved by the facts. Certainly, among the ancient philosophers, living without the Faith, they who were reckoned the wisest erred most harmfully in many things. Though they taught the truth about some things, yet you know how often they taught that which was false and absurd. You know how many uncertain things and doubtful things they handed down about the true nature of the Godhead, the first beginning of creation, the government of the world, God's knowledge of the future, the cause and principle of evil, the last end of man, everlasting beatitude, virtues and vices, as also about other subjects, of which a true and certain knowledge is above everything necessary for man.

On the other hand, the first Fathers and Doctors of the Church understood clearly from the counsel of the will of God that the restorer of human knowledge is Christ, who is the "power of God and the wisdom of God," and "in whom are hidden all the treasures of wisdom and knowledge." They undertook to examine thoroughly the books of these wise men of old, and to compare their opinions with the teaching of Revelation. With prudent choice they accepted all the true words and wise thoughts with which they met; but the rest they either set right or cast utterly away. As God, in His careful foresight for the defence of His Church against the rage of tyrants, raised up the martyrs, very strong and lavish of their mighty souls; so against philosophers, falsely so called, and against heretics, He raised up men great in wisdom to defend even by the help of human reason the treasure of revealed truth. From the very beginning of the Church, indeed, Catholic doctrine has found enemies most hostile to it, who have derided the dogmas and teachings of Christians. They have laid down such doctrines as these: That there are many gods; that the matter of which the world is made has neither beginning nor cause; that the course of events is governed by a certain blind force and inevitable necessity; and that it is not ruled by the counsel of the providence of God. Wise men, whom we call Apologists, have in due course attacked these teachers of insane doctrine, and, with Faith for their guide, have drawn arguments from human wisdom itself. They have in this way proved that one God, highest in every kind of perfection, is to be worshipped; that all things have been made out of nothing by His almighty power; that they are all sustained by His wisdom; and that each one is directed and moved towards its own end.

Among these, St. Justin Martyr claims for himself the first place. Having frequented the most celebrated schools of learning among the Greeks that he might try what they were, he learned, as he himself acknowledges, that he could drink in the truth with full mouth only from revealed doctrines. These he embraced with all the eagerness of his soul; stripped off the calumnies that hung round them; defended them vigorously and fully before the Roman Emperors; and reconciled with them many sayings of the Greek philosophers. In that time the same work was also done exceedingly well by Quadratus, Aristides, Hermias, and Athenagoras. In the same cause glory not less than theirs was gained by the Bishop of Lyons, Irenaeus, the invincible martyr. He refuted with power the wicked teaching of the Easterns, scattered as it was by the help of the Gnostics throughout the bounds of the Roman Empire. St. Jerome says of him: "He explained . . . the beginnings of heresies one by one, and pointed out from what fountains of the philosophers they flowed."

Again, there is no one who does not know the disputations of Clement of Alexandria, which the same St. Jerome thus mentions with honour: "Is there anything that is not learned in them? Is there anything not drawn from the depth of philosophy?" He himself also wrote books of an incredible variety, which are of the greatest use in building up a history of philosophy, in rightly exercising the art of dialectics, and in establishing the harmony that exists between reason and faith. Origen followed him, renowned among the teachers of the Alexandrine school, and deeply learned in the doctrine of the Greeks and the Easterns. He wrote a very great number of books, and spent much labour upon them. Wondrously, just at the right time, they explained the Holy Scriptures, and threw light on our sacred dogmas. It is true that these books, at least in their present state, are not altogether free from errors; yet they embrace great force of teaching, by which natural truths are increased in number and in strength. Tertullian, too, fights against the heretics by the authority of Scripture. Then changing his weapons, he fights against the philosophers with arguments of philosophy. With so much acuteness and learning does he refute them, that he answers them openly and confidently: "Neither about science nor about learning are we, as you think, on an equal footing." Arnobius also in his books against the Gentiles, and Lactantius in his Institutions especially, strive earnestly with like eloquence and strength to persuade men to accept the dogmas and commands of Catholic wisdom. They do not overthrow philosophy, according to the way of the Academy; but partly by their own weapons, and partly by weapons taken from the agreement of philosophers among themselves, they convince them. The great Athanasius and Chrysostom, first of preachers, have left writings about the soul of man, about the Attributes of God, and other questions of the greatest moment. These in the judgment of all are so excellent that it seems as if scarcely anything could be added to their subtlety and exhaustiveness. Not to be too prolix in mentioning them one by one, we add to the number of these most illustrious men of whom we have spoken the great Basil and the two Gregories. From

Athens, then the home of the highest culture, they went forth equipped with the panoply of philosophy. Having acquired all their riches of learning by most ardent study, they used them to refute the heretic, and to build up the faithful.

But it is Augustine who seems to have borne away the palm from all. With a towering intellect, and a mind full to overflowing of sacred and profane learning, he fought resolutely against all the errors of his age, with the greatest faith and equal knowledge. What teaching of philosophy did he pass over? Nay, what was there into which he did not search thoroughly? Did he not do this when he was explaining to believers the deepest mysteries of the Faith, and defending them against the furious attacks of the adversaries? or when, after destroying the fictions of Academics and Manichaeans, he made safe the foundations of human knowledge and their certainty, searching out also to the furthest point the reason and origin and causes of those evils by which man is oppressed? With what copiousness and with what subtlety did he write about the angels, and the soul, and the human mind; about the will and free-will; about religion and the blessed life; about time and eternity; about the nature of all changeable bodies! Afterwards, among the Easterns, John of Damascus followed in the footsteps of Basil and Gregory Nazianzen; while in the West, Boethius and Anselm, setting forth the doctrines of Augustine, greatly enriched the domain of philosophy.

Then .the Doctors of the Middle Ages, whom we call Scholastics, set themselves to do a work of very great magnitude. There are rich and fruitful crops of doctrine scattered everywhere in the mighty volumes of the Holy Fathers. The aim of the Scholastics was to gather these together diligently, and to store them up, as it were, in one place, for the use and convenience of those that come after.

What the origin of the Scholastic discipline was, what were also its characteristics and its value, it will be well, Venerable Brothers, to set forth more fully here in the words of a man of the greatest wisdom—our predecessor Sixtus V: "By the Divine gift of Him, Who alone gives the spirit of knowledge and wisdom and understanding, and Who, through the ages, according to her needs, enriches His Church with new gifts, and surrounds her with new safeguards, our ancestors, being men exceedingly wise, developed the study of Scholastic Theology. There were especially two glorious Doctors, teachers of this famous science—that is, the angelic St. Thomas, and the seraphic St. Bonaventure. With surpassing abilities, with ceaseless study, with laborious toil and long watchings, they worked it out and adorned it. They arranged it in the very best way, unfolded it brilliantly in many methods, and then handed it on to their successors."

The knowledge and the exercise of this science of salvation have certainly always brought the very greatest help to the Church; whether it be for the right understanding and interpretation of Scripture, or for reading and expounding the Fathers with greater safety and profit, or for laying bare and answering different errors and heresies. This doctrine flows from the brimming fountain of the Sacred Scriptures, of the Supreme Pontiffs, and of Holy Fathers and Councils. Now, indeed, in these last days, it is in the highest degree necessary to refute heresies and confirm the dogmas of the Catholic faith. For now have come those dangerous times of which the Apostle speaks. Now men, blasphemous, proud, deceivers, go from bad to worse, wandering from the truth themselves and leading others into error. These words might seem to embrace only the Scholastic Theology; but it is plain that they are also to be taken in reference to philosophy and its praise.

Scholastic Theology has splendid gifts, which make it very formidable to enemies of the truth; as the same Pontiff tells us. "It has," he says, "an apt coherence of facts and causes, connected with one another; an order and arrangement, like soldiers drawn up in battle array; definitions and distinctions very lucid; unanswerableness of argument and acute disputations. By these the light is divided from the darkness, and truth from falsehood. The lies of heretics, wrapped up in many wiles and fallacies, being stripped of their coverings, are bared and laid open." But these great and wondrous gifts can only be found in a right use of that philosophy which the masters of Scholasticism, of set purpose and with wise counsel, were everywhere accustomed to use even in their theological disputations.

Moreover, it is the proper and singular gift of Scholastic theologians to bind together human knowledge and Divine knowledge in the very closest bonds. For this reason, truly the theology in which they excelled could never have gained so much honour and praise from the judgment of men as it did, if they had used a system of philosophy which was maimed, or imperfect, or shallow.

Now far above all other Scholastic Doctors towers Thomas Aquinas, their master and prince. Cajetan says truly of him: "So great was his veneration for the ancient and sacred Doctors that he may be said to have gained a perfect understanding of them all." Thomas gathered together their doctrines like the scattered limbs of a body, and moulded them into a whole. He arranged them in so wonderful an order, and increased them with such great additions, that rightly and deservedly he is reckoned a singular safeguard and glory of the Catholic Church. His intellect was docile and subtle; his memory was ready and tenacious; his life was most holy; and he loved the truth alone. Greatly enriched as he was with the science of God and the science of man, he is likened to the sun; for he warmed the whole earth with the fire of his holiness, and filled the whole earth with the splendour of his teaching. There is no part of philosophy which he did not handle with acuteness and solidity. He wrote about the laws of reasoning; about God and incorporeal substances; about man and other things of sense;

and about human acts and their principles. What is more, he wrote on these subjects in such a way that in him not one of the following perfections is wanting: a full selection of subjects; a beautiful arrangement of their divisions; the best method of treating them; certainty of principles; strength of argument; perspicuity and propriety in language; and the power of explaining deep mysteries.

Besides these questions and the like, the Angelic Doctor, in his speculations, drew certain philosophical conclusions as to the reasons and principles of created things. These conclusions have the very widest reach, and contain, as it were, in their bosom the seeds of truths wellnigh infinite in number. These have to be unfolded with most abundant fruits in their own time by the teachers who come after him. As he used his method of philosophizing, not only in teaching the truth, but also in refuting error, he has gained this prerogative for himself. With his own hand he vanquished all errors of ancient times; and still he supplies an armoury of weapons which brings us certain victory in the conflict with falsehoods ever springing up in the course of years.

Moreover, carefully distinguishing reason from Faith, as is right, and yet joining them together in a harmony of friendship, he so guarded the rights of each, and so watched over the dignity of each, that, as far as man is concerned, reason can now hardly rise higher than she rose, borne up in the flight of Thomas; and Faith can hardly gain more helps and greater helps from reason than those which Thomas gave her.

For these causes, especially in former days, men of the greatest learning and worthy of the highest praise both in theology and philosophy, having sought out with incredible diligence the immortal writings of Thomas, surrendered themselves to his angelic wisdom, not so much to be taught by his words, as to be altogether nourished by them. It is plain also that nearly all founders and lawgivers and religious Orders have bidden their children study the doctrines of Thomas, and very religiously adhere to them, giving a caution that it will be allowed to none to deviate ever so little from the footsteps of so great a man. To pass by the Dominican family which, as it were, by a right of its own, glories in this greatest of teachers, the statutes of each Order testify that Benedictines, Carmelites, Augustinians, the Society of Jesus, and many other holy Orders, are bound by this law.

Now our mind flies with great delight to those very celebrated universities and schools which formerly flourished in Europe: such as Paris, Salamanca, Alcala, Douai, Toulouse, Louvain, Padua, Bologna, Naples, Coimbra, and very many others. No one is ignorant that the reputation of these universities grew by age; that their opinions were asked when weighty issues were at stake; and that those opinions had great influence everywhere. But it is also well known that, in those illustrious abodes of human learning, Thomas reigned as a ruler in his own kingdom. The minds of all, both teachers and hearers, with wondrous consent found rest in the guidance and authority of one Angelic Doctor.

But further—and this is of greater importance—the Roman Pontiffs, our predecessors, bore witness to the wisdom of Thomas Aquinas with praises singularly strong, and with most abundant testimonies. Clement VI, Nicholas V, Benedict XIII, and others, testify that the whole Church was enlightened by his admirable teaching. Pius V acknowledges that heresies are confounded and exposed and scattered by his doctrine, and that by it the whole world is daily freed from pestilent errors. Others, with Clement XII, say that most fruitful blessings have flowed from his writings on the whole Church. They affirm also that the same honour has to be given to him as to the greatest Doctors of the Church, such as Gregory and Ambrose, and Augustine and Jerome. Others did not hesitate to set forth St. Thomas as a standard and teacher to universities and great schools of learning, saying that they might safely follow him. On this point the words of Blessed Urban V to the University of Toulouse seem to be most worthy of mention: "It is our will, and by the authority of these letters we enjoin on you, that you follow the doctrine of Blessed Thomas as true and Catholic, and strive to unfold it with your whole strength." This example of Urban was followed by Innocent XII in the University of Louvain, and by Benedict XIV in the Dionysian College of Granada. To these judgments of the Pontiffs about Thomas there is added, as a crown, the testimony of Innocent VI: "His doctrine above all other doctrine, with the one exception of the Holy Scriptures, has such a propriety of words, such a method of explanation, such a truth of opinions, that no one who holds it will ever be found to have strayed from the path of truth; whereas anyone who has attacked it has always been suspected as to the truth."

Moreover, Oecumenical Councils, made glorious by the flower of wisdom gathered from the whole world, always strove with great care to give singular honour to Thomas Aquinas. In the Councils of Lyons, of Vienne, of Florence, of the Vatican, you may say that Thomas was present at the deliberations and decrees of the Fathers, and almost that he presided at them, contending against the errors of Greeks and heretics and rationalists, with a power from which there was no escape, and with a most auspicious result.

But we now come to the greatest glory of Thomas—a glory which is altogether his own, and shared with no other Catholic Doctor. In the midst of the Council of Trent, the assembled Fathers so willing it, the *Summa* of Thomas Aquinas lay open on the altar, with the Holy Scriptures and the decrees of the Supreme Pontiffs, that from it might be sought counsel and reasons and answers.

Lastly, another crown seems to have been kept for this peerless man— that is, the way in which he extorts homage, praise, and admiration even from the enemies of the Catholic name. It is well known that there have not been wanting heresiarchs who openly said that, if the doctrine of Thomas Aquinas could only be got rid of, they could "easily give battle to other Catholic Doctors, and overcome them, and so scatter the Church." A vain hope indeed, but no vain testimony!

For these reasons, Venerable Brothers, so often as We look at the goodness, the force, and the exceedingly great usefulness of that philosophical doctrine in which our fathers took such delight, We judge that it has been rashly done when this doctrine has not always, and everywhere, been held in its own rightful honour. Especially do We judge this to be the case, since it is plain that long use and the judgment of the greatest men, and, what is more than all, the consent of the Church, have favoured the Scholastic method. Here and there a certain new kind of philosophy has taken the place of the old doctrine; and because of this, men have not gathered those desirable and wholesome fruits which the Church and civil society itself could have wished. The aggressive innovators of the sixteenth century have not hesitated to philosophize without any regard whatever to the Faith, asking, and conceding in return, the right to invent anything that they can think of, and anything that they please. From this it quickly followed, of course, that systems of philosophy were multiplied beyond all reason, and that there sprang up conflicting opinions and diverse opinions even about some of the chief things which are within human knowledge. From a multitude of opinions men very often pass to uncertainty and doubt; while there is no one who does not see how easily their minds glide from doubt into error.

But, since man is drawn by imitation, we have seen these novelties lay hold of the minds of some Catholic philosophers, who, undervaluing the inheritance of ancient wisdom, have chosen rather to invent new things than to extend and perfect the old by new truths, and that certainly with unwise counsel, and not without loss to science; for such a manifold kind of doctrine has only a shifting foundation, resting as it does on the authority and will of individual teachers. For this reason it does not make philosophy firm and strong and solid, like the old philosophy, but, on the contrary, makes it weak and shallow.

When We say this, however, We do not condemn those learned and able men who bring their industry and their knowledge, and the riches of new discoveries, to the aid of philosophy; for We clearly see that such a course tends to the increase of learning. But with great care we must guard against spending the whole of our attention, or even the chief part of it, on such studies as these, and on such instruction.

Let the same judgment be formed about Sacred Theology. This may well be aided and illustrated by many helps of erudition; but it is altogether necessary that it should be treated in the weighty manner of the Scholastics, in order that it may continue to be the "unassailable bulwark of the faith," by the forces of reason and revelation thus united in it.

Students of philosophy, therefore, not a few, giving their minds lately to the task of setting philosophy on a surer footing, have done their utmost, and are doing their utmost, to restore to its place the glorious teaching of Thomas Aquinas, and to win for it again its former renown.

That many of your order, Venerable Brothers, are with like will following promptly and cheerfully in the same path, We know to the great gladness of Our heart. While We praise these much, We exhort them to go on in the way that they have begun. To the rest of you, one by one, We give this word of counsel: there is nothing which We have longer wished for and desired than that you should give largely and abundantly to youths engaged in study the pure streams of wisdom which flow from the Angelic Doctor as from a perennial and copious spring.

Our reasons for wishing this so earnestly as We do are many.

First, in our times, the Christian Faith is commonly opposed by the wiles and craft of a certain deceitful kind of wisdom. All young men, therefore, and especially those who are growing up as the hope of the Church, ought to be fed with healthful and strong food of doctrine. Thus, being mighty in strength, and possessing an armoury in which all needful weapons may be found, they will learn by experience to treat the cause of religion with power and wisdom, according to the admonition of the Apostle, "being ready always to satisfy everyone that asketh you a reason of that hope which is in you": and being "able to exhort in sound doctrine and to convince the gainsayers."

Next, there are many who, with minds alienated from the Faith, hate all Catholic teaching, and say that reason alone is their teacher and guide. To heal these men of their unbelief, and to bring them to grace and the Catholic Faith, We think that nothing, after the supernatural help of God, can be more useful in these days than the solid doctrine of the Fathers and the Scholastics. They teach firm foundations of Faith, its Divine origin, its certain truth, the arguments by which it is commended to men, the benefits that it has conferred on the human race, and its perfect harmony with reason. They teach all such truths with a weight of evidence and a force that may well persuade even minds unwilling and hostile in the highest degree.

Again, we all see the great dangers which threaten family life, and even civil society itself, because of the pestilence of perverse opinions. Truly all civil society would be much more tranquil and much safer if healthier teaching were given in universities and schools; a doctrine more in unison with the perpetual teaching office (*magisterium*) of the Church, such as is contained in the volumes of Thomas Aquinas. He disputes about the true nature of liberty, which, in these days, is passing into lawlessness; about the Divine origin of all authority; about laws and their binding force; about the paternal and just government of sovereign princes, with our obedience to higher powers, and the common love that should be among all. The words of Thomas about these things, and others of a like nature, have the greatest strength, indeed a resistless strength, to overthrow the principles of this new jurisprudence, which is manifestly dangerous to the peaceful order of society and the public safety.

Lastly, from the restoration of philosophical teaching as it has been set forth by Us, all human sciences ought to gather hope of improvement, and the promise of a very great safeguard. For from philosophy, as from a guiding wisdom, the beneficent arts have hitherto derived a healthy method and a right measure. They have, moreover, drunk a vital spirit from it as from a common fountain of life. It is proved by fact and constant experience that the liberal arts have been most flourishing when the honour of philosophy has stood inviolate, and when its judgment has been held for wisdom: but that they have lain neglected and almost obliterated when declining philosophy has been enveloped in errors and absurdities.

Hence, also, the physical sciences, which now are held in so much repute, and everywhere draw to themselves a singular admiration, because of the many wonderful discoveries made in them, would not only take no harm from a restoration of the philosophy of the ancients, but would derive great protection from it. For the fruitful exercise and increase of these sciences it is not enough that we consider facts and contemplate Nature. When the facts are well known we must rise higher, and give our thoughts with great care to understanding the nature of corporeal things, as well as to the investigation of the laws which they obey, and of the principles from which spring their order, their unity in variety, and their common likeness in diversity. It is marvellous what power and light and help are given to these investigations by Scholastic philosophy, if it be wisely used.

On this point it is well to call one thing to your minds. It is only by the highest injustice that any jealousy of the progress and increase of natural sciences is laid, as a fault, at the door of that philosophy. When the Scholastics, following the teaching of the Holy Fathers, everywhere taught throughout their anthropology that the human understanding can only rise to the knowledge of immaterial things by things of sense, nothing could be more useful for the philosopher than to investigate carefully the secrets of Nature, and to be conversant, long and laboriously, with the study of physical science. Indeed, they themselves prove this by their works. Thomas, and Blessed Albert the Great, and other princes of the Scholastics, did not so give themselves up to the study of philosophy, as to have little care for the knowledge of natural things. Nay, on this matter there are not a few of their words and discoveries which modern teachers approve and acknowledge to be in harmony with truth. Besides, in this very age, many distinguished teachers of physical sciences openly bear witness that there is no contradiction, truly so called, between the certain and proved conclusions of recent physics, and the philosophical principles of the Schools.

We, therefore, while We declare that everything wisely said should be received with willing and glad mind, as well as everything profitably discovered or thought out, exhort all of you, Venerable Brothers, with the greatest earnestness to restore the golden wisdom of St. Thomas, and to spread it as far as you can, for the safety and glory of the Catholic Faith, for the good of society, and for the increase of all the sciences. We say the wisdom of St. Thomas; for it is not by any means in our mind to set before this age, as a standard, those things which may have been inquired into by Scholastic Doctors with too great subtlety; or anything taught by them with too little consideration, not agreeing with the investigations of a later age; or, lastly, anything that is not probable.

Let, then, teachers carefully chosen by you do their best to instil the doctrine of Thomas Aquinas into the minds of their hearers; and let them clearly point out its solidity and excellence above all other teaching. Let this doctrine be the light of all places of learning which you may have already opened, or may hereafter open. Let it be used for the refutation of errors that are gaining ground.

But lest the false should be drunk instead of the true; or lest that which is unwholesome should be drunk instead of that which is pure; take care that the wisdom of Thomas be drawn from his own fountain, or at any rate from those streams which, in the certain and unanimous opinion of learned men, yet flow whole and untainted, inasmuch as they are led from the fountain itself. Take care, moreover, that the minds of the young be kept from streams which are said to have flowed from thence, but in reality have been fed by unhealthy waters from other springs.

Well do we know that all our work will be vain, unless, Venerable Brothers, He bless our common efforts, Who in the Divine Scriptures is called the "God of all knowledge." By those same Scriptures we are warned, that "every best gift and every perfect gift is from above, coming down from the Father of lights." Again, "If any of you want wisdom, let him ask of God, who giveth to all men abundantly and upbraideth not; and it shall be given him."

In this matter, then, let us follow the example of the Angelic Doctor, who never began to read or to write without seeking for God's help by prayer; and who in simplicity acknowledged that all his learning had come to him, not so much from his own study and toil, as immediately from God. With humble and united prayer, therefore, let us all together beseech God fervently to pour out the spirit of knowledge and understanding on the sons of the Church, and to open their minds to the understanding of wisdom.

Also, that we may receive more abundant fruits of the goodness of God, use that patronage which is most powerful with Him; that is, the patronage of the Blessed Virgin Mary, who is called the Seat of Wisdom. Secure also, as intercessors, Blessed Joseph, the pure Spouse of the Virgin; and Peter and Paul, the chiefs of the Apostles, who renewed the whole world with truth, when it was corrupted by the uncleanness and the contagion of errors, and who filled it with the light of the wisdom which is from Heaven.

Lastly, in hope, trusting to the help of God and relying on your pastoral zeal, to all of you, Venerable Brothers, to all the clergy, and all the people committed to the care of each, we give, with great love in the Lord, our Apostolical blessing, the earnest of heavenly gifts, and the witness of our special goodwill.

Given at Rome, at St. Peter's, this 4th day of August, 1879, in the second year of our Pontificate.

LEO, PP. XIII.

6 · NIETZSCHE

Friedrich Nietzsche was born at Röcken, in the Prussian province of Saxony, in 1844. He became a professor of classical philology at the University of Basel, Switzerland, in 1869, but resigned ten years later, pleading his poor health. For the next ten years, he spent his summers in Switzerland and his winters in Italy, devoting himself entirely to writing. In January 1889, he collapsed in the street and suffered a complete physical and mental breakdown. He did not die until 1900 but did not regain his lucidity or write anything further.

Of his early essays, *The Birth of Tragedy* (1872) is the best known. His major works are: *Thus Spoke Zarathustra** (1883-92), *Beyond Good and Evil* (1886), *Toward a Genealogy of Morals* (1887), *The Twilight of the Idols** (1889), *The Antichrist** (1895), *Ecce Homo* (1908), and *Nietzsche contra Wagner** (1895). These books were completed in the order in which they are listed, the last of them late in 1888; but some of them were not published until later. The dates of the first German editions are given in parentheses. An asterisk (*) means that a complete translation may be found in *The Portable Nietzsche* (The Viking Press, 1954, paperback ed. 1958), from which the following selections are taken. They comprise sections 29-31, 35-41, and 45 of *The Antichrist*, written in 1888 and first published in 1895.

The Will to Power, sometimes erroneously designated as Nietzsche's last work, is a collection of some of his notes in a topical arrangement not his own. Many of these notes are extremely interesting, but *The Antichrist* was written later.

The Antichrist

29

*W*hat concerns *me* is the psychological type of the Redeemer. After all, this could be contained in the Gospels despite the Gospels, however mutilated or overloaded with alien features: as Francis of Assisi is preserved in his legends, despite his legends. *Not* the truth concerning what he did, what he said, how he really died; but the question *whether* his type can still be exhibited at all, whether it has been "transmitted."

The attempts I know to read the *history* of a "soul" out of the Gospels seem to me proof of a contemptible psychological frivolity. M. Renan, that buffoon *in psychologicis*, has introduced the two most inappropriate concepts possible into his explanation of the Jesus type: the concept of *genius* and the concept of the *hero* ("*héros*"). But if anything is unevangelical it is the concept of the hero. Just the opposite of all wrestling, of all feeling-oneself-in-a-struggle, has here become instinct: the incapacity for resistance becomes morality here ("resist not evil"—the most profound word of the Gospels, their key in a certain sense), blessedness in peace, in gentleness, in not *being able* to be an enemy. What are the "glad tidings"? True life, eternal life, has been found—it is not promised, it is here, it is *in you:* as a living in love, in love without subtraction and exclusion, without regard for station. Everyone is the child of God—Jesus definitely presumes nothing for himself alone —and as a child of God everyone is equal to everyone. To make a *hero* of Jesus! And even more, what a misunderstanding is the word "genius"! Our whole concept, our cultural concept, of "spirit" has no meaning whatever in the world in which Jesus lives. Spoken with the precision of a physiologist, even an entirely different word would still be more nearly fitting here—the word *idiot.*[1]

We know a state in which the *sense of touch* is pathologically excitable and shrinks from any contact, from grasping a solid object. One should translate such a physiological *habitus* into its ultimate consequence—an instinctive hatred of every reality, a flight into "what cannot be grasped," "the incomprehensible," an aversion to every formula, to every concept of time and space, to all that is solid, custom, institution, church; a being at home in a world which is no longer in contact with any kind of reality, a merely "inner" world, a "true" world, an "eternal" world. "The kingdom of God is *in you.*"

30

The instinctive hatred of reality: a consequence of an extreme capacity for suffering and excitement which no longer wants any contact at all because it feels every contact too deeply.

The instinctive exclusion of any antipathy, any hostility, any boundaries or divisions in man's feelings: the consequence of an extreme capacity for suffering and excitement which experiences any resistance, even any compulsion to resist, as unendurable *displeasure* (that is, as *harmful*, as something against which the instinct of self-preservation *warns* us); and finds blessedness (pleasure) only in no longer offering any resistance to anybody, neither

---

[1] The last three words were suppressed by Nietzsche's sister when she first published *The Antichrist* in 1895, in Volume VIII of the Collected Works. They were first made public by Hofmiller in 1931, to prove that Nietzsche must have been insane when he wrote the book. But he was, of course, thinking of Dostoevski's *The Idiot.* The references to Dostoevski in section 31 below and in section 45 of *Twilight of the Idols* should also be noted. The word "idiot" assumes a sudden significance in Nietzsche's work after his discovery of Dostoevski: see section 5 of *The Wagner Case;* section 7 in chapter 2 of *Twilight of the Idols;* sections 11, 26, 31, 42, 51-53 of *The Antichrist;* section 2 of "The Wagner Case" in *Ecce Homo;* sections 2 and 3 of *Nietzsche contra Wagner;* the letters to Brandes and Strindberg, dated October 20 and December 7, 1888; and note 734 in *The Will to Power.*

to evil nor to him who is evil—love as the only, as the *last* possible, way of life.

These are the two *physiological realities* on which, out of which, the doctrine of redemption grew. I call this a sublime further development of hedonism on a thoroughly morbid basis. Most closely related to it, although with a generous admixture of Greek vitality and nervous energy, is Epicureanism, the pagan doctrine of redemption. Epicurus, a *typical decadent*—first recognized as such by me. The fear of pain, even of infinitely minute pain—that can end in no other way than in a *religion of love*.

31

I have already given my answer to the problem. Its presupposition is that the Redeemer type is preserved for us only in extensive distortion. This distortion is very probable in any case; for several reasons, such a type could not remain pure, whole, free from accretions. He must show traces of the milieu in which he moved as a foreign figure; and even more of the history, the *fate* of the first Christian community, from which the type was enriched, retroactively, with features which are comprehensible only in terms of later polemics and propaganda purposes.

That queer and sick world into which the Gospels introduce us—as in a Russian novel, a world in which the scum of society, nervous disorders, and "childlike" idiocy seem to be having a rendezvous—must at all events have *coarsened* the type: in order to be able to understand anything of it, the first disciples, in particular, first translated into their own crudity an existence which was wholly embedded in symbols and incomprehensibilities—for them the type did not *exist* until it had been reshaped in better-known forms. The prophet, the Messiah, the future judge, the moral teacher, the miracle man, John the Baptist—each another chance to misconstrue the type.

Finally, let us not underestimate the *proprium* of all great, and especially sectarian, veneration: it blots out the original, often painfully strange features and idiosyncrasies of the venerated being—*it does not even see them*. It is regrettable that a Dostoevski did not live near this most interesting of all decadents—I mean someone who would have known how to sense the very stirring charm of such a mixture of the sublime, the sickly, and the childlike.

A final consideration: as a type of decadence, the type *might* actually have been peculiarly manifold and contradictory. Such a possibility cannot be excluded altogether. Nevertheless, everything speaks against this: precisely the tradition would have to be curiously faithful and objective in this case—and we have reasons for supposing the opposite. Meanwhile there is a gaping contradiction between the sermonizer on the mount, lake, and meadow, whose appearance seems like that of a Buddha on soil that is not at all Indian, and that fanatic of aggression, that mortal enemy of theologians and priests, whom Renan's malice has glorified as *le grand maître en ironie*. I myself have no doubt that the generous dose of gall (and even of *esprit*) first flowed into the type of the Master from the excited state of Christian propaganda; after all, the unscrupulousness of all sectarians, when it comes to constructing their own *apology* out of their master, is only too well known. When the first community needed a judging, quarreling, angry, malignantly sophistical theologian, *against* theologians, it *created* its "God" according to its needs—just as it put into his mouth, without any hesitation, those wholly unevangelical concepts which now it cannot do without: "the return," the "Last Judgment," every kind of temporal expectation and promise.

35

This "bringer of glad tidings" died as he had lived, as he had taught—*not* to "redeem men" but to show how one must live. This practice is his legacy to mankind: his behavior before the judges, before the catchpoles, before the accusers and all kinds of slander and scorn—his behavior on the *cross*. He does not resist, he does not defend his right, he takes no step which might ward off the worst; on the contrary, he *provokes* it. And he begs, he suffers, he loves *with* those, *in* those, who do him evil. *Not* to resist, *not* to be angry, *not* to hold responsible—but to resist not even the evil one—to *love* him.

36

Only we, we spirits who have *become free*, have the presuppositions for understanding something that nineteen centuries have misunderstood: that integrity which, having become instinct and passion, wages war against the "holy lie" even more than against any other lie. Previous readers were immeasurably far removed from our loving and cautious neutrality, from that discipline of the spirit which alone makes possible the unriddling of such foreign, such tender things: with impudent selfishness they always wanted only their own advantage; out of the opposite of the evangel the church was constructed.

If one were to look for signs that an ironical divinity has its fingers in the great play of the world, one would find no small support in the *tremendous question mark* called Christianity. Mankind lies on its knees before the opposite of that which was the origin, the meaning, the *right* of the evangel; in the concept of "church" it has pronounced holy precisely what the "bringer of the glad tidings" felt to be *beneath* and *behind* himself—one would look in vain for a greater example of *world-historical irony*.

37

Our age is proud of its historical sense: How could it ever make itself believe the nonsense that at the beginning of Christianity there stands the *crude fable of the miracle worker and Redeemer*—and that everything spiritual and symbolical represents only a later development? On the contrary: the history of Christianity, beginning with the death on the cross, is the history of the misunderstanding, growing cruder with every step, of an *original* symbolism. With every diffusion of Christianity to still broader, still cruder masses of people, more and more lacking in the presuppositions to which it owed its birth, it became more necessary to *vulgarize,* to *barbarize* Christianity: it has swallowed doctrines and rites of all the *subterranean* cults of the *imperium Romanum* as well as the nonsense of all kinds of diseased reason. The destiny of Christianity lies in the necessity that its faith had to become as diseased, as base and vulgar, as the needs it was meant to satisfy were diseased, base, and vulgar. In the church, finally, *diseased barbarism* itself gains power—the church, this embodiment of mortal hostility against all integrity, against all *elevation* of the soul, against all discipline of the spirit, against all frank and gracious humanity. *Christian* values—*noble* values: only we, we spirits who have *become free,* have restored this contrast of values, the greatest that there is!

38

At this point I do not suppress a sigh. There are days when I am afflicted with a feeling blacker than the blackest melancholy—*contempt of man.* And to leave no doubt concerning what I despise, whom I despise: it is the man of today, the man with whom I am fatefully contemporaneous. The man of today—I suffocate from his unclean breath. My attitude to the past, like that of all lovers of knowledge, is one of great tolerance, that is, *magnanimous* self-mastery: with gloomy caution I go through the madhouse world of whole millennia, whether it be called "Christianity," "Christian faith," or "Christian church"—I am careful not to hold mankind responsible for its mental disorders. But my feeling changes, breaks out, as soon as I enter modern times, *our* time. Our time *knows better.*

What was formerly just sick is today indecent—it is indecent to be a Christian today. *And here begins my nausea.* I look around: not one word has remained of what was formerly called "truth"; we can no longer stand it if a priest as much as uses the word "truth." If we have even the smallest claim to integrity, we must know today that a theologian, a priest, a pope, not merely is wrong in every sentence he speaks, but *lies*—that he is no longer at liberty to lie from "innocence" or "ignorance." The priest too knows as well as anybody else that there is no longer any "God," any "sinner," any "Redeemer"—that "free will" and "moral world order" are *lies:* seriousness, the profound self-overcoming of the spirit, no longer permits anybody *not* to know about this.

All the concepts of the church have been recognized for what they are, the most malignant counterfeits that exist, the aim of which is to devalue nature and natural values; the priest himself has been recognized for what he is, the most dangerous kind of parasite, the real poison-spider of life. We know, today our *conscience* knows, what these uncanny inventions of the priests and the church are really worth, *what ends they served* in reducing mankind to such a state of self-violation that its sight can arouse nausea: the concepts "beyond," "Last Judgment," "immortality of the soul," and "soul" itself are instruments of torture, systems of cruelties by virtue of which the priest became master, remained master.

Everybody knows this, *and yet everything continues as before*. Where has the last feeling of decency and self-respect gone when even our statesmen, an otherwise quite unembarrassed type of man, anti-Christians through and through in their deeds, still call themselves Christians today and attend communion? A young prince at the head of his regiments, magnificent as an expression of the selfishness and conceit of his people—but, *without* any shame, confessing himself a Christian! *Whom* then does Christianity negate? *What* does it call "world"? That one is a soldier, that one is a judge, that one is a patriot; that one resists; that one sees to one's honor; that one seeks one's advantage; that one is proud. Every practice of every moment, every instinct, every valuation that is translated into *action* is today anti-Christian: what a *miscarriage of falseness* must modern man be, that he is *not ashamed* to be called a Christian in spite of all this!

39

I go back, I tell the *genuine* history of Christianity. The very word "Christianity" is a misunderstanding: in truth, there was only *one* Christian, and he died on the cross. The "evangel" *died* on the cross. What has been called "evangel" from that moment was actually the opposite of that which *he* had lived: *"ill* tidings," a *dysangel*. It is false to the point of nonsense to find the mark of the Christian in a "faith," for instance, in the faith in redemption through Christ: only Christian *practice*, a life such as he *lived* who died on the cross, is Christian.

Such a life is still possible today, for certain people even necessary: genuine, original Christianity will be possible at all times.

Not a faith, but a doing; above all, a *not* doing of many things, another state of *being*. States of consciousness, any faith, considering something true, for example—every psychologist knows this—are fifth-rank matters of complete indifference compared to the value of the instincts: speaking more strictly, the whole concept of spiritual causality is false. To reduce being a Christian, Christianism, to a matter of considering something true, to a mere phenomenon of consciousness, is to negate Christianism. *In fact, there have been no Christians at all*. The "Christian," that which for the last two thousand years has been called a Christian, is merely a psychological self-misunderstanding. If one looks more closely, it was, in spite of all "faith," only the instincts that ruled in him—and *what instincts!*

"Faith" was at all times, for example, in Luther, only a cloak, a pretext, a *screen* behind which the instincts played their game—a shrewd *blindness* about the dominance of *certain* instincts. "Faith"—I have already called it the characteristic Christian *shrewdness*—one always *spoke* of faith, but one always *acted* from instinct alone.

In the Christian world of ideas there is nothing that has the least contact with reality—and it is in the instinctive hatred of reality that we have recognized the only motivating force at the root of Christianity. What follows from this? That *in psychologicis* too, the error here is radical, that it is that which determines the very essence, that it is the *substance*. One concept less, one single reality in its place—and the whole of Christianity hurtles down into nothing.

Viewed from high above, this strangest of all facts—a religion which is not only dependent on errors but which has its inventiveness and even its genius *only* in harmful errors, *only* in errors which poison life and the heart—is really a *spectacle for gods,* for those gods who are at the same time philosophers and whom I have encountered, for example, at those famous dialogues on Naxos. The moment *nausea* leaves them (*and* us!), they become grateful for the spectacle of the Christian: perhaps the miserable little star that is called earth deserves a divine glance, a divine sympathy, just because of *this* curious case. For let us not underestimate the Christian: the Christian, false *to the point of innocence*, is far above the ape—regarding Christians, a well-known theory of descent becomes a mere compliment.

40

The catastrophe of the evangel was decided with the death—it was attached to the "cross." Only the death, this unexpected, disgraceful death, only the cross which was generally reserved for the rabble—only this horrible paradox confronted the disciples with the real riddle: "*Who was this? What was this?*" Their profoundly upset and insulted feelings, and their suspicion that such a death might represent the *refutation* of their cause, the terrible question mark, "Why in this manner?"—this state is only too easy to understand. Here everything *had* to be necessary, had to have meaning, reason, the highest reason; a disciple's love knows no accident. Only now the cleft opened up: "*Who* killed him? *Who* was his natural enemy?" This question leaped forth like lightning. Answer: *ruling* Jewry, its highest class. From this moment one felt oneself in rebellion against the existing order, and in retrospect one understood Jesus to have been *in rebellion against the existing order.* Until then this warlike, this No-saying, No-doing trait had been *lacking* in his image; even more, he had been its opposite.

Evidently the small community did *not* understand the main point, the exemplary character of this kind of death, the freedom, the superiority over any feeling of *ressentiment:* a token of how little they understood him altogether! After all, Jesus could not intend anything with his death except to give publicly the strongest exhibition, the *proof* of his doctrine. But his disciples were far from *forgiving* this death—which would have been evangelic in the highest sense—or even from offering themselves for a like death in gentle and lovely repose of the heart. Precisely the most unevangelical feeling, *revenge*, came to the fore again. The matter could not possibly be finished with this death: "retribution" was needed, "judgment" (and yet, what could possibly be more unevangelical than "retribution," "punishment," "sitting in judgment"!). Once more the popular expectation of a Messiah came to the foreground; a historic moment was envisaged: the "kingdom of God" comes as a judgment over his enemies.

But in this way everything is misunderstood: the "kingdom of God" as the last act, as a promise! After all, the evangel had been precisely the presence, the fulfillment, the *reality* of this "kingdom." Just such a death was this very "kingdom of God." Now for the first time all the contempt and bitterness against the Pharisees and theologians were carried into the type of the Master—and in this way he himself was made into a Pharisee and theologian! On the other hand, the frenzied veneration of these totally unhinged souls no longer endured the evangelic conception of everybody's equal right to be a child of God, as Jesus had taught: it was their revenge to *elevate* Jesus extravagantly, to sever him from themselves—precisely as the Jews had formerly, out of revenge against their enemies, severed their God from themselves and elevated him. The one God and the one Son of God—both products of *ressentiment*.

41

And from now on an absurd problem emerged: "How *could* God permit this?" To this the deranged reason of the small community found an altogether horribly absurd answer: God gave his son for the remission of sins, as a *sacrifice*. In one stroke, it was all over with the evangel! The *trespass sacrifice*—in its most revolting, most barbarous form at that, the sacrifice of the *guiltless* for the sins of the guilty! What gruesome paganism!

Jesus had abolished the very concept of "guilt"—he had denied any cleavage between God and man; he *lived* this unity of God and man as his "glad tidings." And *not* as a prerogative! From now on there enters into the type of the Redeemer, step by step, the doctrine of judgment and return, the doctrine of death as a sacrificial death, the doctrine of the *resurrection* with which the whole concept of "blessedness," the whole and only actuality of the evangel, is conjured away—in favor of a state after death.

Paul, with that rabbinical impudence which distinguishes him in all things, logicalized this conception, this *obscenity* of a conception, in this way: "*If Christ was not resurrected from the dead, then our faith is vain.*" And all at once the evangel became the most contemptible of all unfulfillable promises, the *impertinent* doctrine of personal immortality. Paul himself still taught it as a *reward*.

45

I give some examples of what these little people put into their heads, what they *put into the mouth* of their master: without exception, confessions of "beautiful souls":

"And whosoever shall not receive you, nor hear you, when ye depart thence, shake off the dust under your feet for a testimony against them. Verily I say unto you, It shall be more tolerable for Sodom and Gomorrah in the day of judgment, than for that city" (Mark 6:11). How *evangelical!*

"And whosoever shall offend one of these little ones that believe in me, it is better for him that a millstone were hanged about his neck, and he were cast into the sea" (Mark 9:42). How *evangelical!*

"And if thine eye offend thee, pluck it out: it is better for thee to enter into the kingdom of God with one eye, than having two eyes to be cast into hell fire: Where their worm dieth not, and the fire is not quenched" (Mark 9:47 f.). It is not exactly the eye which is meant.

"Verily I say unto you, That there be some of them that stand here, which shall not taste of death, till they have seen the kingdom of God come with power" (Mark 9:1). Well *lied*, lion!

"Whosoever will come after me, let him deny himself, and take up his cross, and follow me. *For—*" (*Note of a psychologist.* Christian morality is refuted by its *For's:* its "reasons" refute—thus is it Christian.) Mark 8:34.

"Judge not, that ye be not judged. . . . With what measure ye mete, it shall be measured to you again" (Matt. 7:1 f.). What a conception of justice and of a "just" judge!

"For if ye love them which love you, what reward have ye? do not even the publicans the same? And if ye salute your brethren only, what do ye more *than others*? do not even the publicans so?" (Matt. 5:46 f.). The principle of "Christian love": in the end it wants to be *paid* well.

"But if ye forgive not men their trespasses, neither will your Father forgive your trespasses" (Matt. 6:15). Very compromising for said "Father."

"But seek ye first the kingdom of God, and his righteousness; and all these things shall be added unto you" (Matt. 6:33). All these things: namely, food, clothing, all the necessities of life. An *error*, to put it modestly. Shortly before this, God appears as a tailor, at least in certain cases.

"Rejoice ye in that day, and leap for joy: for, behold, your reward is great in heaven: for in the like manner did their fathers unto the prophets" (Luke 6:23). *Impertinent* rabble! They compare themselves with the prophets, no less.

"Know ye not that ye are the temple of God, and that the Spirit of God dwelleth in you? If any man defile the temple of God, him shall God destroy; for the temple of God is holy, which temple ye are" (Paul, I Cor. 3:16 f.). This sort of thing one cannot despise enough.

"Do ye not know that the saints shall judge the world? and if the world shall be judged by you, are ye unworthy to judge the smallest matters?" (Paul, I Cor. 6:2). Unfortunately not merely the talk of a lunatic. This *frightful swindler* continues literally: "Know ye not that we shall judge angels? how much more things that pertain to this life!"

"Hath not God made foolish the wisdom of this world? For after that the world by its wisdom knew not God in his wisdom, it pleased God by foolish preaching to make blessed them that believe in it. . . . Not many wise men after the flesh, not many mighty, not many noble, are called. But God hath chosen the foolish things of the world to ruin the wise; and God hath chosen the weak things of the world to ruin what is strong; And base things of the world, and things which are despised, hath God chosen, yea, and what is nothing, to bring to nought what is something: That no flesh should glory in his presence" (Paul, I Cor. 1:20 *ff.*).[1] To understand this passage, a first-rate document for the psychology of every chandala morality, one should read the first inquiry in my *Genealogy of Morals:* there the contrast between a *noble* morality and a chandala morality, born of *ressentiment* and impotent vengefulness, was brought to light for the first time. Paul was the greatest of all apostles of vengeance.

[1] Nietzsche quotes Luther's translation, and some departures from the King James Bible were found necessary in this quotation because some of its phrases are echoed in subsequent sections.

7 · CLIFFORD

William Kingdon Clifford was born at Exeter, England, in 1845. He was elected a fellow of Trinity College, Cambridge, in 1868, and appointed professor of mathematics at University College, London, in 1871. He was elected a fellow of the Royal Society in 1874. Only thirty-three years old, he died of consumption in 1879, at Madeira.

His works include *Seeing and Thinking* (1879), *Elements of Dynamic* (1879-87), *Mathematical Papers* (1882), and *The Common Sense of the Exact Sciences* (1885). "The Ethics of Belief," reprinted here, comes from the second volume of *Lectures and Essays* (1879), and was originally published in *Contemporary Review*, January, 1877.

The Ethics of Belief

I. THE DUTY OF INQUIRY

A shipowner was about to send to sea an emigrant-ship. He knew that she was old, and not over-well built at the first; that she had seen many seas and climes, and often had needed repairs. Doubts had been suggested to him that possibly she was not seaworthy. These doubts preyed upon his mind, and made him unhappy; he thought that perhaps he ought to have her thoroughly overhauled and refitted, even though this should put him to great expense. Before the ship sailed, however, he succeeded in overcoming these melancholy reflections. He said to himself that she had gone safely through so many voyages and weathered so many storms that it was idle to suppose she would not come safely home from this trip also. He would put his trust in Providence, which could hardly fail to protect all these unhappy families that were leaving their fatherland to seek for better times elsewhere. He would dismiss from his mind all ungenerous suspicions about the honesty of builders and contractors. In such ways he acquired a sincere and comfortable conviction that his vessel was thoroughly safe and seaworthy; he watched her departure with a light heart, and benevolent wishes for the success of the exiles in their strange new home that was to be; and he got his insurance-money when she went down in mid-ocean and told no tales.

What shall we say of him? Surely this, that he was verily guilty of the

death of those men. It is admitted that he did sincerely believe in the sound-
ness of his ship; but the sincerity of his conviction can in no wise help him,
because *he had no right to believe on such evidence as was before him.* He
had acquired his belief not by honestly earning it in patient investigation,
but by stifling his doubts. And although in the end he may have felt so sure
about it that he could not think otherwise, yet inasmuch as he had knowingly and willingly worked himself into that frame of mind, he must be
held responsible for it.

Let us alter the case a little, and suppose that the ship was not unsound
after all; that she made her voyage safely, and many others after it. Will
that diminish the guilt of her owner? Not one jot. When an action is once
done, it is right or wrong for ever; no accidental failure of its good or evil
fruits can possibly alter that. The man would not have been innocent, he
would only have been not found out. The question of right or wrong has
to do with the origin of his belief, not the matter of it; not what it was, but
how he got it; not whether it turned out to be true or false, but whether
he had a right to believe on such evidence as was before him.

There was once an island in which some of the inhabitants professed a
religion teaching neither the doctrine of original sin nor that of eternal
punishment. A suspicion got abroad that the professors of this religion had
made use of unfair means to get their doctrines taught to children. They
were accused of wresting the laws of their country in such a way as to remove children from the care of their natural and legal guardians; and even
of stealing them away and keeping them concealed from their friends and
relations. A certain number of men formed themselves into a society for the
purpose of agitating the public about this matter. They published grave
accusations against individual citizens of the highest position and character,
and did all in their power to injure these citizens in the exercise of their pro-
fessions. So great was the noise they made, that a Commission was appointed
to investigate the facts; but after the Commission had carefully inquired
into all the evidence that could be got, it appeared that the accused were innocent. Not only had they been accused on insufficient evidence, but the
evidence of their innocence was such as the agitators might easily have
obtained, if they had attempted a fair inquiry. After these disclosures the
inhabitants of that country looked upon the members of the agitating
society, not only as persons whose judgment was to be distrusted, but also
as no longer to be counted honourable men. For although they had sincerely
and conscientiously believed in the charges they had made, yet *they had
no right to believe on such evidence as was before them.* Their sincere convictions, instead of being honestly earned by patient inquiring, were stolen
by listening to the voice of prejudice and passion.

Let us vary this case also, and suppose, other things remaining as before,
that a still more accurate investigation proved the accused to have been

really guilty. Would this make any difference in the guilt of the accusers? Clearly not; the question is not whether their belief was true or false, but whether they entertained it on wrong grounds. They would no doubt say, "Now you see that we were right after all; next time perhaps you will believe us." And they might be believed, but they would not thereby become honourable men. They would not be innocent, they would only be not found out. Every one of them, if he chose to examine himself *in foro conscientiae*, would know that he had acquired and nourished a belief, when he had no right to believe on such evidence as was before him; and therein he would know that he had done a wrong thing.

It may be said, however, that in both of these supposed cases it is not the belief which is judged to be wrong, but the action following upon it. The shipowner might say, "I am perfectly certain that my ship is sound, but still I feel it my duty to have her examined, before trusting the lives of so many people to her." And it might be said to the agitator, "However convinced you were of the justice of your cause and the truth of your convictions, you ought not to have made a public attack upon any man's character until you had examined the evidence on both sides with the utmost patience and care."

In the first place, let us admit that, so far as it goes, this view of the case is right and necessary; right, because even when a man's belief is so fixed that he cannot think otherwise, he still has a choice in regard to the action suggested by it, and so cannot escape the duty of investigating on the ground of the strength of his convictions; and necessary, because those who are not yet capable of controlling their feelings and thoughts must have a plain rule dealing with overt acts.

But this being premised as necessary, it becomes clear that it is not sufficient, and that our previous judgment is required to supplement it. For it is not possible so to sever the belief from the action it suggests as to condemn the one without condemning the other. No man holding a strong belief on one side of a question, or even wishing to hold a belief on one side, can investigate it with such fairness and completeness as if he were really in doubt and unbiased; so that the existence of a belief not founded on fair inquiry unfits a man for the performance of this necessary duty.

Nor is that truly a belief at all which has not some influence upon the actions of him who holds it. He who truly believes that which prompts him to an action has looked upon the action to lust after it, he has committed it already in his heart. If a belief is not realized immediately in open deeds, it is stored up for the guidance of the future. It goes to make a part of that aggregate of beliefs which is the link between sensation and action at every moment of all our lives, and which is so organized and compacted together that no part of it can be isolated from the rest, but every new addition modifies the structure of the whole. No real belief, however trifling and fragmentary it may seem, is ever truly insignificant; it prepares us to receive more of its like, confirms those which resembled it before, and weakens others; and so gradually it lays a stealthy train in our inmost thoughts, which may some day explode into overt action, and leave its stamp upon our character for ever.

And no one man's belief is in any case a private matter which concerns himself alone. Our lives are guided by that general conception of the course of things which has been created by society for social purposes. Our words, our phrases, our forms and processes and modes of thought, are common property, fashioned and perfected from age to age; an heirloom which every succeeding generation inherits as a precious deposit and a sacred trust to be handed on to the next one, not unchanged but enlarged and purified, with some clear marks of its proper handiwork. Into this, for good or ill, is woven every belief of every man who has speech of his fellows. An awful privilege, and an awful responsibility, that we should help to create the world in which posterity will live.

In the two supposed cases which have been considered, it has been judged wrong to believe on insufficient evidence, or to nourish belief by suppressing doubts and avoiding investigation. The reason of this judgment is not far to seek: it is that in both these cases the belief held by one man was of great importance to other men. But forasmuch as no belief held by one man, however seemingly trivial the belief, and however obscure the believer, is ever actually insignificant or without its effect on the fate of mankind, we have no choice but to extend our judgment to all cases of belief whatever. Belief, that sacred faculty which prompts the decisions of our will, and knits into harmonious working all the compacted energies of our being, is ours not for ourselves, but for humanity. It is rightly used on truths which have been established by long experience and waiting toil, and which have stood in the fierce light of free and fearless questioning. Then it helps to bind men together, and to strengthen and direct their common action. It is desecrated when given to unproved and unquestioned statements, for the solace and private pleasure of the believer; to add a tinsel splendour to the plain straight road of our life and display a bright mirage beyond it; or even to drown the common sorrows of our kind by a self-deception which allows them not only to cast down, but also to degrade us. Whoso would deserve well of his fellows in this matter will guard the purity of his belief with a very fanaticism of jealous care, lest at any time it should rest on an unworthy object, and catch a stain which can never be wiped away.

It is not only the leader of men, statesman, philosopher, or poet, that owes this bounden duty to mankind. Every rustic who delivers in the village alehouse his slow, infrequent sentences, may help to kill or keep alive the fatal superstitions which clog his race. Every hard-worked wife of an artisan may transmit to her children beliefs which shall knit society together, or rend it in pieces. No simplicity of mind, no obscurity of station, can escape the universal duty of questioning all that we believe.

It is true that this duty is a hard one, and the doubt which comes out of it is often a very bitter thing. It leaves us bare and powerless where we thought that we were safe and strong. To know all about anything is to know how to deal with it under all circumstances. We feel much happier and more secure when we think we know precisely what to do, no matter what happens, than when we have lost our way and do not know where to turn. And if we have supposed ourselves to know all about anything, and to be capable of doing what is fit in regard to it, we naturally do not like to find that we are really ignorant and powerless, that we have to begin again at the beginning, and try to learn what the thing is and how it is to be dealt with—if indeed anything can be learnt about it. It is the sense of power attached to a sense of knowledge that makes men desirous of believing, and afraid of doubting.

This sense of power is the highest and best of pleasures when the belief on which it is founded is a true belief, and has been fairly earned by investigation. For then we may justly feel that it is common property, and hold good for others as well as for ourselves. Then we may be glad, not that *I* have learned secrets by which I am safer and stronger, but that *we men* have got mastery over more of the world; and we shall be strong, not for ourselves, but in the name of Man and in his strength. But if the belief has been accepted on insufficient evidence, the pleasure is a stolen one. Not only does it deceive ourselves by giving us a sense of power which we do not really possess, but it is sinful, because it is stolen in defiance of our duty to mankind. That duty is to guard ourselves from such beliefs as from a pestilence, which may shortly master our own body and then spread to the rest of the town. What would be thought of one who, for the sake of a sweet fruit, should deliberately run the risk of bringing a plague upon his family and his neighbours?

And, as in other such cases, it is not the risk only which has to be considered; for a bad action is always bad at the time when it is done, no matter what happens afterwards. Every time we let ourselves believe for unworthy reasons, we weaken our powers of self-control, of doubting, of judicially and fairly weighing evidence. We all suffer severely enough from the maintenance and support of false beliefs and the fatally wrong actions which they lead to, and the evil born when one such belief is entertained is great and wide. But a greater and wider evil arises when the credulous character is maintained and supported, when a habit of believing for unworthy reasons is fostered and made permanent. If I steal money from any person, there may be no harm done by the mere transfer of possession; he may not feel the loss, or it may prevent him from using the money badly. But I cannot help doing this great wrong towards Man, that I make myself dishonest. What hurts society is not that it should lose its property, but that it should become a den of thieves; for then it must cease to be society. This is why we ought not to do evil that good may come; for at any rate this great evil has come, that we have done evil and are made wicked thereby. In like manner, if I let myself believe anything on insufficient evidence, there may be no great harm done by the mere belief; it may be true after all, or I may never have occasion to exhibit it in outward acts. But I cannot help doing this great wrong towards Man, that I make myself credulous. The danger to society is not merely that it should believe wrong things, though that is great enough; but that it should become credulous, and lose the habit of testing things and inquiring into them; for then it must sink back into savagery.

The harm which is done by credulity in a man is not confined to the fostering of a credulous character in others, and consequent support of false beliefs. Habitual want of care about what I believe leads to habitual want of care in others about the truth of what is told to me. Men speak the truth to one another when each reveres the truth in his own mind and in the other's mind; but how shall my friend revere the truth in my mind when I myself am careless about it, when I believe things because I want to believe them, and because they are comforting and pleasant? Will he not learn to cry, "Peace," to me, when there is no peace? By such a course I shall surround myself with a thick atmosphere of falsehood and fraud, and in that I must live. It may matter little to me, in my cloud-castle of sweet illusions and darling lies; but it matters much to Man that I have made my neighbours ready to deceive. The credulous man is father to the liar and the cheat; he lives in the bosom of this his family, and it is no marvel if he should become even as they are. So closely are our duties knit together, that whoso shall keep the whole law, and yet offend in one point, he is guilty of all.

To sum up: it is wrong always, everywhere, and for anyone, to believe anything upon insufficient evidence.

If a man, holding a belief which he was taught in childhood or persuaded of afterwards, keeps down and pushes away any doubts which arise about it in his mind, purposely avoids the reading of books and the company of men that call in question or discuss it, and regards as impious those questions which cannot easily be asked without disturbing it—the life of that man is one long sin against mankind.

If this judgment seems harsh when applied to those simple souls who have never known better, who have been brought up from the cradle with a horror of doubt, and taught that their eternal welfare depends on *what* they believe, then it leads to the very serious question, *Who hath made Israel to sin?*

It may be permitted me to fortify this judgment with the sentence of Milton[1]—

"A man may be a heretic in the truth; and if he believe things only because his pastor says so, or the assembly so determine, without knowing other reason, though his belief be true, yet the very truth he holds becomes his heresy."

And with this famous aphorism of Coleridge[2]—

"He who begins by loving Christianity better than Truth, will proceed by loving his own sect or Church better than Christianity, and end in loving himself better than all."

Inquiry into the evidence of a doctrine is not to be made once for all, and then taken as finally settled. It is never lawful to stifle a doubt; for either it can be honestly answered by means of the inquiry already made, or else it proves that the inquiry was not complete.

"But," says one, "I am a busy man; I have no time for the long course of study which would be necessary to make me in any degree a competent judge of certain questions, or even able to understand the nature of the arguments." Then he should have no time to believe.

II. THE WEIGHT OF AUTHORITY

Are we then to become universal sceptics, doubting everything, afraid always to put one foot before the other until we have personally tested the firmness of the road? Are we to deprive ourselves of the help and guidance of that vast body of knowledge which is daily growing upon the world, because neither we nor any other one person can possibly test a hundredth part of it by immediate experiment or observation, and because it would not be completely proved if we did? Shall we steal and tell lies because we have had no personal experience wide enough to justify the belief that it is wrong to do so?

There is no practical danger that such consequences will ever follow from scrupulous care and self-control in the matter of belief. Those men who have most nearly done their duty in this respect have found that certain great principles, and these most fitted for the guidance of life, have stood out more and more clearly in proportion to the care and honesty with which they were tested, and have acquired in this way a practical certainty. The beliefs about right and wrong which guide our actions in dealing with men in society, and the beliefs about physical nature which guide our actions in dealing with animate and inanimate bodies, these never suffer from investigation; they can take care of themselves, without being propped up by "acts of faith," the clamour of paid advocates, or the suppression of contrary evidence. More-

---

[1] *Areopagitica.*
[2] *Aids to Reflection.*

over there are many cases in which it is our duty to act upon probabilities, although the evidence is not such as to justify present belief; because it is precisely by such action, and by observation of its fruits, that evidence is got which may justify future belief. So that we have no reason to fear lest a habit of conscientious inquiry should paralyse the actions of our daily life.

But because it is not enough to say, "It is wrong to believe on unworthy evidence," without saying also what evidence is worthy, we shall now go on to inquire under what circumstances it is lawful to believe on the testimony of others; and then, further, we shall inquire more generally when and why we may believe that which goes beyond our own experience, or even beyond the experience of mankind.

In what cases, then, let us ask in the first place, is the testimony of a man unworthy of belief? He may say that which is untrue either knowingly or unknowingly. In the first case he is lying, and his moral character is to blame; in the second case he is ignorant or mistaken, and it is only his knowledge or his judgment which is in fault. In order that we may have the right to accept his testimony as ground for believing what he says, we must have reasonable grounds for trusting his *veracity*, that he is really trying to speak the truth so far as he knows it; his *knowledge*, that he has had opportunities of knowing the truth about this matter; and his *judgment*, that he has made proper use of those opportunities in coming to the conclusion which he affirms.

However plain and obvious these reasons may be, so that no man of ordinary intelligence, reflecting upon the matter, could fail to arrive at them, it is nevertheless true that a great many persons do habitually disregard them in weighing testimony. Of the two questions, equally important to the trustworthiness of a witness, "Is he dishonest?" and "May he be mistaken?" the majority of mankind are perfectly satisfied if *one* can, with some show of probability, be answered in the negative. The excellent moral character of a man is alleged as ground for accepting his statements about things which he cannot possibly have known. A Mohammedan, for example, will tell us that the character of his Prophet was so noble and majestic that it commands the reverence even of those who do not believe in his mission. So admirable was his moral teaching, so wisely put together the great social machine which he created, that his precepts have not only been accepted by a great portion of mankind, but have actually been obeyed. His institutions have on the one hand rescued the Negro from savagery, and on the other hand have taught civilization to the advancing West; and although the races which held the highest forms of his faith, and most fully embodied his mind and thought, have all been conquered and swept away by barbaric tribes, yet the history of their marvellous attainments remains as an imperishable glory to Islam. Are we to doubt the word of a man so great and so good? Can we suppose that this magnificent genius, this splendid moral hero, has lied to us about the most solemn and sacred matters? The testimony of Mohammed is clear, that there is but one God, and that he, Mohammed, is his prophet; that if we believe in him we shall enjoy everlasting felicity, but that if we do not we shall be damned. This testimony rests on the most awful of foundations, the revelation of heaven itself; for was he not visited by the angel Gabriel, as he fasted and prayed in his desert cave, and allowed to enter into the blessed fields of Paradise? Surely God is God and Mohammed is the Prophet of God.

What should we answer to this Mussulman? First, no doubt, we should be tempted to take exception against his view of the character of the Prophet and the uniformly beneficial influence of Islam: before we could go with him altogether in these matters it might seem that we should have to forget many terrible things of which we have heard or read. But if we chose to grant him all these assumptions, for the sake of argument, and because it is difficult both for the faithful and for infidels to discuss them fairly and without passion, still we should have something to say which takes away the ground of his belief, and therefore shows that it is wrong to entertain it. Namely this: the character of Mohammed is excellent evidence that he was honest and spoke the truth so far as he knew it; but it is no evidence at all that he knew what the truth was. What means could he have of knowing that the form which appeared to him to be the angel Gabriel was not a hallucination, and that his apparent visit to Paradise was not a dream? Grant that he himself was fully persuaded and honestly believed that he had the guidance of heaven, and was the vehicle of a supernatural revelation, how could he know that this strong conviction was not a mistake? Let us put ourselves in his place; we shall find that the more completely we endeavour to realize what passed through his mind, the more clearly we shall perceive that the Prophet could have had no adequate ground for the belief in his own inspiration. It is most probable that he himself never doubted of the matter, or thought of asking the question; but we are in the position of those to whom the question has been asked, and who are bound to answer it. It is known to medical observers that solitude and want of food are powerful means of producing delusion and of fostering a tendency to mental disease. Let us suppose, then, that I, like Mohammed, go into desert places to fast and pray; what things can happen to me which will give me the right to believe that I am divinely inspired? Suppose that I get information, apparently from a celestial visitor, which upon being tested is found to be correct. I cannot be sure, in the first place, that the celestial visitor is not a figment of my own mind, and that the information did not come to me, unknown at the time to my consciousness, through some subtle channel of sense. But if my visitor were a real visitor, and for a long time gave me information which was found to be trustworthy, this would indeed be good ground for trusting him in the future as to such matters as fall within human powers of verification; but it would not be ground for trusting his testimony as to any other matters. For although his tested character would justify me in believing that he spoke the truth so far as he knew, yet the same question would present itself—what ground is there for supposing that he knows?

Even if my supposed visitor had given me such information, subsequently verified by me, as proved him to have means of knowledge about verifiable matters far exceeding my own; this would not justify me in believing what he said about matters that are not at present capable of verification by man. It would be ground for interesting conjecture, and for the hope that, as the fruit of our patient inquiry, we might by-and-by attain to such a means of verification as should rightly turn conjecture into belief. For belief belongs to man, and to the guidance of human affairs: no belief is real unless it guide our actions, and those very actions supply a test of its truth.

But, it may be replied, the acceptance of Islam as a system is just that action which is prompted by belief in the mission of the Prophet, and which will serve for a test of its truth. Is it possible to believe that a system which has succeeded so well is really founded upon a delusion? Not only have individual saints found joy and peace in believing, and verified those spiritual experiences which are promised to the faithful, but nations also have been raised from savagery or barbarism to a higher social state. Surely we are at liberty to say that the belief has been acted upon, and that it has been verified.

It requires, however, but little consideration to show that what has really been verified is not at all the supernal character of the Prophet's mission, or the trustworthiness of his authority in matters which we ourselves cannot test, but only his practical wisdom in certain very mundane things. The fact that believers have found joy and peace in believing gives us the right to say that the doctrine is a comfortable doctrine, and pleasant to the soul; but it does not give us the right to say that it is true. And the question which our conscience is always asking about that which we are tempted to believe is not, "Is it comfortable and pleasant?" but, "Is it true?" That the Prophet preached certain doctrines, and predicted that spiritual comfort would be found in them, proves only his sympathy with human nature and his knowledge of it; but it does not prove his superhuman knowledge of theology.

And if we admit for the sake of argument (for it seems that we cannot do more) that the progress made by Moslem nations in certain cases was really due to the system formed and sent forth into the world by Mohammed, we are not at liberty to conclude from this that he was inspired to declare the truth about things which we cannot verify. We are only at liberty to infer the excellence of his moral precepts, or of the means which he devised for so working upon men as to get them obeyed, or of the social and political machinery which he set up. And it would require a great amount of careful examination into the history of those nations to determine which of these things had the greater share in the result. So that here again it is the Prophet's knowledge of human nature, and his sympathy with it, that are verified; not his divine inspiration, or his knowledge of theology.

If there were only one Prophet, indeed, it might well seem a difficult and even an ungracious task to decide upon what points we would trust him, and on what we would doubt his authority; seeing what help and furtherance all men have gained in all ages from those who saw more clearly, who felt more strongly, and who sought the truth with more single heart than their weaker brethren. But there is not only one Prophet; and while the consent of many upon that which, as men, they had real means of knowing and did know, has endured to the end, and been honourably built into the great fabric of human knowledge, the diverse witness of some about that which they did not and could not know remains as a warning to us that to exaggerate the prophetic authority is to misuse it, and to dishonour those who have sought only to help and further us after their power. It is hardly in human nature that a man should quite accurately gauge the limits of his own insight; but it is the duty of those who profit by his work to consider carefully where he may have been carried beyond it. If we must needs embalm his possible errors along with his solid achievements, and use his authority as an excuse for believing what he cannot have known, we make of his goodness an occasion to sin.

To consider only one other such witness: the followers of the Buddha have at least as much right to appeal to individual and social experience in support of the authority of the Eastern saviour. The special mark of his religion, it is said, that in which it has never been surpassed, is the comfort and consolation which it gives to the sick and sorrowful, the tender sympathy with which it soothes and assuages all the natural griefs of men. And surely no triumph of social morality can be greater or nobler than that which has kept nearly half the human race from persecuting in the name of religion. If we are to trust the accounts of his early followers, he believed himself to have come upon earth with a divine and cosmic mission to set rolling the wheel of the law. Being a prince, he divested himself of his kingdom, and of his free will became acquainted with misery, that he might learn how to meet and subdue it. Could such a man speak falsely about solemn things? And as for his knowledge, was he not a man miraculous with powers more than man's? He was born of woman without the help of man; he rose into the air and was transfigured before his kinsmen; at last he went up bodily into heaven from the top of Adam's Peak. Is not his word to be believed in when he testifies of heavenly things?

If there were only he, and no other, with such claims! But there is

Mohammed with his testimony; we cannot choose but listen to them both. The Prophet tells us that there is one God, and that we shall live for ever in joy or misery, according as we believe in the Prophet or not. The Buddha says that there is no God, and that we shall be annihilated by-and-by if we are good enough. Both cannot be infallibly inspired; one or the other must have been the victim of a delusion, and thought he knew that which he really did not know. Who shall dare to say which? and how can we justify ourselves in believing that the other was not also deluded?

We are led, then, to these judgments following. The goodness and greatness of a man do not justify us in accepting a belief upon the warrant of his authority, unless there are reasonable grounds for supposing that he knew the truth of what he was saying. And there can be no grounds for supposing that a man knows that which we, without ceasing to be men, could not be supposed to verify.

If a chemist tells me, who am no chemist, that a certain substance can be made by putting together other substances in certain proportions and subjecting them to a known process, I am quite justified in believing this upon his authority, unless I know anything against his character or his judgment. For his professional training is one which tends to encourage veracity and the honest pursuit of truth, and to produce a dislike of hasty conclusions and slovenly investigation. And I have reasonable ground for supposing that he knows the truth of what he is saying, for although I am no chemist, I can be made to understand so much of the methods and processes of the science as makes it conceivable to me that, without ceasing to be man, I might verify the statement. I may never actually verify it, or even see any experiment which goes towards verifying it; but still I have quite reason enough to justify me in believing that the verification is within the reach of human appliances and powers, and in particular that it has been actually performed by my informant. His result, the belief to which he has been led by his inquiries, is valid not only for himself but for others; it is watched and tested by those who are working in the same ground, and who know that no greater service can be rendered to science than the purification of accepted results from the errors which may have crept into them. It is in this way that the result becomes common property, a right object of belief, which is a social affair and matter of public business. Thus it is to be observed that his authority is valid because there are those who question it and verify it; that it is precisely this process of examining and purifying that keeps alive among investigators the love of that which shall stand all possible tests, the sense of public responsibility as of those whose work, if well done, shall remain as the enduring heritage of mankind.

But if my chemist tells me that an atom of oxygen has existed unaltered in weight and rate of vibration throughout all time, I have no right to believe this on his authority, for it is a thing which he cannot know without ceasing to be man. He may quite honestly believe that this statement is a fair inference from his experiments, but in that case his judgment is at fault. A very simple consideration of the character of experiments would show him that they never can lead to results of such a kind; that being themselves only approximate and limited, they cannot give us knowledge which is exact and universal. No eminence of character and genius can give a man authority enough to justify us in believing him when he makes statements implying exact or universal knowledge.

Again, an Arctic explorer may tell us that in a given latitude and longitude he has experienced such and such a degree of cold, that the sea was of such a depth, and the ice of such a character. We should be quite right to believe him, in the absence of any stain upon his veracity. It is conceivable that we might, without ceasing to be men, go there and verify his statement; it can be tested by the witness of his companions, and there is adequate ground for supposing that he knows the truth of what he is saying. But if an old whaler tells us that the ice is three hundred feet thick all the way up to the Pole, we shall not be justified in believing him. For although the statement may be capable of verification by man, it is certainly not capable of verification by *him*, with any means and appliances which he has possessed; and he must have persuaded himself of the truth of it by some means which does not attach any credit to his testimony. Even if, therefore, the matter affirmed is within the reach of human knowledge, we have no right to accept it upon authority unless it is within the reach of our informant's knowledge.

What shall we say of that authority, more venerable and august than any individual witness, the time-honoured tradition of the human race? An atmosphere of beliefs and conceptions has been formed by the labours and struggles of our forefathers, which enables us to breathe amid the various and complex circumstances of our life. It is around and about us and within us; we cannot think except in the forms and processes of thought which it supplies. Is it possible to doubt and to test it? and if possible, is it right?

We shall find reason to answer that it is not only possible and right, but our bounden duty; that the main purpose of the tradition itself is to supply us with the means of asking questions, of testing and inquiring into things; that if we misuse it, and take it as a collection of cut-and-dried statements, to be accepted without further inquiry, we are not only injuring ourselves here, but by refusing to do our part towards the building up of the fabric which shall be inherited by our children, we are tending to cut off ourselves and our race from the human line.

Let us first take care to distinguish a kind of tradition which especially requires to be examined and called in question, because it especially shrinks from inquiry. Suppose that a medicine-man in Central Africa tells his tribe that a certain powerful medicine in his tent will be propitiated if they kill their cattle; and that the tribe believe him. Whether the medicine was propitiated or not, there are no means of verifying, but the cattle are gone. Still the belief may be kept up in the tribe that propitiation has been effected in this way; and in a later generation it will be all the easier for another medicine-man to persuade them to a similar act. Here the only reason for belief is that everybody has believed the thing for so long that it must be true. And yet the belief was founded on fraud, and has been propagated by credulity. That man will undoubtedly do right, and be a friend of men, who shall call it in question and see that there is no evidence for it, help his neighbours to see as he does, and even, if need be, go into the holy tent and break the medicine.

The rule which should guide us in such cases is simple and obvious enough: that the aggregate testimony of our neighbours is subject to the same conditions as the testimony of any one of them. Namely, we have no right to believe a thing true because everybody says so, unless there are good grounds for believing that some one person at least has the means of knowing what is true, and is speaking the truth so far as he knows it. However many nations and generations of men are brought into the witness-box, they cannot testify to anything which they do not know. Every man who has accepted the statement from somebody else, without himself testing and verifying it, is out of court; his word is worth nothing at all. And when we get back at last to the true birth and beginning of the statement, two serious questions must be disposed of in regard to him who first made it: was he mistaken in thinking that he *knew* about this matter, or was he lying?

This last question is unfortunately a very actual and practical one even to us at this day and in this country. We have no occasion to go to La Salette, or to Central Africa, or to Lourdes, for examples of immoral and debasing superstition. It is only too possible for a child to grow up in London surrounded by an atmosphere of beliefs fit only for the savage, which have in our own time been founded in fraud and propagated by credulity.

Laying aside, then, such tradition as is handed on without testing by successive generations, let us consider that which is truly built up out of the common experience of mankind. This great fabric is for the guidance of our thoughts, and through them of our actions, both in the moral and in the material world. In the moral world, for example, it gives us the conceptions of right in general, of justice, of truth, of beneficence, and the like. These are given as conceptions, not as statements or propositions; they answer to certain definite instincts, which are certainly within us, however they came there. That it is right to be beneficent is matter of immediate personal experience; for when a man retires within himself and there finds something, wider and more lasting than his solitary personality, which says, "I want to do right," as well as, "I want to do good to man," he can verify by direct observation that one instinct is founded upon and agrees fully with the other. And it is his duty so to verify this and all similar statements.

The tradition says also, at a definite place and time, that such and such actions are just, or true, or beneficent. For all such rules a further inquiry is necessary, since they are sometimes established by an authority other than that of the moral sense founded on experience. Until recently, the moral tradition of our own country—and indeed of all Europe—taught that it was beneficent to give money indiscriminately to beggars. But the questioning of this rule, and investigation into it, led men to see that true beneficence is that which helps a man to do the work which he is most fitted for, not that which keeps and encourages him in idleness; and that to neglect this distinction in the present is to prepare pauperism and misery for the future. By this testing and discussion, not only has practice been purified and made more beneficent, but the very conception of beneficence has been made wider and wiser. Now here the great social heirloom consists of two parts: the instinct of beneficence, which makes a certain side of our nature, when predominant, wish to do good to men; and the intellectual conception of beneficence, which we can compare with any proposed course of conduct and ask, "Is this beneficent or not?" By the continual asking and answering of such questions the conception grows in breadth and distinctness, and the instinct becomes strengthened and purified. It appears then that the great use of the conception, the intellectual part of the heirloom, is to enable us to ask questions; that it grows and is kept straight by means of these questions; and if we do not use it for that purpose we shall gradually lose it altogether, and be left with a mere code of regulations which cannot rightly be called morality at all.

Such considerations apply even more obviously and clearly, if possible, to the store of beliefs and conceptions which our fathers have amassed for us in respect of the material world. We are ready to laugh at the rule of thumb of the Australian, who continues to tie his hatchet to the side of the handle, although the Birmingham fitter has made a hole on purpose for him to put the handle in. His people have tied up hatchets so for ages: who is he that he should set himself up against their wisdom? He has sunk so low that he cannot do what some of them must have done in the far distant past—call in question an established usage, and invent or learn something better. Yet here, in the dim beginning of knowledge, where science and art are one, we find only the same simple rule which applies to the highest and deepest growths of that cosmic Tree; to its loftiest flower-tipped branches as well as to the profoundest of its hidden roots; the rule, namely, that what is stored up and handed down to us is rightly used by those who act as the makers acted, when they stored it up; those who use it to ask further questions, to examine, to investigate; who try honestly and solemnly to find out what is the right way of looking at things and of dealing with them.

A question rightly asked is already half answered, said Jacobi; we may add that the method of solution is the other half of the answer, and that the actual result counts for nothing by the side of these two. For an example let us go to the telegraph, where theory and practice, grown each to years of discretion, are marvellously wedded for the fruitful service of men. Ohm found that the strength of an electric current is directly proportional to the strength of the battery which produces it, and inversely as the length of the wire along which it has to travel. This is called Ohm's law; but the result, regarded as a statement to be believed, is not the valuable part of it. The first half is the question: what relation holds good between these quantities? So put, the question involves already the conception of strength of current, and of strength of battery, as quantities to be measured and compared; it hints clearly that these are the things to be attended to in the study of electric currents. The second half is the method of investigation; how to measure these quantities, what instruments are required for the experiment, and how are they to be used? The student who begins to learn about electricity is not asked to believe in Ohm's law: he is made to understand the question, he is placed before the apparatus, and he is taught to verify it. He learns to do things, not to think he knows things; to use instruments and to ask questions, not to accept a traditional statement. The question which required a genius to ask it rightly is answered by a tyro. If Ohm's law were suddenly lost and forgotten by all men, while the question and the method of solution remained, the result could be rediscovered in an hour. But the result by itself, if known to a people who could not comprehend the value of the question or the means of solving it, would be like a watch in the hands of a savage who could not wind it up, or an iron steamship worked by Spanish engineers.

In regard, then, to the sacred tradition of humanity, we learn that it consists, not in propositions or statements which are to be accepted and believed on the authority of the tradition, but in questions rightly asked, in conceptions which enable us to ask further questions, and in methods of answering questions. The value of all these things depends on their being tested day by day. The very sacredness of the precious deposit imposes upon us the duty and the responsibility of testing it, of purifying and enlarging it to the utmost of our power. He who makes use of its results to stifle his own doubts, or to hamper the inquiry of others, is guilty of a sacrilege which centuries shall never be able to blot out. When the labours and questionings of honest and brave men shall have built up the fabric of known truth to a glory which we in this generation can neither hope for nor imagine, in that pure and holy temple he shall have no part nor lot, but his name and his works shall be cast out into the darkness of oblivion for ever.

III. THE LIMITS OF INFERENCE

The question in what cases we may believe that which goes beyond our experience, is a very large and delicate one, extending to the whole range of scientific method, and requiring a considerable increase in the application of it before it can be answered with anything approaching to completeness. But one rule, lying on the threshold of the subject, of extreme simplicity and vast practical importance, may here be touched upon and shortly laid down.

A little reflection will show us that every belief, even the simplest and most fundamental, goes beyond experience when regarded as a guide to our actions. A burnt child dreads the fire, because it believes that the fire will burn it to-day just as it did yesterday; but this belief goes beyond experience, and assumes that the unknown fire of to-day is like the known fire of yesterday. Even the belief that the child was burnt yesterday goes beyond *present* experience, which contains only the memory of a burning, and not the burning itself; it assumes, therefore, that this memory is trustworthy, although we know that a memory may often be mistaken. But if it is to be used as a guide to action, as a hint of what the future is to be, it must assume something about that future, namely, that it will be consistent with the supposition that the burning really took place yesterday; which is going beyond experience. Even the fundamental "I am," which cannot be doubted, is no guide to action until it takes to itself "I shall be," which goes beyond experience. The question is not, therefore, "May we believe what goes beyond experience?" for this is involved in the very nature of belief; but "How far and in what manner may we add to our experience in forming our beliefs?"

And an answer, of utter simplicity and universality, is suggested by the example we have taken: a burnt child dreads the fire. We may go beyond experience by assuming that what we do not know is like what we do know; or, in other words, we may add to our experience on the assumption of a uniformity in nature. What this uniformity precisely is, how we grow in the knowledge of it from generation to generation, these are questions which for the present we lay aside, being content to examine two instances which may serve to make plainer the nature of the rule.

From certain observations made with the spectroscope, we infer the existence of hydrogen in the sun. By looking into the spectroscope when the sun is shining on its slit, we see certain definite bright lines: and experiments made upon bodies on the earth have taught us that when these bright lines are seen hydrogen is the source of them. We assume, then, that the unknown bright lines in the sun are like the known bright lines of the laboratory, and that hydrogen in the sun behaves as hydrogen under similar circumstances would behave on the earth.

But are we not trusting our spectroscope too much? Surely, having found it to be trustworthy for terrestrial substances, where its statements can be verified by man, we are justified in accepting its testimony in other like cases; but not when it gives us information about things in the sun, where its testimony cannot be directly verified by man?

Certainly, we want to know a little more before this inference can be justified; and fortunately we do know this. The spectroscope testifies to exactly the same thing in the two cases; namely, that light-vibrations of a certain rate are being sent through it. Its construction is such that if it were wrong about this in one case, it would be wrong in the other. When we come to look into the matter, we find that we have really assumed the matter of the sun to be like the matter of the earth, made up of a certain number of distinct substances; and that each of these, when very hot, has a distinct rate of vibration, by which it may be recognized and singled out from the rest. But this is the kind of assumption which we are justified in using when we add to our experience. It is an assumption of uniformity in nature, and can only be checked by comparison with many similar assumptions which we have to make in other such cases.

But is this a true belief, of the existence of hydrogen in the sun? Can it help in the right guidance of human action?

Certainly not, if it is accepted on unworthy grounds, and without some understanding of the process by which it is got at. But when this process is taken in as the ground of the belief, it becomes a very serious and practical matter. For if there is no hydrogen in the sun, the spectroscope—that is to say, the measurement of rates of vibration—must be an uncertain guide in recognizing different substances; and consequently it ought not to be used in chemical analysis—in assaying, for example—to the great saving of time, trouble, and money. Whereas the acceptance of the spectroscopic method as trustworthy has enriched us not only with new metals, which is a great thing, but with new processes of investigation, which is vastly greater.

For another example, let us consider the way in which we infer the truth of an historical event—say the siege of Syracuse in the Peloponnesian war. Our experience is that manuscripts exist which are said to be and which call themselves manuscripts of the history of Thucydides; that in other manuscripts, stated to be by later historians, he is described as living during the time of the war; and that books, supposed to date from the revival of learning, tell us how these manuscripts had been preserved and were then acquired. We find also that men do not, as a rule, forge books and histories without a special motive; we assume that in this respect men in the past were like men in the present; and we observe that in this case no special motive was present. That is, we add to our experience on the assumption of a uniformity in the characters of men. Because our knowledge of this uniformity is far less complete and exact than our knowledge of that which obtains in physics, inferences of the historical kind are more precarious and less exact than inferences in many other sciences.

But if there is any special reason to suspect the character of the persons who wrote or transmitted certain books, the case becomes altered. If a group of documents give internal evidence that they were produced among people who forged books in the names of others, and who, in describing events, suppressed those things which did not suit them, while they amplified such as did suit them; who not only committed these crimes, but gloried in them as proofs of humility and zeal; then we must say that upon such documents no true historical inference can be founded, but only unsatisfactory conjecture.

We may, then, add to our experience on the assumption of a uniformity in nature; we may fill in our picture of what is and has been, as experience gives it us, in such a way as to make the whole consistent with this uniformity. And practically demonstrative inference—that which gives us a right to believe in the result of it—is a clear showing that in no other way than by the truth of this result can the uniformity of nature be saved.

No evidence, therefore, can justify us in believing the truth of a statement which is contrary to, or outside of, the uniformity of nature. If our experience is such that it cannot be filled up consistently with uniformity, all we have a right to conclude is that there is something wrong somewhere; but the possibility of inference is taken away; we must rest in our experience, and not go beyond it at all. If an event really happened which was not a part of the uniformity of nature, it would have two properties: no evidence could give the right to believe it to any except those whose actual experience it was; and no inference worthy of belief could be founded upon it at all.

Are we then bound to believe that nature is absolutely and universally uniform? Certainly not; we have no right to believe anything of this kind. The rule only tells us that in forming beliefs which go beyond our experience, we may make the assumption that nature is practically uniform so far as we are concerned. Within the range of human action and verification, we may form, by help of this assumption, actual beliefs; beyond it, only those hypotheses which serve for the more accurate asking of questions.

To sum up:—

We may believe what goes beyond our experience, only when it is inferred from that experience by the assumption that what we do not know is like what we know.

We may believe the statement of another person, when there is reasonable ground for supposing that he knows the matter of which he speaks, and that he is speaking the truth so far as he knows it.

It is wrong in all cases to believe on insufficient evidence; and where it is presumption to doubt and to investigate, there it is worse than presumption to believe.

William James was born in New York City in 1842. He received an M.D. from Harvard in 1870 and, two years later, began his teaching career at Harvard as a lecturer in anatomy and physiology. From 1880 until his death in 1910, he taught philosophy and psychology.

His *Principles of Psychology* (2 vols., 1890) remains one of his major works. It was followed by *The Will to Believe and Other Essays* (1897), *The Varieties of Religious Experience* (1902), *Pragmatism: A New Name for Some Old Ways of Thinking* (1907), *A Pluralistic Universe* (1909), and *Essays in Radical Empiricism* (1912).

"The Will to Believe" was originally an address delivered before the Philosophical Clubs of Yale and Brown Universities. It was first published in the *New World*, June 1896, and then, in 1897, reprinted in the above-mentioned collection. It will be noted that James explicitly refers to Clifford's essay, reprinted above.

The Will to Believe

In the recently published Life by Leslie Stephen of his brother, Fitz-James, there is an account of a school to which the latter went when he was a boy. The teacher, a certain Mr. Guest, used to converse with his pupils in this wise: "Gurney, what is the difference between justification and santification?—Stephen, prove the omnipotence of God!" etc. In the midst of our Harvard freethinking and indifference we are prone to imagine that here at your good old orthodox College conversation continues to be somewhat upon this order; and to show you that we at Harvard have not lost all interest in these vital subjects, I have brought with me to-night something like a sermon on justification by faith to read to you,—I mean an essay in justification *of* faith, a defence of our right to adopt a believing attitude in religious matters, in spite of the fact that our merely logical intellect may not have been coerced. "The Will to Believe," accordingly, is the title of my paper.

I have long defended to my own students the lawfulness of voluntarily adopted faith; but as soon as they have got well imbued with the logical spirit, they have as a rule refused to admit my contention to be lawful philosophically, even though in point of fact they were personally all the time chock-full of some faith or other themselves. I am all the while, however, so profoundly convinced that my own position is correct, that your invitation has seemed to me a good occasion to make my statements more clear. Perhaps your minds will be more open than those with which I have hitherto had to deal. I will be as little technical as I can, though I must begin by setting up some technical distinctions that will help us in the end.

I

Let us give the name of *hypothesis* to anything that may be proposed to our belief; and just as the electricians speak of live and dead wires, let us speak of any hypothesis as either *live* or *dead*. A live hypothesis is one which appeals as a real possibility to him to whom it is proposed. If I ask you to believe in the Mahdi, the notion makes no electric connection with your nature,—it refuses to scintillate with any credibility at all. As an hypothesis it is completely dead. To an Arab, however (even if he be not one of the Mahdi's followers), the hypothesis is among the mind's possibilities: it is alive. This shows that deadness and liveness in an hypothesis are not intrinsic properties, but relations to the individual thinker. They are measured by his willingness to act. The maximum of liveness in an hypothesis means willingness to act irrevocably. Practically, that means belief; but there is some believing tendency wherever there is willingness to act at all.

Next, let us call the decision between two hypotheses an *option*. Options may be of several kinds. They may be—1, *living* or *dead;* 2, *forced* or *avoidable;* 3, *momentous* or *trivial;* and for our purposes we may call an option a *genuine* option when it is of the forced, living, and momentous kind.

1. A living option is one in which both hypotheses are live ones. If I say to you: "Be a theosophist or be a Mohammedan," it is probably a dead option, because for you neither hypothesis is likely to be alive. But if I say: "Be an agnostic or be a Christian," it is otherwise: trained as you are, each hypothesis makes some appeal, however small, to your belief.

2. Next, if I say to you: "Choose between going out with your umbrella or without it," I do not offer you a genuine option, for it is not forced. You can easily avoid it by not going out at all. Similarly, if I say, "Either love me or hate me," "Either call my theory true or call it false," your option is avoidable. You may remain indifferent to me, neither loving nor hating, and you may decline to offer any judgment as to my theory. But if I say, "Either accept this truth or go without it," I put on you a forced option, for there is no standing place outside of the alternative. Every dilemma based on a complete logical disjunction, with no possibility of not choosing, is an option of this forced kind.

3. Finally, if I were Dr. Nansen and proposed to you to join my North Pole expedition, your option would be momentous; for this would probably

be your only similar opportunity, and your choice now would either exclude you from the North Pole sort of immortality altogether or put at least the chance of it into your hands. He who refuses to embrace a unique opportunity loses the prize as surely as if he tried and failed. *Per contra*, the option is trivial when the opportunity is not unique, when the stake is insignificant, or when the decision is reversible if it later prove unwise. Such trivial options abound in the scientific life. A chemist finds an hypothesis live enough to spend a year in its verification: he believes in it to that extent. But if his experiments prove inconclusive either way, he is quit for his loss of time, no vital harm being done.

It will facilitate our discussion if we keep all these distinctions well in mind.

II

The next matter to consider is the actual psychology of human opinion. When we look at certain facts, it seems as if our passional and volitional nature lay at the root of all our convictions. When we look at others, it seems as if they could do nothing when the intellect had once said its say. Let us take the latter facts up first.

Does it not seem preposterous on the very face of it to talk of our opinions being modifiable at will? Can our will either help or hinder our intellect in its perceptions of truth? Can we, by just willing it, believe that Abraham Lincoln's existence is a myth, and that the portraits of him in McClure's Magazine are all of some one else? Can we, by any effort of our will, or by any strength of wish that it were true, believe ourselves well and about when we are roaring with rheumatism in bed, or feel certain that the sum of the two one-dollar bills in our pocket must be a hundred dollars? We can *say* any of these things, but we are absolutely impotent to believe them; and of just such things is the whole fabric of the truths that we do believe in made up,—matters of fact, immediate or remote, as Hume said, and relations between ideas, which are either there or not there for us if we see them so, and which if not there cannot be put there by any action of our own.

In Pascal's Thoughts there is a celebrated passage known in literature as Pascal's wager. In it he tries to force us into Christianity by reasoning as if our concern with truth resembled our concern with the stakes in a game of chance. Translated freely his words are these: You must either believe or not believe that God is—which will you do? Your human reason cannot say. A game is going on between you and the nature of things which at the day of judgment will bring out either heads or tails. Weigh what your gains and your losses would be if you should stake all you have on heads, or God's existence: if you win in such case, you gain eternal beatitude; if you lose, you lose nothing at all. If there were an infinity of chances, and only one for God in this wager, still you ought to stake your all on God; for though you surely risk a finite loss by this procedure, any finite loss is reasonable, even a certain one is reasonable, if there is but the possibility of infinite gain. Go, then, and take holy water, and have masses said; belief will come and stupefy your scruples,—*Cela vous fera croire et vous abêtira.* Why should you not? At bottom, what have you to lose?

You probably feel that when religious faith expresses itself thus, in the language of the gaming-table, it is put to its last trumps. Surely Pascal's own personal belief in masses and holy water had far other springs; and this celebrated page of his is but an argument for others, a last desperate snatch at a weapon against the hardness of the unbelieving heart. We feel that a faith in masses and holy water adopted wilfully after such a mechanical calculation would lack the inner soul of faith's reality; and if we were ourselves in the place of the Deity, we should probably take particular pleasure in cutting off believers of this pattern from their infinite reward. It is evident that unless there be some pre-existing tendency to believe in masses and holy water, the option offered to the will by Pascal is not a living option. Certainly no Turk ever took to masses and holy water on its account; and even to us Protestants these means of salvation seem such foregone impossibilities that Pascal's logic, invoked for them specifically, leaves us unmoved. As well might the Mahdi write to us, saying, "I am the Expected One whom God has created in his effulgence. You shall be infinitely happy if you confess me; otherwise you shall be cut off from the light of the sun. Weigh, then, your infinite gain if I am genuine against your finite sacrifice if I am not!" His logic would be that of Pascal; but he would vainly use it on us, for the hypothesis he offers us is dead. No tendency to act on it exists in us to any degree.

The talk of believing by our volition seems, then, from one point of view, simply silly. From another point of view it is worse than silly, it is vile. When one turns to the magnificent edifice of the physical sciences, and sees how it was reared; what thousands of disinterested moral lives of men lie buried in its mere foundations; what patience and postponement, what choking down of preference, what submission to the icy laws of outer fact are wrought into its very stones and mortar; how absolutely impersonal it stands in its vast augustness,—then how besotted and contemptible seems every little sentimentalist who comes blowing his voluntary smoke-wreaths, and pretending to decide things from out of his private dream! Can we wonder if those bred in the rugged and manly school of science should feel like spewing such subjectivism out of their mouths? The whole system of loyalties which grow up in the schools of science go dead against its toleration; so that it is only natural that those who have caught the scientific fever should pass over to the opposite extreme, and write sometimes as if the incorruptibly truthful intellect ought positively to prefer bitterness and unacceptableness to the heart in its cup.

> It fortifies my soul to know
> That, though I perish, Truth is so—

sings Clough, while Huxley exclaims: "My only consolation lies in the reflection that, however bad our posterity may become, so far as they hold by the plain rule of not pretending to believe what they have no reason to believe, because it may be to their advantage so to pretend [the word 'pretend' is surely here redundant], they will not have reached the lowest depth of immorality." And that delicious *enfant terrible* Clifford writes: "Belief is desecrated when given to unproved and unquestioned statements for the solace and private pleasure of the believer. . . . Whoso would deserve well of his fellows in this matter will guard the purity of his belief with a very fanaticism of jealous care, lest at any time it should rest on an unworthy object, and catch a stain which can never be wiped away. . . . If [a] belief has been accepted on insufficient evidence [even though the belief be true, as Clifford on the same page explains] the pleasure is a stolen one. . . . It is sinful because it is stolen in defiance of our duty to mankind. That duty is to guard ourselves from such beliefs as from a pestilence which may shortly master our own body and then spread to the rest of the town. . . . It is wrong always, everywhere, and for every one, to believe anything upon insufficient evidence."

III

All this strikes one as healthy, even when expressed, as by Clifford, with somewhat too much of robustious pathos in the voice. Free-will and simple wishing do seem, in the matter of our credences, to be only fifth wheels to the coach. Yet if any one should thereupon assume that intellectual insight is what remains after wish and will and sentimental preference have taken wing, or that pure reason is what then settles our opinions, he would fly quite as directly in the teeth of the facts.

It is only our already dead hypotheses that our willing nature is unable to bring to life again. But what has made them dead for us is for the most part a previous action of our willing nature of an antagonistic kind. When I say "willing nature," I do not mean only such deliberate volitions as may have set up habits of belief that we cannot now escape from,—I mean all such factors of belief as fear and hope, prejudice and passion, imitation and partisanship, the circumpressure of our caste and set. As a matter of fact we find ourselves believing, we hardly know how or why. Mr. Balfour gives the name of "authority" to all those influences, born of the intellectual climate, that make hypotheses possible or impossible for us, alive or dead. Here in this room, we all of us believe in molecules and the conservation of energy, in democracy and necessary progress, in Protestant Christianity and the duty of fighting for "the doctrine of the immortal Monroe," all for no reasons worthy of the name. We see into these matters with no more inner clearness, and probably with much less, than any disbeliever in them might possess. His unconventionality would probably have some grounds to show for its conclusions; but for us, not insight, but the *prestige* of the opinions, is what makes the spark shoot from them and light up our sleeping magazines of faith. Our reason is quite satisfied, in nine hundred and ninety-nine cases out of every thousand of us, if it can find a few arguments that will do to recite in case our credulity is criticised by some one else. Our faith is faith in some one else's faith, and in the greatest matters this is most the case. Our belief in truth itself, for instance, that there is a truth, and that our minds and it are made for each other,—what is it but a passionate affirmation of desire, in which our social system backs us up? We want to have a truth; we want to believe that our experiments and studies and discussions must put us in a continually better and better position towards it; and on this line we agree to fight out our thinking lives. But if a pyrrhonistic sceptic asks us *how we know* all this, can our logic find a reply? No! certainly it cannot. It is just one volition against another,— we willing to go in for life upon a trust or assumption which he, for his part, does not care to make.[1]

As a rule we disbelieve all facts and theories for which we have no use. Clifford's cosmic emotions find no use for Christian feelings. Huxley belabors the bishops because there is no use for sacerdotalism in his scheme of life. Newman, on the contrary, goes over to Romanism, and finds all sorts of reasons good for staying there, because a priestly system is for him an organic need and delight. Why do so few "scientists" even look at the evidence for telepathy, so called? Because they think, as a leading biologist, now dead, once said to me, that even if such a thing were true, scientists ought to band together to keep it suppressed and concealed. It would undo the uniformity of Nature and all sorts of other things without which scientists cannot carry on their pursuits. But if this very man had been shown something which as a scientist he might *do* with telepathy, he might not only have examined the evidence, but even have found it good enough. This very law which the logicians would impose upon us— if I may give the name of logicians to those who would rule out our willing nature here—is based on nothing but their own natural wish to exclude all elements for which they, in their professional quality of logicians, can find no use.

Evidently, then, our non-intellectual nature does influence our convic-

[1] Compare the admirable p. 310 in S. H. Hodgson's *Time and Space*, London, 1865.

tions. There are passional tendencies and volitions which run before and others which come after belief, and it is only the latter that are too late for the fair; and they are not too late when the previous passional work has been already in their own direction. Pascal's argument, instead of being powerless, then seems a regular clincher, and is the last stroke needed to make our faith in masses and holy water complete. The state of things is evidently far from simple; and pure insight and logic, whatever they might do ideally, are not the only things that really do produce our creeds.

IV

Our next duty, having recognized this mixed-up state of affairs, is to ask whether it be simply reprehensible and pathological, or whether, on the contrary, we must treat it as a normal element in making up our minds. The thesis I defend is, briefly stated, this: *Our passional nature not only lawfully may, but must, decide an option between propositions, whenever it is a genuine option that cannot by its nature be decided on intellectual grounds; for to say, under such circumstances, "Do not decide, but leave the question open," is itself a passional decision,—just like deciding yes or no,—and is attended with the same risk of losing the truth.* The thesis thus abstractly expressed will, I trust, soon become quite clear. But I must first indulge in a bit more of preliminary work.

V

It will be observed that for the purposes of this discussion we are on "dogmatic" ground,—ground, I mean, which leaves systematic philosophical scepticism altogether out of account. The postulate that there is truth, and that it is the destiny of our minds to attain it, we are deliberately resolving to make, though the sceptic will not make it. We part company with him, therefore, absolutely, at this point. But the faith that truth exists, and that our minds can find it, may be held in two ways. We may talk of the *empiricist* way and of the *absolutist* way of believing in truth. The absolutists in this matter say that we not only can attain to knowing truth, but we can *know when* we have attained to knowing it; while the empiricists think that although we may attain it, we cannot infallibly know when. To *know* is one thing, and to know for certain *that* we know is another. One may hold to the first being possible without the second; hence the empiricists and the absolutists, although neither of them is a sceptic in the usual philosophic sense of the term, show very different degrees of dogmatism in their lives.

If we look at the history of opinions, we see that the empiricist tendency has largely prevailed in science, while in philosophy the absolutist tendency has had everything its own way. The characteristic sort of happiness, indeed, which philosophies yield has mainly consisted in the conviction felt by each successive school or system that by it bottom-certitude had been attained. "Other philosophies are collections of opinions, mostly false; *my* philosophy gives standing-ground forever,"—who does not recognize in this the key-note of every system worthy of the name? A system, to be a system at all, must come as a *closed* system, reversible in this or that detail, perchance, but in its essential features never!

Scholastic orthodoxy, to which one must always go when one wishes to find perfectly clear statement, has beautifully elaborated this absolutist conviction in a doctrine which it calls that of "objective evidence." If, for example, I am unable to doubt that I now exist before you, that two is less than three, or that if all men are mortal then I am mortal too, it is because these things illumine my intellect irresistibly. The final ground of this objective evidence possessed by certain propositions is the *adaequatio intellectûs nostri cum rê.* The certitude it brings involves an *aptitudinem ad extorquendum certum assensum* on the part of the truth envisaged, and on the side of the subject a *quietem in cognitione,* when once the object is mentally received, that leaves no possibility of doubt behind; and in the whole transaction nothing operates but the *entitas ipsa* of the object and the *entitas ipsa* of the mind. We slouchy modern thinkers dislike to talk in Latin,—indeed, we dislike to talk in set terms at all; but at bottom our own state of mind is very much like this whenever we uncritically abandon ourselves: You believe in objective evidence, and I do. Of some things we feel that we are certain: we know, and we know that we do know. There is something that gives a click inside of us, a bell that strikes twelve, when the hands of our mental clock have swept the dial and meet over the meridian hour. The greatest empiricists among us are only empiricists on reflection: when left to their instincts, they dogmatize like infallible popes. When the Cliffords tell us how sinful it is to be Christians on such "insufficient evidence," insufficiency is really the last thing they have in mind. For them the evidence is absolutely sufficient, only it makes the other way. They believe so completely in an anti-christian order of the universe that there is no living option: Christianity is a dead hypothesis from the start.

VI

But now, since we are all such absolutists by instinct, what in our quality of students of philosophy ought we to do about the fact? Shall we espouse and indorse it? Or shall we treat it as a weakness of our nature from which we must free ourselves, if we can?

I sincerely believe that the latter course is the only one we can follow as reflective men. Objective evidence and certitude are doubtless very fine ideals to play with, but where on this moonlit and dream-visited planet are they found? I am, therefore, myself a complete empiricist so far as my theory of human knowledge goes. I live, to be sure, by the practical faith that we must go on experiencing and thinking over our experience, for only thus can our opinions grow more true; but to hold any one of them —I absolutely do not care which—as if it never could be reinterpretable or corrigible, I believe to be a tremendously mistaken attitude, and I think that the whole history of philosophy will bear me out. There is but one indefectibly certain truth, and that is the truth that pyrrhonistic scepticism itself leaves standing,—the truth that the present phenomenon of consciousness exists. That, however, is the bare starting-point of knowledge, the mere admission of a stuff to be philosophized about. The various philosophies are but so many attempts at expressing what this stuff really is. And if we repair to our libraries what disagreement do we discover! Where is a certainly true answer found? Apart from abstract propositions of comparison (such as two and two are the same as four), propositions which tell us nothing by themselves about concrete reality, we find no proposition ever regarded by any one as evidently certain that has not either been called a falsehood, or at least had its truth sincerely questioned by some one else. The transcending of the axioms of geometry, not in play but in earnest, by certain of our contemporaries (as Zöllner and Charles H. Hinton), and the rejection of the whole Aristotelian logic by the Hegelians, are striking instances in point.

No concrete test of what is really true has ever been agreed upon. Some make the criterion external to the moment of perception, putting it either in revelation, the *consensus gentium,* the instincts of the heart, or the systematized experience of the race. Others make the perceptive moment its own test,—Descartes, for instance, with his clear and distinct ideas guaranteed by the veracity of God; Reid with his "common-sense"; and Kant with his forms of synthetic judgment *a priori.* The inconceivability of the opposite; the capacity to be verified by sense; the possession of complete organic unity or self-relation, realized when a thing is its own other,—are standards which, in turn, have been used. The much lauded objective evidence is never triumphantly there; it is a mere aspiration or *Grenzbegriff,* marking the infinitely remote ideal of our thinking life. To claim that certain truths now possess it, is simply to say that when you think them true and they *are* true, then their evidence is objective, otherwise it is not. But practically one's conviction that the evidence one goes by is of the real objective brand, is only one more subjective opinion added to the lot. For what a contradictory array of opinions have objective evidence and absolute certitude been claimed! The world is rational through and through,— its existence is an ultimate brute fact; there is a personal God,—a personal God is inconceivable; there is an extra-mental physical world immediately known,—the mind can only know its own ideas; a moral imperative exists,

—obligation is only the resultant of desires; a permanent spiritual principle is in every one,—there are only shifting states of mind; there is an endless chain of causes,—there is an absolute first cause; an eternal necessity,—a freedom; a purpose,—no purpose; a primal One,—a primal Many; a universal continuity,—an essential discontinuity in things; an infinity,—no infinity. There is this,—there is that; there is indeed nothing which some one has not thought absolutely true, while his neighbor deemed it absolutely false; and not an absolutist among them seems ever to have considered that the trouble may all the time be essential, and that the intellect, even with truth directly in its grasp, may have no infallible signal for knowing whether it be truth or no. When, indeed, one remembers that the most striking practical application to life of the doctrine of objective certitude has been the conscientious labors of the Holy Office of the Inquisition, one feels less tempted than ever to lend the doctrine a respectful ear.

But please observe, now, that when as empiricists we give up the doctrine of objective certitude, we do not thereby give up the quest or hope of truth itself. We still pin our faith on its existence, and still believe that we gain an ever better position towards it by systematically continuing to roll up experiences and think. Our great difference from the scholastic lies in the way we face. The strength of his system lies in the principles, the origin, the *terminus a quo* of his thought; for us the strength is in the outcome, the upshot, the *terminus ad quem*. Not where it comes from but what it leads to is to decide. It matters not to an empiricist from what quarter an hypothesis may come to him: he may have acquired it by fair means or by foul; passion may have whispered or accident suggested it; but if the total drift of thinking continues to confirm it, that is what he means by its being true.

VII

One more point, small but important, and our preliminaries are done. There are two ways of looking at our duty in the matter of opinion,—ways entirely different, and yet ways about whose difference the theory of knowledge seems hitherto to have shown very little concern. *We must know the truth;* and *we must avoid error.*—these are our first and great commandments as would-be knowers; but they are not two ways of stating an identical commandment, they are two separable laws. Although it may indeed happen that when we believe the truth *A*, we escape as an incidental consequence from believing the falsehood *B*, it hardly ever happens that by merely disbelieving *B* we necessarily believe *A*. We may in escaping *B* fall into believing other falsehoods, *C* or *D*, just as bad as *B*; or we may escape *B* by not believing anything at all, not even *A*.

Believe truth! Shun error!—these, we see, are two materially different laws; and by choosing between them we may end by coloring differently our whole intellectual life. We may regard the chase for truth as paramount, and the avoidance of error as secondary; or we may, on the other hand, treat the avoidance of error as more imperative, and let truth take its chance. Clifford, in the instructive passage which I have quoted, exhorts us to the latter course. Believe nothing, he tells us, keep your mind in suspense forever, rather than by closing it on insufficient evidence incur the awful risk of believing lies. You, on the other hand, may think that the risk of being in error is a very small matter when compared with the blessings of real knowledge, and be ready to be duped many times in your investigation rather than postpone indefinitely the chance of guessing true. I myself find it impossible to go with Clifford. We must remember that these feelings of our duty about either truth or error are in any case only expressions of our passional life. Biologically considered, our minds are as ready to grind out falsehood as veracity, and he who says, "Better go without belief forever than believe a lie!" merely shows his own preponderant private horror of becoming a dupe. He may be critical of many of his desires and fears, but this fear he slavishly obeys. He cannot imagine any one questioning its binding force. For my own part, I have also a horror of being duped; but I can believe that worse things than being duped may happen to a man in this world: so Clifford's exhortation has to my ears a thoroughly fantastic sound. It is like a general informing his soldiers that it is better to keep out of battle forever than to risk a single wound. Not so are victories either over enemies or over nature gained. Our errors are surely not such awfully solemn things. In a world where we are so certain to incur them in spite of all our caution, a certain lightness of heart seems healthier than this excessive nervousness on their behalf. At any rate, it seems the fittest thing for the empiricist philosopher.

VIII

And now, after all this introduction, let us go straight at our question. I have said, and now repeat it, that not only as a matter of fact do we find our passional nature influencing us in our opinions, but that there are some options between opinions in which this influence must be regarded both as an inevitable and as a lawful determinant of our choice.

I fear here that some of you my hearers will begin to scent danger, and lend an inhospitable ear. Two first steps of passion you have indeed had to admit as necessary,—we must think so as to avoid dupery, and we must think so as to gain truth; but the surest path to those ideal consummations, you will probably consider, is from now onwards to take no further passional step.

Well, of course, I agree as far as the facts will allow. Wherever the option between losing truth and gaining it is not momentous, we can throw the chance of *gaining truth* away, and at any rate save ourselves from any chance of *believing falsehood*, by not making up our minds at all till objective evidence has come. In scientific questions, this is almost always the case; and even in human affairs in general, the need of acting is seldom so urgent that a false belief to act on is better than no belief at all. Law courts, indeed, have to decide on the best evidence attainable for the moment, because a judge's duty is to make law as well as to ascertain it, and (as a learned judge once said to me) few cases are worth spending much time over: the great thing is to have them decided on *any* acceptable principle, and got out of the way. But in our dealings with objective nature we obviously are recorders, not makers, of the truth; and decisions for the mere sake of deciding promptly and getting on to the next business would be wholly out of place. Throughout the breadth of physical nature facts are what they are quite independently of us, and seldom is there any such hurry about them that the risks of being duped by believing a premature theory need be faced. The questions here are always trivial options, the hypotheses are hardly living (at any rate not living for us spectators), the choice between believing truth or falsehood is seldom forced. The attitude of sceptical balance is therefore the absolutely wise one if we would escape mistakes. What difference, indeed, does it make to most of us whether we have or have not a theory of the Röntgen rays, whether we believe or not in mind-stuff, or have a conviction about the causality of conscious states? It makes no difference. Such options are not forced on us. On every account it is better not to make them, but still keep weighing reasons *pro et contra* with an indifferent hand.

I speak, of course, here of the purely judging mind. For purposes of discovery such indifference is to be less highly recommended, and science would be far less advanced than she is if the passionate desires of individuals to get their own faiths confirmed had been kept out of the game. See for example the sagacity which Spencer and Weismann now display. On the other hand, if you want an absolute duffer in an investigation, you must, after all, take the man who has no interest whatever in its results: he is the warranted incapable, the positive fool. The most useful investigator, because the most sensitive observer, is always he whose eager interest in one side of the question is balanced by an equally keen nervousness lest he become deceived.[1] Science has organized this nervousness into a regular *technique*, her so-called method of verification; and she has fallen so deeply in love with the method that one may even say she has ceased to care for truth by itself at all. It is only truth as technically verified that interests her. The truth of truths might come in merely affirmative form, and she would

[1] Compare Wilfrid Ward's Essay, "The Wish to Believe," in his *Witnesses to the Unseen*, Macmillan & Co., 1893.

decline to touch it. Such truth as that, she might repeat with Clifford, would be stolen in defiance of her duty to mankind. Human passions, however, are stronger than technical rules. "Le coeur a ses raisons," as Pascal says, "que la raison ne connaît pas"; and however indifferent to all but the bare rules of the game the umpire, the abstract intellect, may be, the concrete players who furnish him the materials to judge of are usually, each one of them, in love with some pet "live hypothesis" of his own. Let us agree, however, that wherever there is no forced option, the dispassionately judicial intellect with no pet hypothesis, saving us, as it does, from dupery at any rate, ought to be our ideal.

The question next arises: Are there not somewhere forced options in our speculative questions, and can we (as men who may be interested at least as much in positively gaining truth as in merely escaping dupery) always wait with impunity till the coercive evidence shall have arrived? It seems *a priori* improbable that the truth should be so nicely adjusted to our needs and powers as that. In the great boarding-house of nature, the cakes and the butter and the syrup seldom come out so even and leave the plates so clean. Indeed, we should view them with scientific suspicion if they did.

I X

Moral questions immediately present themselves as questions whose solution cannot wait for sensible proof. A moral question is a question not of what sensibly exists, but of what is good, or would be good if it did exist. Science can tell us what exists; but to compare the *worths*, both of what exists and of what does not exist, we must consult not science, but what Pascal calls our heart. Science herself consults her heart when she lays it down that the infinite ascertainment of fact and correction of false belief are the supreme goods for man. Challenge the statement, and science can only repeat it oracularly, or else prove it by showing that such ascertainment and correction bring man all sorts of other goods which man's heart in turn declares. The question of having moral beliefs at all or not having them is decided by our will. Are our moral preferences true or false, or are they only odd biological phenomena, making things good or bad for *us*, but in themselves indifferent? How can your pure intellect decide? If your heart does not *want* a world of moral reality, your head will assuredly never make you believe in one. Mephistophelian scepticism, indeed, will satisfy the head's play-instincts much better than any rigorous idealism can. Some men (even at the student age) are so naturally cool-hearted that the moralistic hypothesis never has for them any pungent life, and in their supercilious presence the hot young moralist always feels strangely ill at ease. The appearance of knowingness is on their side, of *naïveté* and gullibility on his. Yet, in the inarticulate heart of him, he clings to it that he is not a dupe, and that there is a realm in which (as Emerson says) all their wit and intellectual superiority is no better than the cunning of a fox. Moral scepticism can no more be refuted or proved by logic than intellectual scepticism can. When we stick to it that there *is* truth (be it of either kind), we do so with our whole nature, and resolve to stand or fall by the results. The sceptic with his whole nature adopts the doubting attitude; but which of us is the wiser, Omniscience only knows.

Turn now from these wide questions of good to a certain class of questions of fact, questions concerning personal relations, states of mind between one man and another. *Do you like me or not?*—for example. Whether you do or not depends, in countless instances, on whether I meet you half-way, am willing to assume that you must like me, and show you trust and expectation. The previous faith on my part in your liking's existence is in such cases what makes your liking come. But if I stand aloof, and refuse to budge an inch until I have objective evidence, until you shall have done something apt, as the absolutists say, *ad extorquendum assensum meum*, ten to one your liking never comes. How many women's hearts are vanquished by the mere sanguine insistence of some man that they *must* love him! he will not consent to the hypothesis that they cannot. The desire for a cerain kind of truth here brings about that special truth's existence; and so it is in innumerable cases of other sorts. Who gains promotions, boons, appointments, but the man in whose life they are seen to play the part of live hypotheses, who discounts them, sacrifices other things for their sake before they have come, and takes risks for them in advance? His faith acts on the powers above him as a claim, and creates its own verification.

A social organism of any sort whatever, large or small, is what it is because each member proceeds to his own duty with a trust that the other members will simultaneously do theirs. Wherever a desired result is achieved by the co-operation of many independent persons, its existence as a fact is a pure consequence of the precursive faith in one another of those immediately concerned. A government, an army, a commercial system, a ship, a college, an athletic team, all exist on this condition, without which not only is nothing achieved, but nothing is even attempted. A whole train of passengers (individually brave enough) will be looted by a few highwaymen, simply because the latter can count on one another, while each passenger fears that if he makes a movement of resistance, he will be shot before any one else backs him up. If we believed that the whole car-full would rise at once with us, we should each severally rise, and train-robbing would never even be attempted. There are, then, cases where a fact cannot come at all unless a preliminary faith exists in its coming. *And where faith in a fact can help create the fact*, that would be an insane logic which should say that faith running ahead of scientific evidence is the "lowest kind of immorality" into which a thinking being can fall. Yet such is the logic by which our scientific absolutists pretend to regulate our lives!

x

In truths dependent on our personal action, then, faith based on desire is certainly a lawful and possibly an indispensable thing.

But now, it will be said, these are all childish human cases, and have nothing to do with great cosmical matters, like the question of religious faith. Let us then pass on to that. Religions differ so much in their accidents that in discussing the religious question we must make it very generic and broad. What then do we now mean by the religious hypothesis? Science says things are; morality says some things are better than other things; and religion says essentially two things.

First, she says that the best things are the more eternal things, the overlapping things, the things in the universe that throw the last stone, so to speak, and say the final word. "Perfection is eternal,"—this phrase of Charles Secrétan seems a good way of putting this first affirmation of religion, an affirmation which obviously cannot yet be verified scientifically at all.

The second affirmation of religion is that we are better off even now if we believe her first affirmation to be true.

Now, let us consider what the logical elements of this situation are *in case the religious hypothesis in both its branches be really true.* (Of course, we must admit that possibility at the outset. If we are to discuss the question at all, it must involve a living option. If for any of you religion be a hypothesis that cannot, by any living possibility be true, then you need go no farther. I speak to the "saving remnant" alone.) So proceeding, we see, first, that religion offers itself as a *momentous* option. We are supposed to gain, even now, by our belief, and to lose by our non-belief, a certain vital good. Secondly, religion is a *forced* option, so far as that good goes. We cannot escape the issue by remaining sceptical and waiting for more light, because, although we do avoid error in that way *if religion be untrue,* we lose the good, *if it be true,* just as certainly as if we positively chose to disbelieve. It is as if a man should hesitate indefinitely to ask a certain woman to marry him because he was not perfectly sure that she would prove an angel after he brought her home. Would he not cut himself off from that particular angel-possibility as decisively as if he went and married some one else? Scepticism, then, is not avoidance of option; it is option of a certain particular kind of risk. *Better risk loss of truth than chance of error,*—that is your faith-vetoer's exact position. He is actively playing his stake as much as the believer is; he is backing the field against the religious hypothesis, just as the believer is backing the religious hypothesis against the field. To preach scepticism to us as a duty until "sufficient evidence" for religion be found, is tantamount therefore to telling us, when in presence of the religious hypothesis, that to yield to our fear of its being error is wiser and better than to yield to our hope that it may be true. It is not intellect against all passions, then; it is only intellect with one passion laying down its law. And by what, forsooth, is the supreme wisdom of this passion warranted? Dupery for dupery, what proof is there that dupery through hope is so much worse than dupery through fear? I, for one, can see no proof; and I simply refuse obedience to the scientist's command to imitate his kind of option, in a case where my own stake is important enough to give me the right to choose my own form of risk. If religion be true and the evidence for it be still insufficient, I do not wish, by putting your extinguisher upon my nature (which feels to me as if it had after all some business in this matter), to forfeit my sole chance in life of getting upon the winning side,—that chance depending, of course, on my willingness to run the risk of acting as if my passional need of taking the world religiously might be prophetic and right.

All this is on the supposition that it really may be prophetic and right, and that, even to us who are discussing the matter, religion is a live hypothesis which may be true. Now, to most of us religion comes in a still further way that makes a veto on our active faith even more illogical. The more perfect and more eternal aspect of the universe is represented in our religions as having personal form. The universe is no longer a mere *It* to us, but a *Thou*, if we are religious; and any relation that may be possible from person to person might be possible here. For instance, although in one sense we are passive portions of the universe, in another we show a curious autonomy, as if we were small active centres on our own account. We feel, too, as if the appeal of religion to us were made to our own active goodwill, as if evidence might be forever withheld from us unless we met the hypothesis half-way. To take a trivial illustration: just as a man who in a company of gentlemen made no advances, asked a warrant for every concession, and believed no one's word without proof, would cut himself off by such churlishness from all the social rewards that a more trusting spirit would earn,—so here, one who should shut himself up in snarling logicality and try to make the gods extort his recognition willy-nilly, or not get it at all, might cut himself off forever from his only opportunity of making the gods' acquaintance. This feeling, forced on us we know not whence, that by obstinately believing that there are gods (although not to do so would be so easy both for our logic and our life) we are doing the universe the deepest service we can, seems parts of the living essence of the religious hypothesis. If the hypothesis *were* true in all its parts, including this one, then pure intellectualism, with its veto on our making willing advances, would be an absurdity; and some participation of our sympathetic nature

would be logically required. I, therefore, for one, cannot see my way to accepting the agnostic rules for truth-seeking, or wilfully agree to keep my
willing nature out of the game. I cannot do so for this plain reason, that *a
rule of thinking which would absolutely prevent me from acknowledging
certain kinds of truth if those kinds of truth were really there, would be an
irrational rule.* That for me is the long and short of the formal logic of the
situation, no matter what the kinds of truth might materially be.

I confess I do not see how this logic can be escaped. But sad experience
makes me fear that some of you may still shrink from radically saying with
me, *in abstracto*, that we have the right to believe at our own risk any
hypothesis that is live enough to tempt our will. I suspect, however, that
if this is so, it is because you have got away from the abstract logical point
of view altogether, and are thinking (perhaps without realizing it) of some
particular religious hypothesis which for you is dead. The freedom to "believe what we will" you apply to the case of some patent superstition; and
the faith you think of is the faith defined by the schoolboy when he said,
"Faith is when you believe something that you know ain't true." I can only
repeat that this is misapprehension. *In concreto*, the freedom to believe can
only cover living options which the intellect of the individual cannot by
itself resolve; and living options never seem absurdities to him who has them
to consider. When I look at the religious question as it really puts itself to
concrete men, and when I think of all the possibilities which both practically and theoretically it involves, then this command that we shall put
a stopper on our heart, instincts, and courage, and *wait*—acting of course
meanwhile more or less as if religion were *not* true[1]—till doomsday, or
till such time as our intellect and senses working together may have raked
in evidence enough,—this command, I say, seems to me the queerest idol
ever manufactured in the philosophic cave. Were we scholastic absolutists, there might be more excuse. If we had an infallible intellect with its
objective certitudes, we might feel ourselves disloyal to such a perfect
organ of knowledge in not trusting to it exclusively, in not waiting for its
releasing word. But if we are empiricists, if we believe that no bell in us
tolls to let us know for certain when truth is in our grasp, then it seems a
piece of idle fantasticality to preach so solemnly our duty of waiting for
the bell. Indeed we *may* wait if we will,—I hope you do not think that I
am denying that,—but if we do so, we do so at our peril as much as if we

[1] Since belief is measured by action, he who forbids us to believe religion to be true,
necessarily also forbids us to act as we should if we did believe it to be true. The whole
defence of religious faith hinges upon action. If the action required or inspired by the
religious hypothesis is in no way different from that dictated by the naturalistic hypothesis, then religious faith is a pure superfluity, better pruned away, and controversy
about its legitimacy is a piece of idle trifling, unworthy of serious minds. I myself believe, of course, that the religious hypothesis gives to the world an expression which
specifically determines our reactions, and makes them in a large part unlike what they
might be on a purely naturalistic scheme of belief.

believed. In either case we *act*, taking our life in our hands. No one of us ought to issue vetoes to the other, nor should we bandy words of abuse. We ought, on the contrary, delicately and profoundly to respect one another's mental freedom: then only shall we bring about the intellectual republic; then only shall we have that spirit of inner tolerance without which all our outer tolerance is soulless, and which is empiricism's glory; then only shall we live and let live, in speculative as well as in practical things.

I began by a reference to Fitz-James Stephen; let me end by a quotation from him. "What do you think of yourself? What do you think of the world? . . . These are questions with which all must deal as it seems good to them. They are riddles of the Sphinx, and in some way or other we must deal with them. . . . In all important transactions of life we have to take a leap in the dark. . . . If we decide to leave the riddles unanswered, that is a choice; if we waver in our answer, that, too, is a choice: but whatever choice we make, we make it at our peril. If a man chooses to turn his back altogether on God and the future, no one can prevent him; no one can show beyond reasonable doubt that he is mistaken. If a man thinks otherwise and acts as he thinks, I do not see that any one can prove that *he* is mistaken. Each must act as he thinks best; and if he is wrong, so much the worse for him. We stand on a mountain pass in the midst of whirling snow and blinding mist, through which we get glimpses now and then of paths which may be deceptive. If we stand still we shall be frozen to death. If we take the wrong road we shall be dashed to pieces. We do not certainly know whether there is any right one. What must we do? 'Be strong and of good courage.' Act for the best, hope for the best, and take what comes. . . . If death ends all, we cannot meet death better."[1]

[1] *Liberty, Equality, Fraternity*, p. 353, 2d ed., London, 1874.

Josiah Royce was born at Grass Valley, California, in 1855. He studied at the University of California and at Johns Hopkins, became an instructor in philosophy at Harvard in 1882, and taught at Harvard until his death in 1916.

He was the leading American exponent of philosophical Idealism, which he espoused in a very large number of works. Among his most important books are *The Religious Aspect of Philosophy* (1885), *The Spirit of Modern Philosophy* (1892), *The Conception of God* (1895), *Studies of Good and Evil* (1898), which includes "The Problem of Job" reprinted here, *The World and the Individual* (1901-4), *The Philosophy of Loyalty* (1908), and *Lectures on Modern Idealism* (1919).

The Problem of Job

*I*n speaking of the problem of Job, the present writer comes to the subject as a layman in theology, and as one ignorant of Hebrew scholarship. In referring to the original core of the Book of Job he follows, in a general way, the advice of Professor C. H. Toy; and concerning the text of the poem he is guided by the translation of Dr. Gilbert. What this paper has to attempt is neither criticism of the book, nor philological exposition of its obscurities, but a brief study of the central problem of the poem from the point of view of a student of philosophy.

The problem of our book is the personal problem of its hero, Job himself. Discarding, for the first, as of possibly separate authorship, the Prologue, the Epilogue and the addresses of Elihu and of the Lord one may as well come at once to the point of view of Job, as expressed in his speeches to his friends. Here is stated the problem of which none of the later additions in our poem offer any intelligible solution. In the exposition of this problem the original author develops all his poetical skill, and records thoughts that can never grow old. This is the portion of our book which is most frequently quoted and which best expresses the genuine experience of suffering humanity. Here, then, the philosophical as well as the human interest of our poem centres.

I

Job's world, as he sees it, is organized in a fashion extremely familiar to us all. The main ideas of this cosmology are easy to be reviewed. The very simplicity of the scheme of the universe here involved serves to bring into clearer view the mystery and horror of the problem that besets Job himself. The world, for Job, is the work of a being who, in the very nature of the case, ought to be intelligible (since he is wise), and friendly to the righteous, since, according to tradition, and by virtue of his divine wisdom itself, this God must know the value of a righteous man. But—here is the mystery—this God, as his works get known through our human experiences of evil, appears to us not friendly, but hopelessly foreign and hostile in his plans and his doings. The more, too, we study his ways with man, the less intelligible seems his nature. Tradition has dwelt upon his righteousness, has called him merciful, has magnified his love towards his servants, has described his justice in bringing to naught the wicked. One has learned to trust all these things, to conceive God in these terms, and to expect all this righteous government from him. Moreover, tradition joins with the pious observation of nature in assuring us of the omnipotence of God. Job himself pathetically insists that he never doubts, for an instant, God's power to do whatever in heaven or earth he may please to do. Nothing hinders God. No blind faith thwarts him. Sheol is naked before him. The abyss has no covering. The earth hangs over chaos because he orders it to do so. His power shatters the monsters and pierces the dragons. He can, then, do with evil precisely what he does with Rahab or with the shades, with the clouds or with the light or with the sea, namely, exactly what he chooses. Moreover, since he knows everything, and since the actual value of a righteous man is, for Job, an unquestionable and objective fact, God cannot fail to know this real worth of righteousness in his servants, as well as the real hatefulness and mischief of the wicked. God knows worth, and cannot be blind to it, since it is as real a fact as heaven and earth themselves.

Yet despite all these unquestioned facts, this God, who can do just what he chooses, "deprives of right" the righteous man, in Job's own case, and "vexes his soul," becomes towards him as a "tyrant," "persecutes" him "with strong hand," "dissolves" him "into storm," makes him a "byword" for outcasts, "casts" him "into the mire," renders him "a brother to jackals," deprives him of the poor joy of his "one day as a hireling," of the little delight that might come to him as a man before he descends hopelessly to the dark world of the shades, "watches over" him by day to oppress, by night to "terrify" him "with dreams and with visions"—in brief, acts as his enemy, "tears" him "in anger," "gnashes upon" him "with his teeth." All these are the expressions of Job himself. On the other hand, as, with equal wonder and horror the righteous Job reports, God on occasion does just the reverse of all this to the notoriously and deliberately wicked who "grow old," "wax mighty in power," "see their offspring established," and their homes "secure from fear." If one turns from this view of God's especially unjust dealings with righteous and with wicked individuals to a general survey of his providential government of the world, one sees vast processes going on, as ingenious as they are merciless, as full of hints of a majestic wisdom as they are of indifference to every individual right.

> A mountain that falleth is shattered,
> And a rock is removed from its place;
> The waters do wear away stones,
> Its floods sweep the earth's dust away;
> And the hope of frail man thou destroyest.
> Thou subdu'st him for aye, and he goes;
> Marring his face thou rejectest him.

Here is a mere outline of the divine government as Job sees it. To express himself thus is for Job no momentary outburst of passion. Long days and nights he has brooded over these bitter facts of experience, before he has spoken at all. Unweariedly, in presence of his friends' objections, he reiterates his charges. He has the right of the sufferer to speak, and he uses it. He reports the facts that he sees. Of the paradox involved in all this he can make nothing. What is clear to him, however, is that this paradox is a matter for reasoning, not for blind authority. God ought to meet him face to face, and have the matter out in plain words. Job fears not to face his judge, or to demand his answer from God. God knows that Job has done nothing to deserve this fury. The question at issue between maker and creature is therefore one that demands a direct statement and a clear decision. "Why, since you can do precisely as you choose, and since you know, as all-knower, the value of a righteous servant, do you choose, as enemy, to persecute the righteous with this fury and persistence of hate?" Here is the problem.

The human interest of the issue thus so clearly stated by Job lies, of course, in the universality of just such experiences of undeserved ill here upon earth. What Job saw of evil we can see ourselves to-day whenever we choose. Witness Armenia. Witness the tornadoes and the earthquakes. Less interesting to us is the thesis mentioned by Job's friends, in the antiquated form in which they state it, although to be sure, a similar thesis, in altered forms, is prevalent among us still. And of dramatic significance only is the earnestness with which Job defends his own personal righteousness. So naïve a self-assurance as is his is not in accordance with our modern conscience, and it is seldom indeed that our day would see any man sincerely using this phraseology of Job regarding his own consciousness of rectitude. But what is to-day as fresh and real to us as it was to our poet is the fact that all about us, say in every child born with an unearned heredity of misery, or in every pang of the oppressed, or in every arbitrary coming of ill fortune, some form of innocence is beset with an evil that the sufferer has not deserved. Job wins dramatic sympathy as an extreme, but for the purpose all the more typical, case of this universal experience of unearned ill fortune. In every such case we therefore still have the interest that Job had in demanding the solution of this central problem of evil. Herein, I need not say, lies the permanent significance of the problem of Job,—a problem that wholly outlasts any ancient Jewish controversy as to the question whether the divine justice always does or does not act as Job's friends, in their devotion to tradition, declare that it acts. Here, then, is the point where our poem touches a question, not merely of an older religion, but of philosophy, and of all time.

I I

The general problem of evil has received, as is well known, a great deal of attention from the philosophers. Few of them, at least in European thought, have been as fearless in stating the issue as was the original author of Job. The solutions offered have, however, been very numerous. For our purposes they may be reduced to a few.

First, then, one may escape Job's paradox by declining altogether to view the world in teleological terms. Evils, such as death, disease, tempests, enemies, fires, are not, so one may declare, the works of God or of Satan, but are natural phenomena. Natural, too, are the phenomena of our desires, of our pains, sorrows and failures. No divine purpose rules or overrules any of these things. That happens to us, at any time, which must happen, in view of our natural limitations and of our ignorance. The way to better things is to understand nature better than we now do. For this view—a view often maintained in our day—there is no problem of evil, in Job's sense at all. Evil there indeed is, but the only rational problems are those of natural laws. I need not here further consider this method, not of solving but of abolishing the problem before us, since my intent is, in this paper, to suggest the possibility of some genuinely teleological answer to Job's question. I mention this first view only to recognize, historically, its existence.

In the second place, one may deal with our problem by attempting any one, or a number, of those familiar and popular compromises between the belief in a world of natural law and the belief in a teleological order, which are all, as compromises, reducible to the assertion that the presence of evil in the creation is a relatively insignificant, and an inevitable, incident of a plan that produces sentient creatures subject to law. Writers who expound such compromises have to point out that, since a burnt child dreads the fire, pain is, on the whole, useful as a warning. Evil is a transient discipline, whereby finite creatures learn their place in the system of things. Again, a sentient world cannot get on without some experience of suffering, since sentience means tenderness. Take away pain (so one still again often insists), take away pain, and we should not learn our share of natural truth. Pain is the pedgogue to teach us natural science. The contagious diseases, for instance, are useful in so far as they lead us in the end to study Bacteriology, and thus to get an insight into the life of certain beautiful creatures of God whose presence in the world we should otherwise blindly overlook! Moreover (to pass to still another variation of this sort of explanation), created beings obviously grow from less to more. First the lower, then the higher. Otherwise there could be no Evolution. And were there no evolution, how much of edifying natural science we should miss! But if one is evolved, if one grows from less to more, there must be something to mark the stages of growth. Now evil is useful to mark the lower stages of evolution. If you are to be, first an infant, then a man, or first a savage, then a civilized being, there must be evils attendant upon the earlier stages of your life—evils that make growth welcome and conscious. Thus, were there no colic and croup, were there no tumbles and crying-spells in infancy, there would be no sufficient incentives to loving parents to hasten the growing robustness of their children, and no motives to impel the children to long to grow big! Just so, cannibalism is valuable as a mark of a lower grade of evolution. Had there been no cannibalism we should realize less joyously than we do what a respectable thing it is to have become civilized! In brief, evil is, as it were, the dirt of the natural order, whose value is that, when you wash it off, you thereby learn the charm of the bath of evolution.

The foregoing are mere hints of familiar methods of playing about the edges of our problem, as children play barefoot in the shallowest reaches of the foam of the sea. In our poem, as Professor Toy expounds it, the speeches ascribed to Elihu contain the most hints of some such way of defining evil, as a merely transient incident of the discipline of the individual. With many writers explanations of this sort fill much space. They are even not without their proper place in popular discussion. But they have no interest for whoever has once come into the presence of Job's problem as it is in itself. A moment's thought reminds us of their superficiality. Pain is useful as a warning of danger. If we did not suffer, we should burn our hands off. Yes, but this explanation of one evil presupposes another, and a still unexplained and greater evil, namely, the existence of the danger of which we need to be thus warned. No doubt it is well that the past sufferings of the Armenians should teach the survivors, say the defenseless women and children, to have a wholesome fear in future of Turks. Does that explain, however, the need for the existence, or for the murderous doings of the Turks? If I can only reach a given goal by passing over a given road, say of evolution, it may be well for me to consent to the toilsome journey. Does that explain why I was created so far from my goal? Discipline, toil, penalty, surgery, are all explicable as means to ends, if only it be presupposed that there exists, and that there is quite otherwise explicable, the necessity for the situations which involve such fearful expenses. One justifies the surgery, but not the disease; the toil, but not the existence of the need for the toil; the penalty, but not the situation which has made the penalty necessary, when one points out that evil is in so many cases medicinal or disciplinary or prophylactic—an incident of imperfect stages of evolution, or the price of a distant good attanied through misery. All such explanations, I insist, trade upon borrowed capital. But God, by hypothesis, is no borrower. He produces his own capital of ends and means. Every evil is explained on the foregoing plan only by presupposing at least an equal, and often a greater and a preëxistent evil, namely, the very state of things which renders the first evil the only physically possible way of reaching a given goal. But what Job wants his judge to explain is not that evil *A* is a physical means of warding off some other greater evil *B*, in this cruel world where the waters wear away even the stones, and where hopes of man are so much frailer than the stones; but why a God who can do whatever he wishes chooses situations where such a heaped-up mass of evil means become what we should call physical necessities to the ends now physically possible.

No real explanation of the presence of evil can succeed which declares evil to be a merely physical necessity for one who desires, in this present world, to reach a given goal. Job's business is not with physical accidents, but with the God who chose to make this present nature; and an answer to Job must show that evil is not a physical but a logical necessity—something whose non-existence would simply contradict the very essence, the very perfection of God's own nature and power. This talk of medicinal and disciplinary evil, perfectly fair when applied to our poor fate-bound human surgeons, judges, jailors, or teachers, becomes cruelly, even cynically trivial when applied to explain the ways of a God who is to choose, not only the physical means to an end, but the very *Physis* itself in which path and goal are to exist together. I confess, as a layman, that whenever, at a funeral, in the company of mourners who are immediately facing Job's own personal problem, and who are sometimes, to say the least, wide enough awake to desire not to be stayed with relative comforts, but to ask that terrible and uttermost question of God himself, and to require the direct answer—that whenever, I say, in such company I have to listen to these half-way answers, to these superficial plashes in the wavelets at the water's edge of sorrow, while the black, unfathomed ocean of finite evil spreads out before our wide-opened eyes—well, at such times this trivial speech about useful burns and salutary medicines makes me, and I fancy others, simply and wearily heartsick. Some words are due to children at school, to peevish patients in the sick-room who need a little temporary quieting. But quite other speech is due to men and women when they are wakened to the higher reason of Job by the fierce anguish of our mortal life's ultimate facts. They deserve either our simple silence, or, if we are ready to speak, the speech of people who ourselves inquire as Job inquired.

III

A third method of dealing with our problem is in essence identical with the course which, in a very antiquated form, the friends of Job adopt. This method takes its best known expression in the doctrine that the presence of evil in the world is explained by the fact that the value of free will in moral agents logically involves, and so explains and justifies, the divine permission of the evil deeds of those finite beings who freely choose to sin, as well as the inevitable fruits of the sins. God creates agents with free will. He does so because the existence of such agents has of itself an infinite worth. Were there no free agents, the highest good could not be. But such agents, because they are free, can offend. The divine justice of necessity pursues such offenses with attendant evils. These evils, the result of sin, must, logically speaking, be permitted to exist, if God once creates the agents who have free will, and himself remains, as he must logically do, a just God. How much ill thus results depends upon the choice of the free agents, not upon God, who wills to have only good chosen, but of necessity must leave his free creatures to their own devices, so far as concerns their power to sin.

This view has the advantage of undertaking to regard evil as a logically necessary part of a perfect moral order, and not as a mere incident of an imperfectly adjusted physical mechanism. So dignified a doctrine, by virtue of its long history and its high theological reputation, needs here no extended exposition. I assume it as familiar, and pass at once to its difficulties. It has its share of truth. There is, I doubt not, moral free will in the universe. But the presence of evil in the world simply cannot be explained by free will alone. This is easy to show. One who maintains this view asserts, in substance, "All real evils are the results of the acts of free and finite moral agents." These agents may be angels or men. If there is evil in the city, the Lord has *not* done it, except in so far as his justice has acted in readjusting wrongs already done. Such ill is due to the deeds of his creatures. But hereupon one asks at once, in presence of any ill, "Who did this?" Job's friends answer: "The sufferer himself; his deed wrought his own undoing. God punishes only the sinner. Every one suffers for his own wrongdoing. Your ill is the result of your crime."

But Job, and all his defenders of innocence, must at once reply: "Empirically speaking, this is obviously, in our visible world, simply not true. The sufferer may suffer innocently. The ill is often undeserved. The fathers sin; the child, diseased from birth, degraded, or a born wretch, may pay the penalty. The Turk or the active rebel sins. Armenia's helpless women and babes cry in vain unto God for help."

Hereupon the reply comes, although not indeed from Job's friends: "Alas! it is so. Sin means suffering; but the innocent may suffer *for* the guilty. This, to be sure, is God's way. One cannot help it. It is so." But therewith the whole effort to explain evil as a logically necessary result of free will and of divine justice alone is simply abandoned. The unearned ills are not justly due to the free will that indeed partly caused them, but to God who declines to protect the innocent. God owes the Turk and the rebel their due. He also owes to his innocent creatures, the babes and the women, his shelter. He owes to the sinning father his penalty, but to the son, born in our visible world a lost soul from the womb, God owes the shelter of his almighty wing, and no penalty. Thus Job's cry is once more in place. The ways of God are not thus justified.

But the partisan of free will as the true explanation of ill may reiterate his view in a new form. He may insist that we see but a fragment. Perhaps the soul born here as if lost, or the wretch doomed to pangs now unearned, sinned of old, in some previous state of existence. Perhaps Karma is to blame. You expiate to-day the sins of your own former existences. Thus the Hindoos varied the theme of our familiar doctrine. This is what Hindoo friends might have said to Job. Well, admit even that, if you like; and what then follows? Admit that here or in former ages the free deed of every present sufferer earned as its penalty every ill, physical or moral, that appears as besetting just this sufferer to-day. Admit that, and what logically follows? It follows, so I must insist, that the moral world itself, which this free-will theory of the source of evil, thus abstractly stated, was to save, is destroyed in its very heart and centre.

For consider. A suffers ill. B sees A suffering. Can B, the onlooker, help his suffering neighbor, A? Can he comfort him in any true way? No, a miserable comforter must B prove, like Job's friends, so long as B, believing in our present hypothesis, clings strictly to the logic of this abstract free-will explanation of the origin of evil. To A he says: "Well, you suffer for your own ill-doing. I therefore simply cannot relieve you. This is God's world of justice. If I tried to hinder God's justice from working in your case, I should at best only postpone your evil day. It would come, for God is just. You are hungry, thirsty, naked, sick, in prison. What can I do about it? All this is your own deed come back to you. God himself, although justly punishing, is not the author of this evil. You are the sole originator of the ill." "Ah!" so A may cry out, "but can you not give me light, insight, instruction, sympathy? Can you not at least teach me to become good?" "No," B must reply, if he is a logical believer in the sole efficacy of the private free will of each finite agent as the one source, under the divine justice, of that agent's ill: "No, if you deserved light or any other comfort, God, being just, would enlighten you himself, even if I absolutely refused. But if you do not deserve light, I should preach to you in vain, for God's justice would harden your heart against any such good fortune as I could offer you from without, even if I spoke with the tongues of men and of angels. Your free will is yours. No deed of mine could give you a good free will, for what I gave you from without would not be *your* free will at all. Nor can any one but you cause your free will to be this or that. A great gulf is fixed between us. You and I, as sovereign free agents, live in God's holy world in sin-tight compartments and in evil-tight compartments too. I cannot hurt you, nor you me. You are damned for your own sins, while all that I can do is to look out for my own salvation." This, I say, is the logically inevitable result of asserting that every ill, physical or moral, that can happen to any agent, is solely the result of that agent's own free will acting under the government of the divine justice. The only possible consequence would indeed be that we live, every soul of us, in separate, as it were absolutely fire-proof, free-will compartments, so that real coöperation as to good and ill is excluded. What more cynical denial of the reality of any sort of moral world could be imagined than is involved in this horrible thesis, which no sane partisan of the abstract and traditional free-will explanation of the source of evil will to-day maintain, precisely because no such partisan really knows or can know what his doctrine logically means, while still continuing to maintain it. Yet whenever one asserts with pious obscurity, that "No harm can come to the righteous," one in fact implies, with logical necessity, just this cynical consequence.

IV

There remains a fourth doctrine as to our problem. This doctrine is in essence the thesis of philosophical idealism, a thesis which I myself feel bound to maintain, and, so far as space here permits, to explain. The theoretical basis of this view, the philosophical reasons for the notion of the divine nature which it implies, I cannot here explain. That is another argument. But I desire to indicate how the view in question deals with Job's problem.

This view first frankly admits that Job's problem is, upon Job's presuppositions, simply and absolutely insoluble. Grant Job's own presupposition that God is a being other than this world, that he is its external creator and ruler, and then all solutions fail. God is then either cruel or helpless, as regards all real finite ill of the sort that Job endures. Job, moreover, is right in demanding a reasonable answer to his question. The only possible answer is, however, one that undertakes to develop what I hold to be the immortal soul of the doctrine of the divine atonement. The answer to Job is: God is not in ultimate essence another being than yourself. He is the Absolute Being. You truly are one with God, part of his life. He is the very soul of your soul. And so, here is the first truth: When you suffer, *your sufferings are God's sufferings*, not his external work, not his external penalty, not the fruit of his neglect, but identically his own personal woe. In you God himself suffers, precisely as you do, and has all your concern in overcoming this grief.

The true question then is: Why does God thus suffer? The sole possible, necessary, and sufficient answer is, Because without suffering, without ill, without woe, evil, tragedy, God's life could not be perfected. This grief is not a physical means to an external end. It is a logically necessary and eternal constituent of the divine life. It is logically necessary that the Captain of your salvation should be perfect through suffering. No outer nature compels him. He chooses this because he chooses his own perfect selfhood. He is perfect. His world is the best possible world. Yet all its finite regions know not only of joy but of defeat and sorrow, for thus alone, in the completeness of his eternity, can God in his wholeness be triumphantly perfect.

This, I say, is my thesis. In the absolute oneness of God with the sufferer, in the concept of the suffering and therefore triumphant God, lies the logical solution of the problem of evil. The doctrine of philosophical idealism is, as regards its purely theoretical aspects, a fairly familiar metaphysical theory at the present time. One may, then, presuppose here as known the fact that, for reasons which I have not now to expound, the idealist maintains that there is in the universe but one perfectly real being, namely, the Absolute, that the Absolute is self-conscious, and that his world is essentially in its wholeness the fulfillment *in actu* of an all-perfect ideal. We ourselves exist as fragments of the absolute life, or better, as partial functions in the unity of the absolute and conscious process of the world. On the other hand, our existence and our individuality are not illusory, but are what they are in an organic unity with the whole life of the Absolute Being. This doctrine once presupposed, our present task is to inquire what case idealism can make for the thesis just indicated as its answer to Job's problem.

In endeavoring to grapple with the theoretical problem of the place of evil in a world that, on the whole, is to be conceived, not only as good, but as perfect, there is happily one essentially decisive consideration concerning good and evil which falls directly within the scope of our own human experience, and which concerns matters at once familiar and momentous as well as too much neglected in philosophy. When we use such words as good, evil, perfect, we easily deceive ourselves by the merely abstract meanings which we associate with each of the terms taken apart from the other. We forget the experiences from which the words have been abstracted. To these experiences we must return whenever we want really to comprehend the words. If we take the mere words, in their abstraction, it is easy to say, for instance, that if life has any evil in it at all, it must needs not be so perfect as life would be were there no evil in it whatever. Just so, speaking abstractly, it is easy to say that, in estimating life, one has to set the good over against the evil, and to compare their respective sums. It is easy to declare that, since we hate evil, wherever and just so far as we recognize it, our sole human interest in the world must be furthered by the removal of evil from the world. And thus viewing the case, one readily comes to say that if God views as not only good but perfect a world in which we find so much evil, the divine point of view must be very foreign to ours, so that Job's rebellious pessimism seems well in order, and Prometheus appears to defy the world-ruler in a genuinely humane spirit. Shocked, however, by the apparent impiety of this result, some teachers, considering divine matters, still misled by the same one-sided use of words, have opposed one falsely abstract view by another, and have strangely asserted that the solution must be in proclaiming that since God's world, the real world, in order to be perfect, must be without evil, what we men call evil must be a mere illusion—a mirage of the human point of view—a dark vision which God, who sees all truth, sees not at all. To God, so this view asserts, the eternal world in its wholeness is not only perfect, but has merely the perfection of an utterly transparent crystal, unstained by any color of ill. Only mortal error imagines that there is any evil. There is no evil but only good in the real world, and that is why God finds the world perfect, whatever mortals dream.

Now neither of these abstract views is my view. I consider them both the result of a thoughtless trust in abstract words. I regard evil as a distinctly real fact, a fact just as real as the most helpless and hopeless sufferer finds it to be when he is in pain. Furthermore, I hold that God's point of view is not foreign to ours. I hold that God willingly, freely, and consciously suffers in us when we suffer, and that our grief is his. And despite all this I maintain that the world from God's point of view fulfills the divine ideal and is perfect. And I hold that when we abandon the one-sided abstract ideas which the words good, evil, and perfect suggest, and when we go back to the concrete experiences upon which these very words are founded, we can see, even within the limits of our own experience, facts which make these very paradoxes perfectly intelligible, and even commonplace.

As for that essentially pernicious view, nowadays somewhat current amongst a certain class of gentle but inconsequent people—the view that all evil is *merely* an illusion and that there is no such thing in God's world—I can say of it only in passing that it is often advanced as an idealistic view, but that, in my opinion, it is false idealism. Good idealism it is to regard all finite experience as an appearance, a hint, often a very poor hint, of deeper truth. Good idealism it is to admit that man can err about truth that lies beyond his finite range of experience. And very good idealism it is to assert that all truth, and so all finite experience, exists in and for the mind of God, and nowhere outside of or apart from God. But it is not good idealism to assert that any facts which fall within the range of finite experience are, even while they are experienced, mere illusions. God's truth is inclusive, not exclusive. What you experience God experiences. The difference lies only in this, that God sees in unity what you see in fragments. For the rest, if one said, "The source and seat of evil is only the error of mortal mind," one would but have changed the name of one's problem. If the evil were but the error, the error would still be the evil, and altering the name would not have diminished the horror of the evil of this finite world.

v

But I hasten from the false idealism to the true; from the abstractions to the enlightening insights of our life. As a fact, idealism does not say: The finite world is, as such, a mere illusion. A sound idealism says, whatever we experience is a fragment, and, as far as it goes, a genuine fragment of the truth of the divine mind. With this principle before us, let us consider directly our own experiences of good and of evil, to see whether they are as abstractly opposed to each other as the mere words often suggest. We must begin with the elementary and even trivial facts. We shall soon come to something deeper.

By good, as we mortals experience it, we mean something that, when it comes or is expected, we actively welcome, try to attain or keep, and regard with content. By evil in general, as it is in our experience, we mean whatever we find in any sense repugnant and intolerable. I use the words repugnant and intolerable because I wish to indicate that words for evil frequently, like the words for good, directly refer to our actions as such. Commonly and rightly, when we speak of evil, we make reference to acts of resistance, of struggle, of shrinking, of flight, of removal of ourselves from a source of mischief—acts which not only follow upon the experience of evil, but which serve to define in a useful fashion what we mean by evil. The opposing acts of pursuit and of welcome define what we mean by good. By the evil which we experience we mean precisely whatever we regard as something to be gotten rid of, shrunken from, put out of sight, of hearing, or of memory, eschewed, expelled, assailed, or otherwise directly or indirectly resisted. By good we mean whatever we regard as something to be welcomed, pursued, won, grasped, held, persisted in, preserved. And we show all this in our acts in presence of any grade of good or evil, sensuous, aesthetic, ideal, moral. To shun, to flee, to resist, to destroy, these are our primary attitudes toward ill; the opposing acts are our primary attitudes towards the good; and whether you regard us as animals or as moralists, whether it is a sweet taste, a poem, a virtue, or God that we look to as good, and whether it is a burn or a temptation, an outward physical foe, or a stealthy, inward, ideal enemy, that we regard as evil. In all our organs of voluntary movement, in all our deeds, in a turn of the eye, in a sigh, a groan, in a hostile gesture, in an act of silent contempt, we can show in endlessly varied ways the same general attitude of repugnance.

But man is a very complex creature. He has many organs. He performs many acts at once, and he experiences his performance of these acts in one highly complex life of consciousness. As the next feature of his life we all observe that he can at the same time shun one object and grasp at another. In this way he can have at once present to him a consciousness of good and a consciousness of ill. But so far in our account these sorts of experience appear merely as facts side by side. Man loves, and he *also* hates, loves this, and hates that, assumes an attitude of repugnance towards one object, while he welcomes another. So far the usual theory follows man's life, and calls it an experience of good and ill as mingled but exclusively and abstractly opposed facts. For such a view the final question as to the worth of a man's life is merely the question whether there are more intense acts of satisfaction and of welcome than of repugnance and disdain in his conscious life.

But this is by no means an adequate notion of the complexity of man's life, even as an animal. If every conscious act of hindrance, of thwarting, of repugnance, means just in so far an awareness of some evil, it is noteworthy that men can have and can show just such tendencies, not only towards external experiences, but towards their own acts. That is, men can be seen trying to thwart and to hinder even their own acts themselves, at the very moment when they note the occurrence of these acts. One can consciously have an impulse to do something, and at that very moment a conscious disposition to hinder or to thwart as an evil that very impulse. If, on the other hand, every conscious act of attainment, of pursuit, of reinforcement, involves the awareness of some good, it is equally obvious that one can show by one's acts a disposition to reinforce or to emphasize or to increase, not only the externally present gifts of fortune, but also one's own deeds, in so far as one observes them. And in our complex lives it is common enough to find ourselves actually trying to reinforce and to insist upon a situation which involves for us, even at the moment of its occurrence, a great deal of repugnance. In such cases we often act as if we felt the very thwarting of our own primary impulses to be so much of a conscious good that we persist in pursuing and reinforcing the very situation in which this thwarting and hindering of our own impulses is sure to arise.

In brief, as phenomena of this kind show, man is being who can to a very great extent find a sort of secondary satisfaction in the very act of thwarting his own desires, and thus assuring for the time his own dissatisfactions. On the other hand, man can to an indefinite degree find himself dissatisfied with his satisfactions and disposed to thwart, not merely his external enemies, but his own inmost impulses themselves. But I now affirm that in all such cases you cannot simply say that man is preferring the less of two evils, or the greater of two goods, as if the good and the evil stood merely side by side in his experience. On the contrary, in such cases, man is not merely setting his acts or his estimates of good and evil side by side and taking the sum of each; but he is making his own relatively primary acts, impulses, desires, the objects of all sorts of secondary impulses, desires, and reflective observations. His whole inner state is one of tension; and he is either making a secondary experience of evil out of his estimate of a primary experience of good, as is the case when he at once finds himself disposed to pursue a given good and to thwart this pursuit as being an evil pursuit; or else he is making a secondary experience of good out of his primary experience of evil, as when he is primarily dissatisfied with his situation, but yet secondarily regards this very dissatisfaction as itself a desirable state. In this way man comes not only to love some things and also to hate other things, he comes to love his own hates and to hate his own loves in an endlessly complex hierarchy of superposed interests in his own interests.

Now it is easy to say that such states of inner tension, where our conscious lives are full of a warfare of the self with itself, are contradictory or absurd states. But it is easy to say this only when you dwell on the words and fail to observe the facts of experience. As a fact, not only our lowest but our highest states of activity are the ones which are fullest of this crossing, conflict, and complex interrelation of loves and hates, of attractions and repugnances. As a merely physiological fact, we begin no muscular act without at the same time initiating acts which involve the innervation of opposing sets of muscles, and these opposing sets of muscles hinder each other's freedom. Every sort of control of movement means the conflicting play of opposed muscular impulses. We do nothing simple, and we will no complex act without willing what involves a certain measure of opposition between the impulses or partial acts which go to make up the whole act. If one passes from single acts to long series of acts, one finds only the more obviously this interweaving of repugnance and of acceptance, of pursuit and of flight, upon which every complex type of conduct depends.

One could easily at this point spend time by dwelling upon numerous and relatively trivial instances of this interweaving of conflicting motives as it appears in all our life. I prefer to pass such instances over with a mere mention. There is, for instance, the whole marvelous consciousness of play, in its benign and in its evil forms. In any game that fascinates, one loves victory and shuns defeat, and yet as a loyal supporter of the game scorns anything that makes victory certain in advance; thus as a lover of fair play preferring to risk the defeat that he all the while shuns, and partly thwarting the very love of victory that from moment to moment fires his hopes. There are, again, the numerous cases in which we prefer to go to places where we are sure to be in a considerable measure dissatisfied; to engage, for instance, in social functions that absorbingly fascinate us despite or even in view of the very fact that, as long as they continue, they keep us in a state of tension which makes us, amongst other things, long to have the whole occasion over. Taking a wider view, one may observe that the greater part of the freest products of the activity of civilization, in ceremonies, in formalities, in the long social drama of flight, of pursuit, or repartee, of contest and of courtesy, involve an elaborate and systematic delaying and hindering of elemental human desires, which we continually outwit, postpone and thwart, even while we nourish them. When students of human nature assert that hunger and love rule the social world, they recognize that the elemental in human nature is trained by civilization into the service of the highest demands of the Spirit. But such students have to recognize that the elemental rules the higher world only in so far as the elemental is not only cultivated, but endlessly thwarted, delayed, outwitted, like a constitutional monarch, who is said to be a sovereign, but who, while he rules, must not govern.

But I pass from such instances, which in all their universality are still, I admit, philosophically speaking, trivial, because they depend upon the accidents of human nature. I pass from these instances to point out what must be the law, not only of human nature, but of every broader form of life as well. I maintain that this organization of life by virtue of the tension of manifold impulses and interests is not a mere accident of our imperfect human nature, but must be a type of the organization of every rational life. There are good and bad states of tension, there are conflicts that can only be justified when resolved into some higher form of harmony. But I insist that, in general, the only harmony that can exist in the realm of the spirit is the harmony that we possess when we thwart the present but more elemental impulse for the sake of the higher unity of experience; as when we rejoice in the endurance of the tragedies of life, because they show us the depth of life, or when we know that it is better to have loved and lost than never to have loved at all, or when we possess a virtue in the moment of victory over the tempter. And the reason why this is true lies in the fact that the more one's experience fulfills ideals, the more that experience presents to one, not of ignorance, but of triumphantly wealthy acquaintance with the facts of manifold, varied and tragic life, full of tension and thereby of unity. Now this is an universal and not merely human law. It is not those innocent of evil who are fullest of the life of God, but those who in their own case have experienced the triumph over evil. It is not those naturally ignorant of fear, or those who, like Siegfried, have never shivered, who possess the genuine experience of courage: but the brave are those who have fears, but control their fears. Such know the genuine virtues of the hero. Were it otherwise, only the stupid could be perfect heroes.

To be sure it is quite false to say, as the foolish do, that the object of life is merely that we may "know life" as an irrational chaos of experiences of good and of evil. But knowing the good in life is a matter which concerns the form, rather than the mere content of life. One who knows life wisely knows indeed much of the content of life; but he knows the good of life in so far as, in the unity of his experience, he finds the evil of his experience not abolished, but subordinated, and in so far relatively thwarted by a control which annuls its triumph even while experiencing its existence.

VI

Generalizing the lesson of experience we may then say: It is logically impossible that a complete knower of truth should fail to know, to experience, to have present to his insight, the fact of actually existing evil. On the other hand, it is equally impossible for one to know a higher good than comes from the subordination of evil to good in a total experience. When one first loving, in an elemental way, whatever you please, himself hinders, delays, thwarts his elemental interest in the interest of some larger whole of experience, he not only knows more fact, but he possesses a higher good than would or could be present to one who was aware neither of the elemental impulse, nor of the thwarting of it in the tension of a richer life. The knowing of the good, in the higher sense, depends upon contemplating the overcoming and subordination of a less significant impulse, which survives even in order that it should be subordinated. Now this law, this form of the knowledge of the good, applies as well to the existence of moral as to that of sensuous ill. If moral evil were simply destroyed and wiped away from the external world, the knowledge of moral goodness would also be destroyed. For the love of moral good is the thwarting of lower loves for the sake of the higher organization. What is needed, then, for the definition of the divine knowledge of a world that in its wholeness is perfect, is not a divine knowledge that shall ignore, wipe out and utterly make naught the existence of any ill, whether physical or moral, but a divine knowledge to which shall be present that love of the world as a whole which is fulfilled in the endurance of physical ill, in the subordination of moral ill, in the thwarting of impulses which survive even when subordinated, in the acceptance of repugnances which are still eternal, in the triumph over an enemy that endures even through its eternal defeat, and in the discovery that the endless tension of the finite world is included in the contemplative consciousness of the repose and harmony of eternity. To view God's nature thus is to view his nature as the whole idealistic theory views him, not as the Infinite One beyond the finite imperfections, but as the being whose unity determines the very constitution, the lack, the tension, and relative disharmony of the finite world.

The existence of evil, then, is not only consistent with the perfection of the universe, but is necessary for the very existence of that perfection. This is what we see when we no longer permit ourselves to be deceived by the abstract meanings of the words good and evil into thinking that these two opponents exist merely as mutually exclusive facts side by side in experience, but when we go back to the facts of life and perceive that all relatively higher good, in the trivial as in the more truly spiritual realm, is known only in so far as, from some higher reflective point of view, we accept as good the thwarting of an existent interest that is even thereby declared to be a relative ill, and love a tension of various impulses which even thereby involves, as the object of our love, the existence of what gives us aversion or grief. Now if the love of God is more inclusive than the love of man, even as the divine world of experience is richer than the human world, we can simply set no human limit to the intensity of conflict, to the tragedies of existence, to the pangs of finitude, to the degree of moral ill, which in the end is included in the life that God not only loves, but finds the fulfillment of the perfect ideal. If peace means satisfaction, acceptance of the whole of an experience as good, and if even we, in our weakness, can frequently find rest in the very presence of conflict and of tension, in the very endurance of ill in a good cause, in the hero's triumph over temptation, or in the mourner's tearless refusal to accept the lower comforts of forgetfulness, or to wish that the lost one's preciousness had been less painfully revealed by death—well, if even we know our little share of this harmony in the midst of the wrecks and disorders of life, what limit shall we set to the divine power to face this world of his own sorrows, and to find peace in the victory over all its ills.

But in this last expression I have pronounced the word that serves to link this theory as to the place of evil in a good world with the practical problem of every sufferer. Job's rebellion came from the thought that God, as a sovereign, is far off, and that, for his pleasure, his creature suffers. Our own theory comes to the mourner with the assurance: "Your suffering, just as it is in you, is God's suffering. No chasm divides you from God. He is not remote from you even in his eternity. He is here. His eternity means merely the completeness of his experience. But that completeness is inclusive. Your sorrow is one of the included facts." I do not say: "God sympathizes with you from without, would spare you if he could, pities you with helpless external pity merely as a father pities his children." I say: "God here sorrows, not *with* but *in* your sorrow. Your grief is identically his grief, and what you know as your loss, God knows as his loss, just in and through the very moment when you grieve."

But hereupon the sufferer perchance responds: "If this is God's loss, could he not have prevented it? To him are present in unity all the worlds; and yet he must lack just this for which I grieve." I respond: "He suffers here that he may triumph. For the triumph of the wise is no easy thing. Their lives are not light, but sorrowful. Yet they rejoice in their sorrow, not, to be sure, because it is mere experience, but because, for them, it becomes part of a strenuous whole of life. They wander and find their home even in wandering.

They long, and attain through their very love of longing. Peace they find in triumphant warfare. Contentment they have most of all in endurance. Sovereignty they win in endless service. The eternal world contains Gethsemane."

Yet the mourner may still insist: "If my sorrow is God's, his triumph is not mine. Mine is the woe. His is the peace." But my theory is a philosophy. It proposes to be coherent. I must persist: "It is your fault that you are thus sundered from God's triumph. His experience in its wholeness cannot now be yours, for you just as you—this individual—are now but a fragment, and see his truth as through a glass darkly. But if you see his truth at all, through even the dimmest light of a glimmering reason, remember, that truth is in fact your own truth, your own fulfillment, the whole from which your life cannot be divorced, the reality that you mean even when you most doubt, the desire of your heart even when you are most blind, the perfection that you unconsciously strove for even when you were an infant, the complete Self apart from whom you mean nothing, the very life that gives your life the only value which it can have. In thought, if not in the fulfillment of thought, in aim if not in attainment of aim, in aspiration if not in the presence of the revealed fact, you can view God's triumph and peace as your triumph and peace. Your defeat will be no less real than it is, nor will you falsely call your evil a mere illusion. But you will see not only the grief but the truth, your truth, your rescue, your triumph."

Well, to what ill-fortune does not just such reasoning apply? I insist: our conclusion is essentially universal. It discounts any evil that experience may contain. All the horrors of the natural order, all the concealments of the divine plan by our natural ignorance, find their general relation to the unity of the divine experience indicated in advance by this account of the problem of evil.

"Yes," one may continue, "ill-fortune you have discovered, but how about moral evil? What if the sinner now triumphantly retorts: 'Aha! So my will is God's will. All then is well with me.'" I reply: What I have said disposes of moral ill precisely as definitely as of physical ill. What the evil will is to the good man, whose goodness depends upon its existence, but also upon the thwarting and the condemnation of its aim, just such is the sinner's will to the divine plan. God's will, we say to the sinner, is your will. Yes, but it is your will thwarted, scorned, overcome, defeated. In the eternal world you are seen, possessed, present, but your damnation is also seen including and thwarting you. Your apparent victory in this world stands simply for the vigor of your impulses. God wills you not to triumph. And that is the use of you in the world—the use of evil generally—to be hated but endured, to be triumphed over through the very fact of your presence, to be willed down even in the very life of which you are a part.

But to the serious moral agent we say: What you mean when you say that evil in this temporal world ought not to exist, and ought to be suppressed, is simply what God means by seeing that evil ought to be and is endlessly thwarted, endured, but subordinated. In the natural world you are the minister of God's triumph. Your deed is his. You can never clean the world of evil; but you can subordinate evil. The justification of the presence in the world of the morally evil becomes apparent to us mortals only in so far as this evil is overcome and condemned. It exists only that it may be cast down. Courage, then, for God works in you. In the order of time you embody in outer acts what is for him the truth of his eternity.

Oscar (Fingal O'Flahertie Wills) Wilde was born at Dublin in 1854. Too often, he is chiefly remembered for the four plays, *Lady Windermere's Fan* (1892), *A Woman of No Importance* (1893), *An Ideal Husband* (1895), and, above all, *The Importance of Being Earnest* (1895). One also recalls that he brought an ill-advised suit for libel against the Marquis of Queensbury, that in the course of the trial it appeared that he was guilty of sodomy, that in 1895 he was sentenced to two years in prison, that he went to France after his release in 1897, a broken man, unable to equal his earlier successes, and that he died in Paris in 1900.

His publications, however, also include *Poems* (1881), *The Canterville Ghost* (1887), *The Happy Prince and Other Tales* (1888), *A House of Pomegranates* (1891), *The Picture of Dorian Gray* (1891), *Salome* (1893; refused a license by the licenser of plays in London, but produced in Paris by Sarah Bernhardt the following year, in French), *The Ballad of Reading Gaol* (1898, written in prison), *De Profundis* (1905, also written in prison), and two letters on prison reform, one of which is included in the selections that follow.

The Doer of Good

It was night-time, and He was alone.

And He saw afar off the walls of a round city, and went towards the city.

And when He came near He heard within the city the tread of the feet of joy, and the laughter of the mouth of gladness, and the loud noise of many lutes. And He knocked at the gate and certain of the gate-keepers opened to Him.

And He beheld a house that was of marble, and had fair pillars of marble before it. The pillars were hung with garlands, and within and without there were torches of cedar. And He entered the house.

And when He had passed through the hall of chalcedony and the hall of jasper, and reached the long hall of feasting, He saw lying on a couch of sea-purple one whose hair was crowned with red roses and whose lips were red with wine.

And He went behind him and touched him on the shoulder, and said to him:

"Why do you live like this?"

And the young man turned round and recognised Him, and made answer, and said: "But I was a leper once, and you healed me. How else should I live?"

And He passed out of the house and went again into the street.

And after a little while He saw one whose face and raiment were painted and whose feet were shod with pearls. And behind her came slowly, as a hunter, a young man who wore a cloak of two colours. Now the face of the woman was as the fair face of an idol, and the eyes of the young man were bright with lust.

And He followed swiftly, and touched the hand of the young man, and said to him: "Why do you look at this woman and in such wise?"

And the young man turned round and recognised Him, and said: "But I was blind once, and you gave me sight. At what else should I look?"

And He ran forward and touched the painted raiment of the woman, and said to her: "Is there no other way in which to walk save the way of sin?"

And the woman turned round and recognised Him, and laughed, and said: "But you forgave me my sins, and the way is a pleasant way."

And He passed out of the city.

And when He had passed out of the city, He saw, seated by the road-side, a young man who was weeping.

And He went towards him and touched the long locks of his hair, and said to him: "Why are you weeping?"

And the young man looked up and recognised Him, and made answer: "But I was dead once, and you raised me from the dead. What else should I do but weep?"

The Master

*A*nd when the darkness came over the earth, Joseph of Arimathea, having lighted a torch of pine-wood, passed down from the hill into the valley. For he had business in his own home.

And kneeling on the flint stones of the Valley of Desolation he saw a young man who was naked and weeping. His hair was the colour of honey, and his body was as a white flower; but he had wounded his body with thorns, and on his hair he had set ashes as a crown.

And he who had great possessions said to the young man who was naked: "I do not wonder that your sorrow is so great, for surely He was a just man."

And the young man answered: "It is not for Him that I am weeping, but for myself. I, too, have changed water into wine, and I have healed the leper and given sight to the blind. I have walked upon the waters, and from the dwellers in the tombs I have cast out devils. I have fed the hungry in the desert where there was no food, and I have raised the dead from their narrow houses; and at my bidding, and before a great multitude of people, a barren fig-tree withered away. All things that this man has done I have done also. And yet they have not crucified me."

The Nightingale and the Rose

"She said that she would dance with me if I brought her red roses," cried the young Student; "but in all my garden there is no red rose."

From her nest in the holm-oak tree the Nightingale heard him, and she looked out through the leaves, and wondered.

"No red rose in all my garden!" he cried, and his beautiful eyes filled with tears. "Ah, on what little things does happiness depend! I have read all that the wise men have written, and all the secrets of philosophy are mine, yet for want of a red rose is my life made wretched."

"Here at last is a true lover," said the Nightingale. "Night after night have I sung to him, though I knew him not: night after night have I told his story to the stars, and now I see him. His hair is dark as the hyacinth-blossom, and his lips are red as the rose of his desire; but passion has made his face like pale ivory, and sorrow has set her seal upon his brow."

"The Prince gives a ball to-morrow night," murmured the young Student, "and my love will be of the company. If I bring her a red rose she will dance with me till dawn. If I bring her a red rose, I shall hold her in my arms, and she will lean her head upon my shoulder, and her hand will be clasped in mine. But there is no red rose in my garden, so I shall sit lonely, and she will pass me by. She will have no heed of me, and my heart will break."

"Here indeed is the true lover," said the Nightingale. "What I sing of, he suffers: what is joy to me, to him is pain. Surely Love is a wonderful thing. It is more precious than emeralds, and dearer than fine opals. Pearls and pomegranates cannot buy it, nor is it set forth in the market-place. It may not be purchased of the merchants, nor can it be weighed out in the balance for gold."

"The musicians will sit in their gallery," said the young Student, "and play upon their stringed instruments, and my love will dance to the sound of the harp and the violin. She will dance so lightly that her feet will not touch the floor, and the courtiers in their gay dresses will throng round her. But with me she will not dance, for I have no red rose to give her"; and he flung himself down on the grass, and buried his face in his hands, and wept.

"Why is he weeping?" asked a little Green Lizard as he ran past him with his tail in the air.

"Why, indeed?" said a Butterfly, who was fluttering about after a sunbeam.

"Why, indeed?" whispered a Daisy to his neighbour, in a soft, low voice.

"He is weeping for a red rose," said the Nightingale.

"For a red rose!" they cried; "how very ridiculous!" and the little Lizard, who was something of a cynic, laughed outright.

But the Nightingale understood the secret of the Student's sorrow, and she sat silent in the oak-tree, and thought about the mystery of Love.

Suddenly she spread her brown wings for flight, and soared into the air. She passed through the grove like a shadow, and like a shadow she sailed across the garden.

In the centre of the grass-plot was standing a beautiful Rose-tree, and when she saw it, she flew over to it, and lit upon a spray.

"Give me a red rose," she cried, "and I will sing you my sweetest song." But the Tree shook its head.

"My roses are white," it answered; "as white as the foam of the sea, and whiter than the snow upon the mountain. But go to my brother who grows round the old sun-dial, and perhaps he will give you what you want."

So the Nightingale flew over to the Rose-tree that was growing round the old sun-dial.

"Give me a red rose," she cried, "and I will sing you my sweetest song." But the Tree shook its head.

"My roses are yellow," it answered; "as yellow as the hair of the mermaiden who sits upon an amber throne, and yellower than the daffodil that blooms in the meadow before the mower comes with his scythe. But go to my brother who grows beneath the Student's window, and perhaps he will give you what you want."

So the Nightingale flew over to the Rose-tree that was growing beneath the Student's window.

"Give me a red rose," she cried, "and I will sing you my sweetest song." But the Tree shook its head.

"My roses are red," it answered; "as red as the feet of the dove, and redder than the great fans of coral that wave and wave in the ocean cavern. But the winter has chilled my veins, and the frost has nipped my buds, and the storm has broken my branches, and I shall have no roses at all this year."

"One red rose is all I want," cried the Nightingale. "Only one red rose! Is there any way by which I can get it?"

"There is a way," answered the Tree; "but it is so terrible that I dare not tell it to you."

"Tell it to me," said the Nightingale, "I am not afraid."

"If you want a red rose," said the Tree, "you must build it out of music by moonlight, and stain it with your own heart's-blood. You must sing to me with your breast against a thorn. All night long you must sing to me, and the thorn must pierce your heart, and your life-blood must flow into my veins, and become mine."

"Death is a great price to pay for a red rose," cried the Nightingale, "and Life is very dear to all. It is pleasant to sit in the green wood, and to watch the Sun in his chariot of gold, and the Moon in her chariot of pearl. Sweet is the scent of the hawthorn, and sweet are the bluebells that hide in the valley, and the heather that blows on the hill. Yet Love is better than Life, and what is the heart of a bird compared to the heart of a man?"

So she spread her brown wings for flight, and soared into the air. She swept over the garden like a shadow, and like a shadow she sailed through the grove.

The young Student was still lying on the grass, where she had left him, and the tears were not yet dry in his beautiful eyes.

"Be happy," cried the Nightingale, "be happy; you shall have your red rose. I will build it out of music by moonlight, and stain it with my own heart's-blood. All that I ask of you in return is that you will be a true lover, for Love is wiser than Philosophy, though she is wise, and mightier than Power, though he is mighty. Flame-coloured are his wings, and coloured like flame is his body. His lips are sweet as honey, and his breath is like frankincense."

The Student looked up from the grass, and listened, but he could not understand what the Nightingale was saying to him, for he only knew the things that are written down in books.

But the Oak-tree understood, and felt sad, for he was very fond of the little Nightingale who had built her nest in his branches.

"Sing me one last song," he whispered; "I shall feel very lonely when you are gone."

So the Nightingale sang to the Oak-tree, and her voice was like water bubbling from a silver jar.

When she had finished her song the Student got up, and pulled a note-book and a lead-pencil out of his pocket.

"She has form," he said to himself, as he walked away through the grove—"that cannot be denied her; but has she got feeling? I am afraid not. In fact, she is like most artists; she is all style, without any sincerity. She would not sacrifice herself for others. She thinks merely of music, and everybody knows that the arts are selfish. Still, it must be admitted that she has some beautiful notes in her voice. What a pity it is that they do not mean anything, or do any practical good." And he went into his room, and lay down on his little pallet-bed, and began to think of his love; and, after a time, he fell asleep.

And when the Moon shone in the heavens the Nightingale flew to the Rose-tree, and set her breast against the thorn. All night long she sang with her breast against the thorn, and the cold crystal Moon leaned down and listened. All night long she sang, and the thorn went deeper and deeper into her breast, and her life-blood ebbed away from her.

She sang first of the birth of love in the heart of a boy and a girl. And on the topmost spray of the Rose-tree there blossomed a marvellous rose, petal followed petal, as song followed song. Pale was it, at first, as the mist that hangs over the river—pale as the feet of the morning, and silver as the wings of the dawn. As the shadow of a rose in a mirror of silver, as the shadow of a rose in a water-pool, so was the rose that blossomed on the topmost spray of the Tree.

But the Tree cried to the Nightingale to press closer against the thorn, "Press closer, little Nightingale," cried the Tree, "or the Day will come before the rose is finished."

So the Nightingale pressed closer against the thorn, and louder and louder grew her song, for she sang of the birth of passion in the soul of a man and a maid.

And a delicate flush of pink came into the leaves of the rose, like the flush in the face of the bridegroom when he kisses the lips of the bride. But the thorn had not yet reached her heart, so the rose's heart remained white, for only a Nightingale's heart's-blood can crimson the heart of a rose.

And the Tree cried to the Nightingale to press closer against the thorn. "Press closer, little Nightingale," cried the Tree, "or the Day will come before the rose is finished."

So the Nightingale pressed closer against the thorn, and the thorn touched her heart, and a fierce pang of pain shot through her. Bitter, bitter was the pain, and wilder and wilder grew her song, for she sang of the Love that is perfected by Death, of the Love that dies not in the tomb.

And the marvellous rose became crimson, like the rose of the eastern sky. Crimson was the girdle of petals, and crimson as a ruby was the heart.

But the Nightingale's voice grew fainter, and her little wings began to beat, and a film came over her eyes. Fainter and fainter grew her song, and she felt something choking her in her throat.

Then she gave one last burst of music. The white Moon heard it, and she forgot the dawn, and lingered on in the sky. The red rose heard it, and it trembled all over with ecstasy, and opened its petals to the cold morning air. Echo bore it to her purple cavern in the hills, and woke the sleeping shepherds from their dreams. It floated through the reeds of the river, and they carried its message to the sea.

"Look, look!" cried the Tree, "the rose is finished now"; but the Nightingale made no answer, for she was lying dead in the long grass, with the thorn in her heart.

And at noon the Student opened his window and looked out.

"Why, what a wonderful piece of luck!" he cried; "here is a red rose! I have never seen any rose like it in all my life. It is so beautiful that I am sure it has a long Latin name"; and he leaned down and plucked it.

Then he put on his hat, and ran up to the Professor's house with the rose in his hand.

The daughter of the Professor was sitting in the doorway winding blue silk on a reel, and her little dog was lying at her feet.

"You said that you would dance with me if I brought you a red rose," cried the Student. "Here is the reddest rose in all the world. You will wear it to-night next your heart, and as we dance together it will tell you how I love you."

But the girl frowned.

"I am afraid it will not go with my dress," she answered; "and, besides, the Chamberlain's nephew has sent me some real jewels, and everybody knows that jewels cost far more than flowers."

"Well, upon my word, you are very ungrateful," said the Student angrily; and he threw the rose into the street, where it fell into the gutter, and a cart-wheel went over it.

"Ungrateful!" said the girl. "I tell you what, you are very rude; and, after all, who are you? Only a Student. Why, I don't believe you have even got silver buckles to your shoes as the Chamberlain's nephew has"; and she got up from her chair and went into the house.

"What a silly thing Love is," said the Student as he walked away. "It is not half as useful as Logic, for it does not prove anything, and it is always telling one of things that are not going to happen, and making one believe things that are not true. In fact, it is quite unpractical, and, as in this age to be practical is everything, I shall go back to Philosophy and study Metaphysics."

So he returned to his room and pulled out a great dusty book, and began to read.

A Letter on Prison Life   THE CASE OF WARDEN MARTIN:
(SOME CRUELTIES OF PRISON LIFE)

The Editor of the "Daily Chronicle"

Sir,—I learn with great regret, through the columns of your paper, that the warder Martin, of Reading Prison, has been dismissed by the Prison Commissioners for having given some sweet biscuits to a little hungry child. I saw

[1] May 28, 1897.

the three children myself on the Monday preceding my release. They had just been convicted, and were standing in a row in the central hall in their prison dress, carrying their sheets under their arms previous to their being sent to the cells allotted to them. I happened to be passing along one of the galleries on my way to the reception room, where I was to have an interview with a friend. They were quite small children, the youngest—the one to whom the warder gave the biscuits—being a tiny little chap, for whom they had evidently been unable to find clothes small enough to fit. I had, of course, seen many children in prison during the two years during which I was myself confined. Wandsworth Prison especially contained always a large number of children. But the little child I saw on the afternoon of Monday, the 17th, at Reading, was tinier than any one of them. I need not say how utterly distressed I was to see these children at Reading, for I knew the treatment in store for them. The cruelty that is practised by day and night on children in English prisons is incredible, except to those that have witnessed it and are aware of the brutality of the system.

People nowadays do not understand what cruelty is. They regard it as a sort of terrible mediaeval passion, and connect it with the race of men like Eccelin da Romano, and others, to whom the deliberate infliction of pain gave a real madness of pleasure. But men of the stamp of Eccelin are merely abnormal types of perverted individualism. Ordinary cruelty is simply stupidity. It is the entire want of imagination. It is the result in our days of stereotyped systems, of hard-and-fast rules, and of stupidity. Wherever there is centralisation there is stupidity. What is inhuman in modern life is officialism. Authority is as destructive to those who exercise it as it is to those on whom it is exercised. It is the Prison Board, and the system that it carries out, that is the primary source of the cruelty that is exercised on a child in prison. The people who uphold the system have excellent intentions. Those who carry it out are humane in intention also. Responsibility is shifted on to the disciplinary regulations. It is supposed that because a thing is the rule it is right.

The present treatment of children is terrible, primarily from people not understanding the peculiar psychology of a child's nature. A child can understand a punishment inflicted by an individual, such as a parent or guardian, and bear it with a certain amount of acquiescence. What it cannot understand is a punishment inflicted by society. It cannot realise what society is. With grown people it is, of course, the reverse. Those of us who are either in prison or have been sent there, can understand, and do understand, what that collective force called society means, and whatever we may think of its methods or claims, we can force ourselves to accept it. Punishment inflicted on us by an individual, on the other hand, is a thing that no grown person endures, or is expected to endure.

The child consequently, being taken away from its parents by people whom it has never seen, and of whom it knows nothing, and finding itself in a lonely and unfamiliar cell, waited on by strange faces, and ordered about and punished by the representatives of a system that it cannot understand, becomes an immediate prey to the first and most prominent emotion produced by modern prison life—the emotion of terror. The terror of a child in prison is quite limitless. I remember once in Reading, as I was going out to exercise, seeing in the dimly lit cell right opposite my own a small boy. Two warders—not unkindly men—were talking to him, with some sternness apparently, or perhaps giving him some useful advice about his conduct. One was in the cell with him, the other was standing outside. The child's face was like a white wedge of sheer terror. There was in his eyes the terror of a hunted animal. The next morning I heard him at breakfasttime crying, and calling to be let out. His cry was for his parents. From time to time I could hear the deep voice of the warder on duty telling him to keep quiet. Yet he was not even convicted of whatever little offence he had been charged with. He was simply on remand. That I knew by his wearing his own clothes, which seemed neat enough. He was, however, wearing prison socks and shoes. This showed that he was a very poor boy, whose own shoes, if he had any, were in a bad state. Justices and magistrates, an entirely ignorant class as a rule, often remand children for a week, and then perhaps remit whatever sentence they are entitled to pass. They call this "not sending a child to prison." It is, of course, a stupid view on their part. To a little child, whether he is in prison on remand or after conviction is not a subtlety of social position he can comprehend. To him the horrible thing is to be there at all. In the eyes of humanity it should be a horrible thing for him to be there at all.

This terror that seizes and dominates the child, as it seizes the grown man also, is of course intensified beyond power of expression by the solitary cellular system of our prisons. Every child is confined to its cell for twenty-three hours out of the twenty-four. This is the appalling thing. To shut up a child in a dimly lit cell, for twenty-three hours out of the twenty-four, is an example of the cruelty of stupidity. If an individual, parent or guardian, did this to a child, he would be severely punished. The Society for the Prevention of Cruelty to Children would take the matter up at once. There would be on all hands the utmost detestation of whomsoever had been guilty of such cruelty. A heavy sentence would, undoubtedly, follow conviction. But our own actual society does worse itself, and to the child to be so treated by a strange abstract force, of whose claims it has no cognisance, is much worse than it would be to receive the same treatment from its father or mother, or some one it knew. The inhuman treatment of a child is always inhuman, by whomsoever it is inflicted. But inhuman treatment by society is to the child the more terrible because there is no appeal. A parent or guardian can be moved, and let out a child from the dark lonely room in which it is confined.

But a warder cannot. Most warders are very fond of children. But the system prohibits them from rendering the child any assistance. Should they do so, as Warder Martin did, they are dismissed.

The second thing from which a child suffers in prison is hunger. The food that is given to it consists of a piece of usually badly-baked prison bread and a tin of water for breakfast at half-past seven. At twelve o'clock it gets dinner, composed of a tin of coarse Indian meal stirabout; and at half-past five it gets a piece of dry bread and a tin of water for its supper. This diet in the case of a strong grown man is always productive of illness of some kind, chiefly, of course, diarrhoea, with its attendant weakness. In fact, in a big prison astringent medicines are served out regularly by the warders as a matter of course. In the case of a child, the child is, as a rule, incapable of eating the food at all. Any one who knows anything about children knows how easily a child's digestion is upset by a fit of crying, or trouble and mental distress of any kind. A child who has been crying all day long, and perhaps half the night, in a lonely dimly lit cell, and is preyed upon by terror, simply cannot eat food of this coarse, horrible kind. In the case of the little child to whom Warder Martin gave the biscuits, the child was crying with hunger on Tuesday morning, and utterly unable to eat the bread and water served to it for its breakfast. Martin went out after the breakfasts had been served, and bought the few sweet biscuits for the child rather than see it starving. It was a beautiful action on his part, and was so recognised by the child, who, utterly unconscious of the regulation of the Prison Board, told one of the senior warders how kind this junior warder had been to him. The result was, of course, a report and a dismissal.

I know Martin extremely well, and I was under his charge for the last seven weeks of my imprisonment. On his appointment at Reading he had charge of Gallery C, in which I was confined, so I saw him constantly. I was struck by the singular kindness and humanity of the way in which he spoke to me and to the other prisoners. Kind words are much in prison, and a pleasant "Good-morning" or "Good-evening" will make one as happy as one can be in a prison. He was always gentle and considerate. I happen to know another case in which he showed great kindness to one of the prisoners, and I have no hesitation in mentioning it. One of the most horrible things in prison is the badness of the sanitary arrangements. No prisoner is allowed under any circumstances to leave his cell after half-past five P.M. If, consequently, he is suffering from diarrhoea, he has to use his cell as a latrine, and pass the night in a most fetid and unwholesome atmosphere. Some days before my release Martin was going the rounds at half-past seven with one of the senior warders for the purpose of collecting the oakum and tools of the prisoners. A man just convicted, and suffering from violent diarrhoea in consequence of the food, as is always the case, asked the senior warder to allow him to empty the slops in his cell on account of the horrible odour of the cell and the possibility of illness again in the night. The senior warder refused absolutely; it was against the rules. The man had to pass the night in this dreadful condition. Martin, however, rather than see this wretched man in such a loathsome predicament, said he would empty the man's slops himself, and did so. A warder emptying a prisoner's slops is, of course, against the rules, but Martin did this act of kindness to the man out of the simple humanity of his nature, and the man was naturally most grateful.

As regards the children, a great deal has been talked and written lately about the contaminating influence of prison on young children. What is said is quite true. A child is utterly contaminated by prison life. But the contaminating influence is not that of the prisoners. It is that of the whole prison system—of the governor, the chaplain, the warders, the lonely cell, the isolation, the revolting food, the rules of the Prison Commissioners, the mode of discipline as it is termed, of the life. Every care is taken to isolate a child from the sight even of all prisoners over sixteen years of age. Children sit behind a curtain in chapel, and are sent to take exercise in small sunless yards— sometimes a stone-yard, sometimes a yard at the back of the mills—rather than that they should see the elder prisoners at exercise. But the only really humanising influence in prison is the influence of the prisoners. Their cheerfulness under terrible circumstances, their sympathy for each other, their humility, their gentleness, their pleasant smiles of greeting when they meet each other, their complete acquiescence in their punishments, are all quite wonderful, and I myself learnt many sound lessons from them. I am not proposing that the children should not sit behind a curtain in chapel, or that they should take exercise in a corner of the common yard. I am merely pointing out that the bad influence on children is not, and could never be, that of the prisoners, but is, and will always remain, that of the prison system itself. There is not a single man in Reading Gaol that would not gladly have done the three children's punishment for them. When I saw them last it was on the Tuesday following their conviction. I was taking exercise at half-past eleven with about twelve other men, as the three children passed near us, in charge of a warder, from the damp, dreary stone-yard in which they had been at their exercise. I saw the greatest pity and sympathy in the eyes of my companions as they looked at them. Prisoners are, as a class, extremely kind and sympathetic to each other. Suffering and the community of suffering makes people kind, and day after day as I tramped the yard I used to feel with pleasure and comfort what Carlyle calls somewhere "the silent rhythmic charm of human companionship." In this, as in all other things, philanthropists and people of that kind are astray. It is not the prisoners who need reformation. It is the prisons.

Of course no child under fourteen years of age should be sent to prison at all. It is an absurdity, and, like many absurdities, of absolutely tragic results. If, however, they are to be sent to prison, during the daytime they should be in a workshop or schoolroom with a warder. At night they should sleep in a dormitory, with a night-warder to look after them. They should be allowed exercise for at least three hours a day. The dark, badly ventilated, ill-smelling prison cells are dreadful for a child, dreadful indeed for any one. One is always breathing bad air in prison. The food given to children should consist of tea and bread-and-butter and soup. Prison soup is very good and wholesome. A resolution of the House of Commons could settle the treatment of children in half an hour. I hope you will use your influence to have this done. The way that children are treated at present is really an outrage on humanity and common sense. It comes from stupidity.

Let me draw attention now to another terrible thing that goes on in English prisons, indeed in prisons all over the world where the system of silence and cellular confinement is practised. I refer to the large number of men who become insane or weak-minded in prison. In convict prisons this is, of course, quite common; but in ordinary gaols also, such as that I was confined in, it is to be found.

About three months ago I noticed amongst the prisoners who took exercise with me a young man who seemed to me to be silly or half-witted. Every prison, of course, has its half-witted clients, who return again and again, and may be said to live in the prison. But this young man struck me as being more than usually half-witted on account of his silly grin and idiotic laughter to himself, and the peculiar restlessness of his eternally twitching hands. He was noticed by all the other prisoners on account of the strangeness of his conduct. From time to time he did not appear at exercise, which showed me that he was being punished by confinement to his cell. Finally, I discovered that he was under observation, and being watched night and day by warders. When he did appear at exercise he always seemed hysterical, and used to walk round crying or laughing. At chapel he had to sit right under the observation of two warders, who carefully watched him all the time. Sometimes he would bury his head in his hands, an offence against the chapel regulations, and his head would be immediately struck up by a warder so that he should keep his eyes fixed permanently in the direction of the Communion-table. Sometimes he would cry—not making any disturbance—but with tears streaming down his face and a hysterical throbbing in the throat. Sometimes he would grin idiot-like to himself and make faces. He was on more than one occasion sent out of chapel to his cell, and of course he was continually punished. As the bench on which I used to sit in chapel was directly behind the bench at the end of which this unfortunate man was placed I had full opportunity of observing him. I also saw him, of course, at exercise continually, and I saw that he was becoming insane, and was being treated as if he was shamming.

On Saturday week last I was in my cell at about one o'clock occupied in cleaning and polishing the tins I had been using for dinner. Suddenly I was startled by the prison silence being broken by the most horrible and revolting shrieks, or rather howls, for at first I thought some animal like a bull or a cow was being unskilfully slaughtered outside the prison walls. I soon realised, however, that the howls proceeded from the basement of the prison, and I knew that some wretched man was being flogged. I need not say how hideous and terrible it was for me, and I began to wonder who it was who was being punished in this revolting manner. Suddenly it dawned upon me that they might be flogging this unfortunate lunatic. My feelings on the subject need not be chronicled; they have nothing to do with the question.

The next day, Sunday 16th, I saw the poor fellow at exercise, his weak, ugly, wretched face bloated by tears and hysteria almost beyond recognition. He walked in the centre ring along with the old men, the beggars, and the lame people, so that I was able to observe him the whole time. It was my last Sunday in prison, a perfectly lovely day, the finest day we had had the whole year, and there, in the beautiful sunlight, walked this poor creature—made once in the image of God—grinning like an ape, and making with his hands the most fantastic gestures, as though he was playing in the air on some invisible stringed instrument, or arranging and dealing counters in some curious game. All the while these hysterical tears, without which none of us ever saw him, were making soiled runnels on his white swollen face. The hideous and deliberate grace of his gestures made him like an antic. He was a living grotesque. The other prisoners all watched him, and not one of them smiled. Everybody knew what had happened to him, and that he was being driven insane—was insane already. After half an hour he was ordered in by the warder, and I supposed punished. At least he was not at exercise on Monday, though I think I caught sight of him at the corner of the stone-yard, walking in charge of a warder.

On the Tuesday—my last day in prison—I saw him at exercise. He was worse than before, and again was sent in. Since then I know nothing of him, but I found out from one of the prisoners who walked with me at exercise that he had had twenty-four lashes in the cookhouse on Saturday afternoon, by order of the visiting justices on the report of the doctor. The howls that had horrified us all were his.

This man is undoubtedly becoming insane. Prison doctors have no knowledge of mental disease of any kind. They are as a class ignorant men. The pathology of the mind is unknown to them. When a man grows insane, they treat him as shamming. They have him punished again and again. Naturally the man becomes worse. When ordinary punishments are exhausted, the doctor reports the case to the justices. The result is flogging. Of course the flogging is not done with a cat-of-nine-tails. It is what is called birching. The instrument is a rod; but the result on the wretched half-witted man may be imagined.

His number is, or was, A. 2.11. I also managed to find out his name. It is Prince. Something should be done at once for him. He is a soldier, and his sentence is one of court-martial. The term is six months. Three have yet to run.

May I ask you to use your influence to have this case examined into, and to see that the lunatic prisoner is properly treated?

No report by the Medical Commissioners is of any avail. It is not to be trusted. The medical inspectors do not seem to understand the difference between idiocy and lunacy—between the entire absence of a function or organ and the diseases of a function or organ. This man A. 2.11. will, I have no doubt, be able to tell his name, the nature of his offence, the day of the month, the date of the beginning and expiration of his sentence, and answer any ordinary simple question; but that his mind is diseased admits of no doubt. At present it is a horrible duel between himself and the doctor. The doctor is fighting for a theory. The man is fighting for his life. I am anxious that the man should win. But let the whole case be examined into by experts who understand brain-disease, and by people of humane feelings who have still some common sense and some pity. There is no reason that the sentimentalist should be asked to interfere. He always does harm.

The case is a special instance of the cruelty inseparable from a stupid system, for the present Governor of Reading is a man of gentle and humane character, greatly liked and respected by all the prisoners. He was appointed in July last, and though he cannot alter the rules of the prison system he has altered the spirit in which they used to be carried out under his predecessor. He is very popular with the prisoners and with the warders. Indeed he has quite altered the whole tone of the prison life. Upon the other hand, the system is, of course, beyond his reach as far as altering its rules is concerned. I have no doubt that he sees daily much of what he knows to be unjust, stupid, and cruel. But his hands are tied. Of course I have no knowledge of his real views of the case of A. 2.11, nor, indeed, of his views on our present system. I merely judge him by the complete change he brought about in Reading Prison. Under his predecessor the system was carried out with the greatest harshness and stupidity.—I remain, Sir, your obedient servant,

OSCAR WILDE

May 27

II · FREUD

Sigmund Freud was born in 1856, at Freiberg (then in Austria-Hungary, now in Czechoslovakia). He grew up in Vienna, studied medicine, received his doctorate in 1881, and then specialized in brain anatomy. In 1885 he was appointed Lecturer in Neuropathology at the University of Vienna.

His first major work was *The Interpretation of Dreams* (1900). It took eight years to sell the initial printing of six hundred copies; but the book went through eight editions and was widely translated before he died in London, a refugee, in 1939, in the third week of World War II.

This book laid the foundations of what Freud called psychoanalysis. He developed his views further in *The Psychopathology of Everyday Life* (1904), *Three Contributions to the Theory of Sex* (1905), and *Totem and Tabu* (1913). His *General Introduction to Psychoanalysis* (1917) remains unsurpassed as an introduction to the field.

After World War I, he re-examined and revised the theoretical foundations of psychoanalysis in *Beyond the Pleasure Principle* (1920) and *The Ego and the Id* (1923); and he offered his reflections on religion and civilization in *The Future of an Illusion* (1927) and *Civilization and Its Discontents* (1930). There are two editions of his collected works in the original German, comprising, respectively, twelve and eighteen volumes.

The following selection comprises Chapters V and VI of *The Future of an Illusion*.

The Future of an Illusion

CHAPTER V

*N*ow to take up again the threads of our enquiry: what is the psychological significance of religious ideas and how can we classify them? The question is at first not at all easy to answer. Having rejected various formulas, I shall take my stand by this one: religion consists of certain dogmas, assertions about facts and conditions of external (or internal) reality, which tell one something that one has not oneself discovered and which claim that one should give them credence. As they give information about what are to us the most interesting and important things in life, they are particularly highly valued. He who knows nothing of them is ignorant indeed, and he who has assimilated them may consider himself enriched.

There are of course many such dogmas about the most diverse things of this world. Every school hour is full of them. Let us choose geography.

We hear there: Konstanz is on the Bodensee. A student song adds: If you don't believe it go and see. I happen to have been there, and can confirm the fact that this beautiful town lies on the shore of a broad stretch of water, which all those dwelling around call the Bodensee. I am now completely convinced of the accuracy of this geographical statement. And in this connection I am reminded of another and very remarkable experience. I was already a man of mature years when I stood for the first time on the hill of the Athenian Acropolis, between the temple ruins, looking out on to the blue sea. A feeling of astonishment mingled with my pleasure, which prompted me to say: then it really is true, what we used to be taught at school! How shallow and weak at that age must have been my belief in the real truth of what I heard if I can be so astonished to-day! But I will not emphasize the significance of this experience too much; yet another explanation of my astonishment is possible, which did not strike me at the time, and which is of a wholly subjective nature and connected with the peculiar character of the place.

All such dogmas as these, then, exact belief in their contents, but not without substantiating their title to this. They claim to be the condensed result of a long process of thought, which is founded on observation and also, certainly, on reasoning; they show how, if one so intends, one can go through this process oneself, instead of accepting the result of it; and the source of the knowledge imparted by the dogma is always added, where it is not, as with geographical statements, self-evident. For instance: the earth is shaped like a globe; the proofs adduced for this are Foucault's pendulum experiment, the phenomena of the horizon and the possibility of circumnavigating the earth. Since it is impracticable, as all concerned realize, to send every school child on a voyage round the world, one is content that the school teaching shall be taken on trust, but one knows that the way to personal conviction is still open.

Let us try to apply the same tests to the dogmas of religion. If we ask on what their claim to be believed is based, we receive three answers, which accord remarkably ill with one another. They deserve to be believed: firstly, because our primal ancestors already believed them; secondly, because we possess proofs, which have been handed down to us from this very period of antiquity; and thirdly, because it is forbidden to raise the question of their authenticity at all. Formerly this presumptuous act was visited with the very severest penalties, and even to-day society is unwilling to see anyone renew it.

This third point cannot but rouse our strongest suspicions. Such a prohibition can surely have only one motive: that society knows very well the uncertain basis of the claim it makes for its religious doctrines. If it were otherwise, the relevant material would certainly be placed most readily at the disposal of anyone who wished to gain conviction for himself. And so we proceed to test the other two arguments with a feeling of mistrust not easily allayed. We ought to believe because our forefathers believed. But these ancestors of ours were far more ignorant than we; they believed in things we could not possibly accept to-day; so the possibility occurs that religious doctrines may also be in this category. The proofs they have bequeathed to us are deposited in writings that themselves bear every trace of being untrustworthy. They are full of contradictions, revisions, and interpolations; where they speak of actual authentic proofs they are themselves of doubtful authenticity. It does not help much if divine revelation is asserted to be the origin of their text or only of their content, for this assertion is itself already a part of those doctrines whose authenticity is to be examined, and no statement can bear its own proof.

Thus we arrive at the singular conclusion that just what might be of the greatest significance for us in our cultural system, the information which should solve for us the riddles of the universe and reconcile us to the troubles of life, that just this has the weakest possible claim to authenticity. We should not be able to bring ourselves to accept anything of as little concern to us as the fact that whales bear young instead of laying eggs, if it were not capable of better proof than this.

This state of things is in itself a very remarkable psychological problem. Let no one think that the foregoing remarks on the impossibility of proving religious doctrines contain anything new. It has been felt at all times, assuredly even by the ancestors who bequeathed this legacy. Probably many of them nursed the same doubts as we, but the pressure imposed on them was too strong for them to have dared to utter them. And since then countless people have been tortured by the same doubts, which they would fain have suppressed because they held themselves in duty bound to believe, and since then many brilliant intellects have been wrecked upon this conflict and many characters have come to grief through the compromises by which they sought a way out.

If all the arguments that are put forward for the authenticity of religious doctrines originate in the past, it is natural to look round and see whether the present, better able to judge in these matters, cannot also furnish such evidence. The whole of the religious system would become infinitely more credible if one could succeed in this way in removing the element of doubt from a single part of it. It is at this point that the activity of the spiritualists comes in; they are convinced of the immortality of the individual soul, and they would demonstrate to us that this one article of religious teaching is free from doubt. Unfortunately they have not succeeded in disproving the fact that the appearances and utterances of their spirits are merely the productions of their own mental activity. They have called up the spirits of the greatest of men, of the most eminent thinkers, but all their utterances and all the information they have received from them have been so foolish and so desperately insignificant that one could find nothing else to believe in but the capacity of the spirits for adapting themselves to the circle of people that had evoked them.

One must now mention two attempts to evade the problem, which both convey the impression of frantic effort. One of them, highhanded in its nature, is old; the other is subtle and modern. The first is the *Credo quia absurdum* of the early Father. It would imply that religious doctrines are outside reason's jurisdiction; they stand above reason. Their truth must be inwardly felt: one does not need to comprehend them. But this *Credo* is only of interest as a voluntary confession; as a decree it has no binding force. Am I to be obliged to believe every absurdity? And if not, why just this one? There is no appeal beyond reason. And if the truth of religious doctrines is dependent on an inner experience which bears witness to that truth, what is one to make of the many people who do not have that rare experience? One may expect all men to use the gift of reason that they possess, but one cannot set up an obligation that shall apply to all on a basis that only exists for quite a few. Of what significance is it for other people that you have won from a state of ecstasy, which has deeply moved you, an imperturbable conviction of the real truth of the doctrines of religion?

The second attempt is that of the philosophy of "As If." It explains that in our mental activity we assume all manner of things, the groundlessness, indeed the absurdity, of which we fully realize. They are called "fictions," but from a variety of practical motives we are led to behave "as if" we believed in these fictions. This, it is argued, is the case with religious doctrines on account of their unequalled importance for the maintenance of human society.[1] This argument is not far removed from the *Credo quia absurdum*. But I think that the claim of the philosophy of "As If" is such as only a philosopher could make. The man whose thinking is not influenced by the wiles of philosophy will never be able to accept it; with the confession of absurdity, of illogicality, there is no more to be said as far as he is concerned. He cannot be expected to forgo the guarantees he demands for all his usual activities just in the matter of his most important interests. I am reminded of one of my children who was distinguished at an early age by a peculiarly marked sense of reality. When the children were told a fairy tale, to which they listened with rapt attention, he would come forward and ask: Is that a true story? Having been told that it was not, he

[1] I hope I am not doing an injustice if I make the author of the philosophy of "As If" represent a point of view that is familiar to other thinkers also. Cp. H. Vaihinger, *Die Philosophie des Als ob*, Siebente und achte Auflage, 1922, S. 68: "We include as fictions not merely indifferent theoretical operations but ideational constructions emanating from the noblest minds, to which the noblest part of mankind cling and of which they will not allow themselves to be deprived. Nor is it our object so to deprive them—for as *practical fictions* we leave them all intact; they perish only as *theoretical truths*" (C. K. Ogden's translation).

would turn away with an air of disdain. It is to be expected that men will soon behave in like manner towards the religious fairy tales, despite the advocacy of the philosophy of "As If."

But at present they still behave quite differently, and in past ages, in spite of their incontrovertible lack of authenticity, religious ideas have exercised the very strongest influence on mankind. This is a fresh psychological problem. We must ask where the inherent strength of these doctrines lies and to what circumstance they owe their efficacy, independent, as it is, of the acknowledgement of the reason.

CHAPTER VI

I think we have sufficiently paved the way for the answer to both these questions. It will be found if we fix our attention on the psychical origin of religious ideas. These, which profess to be dogmas, are not the residue of experience or the final result of reflection; they are illusions, fulfilments of the oldest, strongest and most insistent wishes of mankind; the secret of their strength is the strength of these wishes. We know already that the terrifying effect of infantile helplessness aroused the need for protection—protection through love—which the father relieved, and that the discovery that this helplessness would continue through the whole of life made it necessary to cling to the existence of a father—but this time a more powerful one. Thus the benevolent rule of divine providence allays our anxiety in face of life's dangers, the establishment of a moral world order ensures the fulfilment of the demands of justice, which within human culture have so often remained unfulfilled, and the prolongation of earthly existence by a future life provides in addition the local and temporal setting for these wish-fulfilments. Answers to the questions that tempt human curiosity, such as the origin of the universe and the relation between the body and the soul, are developed in accordance with the underlying assumptions of this system; it betokens a tremendous relief for the individual psyche if it is released from the conflicts of childhood arising out of the father complex, which are never wholly overcome, and if these conflicts are afforded a universally accepted solution.

When I say that they are illusions, I must define the meaning of the word. An illusion is not the same as an error, it is indeed not necessarily an error. Aristotle's belief that vermin are evolved out of dung, to which ignorant people still cling, was an error; so was the belief of a former generation of doctors that *tabes dorsalis* was the result of sexual excess. It would be improper to call these errors illusions. On the other hand, it was an illusion on the part of Columbus that he had discovered a new sea-route to India. The part played by his wish in this error is very clear. One may describe as an illusion the statement of certain nationalists that the Indo-

Germanic race is the only one capable of culture, or the belief, which only psycho-analysis destroyed, that the child is a being without sexuality. It is characteristic of the illusion that it is derived from men's wishes; in this respect it approaches the psychiatric delusion, but it is to be distinguished from this, quite apart from the more complicated structure of the latter. In the delusion we emphasize as essential the conflict with reality; the illusion need not be necessarily false, that is to say, unrealizable or incompatible with reality. For instance, a poor girl may have an illusion that a prince will come and fetch her home. It is possible; some such cases have occurred. That the Messiah will come and found a golden age is much less probable; according to one's personal attitude one will classify this belief as an illusion or as analogous to a delusion. Examples of illusions that have come true are not easy to discover, but the illusion of the alchemists that all metals can be turned into gold may prove to be one. The desire to have lots of gold, as much gold as possible, has been considerably damped by our modern insight into the nature of wealth, yet chemistry no longer considers a transmutation of metals into gold as impossible. Thus we call a belief an illusion when wish-fulfilment is a prominent factor in its motivation, while disregarding its relations to reality, just as the illusion itself does.

If after this survey we turn again to religious doctrines, we may reiterate that they are all illusions, they do not admit of proof, and no one can be compelled to consider them as true or to believe in them. Some of them are so improbable, so very incompatible with everything we have laboriously discovered about the reality of the world, that we may compare them— taking adequately into account the psychological differences—to delusions. Of the reality value of most of them we cannot judge; just as they cannot be proved, neither can they be refuted. We still know too little to approach them critically. The riddles of the universe only reveal themselves slowly to our enquiry, to many questions science can as yet give no answer; but scientific work is our only way to the knowledge of external reality. Again, it is merely illusion to expect anything from intuition or trance; they can give us nothing but particulars, which are difficult to interpret, about our own mental life, never information about the questions that are so lightly answered by the doctrines of religion. It would be wanton to let one's own arbitrary action fill the gap, and according to one's personal estimate declare this or that part of the religious system to be more or less acceptable. These questions are too momentous for that; too sacred, one might say.

At this point it may be objected: well, then, if even the crabbed sceptics admit that the statements of religion cannot be confuted by reason, why should not I believe in them, since they have so much on their side—tradition, the concurrence of mankind, and all the consolation they yield? Yes, why not? Just as no one can be forced into belief, so no one can be forced into unbelief. But do not deceive yourself into thinking that with such ar-

guments you are following the path of correct reasoning. If ever there was
a case of facile argument, this is one. Ignorance is ignorance; no right to
believe anything is derived from it. No reasonable man will behave so frivo-
lously in other matters or rest content with such feeble grounds for his
opinions or for the attitude he adopts; it is only in the highest and holiest
things that he allows this. In reality these are only attempts to delude oneself or other people into the belief that one still holds fast to religion, when
one has long cut oneself loose from it. Where questions of religion are concerned people are guilty of every possible kind of insincerity and intellectual misdemeanour. Philosophers stretch the meaning of words until they
retain scarcely anything of their original sense; by calling "God" some
vague abstraction which they have created for themselves, they pose as
deists, as believers, before the world; they may even pride themselves on
having attained a higher and purer idea of God, although their God is
nothing but an insubstantial shadow and no longer the mighty personality
of religious doctrine. Critics persist in calling "deeply religious" a person
who confesses to a sense of man's insignificance and impotence in face of
the universe, although it is not this feeling that constitutes the essence of
religious emotion, but rather the next step, the reaction to it, which seeks
a remedy against this feeling. He who goes no further, he who humbly
acquiesces in the insignificant part man plays in the universe, is, on the contrary, irreligious in the truest sense of the word.

It does not lie within the scope of this enquiry to estimate the value of
religious doctrines as truth. It suffices that we have recognized them, psy-
chologically considered, as illusions. But we need not conceal the fact that
this discovery strongly influences our attitude to what must appear to
many the most important of questions. We know approximately at what
periods and by what sort of men religious doctrines were formed. If we
now learn from what motives this happened, our attitude to the problem
of religion will suffer an appreciable change. We say to ourselves: it would
indeed be very nice if there were a God, who was both creator of the
world and a benevolent providence, if there were a moral world order and
a future life, but at the same time it is very odd that this is all just as we
should wish it ourselves. And it would be still odder if our poor, ignorant,
enslaved ancestors had suceeded in solving all these difficult riddles of the
universe.

Morris (Raphael) Cohen was born at Minsk, Russia, in 1880. He came to the United States in 1892. His long career as a teacher at the College of the City of New York began in 1902. At first he taught mathematics, but from 1912 until his retirement in 1938 he served as a professor of philosophy. After his retirement, he taught philosophy at the University of Chicago. He died in 1947.

His books include *Reason and Nature* (1931), *Law and the Social Order* (1933), *An Introduction to Logic and Scientific Method* (1934, with Ernest Nagel), *A Preface to Logic* (1945), *The Faith of a Liberal* (1946), *The Meaning of Human History* (1947), and *A Dreamer's Journey: The Autobiography of Morris Raphael Cohen* (1949).

The following essay is reprinted, unabridged, from *The Faith of a Liberal*. The substance of the essay appeared originally as a contribution to the symposium volume, *Religion Today, a Challenging Enigma*, edited by Arthur L. Swift, Jr. (1933).

The Dark Side of Religion

*T*he *advocatus diaboli*, as you know, is not a lawyer employed by the Prince of Darkness. He is a faithful member of the Church whose duty it is, when it is proposed to canonize a saint, to search out all the opposing considerations and to state them as cogently as possible. This wise institution compels the advocates of canonization to exert themselves to develop arguments vigorous enough to overcome all objections. In this symposium on religion, I am asked to serve as *advocatus diaboli:* to state the Dark Side so that those who follow may have definite positions to attack and may thus more fully develop the strength of their case.

While there have not been wanting atheists and other freethinkers who have attacked religion root and branch, these assailants have often shared the indiscriminate or fanatical intensity which has characterized so many upholders of religion. It has therefore been possible to pass over the argument of men like Voltaire, Bradlaugh, or Ingersoll, as inaccurate, superficial, and too one-sided. The truth, however, is that religion is something about which men generally are passionate; and it is as difficult to be patient with those who paint its defects as it is to listen attentively to those who point out our most intimate failings or the shortcoming of those we love most dearly, of our family or of our country. Indeed, to most people religion is just a matter of loyalty to the accepted ways hallowed by our ancestors; and to discuss it at all critically is just bad taste, very much as if a funeral orator were to treat us to a psychoanalysis of our lamented friend.

A curious illustration of the confusion resulting from the absence of a critical discriminating attitude in the discussion of religion is the fact that the heterodox opponent of the established religion has often much more real faith than most of its followers. Thus Theodore Roosevelt was probably representative of Christian America when he referred to Tom Paine as "a filthy little atheist." Yet a comparison of their respective writings can leave little doubt that Paine had far more faith than his contemner in a personal God, in the immortality of the soul, and in moral compensation hereafter. But Theodore Roosevelt never said a word against established religion or the church and so remained respectable—though his conception of religion as identical with such good works as the taking of Panama and the building of the Canal[1] literally ignores the whole spiritual essence of the historic Christianity which our churches profess. The common identification of religion with the unquestioning acceptance of traditional conventions or good manners is shown in the popular distrust of anyone who thinks about religion seriously enough to change his religious affiliations or to depart from the religion of his fathers. Even lower in general esteem are those who think out a religion for themselves. Thus the Russians say: "The Tatars received their religion [Mohammedanism] from God like the color of their skins; but the Molokans are Russians who have invented their faith."[2]

The general disinclination to conscientious or scrupulously logical examination of religious beliefs is shown by the way even educated people judge religious doctrine by their labels rather than by their content. Thus we talk about Spinoza as a God-intoxicated man because he used the *word* "God" and the language of traditional piety. But those who repeat his opposition to that anthropomorphic theism which is the essence of all popular religion, and who do not write nature with a capital N, are just atheists. Indeed a writer who has made a considerable impression on our contemporary public by his books on religion identifies the latter with a belief in *Something*. What should we have thought of his doctrine if we merely heard it, or if we had only one case of type?

One of the effective ways of avoiding any real discussion of religion or discriminating its darker from its brighter side is to define or identify it as "our highest aspiration." This is very much like defining a spouse as the essence of perfection or our country as the home of the brave and the free. Some particular religion, like some particular wife or country, may perhaps deserve the praise. But we must first be able to identify our object before we can tell whether the praise is entirely deserved. To define religion as our highest aspiration, and then to speak of Christianity, Islam, or Judaism

[1] See his Noble Lectures at Harvard.   [2] D. M. Wallace, *Russia*, chapter 10.

as a religion, is obviously to beg the whole question by a verbal trick of definition.

In the interests of intellectual honesty we must also reject the identification of religion with the mere sentiment of benevolence or with altruistic conduct.

This is the favorite vice of our modernists and of scientific leaders like Millikan who try to harmonize religion with science in general (not with their own special field). We may dismiss these harmonizers as plainly ignorant of the history of religion. For to identify all religion with vague altruism[1] rules out not only all the historic tribal and national religions, Hinduism, and most of the Old Testament, but also Christianity of the Orthodox, Catholic, and Fundamentalist-Protestant type. All post-Hellenic cults have insisted on sacraments like baptism and on the acceptance of dogmas about the Trinity, the Incarnation, the Fall of Man, the Atonement, eternal Hell, etc. Worse than that! This "liberal" or nondogmatic view is logically bound to apply the term "religious" to philanthropic atheists and Communists who, in the interests of humanity and to stop the exploitation of the masses by the clergy, are the avowed enemies of all religion. And indeed there are many who do speak of Communism as a religion. But this surely is to cause hopeless confusion. There is no real liberalism in ignoring the historical meaning of words; and no one who knows anything of the historical and general use of the word "religion" can well use it to include atheists like Shelley or Lenin and exclude men like Torquemada, Calvin, and Jonathan Edwards. Such "liberalism" does not really strengthen the case for religion. Consider the vast varieties of religions ancient and modern. Are they all expressions of our highest aspirations? Is each one an effort at universal benevolence? If so, why do they differ? And since they do differ, and each regards the others as inferior, can they all be true? Nor is the case improved if we say that each religious group seeks what is highest or noblest, for there can be no question that error, ignorance, stupidity, and fanatical prejudice enter into what men think.

Instead, then, of darkening counsel by beginning with arbitrary and confusing definitions of religion, let us recognize that the term "religion" is generally used and understood to apply to Christianity, Judaism, Islam, Hinduism, etc., and that these represent certain forms of organized life in which beliefs about God and a supernatural realm enter more or less articulately. Religion is first of all something that makes people do something when children are born, when they become mature, when they marry, and when they die. It makes people go to church, sacrifice, fast, feast, or pray. A religion that does not get so organized or embodied in life is a mere ghost, the creature of a cultivated imagination. Generally speaking, people get these habits by social heredity, according to the community in which

[1] See J. M. and M. C. Coulter, *Where Evolution and Religion Meet.*

they are born. The beliefs thus involved are more or less tacitly assumed. But such tacit beliefs do become at times explicit, and when this happens men cling to the verbal formula with the most amazing intensity and tenacity. Men are willing to burn others and to be burned themselves on the question whether they should cross themselves with one finger or two, or whether God is one person of various aspects or natures, or three persons of one substance.

Now if we thus view religion as an historic phenomenon in human life, we are prepared to believe—from what we know of human nature and history—that religion like all other social institutions has its darker as well as its brighter side.

I. RELIGION STRENGTHENS SUPERSTITION AND HINDERS SCIENCE OR THE SPIRIT OF TRUTH-SEEKING

Since the days of the Greek philosopher Xenophanes, theistic religion has been accused of foolish anthropomorphism. And since Epicurus and Lucretius it has been identified by many thinkers with superstition. Eighteenth- and nineteenth-century writers like Voltaire, Gibbon, and Condorcet, Lecky, Draper, and A. D. White have so traced the history of the conflict between scientific enlightenment and religious obscurantism as to make this point a commonplace. But the attempt has been made to make it appear that this conflict is not between religion and science, but between the latter and theology. This seems to me a cheap and worthless evasion. In the first place, none of the religions that are in the field today ever have dispensed or can dispense with all theology. What would be left today of Christianity, Judaism, or Islam without a belief in a personal God to whom we can pray? In the second place, we do not understand the roots of religion if we do not see that the historic opposition to science has not been a vagary of wicked theologians but has risen out of the very spirit which has animated most, if not all, of the religions which have appeared in history. We must start with the fact that with rare exceptions men cling to the religion in which they are born and to which they have been habituated from childhood. We inherit our traditional ritual with its implicit faith and emotional content almost with our mother's milk; and we naturally cling to it as passionately as we do to all things which have thus become part of our being, our family, our country, or our language. When religious opinion becomes formulated, it naturally expresses itself in absolute claims. Doubts are the fruit of reflection. To one brought up in a Mohammedan village, it would sound blasphemous to say that there probably is a God, Allah, and that he is probably more benevolent than malevolent; and that Mohammed has a fairly good claim to be the most reliable of prophets. Similar considerations hold in the case of every other simple religious person. But science regards all established truths (other than the logical methods of proof and verification) as subject to possible doubt and correction. Consider the attitude of a simple man or woman to anyone who offers to prove that we come from an inferior stock, or that our country is inferior in merit to its traditional rivals. Who can doubt that the first and most patent reaction will be resentment rather than intellectual curiosity? And the same is bound to be our attitude as regards religion, so long as the latter integrates in simple piety all traditional and habitual loyalties to the sources of our being. Thus arises the fierce intolerance of religion as contrasted with the cultivated open-mindedness of science. To religion, agreement is a practical and emotional necessity, and doubt is a challenge and an offense. We cannot tolerate those who wish to interfere or break up the hallowed customs of our group. Science, on the other hand, is a game in which opposing claims only add zest and opportunity. If the foundations of Euclidean geometry or Newtonian physics are suddenly questioned, some individual scientists may show their human limitations; but science as a whole has its field widened thereby, great enthusiasm is created for new investigations, and the innovators are objects of grateful general homage. Science does not need, therefore, to organize crusades to kill off heretics or unbelievers. Science, like art, enjoys its own activity and this enjoyment is not interfered with by anyone who obstinately refuses to join the game or scoffs at what the scientist has proved. The scientific banquet is not spoiled by our neighbors' refusing to enjoy it.

Thus it comes to pass that religion passionately clings to traditional beliefs which science may overthrow to satisfy its insatiable curiosity and its desire for logical consistency. The conflict between religion and science is thus a conflict between (on the one hand) loyalty to the old and (on the other) morally neutral curiosity about everything.

Let us glance at some actual forms of superstition that have been strengthened by religion.

(*1*) *Demoniac Possession.* Whatever be our theories as to the origin of religion, there can be no doubt about the antiquity and persistence of the belief in disembodied spirits, benevolent and malevolent; and all existing religions involve the belief in such supernatural beings, called gods, ghosts, spirits of ancestors, demons, angels, etc. Organized religion is largely based on and develops credulity in this domain. It insists on certain approved ways of conciliating these spirits or obtaining their favor by some ritual of sacrifices, prayer, incantations, the wearing of amulets, or the like. Priests are experts in these rituals, and their influence is certainly not to destroy the belief on which their occupation rests. Consider, for instance, the oracle at Delphi, based on the belief that the raving priestess was possessed by the God Apollo who spoke through her. Religious people like Plato or the Platonic Socrates believed this and held the oracle in great awe. Yet even contemporaries realized that the managing priests were manipulating the final answer under the guise of interpreting the raving utterances of the priestess. The sober Thucydides went out of his way to remark on the only occasion on which the oracle guessed right. Similar observations may be made about the raving prophets mentioned in the Book of Samuel. We find their analogue today in the dancing dervishes of Islam.

One form of this superstition of demoniac possession plays a prominent role in the New Testament. The power of Jesus and his disciples to cast out devils was obviously regarded by the writers of the Gospels as a chief pillar of the Christian claim. The New Testament, to be sure, did not originate this ancient theory of the nature of certain mental aberrations; but its authority has certainly hindered the effort to dispel this superstitious view of the cause of insanity and hysteria—a view that resulted in a most horrible treatment of the sick.

(*2*) *Witchcraft.* The fear of witchcraft is a natural outcome of the belief in spirits and in the possibility of controlling or using them. If religion did not originate this superstition, it certainly did a good deal to strengthen it. Indeed, Protestant as well as Catholic Christianity at one time bitterly persecuted those who did not believe in the efficacy of witchcraft. For the writers of the Bible certainly believed that witches could recall even the prophets from the dead; and the Mosaic law specifically commanded that witches should be put to death.[1]

The effects of this Biblical command were quite horrible. Not only were thousands burned within a short time at Trèves, but the torture of those suspected (in order to make them confess) was perhaps even more frightful. The victims of mere suspicion had their bones broken, were deprived of all water, and suffered unmentionable cruelties. Perhaps even worse was the resulting general insecurity and the terrible feeling of fear and of distrust. Yet so clear was the Biblical injunction that enlightened men like More, Casaubon, and Cudworth denounced those who disbelieved in witchcraft. For to give up the belief in witchcraft is to give up the infallibility of the Bible.

(*3*) *Magic.* Closely related to witchcraft is magic.

Recent writers like Frazer are inclined to draw a sharp distinction between magic and religion. But though the Church hindered the progress of physics, chemistry, and medicine by persecuting magicians,[2] the belief that the course of nature could be changed by invoking supernatural agencies or spirits is common to both religion and magic. The magician cures you by an incantation, pronouncing a strange formula; the priest or rabbi does it by a blessing; the saint does it posthumously to anyone who touches his relics. The magician brings rain by rubbing a stick, the priest by a prayer. If a formula or ritual invokes the accepted god and is performed by the author-

[1] Exod. 22:18; Lev. 20:27.   [2] It burned Peter of Abano even after his death.

ized person, it is religion. If the god, the act, or the agent is not an authorized one, the first is referred to as a devil, the second as a sacrilege, and the third as a magician. The Church itself regarded the pagan deities as demons. Both religion and magic generally involve the influence of the supernatural—though the magicians more frequently studied the physical or medicinal properties of the substances they used. The fetish-worshiper attaches magical potency to stones, but so does the Bible. Touching the Ark, even with the most worshipful intention, brings death.[1] Christianity frowns on idol-worshiping but it still attaches supernatural power to certain objects like the cross, relics of saints, etc. Holy water wards off devils. Miracles are a part of Christian faith and are offered as evidence of its truth. But the evidence in favor of the Virgin Birth, of the stopping of the sun and the moon at Ajalon, or of the Resurrection, etc., cannot support its own weight. A small part of mankind finds it adequate, and this only because of the fear of being damned or anathematized for unbelief. It is inconceivable that an impartial court would convict anybody on such evidence. In fact, no event would be considered miraculous if the evidence in its favor were as cogent as that which makes us believe wonderful but natural occurrences.

Another religious belief that the progress of science has shown to be superstition—i.e., to have no basis in rational evidence—is that the rainbow, comets, and other meteorological phenomena are not natural events but special portents to warn mankind against sin.[2]

(4) *Opposition to Science.* It is not necessary for me to recount the fight of Christianity against the Copernican astronomy, against modern geology or biology, or against the scientific treatment of Biblical history. They have become commonplace, and I may merely refer to the works of Lecky, Draper, A. D. White, and Benn. The point to be noted is that the old adherents of religion did not want to know the truth, and that their religion did not encourage them to think it worth while to seek any truth other than their accepted particular faith. Religious truth is absolute and its possession makes everything else unimportant. Hence religion never preaches the duty of critical thought, of searching or investigating supposed facts.

From this point of view it is interesting to read the testimony of Bishop Colenso as to what led him to write his book on the Pentateuch. When he tried to teach Biblical history to the South African natives, he was amazed at the obvious contradictions which these simple savages discovered in the various accounts of the patriarchs. Yet millions of astute and learned Christians had not noticed these discrepancies.

Consider, for instance, the Biblical statement that the hare chews the cud. This can easily be tested. Does your orthodox Christian do that? This disinclination to question things also appears, of course, elsewhere; but no-

[1] II Sam. 6:6-7.   [2] Gen. 9:13; Joel 2:30, 31.

where so emphatically and persistently as in the field of religion. Believe in the Koran or be damned forever!

Not only does religion fail to regard critical intelligence and the search for natural truth as a virtue, but the ideal which it holds up frequently makes light of truth itself. Even when God lays down a moral law, He is Himself above the moral law. He sends a lying spirit to Ahab, and his Church for a long time did not think a promise to heretics binding. In the fourth century organized Christianity adopted the view that deceit and lying were virtues if in the interests of the Church (*cf*. Mosheim). The duty of truthfulness is much more exemplified in science than in religion.

In this respect "liberal" modernism seems intellectually much more corrupting than orthodox Fundamentalism. Confronted by natural absurdities —such as the sun and the moon stopping in their course, or the hare chewing the cud—the Fundamentalist can still say: "I believe in the word of the Spirit more than in the evidence offered by the eyes of my corruptible flesh." This recognizes a clear conflict; and the intellectual hara-kiri of the Fundamentalist is a desperate venture that can appeal only to those whose faith is already beyond human reason or evidence. But the modernist who gives up the infallibility of the Bible in matters of physics, and tries to keep it in matters of faith and morals, has to resort to intellectually more corrupting procedure. By "liberal" and unhistorical interpretations he tries—contrary to the maxim of Jesus—to pour new wine into old bottles and then pretend that the result *is* the ancient wine of moral wisdom.

In any case, religion makes us cling to certain beliefs, and often corrupts our sense of logical evidence by making us afraid to regard arguments in favor of religion as inconclusive or to view arguments against it as at all probative. The will to believe even contrary to demonstrative evidence, *credo quia absurdum*, is often lauded as a religious virtue.

It has often been claimed that the superstitions of religion are merely the current superstitions of the people who at the time profess that religion. If this were true, it would only prove that religion is powerless to stop superstition—that it is intellectually parasitic and not creative. But the intimate connection between religion and supernaturalism, and the passionate attachment to the old ways which every religion intensifies, cannot but strengthen superstition and hinder the progress of science towards the attainment of new truth as to human affairs. And this is altogether independent of the personal profit in power, prestige, or even revenue which leads many in and outside of the churches to exploit the credulity of the multitude.

II. RELIGION AS AN ANTI-MORAL FORCE

It is often claimed that religion is the protector of morals and that the breakdown of the former inevitably leads to a breakdown of the latter. While there may be some correlation or coincidence between periods of moral change and periods of religious change, there is no evidence at all for the assumption that the abandonment of any established religion leads to an enduring decline in morality. There is more evidence to the contrary. Those who break away from religion are often among the most high-minded members of the community. The chaplains of our prisons do not complain of the prevalence of atheism or lack of religious affiliation among the criminals to whom they minister, while there certainly has been uncontested complaint that religious leaders, high priests, popes, and cardinals have led rapacious and most licentious lives. As faithful a son of the church as Dante puts popes in Hell, and it was in an age of general religious faith that Boccaccio put into the mouth of a Jew the *mot* that the Church of Rome must be of divine origin or it could not stand despite such government. But this is an ungracious task from which we may well turn.

Let us look at the matter more philosophically. What do we mean by morality? Generally we mean those rules of conduct that appeal to people as generally conducive to a decent human life. It follows therefore that, as the conditions of human life change, the content of wise moral rules must change accordingly. Religion, being passionate and absolute in its claim, formulates moral rules as inflexible taboos. It thus prevents needed change and causes tension and violent reaction. But science, studying the principles involved, can distinguish the permanent elements of human organization and safeguard them amidst necessary adjustments to new situations. It is secular social science and philosophy rather than religion that have the wisdom to see the necessity of conserving human values in the very process of facilitating desirable changes.

The absolute character of religious morality has made it emphasize the sanctions of fear—the terrifying consequences of disobedience. I do not wish to ignore the fact that the greatest religious teachers have laid more stress on the love of the good for its own sake. But in the latter respect they have not been different from such great philosophers as Democritus, Aristotle, or Spinoza, who regarded morality as its own reward, like the proper playing of a musical instrument. But the great body of established religions have emphasized extraneous punishment. In the religion of the Old Testament, as in that of almost all Oriental and classic Greek and Roman religions, the punishment meted out to the individual or people is entirely temporal, and the rewards of virtue are in the form of material prosperity. When people realize that this is not true, that the wicked do prosper and that, contrary to the pious Psalmist, not only the righteous but their children are often in want of bread, they either put the whole thing in the realm of theological mystery (as in the Book of Job) or else resort to the pious fiction that the bad man is troubled by his conscience. But the latter is obviously not true. Only those who are trained by religion to cultivate their conscience are troubled that way. The bad man gloats over his evil if he succeeds, and is sorry only if he fails. For this reason, Judaism, Christianity, and Islam have developed and stressed the doctrine of Hell, of eternal and most terrifying punishment. But it is doubtful whether the deterrent value of all these terrors is really large. Living in the presence of a constant terror does not eliminate carelessness. At best, fear secures only conformity. The development of enlightened inclination or disposition depends on educational wisdom and science. Some religions have talked much about love. But the predominant emphasis on the motive of fear for the enforcement of absolute commands has made religious morality develop the intensest cruelty that the human heart has known.

Religion has made a virtue of cruelty. Bloody sacrifices of human beings to appease the gods fill the pages of history. In ancient Mexico we have the wholesale sacrifice of prisoners of war as a form of the national cultus. In the ancient East we have the sacrifice of children to Moloch. Even the Greeks were not entirely free from this religious custom, as the story of the sacrifice of Iphigenia by her father testifies. Let us note that while the Old Testament prohibits the ancient Oriental sacrifice of the first-born, it does not deny its efficacy in the case of the King of Moab (II Kings 3:2) nor is there any revulsion at the readiness with which Abraham was willing to sacrifice his son Isaac. In India it was the religious duty of the widow to be burned on the funeral pyre of her late husband. And while Christianity formally condemned human sacrifice, it revived it in fact under the guise of burning heretics. I pass over the many thousands burned by order of the Inquisition, and the record of the hundreds of people burned by rulers like Queen Mary for not believing in the Pope or in transubstantiation. The Protestant Calvin burned the scholarly Servetus for holding that Jesus was "the son of the eternal God" rather than "the eternal son of God." And in our own Colonial America, heresy was a capital offense.[1]

Cruelty is a much more integral part of religion than most people nowadays realize. The Mosaic law commands the Israelites, whenever attacking a city, to kill all the males, and all females who have known men. The religious force of this is shown when Saul is cursed and his whole dynasty is destroyed for leaving one prisoner, King Agag, alive. Consider that tender psalm, "By the rivers of Babylon." After voicing the pathetic cry "How can we sing the songs of Jehovah in a foreign land?" it goes on to curse Edom, and ends "Happy shall he be, that taketh and dasheth thy little ones against the rock." Has there been any religious movement to expurgate this from the religious service of Jews and Christians? Something of the spirit of this intense hatred for the enemies of God (i.e., those not of our own religion) has invented and developed the terrors of Hell, and condemned almost all of mankind to suffer them eternally—all, that is, except a few members of our

---

[1] This, of course, is based on the Bible: Deut. 17:2-5 and 18:20.

own particular religion. Worst of all, it has regarded these torments as adding to the beatitude of its saints.[1] The doctrine of a loving and all-merciful God professed by Christianity or Islam has not prevented either one from preaching and practicing the duty to hate and persecute those who do not believe. Nay, it has not prevented fierce wars between diverse sects of these religions, such as the wars between Shiites, Sunnites, and Wahabites, between Greek Orthodox, Roman Catholics, and Protestants.

The fierce spirit of war and hatred is not of course entirely due to religion. But religion *has* made a *duty* of hatred. It preached crusades against Mohammedans and forgave atrocious sins to encourage indiscriminate slaughter of Greek Orthodox as well as of Mohammedan populations. It also preached crusades against Albigenses, Waldenses, and Hussite Bohemians. And what is more heartrending than the bloody wars between the two branches of the Hussites over the question of the communion in two kinds? This war desolated and ruined Bohemia.

The Inquisition is fortunately now a matter of the past. Let us not forget, however, that the Church has not abandoned its right and duty to exterminate heretics; and it will doubtless perform its duty when conditions permit it. Spanish and Portuguese saints have expressed deep religious ardor in burning heretics.[2] Ingenuity in inventing means of torture was the outcome of religious zeal on the part of the pious clergy who belonged to the Office of the Holy Inquisition.

The essential cruelty of religious morality shows itself in the peculiar fervor with which Protestant Puritans hate to see anyone enjoy himself on Sunday. Our "Blue Sunday" legislation is directed against the most innocent kinds of enjoyment—against open-air games like baseball, concerts, or theatrical plays. And while there may be some serious social considerations in favor of liquor prohibition, there is little doubt that an element of sadism, a hatred of seeing others enjoying beer or wine, is one of the motives which actuate religious fanatics. For that is in the great historic tradition of the Protestant Church.

Cruel persecution and intolerance are not accidents, but grow out of the very essence of religion, namely, its absolute claims. So long as each religion claims to have absolute, supernaturally revealed truth, all other religions are sinful errors. Despite the fact that some religions speak eloquently of universal brotherhood, they have always in fact divided mankind into sects, while science has united them into one community, which desires to profit by enlightenment. Even when a religion like Christianity or Islam sweeps over diverse peoples and temporarily unites them into one, its passionate nature inevitably leads to the development of sects and heresies. There is no

---

[1] Tertullian, Saint Augustine, and Saint Thomas are among those who have so expressed themselves. See *Summa Theologica Suppl.*, Qu. 94, Art. I.

[2] In our time Unamuno, while not orthodox, defended the Inquisition because he would not accept the secular rationalism which abolished it.

drearier chapter in the history of human misery than the unusually bloody internecine religious or sectarian wars which have drenched in blood so much of Europe, Northern Africa, and Western Asia.

Even in our own day, a common religion of Christian love does not prevent war between Christian nations. Rather do the churches encourage the warlike spirit and pray for victory. If the conflict among the various creeds of Christianity in our own country is not so bloody, it is not because the spirit of intolerance has disappeared. The Ku Klux Klan and the incidents of our presidential campaign in 1928 are sufficient indications to the contrary. The disappearance of religious persecution is rather due to the fact that those who would persecute do not any longer have adequate power. It is the growth of science, making possible free intercourse among different peoples which has led to that liberation which abolished the Inquisition and has made it possible for freethinkers to express their views without losing their civic and political rights.

The complacent assumption which identifies religion with higher morality ignores the historic fact that there is not a single loathsome human practice that has not at some time or other been regarded as a religious duty. I have already mentioned the breaking of promises to heretics. But assassination and thuggery (as the words themselves indicate), sacred prostitution (in Babylonia and India), diverse forms of self-torture, and the verminous uncleanliness of saints like Thomas a Becket, have all been part of religion. The religious conception of morality has been a legalistic one. Moral rules are the commands of the gods. But the latter are sovereigns and not themselves subject to the rules which they lay down for others according to their own sweet wills.

In all religions, the gods have been viewed as subject to flattery. They can be persuaded to change their minds by sacrifices and prayers. A god who responds to the prayers of the vast majority of people cannot be on a much higher moral plane than those who address him. And what would become of religion, to the majority, if prayers and sacrifices were cut out?

It is doubtless true that some of the noblest moral maxims have been expressed by religious teachers—the Buddha, the Hebrew prophets, Jesus, and Mohammed. But in organized religion, these maxims have played but an ornamental part. How much of the profound disillusion and cultivated resignation of Prince Gautama is to be found in the daily practice of the Bhikhus or beggar monks, or the common ritual of prayer-wheels and talismanic statuettes of the Buddha? This, however, is too long a theme. It would require an examination of the actual practices of the various religions which would exhaust many hours.

Let me, however, consider one point. It is often alleged that the later Hebrew prophets beginning with Amos were the first to introduce a strictly moral conception of God. "An honest God's the noblest work of man." Now it is true that men like Amos, Isaiah, and Micah did among other themes preach social righteousness, feeding the widow and orphan, rather than the national cultus of Sabbaths, holy days, and sacrifices. But will anyone dare to assert that the feeding of widows and orphans, and similar deeds of mercy, constitute the distinguishing essence of the Jewish religion? Surely others before and after the prophets believed and practiced such admirable commandments. Some of the philosophers even ventured to discuss and generalize them so that we might have some clew as to when a given act *is* just and merciful, and when it is not. Yet if a Greek or a Persian should "do justice, love mercy, and walk humbly with God" (the last defined, let us say, in Aristotelian or Spinozistic terms), would he be regarded as a Jew in religion? Surely not so much as one who should be rather negligent in regard to justice and mercy, but should practice circumcision and observe the dietary laws, the laws of the Sabbath and of the Day of Atonement, etc. So also a Persian who in fact believed in the ethical commands of Jesus would not be considered a Christian in religion if he had not been baptized into any church, and did not subscribe to the doctrine of the Trinity or the Virgin Birth. Admirable moral practices on the part of a Hindu or an Inca would not make either of them a Christian. One's religion is judged by the organized group or church of which he is a member. My revered teacher Josiah Royce has justly identified religion, and especially Christianity, with communal life.

In the struggle for social justice, what has been the actual influence of religion? Here the grandiose claims of religious apologists are sadly belied by historic facts. The frequent claim that Christianity abolished slavery has nothing but pious wishes to support it. Indeed, in our own country, the clergy of the South was vigorously eloquent in defense of slavery as a divine institution. Nor was it the Church that was responsible for the initiation of the factory legislation that mitigated the atrocious exploitation of human beings in mines and mills. It was not the Church that initiated the movement to organize workmen for mutual support and defense, or that originated the effort to abolish factual slavery when men were paid in orders on company stores—a practice that has prevailed in some of our own states. The Church has generally been on the side of the powerful classes who have supported it—royalists in France, landowners in England, the *cientifico* or exploiting class in Mexico, etc. Here and there some religious leader or group has shown sympathy with the oppressed; but the Church as a whole has property interests which affiliate it with those in power.

III. RELIGION AND THE EMOTIONAL LIFE

Kant has regarded religion as concerned with the great question of *What We Can* (ultimately) *Hope For*. In so far as hopes are resolutions, they are irrefutable by logical arguments. For arguments can only appeal to accepted premises. But hopes may be illusory or ill-founded—they may even attach to what is demonstrably impossible. Such, in the light of modern science, is the hope of the actual resurrection of the body. But what is more important is that many of the hopes that religion has held out to men—e.g., the Mohammedan heaven—are now seen as thoroughly unworthy and even sordid.

Does religion enrich the emotional life? It is customary to speak of religion as if it were always a consolation to the bereaved and a hope in times of trial and distress. Doubtless it often is so. Let us not forget, however, the great fact that religion is based on fear and promotes it. The fear of the Lord is the beginning of religious wisdom, and, while the Lord is sometimes merciful, he is also a God of Vengeance, visiting the sins of the fathers upon the children to the third and fourth generations. The fires of Hell or other forms of divine punishment are a source of real fear whenever and wherever religion has a powerful grip on people generally. Indeed, when the belief in the Devil or evil gods tends to wane, the belief in a personal god tends to evaporate.

The gods are jealous of human happiness. Schiller has portrayed this in *The Ring of Polycrates,* following the good authority of Herodotus and others. When Jehovah is angry at David, he sends a plague killing seventy thousand innocent Israelites. Indeed, throughout the books of Judges, Samuel, and Kings, we have numerous instances of Jehovah's action being above the moral law. In the Book of Job the question is put directly: "Who is man that he dare pass judgment on God's ways?" God's ways are beyond us and nothing is secure for us.

It is the keen dread of the gods and their wanton interference in human affairs that has made men like Lucretius hail the Epicurean philosophy with joy as a great emancipation from continual fear.

Many of the supposedly spiritual comforts of religion are meretricious. The great elation which people experience when they "get religion" is often a morally disintegrating force, as all forms of irrational or uncontrolled excitement are likely to be. We can see this effect in the religious orgies of Semitic times, euphemistically referred to as "rejoicing before the Lord." And we have ample records in America of the breakdown of morale as a result of the hysteria engendered by ignorant revivalist preachers, leading at times to sexual frenzies. Nor is this a new note in religion. Among the Mohammedans, where the sex element is rigorously removed from religious ritual, frenzies take the form of dervish dancing, which results in complete loss of self-control. Such organized hysteria is to be found in all religions.

No one can read religious literature without being struck by the abject terror that the notion of sin has aroused in human consciousness. Religious sin is not something that mortal man can avoid. It is a terrible poison which infects the air we breathe and every fiber of our flesh and blood. For our very existence in the flesh is sinful. How can we avoid this body of death and corruption? This is the terrible cry which rings through the ages in the penitential prayers of the Assyro-Babylonians, Buddhists, Hebrews, medieval monks, and Calvinistic preachers.

> Quid sum miser tunc dicturus,
> Quem patronum rogaturus,
> Cum vix iustus sit securus?

Religion has encouraged men to dwell on the torments of Hell and to inflict on themselves diverse spiritual agonies (see *The Spiritual Exercises* of Saint Ignatius Loyola).

Religion breeds terrors of all sorts. Who, for instance, would worry about the appearance of Halley's Comet if pious readers of the Bible did not conclude that this was a warning from heaven and a portent of evil to come? Yet Europe suffered the most agonizing terror, the veriest paroxysm of fear, because of it. This fear strengthened ecclesiastical tyranny and hatred against unbelievers when the pope himself exorcised that distressing sign in the sky.

Consider the terrors which the religious belief in demons and their control of earthly affairs has aroused in the daily lives of simple-minded men and women. We think it cruel to frighten children by threats of the "bogey man"; yet religion has systematically frightened most of mankind through the doctrine of demons, who have the power to make us sin when we do not know it and to torture us at their evil pleasure. What greater terror can there be than the fear of having witchcraft or even a powerful prayer or curse directed against you by some unsuspected enemy? Perhaps the fear of not believing in miracles which seem to us impossible and thus being guilty of mortal heresy is not now widespread. But it is of the essence of religious thought even today that, unless you can get yourself to believe certain inherently improbable propositions, you must abandon all hope. And how can anyone be free from all doubts when opposed views are actively expressed by some of our most respected fellow men?

Consider also the tragedy of enforcing monastic celibacy on young people because their parents promised them to the Church. Or consider, on the other hand, the opposite harms to family life resulting from the Church's opposition to birth control, no matter how rationally indicated by hygiene and common decency. Whatever motivates the Church's opposition, the source of its strength on this point is the old religious taboo against touching the gates of life and death, a taboo which science daily disregards. This taboo shows itself in the prohibition of any form of euthanasia or suicide, no matter how hideous or tortured life becomes. Even supposedly liberal clergymen are ready with unfeeling arrogance to brand as a coward anyone unfortunate enough to find life unbearable. But despite the depth of this religious fear of touching the gates of life and death, we do not or cannot carry it out consistently. We do control the birth rate and the death rate of any community by economic sanitary and political measures. By excluding the Chinese from our own country and confining them to their inadequate lands we force many of them into starvation. The Church does not condemn this way of controlling the birth or death rate. It does not even condemn the wholesale death-dealing and birth-prevention of war.

While religion has encouraged certain feasts and holidays, it has not been the active friend of that more steady enjoyment of life which comes from developing the industrial and the fine arts. The Old Testament and the Koran, with their prohibition against graven images, have repressed sculpture and representative painting; and the record of the Christian Church for the two thousand years of its existence hardly supports the contention that it has been the mother and patroness of the fine arts. The monasteries, to be sure, developed the art of illuminating manuscripts, and many magnificent structures were erected by bishops and popes like Leo X, who in their personal lives openly flouted the Christian religion. But when did religion or church do anything to nurse the arts and bring them into the homes of the great mass of people? Censorship rather than active encouragement has been the Church's attitude.

In regard to the terrors as well as the superstitions and immoralities of religion, it will not do to urge that they are due only to the imperfections of the men who professed the various religions. If religion cannot restrain evil, it cannot claim effective power for good. In fact, however, the evidence indicates that religion has been effective for evil. It might be urged that certain terrors have likewise been aroused by popular science—e.g., the needless terrors of germs, the absurd and devastating popular theories of diet, etc. But the latter are readily corrigible. Indeed it is the essence of science to corrct the errors which it may originate. Religion cannot so readily confess error, and the terrors with which it surrounds the notion of sin are felt with a fatality and an intensity from which science and art are free.

I have spoken of the dark side of religion and have thus implied that there is another side. But if this implication puts me out of the class of those who are unqualified opponents of all that has been called religion, I do not wish to suggest that I am merely an advocate, or that I have any doubts as to the justice of the arguments that I have advanced. Doubtless some of my arguments may turn out to be erroneous, but at present I hold them all in good faith. I believe that this dark side of religion is a reality, and it is my duty on this occasion to let those who follow me do justice to the other side. But if what I have said has any merit, those who wish to state the bright side of religion must take account of and not ignore the realities which I have tried to indicate. This means that the defense of religion must be stated in a spirit of sober regard for truth, and not as a more or less complacent apology for beliefs which we are determined not to abandon. Anyone can, by assuming his faith to be the truth, argue from it more or less plausibly and entirely to his own satisfaction. But that is seldom illuminating or strengthening. The real case for religion must show compelling reasons why, despite the truths that I have sought to display, men who do not believe in religion should change their views. If this be so, we must reject such apologies for religion as Balfour's *Foundations of Belief*. One who accepts the Anglican Church may regard such a book as a sufficient defense. But in all essentials it is a subtle and urbane, but none the less complacent, begging of all the serious questions in the case. For similar reasons also I think we must reject the apology for religion advanced by my revered and beloved teacher William James.

Let us take up his famous essay on "The Will To Believe." Consider in the first place his argument that science (which is organized reason) is inapplicable in the realm of religion, because to compare values or worths "we must consult not science but what Pascal calls our heart."[1] But if it were true that science and reason have no force in matters of religion, why argue at all? Why all these elaborate reasons in defense of religion? Is it not because the arguments of men like Voltaire and Huxley did have influence that men like De Maistre and James tried to answer them? Who, the latter ask, ever heard of anyone's changing his religion because of an argument? It is not necessary for me to give a list of instances from my own knowledge. Let us admit that few men confess themselves defeated or change their views in the course of any one argument. Does this prove that arguments have no effect? Do not men frequently use against others the very arguments which at first they professed to find unconvincing? The fact is that men do argue about religion, and it is fatuous for those who argue on one side to try also to discredit *all* rational arguments. It seems more like childish weakness to kick against a game or its rules when you are losing in it. And it is to the great credit of the Catholic Church that it has categorically condemned fideism or the effort to eliminate reason from religion. Skepticism against reason is not a real or enduring protection to religion. Its poison, like that of the Nessus shirt, finally destroys the faith that puts it on. Genuine faith in the truth is confident that it can prove itself to universal reason.

Let us look at the matter a little closer.

James argues that questions of belief are decided by our will. Now it is true that one can say: "I do not wish to argue. I want to continue in the belief that I have." But is not the one who says this already conscious of a certain weakness in his faith which might well be the beginning of its disintegration? The man who has a robust faith in his friend does not say, "I want to believe that he is honest," but "I know that he is honest, and any doubt about it is demonstrably false or unreasonable." To be willing to put your case and its evidence before the court of reason is to show real confidence in it.

But James argues that certain things are beloved not on the basis of ra-

[1] See above, p. 233—ED.

tional or scientific weighing of evidence, but on the compulsion of our passional nature. This is true. But reflection may ease the passional compulsion. And why not encourage such reflection?

The history of the last few generations has shown that many have lost their faith in Christianity because of reflection induced by Darwinism. Reflection on the inconsistencies of the Mosaic chronology and cosmology has shown that these do not differ from other mythologies; and this has destroyed the belief of many in the plenary inspiration of the Bible. It is therefore always possible to ask: Shall I believe a given religious proposition as the absolute truth, or shall I suspend final decision until I have further evidence? I must go to church or stay out. But I may do the latter at least without hiding from myself the inadequacy of my knowledge or of the evidence. In politics I vote for X or Y without necessarily getting myself into the belief that my act is anything more than a choice of probabilities. I say: Better vote for X than Y; although if I knew more (for which there is no time) I might vote the other way. In science I choose on the basis of all the available evidence but expressly reserve the possibility that future evidence may make me change my view. It is difficult to make such reservations within any religious system. But it is possible to remain permanently skeptical or agnostic with regard to religion itself and its absolute claims.

The momentous character of the choice in regard to religion may be dissolved by reflection which develops detachment or what James calls lightheartedness. What is the difference between believing in one religion or in another or in none? A realization of the endless variety of religious creeds, of the great diversity of beliefs that different people hold to be essential to our salvation, readily liberates us from the compulsion to believe in every Mullah that comes along or else fear eternal damnation. James draws a sharp distinction between a living and a nonliving issue. To him, I suppose, the question of whether to accept Judaism, Islam, or Buddhism was not a living one. But the question whether to investigate so-called psychical phenomena as proofs of immortality was a living one. But surely reflection may change the situation, and a student of religion may come to feel that James's choice was arbitrary and untenable.

The intensification of the feeling that religious issues are important comes about through the assumption that my eternal salvation depends upon my present choice, or—at most—on what I do during the few moments of my earthly career. There is remarkably little evidence for this assumption. If our life is eternal, we may have had more chances before and we may have more later. Why assume that the whole of an endless life is determined by an infinitesimal part of it? From this point of view, men like Jonathan Edwards, to whom eternal Hell is always present and who makes an intense religious issue out of every bite of food, appears to be just unbalanced, and in need of more play in the sunshine and fresh air and perhaps a little more sleep. I mention Jonathan Edwards because his life and teachings enable us to turn the tables on religion by what James regards as the great pragmatic argument in its favor. Accept it, James says, and you will be better off at once.[1] As most religions condemn forever those who do not follow them, it is as risky to accept any one as none at all. And it is possible to take the view that they are all a little bit ungracious, too intense, and too sure of what in our uncertain life cannot be proved. Let us better leave them all alone and console ourselves with the hypothesis—a not altogether impossible one—that the starry universe and whatever gods there be do not worry about us at all, and will not resent our enjoying whatever humane and enlightened comfort and whatever vision of truth and beauty our world offers us. Let us cultivate our little garden. The pretended certainties of religion do not really offer much more. This is of course not a refutation of religion, or of the necessity which reflective minds find to grapple with it. But it indicates that there may be more wisdom and courage as well as more faith in honest doubt than in most of the creeds.

[1] See above, pp. 235 ff.—ED.

13 · ENSLIN

Morton Scott Enslin was born at Somerville, Massachusetts, in 1897. He was professor of New Testament at Crozer Theological Seminary from 1924 to 1954, and edited the *Crozer Quarterly* from 1941 to 1952. In 1954 he accepted a call to the Theological School, St. Lawrence University. In 1945 he was president of the Society of Biblical Literature and Exegesis; in 1952 he was president of the American Theological Society.

His major works are *The Ethics of Paul* (1930), *Christian Beginnings* (1938; Harper Torchbook ed. in two vols., the third part, pp. 201-533, under the title, *The Literature of the Christian Movement*), and *The Prophet from Nazareth* (1961).

All of the following selections come from *The Literature of the Christian Movement*.

The New Testament

THE GOSPEL ACCORDING TO MATTHEW

The gospel of Matthew has been described as a "manual of the life of Christ and of biblical theology." This is a singularly apt designation, for it emphasizes the characteristic of the writing which is most obvious, namely, that it is at once systematic and comprehensive and intended for church use. It is carefully arranged, with topics easily remembered. Of all the gospels its outline and content are the most easily remembered. It implies an organized church life with a well-defined moral code. Throughout the book the comparison between the first great lawgiver, Moses, and his far greater successor are too apparent to be accidental. Both had been miraculously preserved at the time of their birth from the machinations of a wicked and suspicious king; both had given their God-inspired legislation from the mountain top. In a word, the Gospel of Matthew may be styled the New Law. As one reads this gospel he feels it is the work of the evangelist. Furthermore, the designation *editor* is a most unhappy one; in every sense of the word he deserves the term *author*. He has used sources, probably more completely than has often been admitted, but he clearly felt perfectly free to interpret, to rearrange, to rewrite drastically, and to suppress. Though his readiness to rearrange is everywhere evident, his fondness for preserving the exact phraseology of his several sources, if at all possible, is equally noticeable. It may be remarked parenthetically that in both these latter respects his habit is precisely the reverse of Luke. He skilfully combines Jesus' sayings into units. The Sermon on the Mount is an excellent example. Here various detached sayings of Jesus—many of which are also preserved in Luke, but for the most part are scattered through that gospel—are assembled into an artistic, closely compacted whole to serve as a sample of Jesus' "teachings." Chapter 13 presents a series of parables, illustrative of another phase of his threefold ministry,[1] *viz.*, "preaching the gospel of the kingdom."

Unlike Mark, who has arranged his material to present vividly the problem of Jesus' death—its historical occasion and its theological purport—and to provide occasional materials, almost in the nature of asides to the reader, to keep this emphasis clear, Matthew's purpose is quite different. Although he utilizes Mark's material almost *in toto*, and thus of necessity preserves many of Mark's emphases, he is not concerned with them. One of the features of this gospel is its structure, noticeably its arrangement in numerical groups—three's, five's, and seven's. Among these may be mentioned the curious arrangement of Jesus' ancestors in three divisions each of fourteen generations;[2] the three temptations; three illustrations of the implicates of Christian righteousness[3] (alms, prayer, fasting); three prohibitions[4] ("do not lay up treasures on earth," "do not judge," "do not give that which is holy to the dogs"); three commands[5] (ask, enter, beware of false prophets); three healings[6] (the leper, the centurion's servant, Peter's mother-in-law); three "fear nots";[7] three prayers in Gethsemane;[8] above all the threefold nature of the ministry—"And Jesus went about in all Galilee, teaching in their synagogues, and preaching the gospel of the kingdom, and healing all manner of disease and all manner of sickness among the people."[9] There are seven woes in the blistering attack on the Pharisees;[10] seven beatitudes;[11] and seven parables in chapter 13. Even more conspicuous is the arrangement of Jesus' words into five blocks of extended sayings, each one followed with a colophon:

And it came to pass, when Jesus had finished these words, the multitudes were astonished at his teaching: for he taught them as one having authority, and not as their scribes (7:28).

---

[1] Cf. the clear-cut statement in Matt. 4:23, expanded and illustrated by the remainder of the book.

[2] It has been pointed out that in the genealogy the emphasis upon Jesus as the son of David is pointed. Furthermore, the name David in Hebrew consists of *three* letters DVD whose numerical value is *fourteen* (4+6+4=14). Is it conceivable that in this we have an early Christian riddle?

[3] Matt. 6:1-18.	[6] Matt. 8:1-15.	[9] Matt. 4:23; cf. 9:35.
[4] Matt. 6:19-7:6.	[7] Matt. 10:26,28,31.	[10] Matt. 23:13-36.
[5] Matt. 7:7-20.	[8] Matt. 26:39-44.	

[11] The beatitude, "Blessed are the meek: for they shall inherit the earth," which in many Mss. follows, in others precedes, "Blessed are they that mourn," is probably to be seen as a later addition on the basis of Ps. 37:11.

And it came to pass when Jesus had finished commanding his disciples, he departed thence to teach and preach in their cities (11:1).

And it came to pass, when Jesus had finished these parables, he departed thence (13:53).

And it came to pass when Jesus had finished these words, he departed from Galilee, and came into the borders of Judea beyond the Jordan (19:1a).

And it came to pass, when Jesus had finished *all* these words, he said unto his disciples, Ye know that after two days the passover cometh, and the son of man is delivered up to be crucified (26:1,2).

That to some degree at least these sections were considered parallel by the author is obvious from the striking similar phraseology of these colophons. It will be necessary on a later page to consider the question of whether this fivefold division goes even deeper into the structure of the gospel, and whether it is more than an accident that we have five (not four or six) such divisions. The significant point at this juncture is that the combination and arrangement of material into blocks was due to Matthew[12] himself and not to any source.

One example will suffice. Chapter 13 contains seven parables. The first (Sower) and third (Mustard Seed) are taken from Mark. It is usually stated that the parable of the Seed Growing Secretly (Mark 4:26-29) which follows that of the Sower and precedes that of the Mustard Seed is omitted by Matthew. It appears to me far more probable that Matthew's second (the Wheat and the Tares) is Matthew's own adaptation of the Markan parable which he places in the same relative position. The fourth (the Leaven) occurs also in Luke and is usually ascribed to the source from which Matthew and Luke independently drew. The remaining three (the Hidden Treasure, the Merchantman and the Pearl, and the Drag-net) are unique to Matthew. Perhaps all three are to be ascribed to other sources available to him, very possibly in oral form, although it appears to me highly probable that the last of these three, because of its identification of the kingdom of heaven with the Christian church, is to be ascribed to Matthew himself, and was suggested to him by such a word as that in Mark 1:17. To these seven he appends another.[13] Its purpose is not further to amplify the mystery of the kingdom, for its introduction and nature are quite different from the preceding. In these concluding words regarding the disciple who grasps in full the teaching it may well be, as Bacon remarks,[14] that we have "an unconscious portrait" of the evangelist himself.

[12] Such references, here and in other sections, to the authors of the gospels by the names which the books now bear, are solely for the sake of convenience and imply nothing as to the identity of the authors.

[13] Matt. 13:51,52.

[14] B. W. Bacon, *Studies in Matthew*, p. 131; cf. p. 217 and frequently. This volume, while highly technical, will prove very rewarding to the serious student of the gospels.

In these parables another trait of the evangelist is revealed—his excessive fondness for identity of phrase and balanced statement. The parables of the Mustard Seed, the Leaven, the Buried Treasure, the Pearl, and the Dragnet all begin with the same phrase "The kingdom is like unto . . ." To the second, third, and fourth of the seven is prefixed either "Another parable set he before them saying" or "Another parable spake he unto them." Precisely the same word—"Repent ye: for the kingdom of heaven is at hand"— stands as the message of both John the Baptist and Jesus.[15] In the Markan story of the calling of the first four disciples the same trait is seen.[16] In the case of both pairs of brothers the inconspicuous parallel, "and . . . *his* brother," should not be overlooked. More striking is the double conclusion,

"And they straightway left $\left\{ \begin{array}{l} \text{the nets,} \\ \text{the boat and their father,} \end{array} \right\}$ and followed him."

In the case of the former Matthew has adopted the Markan statement. His love of balance leads him to repeat it at the end in preference to Mark's slightly different phrase. In the temple, Matthew tells us, the children cried out, "Hosanna to the son of David,"[17] thus repeating the shout of the crowd at the Triumphal Entry—in the form which Matthew had there used.[18] Even more noticeable is the repeated word, "Ye have heard that it was said . . . ,"[19] or the balance, "Ye are the salt of the earth" . . . "Ye are the light of the world."[20] Closely allied to these—and the list could be greatly increased—is the fondness for balanced statement. For example, to the statement that Jesus was in the wilderness forty days, Matthew alone feels it necessary to add "and forty nights."[21] To the word, apparently taken from Mark 11:25, which Matthew suffixes to the Lord's Prayer—"For if ye forgive men their trespasses, your heavenly Father will also forgive you"[22]—he provides the balanced opposite, "But if ye forgive not men their trespasses, neither will your heavenly Father forgive your trespasses."[23]

Matthew is dependent upon Mark not only for his general outline, but for his narrative material. He utilizes all of Mark and has practically no other narrative material. The only two incidents *outside* of Mark are (1) the genealogy and birth story, and (2) the curious legend of the Coin in the Fish's Mouth (17:24-27). All the other additions are simply expansions of Markan material, and are joined to it as the "mistletoe to the oak" (Streeter). Examples of this are the stories of Peter walking on the water (14:28-31), the end of Judas (27:3-10), the message and dream of Pilate's wife (27:19), Pilate's washing his hands (27:24,25), the raising of the bodies of the saints who had fallen asleep (27:52,53), and the guard at the

---

[15] Matt. 3:2; 4:17.
[16] Matt. 4:18-22; Mark 1:16-20.
[17] Matt. 21:15.
[18] Matt. 21:9.
[19] Matt. 5:21,27,33,38,43.
[20] Matt. 5:13,14.
[21] Matt. 4:1.
[22] Matt. 6:14.
[23] This latter word, while occurring in some Mss. as Mark 11:26 is demonstrably an interpolation from Matthew.

tomb (27:63-66). All of these are simply haggadic expansions of the Markan narrative and indicate no independence of origin. From this a general working principle emerges: While Mark's narrative is not to be accepted uncritically as a plain chronicle of actual facts, but must be closely examined, Matthew's additions are palpably legendary.

The two exceptions mentioned in the last paragraph are somewhat different and deserve a special word. His inclusion of the genealogy and birth story is certainly not due to any desire to write a fuller biography—if possible, Matthew is even less a biography than Mark. It is probably fair to call it a reply to calumny. Not only the reference to the fulfilment of prophecy (1:22) but the mention of the women—Tamar, Rahab, Ruth, Bathsheba—appear to be an attempt to answer anti-Christian slander, notably Jewish, of Mary.[24] For suggestions as to the ultimate sources of the story and the possibility of its being an "international myth," the student may be referred to Bacon's *Studies in Matthew*, pp. 145-154. His story of the Coin in the Fish's Mouth is apparently a bit of Jewish Christian Haggada, reflecting the problem which Jewish Christians faced in regard to the temple tax. Should they refuse to pay it, on the ground that they were no longer Jews, they would become involved in all sorts of difficulty, especially with their Jewish friends. Nor is this (necessarily) an indication that the story antedates the year 70, for after the destruction of the temple the tax was still collected by Rome for her own purposes. On the other hand, that Matthew is the author of this fable is by no means necessary nor perhaps even probable.

For the rest of his narrative material Mark is the sole source of information,[25] but, though he uses it almost in its entirety, he not only often compresses the narrative, omitting many picturesque details,[26] and by no means preserves the vividness and dramatic quality of the earlier account, but also has no hesitation at all in revamping it drastically so that at times its final form is superficially quite different from its source. That the parable of the Wheat and Tares is to be seen as the Matthaean adaptation of Mark's parable of the Seed Growing Secretly which occurs in the same relative position—between the parables of the Sower and the Mustard Seed—has already been suggested. Occasionally the shortening of the narrative or the rearrangement of material involves Matthew in difficulties. A case in point is the statement of Antipas' judgment about Jesus. In Mark the story of Jesus' rejection in Nazareth because of the people's unbelief (Mark 6:1-6a) is followed by the story of the sending out of the Twelve and their success

---

[24] For evidence of such slander see the material assembled by Herford in his volume, *Christianity in Talmud and Midrash*, and also Origen, *c. Celsum* i,28,32,33,39.

[25] The evidence that this source was the canonical Mark, not an earlier version or a source common to both Matthew and Mark, will be presented in chapter 43 [312 f. below].

[26] Cf., for example, the abbreviation in Matthew's version of Mark 1:29-31; his omission of the word that Jesus was "in the stern . . . on the cushion" (Mark 4:38); that the swine numbered "about two thousand" (Mark 5:13); and that the grass was "green" (Mark 6:39).

(6:6b-13). Then appropriately enough comes the mention of Antipas' concern because of this fame of Jesus (6:14-16), which of course had been noised abroad by his disciples. But Matthew has followed the story of the call of the Twelve by that of their mission, and thus passes directly from the incident of the rejection of Jesus at Nazareth to Herod's amazement at his fame (Matt. 13:53-58; 14:1,2). Without the Markan clue there is thus the patent absurdity in Matthew's account: Antipas thinks Jesus is John the Baptist risen from the dead, because Jesus had been rejected! The exorcism of Mark 1:23-28 is omitted by Matthew in his shortening of the whole Markan section (1:16-39), but is compensated for, since in his version of the story of the Gadarene demoniac (Mark 5:1-20) he has two demoniacs cured (8:24-34). Or again, he omits the story of the blind man (Mark 8:22-26)—was it because it was too gradual a miracle?—but has Jesus heal *two* blind men for Mark's Bartimaeus (20:29-34=Mark 10:46-52). Similarly he omits Mark's story of the Deaf Mute (Mark 7:32-37), perhaps because in the story the mechanics of the miracle were stressed, but in 12:22-24 he gives a parallel story and states that this man was also blind. Thus none of the Markan material is actually neglected, although it is often distinctly revamped. To this there is one exception. The story of the Widow's Mites (Mark 12:41-44) is omitted. This was perhaps dropped out between the two great apocalyptic sections as an inconsequential matter. At times he disapproves of a slant of Mark's, and makes a real substitution. A good case in point is in the story of John's reproof by Jesus for attempting to hinder those "who followed not us"—"For he that is not against us is for us" (Mark 9:38-41). This Matthew omits, apparently disapproving of such an attitude, opposed as it is to the teaching of Matt. 7:21-23. But it is to be observed that in 12:30 he has the converse of Mark 9:40, that is, "He that is not with me is against me," which is precisely the attitude which Mark has Jesus reprove; while, furthermore, Mark 9:41 is salvaged and appears in Matt. 10:42, which in turn follows hard upon 10:40, which is adapted from Mark 9:37 (the verse immediately preceding the "omitted" Markan section). Thus Matthew cannot be said to have neglected the section. He salvaged as much of it as he could, and then continued with the Markan narrative (Matt. 18:6=Mark 9:42). . . .

But though Matthew is dependent upon Mark for narrative material and, as will be seen in a later chapter, for his general order or framework, this accounts for only about half of the gospel. In addition to narrative he presents a large quantity of the sayings in the form of discourse and parable, grouped into five blocks, each of which concludes with a set phrase, "And it came to pass, when . . . ," which, according to Bacon, also serves to introduce the next block of narrative, which latter in turn leads up to the next discourse. It is widely conceded that these five discourses are composite. (1) The first comprises chapters 5-7 and is popularly known as the Sermon on the Mount. This designation has contributed to the widespread notion that it is essentially a sermon preached by Jesus, and many fanciful and unfounded conclusions have been drawn. The sermon deserves careful study, but as an example of the homiletic skill of Matthew, not Jesus. Bacon designates it "Concerning Discipleship";[27] Ropes, "Life of a Disciple of Jesus."[28] Both of these descriptions are apt and free from ambiguity. I am inclined, however, to call it the "Essence of the New Law." To a degree it is similar to the section in Luke 6:24-49, but with a quite different emphasis. Actually the conclusions one reaches regarding the relationship of these Matthaean and Lucan sections are of the utmost importance in the perplexing larger question of the relationship of the two gospels. Bacon has caught the exact difference between the two in his word: "Matthew legislates; Luke proclaims glad tidings." Matthew insists that the great reward in heaven is promised *in consequence* of the scrupulous keeping of the new law by Christians, a law characterized by a righteousness superior to that of the Pharisees. Luke, on the contrary, stresses the fact that in spite of the present difficulties they will gain the kingdom; that is, as over against those who are apparently now in high favour, the Christians are the true elect of God. . . .

THE GOSPEL ACCORDING TO LUKE

. . . The reluctance of Matthew to represent Jesus as moved by human emotions, as sorrow, anger, love, and his frequent omission of those touches in his revision of the Markan account have already been noted. An even more careful pruning out of these is to be seen in Luke, who cancels several which had not offended Matthew. For example, he omits Mark's word that at the feeding of the Five Thousand Jesus was moved with compassion (9:11 = Mark 6:34). Following Peter's confession the disciples as a whole are bidden to keep silent, but the specific rebuke to Peter with which the Markan section closes (Mark 8:32,33) is entirely omitted from the Lucan version. In the account of the Passion Luke takes care to tell the story in such a manner that it will be clear that Jesus was condemned not as a malefactor, as were the two who were crucified with him (23:32), but as the Messiah. In the trial before the Sanhedrin there is no mention of the alleged threat to destroy the temple as in the Markan account (Mark 14:55-61), but simply the query, "If thou art the Christ, tell us" (22:67). Similarly, in place of the gibe of the bystanders at the cross, "Ha! thou that destroyest the temple, and buildest it in three days, save thyself, and come down from the cross" (Mark 15:29), Luke has "If thou art the king of the Jews, save

[27] *Op. cit.*, p. 269.
[28] *The Synoptic Gospels*, p. 48. The student will find this little book of immense value.

thyself" (23:37). The vivid story in Mark of the Cleansing of the Temple, the overturned tables and benches, the refusal to allow any man to carry a vessel through the temple (Mark 11:15-19), is drastically shortened and presented without any show of violence (19:45-48). The spitting on Jesus (Mark 14:65) and the scourging by command of the Roman governor (Mark 15:15) go unnoticed. Furthermore, he recasts Mark's account of two meetings of the Sanhedrin (Mark 14:53 ff. and 15:1) to one, occurring in the early morning. To this, however, he adds the story of another trial before Herod, quite unnoticed by Mark. It was at this meeting that Jesus was decked out in royal garb and insulted (23:6-16; contrast Mark 15:16-20). That in this alteration we are to see evidence that Luke is drawing on extra non-Markan material appears to me improbable. Acts 4:25 ff. with its quotation of Psalm 2, which refers to "the *kings* of the earth and the *rulers* in array against the Lord and against his Anointed," would appear to provide a sufficient ground for the alteration.

The gospel is carefully written, and is far harder to remember than Matthew, where the systematic—one might almost say, the bony—structure is always evident. These corners and joints are all painstakingly smoothed down into a literary whole. It is written in excellent Greek. The preface is classical Greek, while the rest of the gospel is idiomatic and smooth. That it is the translation of an Aramaic original is quite unlikely. There are frequent traces reminiscent of the Semitic genius, but these appear to me adequately explained as due to the author's use of Aramaic sources. Nor should we neglect the possibility that the author has deliberately sought to give to his narrative local colour.

That Luke had become possessed of some new materials, notably in the story of the Passion, is often asserted, and to a limited degree is perhaps not improbable. But it is very easy to overemphasize this element and to seek to explain the variation from Mark as due to his use of some substantial parallel non-Markan account. This appears to me highly questionable. The striking thing—and this is perhaps even truer of Matthew—is the apparent paucity of non-Markan material available to our author. As one studies the gospels he is more and more impressed by the almost complete dependence of the latter two upon the former. It is very easy to overstress the "many" who Luke says had preceded him. Today it is the fashion to talk about "editors," and to explain all variations as being due to a different source, of which "sources" ingenious scholars have discovered a surprisingly large number which give them great aid and comfort.

For the most part Luke has reproduced the Markan order, has incorporated or compensated for most of the Markan material, and except in the Passion and Resurrection narratives has limited his changes for the most part to abbreviations of the fuller Mark or to improvements of the style. Several Markan sections are omitted, usually, however, because Luke appears to have had a parallel narrative available which he preferred. Nor should it be overlooked that, occasionally, at least, his own ingenuity had been solely responsible for the preferred parallel. A few examples will suffice: He omits Mark 6:1-6 because he has already made use of the incident in an earlier connexion (4:16-30). The question of the Scribe in Jerusalem, which Mark[29] presents as the third of a similar series, is omitted because he has already utilized it as the setting for the parable of the Good Samaritan (10:25-28). It is to be noted, however, that he has not scrupled to use the *Scribe's* reply (Mark 12:32) as the pleased rejoinder of the *Scribes* to Jesus' neat tripping of the Sadducees (Luke 20:39), while Mark's final word, "And no man after that durst ask him any question,"[30] is drawn forward similarly to close Luke's shortened series (20:40). Surely the use of this dialogue to introduce the parable is obviously secondary. The Scribe has asked for a definition of his neighbour: Who is the man whom he is to love as himself, that is, who is to be the *object* of his benevolence? This the parable does not answer. Rather, as the query, "Who showed himself neighbour?" reveals, the matter is inverted. "Neighbour" is used in the sense of one who himself showed benevolence, that it, the *subject* of the action. It would hence appear that Luke had himself built this setting to "tie" the parable in to his narrative.

An essentially similar situation is found in the Markan story of the Anointing at Bethany (Mark 14:3-9). This Luke omits, for he has used the material earlier in a story which he constructed to serve as the situation for the parable of the Two Debtors (Luke 7:36-50). Apparently the reason for the Lucan location is the reference, two verses earlier, to Jesus eating and drinking (7:34). The secondary nature of the resulting story is evident: strange, indeed, is the behaviour of the host who invites Jesus but is neglectful of the ordinary duties of a host; unnatural, too, is the discourtesy involved in the comment of Jesus, a guest in the house, regarding his host's omission. But more serious than this is the confusion in the story. Plainly the teaching of the story is: The woman anointed Jesus because she loved him, and hence because of this love was forgiven. But the parable strangely inverts the point: the debtors love the master because he had forgiven them. And again, had Simon provided water and oil, this would not have exhibited his love, great or small, but would have been simply part of his duty as a host. That Luke was not dependent upon Mark for the story, but simply utilized it and cancelled its later Markan doublet is perhaps not impossible, but appears to me on the whole improbable. He is always anxious to tie in his extra-Markan material (here the parable of the Debtors); this story provides the means. The host in each case is Simon. Luke makes him a Pharisee, and places the story in Galilee instead of Bethany in Judea. Simon's leprosy is not mentioned; the "woman" of Mark is made a "sinner," apparently because the debtors were "forgiven."[31]

. . . One step leads logically and continuously to the next. In earlier articles[32] I have tried to show how this dominating interest led him to produce narrative material from the scantiest sources. Is it necessary to assume that he had before him a source which told of the trip from Nazareth to Bethlehem made necessary by an imaginary census? Is it not more probable that the account is his own creation in order to harmonize the two variant traditions, both of which he accepted, that Jesus' family had from the earliest years lived in Nazareth and yet that their child had been born in Bethlehem? Or again, it appears to me that the account in Acts of the connexion of Paul with the stoning of Stephen has no historical foundation. It was in Jerusalem that the Christian mission to gentile lands arose, and it was Stephen's death that had caused this beginning. Paul was the one who above all others was instrumental in the movement. Therefore Paul is transferred from Damascus to Jerusalem and enters the story at this crucial moment. . . .

THE ACTS OF THE APOSTLES

. . . What appears to me the most serious difficulty in believing that the picture of Paul drawn in Acts was produced by a friend and companion is the curiously unsatisfactory way the story of his conversion is told. Three times the story is given.[33] Not only are the details different and mutually contradictory in the three accounts, but they minimize, or at least fail to emphasize, the one point that Paul apparently felt all-important, *viz.*, that he had *seen* the Lord.[34] In the Acts account he hears a voice, a light shines forth, but there is a complete silence as to the actual vision. This to me is very serious. To be sure, it is possible to harmonize the pictures by stressing the word that the *men with him* beheld no man (9:7)—hence that Paul did —but that a friend of Paul's should have so subordinated this all-important point and should have been so vague about the whole happening appears to me quite unlikely.

Nor should it be overlooked that there is a complete silence in the Acts

[31] The Johannine version of this story (John 12:1-8) is dependent upon both Mark and Luke. It occurs in Bethany toward the end of the ministry (Mark), but in the home of Lazarus, and the woman is not a sinner, but Mary. (Is the Lazarus touch due to the blending of the elements, Simon "the leper" with a Lazarus, "full of sores" (Luke 16:20)?) John is dependent upon the Lucan account for the touch that the woman anointed Jesus' *feet* (not his *head* as in Mark), but though she wipes them with her hair, there is no mention of her tears—why should she weep? she is no sinner—which had made the act natural in Luke.

[32] "Paul and Gamaliel," *Journal of Religion*, July, 1927; "The Ascension Story," *Journal of Biblical Literature*, 1928, Parts 1 and 2.

[33] Acts 9:1-19; 22:6-16; 26:12-18.

[34] I Cor. 9:1; 15:8; and probably Gal. 1:12,16; II Cor. 12:1-5.

account about the very considerable collection which Paul had been at such pains to collect for the poor saints in Jerusalem. Could a companion of Paul have overlooked this or have considered it so incidental as unworthy of mention? It does not appear to me legitimate to lay much stress on the author's failure to understand Paul's theology. Few early Christians did. But the completely different emphasis throughout the book on the significance of Jesus' death is after all surprising. In Acts it is simply a horrid crime which the Jews had wrought, and quite in keeping with the earlier acts of their fathers. For Paul it was the all-central point: the means of salvation. That the author should have failed to incorporate that distinctive note in the earlier pages of his book is perhaps not surprising. He might well have sought to preserve the flavour of the earlier, pre-Pauline, preaching. But that there should have been no hint in the speeches in the mouth of Paul himself of the one point that he apparently never ceased to stress and which any travel companion must have heard so often is to me most unlikely. And finally, there is the amazing failure even to hint that Paul had ever written letters to his churches. Surely he must have known that Paul had carried on an extensive correspondence. Why did he fail to mention it? This point, rarely considered in modern discussions of the identity of the author, appears to me of great significance as a weighty, if not fatal, objection to the view that he was a travel companion of Paul's.

Thus I find myself forced to feel that the lack of exact knowledge of the details of Paul's career even in the period during which the author of the "We passages" was with him and the evident readiness to transform and rewrite his sources of information in the light of his philosophy of history exclude the author from having been the companion of Paul, who penned the diary notes. Rather the author used various sources from which he produced his writing. One of them was a series of entries, quite fragmentary in extent, from a diary of an erstwhile travel companion, which he skilfully utilizes, choosing, for reasons about which we can raise guesses but can never know, to preserve the personal "we" touch. It may perhaps be remarked that had the author with his obvious literary skill meant by this touch to indicate his own appearance in the story, he might well have done it in a more finished and natural manner. Nor is it fair to say that in the "We passages" we find a fresher, more vivid tone. Aside from the curious *we's* there is nothing in the accounts which might not well have come from one who knew the country he was describing and knew how to write convincingly.

Several scholars, notably Hobart and Harnack, have seen distinct traces in Luke and Acts that the author was a physician; hence, since the Luke who had been with Paul was a physician,[35] have discovered fresh proof of the justice of the traditional view that it was this Luke who wrote the books.

[35] Col. 4:14.

Professor Cadbury has, however, completely exploded this fallacy of the alleged medical language in Luke-Acts[36] by demonstrating that there was no technical phraseology available for the ancient physician, comparable to that of the present-day medical jargon, and by showing that all of the words and phrases eagerly pounced upon by Hobart and his pedissequi were in common use by such writers as Aristophanes and Lucian, who, to say the least, had never received a doctor's degree. Were it not for the accidental reference of Paul to "Luke, the beloved physician," it is extremely possible that the famous but enigmatic author might have come down to us not in doctor's robes, but in the garb of a sea captain.

One final word with regard to the literary craftsmanship of the author must be mentioned. No classical student will need to be warned that the speeches in the book of Acts are the free composition of the author, precisely as are those of Josephus, Philo, Thucydides, or Livy. Thucydides gives us a terse but frank statement of this ancient custom:

As to the speeches that were made by different men, either when they were about to begin the war or when they were already engaged therein, it has been difficult to recall with strict accuracy the words actually spoken, both for me as regards that which I myself heard, and for those who from various other sources have brought me reports. Therefore the speeches are given in the language in which, as it seemed to me, the several speakers would express, on the subjects under consideration, the sentiments most befitting the occasion, though at the same time I have adhered as closely as possible to the general sense of what was actually said.[37]

In the light of this statement the student will not be perplexed by the marked similarities between all the speeches—be they of a Peter, a Stephen, or a Paul. It will not be necessary to debate whether Paul has been "petronized" or Peter has been "paulinized"; rather, it is clear that all of them have been "lucanized." Their marked sameness of tone, their smoothness and freedom from the little idiosyncrasies which stamp the man himself, the surprising fact that the author knows on occasion what was said in secret council (4:15-17), the providential preservation of the letter of Claudius Lysias to Felix with its highly satisfactory and sympathetic statement of Paul's innocence (23:26-30) require no *tour de force* of laboured explanation. These speeches may well give us a fair picture of early Christian thought and even of the kind of preaching that the early Christians heard—or that Luke thought they ought to have heard—but the cautious student will be slow to use them as sources of knowledge for reconstructing a life of Peter or of Paul. As was remarked on an earlier page, Stephen's famous speech to his accusers does not remotely answer the charges brought against

[36] *The Style and Literary Method of Luke*, pp. 39-72; *Journal of Biblical Literature*, 1926, pp. 190-209.
[37] *de Bello P.* 1,22 (quoted by Cadbury, *The Making of Luke-Acts*, p. 185).

him. It is simply a tirade—whether justified or not is of no consequence at the moment—against the Jews who had from the beginning persecuted God's saints. This theme was very likely a favourite one in early Christian preaching and finds constant expression not alone in the speeches of Peter—

> Let all the house of Israel therefore know assuredly, that God hath made him both Lord and Christ, this Jesus *whom ye crucified*[38]—

but in many of the words now found in the mouth of Jesus, especially as recorded by Matthew.

Occasionally Luke's desire to use the speeches as a convenient means for providing necessary information for the readers gives a distinctly artificial appearance to the utterance. Thus in Peter's first speech he is made to describe to his fellow Jews in Jerusalem an incident which had purportedly just happened and which they must have known as well as did he in the following amazing language:

> And it *became known* to all *the dwellers at Jerusalem,* in so much that *in their language* that field *was called* Akeldama, that is, The field of blood.[39]

None of the speeches attributed to Paul reveal the Paul known to us from the letters. This fact, as has been remarked, is of no small weight in the problem of authorship. Even in the farewell speech of Paul to the Ephesian elders at Miletus (20:18-35)—a speech regarded by some critics as distinctly different from the others and perhaps an actual part of the "We source"— the stereotyped prophecy of impending evil— .

> I know that after my departing grievous wolves shall enter in among you, not sparing the flock; and from among your own selves shall men arise, speaking perverse things, to draw away the disciples after them—

is so precisely similar to the tenor of the Pastoral Epistles, Jude, II Peter, Matt. 5:10-12; 10:16-23 that it does not appear rash to consider it a prophecy *post eventum.*

Nor should it be overlooked that occasionally in the mouths of the speakers are found both improbable sentiments and impossible statements. The speech of James at the council in Jerusalem (15:13-21) is an example of the one; the temperate and oft-cited advice of Gamaliel (5:34-39) of the other. James is made to quote Amos 9:11,12 in very free paraphrase of the Septuagint. The Hebrew read:

> In that day will I raise up the tabernacle of David that is fallen, and close up the breaches thereof; and I will raise up its ruins, and I will build it as in the days

---

[38] Acts 2:36; cf. 2:23; 3:15; 4:10.   [39] Acts 1:19.

of old; that they may possess the remnant of Edom, and *all the nations that are called by my name*, saith Jehovah that doeth this.

That is, that Israel may possess Edom and the other nations. But James is made to say,

. . . *that the residue of men* may seek after the Lord, and *all the gentiles, upon whom my name is called.* . . .

That the historic James used the Septuagint is most unlikely; surely Gal. 2:11 ff. makes it highly improbable that this utterance represents James' attitude, to say nothing of his words.[40] In the other passage Gamaliel is made to refer to the rebellion of Theudas which had occurred "before these days" and which, he goes on to say, was later followed by the insurrection and death of Judas of Galilee. Now Theudas raised his rebellion in the days of Fadus and not earlier than 44 A.D., that is, several years *later* than the difficulty which prompted Gamaliel to speech. Furthermore, Judas of Galilee raised his rebellion not *after* Theudas, but nearly forty years *before* (6 A.D.). Why Luke made this historical error may be deferred to a later paragraph; that this speech can scarcely be construed as a verbatim record of Gamaliel's word is evident. Thus the only safe conclusion with regard to the several speeches would appear to be that they are the author's free composition, as was true of those of all ancient historians. They are not to be used as source material in any moot point. They may occasionally have historic value, but we are not safe in using them unless they agree exactly with something else, the authority for which is unquestioned, and in that case they are super-fluous.

Little more need be said about the probable date of Acts. As has already been argued in the previous chapter, there appears good reason to date the Gospel of Luke about 100 A.D. The book of Acts is at least not earlier. The apologetic tone, which is even clearer in Acts than in the gospel, suggests a date when it was necessary to justify Christianity in the eyes of Rome. Thus the unwillingness of the author to chronicle the deaths of Peter, and especially of Paul, without any corresponding story of their subsequent resurrection triumph may well provide as satisfactory an explanation of the enigmatic end of the book as does the assumption of Torrey and Harnack that the silence was due to the fact that Paul's death had not occurred when Luke for the last time dipped his pen in the inkhorn. The representation of the apostles as a college of officials charged with oversight over the other groups; their refusal to leave Jerusalem under pressure (8:1); the interpretation of the incident of Peter and Cornelius in the light of the later "open

---

[40] This is a powerful argument against the contention that Luke is dependent upon Aramaic sources, not to mention a continuous Aramaic document.

membership" practice; the indications of the organized form Christianity was coming to possess, with presbyters (11:30; 14:23) and ordination (6:6); the legendary accretions, already mentioned, even to the figure of Paul—all this suggests the lapse of many years. And finally, there is always the lingering possibility—some scholars consider it a probability—that Luke had some familarity with the *Antiquities* of Josephus (93-94 A.D.). This assumption rests on two misstatements—one in Acts, the other in Luke. The first, Gamaliel's strange confusion regarding the dates of Theudas and Judas of Galilee, has already been remarked. How could Luke have made such a mistake? It is to be observed that in the *Antiquities* the account of the downfall of Theudas is immediately followed by the words:

> The *sons of Judas of Galilee* were now slain; I mean of that Judas who caused the people to revolt when Quirinius came to take an account of the estates of the Jews as we showed in a former book.[41]

Is not a careless reading (or faulty memory) of this section responsible for Luke's anachronism and mistakes in order—that is, he failed to remember the fact that it was not *Judas* but *Judas'* sons whose deaths were mentioned as subsequent to Theudas? . . .

THE SYNOPTIC PROBLEM

. . . For the moment the point of significance is that it was essentially our Mark[42] from which Matthew and Luke drew nearly their entire narrative matter, approximately half their whole content. This material is commonly styled the "triple tradition," *i.e.*, the matter common to all three. Mark was the source for it, and the only guarantee of its historical accuracy. That Matthew and Luke subsequently repeat it by no means gives it the threefold attestation so often enthusiastically supposed.

In addition to the material which occurs in all three Synoptists (or in Mark and either Matthew or Luke) there are numerous passages where Matthew and Luke agree but where Mark is wanting. And not infrequently in these passages, styled conveniently the "double tradition," the verbal agreements are very striking. Thus, to take but one example, the scalding word of John the Baptist, save for three trifling variations, is reported in identical words by Matthew 3:7-10 and Luke 3:7-9. How are these agreements to be explained? The explanation in favour with the great majority of scholars today is a second source from which both Matthew and Luke independently drew, and which is ordinarily styled Q. . . .

---

[41] *Antt.* 20,5,1.
[42] The word "essentially" is employed because the text of Mark, as of the other gospels, may well have undergone certain corruptions due to errors in copying, both accidental and intentional.

But I find myself more and more skeptical not about the age of Q but of its very existence, and am inclined to feel that it is an unnecessary and unwarranted assumption serving to account for material common to Matthew and Luke which can be more satisfactorily explained on the hypothesis that one of them used the other. And it appears to me highly probable that Luke was the one who did the borrowing. To be sure, the reference in his preface to the many who had "taken in hand to draw up a narrative" does not demand that our Matthew was one of them. On the other hand, it is not unlikely. . . .

Furthermore, just as considerable material which was formerly marked "Matthew special" or "Luke special" may not unreasonably be considered the evangelists' own revamping or rewriting of Markan matter, so I am inclined to feel that a fresh study of the special material of Luke in the light of its being a possible adaptation of Matthew would not be wasted. Thus, for example, it might well be considered if Luke's parable of the Prodigal Son is not actually his own revision of the parable of the Two Sons, as recorded by Matthew (21:28-32). . . .

THE GOSPEL ACCORDING TO JOHN

While Matthew, Mark, and Luke stand so close together, despite their many differences, that the thoughtful reader, even without any technical knowledge of Synoptic criticism, is struck by their similarity of expression and choice of material, the Gospel of John, or as many writers prefer to call it, the Fourth Gospel, is widely different. More than ninety per cent of its material falls outside the Synoptist tradition. This one fact alone makes it valueless to attempt a "harmony" of the four gospels. In former years such were made, but they are not worth the paper they are printed on, unless the few Johannine parallels or reminiscences be subordinated to footnotes or appendix. The attempt to weave all four together is utterly perverse and cannot fail to result in complete confusion. . . .

The miracles are frankly and avowedly signs—stupendous, marvelous manifestations of power intended to compel this belief. The theory of Mark that Jesus deliberately sought to hide his power from the outside world, and constantly bade those upon whom cures had been wrought, "Tell it to no man," is completely reversed in John. Rather, Jesus always performs his miracles at the precise moment when their effect will be the greatest. . . .

The genuine contrasts with the Synoptists are many and significant. Perhaps the most striking is the totally different order of events. In the Synoptists Jesus' ministry is confined to Galilee. Apart from a few obscure references which probably can be explained there is no trace of any visit to Jerusalem during the ministry until the final tragic journey which ended in his death. The length of the ministry appears also to have been brief—at least they indicate nothing to lead the reader to assume that it was more than a few months. In the Fourth Gospel all is changed. The scene has been shifted from Galilee to Jerusalem and its environs in Judea. From Jerusalem there are a few brief excursions up into Galilee,[43] but regularly concluded with a return to Jerusalem to this feast or that. Indeed, Jesus' word about a prophet having no honour in his own country and the implied favour of the Galileans (4:44 f.) might even suggest that Judea, not Galilee, was his *patris*. Against this, however, is the query of Nathanael (1:46) and the repeated reference to Jesus of Nazareth.[44] Again, his family appears at home, or at least with him, in Galilee.[45] The mention of at least three, perhaps four, Passovers suggests that the ministry was of two or three years' duration. . . .

The picture of Jesus is that of a figure quite distinct from all around him. The "Jews" are his enemies; this term, constantly on the lips of the author,[46] is always a reproach and with no suggestion that Jesus himself was a Jew.[47] At the very beginning it is announced: "He came unto his own, and they that were his own received him not" (1:11). So he speaks of "your" law (8:17; 10:34); he can even say: "But this cometh to pass, that the word may be fulfilled that is written in *their* law. They hated me without a cause" (15:25). He is in the world, but is not of the world. Even to his disciples he never speaks of "Our Father"; it is always "My Father" or "Your Father." To Mary Magdalene he can say, "Go unto my brethren, and say to them, I ascend unto *my Father and your Father, and my God and your God*" (20:17).

So it is with the miracles. As has been remarked, the author aptly designates them as *signs* intended to compel belief. The kind-hearted teacher—whom at least modern ingenuity has discovered in the Synoptists—who walks about the Galilean hills and lays his hand in sympathy upon the sick and distressed because his Saviour heart was stirred by their suffering, has vanished. Instead there walks about a majestic and almost aloof figure whose miracles are tremendous signs, not called forth by any sympathy for the afflicted, but precisely to show his tremendous power. Thus it is to be noted that Jesus never takes advice from those about him. Even if he later does precisely what he is advised to do, he is yet made to do it in such a way that it is evident he is doing it solely on his own initiative. Examples of this may be seen in his rejoinder to his mother at Cana (2:4) or in his attitude at learning of the sickness of Lazarus (11:6). The most striking is his attitude toward his brothers' advice: They urge him to go to the feast; he replies,

---

[43] John 2:1-12; 4:43-5:1; 6:1-7:14.   [45] John 2:1; 7:3.

[44] John 18:5,7; 19:19; cf. also 7:41,52.

[46] It is employed seventy times in John as against five in Matthew, six in Mark, and five in Luke.

[47] Cf. John 2:18,20; 5:16; 6:41 and frequently.

"Go ye up unto the feast: I go not up unto this feast." Then after their departure he went up also.[48]

When word comes that Lazarus is sick, instead of hastening to his friend, he waits, lets him die, waits again until he is three days dead, then comes and raises him. The author's reason for this delay is transparent. The Jewish view about death is revealed in one of the Midrashim:[49]

> Bar Qappara taught: The entire intensity of the mourning is reserved for the third day. Three days long the soul hovers about the grave. It thinks that it will return (into the body). When, however, it sees that the colour (appearance) of its face has changed, then it departs and leaves it.

Thus Martha is made to say, "Lord, by this time the body decayeth; for he hath been dead four days."[50] No reader may object that the raising of Lazarus was that of a man who had not actually died. To the gratuitous remark, often made, that the word, "Jesus wept" (11:35), suggests Jesus' sympathy for Lazarus, it need only be remarked that the author reveals quite the contrary by his explicit rejoinder: "The Jews therefore said, Behold how he loved him!" No clearer evidence could be desired. The Jews invariably misunderstood and misinterpreted every word and deed of Jesus. His tears are not of sorrow, but of anger: These Jews in their unbelief have dared to weep for the dead in the presence of him, the Lord of life. The whole point to the story is given in Jesus' words:

> I am the resurrection and the life: he that believeth on me, though he die, yet shall he live; and whosoever liveth and believeth on me shall never die.[51]

By their tears the Jews have shown their unbelief. Thus Lazarus is raised, not out of love for Lazarus, but as Jesus is made expressly to say, "that they may believe that thou didst send me" (11:41-43). The whole scene is one of slow and impressive dignity. The same may be said of the curiously artificial story of the miracle at Cana.[52] The emphasis upon Jesus' aloofness and the lavish display—150 gallons of wine when the feast was drawing to a close!—but express the author's confidence that the old system was being supplanted by the new at the touch of Jesus.

The miracles are few in number—only nine in all—but tremendous in nature. . . .

Jesus never speaks to help his hearers to solve the riddle of life, but

---

[48] John 7:1-13, especially verses 8 and 10.

[49] Genesis R. 100,64a, cited by Strack und Billerbeck, *Kommentar zum Neuen Testament aus Talmud und Midrasch*, Vol. II, p. 544.

[50] John 11:39.

[51] John 11:25,26.

[52] John 2:1-11. Note (1) the mother's confidence, although it is later stated that this was the first miracle performed by Jesus; while in Mark 3:21 it is implied that his mother had no lively confidence; (2) the unfilial word of Jesus; (3) the presumption of the visiting woman in giving orders to the servants; (4) their obedience to her.

always to reveal his own omniscience or to discuss the central point, his own nature. While in the Synoptists he regularly speaks of the kingdom of God, in John the emphasis is not on the kingdom at all—only twice is the phrase used, and then quite incidentally (3:3,5)—but on himself, the king. . . .

The writing is priceless as an indication of the type of thought early Christianity produced, well nigh worthless, however, for the historian who desires to glimpse the Jesus of history. That in the date of the Last Supper the Gospel of John preserves the correct date—namely, that this meal was not the Passover, but held on the evening before—is probable. But this alteration of the tradition was not due to a desire for historical accuracy, but solely because it suited his theological purpose to make Jesus—the true Lamb of God, the Christian's everlasting Passover—die just as the paschal lambs were being slaughtered. The geographical and chronological touches might at first seem to evidence an accurate knowledge on the part of the author. Thus the references to "Bethany beyond the Jordan" (1:28); to "Ænon near to Salim, because there was much water there" (3:23); to Jesus walking about in "Solomon's porch" (10:23); to his two-day visit in Samaria (4:40,43), to its being the "midst of the feast" when Jesus went up to Jerusalem (7:14)—these might tempt one to assume familiarity with the events described. But they are far from conclusive and prove little. Any pilgrim to the holy sites in Palestine at the beginning of the second century —an ancient forerunner of the modern Cook's tour—could easily have acquired such local colour. The thrice-repeated statement that Caiaphas was "high-priest for that year" (11:49,51; 18:13) would certainly imply that his knowledge of things Palestinian was not profound. . . . On the other hand, the famous story of the Woman Taken in Adultery (7:53-8:11) is universally regarded as a comparatively late interpolation. The textual evidence leaves no question. The four earliest uncial manuscripts omit it, as do many of the minuscules; such fathers as Origen, Eusebius, Chrysostom, Cyril of Alexandria, and Theophylact did not read it in their copies of John. Euthymius (*ca.* 1100 A.D.), the first of the Greek expositors to consider the question, states,

> It is necessary to observe that the section is either not found in the accurate manuscripts or is obelized. From this it appears to be an addition and appendage.[53]

A whole group of manuscripts—the so-called Ferrar group—have it not in John but after Luke 21:38. Other manuscripts and versions place it after John 7:36 or 7:44, or at the end of the gospel. Furthermore, the style is utterly unlike that of the Fourth Gospel. Eusebius says that Papias expounded "a story about a woman who was accused before the Lord of many

---

[53] Quoted by W. Bauer, *Das Johannesevangelium, in loc.*

sins, which the Gospel according to the Hebrews contains.[54] How this story came to lodge in the Western text at this point is one of the many enigmas as yet unanswered.

In concluding this section upon the nature and characteristics of the Fourth Gospel it may be repeated that it has a heaviness and artificiality vastly different from the Synoptic accounts. The reason why this gospel is so popular despite its turgidly, often tiresomely, repetitious style is partly due to its several favourite quotations, partly to the fact that we read it in the light of the Synoptists. The simple, unaffected, generous, tender-hearted figure discerned in those accounts is read into the statelier, more tremendous, but not in itself especially pleasing, figure of the Johannine Christ. What we admire is not the Jesus of the Fourth Gospel but the conflate of the two. Should we by a miracle lose our Synoptists and all remembrance of them, I believe many would find the Gospel of John shorn of much of its former charm. . . .

Thus I am definitely inclined to the view that tradition tells us nothing about the actual author, and that all attempts to see the Galilean fisherman as author, in any degree of remove, of this highly theological and apologetic brochure are unwarranted and misleading. The little that we can learn about the personality of the author does not come from surmises, but from the gospel itself—and it is surprisingly meagre. He is a deeply religious man; is acquainted with the Alexandrian philosophy (at least he makes use of the concept of Logos, popularized by Philo, and expanded by the Christian catechetical teachers of that city: Pantaenus, Clement, and Origen); knows the Synoptic gospels and occasionally utilizes some of their material, but without evidencing the slightest feeling that they are inspired Scripture; is influenced, probably deeply influenced, by Paul, although he does not scruple to alter some of that master's central notes. For example, he lays his emphasis on the life of Christ rather than on his death. Thus for him the resurrection was not the proof of Jesus' divine character as it had been for Paul. His life had proved this beyond the peradventure of a doubt. The resurrection marked the beginning of the ever-widening and abiding activity of Jesus. From all these sources he drew, but he drew far more deeply on his own deep and abiding convictions. Today we find it necessary to find a definite "source" for every utterance and idea that our gospel writers expressed, and we hesitate to postulate any originality of thought for any of them. If we deprive our author of *this* source, we simply fail to understand him. In the last analysis the kind of Jesus whom he is depicting is the kind of Jesus whom he knows and whom the church knows. To do this he may at times utilize materials, which because they are earlier than he, we call "historic"; but he does not hesitate to rework and recast them to make his portrait the clearer.

[54] *Hist. Eccl.* iii,39,17.

Martin Niemöller was born at Lippstadt, Germany, in 1892, the son of a clergyman. He joined the navy in 1910, and served as a U-boat commander during World War I. After the War he studied theology, and was ordained in 1924. He took over a church in Berlin-Dahlem in 1931. When Hitler became Chancellor in 1933, Niemöller helped to organize the Pfarrer-Notbund, an emergency association of Protestant ministers that soon developed into the so-called Confessing Church.

Niemöller's heroic stance during these years finds perfect expression in the book, *Dennoch getrost: Die letzten 28 Predigten des Pfarrers Martin Niemöller, vor seiner Verhaftung gahalten in den Jahren 1936 und 1937 in Berlin-Dahlem,* published in Switzerland in 1939. It has been translated under the title, *The Gestapo Defied;* and the first sermon as well as the last two from this volume are here reprinted. As the German title indicates, the final two sermons were the last he delivered before the Gestapo arrested him.

Acquitted by a court, Niemöller was taken into "protective custody" (to protect him from the alleged wrath of the German people at his acquittal) and sent, first, to the concentration camp at Sachsenhausen, then to that at Dachau. Since his liberation in 1945, he has held many posts and received many honors. In 1948 he became president of the Evangelical Church in Hessen and Nassau.

The Wedding Garment

(20TH SUNDAY AFTER TRINITY)

25th October, 1936   Church of Jesus Christ

And Jesus answered and spake unto them again by parables, and said, The Kingdom of heaven is like unto a certain king, which made a marriage for his son,

And sent forth his servants to call them that were bidden to the wedding: and they would not come.

Again, he sent forth other servants, saying, Tell them which are bidden, Behold, I have prepared my dinner: my oxen and my fatlings are killed, and all things are ready: come unto the marriage.

But they made light of it, and went their ways, one to his farm, another to his merchandise:

And the remnant took his servants, and entreated them spitefully, and slew them.

But when the king heard thereof, he was wroth: and he sent forth his armies, and destroyed those murderers, and burned up their city.

Then saith he to his servants, The wedding is ready, but they which were bidden were not worthy.

Go ye therefore into the highways, and as many as ye shall find, bid to the marriage.

So those servants went out into the highways, and gathered together all as many as they found, both bad and good: and the wedding was furnished with guests.

And when the king came in to see the guests, he saw there a man which had not on a wedding garment:

And he saith unto him, Friend, how camest thou in hither not having a wedding garment? And he was speechless.

Then said the king to the servants, Bind him hand and foot, and take him away, and cast him into outer darkness; there shall be weeping and gnashing of teeth.

For many are called, but few are chosen.

[Matt. 22:1-14]

"*M*any are called, but few are chosen."

Jesus' parable of the marriage of the king's son begins in the spaciousness of the world-embracing sovereignty of God, and it leads us in the end into the narrow confines of a purely personal issue. The self-same king who has sent out his armies to punish those who have made light of him, and to enforce obedience to his authority, finally stands face to face with that one wretched man who has come in from the highway; and the glare of the burning city, set ablaze by order of the king, pales before the solemnity of the encounter.

Dear friends, it is easy to interpret the first part of the parable, and, from the fate of the people of Israel who made light of the king's invitation, to draw conclusions regarding the punishment which threatens our own nation if it does not or will not heed the call. If we draw such a conclusion, it is an obvious one. Luther did so again and again in his preaching, pointing out the neglect of God's invitation as the sin of sins, surpassing all others: "to stroll in the market-place or before the city gate, and lounge in the tavern and in the gaming-houses, at church-time," was how Luther put it. But I believe that we lose our inclination for this comparison when we see that its sharp knife-edge could be turned against ourselves and not against others. "Many are called, but few are chosen."

"The kingdom of heaven is like unto a certain king which made a marriage for his son." These glad tidings tell us that the breach between the Creator and the creation is closing, that the time of separation and longing is at an end, and that God Himself is making a new beginning. The son and the bride, the Lord Jesus Christ and His community, God and Man . . . I repeat, God and Man . . . God and I. It is to the feast of reconciliation, the feast of peace, that God is inviting us; and that is why He calls to us, through the message of the Apostles: "Be ye reconciled to God." That is the king's invitation. You would think that every one would accept the invitation joyfully. And yet Israel did not accept it; Israel paid no heed to

the call, but went its own way and shook off those who importuned it
with such an exhortation.

But the call has resounded further, and, dear brethren, there is none
among us who can say that it has not reached him. It was there first of all
on the day of baptism: "Thou art mine." On the day I was confirmed I
heard the call as though it were addressed to me personally: "My son, give
Me thy heart." And how often have we been called during Holy Communion: "Come, all things are ready." And when we try to think of all
the times when God has been near us, when He has called us as our Saviour
and our gracious Lord, when, with threats or entreaties, He has made Himself known to us in the walks of our lives, who would dare to say: "I
have not yet heard the call"?

The question is whether we have heard the call in such a way that we
have accepted it. Sunday after Sunday we are invited to His table, but how
often have we come? How often has it not been a case of: "They went
their ways, one to his farm, another to his merchandise"? Sunday after Sunday we hear God calling us in the preaching of His word, but how often
do our hearts go their own way, absorbed in their own cares, thoughts
and desires? How often does the call lay hold upon us, and we make every
conceivable effort to frustrate the plans which God has for us? Dear
brethren, I ask you, is that anything else but what we have here: "the
remnant took His servants and entreated them spitefully and slew them"?

And so to-day let us learn that there is a time when it is too late, because
none of us knows, after all, whether the moment which we are allowing to
slip past is our last or not; because none of us knows whether God's patience
may end that very moment or not, and there will only remain God's
anger: "The king was wroth." "The wedding is ready, but they which
were bidden were not worthy."

What, then, are we waiting for? The wedding is ready, nothing is lacking. As far as God is concerned, everything has been done. He has bridged
the gulf between Him and us; He has sent His son and brought Him back
from the dead for us, so that we shall believe: "His love is greater than
our—than my—guilt; His life is greater and stronger than my death." We
must die unto sin and live with Him into righteousness. It no longer matters
whether we are good or bad. God calls us, as we heard from the altar: "I
will blot out thy transgressions for My sake. I will do it!" Between Him
and us stands only the crucified Christ, calling: "Come unto Me, all ye that
labour and are heavy laden, and I will give you rest."

It depends upon ourselves whether we hear or not, whether we come
or stay where we are. The choice should not be a difficult one for us, because our souls know how hollow and incomplete is a life without God.
The messenger is there and we hear the message. Yes, friends, the very reason for our coming here to-day is that we feel we need God—the living

God—more than we need our daily bread. We come because we see that our lives dissolve into foolishness and fritter themselves away if God does not sustain us. Many are called—we are all called. We should rejoice that the time of deafness and indifference is over, that God's call reaches us anew; and last, but not least, we should rejoice because we see the judgment on those who have made light of that call—yes, to-day, we see something of that judgment: "Be not deceived; God is not mocked; for whatsoever a man soweth, that shall he also reap." To-day our eyes see a little of that. But, dear friends, this glimpse of what happens to others must not make us feel secure—assuredly not. Our salvation does not depend upon our acknowledging God when others deny Him. To-day many voices are heard to declare that the crux of the matter is that we have a God in contrast to others who have no God. Thus the German nation is played off against other nations. It is a case of choosing, they say, between godlessness and subjection to God; between atheism and religion. It does not matter what this religion looks like: the form, we are told, is unimportant. Each must, in the oft misunderstood and misapplied words of Frederick the Great, "work out his own salvation." The garment, they say, is of no consequence.

That is a man-made thought, but it will not do the moment the living God approaches us. "Friend, how camest thou in hither not having a wedding garment?" In this context the question may seem to us an arbitrary one. We doubt whether this invitation really applies to every one or whether it is intended only for the honest and respectable people. We doubt whether it is seriously meant. Does not this man come in from the highway just like the other guests? How is he supposed to have a wedding garment? Our fathers used to explain this parable by quoting an Eastern custom whereby the giver of the feast ordered a festive garment to be handed to his guests. The second half of the parable must thus be understood to mean that the King of Heaven desires to see us in the garment which he presents to us; for His majesty's sake He will not tolerate our appearing before Him otherwise. The garment is *not* a matter of indifference to Him.

The man in the parable had indeed accepted the invitation and had come to the marriage feast. He had not made light of the call, but he had made light of his host's gift. And so the judgment follows: "Cast him into outer darkness." He was called but not chosen! Brothers and sisters, God is calling us, as we are, from the highway; but He does not wish to see us as we are: He wishes to see us in the garment which He bestows upon us. We must therefore believe: "Repent ye and believe the Gospel." "Repent": that means we must put off our own garment, even though it still suits us tolerably well, and still looks fairly good. We cannot pass muster before God clad in our own righteousness. "Believe in the Gospel": that means, we must put on the garment which is presented to us and which covers our sin and wraps us in His mercy and His righteousness. Thus and in no other raiment does God wish to see us at His table. Otherwise His invitation avails us nothing. "How camest thou in hither, having no wedding garment?" This garment of ours will not do—we suddenly see that it is covered with stains and full of holes. But by that time it is too late. "Cast him into outer darkness!"

Dear friends, perhaps we do not refuse God's gift, in which the Lord Jesus Christ has brought us God's righteousness. Perhaps we do not refuse it; but we are so familiar with it that we accept it and make no use of it. Perhaps we go in and merely take the wedding garment over our arm. Year in, year out, we go to church, to divine service, to the table which God has spread for us, and take what we can, without noticing what a dangerous game that is. We forget what we are doing: namely, evading a personal issue. But in the end the need to decide the issue comes upon us suddenly, like a thief in the night.

Dear friends, that is the real temptation for us church Christians. I do not speak of those who come to church to hear something special or interesting, something that is not in the newspapers. "Verily they have their reward." Nor do I speak of those who come to spy, to catch the Lord Jesus Christ and to nail Him to the cross. They too have their reward. I am thinking of us who come again and again and cannot make up our minds to say good-bye to our own self-righteousness, so that we may give ourselves up wholly to the merciful grace of God.

"Many are called but few are chosen." Do we belong—no, do you belong—no, do *I* belong to those chosen few, who build their hope and their trust wholly upon grace, because they know that Christ the Lord won God's grace for us on the cross? May God help us, we pray, to believe and to learn to profess our belief:

> Christ's precious blood and righteousness
> My jewels are, my festive dress.
> Clad in this glorious robe of grace
> Boldly I'll stand before God's face.

The Salt of the Earth

(4TH SUNDAY AFTER TRINITY)

19th June, 1937   Church of Jesus Christ

Ye are the salt of the earth: but if the salt have lost its savour, wherewith shall it be salted? it is thenceforth good for nothing, but to be cast out, and to be trodden under foot of men.

Ye are the light of the world. A city that is set on an hill cannot be hid.

Neither do men light a candle, and put it under a bushel, but on a candlestick; and it giveth light unto all that are in the house.

Let your light so shine forth before men, that they may see your good works, and glorify your Father which is in heaven.

[Matt. 5:13-16]

*A*nd now, dear brothers and sisters, to-night, in this hour of worship that brings the week to a close, we cannot help remembering, in silent intercession, those who belong to our congregation, to the company of Christ's disciples, and who cannot be here in the congregation with us this evening. We hear the names of those who for the Gospel's sake are hampered in their freedom or robbed of it.

(Here follows the five minutes' reading of the intercessory list, that is of those who have been forbidden to speak, or evicted or arrested.)

Dear brethren, this list has now become shockingly long: it includes—if I have counted rightly—72 or 73 names, known or unknown, names of pastors and church members, names of men and of women, names of young and of old. No one in the German Fatherland can say whether the number is complete and each of us has a foreboding that it may become larger still, as it has grown from day to day in the week which is now ending.

What are these pastors and church members accused of? During the last four years we have been taught to have an extremely bad opinion of all those who have been taken into custody as members of the Church; and when we hear of someone or other who has come into contact with the police we are inclined to think of the things that are being broadcast to-day in the newspapers. God be praised and thanked: our brothers and sisters cannot be reproached with the slightest trace of anything conventionally reprehensible; but, on the contrary, these people have all been banished from their homes, condemned to be silent and thrown into prison, because they considered it their duty and because they claimed that the Evangelical Church had the right to denounce attacks against the Christian faith freely and publicly as attacks, to denounce the decline from Christian faith quite openly as a decline, and to denounce interference with Christian worship fearlessly as interference. There is not one among them against whom another reproach can be levelled; and our brothers and sisters can rest assured that the repulsion of attacks on the Christian faith, the publications of secessions from the Church, and the collection of offerings—these are the three things in question to-day—they can rest assured and can plead that these things have always been the uncontested right of the Christian Church and that the Führer has solemnly guaranteed and has always confirmed this right of the Church and that up to the present day there is no law which restricts this right. Our brothers and sisters can plead that they have been appointed by a higher power, Who calls upon us through His Word to resist the propaganda of unbelief, Who warns the church against defection, and bids them to make intercession for those who have fallen away from the faith, and Who has ordered us to take up an offering—and a money-offering at that—for the needs of the congregation.

And so what is happening to-day to our brothers and sisters brings us up against an unequivocal question, and that question is: "Has the Church of Christ, in its members and office-bearers, still the right to-day which the Führer has confirmed with his word—with his *word of honour*—the right to allow us to defend ourselves against attacks on the Church, or are the people right who forbid us—the Christian community—to defend ourselves against unbelief and make it impossible for us to do so, and cast into prison the people who do defend themselves?" This is the problem in the case of the Chief Pastor, Dr. Jannasch, and in the cases of Pastor Busch and Pastor Held in Essen. They *publicly* repulsed public attacks and were on that account put in prison.

The question is this: "Has the Church of Christ still the right to tell the congregation that members of the congregation have fallen away from the faith, or are the people right who forbid us to carry out this charge and make it impossible for us to do so?" Brothers and sisters, that is the position in which Pastor Niesel finds himself, and the arrested members of the Prussian Council of Brethren—if I count correctly, there are eight of them in all—have declared: "The names of those who have left the church should be made known to the Christian congregation and it is not right to forbid this." Brothers and sisters, the question is quite simple: is the congregation to be allowed to learn who has left the church and may it be called upon to offer prayers of intercession for the deserters; or is that not allowed?

And the third question is this: "Does the Führer's word still hold good?" Has the Church the right—and this right has been guaranteed it from ancient times—to collect alms in the congregation, or can this right to bring offerings in accordance with the will of Christ be forbidden it by the stroke of a pen on the part of a minister—or even of two ministers? No one has yet been imprisoned because of this ban, but a notice appeared in the newspaper the day before yesterday to the effect that collections may no longer be taken unless they are sanctioned by the church authorities set up by the state.

Brothers and sisters, if I refer to these external matters I do so because no one knows to-day if or when he may have another opportunity of telling the Christian community whether the Führer's word holds good, or whether the words of others who order the opposite of what has been promised to the Church of Christ, to the Evangelical Church, hold good. We cannot get away from this question. And as long as one man is left in prison, as long as one man remains evicted, as long as one man is forbidden to speak because he has replied to attacks against the Church or because he has quite clearly called desertion of the faith desertion, or has been put in prison for collecting offerings, the question as to whether the word of the Führer holds good is answered in the negative.

Dear brethren, in this situation, of which we may well say that it could not possibly be darker or more insecure—the remainder of the Prussian Council of Brethren wander about Germany as homeless fugitives. Frau Asmussen was cross-examined for hours to-day at the Alexanderplatz, after she had had to wait for four hours for her trial, because she could not give information as to her husband's whereabouts; for they would like to put the rest of the members of the Prussian Council of Brethren under lock and key. The Prussian Church is without a leader, the service rooms of the Prussian Church leaders are locked, the typewriters have been taken away from them and they have no money—in such a siuation these words strike us as rather peculiar: "Ye are the salt of the earth; ye are the light of the world."

When I read these words to-day, they became really new to me, and I had to go back and reread them; and I had a feeling of inward relief when I found the words which I knew preceded them and which I had also long known theoretically to be in the fifth chapter of Matthew: "Blessed are ye, when men shall revile you, and persecute you, and shall say all manner of evil against you falsely, for my sake. Rejoice, and be exceeding glad: for great is your reward in heaven: for so persecuted they the prophets which were before you!" And then it goes on: "Ye are the salt of the earth; ye are the light of the world!" as though there were no gap between the persecution of the community of Jesus Christ and the "Ye are the salt of the earth; ye are the light of the world," but as though they were directly connected. I must say that in this sequence of ideas contained in this passage of the Bible—which I have known since I was a boy—I to-day realized for the first time that the Lord Jesus Christ is telling His disciples: "You will be reviled and persecuted, you will be slandered and that falsely," and immediately He adds: "Ye are the salt of the earth; ye are the light of the world."

Yet, brothers and sisters, there is something there that does not fit in with our troubles. "Ye are the salt of the earth." The Lord Jesus Christ does not mean, however, that we are to take care to distribute the salt among the people, but He draws our attention to another responsibility: "But if the salt have lost its savour, wherewith shall it be salted?" Our responsibility is not how we shall pass on the salt, but we are to see that the salt really is and continues to be salt, so that the Lord Jesus Christ—who is, as one might say, the cook in charge of this great brew—can utilize the salt for His purposes.

Brothers and sisters, in reply to the question of whether it is possible for the Lord Jesus Christ to render practical service to our people to-day I must say: I see no possible way in which service can be carried out to-day, among the people, or in which the salt can be used among the people. But, brothers and sisters, that is not our concern, it is the Lord Jesus's. We have only to see that the salt does not lose its savour, that it does not lose its power. What does that mean?

The problem with which we have to deal is how to save the Christian community at this moment from the danger of being thrown into the same pot as the world: that is to say: it must keep itself distinct from the rest of the world by virtue of its "saltness." How does Christ's community differ from the world?

We have come through a time of peril—and we are not finished with it yet—when we were told: "Everything will be quite different when you as a Church cease to have such an entirely different flavour: when you cease to practise preaching which is the opposite of what the world around you preaches. You really must suit your message to the world; you really must bring your creed into harmony with the present. Then you will again become influential and powerful."

Dear brethren, that means: The salt loses its savour. It is not for us to worry about how the salt is employed, but to see that it does not lose its savour; to apply an old slogan of four years ago: "The Gospel must remain *the Gospel;* the Church must remain *the Church;* the Creed must remain *the Creed;* Evangelical Christians must remain *Evangelical* Christians." And we must not—for Heaven's sake—make a German Gospel out of the Gospel; we must not—for Heaven's sake—make a *German* Church out of Christ's Church; we must not—for God's sake—make *German* Christians out of the Evangelical Christians!

That is our responsibility: "Ye are the salt of the earth." It is precisely when we bring the salt into accord and harmony with the world that we make it impossible for the Lord Jesus Church, through His Church, to do anything in our nation. But if the salt remains salt, we may trust Him with it: He will use it in such a way that it becomes a blessing.

And the other picture which the Lord Jesus Christ holds up to us: "Ye are the light of the world": we hear these words and are reminded by them that we worry about something that ceases to exist in the presence of the Lord Jesus Christ. What are we worrying about? When I read out the names, a little while ago, did we not think: "Alas and alack, will this wind, this storm, that is going through the world just now, not blow out the Gospel candle? We must therefore take the message in out of the storm and put it in a safe nook."

It is only during these days that I have realized—that I have understood—what the Lord Jesus Christ means when He says: "Do not take up the bushel! I have not lit the candle for you to put it under the bushel, in order to protect it from the wind. Away with the bushel! The light should be placed upon a candlestick! It is not your business to worry about whether the light is extinguished or not by the draught." We are not to worry whether the light is extinguished or not; that is His concern: we are only to see that the light is not hidden away—hidden away perhaps with a noble intent, so that we may bring it out again in calmer times—no: "Let your light shine before men!"

Brothers and sisters, that is the strange pass to which we have been brought to-day. It has come to this: we are being accosted on all sides, by statesmen as well as by "the man in the street," who tell us: "For God's sake, do not speak so loudly or you will land in prison. Pray do not speak so plainly: surely you can also say all that in a more obscure fashion!" Brothers and sisters, we are *not allowed* to put our light under a bushel: if we do so, we are disobedient; but we have received our commission from Him Who is the light of the world. He does not need us as wicks, He can take other wicks as well, other men on whom He can set up His light as on a candlestick.

The silent Church which no longer says *for what purpose* it exists—*that* is our service; but it is no business of ours whether the Church continues to live and is not put to death, or whether the light is blown out or not. "He that findeth his life shall lose it: and he that loseth his life for my sake shall find it." And that is true of the life of the congregation exactly as it holds good for the life of the individual Christian. Surely the practical meaning of this is: I *must* speak thus once again to-day, for perhaps I shall no longer be able to do so next Sunday: I *have* to tell you that to-day once again as plainly as I can, for who knows what next Sunday may bring forth? But it is our *duty* to speak: on this charge of ours depends the promise, it depends upon it whether God will keep His word and keep alive the light— "the poor flickering candle of the Gospel" as Dr. Martin Luther calls it— in our nation; and that depends upon whether we are ready to do what we are bidden and to preach the message and to let the light shine forth. And the Lord Jesus Church has given us still a third picture of the church. "Ye are the salt of the earth. Ye are the light of the world." And lastly: "A city that is set on an hill cannot be hid." And this image, which gleams through the text once, is intended to direct our attention away from the salt-cask and the candlestick to the city on the hill. The salt disappears when it is sprinkled on anything. The candle burns down. Thus shall the Christian community be consumed in the service of its Lord. But the city that is eternal is firmly founded upon a holy hill. In the confusion and distress of our days this hope is held out to us: God's city is firmly established!

Dear friends, it is in our service and in this obligation not to cease our efforts on behalf of the preaching of the Word that the Word of the Lord Jesus Christ is fulfilled to us. We are the city on the hill which has been promised that even the gates of Hell will not prevail against it. And then it is not a case of: "Every mountain and hill shall be made low," but the other words hold good: "My grace shall not forsake thee, saith the Lord, thy God of mercy."

There is a rumour current throughout Germany—a rumour emanating from the German Christians of Thüringia—that to-morrow week the church elections will take place, unexpectedly, on telegraphed instructions. But a week is a long time: we do not know exactly. Dear brothers and sisters, if we are now embarking upon the church elections at a time when the Confessional Church throughout Prussia has been robbed of its leaders, that may be a source of great distress and anxiety, and the coming week may be much harder and more difficult still than the oppression of this week which is to-day ending by God's grace; and we ask where is the hope which will sustain us through the distress of the times—this distress which grows and grows and is now reaching a climax?

The city of God cannot remain hidden. Brothers and sisters, the city of God will not be blown down by the storm. It will not be conquered even though the enemy take its outer walls. The city of God will stand, because its strength comes from on high, because the Lamb is with it, and so it will remain firmly established.

This morning I said to my brethren, my colleagues in Berlin: "Perhaps we have reached the point to-day where, after four years of being guided and kept faithful to our Creed, God is asking us for proof that we can also find the way alone now, that we have not allied ourselves with men, but with the one Lord Who is and ever will be the chief shepherd of His sheep."

And so when it comes to the election, we shall not mix up the salt, we shall not put the light into the corner, but we shall say: "Heaven and earth *may* pass away, as the Word of God says, Heaven and earth *shall* pass away—but the Word of God does *not* pass away!" Brothers and sisters, we will place our trust in that. Happy is he who accepts the sign of grace, who has learned to rely upon it and to establish himself upon it *alone*, so that he stands fast and is firmly established though the storms may roar and the waters rise.

And may God help us all to learn this trust!

Gamaliel

(*5TH SUNDAY AFTER TRINITY*)

27th June, 1937   Church of Jesus Christ
(The Lord shall yet comfort Zion)

When they heard that, they were cut to the heart, and took counsel to slay them.

Then stood there up one in the council, a Pharisee, named Gamaliel, a doctor of the law, had in reputation among all the people, and commanded to put the apostles forth a little space;

And said unto them, Ye men of Israel, take heed to yourselves what ye intend to do as touching these men.

For before these days rose up Theudas, boasting himself to be somebody; to whom a number of men, about four hundred, joined themselves: who was slain; and all, as many as obeyed him, were scattered, and brought to nought.

After this man rose up Judas of Galilee in the days of the taxing, and drew away much people after him: he also perished; and all, even as many as obeyed him, were dispersed.

And now I say unto you, Refrain from these men, and let them alone: for if this counsel or this work be of men, it will come to nought:

But if it be of God, ye cannot overthrow it; lest haply ye be found even to fight against God.

And to him they agreed: and when they had called the apostles, and beaten them, they commanded that they should not speak in the name of Jesus, and let them go.

And they departed from the presence of the council, rejoicing that they were counted worthy to suffer shame for his name.

And daily in the temple, and in every house, they ceased not to teach and preach Jesus Christ.

[Acts 5:33-42]

*T*his was an extremely critical moment in the life of the young Church: the Apostles have in every way broken the ban so solemnly laid upon their preaching, nay more, they have in every way acknowledged this breach of the ban: "One *must obey* God rather than men." Yes, the Apostles have even, in the subsequent trial, taken the offensive and charged their judges, the members of the council, with the murder of the Saviour—and have found them guilty of it: "Him ye slew and hanged on a tree"; after which they have offered them the message of repentance and the forgiveness of sins. And that is where our text begins: "When they heard that, they were cut to the heart, and took counsel to kill them."

At this moment Gamaliel steps forward, and we really must admit that it was thanks to his intervention that the Apostles were set free and the young Church was able to go on living and to carry on its ministry. And for that reason it is and always must be something like gratitude that we, as Christian men and women, feel for this man who was beyond doubt a clever and respected and godly man; and we as Christ's community could wish that in the critical days through which we are passing at present, there was one single, respected, leading man to-day—a man like Gamaliel, "had in reputation among the people" as a clever man; a respectable man like Gamaliel; a godly man like Gamaliel, who might call for caution, for truthfulness, for reverence with regard to God's will. Perhaps if we had such a man, he would be listened to to-day; perhaps people would not be so ready to carry out executions, moral executions, as is done in the notice which appeared in Friday evening's newspaper under the heading: "Incitement to insubordination"; and then comes something about the Evangelical Church. The Prussian Council of Brethren will define their position and say a word with regard to this article. For my part, I have only one thing to say to-day on the subject, because I must say it. When at the end of this newspaper article, which is written to make trouble, it says: "Yet another clergyman escaped arrest by taking to flight," this remark can apply to no one else but our brother pastor, Asmussen. A week ago Asmussen went on leave and left Berlin, on my personal advice and on the explicit instructions of his superiors, the Prussian Council of Brethren. He neither received a subpoena nor was there any question of a warrant for his arrest having been issued. It is a deliberate misrepresentation for anyone to say: "He escaped arrest by taking to flight," and I have written to the Reich Minister of Justice and officially informed him: "Pastor Asmussen will naturally be at your service as soon as a writ of subpoena is served against him or a warrant issued for his arrest." The Reich Minister of Justice has answered me: "We have sent a copy of your letter to the Secret Police, as the matter belongs to their department." So all the authorities concerned know what's what!

We have as little thought and as little hope as the Apostles had of escaping from the clutches of the powers-that-be by our own efforts; and we have certainly as little intention as they had of obeying the human command to keep silent regarding what the Lord our God orders us to say; for, as long as the world shall last, one must obey God rather than men!

That, friends, is the question at stake to-day in the long list of men and women who have been arrested; and there are not only four, to whom the newspaper makes guarded reference—there are, if I know them all, forty-eight people in prison to-day, and in this situation Gamaliel's advice is very shrewd counsel: "Please have patience! Please do not be in too great a hurry; because when all is said and done it is not wise to make martyrs for a cause which one is trying to put down!" In this situation that would be a morally immaculate piece of advice to-day too, because it is neither moral nor seemly to fight convictions with the sword, that is, with external might and power. And Gamaliel's advice is also a godly piece of advice, because, after all, it is ungodly for a human court to try to anticipate God's opinion and to forestall His judgment, which, when all is said and done, we do not know!

And so, dear friends, it might seem to us that the advice of a new Gamaliel might possibly help us to-day and that the proclamation of a real freedom of creed and conscience might perhaps benefit us to-day.

But, dear brethren, let us not deceive ourselves! You remember, the Council in Jerusalem accepted Gamaliel's proposal with respect to freedom of faith and conscience. It let the prisoners go free, all of them; but *not* without a beating and *not* without a new ban on their preaching: they beat them and commanded them "that they should not speak in the name of Jesus (that is, a ban was put upon their preaching) and let them go." And in the very next chapter, when we read on in "Acts," the lightning of the first great persecution of the Christians begins to play: the persecution that is characterized by the name of Stephen. It is no mere accident that the driving power behind this persecution is precisely a pupil of Gamaliel, his favourite pupil even, Saul of Tarsus.

Obviously that tolerance for which Gamaliel here breaks a lance is quite impossible as far as the Christian faith and the preaching of the Christian message are concerned: obviously one cannot be neutral and wait to see how the matter will turn out before taking up one's final stand according to the result. Gamaliel, with all his shrewdness, with all his good reputation, with all his piety, is making a mistake: that is, he thinks that the downfall of Jesus of Nazareth has already been settled and accomplished with the crucifixion; he thinks that this affair will develop along the same lines as the two examples which he quotes, viz. the risings of Theudas and Judas, and that they are dealing here with a new rising about the results of which nothing can yet be said.

But actually, as we know, the Apostles preach the opposite of what Gamaliel thinks and believes and does; actually these Apostles do not preach themselves, but Jesus of Nazareth, the crucified and risen Saviour; that is, they preach that the cause which they represent as their cause has already been decided by God and that the decision does not lie in the future, and that nothing about it can be changed by any visible success or failure. They preach that Jesus Christ is the living Lord of His community and that the decision—whether one acknowledges it or rejects it—no longer depends upon any future sign, or upon any success or failure, or upon any special indication; nor can it be made dependent upon any of these things. They preach: He who does not choose to believe in this Lord when he is told the story of the Cross, decides against Him, even when he thinks he has not yet made his choice or taken his stand. It is as Jesus says: "He who is not with Me is against Me!" and that excludes all neutrality. The message of the Cross puts the question: "Either-or?" and it is a case of deciding whether we shall believe or not believe, whether we shall stand or fall, whether we shall choose salvation or perdition, life or death, and this decision must be made not in the future but *here and now*; and so all neutrality—even a neutrality such as Gamaliel's and even the best-intentioned neutrality—must become hostility, when God can use even this neutrality—as he uses Gamaliel's advice here—as everything must serve His purpose—to carry out His will upon earth.

For us, dear brethren—we must not deceive ourselves—for us Christian men and women Gamaliel's advice: "If it be of men, it will come to nought;

but if it be of God, ye cannot overcome it," means a great temptation, however good and honest and godly it may be intended to be, and however well God has used it and can use it even to-day to help His Church and to attain His ends. Gamaliel's advice might persuade us to look upon human counsel and human work, to look upon what is visible, upon the result, and to found our faith in some way—as they say—upon practical experience. And this temptation has more power over us than we ourselves perhaps admit. We know that for more than a hundred years there has been a great talk of practical experience among Evangelical Christians. Now, when trouble and trials come, we are too apt to be tempted to conclude from the sorrows through which we are passing: "So everything is going wrong after all; so God is not with us; so the world does not believe in God; so the work for which we stand is not from God; so it is not worth bothering about the matter! There is no doubt about it, everything is futile and vain!"

Dear friends, there lies a great danger. We must not forget that God brings about our salvation through the *cross* of His Son—not through Christ's success but through His death. We must not forget that He bestows this salvation upon us by letting us hear and believe the *message of the cross*. We must not forget that there is nothing else in Heaven or on earth —though an angel from Heaven should proclaim it—save this Word of the cross on which we can and may base and establish our faith. We must remember at this time of special testing and tribulation that every other attempt to consolidate and to establish our faith on a different basis, every furtive glance at success or failure, at any other counsel and sustenance and support for our faith, has the opposite effect to what we hope, namely, we sink and perish, our faith is shipwrecked and we are swallowed up in unbelief.

The cross of Jesus—truly that is failure and ruin and utter desolation, and our eyes can see nought else there; and if we agree with Gamaliel, then we conclude: "So this counsel and this work are of men!" And in that case the message of the cross means nothing to us: we cannot see it, it is only something we hear preached. But the Gospel, the Word *alone*, says: "It is *precisely here* that God's love triumphs, and it is precisely here that God reveals Himself through His Word and Holy Spirit and bestows faith upon the believer; here is God's counsel and God's work and he who believes receives of this counsel and this faith!"

Friends, the sufferings and the shame of Christ's community—the suffering and the shame which we have to bear when we side with the crucified Man of Nazareth—that is truly failure, that is assuredly trouble and distress; and we feel depression and doubt—and none of us is free from them—creeping into our souls after hearing Gamaliel's counsel. Is our faith a delusion? Is our faith only the counsel and the work of men, after all?

But the Gospel says otherwise. Jesus Christ says: "Blessed are ye when men shall revile you and persecute you for My sake." And faith hears that, and faith clings to that promise, and faith is happy and comforted, as Jesus bade it: "Rejoice and be exceeding glad!"

But, brothers and sisters, can this *really* be so? Can we be happy and comforted in our faith? We see to-day that this matter of a happy and comforted faith is no child's play, that it is not enough to be able to quote passages from the Bible; that we do not go far with a little inspired protestation and our usual normal measure of inextinguishable optimism, and that we have reached the point where we cannot resist alone, without help.

The oppression is growing, and anyone who has had to submit to the Tempter's machine-gun fire during this last week thinks differently from what he did even three weeks ago. I have in mind how on Wednesday the Secret Police forced their way into the locked church at Friedrichwerder and in the vestry arrested eight members of the Reich Council of Brethren who were holding a meeting there, and took them away. I have in mind how yesterday at Saarbrücken six women and a male member of the congregation were taken into custody because they were distributing an election leaflet of the Confessional Church, at the request of the Council of Brethren. I say to you: anyone who knows these things and who has actually had to suffer these things, is not far from uttering the Prophet's words—indeed such a one would fain say with the Prophet: "It is enough —no, it is too much!—now, O Lord, take away my life!"

And anyone who has the experience I had the night before last at an evening Communion service and sees beside him nothing less than three young members of the Secret Police who have come in their official capacity to spy upon the community of Jesus Christ in their praying, singing and preaching—three young men who were also assuredly baptized once upon a time in the name of the Lord Jesus Christ and who also assuredly vowed loyalty to their Saviour at the confirmation altar, and whose office and duty it now is to set traps for the community of Jesus Christ—anyone who sees that cannot escape so easily from the shame of the Church; he cannot pass the matter off with a pious phrase and an inspired protest: such a sight may cost him a sleepless and most certainly a restless night, and he may even cry from the depths of his despair. "Lord, have mercy upon me!"

And we are remembering that over yonder in the Annenkirche the pulpit stands empty to-day because our brother and pastor, Fritz Müller, along with forty-seven other Christian brothers and sisters of our Evangelical Church, is being kept in custody because of church matters; and at the same time we remember that in the church, even in the so-called Confessional Church and even in our own congregation, people are saying: "They are possibly not quite innocent, you know; they probably have something political chalked up against them!" And now the press has begun its defamatory campaign and in the week which begins to-day the first summary proceedings will take place.

Yes, dear friends—what then? Shall we be happy and comforted or despondent and intimidated? There is in truth nothing left for us but to put our trust in the Word of the crucified Saviour and to cling to this crucified Saviour Himself and to learn to say, in simple and therefore assured faith, the a b c of Christian belief: "I can rejoice, because within my heart Thy name and Cross *alone* shed their radiant beams continually!" And it may take some time for the knowledge: "We can be happy," to become the truth: "We are happy," and for us actually to be as happy as the Apostles, who "departed from the presence of the council, rejoicing that they were counted worthy to suffer shame" for Christ's sake. It may cost us a considerable effort to rejoice because we must suffer: this is not an easy path to tread nor is this walk a pleasure outing. It is an exposed road and those who follow it are told: "If any man will come after Me, let him deny himself, and take up his *cross*—daily—and follow Me." It may be a good thing that this is no pleasure excursion and that the way of the Cross cannot be learned overnight. It may be just as well that the road is long and difficult, otherwise we might confuse our pious moods, our loyalty to our convictions, our manly courage and whatever else the idols may be called, with *faith*, which is a gracious gift from God and which He bestows upon us through the Holy Ghost; but on this long and difficult road we may learn, in the bitterness of tribulation, to pay attention to the Word of our Lord, and so we may begin in earnest to hear and preach and teach the Word of the Cross, the Gospel of Jesus Christ, without ceasing.

Our duty to-day—and we have no other—is that we should be like the Apostles who, when a new embargo was laid upon their preaching, went forth and did not cease to preach the Gospel of Jesus Christ, the message of the Cross; and we can preach it only by learning it, and we can teach it only by listening to it ourselves; for it is by this Word—and by this Word alone—that our faith lives, our faith that is joy; and from this faith flows the joy that keeps us upright beneath the Cross and steadies us upon our feet: this joy is happy beneath the Cross and confesses that it owes its life to the Cross.

Dear friends, man does not live by bread alone, but by the Word of God! And so we can only pray with the disciples:

"Lord, give us, give Thy community, give Thy Christian people now and at all times such bread!"

Malcolm (Vivian) Hay was born in 1881, a Scot. He fought in World War I, and in 1916 published a book recounting some of his experiences: *Wounded and a Prisoner of War.* After the War, he wrote *A Chain of Error in Scottish History* (1927), *The Blairs Papers* (1929), *The Jesuits and the Popish Plot* (1934), and *The Enigma of James II* (1938).

During World War II, Hay edited a monthly periodical for prisoners of war. Hearing of the Nazis' massacres of the Jews, he studied Jewish history and Hebrew; and after the War, he went to Palestine. When British civilians not there on official business were ordered to leave the country in 1947, he "went underground" and, though a Catholic, remained at Rehovot as "Rabbi Hai." After his return to Scotland, he published *The Foot of Pride: The Pressure of Christendom on the People of Israel for 1900 Years* (1950). The book traces anti-Semitism from the age of the New Testament to the establishment of the State of Israel. When it was reissued as a Beacon paperback, under the title *Europe and the Jews* (1960), I was given the opportunity to express my admiration in a preface, "History and Honesty."

Further information about Malcolm Hay may be found in Thomas Sugrue's illuminating introduction to that volume. What follows is the first chapter, uncut; only the footnotes have been omitted.

Europe and the Jews

THE GOLDEN MOUTH

*M*en are not born with hatred in their blood. The infection is usually acquired by contact; it may be injected deliberately or even unconsciously, by parents, or by teachers. Adults, unless protected by the vigor of their intelligence, or by a rare quality of goodness, seldom escape contagion. The disease may spread throughout the land like the plague, so that a class, a religion, a nation, will become the victim of popular hatred without anyone knowing exactly how it all began; and people will disagree, and even quarrel among themselves, about the real reason for its existence; and no one foresees the inevitable consequences.

For hatred dealeth perversely, as St. Paul might have said were he writing to the Corinthians at the present time, and is puffed up with pride; rejoiceth in iniquity; regardeth not the truth. These three things, therefore, corrupt the world: disbelief, despair, and hatred—and of these, the most dangerous of all is hatred.

In the spring of 1945, three trucks loaded with eight to nine tons of human ashes, from the Sachsenhausen concentration camp, were dumped into a canal in order to conceal the high rate of Jewish executions. When a German general was asked at Nuremburg how such things could happen, he replied: "I am of the opinion that when for years, for decades, the doctrine is preached that Jews are not even human, such an outcome is inevitable." This explanation, which gets to the root of the matter, is, however, incomplete. The doctrine which made such deeds inevitable had been preached, not merely for years or for decades, but for many centuries; more than once during the Middle Ages it threatened to destroy the Jewish people. "The Jews," wrote Léon Bloy, "are the most faithful witnesses, the most authentic remainders, of the candid Middle Ages which hated them for the love of God, and so often wanted to exterminate them." In those days the excuse given for killing them was often that they were "not human," and that, in the modern German sense, they were "non-adaptable"; they did not fit into the mediaeval conception of a World State.

The German crime of genocide—the murder of a race—has its logical roots in the mediaeval theory that the Jews were outcasts, condemned by God to a life of perpetual servitude, and it is not, therefore, a phenomenon completely disconnected from previous history. Moreover, responsibility for the nearly achieved success of the German plan to destroy a whole group of human beings ought not to be restricted to Hitler and his gangsters, or to the German people. The plan nearly succeeded because it was allowed to develop without interference.

"It was an excellent saying of Solon's," wrote Richard Bentley, "who when he was asked what would rid the world of injuries, replied: 'If the bystanders would have the same resentment with those that suffer wrong.'" The responsibility of bystanders who remained inactive while the German plan proceeded was recognized by one European statesman, by the least guilty of them all, Jan Masaryk, who had helped to rescue many thousands from the German chambers of death. Masaryk said:

I am not an expert on the Near East and know practically nothing about pipe-lines. But one pipe-line I have watched with horror all my life; it is the pipe-line through which, for centuries, Jewish blood has flowed sporadically, and with horrible, incessant streams from 1933 to 1945. I will not, I cannot, forget this unbelievable fact, and I bow my head in shame as one of those who permitted this greatest of wholesale murders to happen, instead of standing up with courage and decision against its perpetrators before it was too late.

Even after the Nuremberg Laws of 1935, every frontier remained closed against Jews fleeing from German terror, although a few were sometimes allowed in by a back door. Bystanders from thirty-two countries attended a conference at Evian, in 1938, to discuss the refugee problem; they formed a Permanent Intergovernmental Department in London to make arrangements for the admission of Jewish immigrants from Germany. The question of saving Jewish children by sending them to Palestine was not on the agenda of the Committee for assistance to refugees. "Up to August, 1939, the Committee had not succeeded in discovering new opportunities of immigration, though negotiations were proceeding with San Domingo, Northern Rhodesia, the Philippines and British Guiana."

An American writer asked in 1938:

> What is to be done with these people, with the millions who are clawing like frantic beasts at the dark walls of the suffocating chambers where they are imprisoned? The Christian world has practically abandoned them, and sits by with hardly an observable twinge of conscience in the midst of this terrible catastrophe. The Western Jews, still potent and powerful, rotate in their smug self-satisfied orbits, and confine themselves to genteel charity.

Until Germany obtained control of the greater part of Western Europe her policy had been directed mainly to compulsory Jewish emigration. But victories in 1940 had opened up new possibilities; and the Jews were therefore driven into ghettos in Poland and neighboring areas, where arrangements were being made for the "final solution," which was proclaimed in 1942, and put into action throughout all Germany and German-occupied territories. "What should be done with them," asked Hans Frank, governor general of occupied Poland, on December 16th, 1941. The German answer was no longer a secret. "I must ask you, gentlemen," said the governor, "to arm yourselves against all feelings of pity. We must annihilate the Jews wherever we find them."

Hitler, in 1941, was still waiting to see what the Christian world was going to do. Had the Allies opened their doors wide, even then, at least a million people, including hundreds of thousands of children, could have been saved. But no doors anywhere were widely opened. Few hearts anywhere were deeply moved. In Palestine, in the corner secured to Jews by the decision of the League of Nations, the entries by land and by sea were guarded by British soldiers and British sailors. Great numbers, especially in Poland, would have fled from the impending terror: *"If only they could,"* wrote Jacques Maritain in 1938, "if only other countries would open their frontiers." The German government at that time, and even after, was not always unwilling, and in 1939 and 1940, was still prepared to let them go on certain conditions. "The Allies were told that if the Jews of Germany were to receive certificates to Palestine, or visas for any other country, they could be saved. Although for Jews to remain in Germany meant certain death, the pieces of paper needed to save human lives were not granted."

These pieces of paper were not provided, even to save the lives of children. In April, 1943, the Swedish government agreed to ask the German government to permit twenty thousand children to leave Germany for Sweden, provided that Sweden should be relieved of responsibility for them after the war. These children would have been saved had the British government given them certificates for Palestine. But even to save twenty thousand children from being slaughtered by the Germans, "it was not possible," said a British minister in the House of Commons, "for His Majesty's Government to go beyond the terms of policy approved by Parliament."

About the same time, in 1943, the Germans were considering an offer by the Red Cross and the British to evacuate seventy thousand children from Rumania to Palestine. Negotiations dragged on with the usual lack of vigor. And the Germans were persuaded by the Mufti of Jerusalem and Raschid Ali Gailani, prime minister of Iraq, who at the time were living, at German expense, in Berlin, to reject the plan. So the seventy thousand children were sent to the gas chambers.

More than a million children, including uncounted thousands of newborn infants, were killed by the Germans; most of them could have been saved had the countries of the world been determined to save them. But the doors remained closed. The children were taken away from their parents and sent, crowded in the death trains, and alone, to the crematoria of Auschwitz and Treblinka, or to the mass graves of Poland and Western Russia.

The German method of burying people in communal pits was a great improvement on the old system, once considered to be inhuman, of making each condemned man dig his own grave. The shooting of about two million people, whose bodies could not be left lying about, presented a difficult problem owing to the shortage of labor. Jewish women and children, weakened by torture and by long internment in concentration camps, were physically incapable of digging; and the men, when put on the list for "special treatment," were, as a rule, reduced to such a condition by hard labor on meager rations that they could hardly walk. The mass grave was an obvious necessity; but the German stroke of genius was the idea of making their victims get into the grave before they were shot, thus saving the labor of lifting two million dead bodies and throwing them in. Many hundreds of these death pits were dug in Central Europe until the Germans began to apply to extermination their well-known scientific efficiency. One of the largest pits, at Kerch, was examined in 1942 by officials of the Russian army:

It was discovered that this trench, one kilometer in length, four meters wide, and two meters deep, was filled to overflowing with bodies of women, children, old men, and boys and girls in their teens. Near the trench were frozen pools of blood. Children's caps, toys, ribbons, torn off buttons, gloves, milkbottles, and rubber comforters, small shoes, galoshes, together with torn off hands and feet, and other parts of human bodies, were lying nearby. Everything was spattered with blood and brains.

What happened at Dulmo, in the Ukraine, reported by a German witness, Hermann Graebe, is one of the grimmest short stories that has ever been told in the bloody record of inhuman history. Graebe was manager of a building contractor's business at Dulmo. On October 5, 1942, he went as usual to his office and there was told by his foreman of terrible doings in the neighborhood. All the Jews in the district, about five thousand of them, were being liquidated. About fifteen hundred were shot every day, out in the open air, at a place nearby where three large pits had been dug, thirty meters long and three meters deep. Graebe and his foreman, who was intensely agitated, got into a car and drove off to the place. They saw a great mound of earth, twice the length of a cricket pitch and more than six feet high—a good shooting range. Near the mound were several trucks packed with people. Guards with whips drove the people off the trucks. The victims all had yellow patches sewn onto their garments, back and front—the Jewish badge. From behind the earth mound came the sound of rifle shots in quick succession. The people from the lorries, men, women and children of all ages, were herded together near the mound by an SS man armed with a dog whip. They were ordered to strip. They were told to put down their clothes in tidy order, boots and shoes, top clothing and underclothing.

Already there were great piles of this clothing, and a heap of eight hundred to a thousand pairs of boots and shoes. The people undressed. The mothers undressed the little children, "without screaming or weeping," reported Graebe, five years after. They had reached the point of human suffering where tears no longer flow and all hope has long been abandoned. "They stood around in family groups, kissed each other, said farewells, and waited." They were waiting for a signal from the SS man with a whip, who was standing by the pit. They stood there waiting for a quarter of an hour, waiting for their turn to come, while on the other side of the earth mound, now that the shots were no longer heard, the dead and dying were being packed into the pit. Graebe said:

I heard no complaints, no appeal for mercy. I watched a family of about eight persons, a man and a woman both about fifty, with their grown up children, about twenty to twenty-four. An old woman with snow-white hair was holding a little baby in her arms, singing to it and tickling it. The baby was cooing with delight. The couple were looking at each other with tears in their eyes. The father was holding the hand of a boy about ten years old and speaking to him softly; the boy was fighting his tears. . . .

Then suddenly came a shout from the SS man at the pit. They were ready to deal with the next batch. Twenty people were counted off, including the family of eight. They were marched away behind the earth mound. Graebe and his foreman followed them. They walked round the mound and saw the tremendous grave, nearly a hundred feet long and nine feet deep. "People were closely wedged together and lying on top of each other so that only their heads were visible. Nearly all had blood running over their shoulders from their heads." They had been shot, in the usual German way, in the back of the neck. "Some of the shot people were still moving. Some were lifting their arms and turning their heads to show that they were still alive."

The pit was already nearly full; it contained about a thousand bodies. The SS man who did the shooting was sitting on the edge of the pit, smoking a cigarette, with a tommy gun on his knee. The new batch of twenty people, the family of eight and the baby carried in the arms of the woman with snow-white hair, all completely naked, were directed down steps cut in the clay wall of the pit, and clambered over the heads of the dead and the dying. They lay down among them. "Some caressed those who were still alive and spoke to them in a low voice." Then came the shots from the SS man, who had thrown away his cigarette. Graebe looked into the pit "and saw the bodies were twitching, and some heads lying already motionless on top of the dead bodies that lay under them."

The Jews who died in this manner at Dulmo were the most fortunate ones. They were spared torture in laboratory tests carried out by German doctors in order to find out how much agony the human body can endure before it dies; they were spared the choking terror of death in the gas chamber where hundreds of people at a time, squeezed together as tightly as the room could hold them, waited for the stream of poison to be turned on, while members of the German prison staff stood listening for ten or fifteen minutes until the screaming ceased, until all sounds had ceased, and they could safely open the door to the dead. And when the door was opened, the torture was not yet over. Four young Jews, whose turn would come perhaps with the next batch, dressed in a special sanitary uniform, with high rubber boots and long leather gauntlets, and provided with grappling irons, were compelled to drag out the pale dead bodies; and another group of young men was waiting to load the bodies onto a cart and drive them to the crematorium; and they knew that their turn, too, would soon come.

Responsibility for these deeds which have dishonored humanity does not rest solely with Hitler and the men who sat in the dock at Nuremberg. Another tribunal will judge the bystanders, some of them in England, who watched the murderous beginnings, and then looked away and in their hearts secretly approved. "The Jewish blood shed by the Nazis," writes J.–P. Sartre, "is upon the heads of all of us."

As Maxim Gorky said more than thirty years ago, one of the greatest crimes of which men are guilty, is indifference to the fate of their fellow men. This responsibility of the indifferent was recognized by Jacques Maritain a few years before the final act of the tragedy. "There seems to be a spirit," he said in 1938, "which, without endorsing excesses committed against Jews . . . and without professing anti-Semitism, regards the Jewish drama with the indifference of the rational man who goes coldly along his way." It was this spirit of indifference, this cold aloofness of the bystanders, which made it possible for Hitler to turn Europe into a Jewish cemetery. Christian responsibility has, however, been recognized by one English bystander who for many years had never failed "to have the same resentment with those that suffer wrong": "In our own day, and within our own civilization," writes Dr. James Parkes, "more than six million deliberate murders are the consequence of the teachings about Jews for which the Christian Church is ultimately responsible, and of an attitude to Judaism which is not only maintained by all the Christian Churches, but has its ultimate resting place in the teaching of the New Testament itself."

Repressing the instinct to make excuses, read the following words written by a survivor of Auschwitz:

German responsibility for these crimes, however overwhelming it may be, is only a secondary responsibility, which has grafted itself, like a hideous parasite, upon a secular tradition, which is a Christian tradition. How can one forget that Christianity, chiefly from the eleventh century, has employed against Jews a policy of degradation and of pogroms, which has been extended—among certain Christian people—into contemporary history, which can be observed still alive to-day in most Catholic Poland, and of which the Hitlerian system has been only a copy, atrociously perfected.

Even in countries where pogroms are unknown, it was the coldness, the indifference of the average man which made the Jewish drama in Europe possible. "I am convinced," wrote Pierre van Paassen, "that Hitler neither could nor would have done to the Jewish people what he has done . . . if we had not actively prepared the way for him by our own unfriendly attitude to the Jews, by our selfishness and by the anti-Semitic teaching in our churches and schools."

The way was prepared by a hatred which has a long history. The inoculation of the poison began long ago in the nurseries of Christendom.

Millions of children heard about Jews for the first time when they were told the story of how Christ was killed by wicked men; killed by the Jews; crucified by the Jews. And the next thing they learned was that God had punished these wicked men and had cursed the whole of their nation for all time, so that they had become outcasts and were unfit to associate with Christians. When these children grew up, some of them quarreled among themselves about the meaning of the word of Christ and about the story of his life, death and resurrection; and others were Christians only in name; but most of them retained enough Christianity to continue hating the perfidious people, the Christ-killers, the deicide race.

Although the popular tradition that "the Jews" crucified Christ goes back to the beginnings of the Christian Church, no justification for it can be found in the New Testament. St. Matthew, St. Mark and St. Luke all took special care to impress upon their readers the fact that the Jewish people, their own people, were not responsible for, and were for the most part ignorant of, the events which led up to the apprehension, the trial and the condemnation of Christ. St. Matthew's account of what happened does not provide any opportunity for people to differ about his meaning. He states quite clearly in his twenty-sixth chapter that "the Jews" had nothing to do with the plot against Christ. He explains who the conspirators were, and why they had to do their work in secret. "Then were gathered together the Chief Priests and the Ancients of the people into the court of the High Priest who is called Caiaphas. And they consulted together that by subtlety they might apprehend Jesus and put him to death." Secrecy was essential to the plans of the plotters because they "feared the multitude" (Matt. 21:46). They were afraid that "the Jews" might find out what was brewing and start a riot.

The plot which ended on Calvary began to take shape for the first time at that gathering in the court of Caiaphas. These men were engaged upon an enterprise which they knew would not meet with public approval. They had no mandate from the Jewish people for what they were about to do. They did not represent the two or three million Jews who at that time lived in Palestine, or another million who lived in Egypt, or the millions more who were scattered all over the Roman Empire. At least three-quarters of all these people lived and died without ever hearing the name of Christ.

The conspirators did not even represent the wishes of the Jewish population in and around Jerusalem. They were afraid, explained Matthew, of arresting Jesus "on the festival day lest there should be a tumult among the people."

They had to act promptly; they had to avoid publicity. They employed the crowd of idlers and ruffians which can be always collected for an evil purpose, to provide a democratic covering for what they proposed to do. This crowd formed a majority of the people present at the trial; these were the men who, when Pilate, the pioneer of appeasement, tried to save Christ from their fury, replied with the fateful words which Matthew recorded in the twenty-seventh chapter of his Gospel: "And the whole people answering said: 'His blood be upon us and upon our children.'" Although "the whole people," as Matthew explained, meant only the people present "who had been persuaded by the High Priest and the Ancients"

(27:20), his text has been used for centuries by countless Christian preachers as a stimulant to hate and an excuse for anti-Jewish pogroms. "O cursed race!" thundered Bossuet from his pulpit, "your prayer will be answered only too effectively; that blood will pursue you even unto your remotest descendants, until the Lord, weary at last of vengeance, will be mindful, at the end of time, of your miserable remnant."

St. Mark, also, records that the Jewish people had nothing to do with the plot and that if they had known about it they would have expressed violent disapproval. "The Chief Priests and the Pharisees sought how they might destroy him. For they feared him because the whole multitude was in admiration of his doctrine" (11:18). "They sought to lay hands upon him, but they feared the people" (12:12). They sought to lay hold on him and kill him, but they said, "not on the festival day, lest there should be a tumult among the people" (14:2).

St. Luke tells the same story with the same emphasis. "And the Chief Priests and the Scribes, and the rulers of the people, sought to destroy him. And they found not what to do to him; for all the people were very attentive to hear him" (19:47, 48). "The Chief Priests and the Scribes sought to lay hands on him . . . but they feared the people" (20:19). "And the Chief Priests and the Scribes sought how they might put Jesus to death; but they feared the people" (22:2).

This Christian tradition, which made "the Jews" responsible for the death of Christ, first took shape in the Fourth Gospel. St. John deals with the historical beginnings of the Christian Church even more fully than with the ending of the era which preceded the foundation of Christianity. Unlike the other evangelists, he wrote as one outside the Jewish world, as one hostile to it. He was already disassimilated. His Gospel contains the first hint of hostility, the first suggestion of a religious Judaeophobia. He almost invariably employs the phrase "the Jews" when the context shows, and the other evangelists confirm, that he is referring to the action or to the opinions of the High Priests and the Ancients.

Whereas Matthew, Mark and Luke all wrote as if they had foreseen, and were trying to refute in advance, the accusation which would be brought against their fellow-countrymen, John, by his repeated use of the phrase "the Jews," puts into the mind of his readers the idea that they were all guilty. Although Matthew, for instance, says that when Jesus healed the man with a withered hand on the Sabbath, "the Pharisees made a consultation how they might destroy him," John, reporting a similar incident, indicts, not the Pharisees, but "the Jews": "*The Jews* therefore said to him that was healed: it is not lawful for thee to take up thy bed . . . therefore did *the Jews* persecute Jesus because he did these things on the Sabbath" (5:10,16).

When John tells the story of the blind man, he begins by relating what the Pharisees said, but after the man received his sight his parents are reported to have "feared *the Jews*," although it is obvious from the context that they feared the Pharisees. In the same chapter, John wrote that "*the Jews* had agreed among themselves that if any man should confess him to be the Christ, he should be put out of the synagogue." This agreement had been reached, not by the Jews, but by the Chief Priests and the Ancients. In the tenth chapter which deals with the action and behavior of this political group, we read that

a dissension rose again among *the Jews* . . . and many of them said: He hath a devil and is mad. . . . In Solomon's Porch *the Jews* therefore came to him and said to him . . . If thou be the Christ tell us plainly. . . . *The Jews* then took up stones to stone him. . . . *The Jews* answered him—For a good work we stone thee not, but for blasphemy.

John was more careful in his choice of words when he described the details of the crucifixion. He laid special emphasis on the fact that Christ was crucified, not by the Jews, but by Roman soldiers. "The soldiers therefore, when they had crucified him took his garments . . . and also his coat . . . they said to one another: Let us not cut it, but let us cast lots for it . . . and the soldiers indeed did these things" (19: 23, 24). Nevertheless, in John's story of the apprehension, trial and death of Christ, responsibility is laid, as much as inference can lay it, on the whole Jewish people; a prominence is given to the action of "the Jews" which the events as recorded by the other evangelists do not justify.

Père Lagrange suggested that John made use of the phrase "the Jews," as a literary device to save constant repetition of the words "High Priests and Pharisees." It is a pity that this interpretation of John's meaning did not occur to any of the early Fathers. When Origen wrote at the beginning of the fourth century that "the Jews . . . nailed Christ to the cross," he also may have meant something different from what he said—but for many centuries his words were taken as literally true by all Christendom. And consequently, as an English historian in our own time has admitted, "The crime of a handful of priests and elders in Jerusalem was visited by the Christian Churches upon the whole Jewish race."

This tradition has been handed on without much respect for the actual facts as related in the Gospels. Thus, in the thirteenth century, a pious monk, Jacques de Vitry, went to the Holy Land, visited the site of Calvary and sat in meditation, as he recorded in his Chronicle, "on the very spot where *the Jews* divided the garments of Christ, and for his tunic cast lots." When, however, mediaeval writers had to report anything which they feared might arouse Christian sympathy for the children of Israel they called them, in such a context, not "Jews" but "Hebrews." Jacques de Vitry, for instance, described how Christ was welcomed on his entry into Jerusalem by "the Hebrews"; this terminology is still used in the Church's liturgy on Palm Sunday: *Plebs Hebraea cum palmis obviam venit.* The mediaeval mystics, in whose writings religious sentiment was exhibited in its most popular form, show how hatred had become the constant companion of devotion. Juliana of Norwich, an English anchoress whose *Sixteen Revelations of Divine Love* (1373) has been described by Dean Inge as "one of the most precious gems of mediaeval sacred literature," excluded from her programme of love only one section of humanity:

> For though the Revelation was made of goodness in which was made little mention of evil, yet I was not drawn thereby from any point of Faith that Holy Church teacheth me to believe. . . . I saw not so properly specified the Jews that did Him to death. Notwithstanding I knew in my Faith that they were accursed and condemned without end, saving those that were converted by grace.

These words read as if they had been added by Juliana at the suggestion of her confessor, or some religious censor who had been shocked by finding that the *Revelations of Divine Love* did not refer to the part which, according to popular mediaeval belief, had been played by Jews personally in the crucifixion of Christ.

This omission was atoned for by Margery Kempe, a slightly later visionary who, in her description of the Passion, which she imagined she had actually witnessed, followed the common conviction that Jews had nailed Christ to the cross. "Sche beheld how the cruel Jewys leydyn his precyows body to the Crosse and sithyn tokyn a long nayle . . . and wyth gret vilnes and cruelnes thei dreuyn it thorw hys hande." Pictures of Jews hammering in the nails helped to encourage both hatred and piety. A writer at the beginning of the sixteenth century mentions "a Church where there was placed a Jew, of wood, before the Saviour, grasping a hammer."

Pious ingenuity reached a new peak in Spain where, in the first quarter of the eighteenth century, two hundred years after all the Jews had been expelled, hatred continued to flourish alongside Christian faith and Christian superstition. A collection of the fables popular in the Middle Ages, printed in 1728, entitled *Centinela Contra Judios*, revived the belief that certain Jews, who were "born with worms in their mouth . . . were descended from a Jewess who ordered the locksmith who made the nails to crucify Christ to make the points blunt so that the pain of crucifixion would be greater." In the seventeenth century a zealous Catholic who was trying to convert Spinoza asked him to remember "the terrible and unspeakably severe punishments by which the Jews were reduced to the last stages of misery and calamity because they were the authors of Christ's crucifixion."

In order to fortify these traditions, Christian commentators tended increasingly to ignore the obvious meaning of the Gospel texts and sometimes substituted the phrase "the Jews" where John himself had written "the High Priests and the Pharisees." Dom Prosper Guéranger, Abbot of Solesmes, seems to have had access to some hitherto unknown source of information about the story of Martha, Mary Magdalene and Lazarus, originally told in John's Gospel. He wrote that "Mary Magdalene knew that the Jews were plotting the death of Jesus—the Holy Ghost inspired her." This account of what happened does not agree with the text of John's Gospel which states that the death of Christ has been plotted, not by the Jews, but by the "High Priests and the Pharisees." (John 11:47.)

In Russia popular Christianity produced a pattern of hate similar to that of Western Europe. When the Czarina Elizabeth (1741-1761) was asked to admit Jews into the country for economic reasons, she replied: "I do not wish to obtain any benefits from the enemies of Christ." More than a hundred years later, in 1890, when Alexander III was shown the draft of an official report recommending some relaxation of the oppression from which the Jews of his empire were suffering, he noted in the margin: "But we must not forget that the Jews crucified Christ." The pious Russians were not allowed to forget: "Representatives of the court clergy publicly preached that a Christian ought not to cultivate friendly relations with a Jew, since it was the command of the Gospel 'to hate the murderers of the Saviour.' "

At the beginning of the present century, Charles Maurras, founder and leader of L'Action Française, thought that the Gospels were not sufficiently anti-Semitic. He preferred to follow the mediaeval tradition. While still professing to be a Catholic, he was prepared to reject the testimony of all the evangelists. "I would not abandon," he wrote, "the learned procession of Councils, Popes and all the modern elite of great men, to put my trust in the gospels of four obscure Jews."

From the earliest times to the present day, readers of the Fourth Gospel, with rare exceptions, have taken the phrase "the Jews" in its literal sense without any shading of meaning. Consequently the whole literature of Christendom has contributed throughout the centuries to consolidate a tradition not sanctioned by the text of the Synoptic Gospels—one that has brought immeasurable suffering upon countless numbers of innocent human beings: the tradition that "the Jewish nation condemned Christ to be crucified." Joseph Klausner writes:

The Jews, *as a nation*, were far less guilty of the death of Jesus than the Greeks, as a nation, were guilty of the death of Socrates; but who now would think of avenging the blood of Socrates the Greek upon his countrymen, the present Greek race? Yet these nineteen hundred years past, the world has gone on avenging the blood of Jesus the Jew upon his countymen, the Jews, who have already paid the penalty, and still go on paying the penalty, in rivers and torrents of blood.

The extent of Jewish responsibility for the apprehension, trial and death of Christ was defined by the highest authority of the Christian Church, St. Peter, whose judgment corrects the bias shown, a generation later, in the Fourth Gospel. The first papal pronouncement on this question was addressed by St. Peter to "Ye men of Israel," a gathering which had assembled in "the Porch which is called Solomon's"; it was addressed to those men only, in that place, and at that time. St. Peter did not acquit these men of guilt; he knew that they had taken some active part in the plot and at the trial; they were, he told them, accessories to the crime. But the final words he used have often been ignored: "And now, brethren, I know you did it through ignorance; as did also your rulers."

Ignorance, defined by Maimonides as "the want of knowledge respecting things the knowledge of which can be obtained," is acceptable as an excuse only when it is not culpable. Abelard, in the twelfth century, may have extended too widely the proposition that where there is ignorance there can be no sin, when he said that the rulers of Israel acted "out of zeal for their law," and should therefore be absolved from all guilt. Christian tradition, especially in the early centuries, practically ignored St. Peter's statement that the "rulers" acted through ignorance. St. John Chrysostom, indeed, flatly contradicted St. Peter when he wrote that "the Jews . . . erred not ignorantly but with full knowledge." Whatever degree of guilt the "rulers" may have incurred, there is surely no justification for excluding them from the benefit of the petition and the judgment of Christ—"Father, forgive them for they know not what they do" (Luke 23:34). In the Gospel text these words refer quite clearly to the Roman soldiers, and not to the Jews.

The belief current in the Middle Ages which Abelard attacked and St. Bernard defended was that "the Jews" were all guilty; that they had acted with deliberate malice; that their guilt was shared by the whole Jewish people, for all time, and that they, and their children's children to the last generation, were condemned to live in slavery as the servants of Christian princes. That was not the doctrine of St. Peter. If Christians had always remembered his words, the history of the Jews in their long exile would perhaps have been very different, and the civilization of the West might not have witnessed the degradation of humanity which was achieved by the Germans in their death camps and gas chambers.

In spite of St. Peter's judgment the popular Christian doctrine has always been that anyone, whether pagan or Christian, who has at any time persecuted, tortured or massacred Jews has acted as an instrument of Divine wrath. A chronicler, writing in the early years of the thirteenth century, admired the patience of God, who "after the Jews had crucified Our Lord, waited for forty-eight years before chastising them." According to Fleury, who wrote, in the first quarter of the eighteenth century, an enormous and still useful ecclesiastical history, God began to take reprisals against the Jews in the year 38 of the Christian era. In that year, anti-Jewish riots broke out in Alexandria. The rioters were secretly encouraged by Flaccus, the Roman commissioner in Egypt, who took no effective measures to prevent the mob from burning down synagogues, breaking into Jewish shops, and scattering the merchandise into the streets of the city. Flaccus showed his "neutrality" by attempting to disarm, not the rioters, but their victims. "He had searches made in the houses of the Jews on the pretext of disarming the nation, and several women were taken away and tormented when they refused to eat swine's flesh." A great number of Jews were murdered, and their bodies dragged through the streets. "In this manner," wrote Fleury in 1732, "divine vengeance began to be manifested against the Jews."

The sacking of Jerusalem and the destruction of the Temple, in the year 70, when more than a million people were massacred with a brutality to which the world has once again become accustomed, were regarded by many pious Christians as part of God's plan of revenge. "The Jews," wrote Sulpicius Severus, "were thus punished and exiled throughout the whole world, for no other account than for the impious hands they laid upon Christ." This interpretation of the event has been repeated for centuries. Bossuet was one of the worst offenders against common sense and historical accuracy. In many of his sermons and in his *Discours sur l'Historie univer-selle*, he publicized the sanguinary details of what he called "Divine vengeance" on the accursed race. And in history books written for the instruction of youth, in 1947, the same thesis of hate is repeated:

> The punishment of the deicide Jews (God-killers) was not long delayed. Thirty-six years after the Savior's death, the Roman Emperor Titus captured Jerusalem and utterly destroyed the Jewish Temple. The Jews, dispersed throughout the world, have never been able to become once more a nation. They have wandered about, regarded as an accursed race, as an object of contempt to other peoples.

There are therefore still some people who believe that the Jews were cursed out of Palestine because they had behaved in a manner displeasing to God. If nations were liable to be dispossessed for such a reason, very few of them would enjoy security of tenure. "The Curse," as J.–P. Sartre has recently pointed out, was "geographical."

Whether or not the events of the year 70 were due to the vengeance of God, what really happened has often been misrepresented. "The Jews" were not driven out of Palestine after the sack of Jerusalem. Yet mediaeval Christendom believed, and many Christian writers today continue to repeat, that they were dispersed at that time. "Titus destroyed the Temple of Herod," writes H. V. Morton, "and scattered the race to the four corners of the world." Having paid this tribute to the sentimental tradition, he refers, a few pages further on, to the revolt of the Jews in Judaea, more than a generation later, which the Romans suppressed with their usual ruthless efficiency: "Julius Severus began a merciless war in which . . . 580,000 persons were slain." Assuming that the Romans slaughtered one-quarter of the population, which is a very generous estimate, about two million Jews must have been living in Palestine fifty years after the sack of the Temple. Titus, therefore, did not "scatter the race to the four corners of the world."

After the destruction of the Temple, the Jewish people were still allowed full rights of domicile in Palestine, with the exception of Jerusalem, and, during the first two or three centuries of the Christian era they lived almost exclusively by working on the land. They had, however, been deprived of their national status: they lost all prospect of recovering it after the political victory of Christianity. Under Christian-Roman rule they had hardly any rights. They were prohibited from serving in the army, and thus, as St. Jerome noted, "they lost their manly bearing." In the fourth and fifth centuries they were directed by the laws of the Christian-Roman Empire into the most degrading occupations and reduced practically to slavery, in order to destroy among them any hope of regaining their social and political freedom.

As a result of such legislation and of pulpit propaganda, the word "Jew," in the second half of the fifth century, was already in common use as an expression of contempt. In the collection of letters and decrees known as the *Codex Theodosianus*, the word was officially given for the first time the opprobrious significance it retained throughout Christendom for more than a thousand years: "Even their name is horrible and hideous." "The very name of Jew," said an English writer at the end of the eighteenth century, "has long been associated in the mind with the idea of everything base, false, despicable, and unprincipled." "All over the world," wrote Bishop Newton in 1765, "the Jews are in all respects treated as if they were of a different species."

The men who planned this humiliation and degradation of the Jewish people were convinced that they were carrying out the will of God. Ecclesiastical historians attributed the sufferings of the Jews, for which the Christians themselves were often responsible, to a divine plan of vengeance. Eusebius, in the first paragraph of his *Church History*, declared that his intention was "to recount the misfortunes which immediately came upon the whole Jewish nation in consequence of their plots against our Savior." Sozomen, a generation later, began his *History* by expressing astonishment at the obstinate refusal of the Jews to accept Christianity. "My mind has often been exercised in inquiring how it is that other men are very ready to believe in God the Word, while the Jews are so incredulous."

They were, indeed, difficult to convince. They refused to be impressed by a whole series of antonishing events which the Christians, apparently, expected everyone to accept as evidence of the truth of Christian doctrine. An example of this Jewish obstinacy is given by the ecclesiastical historian. Socrates, who recorded that when the Jews were attempting to rebuild the Temple at Jerusalem, in the reign of the Emperor Julian, "luminous impressions of a cross appeared imprinted on their garments, which at daybreak they in vain atempted to rub or wash out." People who refused to be convinced by the story of such a remarkable manifestation were clearly unfit to live in a Christian society. Some of the faithful thought that such obstinacy should be punished by death, and that to kill Jews was pleasing to God.

More in conformity with modern usage was the excuse, when killings on a large scale had taken place, that the Jews were the aggressors and that the Christians had massacred them in self-defense. Where the Jews were locally strong enough, they may sometimes have been the first to start a riot. But the story of their expulsion from Alexandria, by St. Cyril, would probably be less edifying, from a Christian point of view, if some Jewish account of the incident had survived. Many of the charges brought against them in the early centuries are based on reports written by their enemies, and it is not easy now to draw the line between history and propaganda. Socrates accused the Jews of tying a Christian boy to a cross, at a place called Inmestar, and then scourging him to death. "The Jewish inhabitants of the place," he explained, "paid the penalty of the wickedness they had committed in their pious sport." The story may have been true, but it may have been invented by some one, and repeated by Socrates, to account for a massacre.

To justify the persecution of Jews, two excuses, therefore, were available to Christians: either the Christians were acting in self-defense, or they were carrying out the will of God. The teaching of the early Fathers made the second excuse plausible. There was no direct incitement to violence. Athanasius did not tell the people to go out and beat up Jews. But he told them that "the Jews were no longer the people of God, but rulers of Sodom and Gomorrah"; and he asked the ominous question: "What is left unfulfilled, that they should now be allowed to disbelieve with impunity?"

When St. Ambrose told his congregations that the Jewish synagogue was "a house of impiety, a receptacle of folly, which God himself has condemned," no one was surprised when the people went off and set fire to one. St. Ambrose accepted responsibility for the outrage. "I declare that I set fire to the synagogue, or at least that I ordered those who did it, that there might not be a place where Christ was denied. If it be objected to me that I did not set the synagogue on fire here, I answer it began to be burnt by the judgment of God." He told the Emperor that people who burnt a synagogue ought not to be punished, such action being a just reprisal because Jews, in the reign of the Emperor Julian, had burnt down

Christian churches. In any case, he added, since the synagogues contained nothing of any value, "what could the Jews lose by the fire?" When they complained to the Emperor, he was indignant at their impertinence. They had no place in a court of law, he declared, because nothing they said could ever be believed. "Into what calumnies will they not break out, who, by false witness, calumniated even Christ!"

The Emperor, however, who did not approve of fire-raising propaganda, endeavored to protect the synagogues from the fury of the mob. He received a letter, from an unexpected quarter, asking him to revoke the orders he had given for punishing the offenders, a letter dispatched from the top of a pillar by St. Simeon Stylites. This ascetic, who achieved distinction by living for thirty-six years on top of a pillar fifty feet high, had given up, as G. F. Abbott remarked, "all worldly luxuries except Jew-hatred." He is not the only saint who was unable to renounce the consolations of anti-Semitism.

In the fourth century the natural goodness of men, and even saintliness, did not always operate for the benefit of Jews. St. Gregory of Nyssa, with the eloquence for which he was famous, composed against them a comprehensive indictment:

> Slayers of the Lord, murderers of the prophets, adversaries of God, haters of God, men who show contempt for the law, foes of grace, enemies of their father's faith, advocates of the devil, brood of vipers, slanderers, scoffers, men whose minds are in darkness, leaven of the Pharisees, assembly of demons, sinners, wicked men, stoners, and haters of righteousness.

Such exaggeration may have been an offense against charity, but it is not so harmful to the soul as the modern hypocrisy which pretends that the early Christian Fathers were invariably models of proper Christian behavior. "Our duty," wrote Basnage in the seventeenth century, "is to excuse the Fathers in their Extravagance, instead of justifying them, lest such forcible Examples should authorize Modern Divines, and confirm the Hatred and Revenge of writers."

St. John Chrysostom, the Golden-Mouthed, one of the greatest of the Church Fathers, spent his life, in and out of the pulpit, trying to reform the world. Christian writers, of varying shades of belief, have agreed in admiring his fervent love for all mankind, in spite of the fact that he was undoubtedly a socialist. "Chrysostom," said a Protestant divine, "was one of the most eloquent of the preachers who, ever since apostolic times, have brought to men the Divine tidings of truth and love." "A bright cheerful gentle soul," wrote Cardinal Newman, "a sensitive heart, a temperament open to emotion and impulse; and all this elevated, refined, transformed by the touch of heaven,—such was St. John Chrysostom."

Yet in this kindly gentle soul of the preacher who brought to men the tidings of truth and love, was hidden a hard core of hatred. "It must be admitted," wrote an honest French hagiographer, "that, in his homilies against the Jews, he allowed himself to be unduly carried away by an occasional access of passion."

A great deal more than this must be admitted.

The violence of the language used by St. John Chrysostom in his homilies against the Jews has never been exceeded by any preacher whose sermons have been recorded. Allowances must, no doubt, be made for the custom of the times, for passionate zeal, and for the fear that some tender shoots of Christian faith might be chilled by too much contact with Jews. But no amount of allowance can alter the fact that these homilies filled the minds of Christian congregations with a hatred which was transmitted to their children, and to their children's children, for many generations. These homilies, moreover, were used for centuries, in schools and in seminaries where priests were taught to preach, with St. John Chrysostom as their model—where priests were taught to hate, with St. John Chrysostom as their model.

There was no "touch of heaven" in the language used by St. John Chrysostom when he was preaching about Jewish synagogues. "The synagogue," he said, "is worse than a brothel . . . it is the den of scoundrels and the repair of wild beasts . . . the temple of demons devoted to idolatrous cults . . . the refuge of brigands and debauchees, and the cavern of devils."

The synagogue, he told his congregations in another sermon, was "a criminal assembly of Jews . . . a place of meeting for the assassins of Christ . . . a house worse than a drinking shop . . . a den of thieves; a house of ill fame, a dwelling of iniquity, the refuge of devils, a gulf and abyss of perdition." And he concluded, exhausted at length by his eloquence: "Whatever name even more horrible could be found, will never be worse than the synagogue deserves."

These sermons have not been forgotten; nor has contempt for Judaism diminished among the Christian congregations since they were first preached more than fifteen hundred years ago: "The Synagogue is nigh to a curse. Obstinate in her error, she refuses to see or to hear; she has deliberately perverted her judgment: she has extinguished within herself the light of the Holy Spirit; she will go deeper and deeper into evil, and at length fall into the abyss." St. John Chyrsostom was right in suggesting that future generations would think of even more horrible insults. "Sympathy for the Jews," wrote Léon Bloy, "is a sign of turpitude. . . . It is impossible to earn the esteem of a dog if one does not feel an instinctive disgust for the Synagogue."

In reply to some Christians who had maintained that Jewish synagogues might be entitled to respect because in them were kept the writings of Moses and the prophets, St. John Chrysostom answered: Not at all! This was a reason for hating them more, because they use these books, but willfully misunderstand their meaning. "As for me, I hate the synagogue. . . . I hate the Jews for the same reason."

It is not difficult to imagine the effect such sermons must have had upon congregations of excitable Orientals. Not only every synagogue, Chrysostom told them, but every Jew, was a temple of the devil. "I would say the same things about their souls." And he said a great deal more. It was unfit, he proclaimed, for Christians to associate with a people who had fallen into a condition lower than the vilest animals. "Debauchery and drunkenness had brought them to the level of the lusty goat and the pig. They know only one thing, to satisfy their stomachs, to get drunk, to kill and beat each other up like stage villains and coachmen."

The clear implication in all this rhetoric is, not that some Jews were living on the level of goats and pigs, but that *all* Jews lived thus because they were Jews. A variation of this theory has always been, and still is, one of the predominant principles of Judaeophobia, and, with a variety of applications, is still accepted, often subconsciously, by many people at the present time.

A typical example of this common prejudice, which is most pernicious when it is unconscious, occurs in a life of St. John Chrysostom, written in 1872 by an English clergyman, W. R. W. Stephens. "Allowing for some exaggeration in the preacher," he said, "the invectives of St. Chrysostom must be permitted to prove that the Jewish residents in Antioch were of a low and vicious order." No doubt most of them were; and so were most of the Christians. But in the mind of St. John Chrysostom, and in the mind of the Rev. Mr. Stephens, the Jews of Antioch lived like goats and pigs because they were Jews; as for the Christians, that was a very different story.

"The mass of the so-called Christian population," explained the Rev. Mr. Stephens, "was largely infected by the dominant vices—inordinate luxury, sensuality, selfish avarice, and display." It would be startling to read in an English newspaper that "the *so-called* Jewish population of London, or Paris, largely infected by the dominant vices of luxury, sensuality and avarice, were dealing extensively in the black market." A Jew never becomes "so-called" when he does anything wrong. If he behaves well, people say that he behaves like a Christian. In the twelfth century, when some Christians behaved badly, St. Bernard of Clairvaux did not describe them as "so-called," he simply said that they behaved like Jews. The wickedness of Jews consists, not in their conduct, but in their Jewishness. This was the doctrine of St. John Chrysostom.

The Jews, he told his congregations, are men possessed by an evil spirit, they are habitual murderers and destroyers. "We should not even salute them, or have the slightest converse with them." He employed in the pulpit every word of abuse that he could think of. He called them "lustful, rapacious, greedy, perfidious robbers." He was the first Christian preacher to apply the word "deicide" to the Jewish nation. The fervor of his hate has perhaps never been surpassed, even in modern times. "The Jews have assassinated the Son of God! How dare you take part in their festivals? . . . you dare to associate with this nation of assassins and hangmen! . . . O Jewish people! A man crucified by your hands has been stronger than you and has destroyed you and scattered you . . ."

All Jews were guilty, they had been punished by God, and the punishment would endure for all time. They were condemned by God, said Chrysostom, to a real hell on earth, condemned to a misery which would endure as long as the world lasted. After describing the misfortunes from which they had suffered under Roman tyranny, planned by a vindictive God, he pointed triumphantly to their present condition. "See how Judaea is a desert, and how all is desolation and ruin in that nation!" He foretold, moreover, that the present calamities would have no end. "Your situation, O Jewish people, becomes more and more disastrous, and one cannot see showing on your foreheads the slightest ray of hope."

Such logic would justify the German race murderers. St. John Chrysostom could have preached a powerful sermon beside the mass grave at Dulmo. He could have explained that a revengeful God had chastised the little Jewish boy who had tried to keep back his tears so that the Germans would not see that he was afraid; and the little baby, and the Jewish family, who all went down into the pit. He did, indeed, provide a suitable text for such a sermon in his "Sixth Homily Against the Jews":

But it was men, says the Jew, who brought these misfortunes upon us, not God. On the contrary it was in fact God who brought them about. If you attribute them to men, reflect again that, even supposing men had dared, they would not have had the power to accomplish them, unless it had been God's will.

Another passage from the same sermon would have been useful to the defense at Nuremberg: "So *whenever* the Jew tells you: It was men who made war on us, it was men who plotted against us, say to him: Men would certainly not have made war unless God had permitted them."

Chrysostom, said Duchesne, "was one of those unyielding Saints in whose eyes principles are made to be put into practice." Immediately after his arrival at Constantinople in 398, he brought his influence to bear on the Emperor, who had granted certain privileges to the Jews, so that all the laws in their favor were suspended. A few years later, when he was driven out of the city, legislation favorable to the Jews was restored. He hated them; and he did his best to make the whole world hate them too. But even this was not enough. You are, he told them, a people whom God has deprived of their inheritance. "Why then did he rob you? Is it not obvious that it was because he hated you, and rejected you once for all?"

When the usual allowances have been made for the manners of the time, pious zeal, oriental imagery, and for any context, setting, or background which might be urged in mitigation, these are words difficult to justify. This condemnation of the people of Israel, in the name of God, was not forgotten. It helped to strengthen the tradition of hate handed on through the Dark Ages and welcomed by mediaeval Christendom, a tradition which has disfigured the whole history of Western Europe.

For many centuries the Jews listened to the echo of those three words of St. John Chrysostom, the Golden-Mouthed: "God hates you."

Karl Barth was born at Basel, Switzerland, in 1886. He held professorships at the German universities of Göttingen, Münster, and Bonn before he left Germany in 1935, two years after Hitler had become Chancellor. Since 1935, Karl Barth has been a professor of theology at the University of Basel.

The number of his publications is prodigious. *Der Römerbrief* (1919; *The Epistle to the Romans*) established his reputation. *Die Auferstehung der Toten* (1924; *The Resurrection of the Dead*) has been very widely discussed, too. His most ambitious undertaking is his *Kirchliche Dogmatik:* the first eight tomes give some idea of the scope of the unfinished work. All of these books have been translated, the last named as *Church Dogmatics.*

A few of Barth's shorter works are available in paperback editions. Our selection is taken from Barth's *Against the Stream: Shorter Post-War Writings 1946-52* (1954).

Emil Brunner was born in Switzerland in 1889 and has been teaching theology in Zurich since 1924. His many books include *Der Mittler* (1927; *The Mediator*) and *Offenbarung und Vernunft* (1941; *Revelation and Reason*).

A Correspondence

AN OPEN LETTER TO KARL BARTH

*M*any will no doubt have read your report on Hungary with as great an interest as I have done. But not a few, including some of your own theological associates, have been extremely surprised by your attitude to the political problems of the Church under Soviet rule. Those who were familiar with the pronouncements on current events which you have issued since the end of the war were aware that your attitude to the great Communist power in the East was, if not friendly, as any rate emphatically sympathetic, and deliberately avoided any harsh outright rejection of Communist pretensions. I myself have only been able to interpret your approach as an after-effect of the satisfaction you felt at the overpowering of the brown monster in which Communist Russia played such a leading part. I had hoped that this mildness would automatically disappear and give way to a more fundamental judgment as soon as the true character of that power had emerged more clearly. I imagined you would undergo the same change of outlook as Reinhold Niebuhr, who only two years ago was expressing doubts about my fundamental rejection of Communist totalitarianism at an important ecumenical conference, but who has since joined the absolute opponents of Communism, particularly since seeing the monster at close quarters in Berlin. What I cannot understand—and it is this that prompts me to write an open letter to you—is why a similar change has not occurred in your attitude—even after the recent events in Prague.

Not only after the end of the war and during the last two years, but even now, you are passing on the watchword that the Church must not allow itself to be dragged into a clear-cut, fundamental opposition to "Communism." You praise the Reformed Hungarians for not "sharing that nervousness about the Russians, the peoples' democracies and the whole problem of Eastern Europe which some people in our own country apparently regard as inevitable." You evidently agree with your pupil Hermann Diem that in its first encounter with the "Communism" of the East the Evangelical Church should not reject it out of hand but wait and see, and be ready to co-operate. I don't know if you even approve of the attitude of your friend Hromadka in Prague, who belongs to the Communist Action Committee and who, although he prophesied only a short time ago in England that there would be no *coup d'état* in Prague, since Czech Communism was different from Russian Communism, was, when the crisis came, ready to co-operate.

All this is inexplicable to those who can see no fundamental difference between Communist and any other brand of totalitarianism, for example Nazism. Naturally we who have taken this line for many years realise that the origins and original motivation of Russian Communism were quite different from those of Nazism. We know too that certain postulates of social justice appear to be fulfilled in Communist totalitarianism. In brief, we know that the red variety of totalitarianism is different from the brown.

The question we want to ask you, however—and when I say "we" I mean not only the Swiss, but also many of your theological friends in Germany, Britain and America—is whether, whatever the differences between the several varieties, totalitarianism as such is a quantity to which the Christian Church can only issue an absolute, unmistakable and passionate "No!", just as you said "No!" to Hitlerism and summoned the Church to say an absolute "No!" Let me make a few observations to establish and explain the question:

1. I was always struck, and probably others were too, by the fact that even at the height of your struggle against Nazism you always evaded the problem of totalitarianism. Passionate and absolute as was your hostility to that incarnation of social injustice, if I am not mistaken, you hardly ever attacked the fundamental illegality and inhumanity inherent in the very nature of totalitarianism as such. This may have struck me more than others,

since as far back as the spring of 1934 I became involved in a sharp exchange with some German theologians at an ecumenical conference in Paris because they refused to swallow my thesis that the totalitarian State is *eo ipso* an unjust, inhuman and godless State. Since then I have repeatedly defended that position, and was therefore never able wholly to agree with the thesis you put forward in Wipkingen in 1938, that National Socialism was "the" political problem of the Church in our time, wholeheartedly as I agreed with you that it was the primary and most urgent problem from a purely political and military point of view.

2. I have been equally struck by the fact that in your utterances and those of your closest friends the problem of the totalitarian State is displaced by two other problems, which I can only regard as concealing the real problem. You talk about "the problem of East and West" and the problem of "Communism."

If the only issue was a "problem of East and West" the Church would certainly do well not to join too ostentatiously in the conversations of the politicians. For "East and West" is undoubtedly not a problem in which the Church as such has anything authoritative to say. But what one must not forget is that there are nations in Eastern Europe today which have been violated and regard themselves as having been violated by a political despotism in the same way as non-German nations did under Hitler. Nazism did not become an "Eastern" problem because Hitler occupied large territories in Eastern Europe. Because a political system subjugates and controls by means of puppet governments the peoples of Russia, the Baltic, Poland and the Balkans, the conflict today has certainly not become one between East and West. That would be the case only if the nations involved had given their consent to the Communist system, and if such consent could be explained on the grounds of traditional modes of thinking in Eastern Europe. Today everyone with eyes to see knows that that is not so. We churchmen really ought not to associate ourselves with such a camouflaging of the truth.

3. The other shift of emphasis is rather better founded, though no less dangerous. People—including yourself—talk simply about the "Communism" which the Church should not reject outright. Certainly the Christian who believes in the Communion of Saints and celebrates Holy Communion, cannot be against "Communism" as such. Among the many possible forms of Communism there are some with thoroughly Christian potentialities. One can indeed argue, as I have often done, that the system that calls itself Communism today would not have become possible if the Church had been more communistic on the lines of the communism we find in the Acts of the Apostles which is inherent in the very nature of the Christian society. What we are dealing with today, however, is a manifestation of the totalitarian State, a totalitarian Communism. This so-called Communism is the logical consequence of totalitarianism. If Hitler did not get as far as total national-

isation, total political and military control until the last years of the war, it only shows what an amateur he was. The "fully matured," the consistent totalitarian State must be "communistic," since one of its essential foundations is the subjugation to the State of the whole of life and the whole of man. And the nationalisation of the whole economic life of the country is the indispensable first step towards the totalitarian State. The question which confronts the Church today is therefore not whether or not it should adopt a fundamentally negative attitude towards "Communism," but whether it can say anything but a passionately fundamental No to the totalitarian State which, to be consistent, must also be communistic.

4. You justify the rejection of a fundamentally negative answer to "Communism" by referring to the social injustice of which there is certainly no lack in the nations of the West. The alternative as it is usually put sounds more imposing: Communism or Capitalism? Of course, the Church cannot and should not deny that there is a great deal of scandalous social injustice in the West. Of course it must fight against all social wrongs with the utmost earnestness and passion. Whether it does well to adopt the slogan of "capitalism" as the embodiment of social evil will depend on whether it knows what it means by capitalism. If it only means an economy which is not nationalised, I would resist the war-cry vigorously. The crucial point, however, is that we must never forget that in the countries not under totalitarian control it is still possible to fight against social injustice, that the fight is being waged and has already achieved a great deal, though nothing like enough.

5. If I am correctly informed, you are still a Socialist. However you interpret the Socialism in which you believe—the English interpretation, for example, is very different from that of our "socialist" Press, and the current German version is quite different from the one in fashion there twenty years ago—one thing cannot be denied: Socialism is engaged in a life and death struggle against "Communism" because and in so far as it is fundamentally and passionately anti-totalitarian. Is it therefore a good thing that this anti-totalitarian Socialism should be attacked in the rear—by churchmen of all people—in its defensive fight against totalitarian Communism? This is the effect of your statement that the well-advised Christian cannot be anti-Communist. Do you mean that Christians must not participate in the common struggle which the bourgeoisie and Socialism are waging against totalitarian Communism? I believe that would amount to a denial of principles which the Christian must never deny. Why not? Well, what is at stake in the struggle against totalitarianism? What is totalitarianism?

6. The totalitarian State is based on, is in fact identical with, the denial of those rights of the person vis-à-vis the State which are usually called human rights. That was the situation in Hitler's State, and it is the same now in the Communist totalitarian State. The individual has no original rights con-

ferred on him as a creature of God. Only the State can establish rights, and the individual only has the rights the State gives him and can take away from him at any time.

The totalitarian State is therefore a State of basic injustice. It is therefore also fundamentally inhuman and a fundamental denial of personal dignity. It is therefore intrinsically godless even though it may, like the Nazi State, tolerate the Church within certain narrow limits, or like Communist totalitarianism, for reasons of expediency keep its openly declared war on religion within certain bounds which just make it possible for the Church to exist.

The totalitarian State is intrinsically atheistic and anti-theistic since, by definition, it claims the total allegiance of man. From this intrinsic nature of totalitarianism all the familiar, ghastly phenomena have resulted which we got to know from the Russian State from 1917-1948, and from the Nazi State from 1933-1945: the G.P.U. and the Gestapo; the concentration camp without legal proceedings; the slave labour of millions; the utter uncertainty of the law, and so on. My question is: can the Church possibly say anything but a passionate and absolute No to totalitarianism? Must it not take its stand just as definitely against "Communism," i.e. against the consistently totalitarian State as against the amateurish Nazi State?

7. You assert that the Communist State realises certain social postulates which the Christian cannot oppose, but must on the contrary welcome. We heard exactly the same argument in the Hitler State—how often they tried to hoodwink us with the marvellous social achievements of the Nazi régime—things which it was impossible flatly to deny and which persuaded the naïve to believe that, in spite of all the horrors, "at bottom" National Socialism was a good thing. It cannot be denied that the Communist State has achieved and is achieving all kinds of valuable things—how else could it continue to exist at all? But as Christians we surely know it is always the devil's way to mix elements of truth in the system of lies and to endue a system of injustice with certain splendid appearances of justice. Are we no longer to fight the system of injustice, which is what the totalitarian State is fundamentally, because it also contains a number of valuable achievements? The dividing up of large estates was certainly a long overdue measure, in the interests of a healthy economy and a free peasantry. And it is also open to debate how far the nationalising of certain branches of economic life is not in the interest of justice and the common weal. Regarding the last point, I am more sceptical than my Socialist friends; but it is a matter that is certainly worth discussing amongst Christians. What is not open to discussion, however, is whether, because of measures such as these, which may be justified in themselves, the system of injustice and inhumanity which totalitarianism is, may be considered a feasible system for Christians.

8. Your friend Hromadka defends the strange view that Communism—meaning the totalitarian Communism which is the only variety we are con-

cerned with today—is a historical necessity, since democracy has proved its inability to survive: therefore the Christian Church must welcome Communism. We heard just the same argument in Switzerland during the worst years of the Hitler régime. I regard it as an utterly dangerous aberration of which a Protestant theologian ought to be thoroughly ashamed. A doubtful piece of historical determinism, shaky in relation to facts and principles alike, is used to confer the status of a normative principle on what amounts to an abdication of ethics and a surrender to the brute force of reality. Since when has the Christian capitulated in the face of "historical necessities"? Certainly there are situations in which the Christian or the Church is powerless to do anything, in which they cannot prevent disasters, in which they cannot redress even the most flagrant injustice, in which they may not even be able to protest publicly without endangering their very existence. All the more reason, surely, why the Church should beware of giving an ethical sanction to something it is powerless to prevent—but that is precisely what Hromadka is doing. What will he, what will his friends have to say for themselves when this totalitarian system that has been forced on their people collapses and is brought to judgment, as the Nazi system was brought to judgment in the Nuremberg Trials? They will stand convicted as collaborators, who not merely co-operated with the power of tyranny and injustice but even set themselves up as its champions!

9. There is one final argument which we find in your utterances and those of your friends: this fundamental attack on "Communism" is something the Catholic Church is engaged in—therefore we Protestants should not join in. I do not feel called upon to defend Catholic politics. I know perfectly well how much the Catholics always pursue their own power-political ends, how much, especially in Hungary, the Catholic Church is defending its former privileges in its struggle against Communism. But when the Catholic Church declares that the totalitarian State, red or brown, is irreconcilable with the Christian faith, why should the Evangelical Church have to stand aside merely because the truth is spoken by the Catholic Church? Did not Catholics and Protestants stand together in the struggle against the Hitler régime, and did you yourself not rejoice in the brave utterances of individual Catholic leaders and heartily agree with them when they condemned the totalitarian State passionately and unconditionally? A doctrine does not become false simply because it is expressed by the Catholic Church even if we always have good reason to reserve to ourselves the right to deviate from the Catholics and interpret and justify the doctrine more closely.

10. One further word about Hungary. I have not visited post-war Hungary, but I am fairly well-informed about what is going on, and I know how many different interpretations of the situation are current there. I know that very many good members of the Reformed Church view with

the utmost consternation these new collaborationist slogans, these tendencies towards a "positive evaluation" which are inspired by Pétain-Tildy, himself a member of the Reformed Church. The Reformed collaborators, even the Reformed fellow-travellers, will have to atone bitterly one day, I was told by someone who has suffered severely under the Communists. And even now many are turning away disillusioned from these members of the Reformed Church, because they feel they are betraying the cause of freedom, human rights, justice and humanity.

I simply cannot grasp why you, of all people, who condemned so severely even a semblance of collaborationism on the part of the Church under Hitler, should now be making yourself the spokesman of those who condemn not merely outward but even inward spiritual resistance, and why you should deride as "nervousness" what is really a horror-struck revulsion from a truly diabolical system of injustice and inhumanity; why you, who were only recently condemning in the most unsparing terms those Germans who withdrew to a purely inward line in the struggle against Hitlerism, and maintained that the Christian duty was simply to proclaim the Word of God under whatever political system, why you now suddenly advocate the very same line and commend the theologians in Hungary who "are occupied not with the rights and wrongs of their present government but simply with the positive tasks of their own Church." Have you now returned, after a fifteen years' intermezzo of theologically political activism, to that attitude of passive unconcern in which, in the first number of *Theologische Existenz heute*, you summoned the Church to apply itself simply to its task of preaching the gospel, "as if nothing had happened"?

I have felt bound to submit this question to you in my own name and in that of many of those who listen to you who are equally disturbed. Mindful of the great influence of whatever you say, you will surely regard it as a duty to give the question a clear answer.

Your EMIL BRUNNER

KARL BARTH'S REPLY

Dear Emil Brunner,—You do not seem to understand. At the moment I am not rousing the Church to oppose Communism and to witness against it, in the same way as I did between 1933 and 1945 in the case of National Socialism; you demand a "clear reply" to the question of how this is to be construed. I will come straight to the point.

Let us begin with a general statement. A certain binding spiritual and theological viewpoint in accordance with its creed is demanded of the Church in the political realm in certain times of need, i.e. when it is called upon to vindicate its faith in the carrying out of its duty according to God's Word, or when it is called upon to give an explanation regarding a definite occurrence. The Church must not concern itself eternally with various "isms" and systems, but with historical realities as seen in the light of the Word of God and of the Faith. Its obligations lie, not in the direction of any fulfilling of the law of nature, but towards its living Lord. Therefore, the Church never thinks, speaks or acts "on principle." Rather it judges spiritually and by individual cases. For that reason it rejects every attempt to systematise political history and its own part in that history. Therefore, it preserves the freedom to judge each new event afresh. If yesterday it travelled along one path, it is not bound to keep to the same path today. If yesterday it spoke from its position of responsibility, then today it should be silent if in this position it considers silence to be the better course. The unity and continuity of theology will best be preserved if the Church does not let itself be discouraged from being up-to-date theologically.

I ask this question: Was it not true that in the years after 1933 up till the end of the war there really was this need? The Central and Western European peoples—first Germany, then the others—had succumbed to Hitler's spell. He had become a spiritual and, almost everywhere, a political source of temptation. He had English, French and American admirers. Did not even Churchill have a few friendly words to say for him? And in Switzerland there were more than two hundred sympathisers, there was a Rudolf Grob, there were innumerable people who were impressed and influenced, though also very many who were frightened and despondent. One of the most important aims of our political authorities was to preserve correct and friendly relations with our powerful neighbour. In the Swiss Zofinger Society there was a serious discussion as to whether it was not time to subject our democratic system, established in 1848 (which event we are triumphantly celebrating today) to a thorough revision. Of the state of the Press one can read in the edifying book by Karl Weber, *Switzerland in the War of Nerves*. How great were the cares of our military directors can be seen from the account of our General, and from the fine book by Lt.-Col. Barbey about the five years he spent in the General's entourage. It was at that time that I made my various attempts to make the Church ready for action against the temptations of National Socialism, in Germany obviously spiritual, in Switzerland obviously political. At that time it had to warn men against tempters, to recall those who had strayed, to rouse the careless, to "confirm the feeble knees," to comfort sorrowing hearts.

Whether the essence of National Socialism consisted in its "totalitarianism" or, according to other views, in its "nihilism," or again in its barbarism, or anti-semitism or whether it was a final, concluding outburst of the militarism which had taken hold on Germany like a madness since 1870— what made it interesting from the Christian point of view was that it was a spell which notoriously revealed its power to overwhelm our souls, to persuade us to believe in its lies and to join in its evildoings. It could and would take us captive with "strong mail of craft and power." We were hypnotised by it as a rabbit by a giant snake. We were in danger of bringing, first incense, and then the complete sacrifice to it as to a false god. That ought not to have been done. We had to object with all our protestantism as though against *the* evil. It was not a matter of declaiming against some mischief, distant and easily seen through. It was a matter of life and death, of resistance against a godlessness which was in fact attacking body and soul, and was therefore effectively masked to many thousands of Christian eyes. For that very reason I spoke then and was not silent. For that very reason I could not forgive the collaborators, least of all those among them who were cultured, decent and well-meaning. In that way I consider that I acted as befits a churchman.

Now a second question: Is it not true that today there is again a state of emergency, this time in the shape of Communism? Has history already repeated itself, in that today we only need to take the remedy (which at that time took long enough to learn) from out of our pockets and to make immediate use of it? In the last few years I have become acquainted with Western Germany and also with the non-Russian sectors of Berlin. Fear, distrust and hatred for the "Eastern monster," as you call it, I met there in abundance, but apart from the German Communists I met no man of whom I received the impression (as one did with almost everybody in 1933) that he felt that this "monster" was a vexation, a temptation, an enticement, or that he was in danger of liking it or of condoning its deeds and of co-operating with it. On the contrary, it was quite clear to everyone, and it was universally agreed that for many reasons there was nothing in it. Is the situation any different here in Switzerland? in France, England or America? Are we not all convinced, whether we have read *I Chose Freedom* or not, that we cannot consider the way of life of the people in Soviet territory and in the Soviet-controlled "peoples' democracies" to be worthy, acceptable or of advantage to us, because it does not conform to our standards of justice and freedom? Who can contradict this? A few Western European Communists! Yet are we in danger of letting ourselves be overwhelmed by this power merely on account of the existence and the activities of these latter? Is there not freedom for every man—and who would not take advantage of this freedom?—to vent his anger against this "monster" to his heart's content, and again and again to bring to light its evils as "thoroughly" and as "passionately" as he wishes? Anyone who would like from me a political disclaimer of its system and its methods may have it at once. However, what is given cheaply can be had cheaply. Surely it would cost no one anything—not even a little thought—certainly nothing more, to add his bundle of faggots to the bonfire? I cannot admit that this is a repetition of the situation and of the tasks during the years 1933-45. For I cannot admit that it is the duty of Christians or of the Church to give theological backing to what every citizen can, with much shaking of his head, read in his daily paper and what is so admirably expressed by Mr. Truman and by the Pope. Has the "East" or whatever we may call it, really such a hold over us that we must needs oppose it with our last breath when the last but one would suffice? No, when the Church witnesses it moves in fear and trembling, not with the stream but against it. Today it certainly has no cause to move against the stream and thus to witness to Communism because it could never be worthy of it, either in its Marxist or its imperialist, or let us say, in its Asiatic aspects. Must the Church then move with the stream and thus side with America and the Vatican, merely because somewhere in the text-books of its professors—ever since 1934—it has rightly been said that "totalitarianism" is a dreadful thing? Where is the spiritual danger and need which the Church would meet if it witnessed to this truth, where is its commission to do so? Whom would it teach, enlighten, rouse, set on the right path, comfort and lead to repentance and a new way of life? Surely not the "Christian" peoples of the West, nor the Americans! Are they not already sure enough of the justice of their cause against Russia without this truth and our Christian support? Surely not the poor Russians and even the poor Communists? For how should they be able to understand what the Western Church, which in the old days and even today has accepted so much "totalitarianism" and has co-operated with it without witnessing against it, claims to have against their Church? Surely not the Christian Churches behind the Iron Curtain? In their struggle with the "monster" it would be no help at all to them if we were to proclaim those well-known truths as energetically as possible, since we are not asked for them anyway, nor would they cost us anything. As it is not possible to give satisfactory answers to these questions, I am of the opinion that the Church today—contrary to its action between 1933 and 1945—ought to stand quietly aloof from the present conflict and not let off all its guns before it is necessary but wait calmly to see whether and in what sense the situation will grow serious again and call for speech. If a definite spiritual crisis were again to develop as it did during the years 1933-45—though we do not yet know from what direction it is likely to come—then a concrete answer would be demanded from us, for which we ourselves should have to pay: then it would be obvious against whom and for whom we should have to witness, and whether and how far we should be prepared for this new emergency. Then something would be at stake other than these eternal truths which you wish me to proclaim. According to my view, we shall then profit more from the first article of the Declaration of Barmen than from your knowledge of the objectionableness of "totalitarianism."

But, however that may be, with this problem in view I met responsible members of the Reformed Church in Hungary and thought that I could encourage them in their attempt to walk along the narrow path midway between Moscow and Rome. I did not take a ruler with me to draw this dividing line, so I could not leave one behind for their use. Their past history, their present situation and their task do not resemble ours, nor those of the Evangelical Church in Germany which is joining in the battle. They have come to an agreement with the new régime and are directing all their energies towards the positive tasks of their Church, and this is not the same as what the central parties, which you esteem so highly, or even the "German Christians," are doing in the battle for the Church in Germany. Incidentally, it is a legend without historical foundation that in 1933 I recommended "passive resistance" when I urged the Germans to fulfil their duties of Christian witness "as though nothing had happened," i.e. ignoring Adolf Hitler's alleged divine revelation. If they had consequently done so, they would have built up against National Socialism a political factor of the first order.

For Hungary, though not only for this country, everything depends on whether the Church, not bound to abstract principles but to its living Lord, will seek and find its own way and also learn to choose freely the time for speech and the time for silence and all the various other times mentioned in Ecclesiastes, Chapter 3, without thereby becoming confused by any law other than that of the gospel.

Your KARL BARTH

Basel
June 6th, 1948

Eugenio Pacelli was born at Rome in 1876. He was ordained priest in 1899, and in 1917 he became titular archbishop of Sardi and papal nuncio to Munich, where Hitler made his first abortive bid for power in 1923. For twelve years, Pacelli served as papal envoy in Germany; after 1920, as nuncio to all of Germany. In 1929 he was created a cardinal, and in 1930 he was appointed Papal Secretary of State. Elected pope in 1939, he assumed the name of Pius XII. He died in 1958, at Castel Gandolfo, near Rome.

The dogma of the Assumption was defined by the Apostolic Constitution *Munificentissimus Deus*, November 2, 1950, and the translation that follows is that of the Official English Version. The encyclical *Humani Generis* bears the date of August 12, 1950, and the translation reprinted here, unabridged, is that of A. C. Cotter, S.J., originally published by the Weston College Press, with the Latin text on facing pages, and with a commentary.

The Dogma of the Assumption

*W*herefore, after We have unceasingly offered Our most fervent prayers to God, and have called upon the Spirit of Truth, for the glory of Almighty God who has lavished His special affection upon the Virgin Mary, for the honor of her Son, the immortal King of the Ages and the Victor over sin and death, for the increase of the glory of that same august Mother, and for the joy and exultation of the entire Church; by the authority of our Lord Jesus Christ, of the blessed Apostles Peter and Paul, and by Our own authority, *We pronounce, declare, and define it to be a divinely revealed dogma: that the Immaculate Mother of God, the ever Virgin Mary, having completed the course of her earthly life, was assumed body and soul into heavenly glory.*

Hence if anyone, which God forbid, should dare wilfully to deny or to call into doubt that which we have defined, let him know that he has fallen away completely from the divine and Catholic Faith. . . .

Humani Generis

ENCYCLICAL LETTER
TO OUR VENERABLE BRETHREN: PATRIARCHS, PRIMATES, ARCHBISHOPS, BISH-
OPS AND OTHER LOCAL ORDINARIES HAVING PEACE AND COMMUNION WITH THE
APOSTOLIC SEE: CONCERNING SOME FALSE OPINIONS WHICH THREATEN TO
UNDERMINE THE FOUNDATIONS OF CATHOLIC DOCTRINE.

PIUS XII, Pope

VENERABLE BRETHREN
Greetings and Apostolic Blessing

1. Discord and error among men on moral and religious matters have always been a cause of deep sorrow to all good men, and above all to the true and loyal sons of the Church, especially today when we see the very principles of Christian culture attacked on all sides.

2. Truth to tell, it is not surprising that discord and error should always have existed outside the fold of Christ. For though, absolutely speaking, human reason can, by its natural powers and light, arrive at a true and certain knowledge of the one personal God whose providence watches over and governs the world, and also of the natural law which the Creator has written in our hearts, still not a few obstacles prevent reason from using its natural ability effectively and profitably. For the truths that have to do with God and the relations between God and men, transcend completely the sensible order, and where there is question of their practical application and guidance, call for self-surrender and self-abnegation. In the acquisition of such truths the human intellect is hampered not only by the impulses of the senses and the imagination, but also by evil passions stemming from original sin. As a result, men readily persuade themselves in such matters that what they do not wish to be true, is false or at least doubtful.

3. It is for this reason that divine revelation must be called morally necessary, so that those religious and moral truths which are not of their nature beyond the reach of reason, may, also in the present condition of the human race, be known by all with ease, with unwavering certitude and without any admixture of error.

4. Furthermore, the human mind may at times experience difficulties in forming a sure judgment about the credibility of the Catholic faith, not-withstanding the wonderful external signs which God has vouchsafed in such profusion, and which suffice to prove with certitude, by the unaided light of natural reason, the divine origin of the Christian religion. For man can, whether from prejudice or passion or bad faith, shut his eyes to the

available evidence of external proofs and be deaf to those supernal whisperings by which God stirs our hearts.

5. Looking around at those outside the fold of Christ, one can easily discern the principal trends which not a few learned men follow. Some are imprudent and indiscreet enough to hold that the so-called theory of evolution, although not yet fully proved even in the domain of natural sciences, explains the origin of all things, and they go so far as to support the monistic and pantheistic notion that the whole world is subject to continual evolution. Communists eagerly seize upon this theory in the hope of depriving the souls of every idea of God and of defending and propagating the more effectively their dialectical materialism.

6. The fictitious tenets of evolution, which repudiate all that is absolute, firm and immutable, have paved the way for the new erroneous philosophy which, a rival of idealism, immanentism and pragmatism, has come to be called existentialism because, forgetful of the immutable essences of things, it concerns itself only with individual existence.

7. There is also a certain false historicism which, refusing to look beyond the random happenings of human life, undermines the foundations of all truth and absolute law in the domain of philosophy as well as in that of Christian dogma.

8. In all this doctrinal confusion it is some consolation to us to see today quite a few of former adherents of rationalism desiring to return to the fountain of divinely revealed truth, acknowledging and professing the Sacred Scriptures as the word of God and as the foundation of theology. At the same time it is a matter of regret that not a few of them, while firmly clinging to the word of God, belittle human reason, and while exalting the authority of God the Revealer, severely spurn the Magisterium of the Church which Christ our Lord instituted to preserve and interpret divine revelation. Such an attitude is plainly at variance with Holy Scripture; but experience, too, reveals its inconsistency; for it often happens that those who are separated from the true Church, complain frankly of their mutual disagreements in matters of doctrine, and thus bear unwilling witness to the necessity of a living Magisterium.

9. Catholic theologians and philosophers, whose solemn duty it is to defend natural and supernatural truth and instil it in the hearts of men, cannot afford to ignore or neglect these doctrines more or less devious. Rather they must understand them well, first because diseases are not properly treated unless they are correctly diagnosed, then, too, because false theories sometimes contain a certain amount of truth ,and finally because the mind is thereby spurred on to examine and weigh certain philosophical or theological doctrines more attentively.

10. Now if our philosophers and theologians merely tried to derive such benefit from the cautious study of these theories, the Magisterium of

the Church would have no reason to intervene. But although we know well that the vast majority of Catholic teachers guard against these errors, there are some, today as in apostolic times, who hanker too much after novelties and who dread being thought ignorant of the latest scientific findings. Tending to withdraw from the guidance of the sacred Magisterium, they are in danger of gradually losing revealed truth and of drawing others along with them into error.

11. There is yet another danger all the more serious because it hides under the appearance of virtue. Many in fact, deploring the discord among men and the prevalent intellectual confusion, yet fired by an imprudent zeal for souls, plunge ahead in their eagerness to break down the barriers that divide good and honest men. They advocate an irenicism which, setting aside the questions that divide men, aims not only at joining forces against the onrush of atheism, but also at bridging contradictions in matters dogmatic. And as in former times there were men who questioned whether the traditional apologetics of the Church did not constitute an obstacle rather than a help to the winning of souls for Christ, so today some go so far as to question seriously whether theology and its method as carried on in our schools with the approval of ecclesiastical authority, should not only be improved, but completely made over, so that the kingdom of Christ could everywhere, among men of every culture and religious persuasion, be propagated more efficaciously.

12. Now if they only meant that ecclesiastical teaching and its method should, through the introduction of new ideas, be adapted to modern conditions and requirements, there would scarcely be any cause for alarm. But fired by an imprudent irenicism, some appear to consider as an obstacle to the restoration of fraternal union, tenets based on the laws and principles promulgated by Christ and on the institutions founded by Him, or those things which serve as ramparts and buttresses of the integrity of the faith, and the destruction of which would indeed bring about the union of all, but only in a common ruin.

13. The new opinions, whether originating from a reprehensible itch of novelty or from a laudable motive, are not always advanced in the same degree, nor with equal clarity, nor in the same terms, nor with unanimity among their sponsors. What is today put forward rather covertly by some, not without precautions and distinctions, will tomorrow be proclaimed from the housetops and without moderation by more venturesome spirits. This is a scandal to many, especially among the young clergy, and detrimental to ecclesiastical authority. And while some caution is as a rule observed in published works, there is less of it in writings intended for private circulation as well as in conferences and lectures. Moreover, these ideas are spread not only among members of the clergy, both secular and regular, and

in seminaries and religious institutes, but also among the laity and especially among those who are engaged in teaching youth.

14. In theology some are out to whittle down as much as possible the content of dogmas, to free dogma itself from a terminology of long standing in the Church and from philosophical concepts employed by Catholic teachers, and to return in the explanation of Catholic doctrine to the modes of expression used in Holy Scripture and by the Fathers. They cherish the hope that when dogma is stripped of the elements which they call extrinsic to divine revelation, fruitful comparisons can be made with the doctrinal opinions of those who are separated from the unity of the Church, and that in this way we shall gradually arrive at a mutual assimilation of Catholic dogma and the tenets of the dissidents.

15. They also assert that such a change of Catholic doctrine would enable us to satisfy a modern need; for it would permit of dogma being expressed in the categories of modern thought, whether of immanentism or idealism or existentialism or any other ism. Some, more daring, affirm that this can and must be done for yet another reason; they claim that the mysteries of faith cannot be expressed by concepts that are adequately true, but only by approximate and ever changeable notions which vaguely hint at the truth, but also necessarily distort it. They do not consider it absurd, but altogether necessary that theology should substitute new concepts in place of the old ones in keeping with the variety of philosophies which it has used as its instruments; they think that theology could thus express in human language the same divine truths by different modes which though somewhat contradictory, may be called equivalent. Finally, they go on to say that the history of dogma consists in tracing the successive forms which were given to revealed truth in accordance with the various theories and speculations as they emerged in the course of centuries.

16. But it is obvious from all we said that such projects not merely lead to what is called dogmatic relativism, but already contain it. The contempt shown for the commonly accepted doctrine and the corresponding terminology is significant enough in this respect. To be sure, the terminology used in the schools and even by the Magisterium of the Church is susceptible of further improvement and refinement; it is also well-known that the Church did not always keep to the same identical terms; it is evident, too, that the Church cannot tie herself to any philosophy that enjoys a brief moment of popularity. But what has been thought out over the centuries and agreed upon by Catholic teachers in the effort to gain some understanding of dogma, surely does not rest on a flimsy foundation of that sort. It rests on principles and conceptions which are inferred from a just apprehension of created things; and in the making of such inferences divine revelation has, like a star, illuminated the human mind through the Church's agency. No wonder that General Councils have not only used but

also sanctioned some of these conceptions, so that it would be wrong to discard them.

17. It would be wrong to neglect or cast aside or rob of their meaning those precious concepts which have been coined and polished in order to express, with ever-increasing accuracy, the truths of faith—a process that has often cost centuries of labor and was carried out by men of uncommon intelligence and sanctity, under the watchful eye of the Magisterium, with light and guidance, too, from the Holy Spirit. To substitute for them conjectural notions and the vague and fluid diction of a new philosophy, which thrive today like the flowers of the field and wilt tomorrow, would indeed be the height of imprudence; dogma itself would become no better than a reed shaken by the wind. Disrespect for the terms and concepts current among scholastic theologians would take all the force out of what is called speculative theology, which has no real validity, they say, inasmuch as it rests on theological reasoning.

18. Worse still, the lovers of novelty easily pass from disdain of scholastic theology to the neglect of and even contempt for the Magisterium of the Church which bestows high authoritative approval on that branch of theology. They represent the Magisterium as a hindrance to progress and an obstacle in the way of science, while certain non-Catholics look upon it as an unjust restraint which prevents better qualified theologians from reforming their science. Now it is true that this sacred Magisterium must remain, in matters of faith and morals, the proximate and universal criterion of truth for every theologian, since to it has been entrusted by Christ our Lord the whole deposit of faith—Sacred Scripture and divine Tradition— to be preserved, guarded and interpreted; but the faithful are also obliged to flee those errors which more or less approach heresy, and accordingly "to keep also the constitutions and decrees by which such evil doctrines are proscribed and forbidden by the Holy See." This duty is sometimes ignored just as if it did not exist. What is expounded in the Encyclicals of the Roman Pontiffs concerning the nature and the constitution of the Church is habitually and deliberately set aside by some with the intent of substituting certain vague notions which they pretend to have found in the ancient Fathers, especially the Greeks. For the Popes, they claim, do not wish to pass judgment on what are matters of dispute among theologians; so recourse must be had to the primitive sources, and the later constitutions and decrees of the Magisterium must be interpreted in accordance with the writings of antiquity.

19. While this may sound clever, it is really a sophism. It is true that as a rule the Popes leave theologians free in those matters on which respectable authorities hold divergent opinions; but, as history teaches, many points that were formerly open to dispute, are so no longer.

20. Nor must it be thought that what is contained in Encyclical letters

does not of itself demand assent, on the pretext that the Popes do not exercise in them the supreme power of their teaching authority. Rather, such teachings belong to the ordinary Magisterium, of which it is also true to say: "He who heareth you, heareth me"; very often, too, what is expounded and inculcated in Encyclical letters, already appertains to Catholic doctrine for other reasons. But if the Supreme Pontiffs in their official acts expressly pass judgment on a matter debated until then, it is obvious to all that the matter, according to the mind and will of the same Pontiffs, cannot be considered any longer a question open for discussion among theologians.

21. It is also true that theologians must always go back to the sources of divine revelation; for it pertains to their office to show how the teachings of the living Magisterium are contained, either explicitly or implicitly, in the Sacred Scriptures and divine Tradition. Besides, each source of divinely revealed doctrine contains so many rich treasures of truth that they can really never be exhausted. Hence it is that study of the sacred sources brings to theology ever new youth, whereas speculation which neglects to delve deeper into the sacred deposit, proves barren, as we know from experience. But this is no reason to put even so-called positive theology on a par with mere history. For together with those sources God has given to His Church a living Magisterium to elucidate and explain what is contained in the deposit of faith only obscurely and, as it were, implicitly. No, the authentic interpretation of the deposit our divine Redeemer did not entrust to the faithful, nor even to theologians, but exclusively to the Magisterium of the Church. If then the Church does exercise this function, as she has often done in the past, either in the ordinary or in an extraordinary way, it is plain how false is a method which would explain what is clear by what is obscure, and that all must follow the opposite procedure. We see now why our predecessor of immortal memory, Pius IX, when explaining that the noblest office of theology is to show how a doctrine defined by the Church is contained in the sources, added these words, and with good reason: "in the same sense in which it has been defined by the Church."

22. To return, however, to the novel doctrines mentioned above, there are also those who propose or suggest theories inimical to the divine authority of Sacred Scripture. For some, audaciously perverting the sense of the Vatican Council's definition that God is the author of Holy Scripture, again put forward the opinion, already condemned more than once, which asserts that immunity from error extends only to those parts of the Bible that treat of God and of moral and religious matters. Besides that, they wrongly speak of a human sense of the Sacred Scriptures beneath which lies hidden the divine sense, the only infallible one according to them. In the interpretation of Scripture they will not take into account the analogy

of faith and the Tradition of the Church. Thus the teachings of the Fathers and the Magisterium would have to be judged by Holy Scripture as interpreted by a purely rational exegesis, whereas Holy Scripture is to be explained according to the mind of the Church which Christ our Lord has appointed guardian and interpreter of the whole deposit of divinely revealed truth.

23. Further, the literal sense of Holy Scripture and its explanation which has been worked out by so many great exegetes under the Church's vigilance, should now, according to their phantasies, yield to a new exegesis which they call symbolic or spiritual, so that the Old Testament, which today is a sealed book in the Church, would at long last be rendered intelligible to all. In this way, they claim, all difficulties would vanish, difficulties which irk only those who cling to the literal sense of Scripture.

24. Everyone sees how foreign all this is to the hermeneutical principles and norms rightly set down by our predecessors of happy memory, Leo XIII in his Encyclical *Providentissimus*, and Benedict XV in the Encyclical *Spiritus Paraclitus*, as also ourselves in the Encyclical *Divino Afflante Spiritu*.

25. It is not surprising that novelties of this sort have already borne their poisoned fruit in almost all branches of theology. It is now doubted that human reason can, without the help of divine revelation and grace, prove the existence of a personal God by arguments drawn from created things; it is denied that the world had a beginning, and it is argued that the creation of the world was necessary since it proceeds from the necessary liberality of divine love; it is denied that God has eternal and infallible foreknowledge of the free actions of men—all this in opposition to the decrees of the Vatican Council.

26. Some also question whether angels are personal beings, and whether matter differs essentially from spirit. Others misinterpret the gratuity of the supernatural order when they pretend that God cannot create intellectual beings without ordering and calling them to the beatific vision. Nor is this all. Disregarding the definitions of the Council of Trent, some pervert the concept of original sin, along with the concept of sin in general, as an offense against God, as well as the idea of satisfaction offered for us by Christ. There are those who insist that the doctrine of transubstantiation as being based on an antiquated philosophic notion of substance, should be so modified that the real presence of Christ in the Holy Eucharist is reduced to a kind of symbolism, whereby the consecrated species would be merely efficacious signs of the spiritual presence of Christ and of His intimate union with the faithful members of His Mystical Body.

27. Some think they are not bound by the doctrine, set forth in our Encyclical letter of a few years ago and based on the sources of revelation, according to which the Mystical Body of Christ and the Roman Catholic Church are one and the same. Some reduce to an empty formula the neces-

sity of belonging to the true Church in order to gain salvation. Others finally infringe on the reasonable character of the credibility of the Christian faith.

28. We know that these and similar errors have crept in among certain of our sons, who are deceived by an indiscreet zeal for souls or by false science. To them we are compelled with a grieving heart to repeat once again truths already well known and to point out, not without anxiety, manifest errors and dangers of error.

29. It is well known how highly the Church esteems human reason for its function to demonstrate with certainty the existence of God, personal and one; to prove beyond doubt from divine signs the foundations of the Christian faith itself; to express properly the law which the Creator has imprinted in the hearts of men; and finally to attain to some understanding, indeed a very fruitful one, of mysteries.

30. But reason can perform these functions safely and adequately only when properly trained; that is, when imbued with that sound philosophy which constitutes a patrimony handed on from earlier Christian ages, and which possesses an added authority of even higher order, since the Magisterium of the Church has weighed in the balance of divine revelation its principles and major assertions slowly elaborated and defined by men of great genius. This philosophy, acknowledged and accepted by the Church, safeguards the genuine validity of human knowledge, the unshaken metaphysical principles of sufficient reason, causality and finality, in a word, the possibility of attaining certain and unchangeable truth.

31. Of course, there are many things in this philosophy which do not touch faith and morals either directly or indirectly, and which the Church leaves therefore to the free discussion of scholars. But this does not apply to many other things, especially to the principles and major assertions just referred to. Even in these fundamental issues, however, it is permissible to clothe our philosophy in fitter and richer dress, to reenforce it with more effective terminology, to divest it of certain scholastic aids found less useful, and to embody in it cautiously the sound fruits of human progress. But never may we subvert it, or contaminate it with false principles, or esteem it merely as a grand but obsolete relic. For truth and its philosophical expression cannot change from day to day, least of all where there is question of the self-evident principles of the human mind or of those assertions which are supported by the wisdom of the ages and agree with divine revelation. Surely, whatever new truth the human mind is able to discover by honest research, cannot contradict truth already acquired; for God, the sovereign Truth, has created the human intellect and guides it, not that it may daily oppose novelties to rightly established truth, but rather that, eliminating errors which may have crept in, it may build truth upon truth in the same order and structure that we perceive to exist in nature, the source

of truth. Let no Catholic then, whether philosopher or theologian, be too hasty in embracing whatever novelty happens to be thought up from day to day, but rather let him weigh it carefully and with a balanced judgment, lest he lose or contaminate the truth he already has, with grave danger and damage to his faith.

32. If all this has been well understood, it is easily seen why the Church demands that future priests be trained in philosophy "according to the method, doctrine and principles of the Angelic Doctor," since, as she well knows from the experience of ages, the method of Aquinas is singularly pre-eminent both for teaching students and for bringing hidden truth to light. She also knows that his doctrine is in perfect harmony with divine revelation, and is most effective for safeguarding the foundations of the faith as well as for reaping, safely and usefully, the fruits of sound progress.

33. How deplorable it is then that this philosophy, received and honored by the Church, is scorned by some who are impudent enough to call it outmoded in form and rationalistic, as they say, in its thought processes. They keep repeating that this our philosophy wrongly maintains the possibility of a metaphysic that is absolutely true; whereas, they say, reality, especially transcendent reality, cannot be expressed better than by disparate propositions which complete one another, even though they are almost contradictory. They concede that the philosophy taught in our schools, with its clear exposition of questions and their solution, with its accurate definitions of terms and clear-cut distinctions, can be useful as a preparation for scholastic theology, and that it was marvelously adapted to the medieval mentality; but they deny that it offers a method of philosophizing suited to the needs of our modern culture. They object also that our *philosophia perennis* is only a philosophy of immutable essences, whereas the contemporary mind must be interested in the existence of individuals and in the incessant flux of life. And while despising our philosophy, they extol others, ancient or modern, oriental or occidental, by which they seem to imply that any kind of philosophy or theory can, with a few additions or corrections if necessary, be harmonized with Catholic dogma. But this is absolutely false, especially where there is question of those fictitious theories which go by the name of immanentism or idealism or materialism, whether historic or dialectic, or also existentialism, whether atheistic or the type that denies at least the validity of metaphysical reasoning. No Catholic can have the least doubt on that score.

34. Finally, they reproach the philosophy taught in our schools that, in explaining the process of cognition, it takes into account the intellect alone, neglecting the function of the will and the emotions. This is simply untrue. Never has Christian philosophy denied the usefulness and efficacy of good dispositions of the whole soul for fully understanding and embracing moral and religious truths. On the contrary, it has always taught that the

lack of such dispositions can be the reason why the intellect, influenced by passions and bad will, may be so darkened that it cannot see straight. Indeed, St. Thomas thinks that the intellect can in some way perceive higher goods of the moral order, whether natural or supernatural, in so far as the soul experiences a certain affective "connaturalness" to them, whether this "connaturalness" be natural or the result of grace; it is clear how much even this somewhat obscure perception can aid reason in its investigations. But it is one thing to admit that the dispositions of the will can help reason to gain a surer and firmer grasp of moral truths; it is quite another thing to say, as these innovators do, that the appetitive and affective faculties have a certain power of intuition, and that man, unable to decide with certainty by using his reason what is to be accepted as true, turns to his will to choose freely among opposite opinions; that would be an incongruous confusion of cognition and an act of the will.

35. It is not surprising that these new theories endanger two philosophical departments which by their nature are closely connected with faith, that is, theodicy and ethics. According to the new views, their function is not to prove with certitude anything about God or any other transcendent being, but rather to show that truths which faith teaches about a personal God and about His precepts, correspond perfectly to the necessities of life, and are therefore to be accepted by all in order to avoid despair and to attain eternal salvation. All of which is evidently contrary to the documents of our predecessors, Leo XIII and Pius X, nor can it be reconciled with the decrees of the Vatican Council. It would indeed be unnecessary to deplore these aberrations from truth if all, even in the domain of philosophy, showed proper reverence for and paid attention to the Magisterium of the Church which has the divinely given mission not only to guard and interpret the deposit of divinely revealed truth, but also to watch over the philosophical sciences lest erroneous theories harm Catholic dogma.

36. Nothing now remains but to say a word about those problems which pertain to what are called the positive sciences, yet are more or less connected with the truths of Christian faith. Not a few demand insistently that Catholic religion take them into account as much as possible. This demand is certainly praiseworthy when there is question of clearly proved facts; but it must be advanced with caution when there is rather question of hypotheses which, while having some sort of scientific foundation, touch on doctrines contained in Sacred Scripture or in Tradition. If such conjectures are directly or indirectly opposed to a doctrine revealed by God, then the demand can in no way be allowed.

37. Accordingly, the Magisterium of the Church does not forbid that the theory of evolution concerning the origin of the human body as coming from pre-existent and living matter—for Catholic faith obliges us to hold that the human soul is immediately created by God—be investigated

and discussed by experts as far as the present state of human sciences and sacred theology allows. However, this must be done so that reasons for both sides, that is, those favorable and those unfavorable to evolution, be weighed and judged with the necessary gravity, moderation and discretion; and let all be prepared to submit to the judgment of the Church to whom Christ has given the mission of interpreting authentically the Sacred Scriptures and of safeguarding the dogmas of faith. On the other hand, those go too far and transgress this liberty of discussion who act as if the origin of the human body from pre-existing and living matter were already fully demonstrated by the facts discovered up to now and by reasoning on them, and as if there were nothing in the sources of divine revelation which demanded the greatest reserve and caution in this controversy.

38. But as regards another conjecture, namely so-called polygenism, the children of the Church by no means enjoy the same liberty. No Catholic can hold that after Adam there existed on this earth true men who did not take their origin through natural generation from him as from the first parent of all, or that Adam is merely a symbol for a number of first parents. For it is unintelligible how such an opinion can be squared with what the sources of revealed truth and the documents of the Magisterium of the Church teach on original sin, which proceeds from sin actually committed by an individual Adam, and which, passed on to all by way of generation, is in everyone as his own.

39. Just as in the biological and anthropological sciences, so also in history there are those who boldly flout the limits and safeguards set up by the Church. Deplorable in particular is a certain fashion of interpreting too freely the historical books of the Old Testament. They wrongly quote in their favor a letter which the Pontifical Commission on Biblical Studies sent not long ago to the Archbishop of Paris. But this letter clearly points out that the first eleven chapters of Genesis, although they do not properly conform to the rules of historical composition used by the great Greek and Latin historians or by the historians of our time, do nevertheless pertain to history in a true sense to be further studied and determined by exegetes; that letter also says that the same chapters contain, in simple and metaphorical language adapted to the mentality of a people of low culture, the principal truths fundamental for our eternal salvation and a popular description of the origin of the human race and the chosen people. For the rest, if the ancient hagiographers have taken anything from popular narratives (and this may be conceded), we must not forget that they did so with the help of divine inspiration which preserved them from error in selecting and appraising those documents.

40. In any case, whatever of popular narratives have found a place in the Sacred Scriptures, must in no way be considered on a par with myths or other such things; these are more the product of an exuberant imagination

than of that striving for truth and simplicity which is so apparent in the Sacred Books, also of the Old Testament, that our hagiographers must be regarded as decidedly superior to the profane writers of antiquity.

41. We are certainly aware that the majority of Catholic teachers, whose studies benefit universities, seminaries and colleges of the religious, are far removed from those errors which are being spread today either openly or covertly, whether through an urge of novelty or through ill-considered plans for an apostolate. But we also know that such new theories can entice the unwary; and therefore we prefer to withstand the very beginnings rather than administer medicine after the disease has grown inveterate.

42. Therefore, after mature reflection and consideration before God, that we may not be wanting in our sacred duty, we charge Bishops and Superiors of religious orders, binding them most seriously in conscience, to watch carefully lest such opinions be aired in schools, in conferences or in writings of any kind, and lest they be taught in any manner whatsoever to clergy or laity.

43. Let professors in ecclesiastical institutes remember that they cannot with tranquil conscience exercise the office of teaching entrusted to them unless they religiously accept the doctrinal norms which we have laid down and exactly observe them in the instruction of their students. Let them likewise instil into the minds and hearts of their pupils the reverence and submission due to the Magisterium of the Church which should guide them in their own daily labor.

44. Let them strive with all their energy and zeal to further the progress of the sciences which they teach; but let them also guard against overstepping the limits which we have established for the protection of the truth of the Catholic faith and doctrine. When face to face with the new problems that are posed by modern culture and progress, let them engage in diligent research, but with the necessary prudence and caution; finally let them not indulge in a false irenicism or think that the dissident and erring can happily be brought back to the bosom of the Church if the whole truth found in the Church is not sincerely taught to all without corruption and diminution.

45. With this hope and relying on your pastoral solicitude, as a pledge of celestial gifts and a sign of our paternal benevolence, We impart with all our heart to each and all of you, Venerable Brethren, as well as to your clergy and people, the Apostolic Blessing.

Given at Rome, at St. Peter's, August 12, 1950, the 12th year of Our Pontificate.

PIUS XII, Pope

Jacques Maritain was born at Paris in 1882. He studied both in France and at the University of Heidelberg, Germany. In 1906 he was converted from Protestantism to Catholicism. Subsequently, he immersed himself more and more in the study of St. Thomas' philosophy, and in time became known as one of the foremost Neo-Thomists.

He has held many positions as a professor and lecturer, including a chair at the Institut Catholique de Paris, to which he was called in 1914, and a professorship in the Department of Philosophy at Princeton University, which he occupied from 1948 until his retirement. From 1945 to 1948, he was French ambassador to the Vatican.

Of his extremely numerous publications, some of the more recent include *St. Thomas Aquinas, Angel of the Schools* (1931; rev. ed. 1958), *The Degrees of Knowledge* (1938), *True Humanism* (1938), *Scholasticism and Politics* (1940), *The Rights of Man and Natural Law* (1943), *Man and the State* (1951), *The Range of Reason* (1952), *Creative Intuition in Art and Poetry* (1953), *On the Philosophy of History* (1957), *Reflections on America* (1958), and *The Responsibility of the Artist* (1960).

Our selection is taken from *Approaches to God* (1954).

The Third Way: BY THE CONTINGENT
AND THE NECESSARY

*A*lthough there is chance in the world (that is, events resulting from the meeting of independent causal series), the indeterminism of modern physics, valuable as it may be on the scientific level, cannot be built up into a philosophical theory. All happenings in the physical world are determined. This, however, does not prevent their being at the same time contingent to one degree or another. If the proximate causes which produce them had been impeded by the intervention of other causal lines in their particular field of action, or if, in the last analysis, the universe were other than it is, they might not have been produced.[1] In a general way a thing is contingent when its nonoccurrence or its not being posited in existence is not an impossibility. This definition can be verified of a thing taken in itself (a star is no more necessary in itself than a glint of light on a stream), even if it is not verified of the thing considered in relation to the causes which produce it (the stars

---

[1] Cf. "Reflections on Necessity and Contingence," *Essays in Thomism*, ed. by Robert E. Brennan, O.P., New York, Sheed & Ward, 1942.

have been produced as a *de facto* necessary result of cosmic evolution). Change implies contingency. A clear sky becomes clouded; being clear or being clouded are for the sky things whose nonoccurrence is possible. Plants and animals, stars and atoms are subject to the universal rhythm of destruction and production; all the forms our eyes perceive are perishable; they can cease to be. In other words they possess existence in a contingent way.

Is there, however, nothing *but* the contingent, nothing *but* what is *able not to be?* Can we by thought eliminate *absolutely all necessity* from things? The hypothesis destroys itself: on the supposition of *pure contingency*, nothing at all would exist.

Imagine a time without beginning or end; imagine that there was nevertheless absolutely nothing necessary, either in time or above time: It is then impossible that there *always* was being, for that for which there is *no necessity* cannot have been *always*. It is inevitable then that at a certain moment nothing would have existed. But "if for one moment there be nothing, there will be nothing eternally,"[1] for nothing can come into existence except through something already existing. And therefore right now nothing would be existing.

There must be, then, something necessary in things. For example, matter, understood as the common substratum of all that is subject to destruction and production, must be itself necessary in its permanence through all changes. There must be necessary laws in nature. In other words, things cannot be contingent absolutely or in all respects; they must contain intelligible structures or natures necessarily demanding certain effects.

The question now arises regarding whatever may be necessary in the world of things, whether it derives its necessity from no other thing, or, in other terms, whether it is necessary through itself (*per se*) or in essence (*per essentiam*).[2] In the latter case, there would be neither change nor contingency in things. For what is necessary *in essence* excludes every kind of contingency and change, and exists of itself with the infinite plenitude of being, since, by definition, it cannot be necessary in one respect only.

But if the necessary in things is not necessary *per se* and in essence, in other words if the necessity of the necessary in things is caused, you can imagine all the causes you wish, each of which, in turn, is itself caused, and

---

[1] Bossuet.

[2] When it comes to perfections that relate to the transcendental order, the phrase *per se* ("through itself") or *per suam essentiam* and the phrase *per essentiam* ("in essence," as I put it) coincide in their application, though they differ in formal meaning. To say that a thing is necessary *per se* or *per suam essentiam* is to say that the predicate "necessary" belongs to this subject (this thing) by virtue of the essence of the latter. To say that a thing is necessary *per essentiam* is to say that the subject (the thing in question) is one with the very essence of this predicate. See Cajetan, in *Sum. Theol.*, I, 6, 3.

it will nevertheless be necessary to stop at a First Cause which accounts for all the necessary there is in things, and whose necessity is not caused, that is to say, a First Cause which is necessary through itself and in essence, in the infinite transcendence of the very act of existence subsisting by itself.

a) Should it be said that the argument is not demonstrative because, supposing that there is absolutely nothing necessary, either in time or above time, one does not have to adopt the hypothesis of an infinite time, but may assume a time finite as to the past; and consequently the argument would not stand because it would be possible that the moment at which nothing would be had not *yet* arrived. The answer is clear.

As an objection this is null and void. For on the hypothesis of a time finite as to the past, the argument bears, as a matter of fact, on the very origin of this time. In fact there would not by hypothesis be any being *chronologically prior* to this time (since it *did* begin). Further, there would not be any being preceding this time by a *priority of nature*, because only a being that is necessary at least in some respect can precede time by a priority of nature, and because it was supposed, in any case, that there is absolutely nothing necessary either beyond time or in time. There would be then *no being* to make the first thing and the first instant at which the time in question presumably began to come into existence.

b) Should it be further alleged that the principle "That for which there is no necessity cannot always be" (*quod possibile est non esse, quandoque non est*) is not self-evident, but only an empirical generalization devoid of intrinsic evidence, what is to be answered?

This principle is in no wise a mere empirical generalization. It is for the intellect an intrinsically obvious principle. It is evident in virtue of the very principle of "reason-for-being" (*raison d'être*). Either a thing is by reason of itself—then it is its own reason; or it is by reason of something else—then it has its reason for being in something else. Correspondingly, a thing is *always* either by reason of itself or by reason of something else. The fact that it never ceases to be has itself a reason. If it is of itself the total reason for its *always* being, then it is necessary by reason of itself. If the reason for its *always* being is something other than itself, then that reason, by the very fact that it guarantees its never ceasing to be, endows it with some kind of necessity.

As noted above, contingent things which do exist in the real world and with which we have to deal always imply a certain bit of necessity, under one aspect or another. They are not the pure contingent. The force of Thomas Aquinas' line of argument comes from the fact that it considers with full metaphysical rigor the hypothesis of the *pure contingent*. In the light of this consideration it becomes obvious that this hypothesis is not tenable. To posit the pure contingent is to imply that nothing exists.

Paul (Johannes) Tillich was born in Germany, near Frankfurt an der Oder, in 1886. He wrote his doctoral dissertation on the philosophy of the old Schelling, who had been one of the leading spirits of German Idealism in his youth, but who later turned against Idealism and influenced existentialism. During World War I, Tillich served as a chaplain. After the War, he taught at Berlin, Marburg, Dresden, and, from 1929 to 1933, at the University of Frankfurt (Frankfurt am Main, not Frankfurt an der Oder). During this period, Tillich was a prominent representative of Christian socialism; and when Hitler became Chancellor in 1933, Tillich accepted a call to the Union Theological Seminary in New York City, where he taught for more than twenty years, exerting an ever-growing influence on American Protestant theology. In 1954 he accepted a call to Harvard University as a University Professor.

His publications are voluminous. *Systematic Theology* (1951-57) is probably his major work, but some of his shorter books, such as *The Courage To Be* (1952), have been read more widely. No other work gives as succinct and revealing a summary of his central ideas as his *Dynamics of Faith* (1957, Harper Torchbook ed. 1958). The central portion of that book is reprinted here.

Symbols of Faith

I. THE MEANING OF SYMBOL

*M*an's ultimate concern must be expressed symbolically, because symbolic language alone is able to express the ultimate. This statement demands explanation in several respects. In spite of the manifold research about the meaning and function of symbols which is going on in contemporary philosophy, every writer who uses the term "symbol" must explain his understanding of it.

Symbols have one characteristic in common with signs; they point beyond themselves to something else. The red sign at the street corner points to the order to stop the movements of cars at certain intervals. A red light and the stopping of cars have essentially no relation to each other, but conventionally they are united as long as the convention lasts. The same is true of letters and numbers and partly even words. They point beyond themselves to sounds and meanings. They are given this special function by convention within a nation or by international conventions, as the mathematical signs. Sometimes such signs are called symbols; but this is unfortunate because it makes the distinction between signs and symbols more difficult. Decisive is the fact that signs do not participate in the reality of that to which they point, while symbols do. Therefore, signs can be replaced for reasons of expediency or convention, while symbols cannot.

This leads to the second characteristic of the symbol: It participates in that to which it points: the flag participates in the power and dignity of the nation for which it stands. Therefore, it cannot be replaced except after an historic catastrophe that changes the reality of the nation which it symbolizes. An attack on the flag is felt as an attack on the majesty of the group in which it is acknowledged. Such an attack is considered blasphemy.

The third characteristic of a symbol is that it opens up levels of reality which otherwise are closed for us. All arts create symbols for a level of reality which cannot be reached in any other way. A picture and a poem reveal elements of reality which cannot be approached scientifically. In the creative work of art we encounter reality in a dimension which is closed for us without such works. The symbol's fourth characteristic not only opens up dimensions and elements of reality which otherwise would remain unapproachable but also unlocks dimensions and elements of our soul which correspond to the dimensions and elements of reality. A great play gives us not only a new vision of the human scene, but it opens up hidden depths of our own being. Thus we are able to receive what the play reveals to us in reality. There are within us dimensions of which we cannot become aware except through symbols, as melodies and rhythms in music.

Symbols cannot be produced intentionally—this is the fifth characteristic. They grow out of the individual or collective unconscious and cannot function without being accepted by the unconscious dimension of our being. Symbols which have an especially social function, as political and religious symbols, are created or at least accepted by the collective unconscious of the group in which they appear.

The sixth and last characteristic of the symbol is a consequence of the fact that symbols cannot be invented. Like living beings, they grow and they die. They grow when the situation is ripe for them, and they die when the situation changes. The symbol of the "king" grew in a special period of history, and it died in most parts of the world in our period. Symbols do not grow because people are longing for them, and they do not die because of scientific or practical criticism. They die because they can no longer produce response in the group where they originally found expression.

These are the main characteristics of every symbol. Genuine symbols are created in several spheres of man's cultural creativity. We have mentioned already the political and the artistic realm. We could add history and, above all, religion, whose symbols will be our particular concern.

II. RELIGIOUS SYMBOLS

We have discussed the meaning of symbols generally because, as we said, man's ultimate concern must be expressed symbolically! One may ask: Why can it not be expressed directly and properly? If money, success or the nation is someone's ultimate concern, can this not be said in a direct way without symbolic language? Is it not only in those cases in which the content of the ultimate concern is called "God" that we are in the realm of symbols? The answer is that everything which is a matter of unconditional concern is made into a god. If the nation is someone's ultimate concern, the name of the nation becomes a sacred name and the nation receives divine qualities which far surpass the reality of the being and functioning of the nation. The nation then stands for and symbolizes the true ultimate, but in an idolatrous way. Success as ultimate concern is not the natural desire of actualizing potentialities, but is readiness to sacrifice all other values of life for the sake of a position of power and social predominance. The anxiety about not being a success is an idolatrous form of the anxiety about divine condemnation. Success is grace; lack of succcess, ultimate judgment. In this way concepts designating ordinary realities become idolatrous symbols of ultimate concern.

The reason for this transformation of concepts into symbols is the character of ultimacy and the nature of faith. That which is the true ultimate transcends the realm of finite reality infinitely. Therefore, no finite reality can express it directly and properly. Religiously speaking, God transcends his own name. This is why the use of his name easily becomes an abuse or a blasphemy. Whatever we say about that which concerns us ultimately, whether or not we call it God, has a symbolic meaning. It points beyond itself while participating in that to which it points. In no other way can faith express itself adequately. The language of faith is the language of symbols. If faith were what we have shown that it is not, such an assertion could not be made. But faith, understood as the state of being ultimately concerned, has no language other than symbols. When saying this I always expect the question: Only a symbol? He who asks this question shows that he has not understood the difference between signs and symbols nor the power of symbolic language, which surpasses in quality and strength the power of any nonsymbolic language. One should never say "only a symbol," but one should say "not less than a symbol." With this in mind we can now describe the different kinds of symbols of faith.

The fundamental symbol of our ultimate concern is God. It is always present in any act of faith, even if the act of faith includes the denial of God. Where there is ultimate concern, God can be denied only in the name of God. One God can deny the other one. Ultimate concern cannot deny its own character as ultimate. Therefore, it affirms what is meant by the word

"God." Atheism, consequently, can only mean the attempt to remove any ultimate concern—to remain unconcerned about the meaning of one's existence. Indifference toward the ultimate question is the only imaginable form of atheism. Whether it is possible is a problem which must remain unsolved at this point. In any case, he who denies God as a matter of ultimate concern affirms God, because he affirms ultimacy in his concern. God is the fundamental symbol for what concerns us ultimately. Again it would be completely wrong to ask: So God is nothing but a symbol? Because the next question has to be: A symbol for what? And then the answer would be: For God! God is symbol for God. This means that in the notion of God we must distinguish two elements: the element of ultimacy, which is a matter of immediate experience and not symbolic in itself, and the element of concreteness, which is taken from our ordinary experience and symbolically applied to God. The man whose ultimate concern is a sacred tree has both the ultimacy of concern and the concreteness of the tree which symbolizes his relation to the ultimate. The man who adores Apollo is ultimately concerned, but not in an abstract way. His ultimate concern is symbolized in the divine figure of Apollo. The man who glorifies Jahweh, the God of the Old Testament, has both an ultimate concern and a concrete image of what concerns him ultimately. This is the meaning of the seemingly cryptic statement that God is the symbol of God. In this qualified sense God is the fundamental and universal content of faith.

It is obvious that such an understanding of the meaning of God makes the discussions about the existence or non-existence of God meaningless. It is meaningless to question the ultimacy of an ultimate concern. This element in the idea of God is in itself certain. The symbolic expression of this element varies endlessly through the whole history of mankind. Here again it would be meaningless to ask whether one or another of the figures in which an ultimate concern is symbolized does "exist." If "existence" refers to something which can be found within the whole of reality, no divine being exists. The question is not this, but: which of the innumerable symbols of faith is most adequate to the meaning of faith? In other words, which symbol of ultimacy expresses the ultimate without idolatrous elements? This is the problem, and not the so-called "existence of God"—which is in itself an impossible combination of words. God as the ultimate in man's ultimate concern is more certain than any other certainty, even that of oneself. God as symbolized in a divine figure is a matter of daring faith, of courage and risk.

God is the basic symbol of faith, but not the only one. All the qualities we attribute to him, power, love, justice, are taken from finite experiences and applied symbolically to that which is beyond finitude and infinity. If faith calls God "almighty," it uses the human experience of power in order to symbolize the content of its infinite concern, but it does not describe a highest being who can do as he pleases. So it is with all the other qualities and with all the actions, past, present and future, which men attribute to God. They are symbols taken from our daily experience, and not information about what God did once upon a time or will do sometime in the future. Faith is not the belief in such stories, but it is the acceptance of symbols that express our ultimate concern in terms of divine actions.

Another group of symbols of faith are manifestations of the divine in things and events, in persons and communities, in words and documents. This whole realm of sacred objects is a treasure of symbols. Holy things are not holy in themselves, but they point beyond themselves to the source of all holiness, that which is of ultimate concern.

III. SYMBOLS AND MYTHS

The symbols of faith do not appear in isolation. They are united in "stories of the gods," which is the meaning of the Greek word "mythos" —myth. The gods are individualized figures, analogous to human personalities, sexually differentiated, descending from each other, related to each other in love and struggle, producing world and man, acting in time and space. They participate in human greatness and misery, in creative and destructive works. They give to man cultural and religious traditions, and defend these sacred rites. They help and threaten the human race, especially some families, tribes or nations. They appear in epiphanies and incarnations, establish sacred places, rites and persons, and thus create a cult. But they themselves are under the command and threat of a fate which is beyond everything that is. This is mythology as developed most impressively in ancient Greece. But many of these characteristics can be found in every mythology. Usually the mythological gods are not equals. There is a hierarchy, at the top of which is a ruling god, as in Greece; or a trinity of them, as in India; or a duality of them, as in Persia. There are savior-gods who mediate between the highest gods and man, sometimes sharing the suffering and death of man in spite of their essential immortality. This is the world of the myth, great and strange, always changing but fundamentally the same: man's ultimate concern symbolized in divine figures and actions. Myths are symbols of faith combined in stories about divine-human encounters.

Myths are always present in every act of faith, because the language of faith is the symbol. They are also attacked, criticized and transcended in each of the great religions of mankind. The reason for this criticism is the very nature of the myth. It uses material from our ordinary experience. It puts the stories of the gods into the framework of time and space although it belongs to the nature of the ultimate to be beyond time and space. Above all, it divides the divine into several figures, removing ultimacy from each of them without removing their claim to ultimacy. This inescapably leads to conflicts of ultimate claims, able to destroy life, society, and consciousness.

The criticism of the myth first rejects the division of the divine and goes beyond it to one God, although in different ways according to the different types of religion. Even one God is an object of mythological language, and if spoken about is drawn into the framework of time and space. Even he loses his ultimacy if made to be the content of concrete concern. Consequently, the criticism of the myth does not end with the rejection of the polytheistic mythology.

Monotheism also falls under the criticism of the myth. It needs, as one says today, "demythologization." This word has been used in connection with the elaboration of the mythical elements in stories and symbols of the Bible, both of the Old and the New Testaments—stories like those of the Paradise, of the fall of Adam, of the great Flood, of the Exodus from Egypt, of the virgin birth of the Messiah, of many of his miracles, of his resurrection and ascension, of his expected return as the judge of the universe. In short, all the stories in which divine-human interactions are told are considered as mythological in character, and objects of demythologization. What does this negative and artificial term mean? It must be accepted and supported if it points to the necessity of recognizing a symbol as a symbol and a myth as a myth. It must be attacked and rejected if it means the removal of symbols and myths altogether. Such an attempt is the third step in the criticism of the myth. It is an attempt which never can be successful, because symbol and myth are forms of the human consciousness which are always present. One can replace one myth by another, but one cannot remove the myth from man's spiritual life. For the myth is the combination of symbols of our ultimate concern.

A myth which is understood as a myth, but not removed or replaced, can be called a "broken myth." Christianity denies by its very nature any unbroken myth, because its presupposition is the first commandment: the affirmation of the ultimate as ultimate and the rejection of any kind of idolatry. All mythological elements in the Bible, and doctrine and liturgy should be recognized as mythological, but they should be maintained in their symbolic form and not be replaced by scientific substitutes. For there is no substitute for the use of symbols and myths: they are the language of faith.

The radical criticism of the myth is due to the fact that the primitive mythological consciousness resists the attempt to interpret the myth of myth. It is afraid of every act of demythologization. It believes that the broken myth is deprived of its truth and of its convincing power. Those who live in an unbroken mythological world feel safe and certain. They resist, often fanatically, any attempt to introduce an element of uncertainty by "breaking the myth," namely, by making conscious its symbolic character. Such resistance is supported by authoritarian systems, religious or political, in order to give security to the people under their control and unchallenged power to those who exercise the control. The resistance against demythologization expresses itself in "literalism." The symbols and myths are understood in their immediate meaning. The material, taken from nature and history, is used in its proper sense. The character of the symbol to point beyond itself to something else is disregarded. Creation is taken as a magic act which happened once upon a time. The fall of Adam is localized on a special geographical point and attributed to a human individual. The virgin birth of the Messiah is understood in biological terms, resurrection and ascension as physical events, the second coming of the Christ as a telluric, or cosmic, catastrophe. The presupposition of such literalism is that God is a being, acting in time and space, dwelling in a special place, affecting the course of events and being affected by them like any other being in the universe. Literalism deprives God of his ultimacy and, religiously speaking, of his majesty. It draws him down to the level of that which is not ultimate, the finite and conditional. In the last analysis it is not rational criticism of the myth which is decisive but the inner religious criticism. Faith, if it takes its symbols literally, becomes idolatrous! It calls something ultimate which is less than ultimate. Faith, conscious of the symbolic character of its symbols, gives God the honor which is due him.

One should distinguish two stages of literalism, the natural and the reactive. The natural stage of literalism is that in which the mythical and the literal are indistinguishable. The primitive period of individuals and groups consists in the inability to separate the creations of symbolic imagination from the facts which can be verified through observation and experiment. This stage has a full right of its own and should not be disturbed, either in individuals or in groups, up to the moment when man's questioning mind breaks the natural acceptance of the mythological visions as literal. If, however, this moment has come, two ways are possible. The one is to replace the unbroken by the broken myth. It is the objectively demanded way, although it is impossible for many people who prefer the repression of their questions to the uncertainty which appears with the breaking of the myth. They are forced into the second stage of literalism, the conscious one, which is aware of the questions but represses them, half consciously, half unconsciously. The tool of repression is usually an acknowledged authority with sacred qualities like the Church or the Bible, to which one owes unconditional surrender. This stage is still justifiable, if the questioning power is very weak and can easily be answered. It is unjustifiable if a mature mind is broken in its personal center by political or psychological methods, split in his unity, and hurt in his integrity. The enemy of a critical theology is not natural literalism but conscious literalism with repression of and aggression toward autonomous thought.

Symbols of faith cannot be replaced by other symbols, such as artistic ones, and they cannot be removed by scientific criticism. They have a genuine standing in the human mind, just as science and art have. Their symbolic character is their truth and their power. Nothing less than symbols and myths can express our ultimate concern.

One more question arises, namely, whether myths are able to express every kind of ultimate concern. For example, Christian theologians argue that the word "myth" should be reserved for natural myths in which repetitive natural processes, such as the seasons, are understood in their ultimate meaning. They believe that if the world is seen as an historical process with beginning, end and center, as in Christianity and Judaism, the term "myth" should not be used. This would radically reduce the realm in which the term would be applicable. Myth could not be understood as the language of our ultimate concern, but only as a discarded idiom of this language. Yet history proves that there are not only natural myths but also historical myths. If the earth is seen as the battleground of two divine powers, as in ancient Persia, this is an historical myth. If the God of creation selects and guides a nation through history toward an end which transcends all history, this is an historical myth. If the Christ —a transcendent, divine being—appears in the fullness of time, lives, dies and is resurrected, this is an historical myth. Christianity is superior to those religions which are bound to a natural myth. But Christianity speaks the mythological language like every other religion. It is a broken myth, but it is a myth; otherwise Christianity would not be an expression of ultimate concern.

John Wisdom was born in 1904, the son of a clergyman. He received his B.A. from Cambridge University in 1924, and in 1952 became professor of philosophy at Cambridge.

His early publications are avowedly the work of one of Wittgenstein's students, and occasionally the world at large gleaned Wittgenstein's views from Wisdom's articles, because Wisdom always took care to give due credit. For all that, Wisdom's originality is unquestioned and equally notable in his style and in his ideas. Among his publications, two volumes of collected articles are particularly noteworthy: *Other Minds* (1952) and *Philosophy and Psycho-Analysis* (1953). The essay reprinted here is found in the latter volume.

John Oulton Wisdom, the author of a book on *The Unconscious Origins of Berkeley's Philosophy*, is John Wisdom's cousin.

Gods

1. The existence of God is not an experimental issue in the way it was. An atheist or agnostic might say to a theist "You still think there are spirits in the trees, nymphs in the streams, a God of the world." He might say this because he noticed the theist in time of drought pray for rain and make a sacrifice and in the morning look for rain. But disagreement about whether there are gods is now less of this experimental or betting sort than it used to be. This is due in part, if not wholly, to our better knowledge of why things happen as they do.

It is true that even in these days it is seldom that one who believes in God has no hopes or fears which an atheist has not. Few believers now expect prayer to still the waves, but some think it makes a difference to people and not merely in ways the atheist would admit. Of course with people, as opposed to waves and machines, one never knows what they won't do next, so that expecting prayer to make a difference to them is not so definite a thing as believing in its mechanical efficacy. Still, just as primitive people pray in a business-like way for rain so some people still pray for others with a real feeling of doing something to help. However, in spite of this persistence of an experimental element in some theistic belief, it remains true that Elijah's method on Mount Carmel of settling the matter of what god or gods exist would be far less appropriate to-day than it was then.

2. *Belief in gods is not merely a matter of expectation of a world to come.*

Someone may say "The fact that a theist no more than an atheist expects prayer to bring down fire from heaven or cure the sick does not mean that there is no difference between them as to the facts, it does not mean that the theist has no expectations different from the atheist's. For very often those who believe in God believe in another world and believe that God is there and that we shall go to that world when we die."

This is true, but I do not want to consider here expectations as to what one will see and feel after death nor what sort of reasons these logically unique expectations could have. So I want to consider those theists who do not believe in a future life, or rather, I want to consider the differences between atheists and theists in so far as these differences are not a matter of belief in a future life.

3. *What are these differences? And is it that theists are superstitious or that atheists are blind?* A child may wish to sit a while with his father and he may, when he has done what his father dislikes, fear punishment and feel distress at causing vexation, and while his father is alive he may feel sure of help when danger threatens and feel that there is sympathy for him when disaster has come. When his father is dead he will no longer expect punishment or help. Maybe for a moment an old fear will come or a cry for help escape him, but he will at once remember that this is no good now. He may feel that his father is no more until perhaps someone says to him that his father is still alive though he lives now in another world and one so far away that there is no hope of seeing him or hearing his voice again. The child may be told that nevertheless his father can see him and hear all he says. When he has been told this the child will still fear no punishment nor expect any sign of his father, but now, even more than he did when his father was alive, he will feel that his father sees him all the time and will dread distressing him and when he has done something wrong he will feel separated from his father until he has felt sorry for what he has done. Maybe when he himself comes to die he will be like a man who expects to find a friend in the strange country where he is going, but even when this is so, it is by no means all of what makes the difference between a child who believes that his father lives still in another world and one who does not.

Likewise one who believes in God may face death differently from one who does not, but there is another difference between them besides this. This other difference may still be described as belief in another world, only this belief is not a matter of expecting one thing rather than another here or hereafter, it is not a matter of a world to come but of a world that now is, though beyond our senses.

We are at once reminded of those other unseen worlds which some philosophers "believe in" and others "deny," while non-philosophers unconsciously "accept" them by using them as models with which to "get the hang of" the patterns in the flux of experience. We recall the timeless entities whose changeless connections we seek to represent in symbols, and the values which stand firm[1] amidst our flickering satisfaction and remorse, and the physical things which, though not beyond the corruption of moth and rust, are yet more permanent than the shadows they throw upon the screen before our minds. We recall, too, our talk of souls and of what lies in their depths and is manifested to us partially and intermittently in our own feelings and the behaviour of others. The hypothesis of mind, of other human minds and of animal minds, is reasonable because it explains for each of us why certain things behave so cunningly all by themselves unlike even the most ingenious machines. Is the hypothesis of minds in flowers and trees reasonable for like reasons? Is the hypothesis of a world mind reasonable for like reasons— someone who adjusts the blossom to the bees, someone whose presence may at times be felt—in a garden in high summer, in the hills when clouds are gathering, but not, perhaps, in a cholera epidemic?

4. *The question "Is belief in gods reasonable?" has more than one source.* It is clear now that in order to grasp fully the logic of belief in divine minds we need to examine the logic of belief in animal and human minds. But we cannot do that here and so for the purposes of this discussion about divine minds let us acknowledge the reasonableness of our belief in human minds without troubling ourselves about its logic. The question of the reasonableness of belief in divine minds then becomes a matter of whether there are facts in nature which support claims about divine minds in the way facts in nature support our claims about human minds.

In this way we resolve the force behind the problem of the existence of gods into two components, one metaphysical and the same which prompts the question "Is there *ever any* behaviour which gives reason to believe in *any* sort of mind?" and one which finds expression in "Are there other mind-patterns in nature beside the human and animal patterns which we can all easily detect, and are these other mind-patterns super-human?"

Such over-determination of a question syndrome is common. Thus, the puzzling questions "Do dogs think?", "Do animals feel?" are partly metaphysical puzzles and partly scientific questions. They are not purely metaphysical; for the reports of scientists about the poor performances of cats in cages and old ladies' stories about the remarkable performances of their pets are not irrelevant. But nor are these questions purely scientific; for the stories never settle them and therefore they have other sources. One other source is the metaphysical source we have already noticed, namely, the difficulty about getting behind an animal's behaviour to its mind, whether it is a non-human animal or a human one.

But there's a third component in the force behind these questions, these disputes have a third source, and it is one which is important in the dispute which finds expression in the words "I believe in God," "I do not." This

[1] In another world, Dr. Joad says in the *New Statesman* recently.

source comes out well if we consider the question "Do flowers feel?" Like the questions about dogs and animals this question about flowers comes partly from the difficulty we sometimes feel over inference from *any* behaviour to thought or feeling and partly from ignorance as to what behaviour is to be found. But these questions, as opposed to a like question about human beings, come also from hesitation as to whether the behaviour in question is *enough* mind-like, that is, is it enough similar to or superior to human behaviour to be called "mind-proving"? Likewise, even when we are satisfied that human behaviour shows mind and even when we have learned whatever mind-suggesting things there are in nature which are not explained by human and animal minds, we may still ask "But are these things sufficiently striking to be called a mind-pattern? Can we fairly call them manifestations of a divine being?"

"The question," someone may say, "has then become merely a matter of the application of a name. And 'What's in a name?'"

5. *But the line between a question of fact and a question or decision as to the application of a name is not so simple as this way of putting things suggests.* The question "What's in a name?" is engaging because we are inclined to answer both "Nothing" and "Very much." And this "Very much" has more than one source. We might have tried to comfort Heloise by saying "It isn't that Abelard no longer loves you, for this man isn't Abelard"; we might have said to poor Mr. Tebrick in Mr. Garnet's *Lady into Fox* "But this is no longer Silvia." But if Mr. Tebrick replied "Ah, but it is!" this might come not at all from observing facts about the fox which we have not observed, but from noticing facts about the fox which we had missed, although we had in a sense observed all that Mr. Tebrick had observed. It is possible to have before one's eyes all the items of a pattern and still to miss the pattern. Consider the following conversation:

" 'And I think Kay and I are pretty happy. We've always been happy.'

"Bill lifted up his glass and put it down without drinking.

" 'Would you mind saying that again?' he asked.

" 'I don't see what's so queer about it. Taken all in all, Kay and I have really been happy.'

" 'All right,' Bill said gently, 'Just tell me how you and Kay have been happy.'

"Bill had a way of being amused by things which I could not understand.

" 'It's a little hard to explain,' I said. 'It's like taking a lot of numbers that don't look alike and that don't mean anything until you add them all together.'

"I stopped, because I hadn't meant to talk to him about Kay and me.

" 'Go ahead,' Bill said. 'What about the numbers.' And he began to smile.

" 'I don't know why you think it's so funny," I said. 'All the things that two people do together, two people like Kay and me, add up to something.

There are the kids and the house and the dog and all the people we have known and all the times we've been out to dinner. Of course, Kay and I do quarrel sometimes but when you add it all together, all of it isn't as bad as the parts of it seem. I mean, maybe that's all there is to anybody's life.'

"Bill poured himself another drink. He seemed about to say something and checked himself. He kept looking at me."[1]

Or again, suppose two people are speaking of two characters in a story which both have read[2] or of two friends which both have known, and one says "Really she hated him," and the other says "She didn't, she loved him." Then the first may have noticed what the other has not although he knows no incident in the lives of the people they are talking about which the other doesn't know too, and the second speaker may say "She didn't, she loved him" because he hasn't noticed what the first noticed, although he can remember every incident the first can remember. But then again he may say "She didn't, she loved him" not because he hasn't noticed the patterns in time which the first has noticed but because though he has noticed them he doesn't feel he still needs to emphasize them with "Really she hated him." The line between using a name because of how we feel and because of what we have noticed isn't sharp. "A difference as to the facts," "a discovery," "a revelation," these phrases cover many things. Discoveries have been made not only by Christopher Columbus and Pasteur, but also by Tolstoy and Dostoievsky and Freud. Things are revealed to us not only by the scientists with microscopes, but also by the poets, the prophets, and the painters. What is so isn't merely a matter of "the facts." For sometimes when there is agreement as to the facts there is still argument as to whether defendant did or did not "exercise reasonable care," was or was not "negligent."

And though we shall need to emphasize how much "There is a God" evinces an attitude to the familiar[3] we shall find in the end that it also evinces some recognition of patterns in time easily missed and that, therefore, difference as to there being any gods is in part a difference as to what is so and therefore as to the facts, though not in the simple ways which first occurred to us.

6. *Let us now approach these same points by a different road.*

6.1. *How it is that an explanatory hypothesis, such as the existence of God, may start by being experimental and gradually become something quite different can be seen from the following story:*

Two people return to their long neglected garden and find among the weeds a few of the old plants surprisingly vigorous. One says to the other "It must be that a gardener has been coming and doing something about these

---

[1] John P. Marquand, *H. M. Pulham, Esq.*, p. 320.
[2] E.g. Havelock Ellis's autobiography.
[3] Charles Leslie Stevenson, "Persuasive Definitions," *Mind*, July, 1938, should be read here. It is very good. [Also in his *Ethics and Language*, Yale, 1945.—Editor.]

plants." Upon inquiry they find that no neighbour has ever seen anyone at work in their garden. The first man says to the other "He must have worked while people slept." The other says "No, someone would have heard him and besides, anybody who cared about the plants would have kept down these weeds." The first man says "Look at the way these are arranged. There is purpose and a feeling for beauty here. I believe that someone comes, someone invisible to mortal eyes. I believe that the more carefully we look the more we shall find confirmation of this." They examine the garden ever so carefully and sometimes they come on new things suggesting that a gardener comes and sometimes they come on new things suggesting the contrary and even that a malicious person has been at work. Besides examining the garden carefully they also study what happens to gardens left without attention. Each learns all the other learns about this and about the garden. Consequently, when after all this, one says "I still believe a gardener comes" while the other says "I don't" their different words now reflect no difference as to what they have found in the garden, no difference as to what they would find in the garden if they looked further and no difference about how fast untended gardens fall into disorder. At this stage, in this context, the gardener hypothesis has ceased to be experimental, the difference between one who accepts and one who rejects it is now not a matter of the one expecting something the other does not expect. What is the difference between them? The one says "A gardener comes unseen and unheard. He is manifested only in his works with which we are all familiar," the other says "There is no gardener" and with this difference in what they say about the gardener goes a difference in how they feel towards the garden, in spite of the fact that neither expects anything of it which the other does not expect.

But is this the whole difference between them—that the one calls the garden by one name and feels one way towards it, while the other calls it by another name and feels in another way towards it? And if this is what the difference has become then is it any longer appropriate to ask "Which is right?" or "Which is reasonable?"

And yet surely such questions *are* appropriate when one person says to another "You still think the world's a garden and not a wilderness, and that the gardener has not forsaken it" or "You still think there are nymphs of the streams, a presence in the hills, a spirit of the world." Perhaps when a man sings "God's in His heaven" we need not take this as more than an expression of how he feels. But when Bishop Gore or Dr. Joad writes about belief in God and young men read them in order to settle their religious doubts the impression is not simply that of persons choosing exclamations with which to face nature and the "changes and chances of this mortal life." The disputants speak as if they are concerned with a matter of scientific fact, or of trans-sensual, trans-scientific and metaphysical fact, but still of fact and still a matter about which reasons for and against may be offered, although no scientific reasons in the sense of field surveys for fossils or experiments on delinquents are to the point.

6.2. *Now can an interjection have a logic?* Can the manifestation of an attitude in the utterance of a word, in the application of a name, have a logic? When all the facts are known how can there still be a question of fact? How can there still be a question? Surely as Hume says ". . . after every circumstance, every relation is known, the understanding has no further room to operate"?[1]

6.3. When the madness of these questions leaves us for a moment *we can all easily recollect disputes which though they cannot be settled by experiment are yet disputes in which one party may be right and the other wrong* and in which both parties may offer reasons and the one better reasons than the other. *This may happen in pure and applied mathematics and logic.* Two accountants or two engineers provided with the same data may reach different results and this difference is resolved not by collecting further data but by going over the calculations again. Such differences indeed share with differences as to what will win a race, the honour of being among the most "settlable" disputes in the language.

6.4. *But it won't do to describe the theistic issue as one settlable by such calculation,* or as one about what can be deduced in this *vertical* fashion from the facts we know. No doubt dispute about God has sometimes, perhaps especially in mediaeval times, been carried on in this fashion. But nowadays it is not and we must look for some other analogy, some other case in which a dispute is settled but not by experiment.

6.5. *In courts of law* it sometimes happens that opposing counsel are agreed as to the facts and are not trying to settle a question of further fact, are not trying to settle whether the man who admittedly had quarrelled with the deceased did or did not murder him, but are concerned with whether Mr. A who admittedly handed his long-trusted clerk signed blank cheques did or did not exercise reasonable care, whether a ledger is or is not a document,[2] whether a certain body was or was not a public authority.

In such cases we notice that the process of argument is not a *chain* of demonstrative reasoning. It is a presenting and representing of those features of the case which *severally co-operate* in favour of the conclusion, in favour of saying what the reasoner wishes said, in favour of calling the situation by the name by which he wishes to call it. The reasons are like

---

[1] Hume, *An Enquiry concerning the Principles of Morals.* Appendix I.

[2] *The Times*, March 2, 1945. Also in *The Times* of June 13, 1945, contrast the case of Hannah v. Peel with that of the cruiser cut in two by a liner. In the latter case there is not agreement as to the facts. See also the excellent articles by Dr. Glanville L. Williams in the *Law Quarterly Review*, "Language and the Law," January, and April, 1945, and "The Doctrine of Repugnancy," October, 1943, January, 1944, and April, 1944. The author, having set out how arbitrary are many legal decisions, needs now to set out how far from arbitrary they are—if his readers are ready for the next phase in the dialectic process.

the legs of a chair, not the links of a chain. Consequently although the discussion is *a priori* and the steps are not a matter of experience, the procedure resembles scientific argument in that the reasoning is not *vertically* extensive but *horizontally* extensive—it is a matter of the cumulative effect of several independent premises, not of the repeated transformation of one or two. And because the premises are severally inconclusive the process of deciding the issue becomes a matter of weighing the cumulative effect of one group of severally inconclusive items against the cumulative effect of another group of severally inconclusive items, and thus lends itself to description in terms of conflicting "probabilities." This encourages the feeling that the issue is one of fact—that it is a matter of guessing from the premises at a further fact, at what is to come. But this is a muddle. *The dispute does not cease to be* a priori *because it is a matter of the cumulative effect of severally inconclusive premises.* The logic of the dispute is not that of a chain of deductive reasoning as in a mathematic calculation. But nor is it a matter of collecting from several inconclusive items of information an expectation as to something further, as when a doctor from a patient's symptoms guesses at what is wrong, or a detective from many clues guesses the criminal. It has its own sort of logic and its own sort of end—the solution of the question at issue is a decision, a ruling by the judge. But it is not an arbitrary decision though the rational connections are neither quite like those in vertical deductions nor like those in inductions in which from many signs we guess at what is to come; and though the decision manifests itself in the application of a name it is no more merely the application of a name than is the pinning on of a medal merely the pinning on of a bit of metal. Whether a lion with stripes is a tiger or a lion is, if you like, merely a matter of the application of a name. Whether Mr. So-and-So of whose conduct we have so complete a record did or did not exercise reasonable care is not merely a matter of the application of a name or, if we choose to say it is, then we must remember that with this name a game is lost and won and a game with very heavy stakes. With the judges' choice of a name for the facts goes an attitude, and the declaration, the ruling, is an exclamation evincing that attitude. But *it is an exclamation which not only has a purpose but also has a logic,* a logic surprisingly like that of "futile," "deplorable," "graceful," "grand," "divine."

6.6. *Suppose two people are looking at a picture or natural scene.* One says "Excellent" or "Beautiful" or "Divine"; the other says "I don't see it." He means he doesn't see the beauty. And this reminds us of how we felt the theist accuse the atheist of blindness and the atheist accuse the theist of seeing what isn't there. And yet surely each sees what the other sees. It isn't that one can see part of the picture which the other can't see. So the difference is in a sense not one as to the facts. And so it cannot be removed by the one disputant discovering to the other what so far he hasn't seen. It isn't that the one sees the picture in a different light and so, as we might say, sees a different picture. Consequently the difference between them cannot be resolved by putting the picture in a different light. And yet surely this is just what can be done in such a case—not by moving the picture but by talk perhaps. To settle a dispute as to whether a piece of music is good or better than another we listen again, with a picture we look again. Someone perhaps points to emphasize certain features and we see it in a different light. Shall we call this "field work" and "the last of observation" or shall we call it "reviewing the premises" and "the beginning of deduction (horizontal)"?

If in spite of all this we choose to say that a difference as to whether a thing is beautiful is not a factual difference we must be careful to remember that there is a procedure for settling these differences and that this consists not only in reasoning and redescription as in the legal case, but also in a more literal re-setting-before with re-looking or re-listening.

6.7. *And if we say as we did at the beginning that when a difference as to the existence of a God is not one as to future happenings then it is not experimental and therefore not as to the facts, we must not forthwith assume that there is no right and wrong about it,* no rationality or irrationality, no appropriateness or inappropriateness, no procedure which tends to settle it, *nor even that this procedure is in no sense a discovery of new facts.* After all even in science this is not so. Our two gardeners even when they had reached the stage when neither expected any experimental result which the other did not, might yet have continued the dispute, each presenting and re-presenting the features of the garden favouring his hypothesis, that is, fitting his model for describing the accepted fact; each emphasizing the pattern he wishes to emphasize. True, in science, there is seldom or never a pure instance of this sort of dispute, for nearly always with difference of hypothesis goes some difference of expectation as to the facts. But scientists argue about rival hypotheses with a vigour which is not exactly proportioned to difference in expectations of experimental results.

The difference as to whether a God exists involves our feelings more than most scientific disputes and in this respect is more like a difference as to whether there is beauty in a thing.

7. *The Connecting Technique.* Let us consider again the technique used in revealing or proving beauty, in removing a blindness, in inducing an attitude which is lacking, in reducing a reaction that is inappropriate. Besides running over in a special way the features of the picture, tracing the rhythms, making sure that this and that are not only seen but noticed, and their relation to each other—besides all this—there are other things we can do to justify our attitude and alter that of the man who cannot see. For features of the picture may be brought out by setting beside it other pictures; just as the merits of an argument may be brought out, proved, by setting beside it other arguments, in which striking but irrelevant features of the original are changed

and relevant features emphasized; just as the merits and demerits of a line of action may be brought out by setting beside it other actions. To use Susan Stebbing's example: Nathan brought out for David certain features of what David had done in the matter of Uriah the Hittite by telling him a story about two sheepowners. This is the kind of thing we very often do when someone is "inconsistent" or "unreasonable." This is what we do in referring to other cases in law. The paths we need to trace from other cases to the case in question are often numerous and difficult to detect and the person with whom we are discussing the matter may well draw attention to connections which, while not incompatible with those we have tried to emphasize, are of an opposite inclination. A may have noticed in B subtle and hidden likenesses to an angel and reveal these to C, while C has noticed in B subtle and hidden likenesses to a devil which he reveals to A.

Imagine that a man picks up some flowers that lie half withered on a table and gently puts them in water. Another man says to him "You believe flowers feel." He says this although he knows that the man who helps the flowers doesn't expect anything of them which he himself doesn't expect; for he himself expects the flowers to be "refreshed" and to be easily hurt, injured, I mean, by rough handling, while the man who puts them in water does not expect them to whisper "Thank you." The Sceptic says "You believe flowers feel" because something about the way the other man lifts the flowers and puts them in water suggests an attitude to the flowers which he feels inappropriate although perhaps he would not feel it inappropriate to butterflies. He feels that this attitude to flowers is somewhat crazy *just as it is sometimes felt that a lover's attitude is somewhat crazy even when this is not a matter of his having false hopes about how the person he is in love with will act.* It is often said in such cases that reasoning is useless. But the very person who says this feels that the lover's attitude is crazy, is inappropriate like some dreads and hatreds, such as some horrors of enclosed places. And often one who says "It is useless to reason" proceeds at once to reason with the lover, nor is this reasoning always quite without effect. We may draw the lover's attention to certain things done by her he is in love with and trace for him a path to these from things done by others at other times[1] which have disgusted and infuriated him. And by this means we may weaken his admiration and confidence, make him feel it unjustified and arouse his suspicion and contempt and make him feel our suspicion and contempt reasonable. It is possible, of course, that he has already noticed the analogies, the connections, we point out and that he has accepted them— that is, he has not denied them nor passed them off. He has recognized them and they have altered his attitude, altered his love, but he still loves. We then feel that perhaps it is we who are blind and cannot see what he can see.

[1] Thus, like the scientist, the critic is concerned to show up the irrelevance of time and space.

8. *Connecting and Disconnecting.* But before we confess ourselves thus inadequate there are other fires his admiration must pass through. For when a man has an attitude which it seems to us he should not have or lacks one which it seems to us he should have then, not only do we suspect that he is not influenced by connections which we feel should influence him and draw his attention to these, but also we suspect he is influenced by connections which should not influence him and draw his attention to these. It may, for a moment, seem strange that we should draw his attention to connections which we feel should not influence him, and which, since they do influence him, he has in a sense already noticed. But we do—such is our confidence in "the light of reason."

Sometimes the power of these connections comes mainly from a man's mismanagement of the language he is using. This is what happens in the Monte Carlo fallacy, where by mismanaging the laws of chance a man passes from noticing that a certain colour or number has not turned up for a long while to an improper confidence that now it soon will turn up. In such cases our showing up of the false connections is a process we call "explaining a fallacy in reasoning." To remove fallacies in reasoning we urge a man to call a spade a spade, ask him what he means by "the State" and having pointed out ambiguities and vaguenesses ask him to reconsider the steps in his argument.

9. *Unspoken Connections. Usually, however, wrongheadedness or wrongheartedness in a situation, blindness to what is there or seeing what is not, does not arise merely from mismanagement of language but is more due to connections which are not mishandled in language, for the reason that they are not put into language at all.* And often these misconnections too, weaken in the light of reason, if only we can guess where they lie and turn it on them. In so far as these connections are not presented in language the process of removing their power is not a process of correcting the mismanagement of language. But it is still akin to such a process; for though it is not a process of setting out fairly what has been set out unfairly, it is a process of setting out fairly what has not been set out at all. And we must remember that the line between connections ill-presented or half-presented in language and connections operative but not presented in language, or only hinted at, is not a sharp one.

Whether or not we call the process of showing up these connections "reasoning to remove bad unconscious reasoning" or not, it is certain that in order to settle in ourselves what weight we shall attach to someone's confidence or attitude we not only ask him for his reasons but also look for unconscious reasons both good and bad; that is, for reasons which he can't put into words, isn't explicitly aware of, is hardly aware of, isn't aware of at all—perhaps it's long experience which he *doesn't* recall which lets him know a squall is coming, perhaps it's old experience which he *can't* recall which makes the cake in the tea mean so much and makes Odette so fascinating.[1]

I am well aware of the distinction between the question "What reasons are there for the belief that S is P?" and the question "What are the sources of beliefs that S is P?" There are cases where investigation of the rationality of a claim which certain persons make is done with very little inquiry into why they say what they do, into the causes of their beliefs. This is so when we have very definite ideas about what is really logically relevant to their claim and what is not. Offered a mathematical theorem we ask for the proof; offered the generalization that parental discord causes crime we ask for the correlation co-efficients. But even in this last case, if we fancy that only the figures are reasons we underestimate the complexity of the logic of our conclusion; and yet it is difficult to describe the other features of the evidence which have weight and there is apt to be disagreement about the weight they should have. In criticizing other conclusions and especially conclusions which are largely the expression of an attitude, we have not only to ascertain what reasons there are for them but also to decide what things are reasons and how much. This latter process of sifting reasons from causes is part of the critical process for every belief, but in some spheres it has been done pretty fully already. In these spheres we don't need to examine the actual processes to belief and distil from them a logic. But in other spheres this remains to be done. Even in science or on the stock exchange or in ordinary life we sometimes hesitate to condemn a belief or a hunch[2] merely because those who believe it cannot offer the sort of reasons we had hoped for. And now suppose Miss Gertrude Stein finds excellent the work of a new artist while we see nothing in it. We nervously recall, perhaps, how pictures by Picasso, which Miss Stein admired and others rejected, later came to be admired by many who gave attention to them, and we wonder whether the case is not a new instance of her perspicacity and our blindness. But if, upon giving all our attention to the work in question, we still do not respond to it, and we notice that the subject matter of the new pictures is perhaps birds in wild places and learn that Miss Stein is a birdwatcher, then we begin to trouble ourselves less about her admiration.

It must not be forgotten that our attempt to show up misconnections in Miss Stein may have an opposite result and reveal to us connections we had missed. Thinking to remove the spell exercised upon his patient by the old stories of the Greeks, the psycho-analyst may himself fall under that spell and find in them what his patient has found and, incidentally, what made the Greeks tell those tales.

10. *Now what happens, what should happen, when we inquire in this way*

[1] Proust, *Swann's Way*, Vol. I, p. 58, Vol. II. Phoenix ed.
[2] Here I think of Mr. Stace's interesting reflections in *Mind*, January, 1945, "The Problems of Unreasoned Beliefs."

into the reasonableness, the propriety of belief in gods? The answer is: A double and opposite-phased change. Wordsworth writes:

> . . . And I have felt
> A presence that disturbs me with the joy
> Of elevated thoughts; a sense sublime
> Of something far more deeply interfused,
> Whose dwelling is the light of setting suns,
> And the round ocean and the living air,
> And the blue sky, and in the mind of man:
> A motion and a spirit, that impels
> All thinking things, all objects of all thought,
> And rolls through all things . . .[1]

We most of us know this feeling. But is it well placed like the feeling that here is first-rate work, which we sometimes rightly have even before we have fully grasped the picture we are looking at or the book we are reading? Or is it misplaced like the feeling in a house that has long been empty that someone secretly lives there still. Wordsworth's feeling *is* the feeling that the world is haunted, that something watches in the hills and manages the stars. The child feels that the stone tripped him when he stumbled, that the bough struck him when it flew back in his face. He has to learn that the wind isn't buffeting him, that there is not a devil in it, that he was wrong, that his attitude was inappropriate. And as he learns that the wind wasn't hindering him so he also learns it wasn't helping him. But we know how, though he learns, his attitude lingers. It is plain that Wordsworth's feeling is of this family.

Belief in gods, it is true, is often very different from belief that stones are spiteful, the sun kindly. For the gods appear in human form and from the waves and control these things and by so doing reward and punish us. But varied as are the stories of the gods they have a family likeness and we have only to recall them to feel sure of the other main sources which co-operate with animism to produce them.

What are the stories of the gods? What are our feelings when we believe in God? They are feelings of awe before power, dread of the thunderbolts of Zeus, confidence in the everlasting arms, unease beneath the all-seeing eye. They are feelings of guilt and inescapable vengeance, of smothered hate and of a security we can hardly do without. We have only to remind ourselves of these feelings and the stories of the gods and goddesses and heroes in which these feelings find expression, to be reminded of how we felt as children to our parents and the big people of our childhood. Writing of a first telephone call from his grandmother, Proust says: ". . . it was rather that this isolation of the voice was like a

[1] *Tintern Abbey.*

symbol, a presentation, a direct consequence of another isolation, that of my grandmother, separated for the first time in my life, from myself. The orders or prohibitions which she addressed to me at every moment in the ordinary course of my life, the tedium of obedience or the fire of rebellion which neutralized the affection that I felt for her were at this moment eliminated. . . . "Granny!" I cried to her . . . but I had beside me only that voice, a phantom, as unpalpable as that which would come to revisit me when my grandmother was dead. 'Speak to me!' but then it happened that, left more solitary still, I ceased to catch the sound of her voice. My grandmother could no longer hear me . . . I continued to call her, sounding the empty night, in which I felt that her appeals also must be straying. I was shaken by the same anguish which, in the distant past, I had felt once before, one day when, a little child, in a crowd, I had lost her."

Giorgio de Chirico, writing of Courbet, says: "The word yesterday envelops us with its yearning echo, just as, on waking, when the sense of time and the logic of things remain a while confused, the memory of a happy hour we spent the day before may sometimes linger reverberating within us. At times we think of Courbet and his work as we do of our own father's youth."

When a man's father fails him by death or weakness how much he needs another father, one in the heavens with whom is "no variableness nor shadow of turning."

We understood Mr. Kenneth Graham when he wrote of the Golden Age we feel we have lived in under the Olympians. Freud says: "The ordinary man cannot imagine this Providence in any other form but that of a greatly exalted father, for only such a one could understand the needs of the sons of men, or be softened by their prayers and be placated by the signs of their remorse. The whole thing is so patently infantile, so incongruous with reality. . . ." "So incongruous with reality"! It cannot be denied.

But here a new aspect of the matter may strike us.[1] For the very facts which make us feel that now we can recognize systems of superhuman, sub-human, elusive, beings for what they are—the persistent projections of infantile phantasies—include facts which make these systems less fantastic. What are these facts? They are patterns in human reactions which are well described by saying that we are as if there were hidden within us powers, persons, not ourselves and stronger than ourselves. That this is so may perhaps be said to have been common knowledge yielded by ordinary observation of people,[2] but we did not know the degree in

---

[1] I owe to the late Dr. Susan Isaacs the thought of this different aspect of the matter, of this connection between the heavenly Father and "the good father" spoken of in psycho-analysis.

[2] Consider Tolstoy and Dostoievsky—I do not mean, of course, that their observation was ordinary.

which this is so until recent study of extraordinary cases in extraordinary conditions had revealed it. I refer, of course, to the study of multiple personalities and the wider studies of psycho-analysts. Even when the results of this work are reported to us that is not the same as tracing the patterns in the details of the cases on which the results are based; and even that is not the same as taking part in the studies oneself. One thing not sufficiently realized is that some of the things shut within us are not bad but good.

Now the gods, good and evil and mixed, have always been mysterious powers outside us rather than within. But they have also been within. It is not a modern theory but an old saying that in each of us a devil sleeps. Eve said: "The serpent beguiled me." Helen says to Menelaus:

> . . . And yet how strange it is!
> I ask not thee; I ask my own sad thought,
> What was there in my heart, that I forgot
> My home and land and all I loved, to fly
> With a strange man? Surely it was not I,
> But Cypris there![1]

Elijah found that God was not in the wind, nor in the thunder, but in a still small voice. The kingdom of Heaven is within us, Christ insisted, though usually about the size of a grain of mustard seed, and he prayed that we should become one with the Father in Heaven.

New knowledge made it necessary either to give up saying "The sun is sinking" or to give the words a new meaning. In many contexts we preferred to stick to the old words and give them a new meaning which was not entirely new but, on the contrary, *practically* the same as the old. The Greeks did not speak of the dangers of repressing instincts but they did speak of the dangers of thwarting Dionysos, of neglecting Cypris for Diana, of forgetting Poseidon for Athena. We have eaten of the fruit of a garden we can't forget though we were never there, a garden we still look for though we can never find it. Maybe we look for too simple a likeness to what we dreamed. Maybe we are not as free as we fancy from

[1] Euripides: *The Trojan Women*, Gilbert Murray's translation. Roger Hinks in *Myth and Allegory in Ancient Art* writes (p. 108): "Personifications made their appearance very early in Greek poetry. . . . It is out of the question to call these terrible beings 'abstractions'. . . . They are real daemons to be worshipped and propitiated. . . . These beings we observe correspond to states of mind. The experience of man teaches him that from time to time his composure is invaded and overturned by some power from outside, panic, intoxication, sexual desire."

> "What use to shoot off guns at unicorns?
> Where one horn's hit another fierce horn grows.
> These beasts are fabulous, and none were born
> Of woman who could lay a fable low."
> —*The Glass Tower*, Nicholas Moore, p. 100.

the old idea that Heaven is a happy hunting ground, or a city with streets of gold. Lately Mr. Aldous Huxley has recommended our seeking not somewhere beyond the sky or late in time but a timeless state not made of the stuff of this world, which he rejects, picking it into worthless pieces. But this sounds to me still too much a looking for another place, not indeed one filled with sweets but instead so empty that some of us would rather remain in the Lamb or the Elephant, where, as we know, they stop whimpering with another bitter and so far from sneering at all things, hang pictures of winners at Kempton and stars of the 'nineties. Something good we have for each other is freed there, and in some degree and for a while the miasma of time is rolled back without obliging us to deny the present.

The artists who do most for us don't tell us only of fairylands. Proust, Manet, Breughel, even Botticelli and Vermeer show us reality. And yet they give us for a moment exhilaration without anxiety, peace without boredom. And those who, like Freud, work in a different way against that which too often comes over us and forces us into deadness or despair,[1] also deserve critical, patient and courageous attention. For they, too, work to release us from human bondage into human freedom.

Many have tried to find ways of salvation. The reports they bring back are always incomplete and apt to mislead even when they are not in words but in music or paint. But they are by no means useless; and not the worst of them are those which speak of oneness with God. But in so far as we become one with Him He becomes one with us. St. John says he is in us as we love one another.

This love, I suppose, is not benevolence but something that comes of the oneness with one another of which Christ spoke.[2] Sometimes it momentarily gains strength.[3] Hate and the Devil do too. And what is oneness without otherness?

[1] Matthew Arnold, *Summer Night.*   [2] St. John 16:21.
[3] "The Harvesters," in Kenneth Graham, *The Golden Age.*

Albert Schweitzer was born in the Alsace, then part of Germany, in 1875. By 1913, when he founded a hospital in Central Africa, at Lambarene, he had established an international reputation both in New Testament studies and in musicology. His work in Africa attracted even more attention than his books on Jesus, Paul, Bach, and the organ; and his philosophic works as well as his autobiographical studies have been read the world over. In 1952, he received the Nobel Peace Prize.

His major works include *Von Reimarus zu Wrede: Eine Geschichte der Leben-Jesu Forschung* (1906; *The Quest of the Historical Jesus*); *Die Mystik des Apostels Paulus* (1930; *The Mysticism of Paul the Apostle*); a two-volume *Philosophy of Civilization* (*Verfall und Wiederaufbau der Kultur* and *Kultur und Ethik*, both 1923); and *Aus Meinem Leben und Denken* (1931; *Out of My Life and Thought*). Many other books by Schweitzer are also available in English.

The essay reprinted here appeared originally as an appendix to E. N. Mozley's *The Theology of Albert Schweitzer* (1950). The original German text appeared three years later in *Schweizerische Theologische Umschau*, February 1953 (XXIII.½), under the title "Die Idee des Reiches Gottes im Verlaufe der Umbildung des eschatologischen Glaubens in den uneschatologischen." According to his British publisher, Schweitzer himself attaches singular importance to this essay.

The Conception of the Kingdom of God in the Transformation of Eschatology

The primitive Christian hope of an immediate coming of the Kingdom of God was based on the teaching of Jesus; yet the fact that it remained unfulfilled did not shatter Christian faith. How was the catastrophe dealt with? What transformation of the faith enabled it to survive the surrender of the original expectation?

Although the eschatological problem has been under discussion for more than a generation, until quite recently only three factors have usually been taken into consideration as determining the development and re-shaping of Christian belief, *viz.*, the struggle for unity, the conflict with second century Gnosticism, and accommodation to Greek metaphysics. But these do not cover the whole ground. A fourth factor was at work, much more strongly than has been admitted, *viz.*, the inescapable abandonment of the early hope of a speedy coming of the Kingdom of God. The effect of this has been studied in detail for the first time by Martin Werner in *Die Entstehung des Christlichen Dogmas.*[1]

The apostle Paul had to wrestle with the problem, but it did not seriously affect him, because he took the view that the coming of the Kingdom was only postponed for a short time. He was thus able to hold to his conviction that the Kingdom must come as the immediate consequence of the self-sacrifice of Jesus on the Cross. His theory is that the Kingdom of God has actually come in the death and resurrection of Jesus, and is actually present, though not yet revealed. Those events inaugurated the transformation of the world of nature into the supernatural world of the Kingdom of God. Through mystical fellowship with the crucified and risen Jesus Christ, believers already share with him the supernatural quality of life in the Kingdom; they are already risen, though they look like ordinary people.

This view enables Paul to distinguish between the coming of the Kingdom and its manifestation. He regards the earlier view, with its hope fixed simply on the future, as falling short of the truth. His whole theology rests on this ante-dating, which is bound up with the assurance that Jesus himself expected the Kingdom to arrive with his resurrection as the result of his death.

The greatest thinker in the early Church thus holds both views side by side; the Kingdom is to come, and it is growing,—and the latter tends to displace the former. But the new view cannot cover the whole ground, because it starts from the theory of a brief postponement, which time will soon disprove. The early Church as a whole rejected this doctrine, holding that the death and resurrection of Jesus simply made it possible for the Kingdom to come some time, and that they must be content to wait for it.

From the second generation onwards the arrival of the Kingdom becomes "one far-off divine event," and in later days it is infinitely far away. This change of necessity affects the nature of the expectation. Originally it held a dominant position at the very centre of the faith; now it falls into the background. Instead of being the very essence of belief, it is now just one article among others.

When the Kingdom was expected immediately, it had a meaning for the present, which it overshadowed. The believer looked for a redemption which would lift him, with the multitude of his fellow-believers, into a world no longer subject to mortality and evil. With such a hope, he felt himself already delivered out of this world. But the Kingdom has no such meaning for the present, when it is imagined as being far away; the believer knows that he is condemned to live out his life in the same old world.

Denial of the world is a different thing when the end is not impending.

[1] Paul Haupt, Bern, 1941.

It presented little difficulty to those for whom the other world was so near; but to those who can cherish no hope of seeing the arrival of the new world, life must mean the denial of this world from first to last. These can have no hope for the world and its inhabitants; hopelessness about the present situation goes along with belief in the coming of the Kingdom of God at the end. Moreover, the fact that the Kingdom is merely something to be waited for has an unfortunate corollary. It made no difference to those who expected it immediately; but it obviously creates an unnatural situation for those whose faith compels them to do nothing but wait for the Kingdom which comes entirely of itself. Both by their denial of the world and by their belief that the Kingdom comes of itself, they are condemned to refrain from all efforts to improve the present situation.

While Christianity has to tread this path, it cannot be to the surrounding Graeco-Roman world what it ought to be. It cannot use its moral energy as power for regenerating the empire and its peoples. It conquers paganism; it becomes the religion of the state. But owing to its peculiar character it must leave the state to its fate. This world is not the dough in which its leaven can work.

The idea of redemption was also affected by the change of outlook. Originally the dominant thought of the Kingdom of God meant that believers shared with one another the blessings of a new creation. But now the experience of the individual took precedence of that of the community. Each separate believer is now concerned with his own redemption. He cares nothing for the future of mankind and of the world. There is something cold and unnatural about the naïve egoism of such piety.

The abandonment of eager expectation meant that Christianity lost the joy which characterised it in the days of Paul and the early Church. It started in bright sunshine, but had to continue its journey in the chilly gloom of a vague and uncertain hope. The idea of the Kingdom of God is no longer at the centre of faith, and this has led to a far-reaching impoverishment.

The substitution of the distant view for the near view of the coming of the Kingdom of God necessitates the elaboration and re-shaping of the faith. Originally the believer expected to come into possession of the blessedness of redemption through immediate admission into the Kingdom opened by the death and resurrection of Jesus. But when these blessings are postponed until the end of time, demands are made of faith which cannot be met by the earlier doctrine of redemption. The old assurance of the immediate attainment of the blessedness of redemption has now faded, and must be replaced by the assurance of a right, secured by the death and resurrection of Jesus, to the blessedness of the Kingdom of God at the end of time. The early Christians thought of redemption and blessedness as different aspects of the same experience. Later they were separated in time, and each came to have its own meaning. Instead of blessedness as such, the believer had the blessedness of being assured of his right to redemption; and this gave him strength to bear the burden of life in this world.

It became necessary, in the development of the doctrine of redemption, to have a comprehensive interpretation of the death and resurrection of Jesus, showing how these guarantee future blessedness to the believer. Faith feels that it must be clear on this point. Christian theology was entirely occupied, in the first centuries, with meeting the demand of faith for a fuller understanding of the death and resurrection of Jesus.

Assurance of a share in the coming blessedness naturally depends upon the assurance of having received the forgiveness of sins and the power of the resurrection already in this present life. Resurrection and acquittal on the Day of Judgment on the ground that sins have already been forgiven: these are the conditions of entrance into the Kingdom of God and its blessedness. Christianity had been the religion of faith in the Kingdom of God; now it became the religion of faith in the resurrection and the forgiveness of sins.

Greek theology is chiefly interested in the problem of reaching certainty with regard to the possession of power to rise again from the dead; in the west it is the forgiveness of sins of which theology wants to make sure. The task was made easier in both cases by the work which Paul had done. He was the first to tackle the question of being actually redeemed before the full revelation of the Kingdom of God; and he solved it in his own way. Later generations, however, could not simply adopt his solution, since they lacked the glowing eschatological expectation which lay behind his doctrine of the possession of eternal life and the forgiveness of sins through mystical union with Christ. But Paul's theology is a magnificent structure, and it provided material which could be used for buildings of another style.

The creators of Greek theology are known to us through their writings: Ignatius, bishop of Antioch, who suffered martyrdom in Rome in the second decade of the second century; Justin Martyr, born in Palestine, who shared the same fate in Rome in 165; and Irenaeus, from Asia Minor, who was made bishop of Lyons in 178.

Their teaching starts from Paul's view of the power of resurrection, which the Spirit imparts to the physical nature of Jesus and of believers. Appropriating this, they develop and re-shape it. Their re-shaping consists in placing the work of the Spirit, which follows upon the death and resurrection of Jesus, in the long continuing course of the natural order, whereas Paul assigned it to the era during which the natural world was being transformed into the supernatural world of the Kingdom of God.

Greek theology only found it possible to assert, as if it were quite obvious, that the Spirit prepares the body for the coming resurrection, because this was stated in Paul's epistles. There was nothing in the primitive Christian doctrine of the Spirit to justify the idea, but Paul's teaching gave it apostolic authority. His sovereign treatment of the Jewish eschatological doctrine of the work of the Spirit gave to the Christian faith something which Greek religious thought could appropriate. Ignatius, Justin and Irenaeus turned the eschatological mysticism of being "in Christ" into Greek mysticism.

The fundamental idea in Greek theology is that the Spirit first entered into union with human flesh in the person of Jesus, and thus gained the power to work upon man's physical nature. This power was further exercised among men after Jesus was separated from the world by his death and resurrection. As a new principle of life, it regenerates men spiritually and physically, so that they are fitted for eventual entrance into the Kingdom of God. The new life, which is for Paul the effect of being already risen with Christ, is regarded by Greek theology as being born again through the Spirit; the theory of dying and rising again with Christ is gone. The effect is the same as it was for Paul, but the sole cause is now said to be the working of the Spirit.

The Greek Fathers agree with Paul that the transformation of believers is due to the death and resurrection of Jesus, but for them it takes place with the Kingdom of God in view, and not, as for him, in the Kingdom already present. According to their teaching, believers live no longer in the world, but in the intermediate realm of the Spirit, until the Kingdom comes. Ignatius and Justin set the seal of martyrdom on this doctrine—noble of its kind—of world-renunciation through the Spirit.

Western theology is mainly concerned with the doctrine of the forgiveness of sins, and its task is to interpret the death of Jesus in such a way that men may find in it forgiveness ever available, ever renewed, for all the lapses of which they become guilty. Only thus can believers have the assurance that their redemption has already been achieved; for them the Kingdom is not at hand, but far away, and the whole of their life in this world has to be lived in the midst of temptation.

Neither Jesus himself nor Paul offers this view of the efficacy of the atoning death on the Cross.

Jesus takes it for granted, in his preaching, that God in his tender mercy guarantees forgiveness to those who truly repent. The Lord's Prayer attaches the condition that the petitioner must have forgiven all his debtors.

Two sayings of Jesus, from the later period of his activity, give an atoning significance to his death:

The Son of man came not to be ministered unto, but to minister, and to give his life a ransom for many. *Mark* 10:45.

This is my blood of the covenant, which is shed for many. *Mark* 14:24. (. . . unto remission of sins. *Matt.* 26:28.)

The atoning value of his death, according to Jesus, does not interfere with the direct flowing of forgiveness from the tender mercy of God, but adds something to it. Its object, as he sees it, is not to enable God to forgive, but to save the faithful from having to pay the penalty of their sins in the tribulation preceding the advent of the Messiah, to put an end to the power of the evil one without exposing them to his final onslaught, and bring in the Kingdom of God without this ghastly prelude.

Jesus undertakes his Passion in order that the last petition of the Lord's prayer may be fulfilled: "Lead us not into temptation, but deliver us from evil." "Temptation" means "trial," and refers to the pre-Messianic tribulation which was to take place before the coming of the Kingdom, according to late Jewish eschatology. The words and deeds of Jesus can only be understood when due attention is paid to his pre-occupation with this dreadful anticipation.

No teaching about the atonement is given by Jesus to his disciples; he demands of them no theory about it, no faith in it. It remains his secret. He neither poses as the coming Messiah nor seeks for faith in himself as such. It is enough that his followers believe in the coming of the Kingdom of God, and prepare for entrance into it by repentance and fulfilment of his higher moral law. Who he is, and what he has done for them will come home to them when the Kingdom is there, and they have entered into it without passing through the great tribulation.

The meaning of the Passion for Jesus himself is rooted in eschatology, its object being to destroy the force of a certain prediction. The many, who are to be ransomed, are believers who await with him the coming of the Kingdom, not mankind as a whole. His own generation is the last. The end of this world is close at hand.

We cannot tell how far the disciples and the first Christians were concerned with the problem of the pre-Messianic tribulation, or how far they were persuaded that for them atonement, having been wrought by the death of Jesus, would not involve this tribulation. After the crucifixion they found themselves in a situation which left no room for that way of thinking. They knew, from the hints which he had given them, that he was the Messiah and Son of Man, about to be revealed in his glory, and that his death effected an atonement, involving their own forgiveness, and the coming of the Kingdom.

Having no precise doctrine of the atonement, the apostles and first believers took the simple view that through his death Jesus had gained the forgiveness of sins for them, and so they would escape condemnation in the judgment which would take place at the coming of the Kingdom of God. Thus the atoning death of Jesus was given a new meaning at the very beginning; the original idea of Jesus himself was displaced by the view that it was actually the necessary condition of the divine forgiveness of sins. This created an insoluble problem. How is it conceivable that God only forgives sins on the ground that Jesus has died? How is such a view to be reconciled with the fact that in the Lord's Prayer Jesus teaches us to ask for forgiveness as if it could only be granted through the mercy of God to those who forgive their debtors?

It was centuries before anybody had the courage to face this problem. The first really to do so was the schoolman, Anselm of Canterbury (1033-1109), in his famous writing, *Cur Deus homo* (Why must God become man?). He argues that God's honour has been damaged by man's sin, and that there can be no forgiveness without satisfaction. This cannot be provided by sinful man. But in his love God means to forgive. Only a human being who is at the same time God, and therefore perfect and sinless, can give adequate satisfaction. Therefore Jesus came into the world, and achieved this through his voluntary death, thus enabling God to act both with justice and with love. All subsequent efforts to solve the problem follow in the track of this completely unsatisfactory explanation.

Those who cannot reconcile their conception of God with a belief that he needs a sacrifice before he can forgive sins are at liberty to look simply to his mercy for forgiveness, and to find redemption in the gift of the Spirit of God through Jesus, whereby we are taken out of this world and brought to God.

The fundamental meaning of the death of Jesus for Paul is that he has thereby brought to an end the dominion of the powers of evil in the world, and set in motion the process, shown in his resurrection, of transforming the natural world into the supernatural. This is in full harmony with the view held by Jesus himself of the effect of his self-sacrifice in death.

Paul is giving expression to the simple early Christian belief in the forgiveness of sins, when he says that God overlooks the sins committed formerly on the ground of the atonement wrought by Jesus (Rom. 3:25), not reckoning them (II Cor. 5:19), and that Jesus delivers believers from the wrath to come (I Thess. 1:10; Rom. 5:9).

But he does not hold to the early view that the death of Jesus makes it possible for the Kingdom to come, and by its atoning efficacy procures forgiveness for believers on the Day of Judgment. His position is that believers are already free from all sins, basing this on his theory that the transformation of the natural world into the supernatural has already begun and is going on in those who die and rise again with Christ. "We are dead to sin." "He that hath died is justified from sin." "Ye are not in the flesh, but in the spirit." (Rom. 6:2, 7; 8:9). Sin no longer comes into consideration for believers who have, with Paul, the assurance that they are sharers in a real and complete forgiveness of sins.

His polemic against those Christians who are still under the sway of the Jewish view that righteousness is earned by practising circumcision and observing the Law leads Paul to fashion the doctrine of justification by faith in Jesus Christ alone. "But now apart from the Law a righteousness of God hath been manifested, . . . even the righteousness of God through faith in Jesus Christ; . . . justified freely by his grace through the redemption that is in Christ Jesus" (Rom. 3:21-24).

This assurance of already possessing the full reality of redemption, which goes so far beyond the experience of the first Christians, rested for Paul on his conviction that believers are already risen again, since union with Jesus, through faith and the power of his death, involves dying and rising again with him; they are already in the Kingdom of God. The righteousness which is the qualification for entrance into the Kingdom is no longer something to be striven after. Believers must have it already through their faith in Jesus; otherwise they could not find themselves sharing in the resurrection, which proves that they are already partakers in the Kingdom of God.

Paul's doctrine is not one of continuous forgiveness, but of full forgiveness. He does not take into consideration the possibility of going on sinning after becoming a believer. But his view of justification by faith alone is of fundamental importance for the later rise and development of the doctrine of continuous forgiveness. This made its appearance when Paul's doctrine was separated from eschatology and from the eschatological mysticism of union with Christ in his death and resurrection.

Early Christianity did not contemplate the possibility that further generations of men would make their appearance upon the earth after the death of Jesus. But that is what happened. So it became necessary to widen the scope of the doctrine of the atonement, in order to make it possible for men, yet to be born, to obtain the forgiveness of sins on becoming believers.

If forgiveness becomes available for men of all ages, it must be thought of as being continuous. That was not necessary at the beginning, when the Kingdom was expected immediately. What men needed then was the forgiveness of sins committed before their conversion. The early Christians' view was that this was procured by the death of Jesus and became theirs in baptism. The presumption was that they would continue sinless during the short period of waiting for the Kingdom. Forgiveness takes place, for them as for Paul, only once (cf. Rom. 3:25). But those who have to live the whole of their life in the natural sinful world need to be assured that believers go on being forgiven again and again for the lapses of which they are guilty in the course of time.

There was, however, a great difficulty in the way of the development of the new doctrine. Baptism could only mean what it had meant from the beginning, *viz.*, the bestowal of forgiveness for past sins. Its character could not be altered, and it remained unaffected by the abandonment of an immediate expectation of the coming of the Kingdom. The problem thus arose as to whether post-baptismal sins can be forgiven at all, and if they can, by what means this is to be accomplished.

At first the possibility was strongly denied. The author of the epistle to the Hebrews, writing between the years 70 and 80, says that "as touching those who were once enlightened . . . and were made partakers of the Holy Spirit, and tasted the good word of God, and the powers of the age to come, and then fell away, it is impossible to renew them again unto repentance, seeing they crucify to themselves the Son of God afresh, and put him to an open shame" (Heb. 6:4-6).

Hermas, a Roman layman, at the beginning of the second century, asserts the possibility of obtaining forgiveness for later sins by means of a second repentance, in addition to that which led to baptism. He does this on the strength of a revelation brought to him by an "Angel of repentance" who appeared to him in the form of a shepherd. In his book, *The Shepherd of Hermas*, which appeared about A.D. 130, he announces that God in his mercy is willing to give believers the possibility of regaining their standing in grace by means of a repeated repentance. The Church could do no other than accept this view, which allowed her to take back sinners whom she had been compelled to excommunicate, after they had renewed their repentance.

But the atoning death of Jesus only happened once; and the same is true of the forgiveness which he procured. The recognition of a forgiveness for sins committed after baptism places the Church in the peculiar position of having to admit that besides the forgiveness made possible by the death of Jesus there is another, not resting on that foundation, but granted directly through God's mercy to those who, by repentance and other good works, are found worthy of this grace. Among good works recognised, in addition to public repentance, as having satisfaction-value are—suffering, which has atoning virtue, faithfulness under persecution, deeds of love, and the conversion of heretics.

The Church is the stewardess of this supplementary forgiveness. She prescribes what the sinner must do in the way of repentance and satisfaction, exercises over-sight, and makes sure how far he has done his duty. When she judges that he can have found forgiveness with God, she takes him back into the congregation. She makes no claim to forgive, but feels herself to be the announcer of the forgiveness which God has granted.

But the matter cannot rest there, with the permission of only one supplementary forgiveness; it gradually comes to repentance procuring forgiveness again and again. And then there is the problem of differentiating between venial sins and those which are too serious to be forgiven. Thus in the course of time the idea of continuous forgiveness was reached.

Augustine (354-430) lays it down as a principle that forgiveness is available within the Church for all sins committed after baptism, provided appropriate satisfaction is made. Outside the Church there is no pardon. Not to believe in the continuous forgiveness of sins within the Church is to commit the sin against the Holy Spirit.

Contemporary new ideas mentioned by Augustine in connexion with continuous forgiveness are that of Purgatory and that of the offering of prayer, alms and the Sacrifice of the Mass by the living on behalf of the dead, that they may find forgiveness.

Purgatory is not punishment in hell, but only a possibility, held out to the sinner after death, of completing, by the endurance of torment, the repentance of which he fell short in his earthly life.

The idea that in the Mass the body and blood of Jesus are offered up afresh as an atoning sacrifice to God appears first in Cyprian, bishop of Carthage, who died as a martyr in 258. Augustine understands this in a purely spiritual sense. The realistic view established itself under Pope Gregory I (590-604), *viz.*, that in the Mass Jesus is offered as a sacrifice sacramentally again and again, to bring the benefit of the atonement to the living and the dead. This sacramental repetition implies that the forgiveness brought about by Jesus on Golgotha avails, not only for sins committed before baptism, but also—as it were by a side-channel—for those committed after. By letting its priests carry out this repetition of the atoning sacrifice of Jesus, the Church helps to establish the view that it brings about and bestows the forgiveness of sins, instead of merely announcing it as something which God does when adequate satisfaction is offered.

Subsequently it became customary for more and more Masses to be celebrated. These were no longer congregational acts of worship, but were only intended to convey the atoning power of the sacramental repetition of the death of Jesus to those, living or dead, on whose behalf they were held. Towards the end of the Middle Ages all Churches had, in addition to the high altar, side-altars at which these special Masses were said.

Continuous forgiveness became generally easier and easier to obtain during the Middle Ages—and more and more dependent upon outward performances. It gradually became the custom to secure exemption from the penance ordered by the priests on the ground of merits or of payments to the Church. Those who took part in the Crusades obtained full exemption. From the twelfth century, those who did not go to war against the infidel could get their indulgence by the payment of money. The Schoolmen justified the dispensation of indulgences by the Popes on the ground that they were the custodians of the accumulated merits of the saints. In the year 1477 Pope Sixtus IV (1471-1484) announced that indulgences were also valid for souls in Purgatory, and would shorten the time of their purification.

It was widely felt at the end of the Middle Ages that this state of affairs was unsatisfactory. But it would not meet the case, simply to reform the doctrine of continuous forgiveness and return to the purity of its original formulation.

Then there appeared on the scene, in Martin Luther (1483-1546), a man of outstanding religious personality, who first objected to the unspiritual practices which had come to be associated with the Church's doctrine of continuous forgiveness, and then proceeded to question its underlying principle.

As a monk, Luther tried to reach the assurance of forgiveness along the orthodox lines. He did not succeed. In his agony, he asked himself whether he was not one of those predestined to damnation, since all his penance, and the absolution which he received, failed to bring him the deliverance for which he looked.

Through Augustine he was led to Paul, whose doctrine of justification by faith alone, without works, was the light which penetrated his darkness. His final spiritual deliverance took place in 1512, and he owed it to Paul. We have the working out of his new conception of continuous forgiveness on the ground of faith in the operation of the atoning death of Jesus, in his lectures at the University of Wittenberg on the Psalms (1513-1515), Romans (1515-1516), Galatians (1516) and Hebrews (1517).

Luther inevitably discovered that the Catholic view of baptism was the basis of the doctrine of continuous forgiveness as dependent on justification by works and not by faith. It was this which ruled out the attribution of continuous forgiveness to the atoning death of Jesus. It was responsible for the view that post-baptismal sins required justification by works to obtain forgiveness.

But the effect of baptism should not be confined to the forgiveness of past sins through Jesus' death; it ought to secure for the believer the possibility of finding continuous forgiveness at the Cross. So Luther propounded the doctrine that baptism "is the beginning and gateway of all grace and forgiveness." The pardon which men need every day is just the renewal of baptismal grace, freely given by God on the ground of faith in the atoning work of Christ.

The conflict between Luther and the Catholic Church turned finally upon the doctrine of baptism. Historically Luther was in the wrong. He intended to restore the simple original doctrine, from which he thought the Church had departed. But it was the Church, and not Luther, that held the old idea of baptism. Religiously, however, his view was right, for it made it possible to believe in the continuous forgiveness of sins as coming directly from God through Christ.

The Catholic doctrine of baptism is the only thing which has been preserved unaltered throughout the centuries from the first age of eschatological faith. It was a big step in the movement away from eschatology when Luther formulated his doctrine of baptism without any reference to the last things.

Luther's doctrine of forgiveness is not identical with Paul's; it is a restatement of it without the primitive eschatology. It was because Paul was the only great thinker in the early Church who saw clearly that redemption, like the Kingdom, was not something in the future, but a present reality, that Luther found in him the substance and the spirit of his own doctrine of salvation now through the continuous forgiveness of sins. The latter meant for him what the nearness of the Kingdom meant for Paul.

So Luther sounds the same note of victory as Paul, a note which had not been heard in Christian preaching since Paul's day. His sense of triumph leads him away from that denial of the world to which the Church was still committed in spite of its weakened eschatology. He does not ask for renunciation of the world as the expression of true Christianity; what he enjoins is faithful performance of daily duties in the way of our earthly calling and the practice of love to our neighbour. He erects an ideal of Christian perfection which attaches real value to the state, to marriage, and to lawful occupations, and views daily labour, however humble, as service required by God. He feels himself moved to agree with the affirmation of life and the world, although he does not break away from that pessimistic judgment of the world which is involved in the later form of eschatology. In this he was prophetic of what was to happen later in the history of Protestantism.

Luther also combines the conservative with the progressive in that he attaches great importance to the acknowledgment that his doctrine agrees with that of the Church of the first centuries, and yet does not make this agreement a rallying point for Protestants, but summons them to study the Gospel in the New Testament, recognising it as their supreme and sole authority.

This principle is the inspiration of free and dauntless search for religious truth. Luther could not measure the scope of this study of the original Gospel and the recognition of its supreme authority; the road, which he opened up, led further afield than he could ever have imagined. And yet, by following this road, Protestantism completed what Luther had begun. His rejection of the Catholic doctrine of continuous forgiveness as based on primitive Christian baptism, in favour of a new one, constitutes the penultimate stage in the movement of Christianity away from eschatology. The last stage is the surrender of the eschatological idea of the Kingdom of God, with the acceptance of a view that is not determined by its relation to the last things. This is the experience destined for Protestantism in its effort to get back to the true Gospel.

What then, is being done to effect this surrender and eliminate eschatology from the conception of the Kingdom? How are matters going?

The fundamental pre-supposition necessary for this change is provided by the existence of a new attitude towards the world. The affirmation and acceptance of the world begin to take their place beside the traditional Christian denial and rejection of it, which resulted from eschatology.

When it first makes its appearance in the fourteenth century, the positive attitude can hardly be described as a philosophy; it consists rather in the rejection of the spirit of the Middle Ages and all that it comprises.

With the contemporary rise and growth of natural science, a more profound level is reached. The order and harmony of the universe come into view as the result of the astronomy of a Copernicus (1473-1543), a Kepler (1571-1630) and a Galileo (1564-1642). Advances in knowledge and skill encourage a belief in progress, and this adds to the strength and vitality of the acceptance of life and the world. The spirit of man acquires an unprecedented confidence in human capacity and creative power in every field. Thus by the time of a Giordano Bruno (1548-1600) the new attitude has attained to the stature of a philosophy.

Clarified and deepened under the influence of the achievements of natural science, the movement then gains strength by appropriating the ethics of later Stoicism, as found in the writings of Cicero (106-43 B.C.) and developed by Seneca (4 B.C.-A.D. 65), Epictetus (b. about A.D. 50) and Marcus Aurelius (120-180). Hugo Grotius (1583-1645) shews how completely the modern acceptance of life and the world is under the influence of the Stoic ideal of humanity. Here is something absolutely new in the intellectual history of Europe: a philosophical acceptance of the world with a moral outlook. Herein lies the differentia of modern European man, as compared with man in earlier times. He has a new intellectual attitude, believing in progress, determined to do all he can to help the world onward and upward, and disposed to universal charity.

The ethical quality of the new outlook makes it acceptable to Christians, who are prepared for it by the ethical teaching of Jesus. For although the latter adopted a negative attitude to life and the world, it did not lose itself in absolute pessimism. That would have involved accepting the ideal of inactivity, whereas Christianity means active love.

The reason why the ethic of Jesus is practical is to be found in the fact that the eschatological denial of the world does not go as far as the Indian.

It does not reject existence as such in favour of non-existence, like the Indian, but only the natural, imperfect, painful world in prospect of the world of the Kingdom of God. Its view is that man must prove and demonstrate his calling to take part in the perfecting of existence by living an active moral life in the natural world. The ethic of Jesus has an affinity with the ethical philosophy of world-acceptance in so far as its ideal is one of activity.

Modern Protestant Christianity takes a long time to break away from world-denial. The hymns of the Church remain under its influence until late in the eighteenth century. Escape from the world provides the leading motif in the cantatas of Johann Sebastian Bach (1685-1750); yet the Protestantism of that time is moving irresistibly in the direction of a philosophy of world-acceptance. It is not conscious of the step that it is taking; the passage from the old to the new is concealed by the fact that there is so much in common between Christianity and ethical world-acceptance. The point of contact is in the ethic: the Stoic ideal of humanity comes very close to Jesus' ideal of love. So the passage of Christianity in the new age from the ethical negative to the ethical positive view takes place without observation and without conflict.

Belief in the Kingdom of God now takes a new lease of life. It no longer looks for its coming, self-determined, as an eschatological cosmic event, but regards it as something ethical and spiritual, not bound up with the last things, but to be realised with the co-operation of men.

In ancient and mediaeval times, Christians had no faith in progress, no urge to go forward, no idea that things could be moving onward and upward; yet it never occurred to them that they were in an unnatural situation so long as their religious life was based on the idea that the Kingdom of God lay far away in the future. It seemed obvious to them that passivity concerning the Kingdom was the only possible attitude.

It is otherwise with those of the new age who are under the influence of the ethical affirmation of the world. What they think is that the Kingdom is something ethical and religious, to be conceived as developing in this world, and requiring ethical effort on the part of believers. This is so obvious to them that they can conceive of no other way of looking at the subject; they understand the Gospels to say that Jesus came into this world to found the Kingdom, and to call men into it as fellow-workers. Just as Luther substituted his non-eschatological view of baptism for that of the early Church, convinced that it was the authentic teaching of the Gospels, so modern Protestantism substitutes its view of the Kingdom of God and its coming for the eschatological view which Jesus presented as if it really represented the original. Historically both are wrong; but religiously both are right.

Only as it comes to be understood as something ethical and spiritual, rather than supernatural, as something to be realised rather than expected, can the Kingdom of God regain, in our faith, the force that it had for Jesus and the early Church. Christianity must have a firm hold of this, if it is to remain true to itself, as it was at the beginning,—religion dominated by the idea of the Kingdom of God. What the Kingdom of God is in reality is shown by the part which it plays in the life of faith. The precise conception which is held of its coming is a matter of secondary consideration. In spite of many fundamental differences from the past, modern Protestant Christianity remains true to the Gospel since it is still the religion of a living faith in the Kingdom of God.

About the end of the eighteenth and the beginning of the nineteenth century, "Lives of Jesus" began to appear, these being the first efforts to reach a historical understanding of his earthly life and teaching. Mention may be made of the works of Johann Jakob Hess (1768-1772)—in three volumes—Franz Volkmar Reinhard (1781), Johann Gottfried Herder (1796), Heinrich Eberhard Gottleib Paulus (1828) and Karl August Hase (1829).

According to these, Jesus appeared before the Jews, whose hopes of the Kingdom of God and the Messiah were materialistic and mundane, as the true Messiah, quite different in character, who made the beginning of a Kingdom of God which meant the control of human life by the Spirit of God. The idea that Jesus spiritualised the Jewish hope of the Kingdom continued to dominate historical and critical theology during the second half of the nineteenth century. It was set forth by Adolf Harnack in his famous lectures at Berlin University in the winter of 1899-1900 under the title, *Das Wesen des Christentums* (What is Christianity?).

Even at that time there were grounds for questioning this idea. More careful study of the documents of later Jewish eschatology revealed the fact that their fundamental conceptions were shared by sayings of Jesus concerning the Kingdom of God and the Messiah. This is specially clear in the records of Matthew and Mark, which in this respect are shown to be the oldest. But it seemed impossible to believe that Jesus should not have held views about the Kingdom of God and his own Messianic calling that were in harmony with the inwardness and depth of his ideal of love.

At the beginning of this century, therefore, the difficulty was overcome by putting forward the theory that the sayings in question were not actually uttered by Jesus. They had been introduced into the tradition by the early Church, which was still under the influence of the later Jewish eschatology. Harnack and others even suggested that Jesus was able to combine elements of that eschatology with his own spiritual view of the Kingdom in some way that is beyond our comprehension.

But already in 1892 Johannes Weiss, of Heidelberg, had shown that it is impossible to differentiate the eschatological view of the Kingdom and the Messiah, held by Jesus, from that of later Judaism—in his study, *Die Predigt Jesu von Reiche Gottes* (The Preaching of Jesus concerning the Kingdom of God), based on Matthew and Mark. I carried Johannes Weiss's argument to its conclusion in my sketch of the life of Jesus, *Das Messianitäts- und Leidensgeheimnis* (1901) and my *Geschichte der Leben-Jesu-Forschung* (1906), showing that eschatology not only coloured the thoughts of Jesus, but also determined his actions.

Those who have the courage to let Matthew and Luke mean what they say must agree that Jesus shared the later Jewish view of the advent of the Kingdom of God, not spiritualising it, but using it as a vehicle for his profound and powerful ideal of love.

It is hard for us to bring ourselves to the point of admitting that Jesus, who is uniquely endowed with the Spirit of God, and is for us the supreme revealer of religious and spiritual truth, does not stand above his age in the way that might seem to be demanded by the significance which he has for all ages.

What we should prefer is that we, and men of every age, might find in Jesus the final truth of religion available in a form that need never be changed. And now we are confronted by the fact that he shared the outlook of an age long past, which is to us mistaken and unacceptable. Why should Christianity have to endure this? Is it not a wound for which there is no balm? Ought we not to maintain the absolute inerrancy of Jesus in matters of religion? Are we not rejecting his authority?

Both Johannes Weiss and I have suffered severely through the compulsion which truth laid upon us to put forward something which was bound to offend Christian faith.

To me, however, Jesus remains what he was. Not for a single moment have I had to struggle for my conviction that in him is the supreme spiritual and religious authority, though his expectation of the speedy advent of a supernatural Kingdom of God was not fulfilled, and we cannot make it our own.

The difficulty can only be overcome by a right apprehension of what is meant by the inerrancy of Jesus.

Our assumption of the limitation of his knowledge does not mean that he had an understanding of nature equal to that attained, or ever attainable, by modern science, but refrained from using it. The historical Jesus stands before us as one who shared naturally the outlook of his time. This is not a pose, but an actual reality. Anything else would involve a dissimulation which we can never associate with him.

If Jesus thinks like his contemporaries about the world and what happens in it, then his view of the coming of the Kingdom of God must resemble that of later Judaism.

It is perfectly clear to any one who studies deeply the way in which progress is achieved in history that what is absolutely new does not easily establish itself, and if, for any reason, it does succeed, it is apt to appear unnatural and questionable. So we must believe that, if Jesus had appeared with a fully spiritualised view of the Kingdom and its coming, his proclamation of it would never have been believed. The ancient world, Jewish, Greek and Roman, would have had no point of contact with such an announcement. To enable it to do its work naturally, every new idea must be in some way embedded in what is old, and thus be linked with that which preceded it. Jesus ends a series of parables of the Kingdom of God with the remarkable saying, "Therefore every scribe who hath been made a disciple to the Kingdom of heaven is like unto a man that is a householder, which bringeth forth out of his treasure things new and old" (Matt. 13:52).

Truth cannot dissociate itself from the time process; it must work within it. Jesus spiritualises the conception of the Kingdom of God, in that he brings it into subjection to his ideal and ethic of love. In due time this transforms the conception of the Kingdom.

Spiritual truth is concerned with the knowledge of what we must become spiritually in order to be in a right relationship to God. It is complete in itself. It is intuitive knowledge of what ought to be in the realm of the spirit. All other knowledge is of a different kind, having to do, not with what happens in us, but with what goes on in the world,—a field in which understanding can only be limited and liable to change.

The conception of the realisation of a spiritual idea on a universal scale is conditioned by the conception of the world and its events which prevails at a particular time. The fact that Jesus thinks of the realisation of the Kingdom of God in a way that is not justified by events does not call in question his authority as a unique revealer of spiritual truth; it only challenges the traditional view of his personality and authority. Christian faith, under the influence of Greek metaphysics, was pleased to confer upon him a divinity and a divine inerrancy to which he made no claim. We shall only deal successfully with the problem of his unfulfilled promise when we turn back to see exactly how he confronts us in the two oldest Gospels. He is so great, that the discovery that he belongs to his age can do him no harm. He remains our spiritual Lord.

All attempts to avoid the admission that Jesus held a view of the Kingdom of God and its coming which was not fulfilled and cannot be adopted by us involve the shirking of the truth. Devotion to truth in this matter is of the essence of spiritual life. Faith which refuses to face indisputable facts is but little faith. Truth is always gain, however hard it is to accommodate ourselves to it. To linger in any kind of untruth proves to be a departure from the straight way of faith.

The modern view of the Kingdom of God and its coming creates a spiritual situation comparable with that of Jesus and his little flock and of the early Church. Again, after many centuries, the Kingdom of God has become a live question. Again mankind as a whole is changing its mind as to what it really means.

Modern faith finds the beginning of the Kingdom of God in Jesus and in the Spirit which came into the world with him. We no longer leave the fate of mankind to be decided at the end of the world. The time in which we live summons us to new faith in the Kingdom of God.

We are no longer content, like the generations before us, to believe in the Kingdom that comes of itself at the end of time. Mankind to-day must either realise the Kingdom of God or perish. The very tragedy of our present situation compels us to devote ourselves in faith to its realisation.

We are at the beginning of the end of the human race. The question before it is whether it will use for beneficial purposes or for purposes of destruction the power which modern science has placed in its hands. So long as its capacity for destruction was limited, it was possible to hope that reason would set a limit to disaster. Such an illusion is impossible to-day, when its power is illimitable. Our only hope is that the Spirit of God will strive with the spirit of the world and will prevail.

The last petition of the Lord's Prayer has again its original meaning for us as a prayer for deliverance from the dominion of the evil powers of the world. These are no less real to us as working in men's minds, instead of being embodied in angelic beings opposed to God. The first believers set their hope solely upon the Kingdom of God in expectation of the end of the world; we do it in expectation of the end of the human race.

The Spirit shows us the signs of the time and their meaning.

Belief in the Kingdom of God makes the biggest demands of all the articles of the Christian faith. It means believing the seemingly impossible,— the conquest of the spirit of the world by the Spirit of God. We look with confidence for the miracle to be wrought through the Spirit.

The miracle must happen in us before it can happen in the world. We dare not set our hope on our own efforts to create the conditions of God's Kingdom in the world. We must indeed labour for its realisation. But there can be no Kingdom of God in the world without the Kingdom of God in our hearts. The starting-point is our determined effort to bring every thought and action under the sway of the Kingdom of God. Nothing can be achieved without inwardness. The Spirit of God will only strive against the spirit of the world when it has won its victory over that spirit in our hearts.

Martin Buber was born in Vienna in 1878. Before 1933, he was a professor at the University of Frankfurt, Germany; from 1938 until his retirement, he was a professor at the Hebrew University in Jerusalem. In Germany he also participated in various adult education projects, and since the War he has lectured in many countries, including the United States. His influence as a teacher has not been confined to his students at Frankfurt and Jerusalem; many others consider him one of the great teachers of his generation.

Hasidim, literally translated, means pious ones; and Hasidism, pietism. The Hasidim whose lore Buber has collected and written about were members of a religious movement founded in the eighteenth century by Israel ben Eliezer (about 1699-1760), whom his disciples called the Baal Shem Tov or Baal Shem, which means Master of the (Good) Name, i.e., the name of God. For a view of Hasidism somewhat different from Buber's, see Scholem's *Major Trends of Jewish Mysticism.* The abiding importance of Buber's *Tales of the Hasidim* and of the following selection does not hinge on the historical accuracy of his interpretations which, though controversial, have their defenders. These stories, even if they should owe something to Buber, are among the great religious stories of all time. And what makes a gem is, not least, the art of cutting.

The Way of Man according to the Teachings of Hasidism was originally published as a separate book and is reprinted here without omission.

The Way of Man According to the Teachings of Hasidism

INTRODUCTION

In most systems of belief the believer considers that he can achieve a perfect relationship to God by renouncing the world of the senses and overcoming his own natural being. Not so the hasid. Certainly, "cleaving" unto God is to him the highest aim of the human person, but to achieve it he is not required to abandon the external and internal reality of earthly being, but to affirm it in its true, God-oriented essence and thus so to transform it that he can offer it up to God.

Hasidism is no pantheism. It teaches the absolute transcendence of God, but as combined with his conditioned immanence. The world is an irradiation of God, but as it is endowed with an independence of existence and striving, it is apt, always and everywhere, to form a crust around itself. Thus, a divine spark lives in every thing and being, but each such spark is enclosed by an isolating shell. Only man can liberate it and re-join it with the Origin: by holding holy converse with the thing and using it in a holy manner, that is, so that his intention in doing so remains directed toward God's transcendence. Thus the divine immanence emerges from the exile of the "shells."

But also in man, in every man, is a force divine. And in man far more than in all other beings it can pervert itself, can be misused by himself. This happens if he, instead of directing it toward its origin, allows it to run directionless and seize at everything that offers itself to it; instead of hallowing passion, he makes it evil. But here, too, a way to redemption is open: he who with the entire force of his being "turns" to God, at this his point of the universe lifts the divine immanence out of its debasement, which he has caused.

The task of man, of every man, according to hasidic teaching, is to affirm for God's sake the world and himself and by this very means to transform both.

I. HEART-SEARCHING

Rabbi Shneur Zalman, the *rav*[1] of Northern White Russia (died 1813), was put in jail in Petersburg, because the *mitnagdim*[2] had denounced his principles and his way of living to the government. He was awaiting trial when the chief of the gendarmes entered his cell. The majestic and quiet face of the rav, who was so deep in meditation that he did not at first notice his visitor, suggested to the chief, a thoughtful person, what manner of man he had before him. He began to converse with his prisoner and brought up a number of questions which had occurred to him in reading the Scriptures. Finally he asked: "How are we to understand that God, the all-knowing, said to Adam: 'Where art thou?'"

"Do you believe," answered the rav, "that the Scriptures are eternal and that every era, every generation and every man is included in them?"

"I believe this," said the other.

"Well then," said the zaddik, "in every era, God calls to every man: 'Where are you in your world? So many years and days of those allotted to you have passed, and how far have you gotten in your world?' God says something like this: 'You have lived forty-six years. How far along are you?'"

When the chief of the gendarmes heard his age mentioned, he pulled himself together, laid his hand on the rav's shoulder, and cried: "Bravo!" But his heart trembled.

What happens in this tale?

At first sight, it reminds us of certain Talmudic stories in which a Roman or some other heathen questions a Jewish sage about a Biblical passage, with

---

[1] Rabbi.   [2] Adversaries (of Hasidism).

a view to exposing an alleged contradiction in Jewish religious doctrine, and receives a reply which either explains that there is no such contradiction or refutes the questioner's arguments in some other way; sometimes, a personal admonition is added to the actual reply. But we soon perceive an important difference between those Talmudic stories and this Hasidic one, though at first the difference appears greater than it actually is. It consists in the fact that in the Hasidic story the reply is given on a different plane from that on which the question is asked.

The chief wants to expose an alleged contradiction in Jewish doctrine. The Jews profess to believe in God as the all-knowing, but the Bible makes him ask questions as they are asked by someone who wants to learn something he does not know. God seeks Adam, who has hidden himself. He calls into the garden, asking where he is; it would thus seem that He does not know it, that it is possbile to hide from Him and, consequently, that He is not all-knowing. Now, instead of explaining the passage and solving the seeming contradiction, the rabbi takes the text merely as a starting point from where he proceeds to reproach the chief with his past life, his lack of seriousness, his thoughtlessness and irresponsibility. An impersonal question which, however seriously it may be meant in the present instance, is in fact no genuine question but merely a form of controversy, calls forth a personal reply or, rather, a personal admonition in lieu of a reply. It thus seems as if nothing had remained of those Talmudic answers but the admonition which sometimes accompanied them.

But let us examine the story more closely. The chief inquires about a passage from the Biblical story of Adam's sin. The rabbi's answer means, in effect: "You yourself are Adam, you are the man whom God asks: 'Where art thou?' " It would thus seem that the answer gives no explanation of the passage as such. In fact, however, it illuminates both the situation of the Biblical Adam and that of every man in every time and in every place. For as soon as the chief hears and understands that the Biblical question is addressed to him, he is bound to realize what it means when God asks: "Where art thou?" whether the question be addressed to Adam or to some other man. In so asking, God does not expect to learn something he does not know; what he wants is to produce an effect in man which can only be produced by just such a question, provided that it reaches man's heart—that man allows it to reach his heart.

Adam hides himself to avoid rendering accounts, to escape responsibility for his way of living. Every man hides for this purpose, for every man is Adam and finds himself in Adam's situation. To escape responsibility for his life, he turns existence into a system of hideouts. And in thus hiding again and again "from the face of God," he enmeshes himself more and more deeply in perversity. A new situation thus arises, which becomes more and more questionable with every day, with every new hideout. This situation can be precisely defined as follows: Man cannot escape the eye of God, but in trying to hide from Him, he is hiding from himself. True, in him too there is something that seeks him, but he makes it harder and harder for that "something" to find him. This is the situation into which God's question falls. This question is designed to awaken man and destroy his system of hideouts; it is to show man to what pass he has come and to awake in him the great will to get out of it.

Everything now depends on whether man faces the question. Of course, every man's heart, like that of the chief in the story, will tremble when he hears it. But his system of hideouts will help to overcome this emotion. For the Voice does not come in a thunderstorm which threatens man's very existence; it is a "still small voice," and easy to drown. So long as this is done, man's life will not become a *way*. Whatever success and enjoyment he may achieve, whatever power he may attain and whatever deeds he may do, his life will remain way-less, so long as he does not face the Voice. Adam faces the Voice, perceives his enmeshment, and avows: "I hid myself"; this is the beginning of man's way. The decisive heart-searching is the beginning of the way in man's life; it is, again and again, the beginning of a human way.

But heart-searching is decisive only if it leads to the way. For there is a sterile kind of heart-searching, which leads to nothing but self-torture, despair and still deeper enmeshment. When the Rabbi of Ger,[1] in expounding the Scriptures, came to the words which Jacob addresses to his servant: "When Esau my brother meets thee, and asks thee, saying, Whose art thou? and whither goest thou? and whose are these before thee?" he would say to his disciples: "Mark well how similar Esau's questions are to the saying of our sages: 'Consider three things. Know whence you came, whither you are going, and to whom you will have to render accounts.' Be very careful, for great caution should be exercised by him who considers these three things: lest Esau ask in him. For Esau, too, may ask these questions and bring man into a state of gloom."

There is a demonic question, a spurious question, which apes God's question, the question of Truth. Its characteristic is that it does not stop at: "Where art thou?" but continues: "From where you have got to, there is no way out." This is the wrong kind of heart-searching, which does not prompt man to turn or put him on the way, but, by representing turning as hopeless, drives him to a point where it appears to have become entirely impossible and lets him go on living only by demonic pride, the pride of perversity.

II. THE PARTICULAR WAY

Rabbi Baer of Radoshitz once said to his teacher, the "Seer" of Lublin: "Show me one general way to the service of God."

[1] Góra Kalwarya near Warsaw.

The zaddik replied: "It is impossible to tell men what way they should take. For one way to serve God is through learning, another through prayer, another through fasting, and still another through eating. Everyone should carefully observe what way his heart draws him to, and then choose this way with all his strength."

In the first place, this story tells us something about our relationship to such genuine service as was performed by others before us. We are to revere it and learn from it, but we are not to imitate it. The great and holy deeds done by others are examples for us, since they show, in a concrete manner, what greatness and holiness is, but they are not models which we should copy. However small our achievements may be in comparison with those of our forefathers, they have their real value in that we bring them about in our own way and by our own efforts.

The *maggid*[1] of Zlotchov[2] was asked by a Hasid: "We are told: 'Everyone in Israel is in duty bound to say: When will my work approach the works of my fathers, Abraham, Isaac and Jacob?' How are we to understand this? How could we ever venture to think that we could do what our fathers did?"

The rabbi expounded: "Just as our fathers founded new ways of serving, each a new service according to his character: one the service of love, the other that of stern justice, the third that of beauty, so each of us in his own way shall devise something new in the light of teachings and of service, and do what has not yet been done."

Every person born into this world represents something new, something that never existed before, something original and unique. "It is the duty of every person in Israel to know and consider that he is unique in the world in his particular character and that there has never been anyone like him in the world, for if there had been someone like him, there would have been no need for him to be in the world. Every single man is a new thing in the world and is called upon to fulfill his particularity in this world. For verily: that this is not done is the reason why the coming of the Messiah is delayed." Every man's foremost task is the actualization of his unique, unprecedented and never-recurring potentialities, and not the repetition of something that another, and be it even the greatest, has already achieved.

The wise Rabbi Bunam once said in old age, when he had already grown blind: "I should not like to change places with our father Abraham! What good would it do God if Abraham became like blind Bunam, and blind Bunam became like Abraham? Rather than have this happen, I think I shall try to become a little more myself."

The same idea was expressed with even greater pregnancy by Rabbi Susya when he said, a short while before his death: "In the world to come I

---

[1] preacher.　　　　　　　　　　　　　[2] town in Eastern Galicia.

shall not be asked: 'Why were you not Moses?' I shall be asked: 'Why were you not Susya?' "

We are here confronted with a doctrine which is based on the fact that men are essentially unlike one another, and which therefore does not aim at making them alike. All men have access to God, but each man has a different access. Mankind's great chance lies precisely in the unlikeness of men, in the unlikeness of their qualities and inclinations. God's all-inclusiveness manifests itself in the infinite multiplicity of the ways that lead to him, each of which is open to one man. When some disciples of a deceased zaddik came to the Seer of Lublin and expressed surprise at the fact that his customs were different from those of their late master, the Seer exclaimed: "What sort of God would that be who has only one way in which he can be served!" But by the fact that each man, starting from his particular place and in a manner determined by his particular nature, is able to reach God, God can be reached by mankind, as such, through its multiple advance by all those different ways.

God does not say: "This way leads to me and that does not," but he says: "Whatever you do may be a way to me, provided you do it in such a manner that it leads you to me." But what it is that can and shall be done by just this person and no other can be revealed to him only in himself. In this matter, as I said before, it would only be misleading to study the achievements of another man and endeavor to equal him; for, in so doing, a man would miss precisely what he and he alone is called upon to do. The Baal-Shem said: "Every man should behave according to his 'rung.' If he does not, if he seizes the 'rung' of a fellow man and abandons his own, he will actualize neither the one nor the other." Thus, the way by which a man can reach God is revealed to him only through the knowledge of his own being, the knowledge of his essential quality and inclination. "Everyone has in him something precious that is in no one else." But this precious something in a man is revealed to him if he truly perceives his strongest feeling, his central wish, that in him which stirs his inmost being.

Of course, in many cases, a man knows this his strongest feeling only in the shape of a particular passion, of the "Evil Urge" which seeks to lead him astray. Naturally, a man's most powerful desire, in seeking satisfaction, rushes in the first instance at objects which lie across his path. It is necessary, therefore, that the power of even this feeling, of even this impulse, be diverted from the casual to the essential, and from the relative to the absolute. Thus a man finds his way.

A zaddik once said: "At the end of Ecclesiastes we read: 'At the end of the matter, the whole is heard: Fear God.' Whatever matter you follow to its end, there, at the end, you will hear one thing: 'Fear God,' and this one thing is the whole. There is no thing in the world which does not point a way to the fear of God and to the service of God. Everything is commandment."

By no means, however, can it be our true task, in the world into which we have been set, to turn away from the things and beings that we meet on our way and that attract our hearts; our task is precisely to get in touch, by hallowing our relationship with them, with what manifests itself in them as beauty, pleasure, enjoyment. Hasidism teaches that rejoicing in the world, if we hallow it with our whole being, leads to rejoicing in God.

One point in the tale of the Seer seems to contradict this, namely, that among the examples of "ways" we find not only eating but also fasting. But if we consider this in the general context of Hasidic teaching, it appears that though detachment from nature, abstinence from natural life, may, in the cases of some men, mean the necessary starting point of their "way" or, perhaps, a necessary act of self-isolation at certain crucial moments of existence, it may never mean the whole way. Some men must begin by fasting, and begin by it again and again, because it is peculiar to them that only by asceticism can they achieve liberation from their enslavement to the world, deepest heart-searching and ultimate communion with the Absolute. But never should asceticism gain mastery over a man's life. A man may only detach himself from nature in order to revert to it again and, in hallowed contact with it, find his way to God.

The Biblical passage which says of Abraham and the three visiting angels: "And he stood over them under the tree and they did eat" is interpreted by Rabbi Susya to the effect that man stands above the angels, because he knows something unknown to them, namely, that eating may be hallowed by the eater's intention. Through Abraham the angels, who were unaccustomed to eating, participated in the intention by which he dedicated it to God. Any natural act, if hallowed, leads to God, and nature needs man for what no angel can perform on it, namely, its hallowing.

III. RESOLUTION

A Hasid of the rabbi of Lublin once fasted from one Sabbath to the next. On Friday afternoon he began to suffer such cruel thirst that he thought he would die. He saw a well, went up to it, and prepared to drink. But instantly he realized that because of the one brief hour he had still to endure, he was about to destroy the work of the entire week. He did not drink and went away from the well. Then he was touched by a feeling of pride for having passed this difficult test. When he became aware of it, he said to himself, "Better I go and drink than let my heart fall prey to pride." He went back to the well, but just as he was going to bend down to draw water, he noticed that his thirst had disappeared. When the Sabbath had begun, he entered his teacher's house. "Patchwork!" the rabbi called to him, as he crossed the threshold.

When in my youth I heard this tale for the first time, I was struck by the harsh manner in which the master treats his zealous disciple. The latter makes his utmost efforts to perform a difficult feat of asceticism. He feels tempted to break off and overcomes the temptation, but his only reward, after all his trouble, is an expression of disapproval from his teacher. It is true that the disciple's first inhibition was due to the power of the body over the soul, a power which had still to be broken, but the second sprang from a truly noble motive: better to fail than, for the sake of succeeding, fall prey to pride. How can a man be scolded for such an inner struggle? Is this not asking too much of a man?

Long afterwards (but still early as a quarter of a century ago), when I myself retold this tale from tradition, I understood that there was no question here of something being asked of a man. The zaddik of Lublin was no friend of asceticism, and the Hasid's fast was certainly not designed to please him, but to lift the Hasid's soul to a higher "rung"; the Seer himself had admitted that fasting could serve this purpose in the initial stage of a person's development and also later, at critical moments of his life. What the master—apparently after watching the progress of the venture with true understanding—says to the disciple means undoubtedly: "This is not the proper manner to attain a higher rung." He warns the disciple of something that perforce hinders him from achieving his purpose. What this is becomes clear enough. The object of the reproof is the advance and subsequent retreat; it is the wavering, shilly-shallying character of the man's doing that make it questionable. The opposite of "patchwork" is work "all of a piece." Now, how does one achieve work "all of a piece"? Only with a united soul.

Again we are troubled by the question whether this man is not being treated too harshly. As things are in this world, one man—"by nature" or "by grace," however one chooses to put it—has a unitary soul, a soul all of a piece, and accordingly performs unitary works, works all of a piece, because his soul, by being as it is, prompts and enables him to do so; another man has a divided, complicated, contradictory soul, and this, naturally, affects his doings: their inhibitions and disturbances originate in the inhibitions and disturbances of his soul; its restlessness is expressed in their restlessness. What else can a man so constituted do than try to overcome the temptations which approach him on the way to what is, at a given time, his goal? What else can he do than each time, in the middle of his doing, "pull himself together," as we say, that is, rally his vacillating soul, and again and again, having rallied it, re-concentrate it upon the goal—and moreover be ready, like the Hasid in the story when pride touches him, to sacrifice the goal in order to save the soul?

Only when, in the light of these questions, we subject our story to renewed scrutiny, do we apprehend the teaching implied in the Seer's criticism. It is the teaching that a man can unify his soul. The man with the divided, complicated, contradictory soul is not helpless: the core of his soul, the divine force in its depths, is capable of acting upon it, changing it, binding the conflicting forces together, amalgamating the diverging elements—is capable of unifying it. This unification must be accomplished *before* a man undertakes some unusual work. Only with a united soul will he be able so to do it that it becomes not patchwork but work all of a piece. The Seer thus reproaches the hasid with having embarked on his venture without first unifying his soul; unity of soul can never be achieved in the middle of the work. Nor should it be supposed that it can be brought about by asceticism; asceticism can purify, concentrate, but it cannot preserve its achievements intact until the attainment of the goal—it cannot protect the soul from its own contradiction.

One thing must of course not be lost sight of: unification of the soul is never final. Just as a soul most unitary from birth is sometimes beset by inner difficulties, thus even a soul most powerfully struggling for unity can never completely achieve it. But any work that I do with a united soul reacts upon my soul, acts in the direction of new and greater unification, leads me, though by all sorts of detours, to a *steadier* unity than was the preceding one. Thus man ultimately reaches a point where he can rely upon his soul, because its unity is now so great that it overcomes contradiction with effortless ease. Vigilance, of course, is necessary even then, but it is a relaxed vigilance.

On one of the days of the Hanukkah feast, Rabbi Nahum, the son of the rabbi of Rishyn,[1] entered the House of Study at a time when he was not expected and found his disciples playing checkers, as was the custom on those days. When they saw the zaddik they were embarrassed and stopped playing. But he gave them a kindly nod and asked: "Do you know the rules of the game of checkers?" And when they did not reply for shyness he himself gave the answer: "I shall tell you the rules of the game of checkers. The first is that one must not make two moves at once. The second is that one may only move forward and not backward. And the third is that when one has reached the last row, one may move wherever one likes."

However, what is meant by unification of the soul would be thoroughly misunderstood if "soul" were taken to mean anything but: the whole man, body and spirit together. The soul is not really united, unless all bodily energies, all the limbs of the body, are united. The Baal-Shem interpreted the Biblical passage: "Whatsoever thy hand finds to do, do it with thy might" to the effect that the deeds one does should be done with every limb, i.e., even the whole of man's physical being should participate in it, no part of him should remain outside. A man who thus becomes a unit of body and spirit—he is the man whose work is all of a piece.

[1] Ružyn (District of Kiev). Rabbi Israel of Rishyn was the founder of the famous "Dynasty of Sadagora."

IV. BEGINNING WITH ONESELF

Once when Rabbi Yitzhak of Vorki was playing host to certain prominent men of Israel, they discussed the value to a household of an honest and efficient servant. They said that a good servant made for good management and cited Joseph at whose hands everything prospered. Rabbi Yitzhak objected. "I once thought that too," he said. "But then my teacher showed me that everything depends on the master of the house. You see, in my youth my wife gave me a great deal of trouble and, though I myself put up with her as best I could, I was sorry for the servants. So I went to my teacher, Rabbi David of Lelov, and asked him whether I should oppose my wife. All he said was: 'Why do you speak to me? Speak to yourself!' I thought over these words for quite a while before I understood them. But I did understand them when I recalled a certain saying of the Baal-Shem: 'There is thought, speech and action. Thought corresponds to one's wife, speech to one's children, and action to one's servants. Whoever straightens himself out in regard to all three will find that everything prospers at his hands.' Then I understood what my teacher had meant: everything depended on myself."

This story touches upon one of the deepest and most difficult problems of our life: the true origin of conflict between man and man.

Manifestations of conflict are usually explained either by the motives of which the quarreling parties are conscious as the occasion of their quarrel, and by the objective situations and processes which underlie these motives and in which both parties are involved; or, proceeding analytically, we try to explore the unconscious complexes to which these motives relate like mere symptoms of an illness to the organic disturbances themselves. Hasidic teaching coincides with this conception in that it, too, derives the problematics of external from that of internal life. But it differs in two essential points, one fundamental and one practical, the latter of which is even more important than the former.

The fundamental difference is that Hasidic teaching is not concerned with the exploration of particular psychical complications, but envisages man as a whole. This is, however, by no means a quantitative difference. For the Hasidic conception springs from the realization that the isolation of elements and partial processes from the whole hinders the comprehension of the whole, and that real transformation, real restoration, at first of the single person and subsequently of the relationship between him and his fellow men, can only be achieved by the comprehension of the whole as a whole. (Putting it paradoxically: the search for the center of gravity shifts it and thereby frustrates the whole attempt at overcoming the problematics involved.) This is not to say that there is no need to consider all the phenomena of the soul; but no one of them should be made so much the center of attention as if everything else could be derived from it; rather, they shall all be made starting points—not singly but in their vital connection.

The practical difference is that in Hasidism man is not treated as an object of examination but is called upon to "straighten himself out." At first, a man should himself realize that conflict-situations between himself and others are nothing but the effects of conflict-situations in his own soul; then he should try to overcome this inner conflict, so that afterwards he may go out to his fellow men and enter into new, transformed relationships with them.

Man naturally tries to avoid this decisive reversal—extremely repugnant to him in his accustomed relationship to the world—by referring him who thus appeals to him, or his own soul, if it is his soul that makes the appeal, to the fact that every conflict involves two parties and that, if he is expected to turn his attention from the external to his own internal conflict, his opponent should be expected to do the same. But just this perspective, in which a man sees himself only as an individual contrasted with other individuals, and not as a genuine person, whose transformation helps toward the transformation of the world, contains the fundamental error which Hasidic teaching denounces. The essential thing is to begin with oneself, and at this moment a man has nothing in the world to care about other than this beginning. Any other attitude would distract him from what he is about to begin, weaken his initiative, and thus frustrate the entire bold undertaking.

Rabbi Bunam taught:

"Our sages say: 'Seek peace in your own place.' You cannot find peace anywhere save in your own self. In the psalm we read: 'There is no peace in my bones because of my sin.' When a man has made peace within himself, he will be able to make peace in the whole world."

However, the story from which I started does not confine itself to pointing out the true origin of external conflicts, i.e., the internal conflict, in a general way. The quoted saying of the Baal-Shem states exactly in what the decisive inner conflict consists. It is the conflict between three principles in man's being and life, the principle of thought, the principle of speech, and the principle of action. The origin of all conflict between me and my fellow men is that I do not say what I mean, and that I do not do what I say. For this confuses and poisons, again and again and in increasing measure, the situation between myself and the other man, and I, in my internal disintegration, am no longer able to master it but, contrary to all my illusions, have become its slave. By our contradiction, our lie, we foster conflict-situations and give them power over us until they enslave us. From here, there is no way out but by the crucial realization: Everything depends on myself; and the crucial decision: I will straighten myself out.

But in order that a man may be capable of this great feat, he must first find his way from the casual, accessory elements of his existence to his own self; he must find his own self, not the trivial ego of the egotistic individual, but the deeper self of the person living in a relationship to the world. And that is also contrary to everything we are accustomed to.

I will close this chapter with an old jest as retold by a zaddik.

Rabbi Hanokh told this story:

There was once a man who was very stupid. When he got up in the morning it was so hard for him to find his clothes that at night he almost hesitated to go to bed for thinking of the trouble he would have on waking. One evening he finally made a great effort, took paper and pencil and as he undressed noted down exactly where he put everything he had on. The next morning, very well pleased with himself, he took the slip of paper in his hand and read: "cap"—there it was, he set it on his head; "pants"—there they lay, he got into them; and so it went until he was fully dressed. "That's all very well, but now where am I myself?" he asked in great consternation. "Where in the world am I?" He looked and looked, but it was a vain search; he could not find himself. "And that is how it is with us," said the rabbi.

V. NOT TO BE PREOCCUPIED WITH ONESELF

Rabbi Hayyim of Zans[1] had married his son to the daughter of Rabbi Eliezer. The day after the wedding he visited the father of the bride and said: "Now that we are related I feel close to you and can tell you what is eating at my heart. Look! My hair and beard have grown white, and I have not yet atoned!"

"O my friend," replied Rabbi Eliezer, "you are thinking only of yourself. How about forgetting yourself and thinking of the world?"

What is said here seems to contradict everything I have hitherto reported of the teachings of Hasidism. We have heard that everyone should search his own heart, choose his particular way, bring about the unity of his being, begin with himself; and now we are told that man should forget himself. But, if we examine this injunction more closely, we find that it is not only consistent with the others but fits into the whole as a necessary link, as a necessary stage, in its particular place. One need only ask one question: "What for?" What am I to choose by particular way for? What am I to unify my being for? The reply is: Not for my own sake. This is why the previous injunction was: to *begin* with oneself. To begin with oneself, but not to end with oneself; to start from oneself, but not to aim at oneself; to comprehend oneself, but not to be preoccupied with oneself.

We see a zaddik, a wise, pious, kindly man, reproach himself in his old

[1] Nowy Sacz in Western Galicia.

age for not yet having performed the true turning. The reply given him is apparently prompted by the opinion that he greatly overrates his sins and greatly underrates the penance he has already done. But what Rabbi Eliezer says goes beyond this. He says, in quite a general sense: "Do not keep worrying about what you have done wrong, but apply the soul-power you are now wasting on self-reproach to such active relationship to the world as you are destined for. You should not be occupied with yourself but with the world."

First of all, we should properly understand what is said here about turning. It is known that turning stands in the center of the Jewish conception of the way of man. Turning is capable of renewing a man from within and changing his position in God's world, so that he who turns is seen standing above the perfect zaddik who does not know the abyss of sin. But turning means here something much greater than repentance and acts of penance; it means that, by a reversal of his whole being, a man who had been lost in the maze of selfishness, where he had always set himself as his goal, finds a way to God, that is, a way to the fulfillment of the particular task for which he, this particular man, has been destined by God. Repentance can only be an incentive to such active reversal; he who goes on fretting himself with repentance, he who tortures himself with the idea that his acts of penance are not sufficient, withholds his best energies from the work of reversal. In a sermon on the Day of Atonement, the Rabbi of Ger warned against self-torture:

"He who has done ill and talks about it and thinks about it all the time does not cast the base thing he did out of his thoughts, and whatever one thinks therein one is, one's soul is wholly and utterly in what one thinks, and so he dwells in baseness. He will certainly not be able to turn, for his spirit will grow coarse and his heart stubborn, and in addition to this he may be overcome by gloom. What would you? Rake the muck this way, rake the muck that way—it will always be muck. Have I sinned, or have I not sinned—what does Heaven get out of it? In the time I am brooding over it I could be stringing pearls for the delight of Heaven. That is why it is written: 'Depart from evil and do good'—turn wholly away from evil, do not dwell upon it, and do good. You have done wrong? Then counteract it by doing right."

But the significance of our story goes beyond this. He who tortures himself incessantly with the idea that he has not yet sufficiently atoned is essentially concerned with the salvation of his soul, with his personal fate in eternity. By rejecting this aim, Hasidism merely draws a conclusion from the teachings of Judaism generally. One of the main points in which Christianity differs from Judaism is that it makes each man's salvation his highest aim. Judaism regards each man's soul as a serving member of God's Creation which, by man's work, is to become the Kingdom of God; thus no soul has its object in itself, in its own salvation. True, each is to know itself, purify itself, perfect itself, but not for its own sake—neither for the sake of its temporal happiness nor for that of its eternal bliss—but for the sake of the work which it is destined to perform upon the world.

The pursuit of one's own salvation is here regarded merely as the sublimest form of self-intending. Self-intending is what Hasidism rejects most emphatically, and quite especially in the case of the man who has found and developed his own self. Rabbi Bunam said: "It is written: 'Now Korah took.' What did he take? He wanted to take himself—therefore, nothing he did could be of any worth." This is why Bunam contrasted the eternal Korah with the eternal Moses, the "humble" man, whose doings are not aimed at himself. Rabbi Bunam taught: "In every generation the soul of Moses and the soul of Korah return. But if once, in days to come, the soul of Korah is willing to subject itself to the soul of Moses, Korah will be redeemed."

Rabbi Bunam thus sees, as it were, the history of mankind on its road to redemption as a process involving two kinds of men, the proud who, if sometimes in the sublimest form, think of themselves, and the humble, who in all matters think of the world. Only when pride subjects itself to humility can it be redeemed; and only when it is redeemed can the world be redeemed.

After Rabbi Bunam's death, one of his disciples—the aforementioned Rabbi of Ger, from whose sermon on the Day of Atonement I quoted a few sentences—remarked: "Rabbi Bunam had the keys to all the firmaments. And why not? A man who does not think of himself is given all the keys."

The greatest of Rabbi Bunam's disciples, a truly tragic figure among the zaddikim, Rabbi Mendel of Kotzk, once said to his congregation: "What, after all, do I demand of you? Only three things: not to look furtively outside yourself, not to look furtively into others, and not to aim at yourselves." That is to say: firstly, everyone should preserve and hallow his own soul in its own particularity and in its own place and not envy the particularity and place of others; secondly, everyone should respect the secret in the soul of his fellow man and not, with brazen curiosity, intrude upon it and take advantage of it; and thirdly, everyone, in his relationship to the world, should be careful not to set himself as his aim.

VI. HERE WHERE ONE STANDS

Rabbi Bunam used to tell young men who came to him for the first time the story of Rabbi Eizik, son of Rabbi Yekel of Cracow. After many years of great poverty which had never shaken his faith in God, he dreamed someone bade him look for a treasure in Prague, under the bridge which leads to the king's palace. When the dream recurred a third time, Rabbi

Eizik prepared for the journey and set out for Prague. But the bridge was guarded day and night and he did not dare to start digging. Nevertheless he went to the bridge every morning and kept walking around it until evening. Finally the captain of the guards, who had been watching him, asked in a kindly way whether he was looking for something or waiting for somebody. Rabbi Eizik told him of the dream which had brought him here from a faraway country. The captain laughed: "And so to please the dream, you poor fellow wore out your shoes to come here! As for having faith in dreams, if I had had it, I should have had to get going when a dream once told me to go to Cracow and dig for treasure under the stove in the room of a Jew—Eizik, son of Yekel, that was the name! Eizik, son of Yekel! I can just imagine what it would be like, how I should have to try every house over there, where one half of the Jews are named Eizik and the other Yekel!" And he laughed again. Rabbi Eizik bowed, traveled home, dug up the treasure from under the stove, and built the House of Prayer which is called "Reb Eizik Reb Yekel's Shul."

"Take this story to heart," Rabbi Bunam used to add, "and make what it says your own: There is something you cannot find anywhere in the world, not even at the zaddik's, and there is, nevertheless, a place where you can find it."

This, too, is a very old story, known from several popular literatures, but thoroughly reshaped by Hasidism. It has not merely—in a superficial sense—been transplanted into the Jewish sphere, it has been recast by the Hasidic melody in which it has been told; but even this is not decisive: the decisive change is that it has become, so to speak, transparent, and that a Hasidic truth is shining through its words. It has not had a "moral" appended to it, but the sage who retold it had at last discovered its true meaning and made it apparent.

There is something that can only be found in one place. It is a great treasure, which may be called the fulfillment of existence. The place where this treasure can be found is the place on which one stands.

Most of us achieve only at rare moments a clear realization of the fact that they have never tasted the fulfillment of existence, that their life does not participate in true, fulfilled existence, that, as it were, it passes true existence by. We nevertheless feel the deficiency at every moment, and in some measure strive to find—somewhere—what we are seeking. Somewhere, in some province of the world or of the mind, except where we stand, where we have been set—but it is there and nowhere else that the treasure can be found. The environment which I feel to be the natural one, the situation which has been assigned to me as my fate, the things that happen to me day after day, the things that claim me day after day—these contain my essential task and such fulfillment of existence as is open to me. It is said of a certain Talmudic master that the paths of heaven were as bright to him as the streets of his native town. Hasidism inverts the order: It is a greater thing if the streets of a man's native town are as bright to him as the paths of heaven. For it is here, where we stand, that we should try to make shine the light of the hidden divine life.

If we had power over the ends of the earth, it would not give us that fulfillment of existence which a quiet devoted relationship to nearby life can give us. If we knew the secrets of the upper worlds, they would not allow us so much actual participation in true existence as we can achieve by performing, with holy intent, a task belonging to our daily duties. Our treasure is hidden beneath the hearth of our own home.

The Baal-Shem teaches that no encounter with a being or a thing in the course of our life lacks a hidden significance. The people we live with or meet with, the animals that help us with our farm work, the soil we till, the materials we shape, the tools we use, they all contain a mysterious spiritual substance which depends on us for helping it toward its pure form, its perfection. It we neglect this spiritual substance sent across our path, if we think only in terms of momentary purposes, without developing a genuine relationship to the beings and things in whose life we ought to take part, as they in ours, then we shall ourselves be debarred from true, fulfilled existence. It is my conviction that this doctrine is essentially true. The highest culture of the soul remains basically arid and barren unless, day by day, waters of life pour forth into the soul from those little encounters to which we give their due; the most formidable power is intrinsically powerlessness unless it maintains a secret covenant with these contacts, both humble and helpful, with strange, and yet near, being.

Some religions do not regard our sojourn on earth as true life. They either teach that everything appearing to us here is mere appearance, behind which we should penetrate, or that it is only a forecourt of the true world, a forecourt which we should cross without paying much attention to it. Judaism, on the contrary, teaches that what a man does now and here with holy intent is no less important, no less true—being a terrestrial indeed, but none the less factual, link with divine being—than the life in the world to come. This doctrine has found its fullest expression in Hasidism.

Rabbi Hanokh said: "The other nations too believe that there are two worlds. They too say: 'In the other world.' The difference is this: They think that the two are separate and severed, but Israel professes that the two worlds are essentially one and shall in fact become one."

In their true essence, the two worlds are one. They only have, as it were, moved apart. But they shall again become one, as they are in their true essence. Man was created for the purpose of unifying the two worlds. He contributes toward this unity by holy living, in relationship to the world in which he has been set, at the place on which he stands.

Once they told Rabbi Pinhas of the great misery among the needy. He listened, sunk in grief. Then he raised his head. "Let us draw God into the world," he cried, "and all need will be stilled."

But is this possible, to draw God into the world? Is this not an arrogant, presumptuous idea? How dare the lowly worm touch upon a matter which depends entirely on God's grace: how much of Himself He will vouchsafe to His creation?

Here again, Jewish doctrine is opposed to that of other religions, and again it is in Hasidism that it has found its fullest expression. God's grace consists precisely in this, that He wants to let Himself be won by man, that He places Himself, so to speak, into man's hands. God wants to come to His world, but He wants to come to it through man. This is the mystery of our existence, the superhuman chance of mankind.

"Where is the dwelling of God?"

This was the question with which the Rabbi of Kotzk surprised a number of learned men who happened to be visiting him.

They laughed at him: "What a thing to ask! Is not the whole world full of His glory?"

Then he answered his own question:

"God dwells wherever man lets Him in."

This is the ultimate purpose: to let God in. But we can let Him in only where we really stand, where we live, where we live a true life. If we maintain holy intercourse with the little world entrusted to us, if we help the holy spiritual substance to accomplish itself in that section of Creation in which we are living, then we are establishing, in this our place, a dwelling for the Divine Presence.

Albert Camus was born in Algeria in 1913. During World War II he was active in the French Resistance and edited the paper *Combat*. His novel, *L'Étranger* (1942; *The Stranger*) attracted wide attention. So did *Le Mythe de Sisyphe* (*The Myth of Sisyphus*), published the same year. His second novel, *La Peste* (1947; *The Plague*), established Camus' international reputation. His major philosophic attempt, *L'Homme Révolté* (1951; *The Rebel*), was well received as a declaration of conscience but not acclaimed by professional philosophers. *La Chute* (1956; *The Fall*) is a brilliant novella after the manner of Dostoevsky's *Notes from Underground;* but, in opposition to Dostoevsky's hero, Camus' has "never felt comfortable except in lofty places," and he has a deep need "to feel above."

Camus received the Nobel Prize for literature in 1957. Early in 1960, he was killed in an automobile accident.

He also published a volume of six short stories, *L'Exil et le Royaume* (1957; *Exile and the Kingdom*), and four plays, issued in English as *Caligula & Three Other Plays* (1958). A collection of his editorials, essays, and miscellaneous pieces, which Camus himself selected from the three volumes of his *Actuelles* (1950, 1953, 1958), was published in English as *Resistance, Rebellion, and Death* (1961). This volume includes "Reflections on the Guillotine"; but the following translation is that which appeared earlier in the *Evergreen Review*, first in 1957, and then once more in 1960. Only the final part of the essay—about one quarter of the whole—is reprinted below.

Reflections on the Guillotine

*W*hat does the death penalty mean for us, half-way through the twentieth century? For the sake of simplification, let us say that our civilization has lost the only values that, to a certain degree, could justify the death penalty, and that it suffers, on the contrary, from every evil that necessitates its suppression. In other words, the abolition of the death penalty should be demanded by the conscious members of our society on grounds of both logic and fidelity to the facts.

Of logic, first of all. To decide that a man must be definitively punished is to deny him any further opportunity whatsoever to make reparation for his acts. It is at this juncture, we repeat, that the arguments for and against capital punishment confront one another blindly, eventuating in a fruitless checkmate. Yet it is exactly here that none of us can afford to be positive, for we are all judges, all party to the dispute. Hence our uncertainty about our right to kill and our impotence to convince others on either side. Unless there is absolute innocence, there can be no supreme judge. Now we have all committed some transgression in our lives, even if this transgression has not put us within the power of the law and has remained an unknown crime: there are no just men, only hearts more or less poor in justice. The mere fact of living permits us to know this, and to add to the sum of our actions a little of the good that might partially compensate for the evil we have brought into the world. This right to live that coincides with the opportunity for reparation is the natural right of every man, even the worst. The most abandoned criminal and the worthiest judge here find themselves side by side, equally miserable and jointly responsible. Without this right, the moral life is strictly impossible. None among us, in particular, is entitled to despair of a single man, unless it be after his death, which transforms his life into destiny and admits of a final judgment. But to pronounce this final judgment before death, to decree the closing of accounts when the creditor is still alive, is the privilege of no man. On these grounds, at least, he who judges absolutely condemns himself absolutely.

Barnard Fallot of the Masuy gang, who worked for the Gestapo, confessed to the entire list of terrible crimes of which he was accused and later went to his death with great courage, declaring himself beyond hope of reprieve: "My hands are too red with blood," he said to one of his fellow prisoners.[1] Public opinion and that of his judges certainly classified him among the irrecoverables, and I would have been tempted to put him in that category myself, had I not read one astonishing piece of evidence: after having declared that he wanted to die bravely, Fallot told the same prisoner: "Do you know what I regret most of all? Not having known sooner about the Bible they gave me here. If I had, I wouldn't be where I am now." It is not a question of surrendering to the sentimentality of conventional imagery and conjuring up Victor Hugo's good convicts. The age of enlightenment, as it is called, wished to abolish the death penalty under the pretext that man was fundamentally good. We know, of course, that he is not (he is simply better or worse). After the last twenty years of our splendid history we know it very well. But it is because man is not fundamentally good that no one among us can set himself up as an absolute judge, for no one among us can pretend to absolute innocence. The verdict of capital punishment destroys the only indisputable human community there is, the community in the face of death, and such a judgment can only be legitimated by a truth or a principle that takes its place above all men, beyond the human condition.

Capital punishment, in fact, throughout history has always been a religious punishment. When imposed in the name of the king, representative of

[1] Jean Bobognano, *Quartier des fauves, prison de Fresnes, Édition du Fuseau.*

God on earth, or by priests, or in the name of a society considered as a sacred body, it is not the human community that is destroyed but the functioning of the guilty man as a member of the divine community which alone can give him his life. Such a man is certainly deprived of his earthly life, yet his opportunity for reparation is preserved. The real judgment is not pronounced in this world, but in the next. Religious values, especially the belief in an eternal life, are thus the only ones on which the death penalty can be based, since according to their own logic they prevent that penalty from being final and irreparable: it is justified only insofar as it is not supreme.

The Catholic Church, for example, has always admitted the necessity of the death penalty. It has imposed the penalty itself, without avarice, at other periods. Today, its doctrines still justify capital punishment, and concede the State the right to apply it. No matter how subtle this doctrine may be, there is at its core a profound feeling which was directly expressed by a Swiss councilor from Fribourg during a discussion of capital punishment by the national council in 1937; according to M. Grand, even the worst criminal examines his own conscience when faced with the actuality of execution. "He repents, and his preparation for death is made easier. The Church has saved one of its members, has accomplished its divine mission. This is why the Church has steadfastly countenanced capital punishment, not only as a means of legitimate protection, but *as a powerful means of salvation.* . . . [My italics.] Without becoming precisely a matter of doctrine, the death penalty, like war itself, can be justified by its quasi-divine efficacity."

By virtue of the same reasoning, no doubt, one can read on the executioner's sword in Fribourg the motto "Lord Jesus, thou art the Judge." The executioner is thereby invested with a divine function. He is the man who destroys the body in order to deliver the soul to its divine judgment, which no man on earth can foresee. It will perhaps be considered that such mottos imply rather outrageous confusions, and certainly those who confine themselves to the actual teachings of Jesus will see this handsome sword as yet another outrage to the body of Christ. In this light can be understood the terrible words of a Russian prisoner whom the executioners of the Tsar were about to hang in 1905, when he turned to the priest who was about to console him with the image of Christ and said: "Stand back, lest you commit a sacrilege." An unbeliever will not fail to remark that those who have placed in the very center of their faith the overwhelming victim of a judicial error should appear more reticent, to say the least, when confronted by cases of legal murder. One might also remind the believer that the emperor Julian, before his conversion, refused to give official posts to Christians because they systematically refused to pronounce the death sentence or to aid in administering it. For five centuries Christians believed that the strict moral teaching of their master forbade them to kill. But the Catholic faith is derived not only from the teachings of Christ, it is nourished by the Old Testament, by Saint Paul, and by the Fathers as well. In particular the immortality of the soul and the universal resurrection of the body are articles of dogma. Hence, capital punishment, for the believer, can be regarded as a provisional punishment which does not in the least affect the definite sentence, but remains a disposition necessary to the terrestrial order, an administrative measure which, far from making an end of the guilty man, can promote, on the contrary, his redemption in heaven. I do not say that all believers follow this reasoning, and I can imagine without much difficulty that most Catholics stand closer to Christ than to Moses or Saint Paul. I say only that the belief in the immortality of the soul has permitted Catholicism to formulate the problem of capital punishment in very different terms, and to justify it.

But what does such a justification mean to the society we live in, a society which in its institutions and manners alike has become almost entirely secular? When an atheist—or skeptic—or agnostic judge imposes the death penalty on an unbelieving criminal, he is pronouncing a definitive punishment that cannot be revised. He sits upon God's throne,[1] but without possessing God's powers and, moreover, without believing in them. He condemns to death, in fact, because his ancestors believed in eternal punishment. Yet the society which he claims to represent pronounces, in reality, a purely eliminative measure, destroys the human community united against death, and sets itself up as an absolute value because it pretends to absolute power. Of course society traditionally assigns a priest to the condemned man, and the priest may legitimately hope that fear of punishment will help effect the condemned man's conversion. Yet who will accept this casuistry as the justification of a punishment so often inflicted and so often received in an entirely different spirit? It is one thing to believe and "therefore know not fear," and another to find one's faith through fear. Conversion by fire or the knife will always be suspect, and one can well understand why the Church renounced a triumph by terror over infidel hearts. In any case, a secularized society has nothing to gain from a conversion concerning which it professes complete disinterest: it enacts a consecrated punishment, and at the same time deprives that punishment of its justification and its utility alike. Delirious in its own behalf, society plucks the wicked from its bosom as if it were virtue personified. In the same way, an honorable man might kill his son who had strayed from the path of duty, saying, "Really, I didn't know what else I could do!" Society thus usurps the right of selection, as if it were nature, and adds a terrible suffering to the eliminative process, as if it were a redeeming god.

To assert, in any case, that a man must be absolutely cut off from society because he is absolutely wicked is the same as saying that society is absolutely good, which no sensible person will believe today. It will not be believed— in fact, it is easier to believe the contrary. Our society has become as diseased

---

[1] The decision of the jury is preceded by the formula "before God and my conscience. . . ."

and criminal as it is only because it has set itself up as its own final justification, and has had no concern but its own preservation and success in history. Certainly it is a secularized society, yet during the nineteenth century it began to fashion a kind of ersatz religion by proposing itself as an object of adoration. The doctrines of evolution, and the theories of selection that accompanied such doctrines, have proposed the future of society as its final end. The political utopias grafted onto these doctrines have proposed, at the end of time, a Golden Age that justifies in advance all intermediary enterprises. Society has grown accustomed to legalizing whatever can minister to its future, and consequently to usurping the supreme punishment in an absolute fashion: it has regarded as a crime and a sacrilege everything that contradicts its own intentions and temporal dogmas. In other words, the executioner, formerly a priest, has become a civil servant. The results surround us. Half-way through the century, our society, which has forfeited the logical right to pronounce the death penalty, must now abolish it for reasons of realism.

Confronted with crime, how does our civilization in fact define itself? The answer is easy: for 30 years crimes of state have vastly exceeded crimes of individuals. I shall not even mention wars—general or local—although blood is a kind of alcohol that eventually intoxicates like the strongest wine. I am referring here to the number of individuals killed directly by the State, a number that has grown to astronomic proportions and infinitely exceeds that of "private" murders. There are fewer and fewer men condemned by common law, and more and more men executed for political reasons. The proof of this fact is that each of us, no matter how honorable he is, can now envisage the *possibility* of someday being put to death, whereas such an eventuality at the beginning of the century would have appeared farcical at best. Alphonse Karr's famous remark, "Let my lords the assassins begin," no longer has any meaning: those who spill the most blood are also those who believe they have right, logic, and history on their side.

It is not so much against the individual killer that our society must protect itself then, as against the State. Perhaps this equation will be reversed in another thirty years. But for the present, a legitimate defense must be made against the State, before all else. Justice and the most realistic sense of our time require that the law protect the individual against a State given over to the follies of sectarianism and pride. "Let the State begin by abolishing the death penalty" must be our rallying cry today.

Bloody laws, it has been said, make bloody deeds. But it is also possible for a society to suffer that state of ignominy in which public behavior, no matter how disorderly, comes no where near being so bloody as the laws. Half of Europe knows this state. We have known it in France and we risk knowing it again. The executed of the Occupation produced the executed of the Liberation whose friends still dream of revenge. Elsewhere, governments charged with too many crimes are preparing to drown their guilt in still greater massacres. We kill for a nation or for a deified social class. We kill for a future society, likewise deified. He who believes in omniscience can conceive of omnipotence. Temporal idols that demand absolute faith tirelessly mete out absolute punishments. And religions without transcendance murder those they condemn en masse and without hope.

How can European society in the twentieth century survive if it does not defend the individual by every means within its power against the oppression of the State? To forbid putting a man to death is one means of publicly proclaiming that society and the State are not absolute values, one means of demonstrating that nothing authorizes them to legislate definitively, to bring to pass the irreparable. Without the death penalty, Gabriel Péri and Brasillach would perhaps be among us still; we could then judge them, according to our lights, and proudly speak out our judgment, instead of which they now judge us, and it is we who must remain silent. Without the death penalty, the corpse of Rajk would not still be poisoning Hungary, a less guilty Germany would be received with better grace by the nations of Europe, the Russian Revolution would not still be writhing in its shame, and the blood of Algeria would weigh less heavily upon us here in France. Without the death penalty, Europe itself would not be infected by the corpses accumulated in its exhausted earth for the last twenty years. Upon our continent all values have been overturned by fear and hatred among individuals as among nations. The war of ideas is waged by rope and knife. It is no longer the natural human society that excercises its rights of repression, but a ruling ideology that demands its human sacrifices. "The lesson the scaffold always provides," Francart wrote, "is that human life ceases to be sacred when it is considered useful to suppress it." Apparently it has been considered increasingly useful, the lesson has found apt pupils, and the contagion is spreading everywhere. And with it, the disorders of nihilism. A spectacular counter-blow is required: it must be proclaimed, in institutions and as a matter of principle, that the human person is above and beyond the State. Every measure which will diminish the pressure of social forces on the individual will also aid in the decongestion of a Europe suffering from an afflux of blood, will permit us to think more clearly, and to make our way toward recovery. The disease of Europe is to believe in nothing and to claim to know everything. But Europe does not know everything, far from it, and to judge by the rebellion and the hope in which we find ourselves today, Europe does believe in something: Europe believes that the supreme misery of man, at its mysterious limit, borders on his supreme greatness. For the majority of Europeans faith is lost, and with it the justifications faith conferred upon the order of punishment. But the majority of Europeans are also sickened by that idolatry of the State which has claimed to replace their lost faith. From now on, with divided goals, certain and uncer-

tain, determined never to submit and never to oppress, we must recognize
both our hope and our ignorance, renounce all absolute law, all irreparable
institutions. We know enough to be able to say that this or that great criminal deserves a sentence of perpetual forced labor. But we do not know
enough to say that he can be deprived of his own future, which is to say,
of our common opportunity for reparation. In tomorrow's united Europe, on
whose behalf I write, the solemn abolition of the death penalty must be the
first article of that European Code for which we all hope.

From the humanitarian idylls of the eighteenth century to its bloody
scaffolds the road runs straight and is easily followed; we all know today's
executioners are humanists. And therefore we cannot be too suspicious of
humanitarian ideologies applied to a problem like that of capital punishment.
I should like to repeat, by way of conclusion, that my opposition to the
death penalty derives from no illusions as to the natural goodness of the
human creature, and from no faith in a golden age to come. On the contrary, the abolition of capital punishment seems necessary to me for reasons
of qualified pessimism, reasons I have attempted to explain in terms of logic
and the most realistic considerations. Not that the heart has not made its contribution to what I have been saying: for anyone who has spent several weeks
among these texts, these memories, and these men—all, intimately or remotely, connected with the scaffold—there can be no question of leaving
their dreadful ranks unaffected by what one has seen and heard. Nevertheless,
I do not believe there is no responsibility in this world for what I have found,
or that one should submit to our modern propensity for absolving victim and
killer in the same moral confusion. This purely sentimental confusion involves more cowardice than generosity, and ends up by justifying whatever
is worst in this world: if everything is blessed, then slave camps are blessed,
and organized murder, and the cynicism of the great political bosses—and
ultimately, blessing everything alike, one betrays one's own brothers. We can
see this happening all around us. But indeed, with the world in its present
condition the man of the twentieth century asks for laws and institutions of
convalescence that will check without crushing, lead without hampering.
Hurled into the unregulated dynamism of history, man needs a new physics,
new laws of equilibrium. He needs, most of all, a reasonable society, not
the anarchy into which his own pride and the State's inordinate powers
have plunged him.

It is my conviction that the abolition of the death penalty will help us
advance toward that society. In taking this initiative, France could propose
its extension on either side of the iron curtain; in any case she could set an
example. Capital punishment would be replaced by a sentence of perpetual
forced labor for criminals judged incorrigible, and by shorter terms for
others. As for those who believe that such punishment is still more cruel than

capital punishment itself, I wonder why, in that case, they do not reserve it for Landru and his like and relegate capital punishment to secondary offenders. One might also add that such forced labor leaves the condemned man the possibility of choosing his death, whereas the guillotine is a point of no return. On the other hand, I would answer those who believe that a sentence of perpetual forced labor is too mild a punishment by remarking first on their lack of imagination and then by pointing out that the privation of liberty could seem to them a mild punishment only to the degree that contemporary society has taught them to despise what liberty they have.[1]

That Cain was not killed, but bore in the sight of all men a mark of reprobation is, in any case, the lesson we should draw from the Old Testament, not to mention the Gospels, rather than taking our inspiration from the cruel examples of the Mosaic law. There is no reason why at least a limited version of such an experiment should not be attempted in France (say for a ten-year period), if our government is still capable of redeeming its vote for alcohol by the great measure in behalf of civilization which total abolition would represent. And if public opinion and its representatives cannot renounce our slothful law which confines itself to eliminating what it cannot amend, at least, while waiting for a day of regeneration and of truth, let us not preserve as it is this "solemn shambles" (in Tarde's expression) which continues to disgrace our society. The death penalty, as it is imposed, even as rarely as it is imposed, is a disgusting butchery, an outrage inflicted on the spirit and body of man. This truncation, this living severed head, these long gouts of blood, belong to a barbarous epoch that believed it could subdue the people by offering them degrading spectacles. Today, when this ignoble death is secretly administered, what meaning can such torture have? The truth is that in an atomic age we kill as we did in the age of steelyards: where is the man of normal sensibility whose stomach is not turned at the mere idea of such clumsy surgery? If the French state is incapable of overcoming its worst impulses to this degree, and of furnishing Europe with one of the remedies it needs most, let it at least reform its means of administering capital punishment. Science, which has taught us so much about killing, could at least teach us to kill decently. An anesthetic which would permit the accused to pass from a state of sleep to death, which would remain within his reach for at least a day so that he could make free use of it, and which in cases of refusal or failure of nerve could then be administered to him,

[1] See also the report on the death penalty made by Representative Dupont to the National Assembly on May 31, 1791: "He [*the assassin*] is consumed by a bitter, burning temper; what he fears above all is repose, a state that leaves him to himself, and to escape it he continually faces death and seeks to inflict it; solitude and his conscience are his real tortures. Does this not tell us what kind of punishment we should impose, to what agonies he is most sensitive? *Is it not in the very nature of the disease that we must seek the remedy which can cure it?*" I italicize this last sentence, which makes this little-known Representative a real precursor of our modern psychological theories.

would assure the elimination of the criminal, if that is what we require, but would also provide a little decency where today there is nothing but a sordid and obscene exhibition.

I indicate these compromises only to the degree that one must sometimes despair of seeing wisdom and the principles of civilization impose themselves upon those responsible for our future. For certain men, more numerous than is supposed, knowing what the death penalty really is and being unable to prevent its application is physically insupportable. In their own way, they suffer this penalty too, and without any justification. If we at least lighten the weight of the hideous images that burden these men, society will lose nothing by our actions. But ultimately even such measures will be insufficient. Neither in the hearts of men nor in the manners of society will there be a lasting peace until we outlaw death.

Angelo Roncalli was born in Sotto il Monte, Bergamo, in the Po valley, on November 25, 1881. He was ordained priest in 1904, served as a professor in Bergamo Seminary and, during the first World War, as an army chaplain. After the war he published several books on religious history, and in 1925 entered the diplomatic service of the Holy See. He was made titular archbishop of Areopolis in Greece in 1925, and of Mesembria in 1934. He served as apostolic delegate in Istanbul and as papal envoy to both Greece and Turkey. In 1944 he became apostolic nuncio to France, a post he held for eight years. Pope Pius XII created him a cardinal on January 12, 1953, and also made him archbishop of Venice and patriarch of Venice. Elected pope on October 28, 1958, after the death of Pius XII, he assumed the name of John XXIII.

It was a commonplace in the eulogies for Pius XII that his successor—and probably also subsequent popes for a long time to come—could not possibly brook comparison with him. Many all but sainted him before he was buried, and then explained that Pope John, almost 77 when elected, was nothing but a compromise candidate who could only be expected to be a place holder. But by the time Pope John died, June 3, 1963, *he* was all but sainted by world opinion; Pius XII was beginning to appear in a very different light; and a consensus had emerged that Pius XII could not brook comparison with his infinitely more lovable successor.

Pope John's permanent achievement is twofold. First, immediately upon his elevation he introduced a new tone which constituted not only an antithesis to the manner of Pius XII but, more important, a striking reversal of the development of the papacy highlighted in the present volume. His warmth and humility captured the imagination and touched the heart of hundreds of millions, non-Catholics as well as his flock. Then, in January 1959, he called a Church Council which became known as the Second Vatican Council and opened in October 1962. (For the First Vatican Council, see pages 12 ff. and 160 ff. above: Pope John's significance can be fully appreciated only against this background.) To this Church Council he invited as observers representatives of Protestant and Eastern Orthodox churches, and by this and many other gestures sought to advance the ecumenical movement. The short selection that follows is the text of his address to these observers on October 13, 1962. (The translation from the original French is that which appeared in the *New York Times* the next day.) Obviously, this short speech gives no adequate idea of the pope's importance, but it catches a little of his distinctive tone and spirit.

This is also the place to add a few words to the selection from Malcolm Hay's *Europe and the Jews* and the discussion of Pope Pius XII's attitude during the Hitler years (see above, pp. 27 ff. and 34). Pope John deleted references to the "perfidious Jews" from the liturgy of the Roman Catholic church and sought to bring about a formal declaration at the Second Vatican Council that the Jews must not be held responsible for the crucifixion of Jesus. He died before this schema was placed before the council, and at the first session after his death there was still sufficient opposition to postpone a vote, but early in 1964 informed sources anticipated that in the fall the council would accept a very forthright statement that would strike at the roots of Christian anti-Semitism.

Meanwhile the discussion of Pope Pius XII's attitude achieved wide prominence through the publication, and performances in Germany, Switzerland, France, England, and the United States, of a play, *The Deputy* (*Der Stellvertreter*) by a young German author, Rolf Hochhuth, born in 1931. Most of the discussion engendered by the play, which is supported by a long appendix that cites and discusses the historical evidence, has quite missed the author's point, although that could hardly be stated more clearly and poignantly than it is stated in the four mottos at the beginning, particularly that from Kierkegaard. It is nice to note that the schema on the Jews and the crucifixion is largely the work of the German Cardinal Bea, and that it was a young German who has succeeded in getting the world to discuss questions that it has long preferred to ignore. Hochhuth lacks Camus's singular charm and hence has been vilified wherever his play has been performed (to be sure, mainly by those who have neither read nor seen it), though what he says at length, in detail, and with documentary support is not so different from Camus's brief and rather general complaint about the church, cited above (pp. 41 f.). One gathers that Hochhuth, like Kierkegaard, feels that there are matters about which one should not speak charmingly and inoffensively.

Insofar as the controversy about Pope Pius XII involves questions of historic fact, illumination must be sought from historians; e.g., from Guenter Lewy's book on *The Catholic Church and Nazi Germany*. Lewy's article on "Pius XII, the Jews, and the German Catholic Church" (published in *Commentary* in February 1964, before the book had appeared) is based on this volume. The article ends: "Finally, one is inclined to conclude that the Pope and his advisors—influenced by the long tradition of moderate anti-Semitism so widely accepted in Vatican circles —did not view the plight of the Jews with a real sense of urgency and moral outrage. . . . Pius XII broke his policy of strict neutrality during World War II to express concern over the German violation of the neutrality of Holland, Belgium, and Luxemburg in May 1940. When some German Catholics criticized him for this action, the Pope wrote the German bishops that neutrality was not synonymous 'with indifference and apathy where moral and humane considerations demanded a candid word.' All things told, did not the murder of several million Jews demand a similarly 'candid word'?"

The Roman Catholic church cannot be expected to answer this rhetorical question officially, nor would it have greatly benefited humanity if Pope John's successor, instead of finding a few words to defend Pope Pius in passing, had condemned his failure to speak out strongly and unequivocally. But the implicit answer of the church is far more staggering and fateful than any such criticism could have been—and it gives some indication of the immense historic impact of Pope John XXIII. Only five years after the death of Pope Pius, a church council (only the second council since the sixteenth century) was seriously considering one of the most far-reaching reinterpretations of sacred history on record; and it seemed possible that in 1964 the church would officially forbid its priests and nuns and teachers the world over to teach their millions of pupils that the Jews must be held responsible for the crucifixion. As has been shown, Pius IX reoriented his church and sought to align it against modernism and liberalism. Pope John may be responsible for a comparable reorientation—toward humanity and inter-faith understanding.

Speech to Non-Catholics

*T*oday's most welcome meeting is to be simple and friendly, respectful and brief.

The first word which rises up in my heart is the prayer taken from the 67th Psalm, which has a lesson for all: *Benedictus Dominus per singulos dies: portat onera nostra Deus, salus nostra.* Blessed be the Lord now and ever. The God who bears our burdens, and wins us the victory.

When in 1952, Pope Pius XII most unexpectedly asked me to become the Patriarch of Venice, I told him that I did not need to reflect very long before accepting the appointment. For in the undertaking there was nothing at all of my own seeking; there was no desire in my heart of being appointed to one office or ministry rather than to another. My episcopal motto fitly provided my answer: *oboedientia et pax.*

And so when, after thirty years in the direct service of the Holy See, I prepared myself to begin a new kind of life and found myself shepherd of the flock of Venice, which I was to tend for the next six years. I reflected and meditated upon those words of the Pslam:

Portat onera nostra, Deus, God who carries us; He carries us, what we are and what we possess; with his treasure in us and with our miseries.

This same thought was present to me when I accepted, four years ago, the succession of St. Peter and it has been so in what has followed right up to the announcement and the preparation of the Council.

In so far as it concerns my humble person, I would not like to claim any special inspiration.

I content myself with the sound doctrine which teaches that everything comes from God. In this sense I have considered this idea of the Council, which began on 11th October to be a heavenly inspiration. I confess to you that it was for me a day of great emotion.

On that providential and historic occasion, I devoted all my attention to my immediate duty of preserving my recollection of praying and giving thanks to God.

But my eye from time to time ranged over the multitude of sons and brothers and suddenly as my glance rested upon your group, on each of you personally, I drew a special comfort from your presence.

I will not say more about that at the moment but will content myself with recording the fact. *Benedictus deus per singulos dies.*

Yet, if you could read my heart, you would perhaps understand much more than words can say.

Can I ever forget the ten years passed at Sofia? Or the ten more at Istanbul and Athens?

They were twenty years of happy and delightful acquaintance with persons I revere and with young people filled with generosity upon whom I looked with affection, even though my work as representative of the Holy Father in the Near East was not explicitly concerned with them.

Then again at Paris, which is one of the crossroads of the world, and was especially so immediately after the end of the last war. I had frequently meetings with Christians of many different denominations.

I cannot remember any occasion on which we were divided on principle nor that there was ever any disagreement on the plane of charity in the common work of helping those in need, which the circumstances of the time made necessary.

We did not haggle, we talked together; we did not have discussions but we bore each other good will.

One day long ago I gave to a venerable and aged prelate of an Oriental church, not in communion with Rome, a medal of the Pontificate of Pius XI.

This gesture was meant to be, and was, a simple act of friendly courtesy.

Not long after, the old man on the point of closing his eyes of the things of this earth requested that when he was dead the medal of the Pope should be put on his breast. I saw it myself and the memory of it still moves me.

I have mentioned this episode deliberately because in its simplicity and innocence it is like a flower of the field which the return of spring allows one to pluck and offer. May the Lord always thus accompany our steps with His grace.

Your welcome presence here and the emotion of our priestly heart—the heart of a Bishop of the Church of God, as we said yesterday before the assembled Council—the emotion of my beloved fellow-workers that there burns in my heart the intention of working and suffering to hasten the hour when for all men the prayer of Jesus at the Last Supper will have reached its fulfilment.

But the Christian virtue of patience is not out of harmony with the equally fundamental virtue of prudence.

And so I say again: *benedictus deus pro singulos dies*. For today let that suffice.

It is now for the Catholic Church to bend herself to her work with calmness and generosity. It is for you to observe her with renewed and friendly attention.

May the inspiration of heavenly grace which moves hearts and rewards good works be upon all of you and all that is yours.

John McTaggart Ellis McTaggart was born in 1866. A slightly younger contemporary of Josiah Royce (see pp. 18 f. and 239 ff. above), he was one of the leading British exponents of Idealism. As a Fellow of Trinity College, Cambridge, he had considerable influence around the turn of the century, and Bertrand Russell and G. E. Moore were under his spell for a short while. Both rebelled against Idealism, and soon after McTaggart's death, in 1925, British philosophy owed far more to this rebellion than it did to McTaggart. Another very distinguished Cambridge philosopher, C. D. Broad, devoted two imposing critical tomes to *An Examination of McTaggart's Philosophy* (1933–1938).

McTaggart's own books include three works on Hegel: *Studies in the Hegelian Dialectic* (1896), *Studies in Hegelian Cosmology* (1901), and *A Commentary on Hegel's Logic* (1910). His metaphysics is set forth in *The Nature of Existence* (2 volumes, 1921–1927). The following selections come from his book, *Some Dogmas of Religion* (1906) and comprise sections 171–79, 210–15, and 225–28. In these selections the emphasis falls not on McTaggart's metaphysics, which is no longer discussed widely, but on his sharp critical analysis of points that are as interesting and important as ever.

Since this material is added only in the second edition, it is conveniently placed at the end of the volume. Otherwise it would find its most fitting place after Royce's essay.

God, Evil, and Immortality

I

171. We now come to the relation of omnipotence to goodness. There is evil in the universe. It is not necessary to inquire how great or how small the amount of evil may be. All that is important for the present discussion is that there is some evil, and this is beyond doubt. A single pang of toothache, a single ungenerous thought, in the midst of a universe otherwise perfectly good, would prove the existence of evil.

The existence of evil is beyond doubt in the sense that no one denies the existence of pain and sin in experience, and that no one denies that pain and sin are, from the point of view of ordinary life, to be considered evil. But it has been asserted that the universe, when looked at rightly, may be completely good. Sometimes the standard is challenged, and it is suggested that pain and sin are really good, though we think them evil. Sometimes our comprehension of the facts is challenged; it is admitted that pain and sin, if they existed, would be bad, but it is maintained that they do not really exist.

The first of these alternatives means complete ethical scepticism. There is no judgement about the good of whose truth we are more certain than the judgement that what is painful or sinful cannot be perfectly good. If we distrust this judgement, we have no reason to put any trust in any judgement of good or evil. In that case we should have no right to call anything or anybody good, and therefore it would be impossible to justify any belief in God, whose definition includes goodness. This objection, therefore, cannot consistently be used, by the believers in an omnipotent God, against the existence of evil.

The second alternative is one which can only be supported by metaphysical arguments of a somewhat abstruse and elaborate nature. To expound and examine these arguments in detail would take us too far from our subject. I will only say briefly that the theory of the unreality of evil now seems to me untenable. Supposing that it could be proved that all that we think evil was in reality good, the fact would still remain that we think it evil. This may be called a delusion or a mistake. But a delusion or mistake is as *real* as anything else. A savage's erroneous belief that the earth is stationary is just as real a fact as an astronomer's correct belief that it moves. The delusion that evil exists, then, is real. But then, to me at least, it seems certain that a delusion or an error which hid from us the goodness of the universe would itself be evil. And so there would be real evil after all. If, again, the existence of the delusion is pronounced to be a delusion, then this second delusion, which would be admitted to be real, must be pronounced evil, since it is now this delusion which deceives us about the true nature of reality, and hides its goodness from us. And so on indefinitely. However many times we pronounce evil unreal, we always leave a reality behind, which in its turn is to be pronounced evil.

172. An omnipotent God is conceived as creating the universe. In that case it seems a natural inference that he is the cause of all the evil in the universe. But some people, who maintain the existence of a creative omnipotent God, maintain also that the choice of the human will between motives has no cause, and, therefore, is not ultimately caused by the creator. They admit, however, that God could have dispensed with the freedom of the human will, if he had chosen to do so.[1]

We may therefore say that an omnipotent God could have prevented all the evil in the universe if he had willed to do so. It is impossible to deny this, if omnipotence is to have any meaning, for to deny it would be to assert that there was something that God could not do if he willed to do it.

173. What bearing has this on the question of God's goodness? It is clear that man may act rightly in permitting evil, and even in directly causing it. It is evil that a child should lose his leg, for the loss deprives him of much happiness, and causes him much pain. But the surgeon who performs the

---

[1] It seems curious that believers in human free will should often accept the argument for God's existence from the necessity of a first cause. If human volition is not completely determined, the law of causality is not universally valid. And, in that case, what force remains in the argument for a first cause?

operation, and the parent who allows it to be performed, may be perfectly justified. For amputation may be the only alternative to evils much greater than those it produces.

And, again, the production of sin may under certain circumstances be justified. Supposing that it were true—fortunately there is no reason to believe that it is true—that employment as an executioner tended to degrade morally a large proportion of those who were employed, it would by no means follow that men ought not to be induced to act as executioners. The evil results which might follow from having no hangman might far outweigh the evil done to morality by having one.

But the justification in these cases depends entirely on the limited powers of the agents. The father and the surgeon, for example, are justified because it is only through the evils of amputation that worse evils can be avoided. If they could have avoided those worse evils by some other course that would not have been evil at all, they would not have been justified in deciding on the amputation.

174. Now the power of an omnipotent God is not limited. He can effect whatever he wills. If he wills to have A without B, he can have A without B, however closely A and B may be connected in the present scheme of the universe. For that scheme also is dependent on his will. It thus appears that his action cannot be justified as the amputation was. It rather resembles that of a father who should first gratuitously break his son's leg, or permit it to be broken, and should then decide for amputation, although a complete cure was possible.

If a man did this we should call him wicked. We do not wait to call a man wicked till he does more evil than good. If a man should, at the risk of his life, save all the crew of a sinking ship but one, and should then, from mere caprice, leave that man to sink, whom he could easily have saved, we should say that he had acted wickedly. Nor is it necessary that a man should do evil for the sake of evil. To desire to attend a concert is not a desire for evil as such, but if I killed a man in order to acquire his ticket, I should have acted wickedly.

Now in what way would the conduct of an omnipotent God, who permitted the existence of evil, differ from the conduct of such men, except for the worse? There are palliations of men's guilt, but what palliations could there be for such a God? A man may have lived a long life of virtue before he fell into sin, or, again, we may have reason to hope that he will repent and amend. But could we have any reason for hoping that the omnipotent God would repent and amend? It seems difficult to imagine such a reason. Again, a man may be excused to some extent for his sin, if ignorance or folly prevents him from realizing the full meaning of his action. But if an omnipotent God is not omniscient (and it seems most natural to suppose that he is), at any rate he could be so if he chose. Or again, a man may have a genuine repugnance for his sin, and only commit it under extreme temptation. A man who betrays his country under torture is less wicked than if he had betrayed it for money. But an omnipotent God can be forced to nothing, and can therefore not be forced to choose between wickedness and suffering.

175. Such conduct, then, as we must attribute to an omnipotent God, would be called wicked in men, although the amount of evil for which any man is responsible is insignificant as compared with the sum of all evil, and although men have in most cases excuses which would not apply to an omnipotent God. Yet this being is still called God, by people who admit that goodness is part of the definition of God. Why is God called good, when his action is asserted to be such as would prove a man to be a monster of wickedness? Two lines of defence have been tried. The first is, in substance, that the omnipotent and good God is not really good, the second that he is not really omnipotent.

The form in which the first is put by its supporters is that goodness in God is of a different nature from what it is in man. Thus Mansel says that 'the infliction of physical suffering, the permission of moral evil' and various other things 'are facts which no doubt are reconcilable, we know not how, with the infinite Goodness of God, but which certainly are not to be explained on the supposition that its sole and sufficient type is to be found in the finite goodness of man.'[2] And he goes on to say that the difference is not one of degree only, but of kind. Pascal is still more plain-spoken: 'What can be more opposed to our wretched rules of justice than the eternal damnation of a child without any will of its own for a sin in which it seems to have had so little share that it was committed six thousand years before the said child came into existence.'[3] Nevertheless Pascal continued to call good, and to worship, a God whom he believed to have done this.

176. But why should the word good be used in two senses absolutely opposed to one another? The senses are not merely different, as they would be if, for example, it was proposed to use the word good to indicate what is generally meant by the word scarlet. For what is called good in God would be called wicked in men, and good and wicked are predicates directly contrary to one another.

Is the alteration to be considered as one of mere caprice? Are the people who say that God is good, while Nero was wicked, in the same position as a man who should call Everest a valley, while he called Snowdon a mountain? It seems to me that there is more than this involved, and that the real ground of the alteration is that good is a word of praise, and that wicked is a word of blame, and that it is felt to be desirable to praise God rather than to blame him.

[2] *Limits of Religious Thought*, fourth edition, Preface, p. xiii.
[3] Works, ed. Brunschvicg, ii, p. 348.

But why is it desirable to praise him? Certainly not for the reasons which make us praise Socrates and blame Nero. For the conduct which in God we call good is conduct for some faint and imperfect approximation to which we blame Nero. What other reason is left? I can only see one—that an omnipotent God is, and will remain, infinitely more powerful than Nero ever was.

On this subject Mill has spoken,[4] and it is unnecessary to quote words which form one of the great turning-points in the religious development of the world. Yet when Mill says that rather than worship such a God he would go to hell, it is possible to raise a doubt. To call such a being good, and to worship him, is to lie and to be degraded. But it is not certain that nothing could be a greater evil than to lie and to be degraded. It is not impossible that God's goodness, as explained by Pascal and Mansel, should include the infliction of such tortures, physical and mental, on one who refused to worship him that they would be a greater evil than lying and degradation. Unless it is said that moral degradation is absolutely incommensurable with suffering—and I doubt if this can be maintained—the case does not seem impossible. Nor need the motive of the worshipper be selfish. The goodness of God, like the wickedness of some men, might include the torture of the culprit's friends as well as of himself.

177. We may doubt, then, whether we should be bound, or justified, in refusing to misapply the predicate good to such an omnipotent being, if the use of the word would diminish our chances of unending torture. But it seems just as likely to increase them. There are, no doubt, men who are prepared to inflict suffering on all who do not flatter them, even when they know that the flattery is empty and undeserved. But, granted that God has some qualities which would be called wicked in men, it does not follow that he has all qualities which would be called wicked in men, and there is no reason to suppose that he has this particular quality. Many men, bad as well as good, are not appeased by such flattery, but rather irritated by it, especially if they know it to be insincere, or to have been insincere when it began. God may resemble these men rather than the others. Indeed, the probability seems to be that he would do so, since pleasure in such flattery is generally a mark of a weak intellect, and even if God's goodness is like our wickedness, it can scarcely be suggested that his wisdom is like our folly. Or, again, God's goodness may induce him to damn us whatever we do, in which case we shall gain nothing by lying.

When everything is so doubtful there does not seem to be the least prudence in flattery. Nor can we rest our actions on any statement made by God as to the conduct which he will pursue. For, if goodness in God is dif-

---

[4] *Examination of Hamilton*, chap. vii. [Reprinted in *The Philosophy of John Stuart Mill*, ed. Marshall Cohen, The Modern Library, pp. 423–441; see especially 435–438. W.K.]

ferent from goodness in us, we should have no reason to believe a statement to be true rather than false, even if it were certain that it came from God. Divine goodness may not exclude the desire to destroy our happiness by false statements.

178. There remains the attempt to save the goodness of an omnipotent God by giving up the reality of his omnipotence, while retaining the name. Various elements in the universe have been taken either as good or as inevitable, and the evil in the universe explained as the necessary consequence of the reality of these elements. Thus, for example, the sin of the universe has been accounted for by the free will of the sinners, and the suffering explained as the necessary consequence, in some way, of the sin. Thus all the evil in the universe, it is asserted, is a necessary consequence of free will, and it is said that free will is so good that God was justified in choosing a universe with all the present evil in it, rather than surrender free will.

Or, again, it is said that it is impossible that there should not be some evil in a universe which was governed according to general laws, and that to be governed according to general laws is so great a perfection in the universe that God did well to choose it with all the evil that it involves.

It seems to me rather difficult to see such supreme value in free will that it would be worth more than the absence of all the present evil of the universe. It might be doubted, even, whether the advantage of unbroken general laws is so great that the evil of the universe would not be cheaply removed at the cost of frequent miracles.[5] But we need not discuss this. For it is quite evident that a God who cannot create a universe in which all men have free will, and which is at the same time free from all evil, is not an omnipotent God, since there is one thing which he cannot do. In the same way, a God who cannot ordain a series of general laws, the uniform working of which would exclude all evil from the universe, is not an omnipotent God.

Or, once more, it is said that a universe without evil would involve in some way the violation of such laws as the law of Contradiction or of Excluded Middle, and that these laws are so fundamental that the existence of evil in the universe is inevitable.

Even if there were any ground for believing that the absence of evil from the universe would violate such laws as these, it is clear that a God who is bound by any laws is not omnipotent, since he cannot alter them. If it is said—as it may very reasonably be said—that these laws are so fundamental that it is unmeaning to speak of a being who is not bound by them, the proper conclusion is not that an omnipotent God is bound by them, but that, if there is a God, he is not omnipotent.

[5] The supporters of this view of the supreme value of unbroken general laws, have often, it may be noted, been men who believed that God did well in permitting the human will to be undetermined, and in working occasional miracles.

It is necessary to emphasize this point because, remarkable as it may appear, it is not an unusual position to maintain that God is absolutely omnipotent, and, at the same time, to believe that there are certain things he cannot do, and even to be quite certain what those things are.[6] As against such a view as this it seems necessary to emphasize the tolerably obvious fact that, if there is anything which God could not do if he wished, he is not omnipotent.

179. It may be said that we are attaching too much importance to a slight inaccuracy of language. If people say that there are certain things which God could not do, then they do not believe him to be omnipotent, and they are simply using the wrong word when they say that they do believe him to be omnipotent.

But then why do they use the word? It seems to me that the confusion of language covers a confusion of thought. Many people are unwilling to accept the idea that God is not omnipotent. It is held to detract from his perfection, and to render it difficult to regard him as the creator of the universe.

And there is another point of grave importance. If God is not omnipotent, the fact that God exists and is good gives us no guarantee that the universe is more good than bad, or even that it is not very bad. If God exists and is good, the universe will of course be as good as he can make it. But, if there are some things that he cannot do, how can we tell that among these impossibilities may not be the impossibility of preventing the world from being more bad than good, or of preventing it from being very bad? If it could be shown that God's power, though limited, was strong enough to prevent this, it could only be by a determination of the precise limits of his power, and, if this could be done at all, it could only be done by an elaborate metaphysical investigation. Such investigations are open to few, and their results are frequently highly controversial. It is not strange that popular theology is unwilling to accept the position that the goodness of the universe can only be proved in such a way.

And thus popular theology has two conflicting impulses. It desires, among other things, to show that the universe is more good than bad—at any rate in the long run. The only means at its disposal for showing this—if it is to remain popular—is its belief in the existence of a God to whose will all evil is repugnant, and who is powerful enough to effect the predominance of good. But if God is to be taken as omnipotent, it is certain that all evil is not repugnant to his will, and if he is to be taken as not omnipotent, it is not certain that he is powerful enough to effect the predominance of good.

The inaccurate use of the word omnipotence hides this dilemma. When popular theology is pressed to reconcile the present existence of evil with the goodness of God, then it pleads that omnipotent does not mean omnipotent, but only very powerful. But when the sceptic has been crushed, and what is

[6] Cp., for example, Flint's *Theism*. The omnipotence of God is asserted: I. 2, III. 1, IX. 2. In VI. 1 and VIII. 1 we find statements of some of the things which God cannot do.

wanted is a belief in the future extinction of evil, then omnipotence slides back into its strict meaning, and it is triumphantly asserted that the cause which has an omnipotent God on its side must certainly win. The confusion is unintentional, no doubt, but it is dangerous.

It seems to me that when believers in God save his goodness by saying that he is not really omnipotent, they are taking the best course open to them, since both the personality and the goodness of God present much fewer difficulties if he is not conceived as omnipotent. But then they must accept the consequences of their choice, and realize that the efforts of a non-omnipotent God in favour of good may, for anything they have yet shown, be doomed to almost total defeat. It is not a very cheerful creed, unless it can be supplemented by some other dogmas which can assure us of God's eventual victory. But it is less depressing and less revolting than the belief that the destinies of the universe are at the mercy of a being who, with the resources of omnipotence at his disposal, decided to make a universe no better than this. . . .

2

210. Another point remains for consideration. If it were proved that there was a person in the universe who greatly excelled all others both in wisdom and power, yet this would not by itself prove the existence of a God. For God has not only to be wise and powerful, but also good. How are we to prove that this director of the universe is good enough to be called God?

In the first place, he could not, as it seems to me, be perfectly good. He is one self in a universe which contains other selves. He is continually acting on them. They, in their turn, are continually acting on him, sometimes helping his plans, sometimes thwarting them, sometimes rejoicing him, sometimes grieving him. Selves in such a union as this form a society. We have to consider, then, the director of the universe as one of a society of selves.

Is it possible that one member of a society should be *completely* perfect while others are not? We see, of course, in everyday life, that people of very different degrees of perfection may be closely united. But I do not see how there can be any unity at all if each is not helped by the perfection, and hindered by the imperfection, of every other. Any hindrance must prevent the person hindered from being quite perfect, and this seems to render God's perfection impossible.

'No doubt,' it might be replied, 'God is not completely perfect—at any rate, as yet. To be perfect he would have to be in perfect harmony with his environment, to be perfectly acquiescent and happy. And this he cannot be in a world which contains sin and pain. But this does not prevent him from being completely perfect *morally*. He can be completely good without being completely happy.'

It is surely, however, a false abstraction to maintain that any cause can work an effect on one aspect of a person's life and leave the others untouched. A person is not a mere aggregate of water-tight compartments. He is essentially a unity, although that unity is manifested in a plurality of activities. And, consequently, nothing can be a hindrance to the perfection of any side of his nature without affecting that unity, and, through it, all the other sides of his nature. One cause, no doubt, may have much more effect on one side of his nature than on other sides, and so the sides may develop unevenly. Thus three people, if arranged in the order of their intellectual perfection, might be placed—*A, B, C;* if in the order of their moral perfection, *B, A, C;* and if in the order of their happiness, *C, A, B.* But every cause must have *some* effect on each aspect of each nature, and so, if any cause exists which causes some imperfection in any aspect of God's nature, it will be impossible to regard him as completely perfect in any respect.

211. The possibility would remain that the director of the universe, although not perfectly good, was very much better than any other person. This would justify us in calling him God. Such a comparative perfection would suffice for worship. If worship is to be anything higher than selfish propitiation of the powerful, it requires that the being worshipped shall be conceived as morally better than the devotee. But, if this is secured, it does not seem essential that it should be accompanied by an assertion of the absolute perfection of the object of worship. Thus the director of the universe, if he exists, may be a God. But it is also possible that he may not be a God. For that would require that he should be distinctly better than the best man. And I do not see that it is impossible that he should be even worse than the worst man. Absolutely bad, indeed, he could not be. Evil, though not a *mere* negation, is nevertheless of a distinctly negative nature, and could only exist as limiting and confining the good. An absolutely bad person—one without any goodness in him—would be an impossibility.

But it is not impossible that the director of the universe should be worse than the worst man. Our only ground of inference as to his moral nature is the present condition of the universe, which would be due largely to his influence. It was admitted that much of what we observe around us in the universe could be easily explained as the means for realizing some end which is good in itself. And if it is to be explained this way, we might argue that the director of the universe must be good. But it seems to me that the facts which we observe could just as easily be explained as the means for realizing some end which is bad in itself. Many of the ends to which facts of the universe appear to be adapted as means are partially good and partially bad. Some of the ends to which the facts of the universe appear to be adapted as means seem to be purely bad. If we believe the director of the universe to be good we say, in the first case, that he brings such ends about for the sake of the good in them, and because the good outweighs the evil with which it is necessarily connected. In the second case, when the ends achieved seem to be purely bad, it is said that in some way which we do not know they may in their turn be indispensable means to some end whose good outweighs their evil.

And all this is quite possible. But then, it seems to me, the contrary hypothesis is also quite possible—that the director of the universe has proposed to himself an end which is distinctly bad. The existence of the good could then be explained in the same way as the existence of evil was by the more cheerful theory. It would be something which the director of the universe unwillingly brought about, because the constitution of the universe prevented him from producing the evil without producing this amount of good also. It would no more prove his goodness than the refreshments administered in the intervals of tortures proved the humanity of the torturers.

Nor would this possibility be removed, even if we could prove that good far outweighs evil in the universe. It would still be possible that the aim of the director of the universe was to produce a much worse result, and that the excess of good merely proved that the conditions under which he worked were unfavourable to his purpose.

212. I cannot see, therefore, that any reason has been given for supposing a director of the universe to be good rather than bad. But even if we assume that he is more good than bad, it would not follow from this that he would be a God. He might be no better than the average good man. The size and complexity of the universe—even of that little part of it which we imperfectly observe—is so enormous that a being who directed it must very greatly excel human beings in wisdom and power. But it is not equally necessary that he should excel them in goodness. For it is not certain that the universe excels the works of men in goodness at all, and still less certain that it excels them very greatly in goodness. Indeed most men would, I imagine, be distinctly relieved if they were certain that good bore as large a proportion to evil in the universe as a whole as it did in the work of such men as Buddha, Aquinas, or Mill. Of course, a universe which was proportionately much more evil than Mill's work *might* have been produced by a person much better than Mill, for the evil *might* have been due almost exclusively to the limitations of his power. But it is also possible that the conditions might have allowed of a better state of things, and that some of the existing evil is due to the defective virtue of the agent.

It is possible, for example, that, while good is attractive to the director of the universe, other things are also attractive. And, when the two attractions lead to different courses, he may sometimes be tempted, like less wise and less powerful persons, and choose the worse alternative. Or, again, to produce the best possible result may well cause him fatigue and pain, and it is possible that the amount of these which he is prepared to encounter is limited. The universe might have been better if his self-sacrifice had been greater.

213. And, once more, if the director of the universe is finite, why should we be certain that there is only one? Many of the facts of experience, while they are compatible with the theory of a single director working under limitations, suggest at least as strongly the idea of several such beings, working in opposition, or possibly—as patriotic Tories work with patriotic Liberals —partly in harmony and partly in opposition. The opposition might be direct, between powers whose ends are intrinsically contrary, or indirect, between powers which had different ends, not intrinsically opposed, but capable of clashing under certain circumstances.

Or, supposing that only one director is at work in the part of the universe which we know, still that part may be very small compared with the whole. How shall we tell that there are not other regions—perhaps separated from ours by vast ungoverned intervals—in which other beings, higher or lower than he whose work we perceive here, are working out other independent and isolated purposes?

There is nothing, perhaps, which should prevent us from giving the name of God to each of several beings simultaneously existing, or to one such being, existing simultaneously with others, who equal him in wisdom and power, but not in goodness. It may not be impossible to revert to polytheism, or to conceive God as striving against other persons who equal him in everything but goodness. But the name of God seems to imply that the person to whom it is applied is of appreciable importance when measured against the whole universe. A person who was only one among millions of similar beings would scarcely be allowed the name. And yet this may be the case with the person, if there is one, to whom we owe all the order and purpose which we can observe in the universe.

214. If we make God to be less than a creator, we make it possible that he should be a person, and that he should be good. And it is sufficiently certain that his wisdom and power would excel our own. But when we come to his relation to the universe, Hume's suggestions are more easily ignored than disproved. 'In a word, Cleanthes, a man who follows your hypothesis, is able, perhaps, to assert, or conjecture, that the universe, sometime, arose from something like design: but beyond that position he cannot ascertain one single circumstance, and is left afterwards to fix every point of his theology by the utmost licence of fancy and hypothesis. This world, for aught he knows, is very faulty and imperfect, compared to a superior standard; and was only the first rude essay of some infant deity, who afterwards abandoned it, ashamed of his lame performance: it is the work only of some dependent, inferior deity; and is the object of derision to his superiors: it is the production of old age and dotage in some superannuated deity; and ever since his death, has run on at adventures, from the first impulse and active force, which it received from him. You justly give signs of horror, Demea, at these strange suppositions: but these, and a thousand more of the same kind, are Cleanthes's

suppositions, not mine. From the moment the attributes of the deity are supposed finite, all these have place.'[7]

2 1 5. Finally, it is necessary once more to emphasize the fact that, if God's moral character is saved by limiting his power, we have no right to be confident as to the eventual victory of those ends in which God is interested. We know that he will work for them, and we know that they will be the more triumphant or the less defeated because of his efforts. But we do not know that they will be completely triumphant. Nor is this all. We do not even know that they will not be almost completely defeated. The fundamental conditions of the universe may prevent it from being anything but very bad, and all that God's utmost efforts may be able to do is to make the inevitable calamity a little less calamitous.

That is all that the doctrine of a non-omnipotent God can give us—a person who fights for the good and who may be victorious. But it is at any rate better than the doctrine of an omnipotent person to whom good and evil are equally pleasing. And it is fortunate that, as we have seen, the more attractive of the two ideas is also the more probable. Indeed, when the non-omnipotent God is also taken as non-creative, there seems to me, as I have said, only one reason why we should not believe in his existence—namely, that there is no reason why we should believe in it. . . .

3

2 2 5. Before leaving our interest in God's works, it may be worth while to discuss the relation of the belief in God to the belief in immortality. These beliefs are often supposed to be logically joined. If the existence of God is accepted, it is often held that from this alone—independent of any alleged revelation on the subject—the immortality of man may be either proved, or, at least, shown to be highly probable. And, on the other hand, it is held that, if the existence of God is rejected, not only has one argument for immortality gone, but there is no chance of proving it at all, or rendering it in the least probable. Atheism must necessarily involve disbelief in immortality.

Let us consider the first of these assertions. Would the certainty of God's existence support the belief in human immortality? If it does so, it must be on account of God's goodness. His wisdom and power might possibly be arguments for proving that he could make man immortal if he wished to do so, but they could throw no light on the question whether he would will to do so or not. The only way of deciding this—and it is a way which is often taken—is to say that immortality is very good, that its absence would

---

[7] *Dialogues concerning Natural Religion*, Part V, *ad fin.* I may remark that it seems to me that Hume's most important contribution to the philosophy of religion is to be found in these Dialogues, and not in the more famous discussion on Miracles in the *Enquiry*.

deprive the universe of almost all its value and significance, and then to argue that God, who is good, could not refuse us this gift.

226. But if immortality is to be proved in this way, it is necessary to be certain that it is good. And this would be difficult. Many people do not desire immortality. There are some who desire no sort of immortality—who would rather cease to exist at the death of their bodies than continue to exist in any way whatever. There are others who would not be unwilling to encounter an immortal life of rest and tranquillity, but who would prefer extinction to an immortality which involved a continuance beyond death of the pain and struggle of this life, even if that struggle should be comparatively short, and should lead to eventual repose. In the far East, again, we find two of the greatest religions of the world teaching that personal immortality is an evil, and that the highest consummation of a wise and virtuous life will lead us to lay down life altogether.

Even if we were able to put these difficulties on one side, and assume that human immortality was certainly good, should we be entitled to base a belief in immortality on a belief in God? I do not see that we are justified in this, whether God is held to be omnipotent or not.

If God is omnipotent, then it is clear, as we saw in Chapter VI, that there are some good things which he does not antecedently will to exist, and some bad things which he does antecedently will to exist. For some good things do not exist, and some bad things do. Now how can we tell that immortality is not one of the good things which he does not will to exist, and the annihilation of persons one of the bad things which he does will to exist? To reply that immortality is better than most things, and annihilation worse than most things may be true, but is irrelevant. For we saw above that, if any evil in the universe was consistent with the goodness of God, it was impossible for us to determine any limits to its amount.

But if God is not omnipotent, then his goodness is no security for immortality. There are some good things which we know that he cannot realize, since we know that they do not exist. How can we be sure that human immortality is not among such things? There are some bad things which we know that he cannot prevent from existing, since they do exist. And among such things may be our annihilation at the death of our bodies.

If immortality can be proved at all, it can only be proved by arguments of a different sort. If we are to do anything, we must be able so to determine the nature of reality as to show that every self is an eternal part of the eternal reality, and that its eternity necessarily manifests itself in an existence throughout all future time, or we must, in some similar way, prove the immortality of the self as a direct consequence of its own nature. Such a line of argument, if possible at all—I believe, as I have said earlier, that it is possible —is difficult and arduous. But nothing less will suffice.

Now it seems clear that such a deduction as this would not be helped by a demonstration of God's existence. If God is taken as director, and not as creator, then my existence is independent of his will. And if my immortality is a consequence of my nature, then my immortality is involved in my existence, and is likewise independent of God's will. And in no other way than by his will could the existence of a directing God be supposed to bear on the question. The mere fact that the universe contained a being who greatly excelled me and all others in perfection could not be a ground for believing that my existence would be unending.

227. If we go back to the hypothesis that God is a creator, and that, among other things, he creates ourselves, then, so far from the existence of God rendering my immortality more probable, it seems to me that it makes it less so. The idea of creation is generally held in a form which makes the created being begin to exist at a point in time, so that there was a time, however distant, when that being had not yet begun to exist. Whether this form is essential to the idea of creation or not, it is the form in which it is almost always found. Indeed the hypothesis of creation is often supported by the assertion that it is impossible for finite beings to have existed through all past time. Now if for every man there was a time when he did not yet exist, I cannot see how his immortality is to be proved. If his relation to the universe is compatible with his non-existence in past time, how shall we be able to prove that his relation with the universe is not compatible with his non-existence in future time? Metaphysics have not yet given us the right to discriminate in this manner between the past and the future.

Of course the difference between the past and the future is very considerable from the point of view of our own interests. We are much more interested in what is about to happen to us than we are in what has happened to us. And this might be important, if the proof of immortality rested on the goodness of the universe or of its creator. To annihilate existing persons might well be a much more serious blemish on the universe than to postpone the creation of persons not yet existent. And so, if immortality could be based on this ground at all, we might prove that a being would never cease to exist in the future, although he had formerly not existed. But we have seen that immortality cannot be based on this ground, and on any other it seems impossible to give any reason why that which was once created should not be again annihilated.[8]

228. Thus we see that there is no logical connexion between the belief in God and the belief in human immortality. And there has not always been a historical connexion. Fichte, in his earlier system at any rate, believed in immortality without believing in God. The same may be said, in my opinion, about Hegel, though this is disputed. Buddhism, again, which has no God, holds immortality to be the natural state of man, from which only the most perfect can escape. And, in modern times, Schopenhauer is in the same

[8] Cp. chap. iv.

position. On the other side we find Lotze. Of all the theists of the nineteenth century he is philosophically the most important. And he regards immortality as quite undemonstrable and as very doubtful.[9]

What is the cause of the opinion that a belief in immortality requires a belief in theism? Partly, perhaps, it is the fact that the majority of theists do believe in immortality, and that the majority of Western believers in immortality are theists. But, in addition to this, it must be remembered that materialism would make any belief in immortality perfectly unreasonable, and that scepticism makes all beliefs unreasonable. Now there is a very common idea that an atheist must either be a materialist or a sceptic, and, therefore, that it is unreasonable for him to believe in immortality. But this, like many other common ideas, is erroneous.

[9] Lotze's defence of theism will be found in his *Microcosmus* (Book IX, chaps. iv and v) and his doctrine of immortality in his *Metaphysics* (Section 245). Both these works are translated into English.

Antony Garrard Newton Flew was born in 1923 and is Professor of Philosophy at The University of North Staffordshire. He has edited *Logic and Language* (2 volumes, 1952–53), *Essays in Conceptual Analysis* (1956), and, together with Alasdair MacIntyre, *New Essays in Philosophical Theology* (1955), which includes the following pieces by Flew himself, Hare, and Mitchell. Flew's own books include *Hume's Philosophy of Belief* (1961).

Richard Marvyn Hare was born in 1919. He is a Fellow of Balliol College, Oxford, and the author of *The Language of Morals* (1952) and *Freedom and Reason* (1963).

Basil Mitchell was born in 1920. He is a Fellow of Keble College, Oxford, and has edited *Faith and Logic* (1957).

The discussion that follows is printed at the end of the volume because it has been added only in the second edition; being based on John Wisdom's essay "Gods" (pp. 391–406 above), it should be read along with that.

Theology and Falsification

A

ANTONY FLEW

*L*et us begin with a parable. It is a parable developed from a tale told by John Wisdom in his haunting and revelatory article 'Gods.'[1] Once upon a time two explorers came upon a clearing in the jungle. In the clearing were growing many flowers and many weeds. One explorer says, 'Some gardener must tend this plot.' The other disagrees, 'There is no gardener.' So they pitch their tents and set a watch. No gardener is ever seen. 'But perhaps he is an invisible gardener.' So they set up a barbed-wire fence. They electrify it. They patrol with bloodhounds. (For they remember how H. G. Wells's *The Invisible Man* could be both smelt and touched though he could not be seen.) But no shrieks ever suggest that some intruder has received a shock. No movements of the wire ever betray an invisible climber. The bloodhounds never give cry. Yet still the Believer is not convinced. 'But there is a gardener, invisible, intangible, insensible to electric shocks, a gardener who has no scent and makes no sound, a gardener who comes secretly to look after the garden which he loves.' At last the Sceptic despairs, 'But what

---

[1] *P.A.S.*, 1944–5, reprinted as Ch. X of *Logic and Language*, Vol I (Blackwell, 1951), and in his *Philosophy and Psychoanalysis* (Blackwell, 1953).

remains of your original assertion? Just how does what you call an invisible, intangible, eternally elusive gardener differ from an imaginary gardener or even from no gardener at all?'

In this parable we can see how what starts as an assertion, that something exists or that there is some analogy between certain complexes of phenomena, may be reduced step by step to an altogether different status, to an expression perhaps of a 'picture preference.'[2] The Sceptic says there is no gardener. The Believer says there is a gardener (but invisible, etc.). One man talks about sexual behaviour. Another man prefers to talk of Aphrodite (but knows that there is not really a superhuman person additional to, and somehow responsible for, all sexual phenomena).[3] The process of qualification may be checked at any point before the original assertion is completely withdrawn and something of that first assertion will remain (Tautology). Mr. Wells's invisible man could not, admittedly, be seen, but in all other respects he was a man like the rest of us. But though the process of qualification may be, and of course usually is, checked in time, it is not always judiciously so halted. Someone may dissipate his assertion completely without noticing that he has done so. A fine brash hypothesis may thus be killed by inches, the death by a thousand qualifications.

And in this, it seems to me, lies the peculiar danger, the endemic evil, of theological utterance. Take such utterances as 'God has a plan,' 'God created the world,' 'God loves us as a father loves his children.' They look at first sight very much like assertions, vast cosmological assertions. Of course, this is no sure sign that they either are, or are intended to be, assertions. But let us confine ourselves to the cases where those who utter such sentences intend them to express assertions. (Merely remarking parenthetically that those who intend or interpret such utterances as crypto-commands, expressions of wishes, disguised ejaculations, concealed ethics, or as anything else but assertions, are unlikely to succeed in making them either properly orthodox or practically effective).

Now to assert that such and such is the case is necessarily equivalent to denying that such and such is not the case.[4] Suppose then that we are in doubt as to what someone who gives vent to an utterance is asserting, or suppose that, more radically, we are sceptical as to whether he is really asserting anything at all, one way of trying to understand (or perhaps it will be to expose)

---

[2] Cf. J. Wisdom, 'Other Minds', *Mind*, 1940; reprinted in his *Other Minds* (Blackwell, 1952).

[3] Cf. Lucretius, *De Rerum Natura*, II, 655-60,

> Hic siquis mare Neptunum Cereremque vocare
> Constituet fruges et Bacchi nomine abuti
> Mavolat quam laticis proprium proferre vocamen
> Concedamus ut hic terrarum dictitet orbem
> Esse deum matrem dum vera re tamen ipse
> Religione animum turpi contingere parcat.

[4] For those who prefer symbolism: $p \equiv \sim\sim p$.

his utterance is to attempt to find what he would regard as counting against, or as being incompatible with, its truth. For if the utterance is indeed an assertion, it will necessarily be equivalent to a denial of the negation of that assertion. And anything which would count against the assertion, or which would induce the speaker to withdraw it and to admit that it had been mistaken, must be part of (or the whole of) the meaning of the negation of that assertion. And to know the meaning of the negation of an assertion, is as near as makes no matter, to know the meaning of that assertion.[5] And if there is nothing which a putative assertion denies then there is nothing which it asserts either: and so it is not really an assertion. When the Sceptic in the parable asked the Believer, 'Just how does what you call an invisible, intangible, eternally elusive gardener differ from an imaginary gardener or even from no gardener at all?' he was suggesting that the Believer's earlier statement had been so eroded by qualification that it was no longer an assertion at all.

Now it often seems to people who are not religious as if there was no conceivable event or series of events the occurrence of which would be admitted by sophisticated religious people to be a sufficient reason for conceding 'There wasn't a God after all' or 'God does not really love us then.' Someone tells us that God loves us as a father loves his children. We are reassured. But then we see a child dying of inoperable cancer of the throat. His earthly father is driven frantic in his efforts to help, but his Heavenly Father reveals no obvious sign of concern. Some qualification is made—God's love is 'not a merely human love' or it is 'an inscrutable love,' perhaps—and we realize that such sufferings are quite compatible with the truth of the assertion that 'God loves us as a father (but, of course, . . .)'. We are reassured again. But then perhaps we ask: what is this assurance of God's (appropriately qualified) love worth, what is this apparent guarantee really a guarantee against? Just what would have to happen not merely (morally and wrongly) to tempt but also (logically and rightly) to entitle us to say 'God does not love us' or even 'God does not exist'? I therefore put to the succeeding symposiasts the simple central questions, 'What would have to occur or to have occurred to constitute for you a disproof of the love of, or of the existence of, God?'

University College of North Staffordshire

ENGLAND

---

[5] For by simply negating $\sim p$ we get $p: \sim \sim p \equiv p$.

B[6]

R. M. HARE

I wish to make it clear that I shall not try to defend Christianity in particular, but religion in general—not because I do not believe in Christianity, but because you cannot understand what Christianity is, until you have understood what religion is.

I must begin by confessing that, on the ground marked out by Flew, he seems to me to be completely victorious. I therefore shift my ground by relating another parable. A certain lunatic is convinced that all dons want to murder him. His friends introduce him to all the mildest and most respectable dons that they can find, and after each of them has retired, they say, 'You see, he doesn't really want to murder you; he spoke to you in a most cordial manner; surely you are convinced now?' But the lunatic replies 'Yes, but that was only his diabolical cunning; he's really plotting against me the whole time, like the rest of them; I know it I tell you.' However many kindly dons are produced, the reaction is still the same.

Now we say that such a person is deluded. But what is he deluded about? About the truth or falsity of an assertion? Let us apply Flew's test to him. There is no behaviour of dons that can be enacted which he will accept as counting against his theory; and therefore his theory, on this test, asserts nothing. But it does not follow that there is no difference between what he thinks about dons and what most of us think about them—otherwise we should not call him a lunatic and ourselves sane, and dons would have no reason to feel uneasy about his presence in Oxford.

Let us call that in which we differ from this lunatic, our respective *bliks*. He has an insane *blik* about dons; we have a sane one. It is important to realize that we have a sane one, not no *blik* at all; for there must be two sides to any argument—if he has a wrong *blik*, then those who are right about dons must have a right one. Flew has shown that a *blik* does not consist in an assertion or system of them; but nevertheless it is very important to have the right *blik*.

Let us try to imagine what it would be like to have different *bliks* about other things than dons. When I am driving my car, it sometimes occurs to me to wonder whether my movements of the steering-wheel will always continue to be followed by corresponding alterations in the direction of the car. I have never had a steering failure, though I have had skids, which must be similar. Moreover, I know enough about how the steering of my car is made, to know the sort of thing that would have to go wrong for the steer-

---

[6] Some references to intervening discussion have been excised—Editors.

ing to fail—steel joints would have to part, or steel rods break, or something—but how do I know that this won't happen? The truth is, I don't know; I just have a *blik* about steel and its properties, so that normally I trust the steering of my car; but I find it not at all difficult to imagine what it would be like to lose this *blik* and acquire the opposite one. People would say I was silly about steel; but there would be no mistaking the reality of the difference between our respective *bliks*—for example, I should never go in a motor-car. Yet I should hesitate to say that the difference between us was the difference between contradictory assertions. No amount of safe arrivals or bench-tests will remove my *blik* and restore the normal one; for my *blik* is compatible with any finite number of such tests.

It was Hume who taught us that our whole commerce with the world depends upon our *blik* about the world; and that differences between *bliks* about the world cannot be settled by observation of what happens in the world. That was why, having performed the interesting experiment of doubting the ordinary man's *blik* about the world, and showing that no proof could be given to make us adopt one *blik* rather than another, he turned to backgammon to take his mind off the problem. It seems, indeed, to be impossible even to formulate as an assertion the normal *blik* about the world which makes me put my confidence in the future reliability of steel joints, in the continued ability of the road to support my car, and not gape beneath it revealing nothing below; in the general non-homicidal tendencies of dons; in my own continued well-being (in some sense of that word that I may not now fully understand) if I continue to do what is right according to my lights; in the general likelihood of people like Hitler coming to a bad end. But perhaps a formulation less inadequate than most is to be found in the Psalms: 'The earth is weak and all the inhabiters thereof: I bear up the pillars of it.'

The mistake of the position which Flew selects for attack is to regard this kind of talk as some sort of *explanation*, as scientists are accustomed to use the word. As such, it would obviously be ludicrous. We no longer believe in God as an Atlas—*nous n'avons pas besoin de cette hypothèse*. But it is nevertheless true to say that, as Hume saw, without a *blik* there can be no explanation; for it is by our *bliks* that we decide what is and what is not an explanation. Suppose we believed that everything that happened, happened by pure chance. This would not of course be an assertion; for it is compatible with anything happening or not happening, and so, incidentally, is its contradictory. But if we had this belief, we should not be able to explain or predict or plan anything. Thus, although we should not be *asserting* anything different from those of a more normal belief, there would be a great difference between us; and this is the sort of difference that there is between those who really believe in God and those who really disbelieve in him.

The word 'really' is important, and may excite suspicion. I put it in, because when people have had a good Christian upbringing, as have most of those who now profess not to believe in any sort of religion, it is very hard to discover what they really believe. The reason why they find it so easy to think that they are not religious, is that they have never got into the frame of mind of one who suffers from the doubts to which religion is the answer. Not for them the terrors of the primitive jungle. Having abandoned some of the more picturesque fringes of religion, they think that they have abandoned the whole thing—whereas in fact they still have got, and could not live without, a religion of a comfortably substantial, albeit highly sophisticated, kind, which differs from that of many 'religious people' in little more than this, that 'religious people' like to sing Psalms about theirs—a very natural and proper thing to do. But nevertheless there may be a big difference lying behind—the difference between two people who, though side by side, are walking in different directions. I do not know in what direction Flew is walking; perhaps he does not know either. But we have had some examples recently of various ways in which one can walk away from Christianity, and there are any number of possibilities. After all, man has not changed biologically since primitive times; it is his religion that has changed, and it can easily change again. And if you do not think that such changes make a difference, get acquainted with some Sikhs and some Mussulmans of the same Punjabi stock; you will find them quite different sorts of people.

There is an important difference between Flew's parable and my own which we have not yet noticed. The explorers do not *mind* about their garden; they discuss it with interest, but not with concern. But my lunatic, poor fellow, minds about dons; and I mind about the steering of my car; it often has people in it that I care for. It is because I mind very much about what goes on in the garden in which I find myself, that I am unable to share the explorers' detachment.

Balliol College
    OXFORD

C

BASIL MITCHELL

*F*lew's article is searching and perceptive, but there is, I think, something odd about his conduct of the theologian's case. The theologian surely would not deny that the fact of pain counts against the assertion that God loves men. This very incompatibility generates the most intractable of theological problems—the problem of evil. So the theologian *does* recognize the fact of pain as counting against Christian doctrine. But it is true that he will not allow it—or anything—to count decisively against it; for he is committed by his faith to trust in God. His attitude is not that of the detached observer, but of the believer.

Perhaps this can be brought out by yet another parable. In time of war in an occupied country, a member of the resistance meets one night a stranger who deeply impresses him. They spend that night together in conversation. The Stranger tells the partisan that he himself is on the side of the resistance—indeed that he is in command of it, and urges the partisan to have faith in him no matter what happens. The partisan is utterly convinced at that meeting of the Stranger's sincerity and constancy and undertakes to trust him.

They never meet in conditions of intimacy again. But sometimes the Stranger is seen helping members of the resistance, and the partisan is grateful and says to his friends, 'He is on our side.'

Sometimes he is seen in the uniform of the police handing over patriots to the occupying power. On these occasions his friends murmur against him: but the partisan still says, 'He is on our side.' He still believes that, in spite of appearances, the Stranger did not deceive him. Sometimes he asks the Stranger for help and receives it. He is then thankful. Sometimes he asks and does not receive it. Then he says, 'The Stranger knows best.' Sometimes his friends, in exasperation, say 'Well, what *would* he have to do for you to admit that you were wrong and that he is not on our side?' But the partisan refuses to answer. He will not consent to put the Stranger to the test. And sometimes his friends complain, 'Well, if *that's* what you mean by his being on our side, the sooner he goes over to the other side the better.'

The partisan of the parable does not allow anything to count decisively against the proposition 'The Stranger is on our side.' This is because he has committed himself to trust the Stranger. But he of course recognizes that the Stranger's ambiguous behaviour *does* count against what he believes about him. It is precisely this situation which constitutes the trial of his faith.

When the partisan asks for help and doesn't get it, what can he do? He can (*a*) conclude that the stranger is not on our side or; (*b*) maintain that he is on our side, but that he has reasons for withholding help.

The first he will refuse to do. How long can he uphold the second position without its becoming just silly?

I don't think one can say in advance. It will depend on the nature of the impression created by the Stranger in the first place. It will depend, too, on the manner in which he takes the Stranger's behaviour. If he blandly dismisses it as of no consequence, as having no bearing upon his belief, it will be assumed that he is thoughtless or insane. And it quite obviously won't do for him to say easily, 'Oh, when used of the Stranger the phrase "is on our side" *means* ambiguous behaviour of this sort.' In that case he would be like the religious man who says blandly of a terrible disaster 'It is God's will.' No, he will only be regarded as sane and reasonable in his belief, if he experiences in himself the full force of the conflict.

It is here that my parable differs from Hare's. The partisan admits that many things may and do count against his belief: whereas Hare's lunatic who has a *blik* about dons doesn't admit that anything counts against his *blik*. Nothing *can* count against *bliks*. Also the partisan has a reason for having in the first instance committed himself, viz. the character of the Stranger; whereas the lunatic has no reason for his *blik* about dons—because, of course, you can't have reasons for *bliks*.

This means that I agree with Flew that theological utterances must be assertions. The partisan is making an assertion when he says, 'The Stranger is on our side.'

Do I want to say that the partisan's belief about the Stranger is, in any sense, an explanation? I think I do. It explains and makes sense of the Stranger's behaviour: it helps to explain also the resistance movement in the context of which he appears. In each case it differs from the interpretation which the others put upon the same facts.

'God loves men' resembles 'the Stranger is on our side' (and many other significant statements, e.g. historical ones) in not being conclusively falsifiable. They can both be treated in at least three different ways: (1) As provisional hypotheses to be discarded if experience tells against them; (2) As significant articles of faith; (3) As vacuous formulae (expressing, perhaps, a desire for reassurance) to which experience makes no difference and which make no difference to life.

The Christian, once he has committed himself, is precluded by his faith from taking up the first attitude: 'Thou shalt not tempt the Lord thy God.' He is in constant danger, as Flew has observed, of slipping into the third. But he need not; and, if he does, it is a failure in faith as well as in logic.

Keble College
OXFORD

D

ANTONY FLEW

*I*t has been a good discussion: and I am glad to have helped to provoke it. But now—at least in *University*—it must come to an end: and the Editors of *University* have asked me to make some concluding remarks. Since it is impossible to deal with all the issues raised or to comment separately upon each contribution, I will concentrate on Mitchell and Hare, as representative of two very different kinds of response to the challenge made in 'Theology and Falsification.'

The challenge, it will be remembered, ran like this. Some theological utterances seem to, and are intended to, provide explanations or express assertions. Now an assertion, to be an assertion at all, must claim that things stand thus and thus; *and not otherwise*. Similarly an explanation, to be an explanation at all, must explain why this particular thing occurs; *and not something else*. Those last clauses are crucial. And yet sophisticated religious people—or so it seemed to me—are apt to overlook this, and tend to refuse to allow, not merely that anything actually does occur, but that anything conceivably could occur, which would count against their theological assertions and explanations. But in so far as they do this their supposed explanations are actually bogus, and their seeming assertions are really vacuous.

Mitchell's response to this challenge is admirably direct, straightforward, and understanding. He agrees 'that theological utterances must be assertions.' He agrees that if they are to be assertions, there must be something that would count against their truth. He agrees, too, that believers are in constant danger of transforming their would-be assertions into 'vacuous formulae.' But he takes me to task for an oddity in my 'conduct of the theologian's case. The theologian surely would not deny that the fact of pain counts against the assertion that God loves men. This very incompatibility generates the most intractable of theological problems, the problem of evil.' I think he is right. I should have made a distinction between two very different ways of dealing with what looks like evidence against the love of God: the way I stressed was the expedient of qualifying the original assertion; the way the theologian usually takes, at first, is to admit that it looks bad but to insist that there is—there must be—some explanation which will show that, in spite of appearances, there really is a God who loves us. His difficulty, it seems to me, is that he has given God attributes which rule out all possible saving explanations. In Mitchell's parable of the Stranger it is easy for the believer to find plausible excuses for ambiguous behaviour: for the Stranger is a man. But suppose the Stranger is God. We cannot say that he would like to help but cannot: God is omnipotent. We cannot say that he would help if he only knew: God is omniscient. We cannot say that he is not responsible for the wickedness of others: God creates those others. Indeed an omnipotent, omniscient God must be an accessory before (and during) the fact to every human misdeed; as well as being responsible for every non-moral defect in the universe. So, though I entirely concede that Mitchell was absolutely right to insist against me that the theologian's first move is to look for an *explanation*, I still think that in the end, if relentlessly pursued, he will have to resort to the avoiding action of *qualification*. And there lies the danger of that death by a thousand qualifications, which would, I agree, constitute 'a failure in faith as well as in logic.'

Hare's approach is fresh and bold. He confesses that 'on the ground marked out by Flew, he seems to me to be completely victorious.' He therefore introduces the concept of *blik*. But while I think that there is room for some such concept in philosophy, and that philosophers should be grateful to Hare for his invention, I nevertheless want to insist that any attempt to analyse Christian religious utterances as expressions or affirmations of a *blik* rather than as (at least would-be) assertions about the cosmos is fundamentally misguided. *First*, because thus interpreted they would be entirely unorthodox. If Hare's religion really is a *blik*, involving no cosmological assertions about the nature and activities of a supposed personal creator, then surely he is not a Christian at all? *Second*, because thus interpreted, they could scarcely do the job they do. If they were not even intended as assertions then many religious activities would become fraudulent, or merely silly. If 'You ought *because* it is God's will' asserts no more than 'You ought,' then the person who prefers the former phraseology is not really giving a reason, but a fraudulent substitute for one, a dialectical dud cheque. If 'My soul must be immortal *because* God loves his children, etc.' asserts no more than 'My soul must be immortal,' then the man who reassures himself with theological arguments for immortality is being as silly as the man who tries to clear his overdraft by writing his bank a cheque on the same account. (Of course neither of these utterances would be distinctively Christian: but this discussion never pretended to be so confined.) Religious utterances may indeed express false or even bogus assertions: but I simply do not believe that they are not both intended and interpreted to be or at any rate to presuppose assertions, at least in the context of religious practice; whatever shifts may be demanded, in another context, by the exigencies of theological apologetic.

One final suggestion. The philosophers of religion might well draw upon George Orwell's last appalling nightmare *1984* for the concept of *doublethink*. '*Doublethink* means the power of holding two contradictory beliefs simultaneously, and accepting both of them. The party intellectual knows that he is playing tricks with reality, but by the exercise of *doublethink* he also satisfies himself that reality is not violated' (*1984*, p. 220). Perhaps religious intellectuals too are sometimes driven to doublethink in order to retain their faith in a loving God in face of the reality of a heartless and indifferent world. But of this more another time, perhaps.

University College of North Staffordshire
ENGLAND

hARpER ✚ tORchbOOKS

American Studies: General

HENRY ADAMS Degradation of the Democratic Dogma. ‡ *Introduction by Charles Hirschfeld.* TB/1450

LOUIS D. BRANDEIS: Other People's Money, *and How the Bankers Use It. Ed. with Intro, by Richard M. Abrams* TB/3081

HENRY STEELE COMMAGER, Ed.: The Struggle for Racial Equality TB/1300

CARL N. DEGLER: Out of Our Past: *The Forces that Shaped Modern America* CN/2

CARL N. DEGLER, Ed.: Pivotal Interpretations of American History
Vol. I TB/1240; Vol. II TB/1241

A. S. EISENSTADT, Ed.: The Craft of American History: *Selected Essays*
Vol. I TB/1255; Vol. II TB/1256

LAWRENCE H. FUCHS, Ed.: American Ethnic Politics TB/1368

MARCUS LEE HANSEN: The Atlantic Migration: 1607-1860. *Edited by Arthur M. Schlesinger. Introduction by Oscar Handlin* TB/1052

MARCUS LEE HANSEN: The Immigrant in American History. *Edited with a Foreword by Arthur M. Schlesinger* TB/1120

ROBERT L. HEILBRONER: The Limits of American Capitalism TB/1305

JOHN HIGHAM, Ed.: The Reconstruction of American History TB/1068

ROBERT H. JACKSON: The Supreme Court in the American System of Government TB/1106

JOHN F. KENNEDY: A Nation of Immigrants. *Illus. Revised and Enlarged. Introduction by Robert F. Kennedy* TB/1118

LEONARD W. LEVY, Ed.: American Constitutional Law: *Historical Essays* TB/1285

LEONARD W. LEVY, Ed.: Judicial Review and the Supreme Court TB/1296

LEONARD W. LEVY: The Law of the Commonwealth and Chief Justice Shaw: *The Evolution of American Law, 1830-1860* TB/1309

GORDON K. LEWIS: Puerto Rico: *Freedom and Power in the Caribbean. Abridged edition* TB/1371

HENRY F. MAY: Protestant Churches and Industrial America TB/1334

RICHARD B. MORRIS: Fair Trial: *Fourteen Who Stood Accused, from Anne Hutchinson to Alger Hiss* TB/1335

GUNNAR MYRDAL: An American Dilemma: *The Negro Problem and Modern Democracy. Introduction by the Author.*
Vol. I TB/1443; Vol. II TB/1444

GILBERT OSOFSKY, Ed.: The Burden of Race: *A Documentary History of Negro-White Relations in America* TB/1405

CONYERS READ, Ed.: The Constitution Reconsidered. *Revised Edition. Preface by Richard B. Morris* TB/1384

ARNOLD ROSE: The Negro in America: *The Condensed Version of Gunnar Myrdal's* An American Dilemma. *Second Edition* TB/3048

JOHN E. SMITH: Themes in American Philosophy: *Purpose, Experience and Community* TB/1466

WILLIAM R. TAYLOR: Cavalier and Yankee: *The Old South and American National Character* TB/1474

American Studies: Colonial

BERNARD BAILYN: The New England Merchants in the Seventeenth Century TB/1149

ROBERT E. BROWN: Middle-Class Democracy and Revolution in Massachusetts, 1691–1780. *New Introduction by Author* TB/1413

JOSEPH CHARLES: The Origins of the American Party System TB/1049

HENRY STEELE COMMAGER & ELMO GIORDANETTI, Eds.: Was America a Mistake? *An Eighteenth Century Controversy* TB/1329

WESLEY FRANK CRAVEN: The Colonies in Transition: 1660-1712† TB/3084

CHARLES GIBSON: Spain in America † TB/3077

CHARLES GIBSON, Ed.: The Spanish Tradition in America + HR/1351

LAWRENCE HENRY GIPSON: The Coming of the Revolution: 1763-1775. † *Illus.* TB/3007

JACK P. GREENE, Ed.: Great Britain and the American Colonies: 1606-1763. + *Introduction by the Author* HR/1477

AUBREY C. LAND, Ed.: Bases of the Plantation Society + HR/1429

JOHN LANKFORD, Ed.: Captain John Smith's America: *Selections* from his Writings ‡ TB/3078

LEONARD W. LEVY: Freedom of Speech and Press in Early American History: *Legacy of Suppression* TB/1109

---

† The New American Nation Series, edited by Henry Steele Commager and Richard B. Morris.
‡ American Perspectives series, edited by Bernard Wishy and William E. Leuchtenburg.
α History of Europe series, edited by J. H. Plumb.
§ The Library of Religion and Culture, edited by Benjamin Nelson.
∥ Researches in the Social, Cultural, and Behavioral Sciences, edited by Benjamin Nelson.
Σ Harper Modern Science Series, edited by James A. Newman.
° Not for sale in Canada.
+ Documentary History of the United States series, edited by Richard B. Morris.
# Documentary History of Western Civilization series, edited by Eugene C. Black and Leonard W. Levy.
Λ The Economic History of the United States series, edited by Henry David et al.
¶ European Perspectives series, edited by Eugene C. Black.
** Contemporary Essays series, edited by Leonard W. Levy.
* The Stratum Series, edited by John Hale.

2

ARNOLD M. PAUL: Conservative Crisis and the Rule of Law: *Attitudes of Bar and Bench, 1887-1895. New Introduction by Author* TB/1415

JAMES S. PIKE: The Prostrate State: *South Carolina under Negro Government.* ‡ *Intro. by Robert F. Durden* TB/3085

WHITELAW REID: After the War: *A Tour of the Southern States, 1865-1866.* ‡ *Edited by C. Vann Woodward* TB/3066

FRED A. SHANNON: The Farmer's Last Frontier: ....*Agriculture, 1860-1897* TB/1348

VERNON LANE WHARTON: The Negro in Mississippi, 1865-1890 TB/1178

American Studies: The Twentieth Century

RICHARD M. ABRAMS, Ed.: The Issues of the Populist and Progressive Eras, 1892-1912 + HR/1428

RAY STANNARD BAKER: Following the Color Line: *American Negro Citizenship in Progressive Era.* ‡ *Edited by Dewey W. Grantham, Jr. Illus.* TB/3053

RANDOLPH S. BOURNE: War and the Intellectuals: *Collected Essays, 1915-1919.* ‡ *Edited by Carl Resek* TB/3043

A. RUSSELL BUCHANAN: The United States and World War II. † *Illus.*
Vol. I TB/3044; Vol. II TB/3045

THOMAS C. COCHRAN: The American Business System: *A Historical Perspective, 1900-1955* TB/1080

FOSTER RHEA DULLES: America's Rise to World Power: 1898-1954. † *Illus.* TB/3021

JEAN-BAPTISTE DUROSELLE: From Wilson to Roosevelt: *Foreign Policy of the United States, 1913-1945. Trans. by Nancy Lyman Roelker* TB/1370

HAROLD U. FAULKNER: The Decline of Laissez Faire, 1897-1917 TB/1397

JOHN D. HICKS: Republican Ascendancy: 1921-1933. † *Illus.* TB/3041

ROBERT HUNTER: Poverty: *Social Conscience in the Progressive Era.* ‡ *Edited by Peter d'A. Jones* TB/3065

WILLIAM E. LEUCHTENBURG: Franklin D. Roosevelt and the New Deal: 1932-1940. † *Illus.* TB/3025

WILLIAM E. LEUCHTENBURG, Ed.: The New Deal: *A Documentary History* + HR/1354

ARTHUR S. LINK: Woodrow Wilson and the Progressive Era: 1910-1917. † *Illus.* TB/3023

BROADUS MITCHELL: Depression Decade: *From New Era through New Deal, 1929-1941* ∧ TB/1439

GEORGE E. MOWRY: The Era of Theodore Roosevelt and the Birth of Modern America: 1900-1912. † *Illus.* TB/3022

WILLIAM PRESTON, JR.: Aliens and Dissenters: *Federal Suppression of Radicals, 1903-1933* TB/1287

WALTER RAUSCHENBUSCH: Christianity and the Social Crisis. ‡ *Edited by Robert D. Cross* TB/3059

GEORGE SOULE: Prosperity Decade: *From War to Depression, 1917-1929* ∆ TB/1349

GEORGE B. TINDALL, Ed.: A Populist Reader: *Selections from the Works of American Populist Leaders* TB/3069

TWELVE SOUTHERNERS: I'll Take My Stand: *The South and the Agrarian Tradition. Intro. by Louis D. Rubin, Jr.; Biographical Essays by Virginia Rock* TB/1072

Art, Art History, Aesthetics

CREIGHTON GILBERT, Ed.: Renaissance Art ** *Illus.* TB/1465

EMILE MALE: The Gothic Image: *Religious Art in France of the Thirteenth Century.* § *190 illus.* TB/344

MILLARD MEISS: Painting in Florence and Siena After the Black Death: *The Arts, Religion and Society in the Mid-Fourteenth Century. 169 illus.* TB/1148

ERWIN PANOFSKY: Renaissance and Renascences in Western Art. *Illus.* TB/1447

ERWIN PANOFSKY: Studies in Iconology: *Humanistic Themes in the Art of the Renaissance. 180 illus.* TB/1077

JEAN SEZNEC: The Survival of the Pagan Gods: *The Mythological Tradition and Its Place in Renaissance Humanism and Art. 108 illus.* TB/2004

OTTO VON SIMSON: The Gothic Cathedral: *Origins of Gothic Architecture and the Medieval Concept of Order. 58 illus.* TB/2018

HEINRICH ZIMMER: Myths and Symbols in Indian Art and Civilization. *70 illus.* TB/2005

Asian Studies

WOLFGANG FRANKE: China and the West: *The Cultural Encounter, 13th to 20th Centuries. Trans. by R. A. Wilson* TB/1326

L. CARRINGTON GOODRICH: A Short History of the Chinese People. *Illus.* TB/3015

DAN N. JACOBS, Ed.: The New Communist Manifesto and Related Documents. *3rd revised edn.* TB/1078

DAN N. JACOBS & HANS H. BAERWALD, Eds.: Chinese Communism: *Selected Documents* TB/3031

BENJAMIN I. SCHWARTZ: Chinese Communism and the Rise of Mao TB/1308

BENJAMIN I. SCHWARTZ: In Search of Wealth and Power: *Yen Fu and the West* TB/1422

Economics & Economic History

C. E. BLACK: The Dynamics of Modernization: *A Study in Comparative History* TB/1321

STUART BRUCHEY: The Roots of American Economic Growth, 1607-1861: *An Essay in Social Causation. New Introduction by the Author.* TB/1350

GILBERT BURCK & EDITORS OF *Fortune:* The Computer Age: *And its Potential for Management* TB/1179

JOHN ELLIOTT CAIRNES: The Slave Power. ‡ *Edited with Introduction by Harold D. Woodman* TB/1433

SHEPARD B. CLOUGH, THOMAS MOODIE & CAROL MOODIE, Eds.: Economic History of Europe: *Twentieth Century* # HR/1388

THOMAS C.COCHRAN: The American Business System: *A Historical Perspective, 1900-1955* TB/1180

ROBERT A. DAHL & CHARLES E. LINDBLOM: Politics, Economics, and Welfare: *Planning and Politico-Economic Systems Resolved into Basic Social Processes* TB/3037

PETER F. DRUCKER: The New Society: *The Anatomy of Industrial Order* TB/1082

HAROLD U. FAULKNER: The Decline of Laissez Faire, 1897-1917 ∧ TB/1397

PAUL W. GATES: The Farmer's Age: *Agriculture, 1815-1860* ∧ TB/1398

WILLIAM GREENLEAF, Ed.: American Economic Development Since 1860 + HR/1353

J. L. & BARBARA HAMMOND: The Rise of Modern Industry. || *Introduction by R. M. Hartwell* TB/1417

3

4

J. M. HUSSEY: The Byzantine World TB/1057
ROBERT LATOUCHE: The Birth of Western Economy: *Economic Aspects of the Dark Ages* °
TB/1290
HENRY CHARLES LEA: The Inquisition of the Middle Ages. || *Introduction by Walter Ullmann* TB/1456
FERDINARD LOT: The End of the Ancient World and the Beginnings of the Middle Ages. *Introduction by Glanville Downev* TB/1044
H. R. LOYN: The Norman Conquest TB/1457
ACHILLE LUCHAIRE: Social France at the time of Philip Augustus. *Intro. by John W. Baldwin* TB/1314
GUIBERT DE NOGENT: Self and Society in Medieval France: *The Memoirs of Guibert de Nogent*. || Edited by John F. Benton TB/1471
MARSILIUS OF PADUA: The Defender of Peace. *The Defensor Pacis. Translated with an Introduction by Alan Gewirth* TB/1310
CHARLES PETET-DUTAILLIS: The Feudal Monarchy in France and England: *From the Tenth to the Thirteenth Century* ° TB/1165
STEVEN RUNCIMAN: A History of the Crusades Vol. I: *The First Crusade and the Foundation of the Kingdom of Jerusalem. Illus.*
TB/1143
Vol. II: *The Kingdom of Jerusalem and the Frankish East 1100-1187. Illus.* TB/1243
Vol. III: *The Kingdom of Acre and the Later Crusades. Illus.* TB/1298
J. M. WALLACE-HADRILL: The Barbarian West: *The Early Middle Ages, A.D. 400-1000*
TB/1061

History: Renaissance & Reformation

JACOB BURCKHARDT: The Civilization of the Renaissance in Italy. *Introduction by Benjamin Nelson and Charles Trinkaus. Illus.*
Vol. I TB/40; Vol. II TB/41
JOHN CALVIN & JACOPO SADOLETO: A Reformation Debate. *Edited by John C. Olin* TB/1239
FEDERICO CHABOD: Machiavelli and the Renaissance TB/1193
THOMAS CROMWELL: Thomas Cromwell on Church and Commonwealth,: *Selected Letters 1523-1540.* ¶ *Ed. with an Intro. by Arthur J. Slavin* TB/1462
R. TREVOR DAVIES: The Golden Century of Spain, 1501-1621 ° TB/1194
J. H. ELLIOTT: Europe Divided, 1559-1598 α °
TB/1414
G. R. ELTON: Reformation Europe, 1517-1559 ° α
TB/1270
DESIDERIUS ERASMUS: Christian Humanism and the Reformation: *Selected Writings. Edited and Translated by John C. Olin* TB/1166
DESIDERIUS ERASMUS: Erasmus and His Age: *Selected Letters. Edited with an Introduction by Hans J. Hillerbrand. Translated by Marcus A. Haworth* TB/1461
WALLACE K. FERGUSON et al.: Facets of the Renaissance TB/1098
WALLACE K. FERGUSON et al.: The Renaissance: *Six Essays. Illus.* TB/1084
FRANCESCO GUICCIARDINI: History of Florence. *Translated with an Introduction and Notes by Mario Domandi* TB/1470
WERNER L. GUNDERSHEIMER, Ed.: French Humanism, 1470-1600. * *Illus.* TB/1473
MARIE BOAS HALL, Ed.: Nature and Nature's Laws: *Documents of the Scientific Revolution* # HR/1420
HANS J. HILLERBRAND, Ed., The Protestant Reformation # HR/1342
JOHAN HUIZINGA: Erasmus and the Age of Reformation. *Illus.* TB/19

JOEL HURSTFIELD: The Elizabethan Nation
TB/1312
JOEL HURSTFIELD, Ed.: The Reformation Crisis
TB/1267
PAUL OSKAR KRISTELLER: Renaissance Thought: *The Classic, Scholastic, and Humanist Strains*
TB/1048
PAUL OSKAR KRISTELLER: Renaissance Thought II: *Papers on Humanism and the Arts*
TB/1163
PAUL O. KRISTELLER & PHILIP P. WIENER, Eds.: Renaissance Essays TB/1392
DAVID LITTLE: Religion, Order and Law: *A Study in Pre-Revolutionary England.* § *Preface by R. Bellah* TB/1418
NICCOLO MACHIAVELLI: History of Florence and of the Affairs of Italy: *From the Earliest Times to the Death of Lorenzo the Magnificent. Introduction by Felix Gilbert* TB/1027
ALFRED VON MARTIN: Sociology of the Renaissance. ° *Introduction by W. K. Ferguson*
TB/1099
GARRETT MATTINGLY et al.: Renaissance Profiles. *Edited by J. H. Plumb* TB/1162
J. E. NEALE: The Age of Catherine de Medici °
TB/1085
J. H. PARRY: The Establishment of the European Hegemony: 1415-1715: *Trade and Exploration in the Age of the Renaissance* TB/1045
J. H. PARRY, Ed.: The European Reconnaissance: *Selected Documents* # HR/1345
BUONACCORSO PITTI & GREGORIO DATI: Two Memoirs of Renaissance Florence: *The Diaries of Buonaccorso Pitti and Gregorio Dati. Edited with Intro. by Gene Brucker. Trans. by Julia Martines* TB/1333
J. H. PLUMB: The Italian Renaissance: *A Concise Survey of Its History and Culture*
TB/1161
A. F. POLLARD: Henry VIII. *Introduction by A. G. Dickens.* ° TB/1249
RICHARD H. POPKIN: The History of Scepticism from Erasmus to Descartes TB/139
PAOLO ROSSI: Philosophy, Technology, and the Arts, in the Early Modern Era 1400-1700. || *Edited by Benjamin Nelson. Translated by Salvator Attanasio* TB/1458
FERDINAND SCHEVILL: The Medici. *Illus.* TB/1010
FERDINAND SCHEVILL: Medieval and Renaissance Florence. *Illus. Vol. I: Medieval Florence*
TB/1090
Vol. II: *The Coming of Humanism and the Age of the Medici* TB/1091
R. H. TAWNEY: The Agrarian Problem in the Sixteenth Century. *Intro. by Lawrence Stone*
TB/1315
H. R. TREVOR-ROPER: The European Witch-craze of the Sixteenth and Seventeenth Centuries and Other Essays ° TB/1416
VESPASIANO: Rennaissance Princes, Popes, and XVth Century: *The Vespasiano Memoirs. Introduction by Myron P. Gilmore. Illus.*
TB/1111

History: Modern European

RENE ALBRECHT-CARRIE, Ed.: The Concert of Europe # HR/1341
MAX BELOFF: The Age of Absolutism, 1660-1815
TB/1062
OTTO VON BISMARCK: Reflections and Reminiscences. *Ed. with Intro. by Theodore S. Hamerow* ¶ TB/1357
EUGENE C. BLACK, Ed.: British Politics in the Nineteenth Century # HR/1427

5

EUGENE C. BLACK, Ed.: European Political History, 1815-1870: *Aspects of Liberalism* ¶ TB/1331

ASA BRIGGS: The Making of Modern England, 1783-1867: *The Age of Improvement* ° TB/1203

D. W. BROGAN: The Development of Modern France ° Vol. I: *From the Fall of the Empire to the Dreyfus Affair* TB/1184 Vol. II: *The Shadow of War, World War I, Between the Two Wars* TB/1185

ALAN BULLOCK: Hitler, A Study in Tyranny. ° *Revised Edition. Illus.* TB/1123

EDMUND BURKE: On Revolution. *Ed. by Robert A. Smith* TB/1401

E. R. CARR: International Relations Between the Two World Wars. 1919-1939 ° TB/1279

E. H. CARR: The Twenty Years' Crisis, 1919-1939: *An Introduction to the Study of International Relations* ° TB/1122

GORDON A. CRAIG: From Bismarck to Adenauer: *Aspects of German Statecraft. Revised Edition* TB/1171

LESTER G. CROCKER, Ed.: The Age of Enlightenment # HR/1423

DENIS DIDEROT: The Encyclopedia: *Selections. Edited and Translated with Introduction by Stephen Gendzier* TB/1299

JACQUES DROZ: Europe between Revolutions, 1815-1848. ° *a Trans. by Robert Baldick* TB/1346

JOHANN GOTTLIEB FICHTE: Addresses to the German Nation. *Ed. with Intro. by George A. Kelly* ¶ TB/1366

FRANKLIN L. FORD: Robe and Sword: *The Re-Louis XIV* TB/1217

ROBERT & ELBORG FORSTER, Eds.: European Society in the Eighteenth Century # HR/1404

C. C. GILLISPIE: Genesis and Geology: *The Decades before Darwin* § TB/51

ALBERT GOODWIN, Ed.: The European Nobility in the Enghteenth Century TB/1313

ALBERT GOODWIN: The French Revolution TB/1064

ALBERT GUERARD: France in the Classical Age: *The Life and Death of an Ideal* TB/1183

JOHN B. HALSTED, Ed.: Romanticism # HR/1387

J. H. HEXTER: Reappraisals in History: *New Views on History and Society in Early Modern Europe* ° TB/1100

STANLEY HOFFMANN et al.: In Search of France: *The Economy, Society and Political System In the Twentieth Century* TB/1219

H. STUART HUGHES: The Obstructed Path: *French Social Thought in the Years of Desperation* TB/1451

JOHAN HUIZINGA: Dutch Civilisation in the 17th Century and Other Essays TB/1453

LIONAL KOCHAN: The Struggle for Germany: *1914-45* TB/1304

HANS KOHN: The Mind of Germany: *The Education of a Nation* TB/1204

HANS KOHN, Ed.: The Mind of Modern Russia: *Historical and Political Thought of Russia's Great Age* TB/1065

WALTER LAQUEUR & GEORGE L. MOSSE, Eds.: Education and Social Structure in the 20th Century. ° *Volume 6 of the Journal* of Contemporary History TB/1339

WALTER LAQUEUR & GEORGE L. MOSSE, Ed.: International Fascism, 1920-1945. ° *Volume 1 of the* Journal of Contemporary History TB/1276

WALTER LAQUEUR & GEORGE L. MOSSE, Eds.: Literature and Politics in the 20th Century. ° *Volume 5 of the* Journal of Contemporary History. TB/1328

WALTER LAQUEUR & GEORGE L. MOSSE, Eds.: The New History: *Trends in Historical Research and Writing Since World War II.* ° *Volume 4 of the* Journal of Contemporary History TB/1327

WALTER LAQUEUR & GEORGE L. MOSSE, Eds.: 1914: *The Coming of the First World War.* ° *Volume3 of the* Journal of Contemporary History TB/1306

C. A. MACARTNEY, Ed.: The Habsburg and Hohenzollern Dynasties in the Seventeenth and Eighteenth Centuries # HR/1400

JOHN MCMANNERS: European History, 1789-1914: *Men, Machines and Freedom* TB/1419

PAUL MANTOUX: The Industrial Revolution in the Eighteenth Century: *An Outline of the Beginnings of the Modern Factory System in England* TB/1079

FRANK E. MANUEL: The Prophets of Paris: *Turgot, Condorcet, Saint-Simon, Fourier, and Comte* TB/1218

KINGSLEY MARTIN: French Liberal Thought in the Eighteenth Century: *A Study of Political Ideas from Bayle to Condorcet* TB/1114

NAPOLEON III: Napoleonic Ideas: *Des Idées Napoléoniennes, par le Prince Napoléon-Louis Bonaparte. Ed. by Brison D. Gooch* ¶ TB/1336

FRANZ NEUMANN: Behemoth: *The Structure and Practice of National Socialism, 1933-1944* TB/1289

DAVID OGG: Europe of the Ancien Régime, 1715-1783 ° *a* TB/1271

GEORGE RUDE: Revolutionary Europe, 1783-1815 ° *a* TB/1272

MASSIMO SALVADORI, Ed.: Modern Socialism # TB/1374

HUGH SETON-WATSON: Eastern Europe Between the Wars, 1918-1941 TB/1330

DENIS MACK SMITH, Ed.: The Making of Italy, 1796-1870 # HR/1356

ALBERT SOREL: Europe Under the Old Regime. *Translated by Francis H. Herrick* TB/1121

ROLAND N. STROMBERG, Ed.: Realism, Naturalism, and Symbolism: *Modes of Thought and Expression in Europe, 1848-1914* # HR/1355

A. J. P. TAYLOR: From Napoleon to Lenin: *Historical Essays* ° TB/1268

A. J. P. TAYLOR: The Habsburg Monarchy, 1809-1918: *A History of the Austrian Empire and Austria-Hungary* ° TB/1187

J. M. THOMPSON: European History, 1494-1789 TB/1431

DAVID THOMSON, Ed.: France: Empire and Republic, 1850-1940 # HR/1387

ALEXIS DE TOCQUEVILLE & GUSTAVE DE BEAUMONT: Tocqueville and Beaumont on Social Reform. *Ed. and trans. with Intro. by Seymour Drescher* TB/1343

G. M. TREVELYAN: British History in the Nineteenth Century and After: *1792-1919* ° TB/1251

H. R. TREVOR-ROPER: Historical Essays TB/1269

W. WARREN WAGAR, Ed.: Science, Faith, and MAN: *European Thought Since 1914* # HR/1362

MACK WALKER, Ed.: Metternich's Europe, 1813-1848 # HR/1361

ELIZABETH WISKEMANN: Europe of the Dictators, 1919-1945 ° *a* TB/1273

JOHN B. WOLF: France: 1814-1919: *The Rise of a Liberal-Democratic Society* TB/3019

Literature & Literary Criticism

JACQUES BARZUN: The House of Intellect TB/1051

6

8